ENCYCLOPEDIA OF PSYCHOLOGY

EDITORS

ENCYCLOPEDIA OF PSYCHOLOGY

Alan E. Kazdin
Editor in Chief

VOLUME 8

AMERICAN PSYCHOLOGICAL ASSOCIATION

OXFORD
UNIVERSITY PRESS

2000

AMERICAN PSYCHOLOGICAL ASSOCIATION
Washington, D.C.

OXFORD
UNIVERSITY PRESS

Oxford New York
Athens Auckland Bangkok Bogotá Buenos Aires Calcutta
Cape Town Chennai Dar es Salaam Delhi Florence Hong Kong Istanbul
Karachi Kuala Lumpur Madrid Melbourne Mexico City Mumbai
Nairobi Paris São Paulo Singapore Taipei Tokyo Toronto Warsaw

and associated companies in
Berlin Ibadan

Published by American Psychological Association
750 First Street, NE, Washington, D.C. 20002-4242
www.apa.org
and
Oxford University Press, Inc.
198 Madison Avenue, New York, New York 10016
www.oup.com

Library of Congress Cataloging-in-Publication Data
Encyclopedia of psychology / Alan E. Kazdin, editor in chief
p. cm.
Includes bibliographical references and index.
1. Psychology—Encyclopedias. I. Kazdin, Alan E.
BF31 .E52 2000 150'.3—dc21 99-055239
ISBN 1-55798-187-6 (set); ISBN 1-55798-657-6 (vol. 8)

AMERICAN PSYCHOLOGICAL ASSOCIATION STAFF

Gary R. VandenBos, Ph.D., *Publisher*
Julia Frank-McNeil, *Commissioning Editor*
Theodore J. Baroody, *Senior Development Editor*
Adrian Harris Forman, *Project Editor*

OXFORD UNIVERSITY PRESS STAFF

Karen Casey, *Publisher*
Claude Conyers, *Commissioning Editor*
Marion Osmun, *Senior Development Editor*
Matthew Giarratano, *Managing Editor*
Peri Zeenkov and Norina Frabotta, *Project Editors*
Nancy Hoagland, *Production Manager*
Jessica Ryan and Will Moore, *Production Editors*
AEIOU, Inc., *Index Editor*
AEIOU, Inc., Linda Berman, Denise McIntyre,
Space Coast Indexers, Inc., Linda Webster, *Indexers*
Suzanne Holt, *Book Design*
Joan Greenfield, *Cover Design*

3 5 7 9 8 6 4 2

Printed in the United States of America
on acid-free paper

T

TABLE ANALYSIS. *See* Analysis of Counts.

TAINE, HIPPOLYTE (1828–1893), French philosopher and historian. Literacy and art critic, philosopher, historian, and psychologist, Taine was one of the best-known intellectuals of the last third of the nineteenth century. His influence is perceptible in an entire generation of writers, notably Maurice Barrès, Charles Maurras, Paul Bourget, Emile Zola and the naturalist school, and Marcel Proust.

Taine scored the highest marks for his year in the entrance examination to the École Normale Supérieure but failed his *agrégation* in philosophy in 1851, when the jury objected to his "Spinozist" tendencies. Posted outside Paris as a secondary-school teacher, he resigned in 1852 and thereafter devoted himself almost exclusively to the 20 or more works that made his name. He was elected to the Académie française in 1878.

Although influenced by the sensationist and associationist philosophers, he was also a romantic fascinated by the variety and complexity of human experience. He first came to notice with *Les philosophes français du XIXe siècle* (French Philosophers of the Nineteenth Century [Paris, 1857]) in which he attacked French spiritualist philosophy, an academic school whose principal representative was Victor Cousin. He came to fame with the program set out in the introduction to his *Histoire de la littérature anglaise* (History of English Litterature [4 vols., Paris, 1863–1864]). There he asserted that the historian must seek to explain systems of thought on the basis of three major causes: race, milieu, and moment. Taine thus adopted the role of psychologist, since understanding history, in his view, implied studying the psychology of its protagonists.

The first edition of his famous treatise on "pure psychology," *De l'intelligence* (On Intelligence [Paris]), appeared in 1870; by 1914, the work had been through 13 editions. In the same year, Théodule Ribot published *La psychologie anglaise contemporaine* (Contemporary English Psychology [Paris]); these two works are considered the founding texts of French "positive" psychology. Taine asserts that psychology is a science of fact and that it must give pride of place to nervous physiology, mental pathology, and all "bizarre" phenomena. Extreme and abnormal cases afford a form of magnification of nervous phenomena analogous to that of the microscope in the physical sciences. Taine also hypothesized that the movement of thought is reducible to the movement of images, a theory famously summarized in his statement that "the mind is a polypary of images." Resolutely idealist, he held that sensation, image, and hallucination are identical in nature, and that "perception is veridical hallucination." In his early research, Alfred Binet sought to confirm this thesis experimentally but subsequently abandoned it in favor of thought without images.

Finally, in 1871, Taine attempted to set out the lessons of the Paris Commune, which horrified him, in a monumental work, *Les origines de la France contemporaine* (The Origins of Contemporary France [1873–1893]). In it, he developed a "psychology applied to history" and, in particular, a psychology of revolutionary crowds. The man in the crowd, Taine believed, returned to a barbaric and even animal state and was subject to mental contagion. Crowds were led by alcoholic criminals, and women were the most bestial elements in the crowd because their mentality was more primitive than men's. This analysis was adopted by reactionary historians and by the crowd psychologists of the late nineteenth century: the Italian Scipio Sighele and the Frenchmen Gabriel Tarde and Gustave Le Bon.

Given his many interests, Taine is not considered a "true" psychologist and is remembered primarily as a historian.

[*Many of the people mentioned in this article are the subjects of independent biographical entries.*]

Bibliography

Carroy, J., & Plas, R. (1993). La méthode pathologique et les origines de la psychologie française au XIXe siècle. *Revue Internationale de Psychopathologie, 12*, 603–612.

Léger, F. (1993). *Monsieur Taine*. Paris: Critérion.

Régine Plas

Translated from French by Chris Miller

TAIWAN. The first psychology laboratory in Taiwan was established in 1928 at Taipei Imperial University, formerly National Taiwan University (NTU), by two Japanese professors, Linuma and Rikimaru, to study the folk psychology of aborigines. This was during the period when Japan was aggressively seeking to colonize its neighbors to the south (e.g., the Philippines). The psychological research was intended to serve the expansionist Japanese government's drive southward. When Taiwan was restored to Nationalist China at the end of World War II, all Japanese were sent back to Japan. The first department of psychology was founded at NTU (which had reverted to its original name) in 1949 by Professor Hsiang-yu Su, a graduate of Beijing University, who was a philosopher by training.

Most professors teaching psychology at colleges or universities during the 1950s were intellectual refugees who had escaped from different provinces of mainland China. Along with some local professors, they resumed the activities of the Chinese Association of Psychological Testing (CAPT) and the Chinese Association for Mental Hygiene (renamed as Mental Health Association in Taiwan, MHAT, since 1992) in 1951 and 1955 respectively. They also organized a Chinese Psychological Association (CPA) in 1953. These three organizations constitute the main bodies of the professional association of psychology on Taiwan, and each of them publishes an official journal: *Psychological Testing* (CAPT), *Chinese Journal of Mental Health* (MHAT), and *Chinese Journal of Psychology* (CPA).

Since Nationalist China was defeated in the Civil War and retreated to this island in 1949, Taiwan had held a chair in the United Nations as the Republic of China and maintained an allied relationship with the United States until the early 1970s. The history of the close connection with the United States has made Taiwan highly dependent on America for educational and academic resources: American textbooks or their translations are widely used in colleges or universities, many teachers were educated in America, and many graduate students also choose American institutions for advanced studies. As a consequence, psychological research in Taiwan is very Americanized: Most scholars find research topics from "hot issues" published in American journals, they apply Western instruments and research methodology to Chinese subjects, and attempt to interpret their research findings in terms of popular American theories. A few of them are able to make breakthroughs in their research and publish their articles in international journals, while most findings of "plain" research are published in local journals.

Taiwan was expelled from the United Nations in 1971, and Chiang Ching-kuo assumed the post of prime minister the next year. He pushed forward the Ten Construction Projects providing infrastructure for rapid economic development thereafter. As a result of industrialization and urbanization, new social problems emerged and called unceasingly for solutions, the social demand for psychologists increased, and many universities began to provide programs for training students in psychology. The population of the psychology community expanded, and the number of published articles accumulated very rapidly. Some scholars began to doubt the adequacy of implementing Western paradigms of research in Chinese society. In December 1981, Academia Sinica sponsored a conference on "Sinicization of Social and Behavioral Sciences." Some social scientists succinctly criticized the popular style of empirical research which mindlessly followed Western paradigms, and Professor Kuo-shu Yang proposed several guidelines for the sinicization of psychological research in Chinese society. However, because each subfield of psychology has its own research tradition for exploring the human mind, their responses to his calling for indigenization have differed.

Experimental Psychology

The mainstream of Taiwanese psychology is very proud to claim itself as a branch of science, so the method of experimentation as well as the field of experimental psychology are supposed to occupy an orthodox status among all subfields of psychology. During the 1960s, a series of experiments were carried out on the process of discrimination, generalization, and classical conditioning. Dr. I. M. Liu was the most outstanding researcher and published many of his works in American journals.

The research paradigm of cognitive psychology was introduced into Taiwan in the early 1970s. It conceptualizes human beings as information processing systems instead of black boxes responding to external stimuli. Because human intelligence is considered universal in its operations and functionings, and since research using the Western spelling system as material for research is specific in its findings, the major task the Taiwanese cognitive psychologists have accomplished is to use monosyllabic Chinese characters as research materials to test the Western theoretical models regarding lexical access, phonetics, character recognition, feature matching, character processing, short-term memory, brain lateralization, sentence comprehension, and problem solving. Many findings of their research has been documented in two books edited by M. H. Bond, *The Psychology of the Chinese People* (1986, see chapter 3) and *The Handbook of Chinese Psychology* (1996, see chapters 2, 3, 4); some of the findings have been incorporated into a textbook on *Cognitive Psychology* by C. M. Cheng (1993).

Psychological Tests

The Chinese have a long history of using psychological tests. The first book on IQ tests was published in Nanking (Lial & Chen, 1921). After CAPT resumed its activities in Taiwan, it published a *Catalogue of Psychological Tests* (1954), which listed 208 psychological tests available at that time.

From 1960 to 1980, numerous psychological tests were translated from English into Chinese, and most of them were revised carefully for the purpose of personnel selection and personnel classification in civil service, military service, and educational placement. *A Bibliographical Guide to Psychological Tests* (CAPT, Taiwan, 1978) listed 130 educational and psychological tests that have been revised and are widely used in Taiwan. Many books on Western theories and methods of psychological testing by professors of Taiwan Normal University and Cheng-chi University had been published. However, because most tests were translated into Chinese without permission of the original author, all unauthorized copies of psychological tests have been abandoned or restricted in noncommercial usage since the Copyright Act was implemented by the Taiwan government in June 1991. It is expected that the incident may stimulate Taiwanese psychologists to reflect upon their situation of overdependency on American resources and develop their own instruments of measurement in the future.

Psychiatry and Clinical Psychology

Chinese people are very pragmatic. In order to deal with problems related to mental health, professional practitioners such as clinical psychologists, social workers, and nurses in mental hospitals were organized to work as a team under the leadership of psychiatrists. They had studied various aspects of this field, including epidemiology and prevalence of mental disorders in various types of communities; psychopathology of cultural-specific syndromes such as *Koro*, psychosomatic complaints, sexual neurosis, Shamanism, alcoholism, and suicide; practices of psychotherapy in different institutions, such as group therapy, occupational therapy, halfway houses, folk therapy, as well as help-seeking behavior of people from different social backgrounds. Students interested in those topics may refer to *Normal and Deviant Behavior in Chinese Culture* (Kleinman & Lin, 1981), *Chinese Societies and Mental Health* (Lin Tseng, & Yeh, 1995) and two books on Chinese psychology edited by Bond (1986, chapter 5; 1996, chapter 26, 27, 28, 29).

However, many culture-specific practices for maintaining mental health are still unknown to the English world. For example, the traditional practices of zen meditation and *qi-gong* (enhancing one's inner strength by voluntary control over one's own muscles and breathing) are very popular in Taiwan, and many psychologists and anthropologists have been attracted by its therapeutic effects, but because such practices were once viewed as "unscientific" or "superstitious," very little research on these topics has been done yet.

Personality and Social Psychology

Social scientists all over the world have long been interested in studying Chinese personality and social behavior, as were Taiwanese psychologists. During the 1960s, various instruments for personality assessment, including the Cattell Sixteen Personality Factor Questionaire, California Personality Inventory, Guilford–Zimmerman Temperament Survey, Maudsley Personality Inventory, and Minnesota Multiphasic Personality Inventory were translated into Chinese, a series of empirical researches were conducted, and abundant data were compiled regarding the structure of the Chinese personality. Y. H. Ko, a professor of clinical psychology at NTU, was the first to insist on doing research with his own instrument, Ko's Mental Health Questionnaire (KMHQ).

Since 1970, the field of research has been expanded to include such topics of social psychology as value change, individual modernity, stereotypes, attributional patterns, life stress, coping styles, etc. The technique of multivariate analysis was introduced and has become a popular method for data analysis since the late 1970s. Nevertheless, most research accomplished during this period was still a "transplantation" of Western paradigms in nature. Dissatisfied with such a situation, K. S. Yang proposed the concept "Sinicization of Psychology" and promoted it as an academic movement. He organized a Research Group of Indigenous Psychology with about 100 members, and since 1993 has published a journal, *Indigenous Psychological Research in Chinese Societies*. As a consequence of his active promotion, the group has accomplished research on such significant aspects of Chinese social behaviors as filial piety, *yuan* (interpersonal affinity), *guanxi* (relationships), *mientze* (face), social-oriented achievement motivation, interpersonal conflict, and leadership and organizational culture. Some of their findings, along with findings of empirical research in the field of personality and social psychology, have been incorporated into Bond's two books on Chinese psychology (1986, chapters 4, 6; 1996, chapters 15, 16, 17, 19, 20, 31).

The author of this article has developed a unique approach to indigenous psychology. In recognition of the fact that scientific progress is made possible through theoretical construction and reconstruction rather than mere accumulation of empirical facts, he has advocated a parallel construction of theoretical models on Chinese social behavior by means of a joint psychological and cultural approach. The structures of theoretical models constructed by these two approaches should be isomorphic and can be integrated on the philosophical ground of constructive realism. Therefore, he constructed a realistically based theoretical model called "Face and Favor: The Chinese Power Game" (Hwang, 1987), and used this model to analyze the structure of the Chinese cultural heritage including Confucianism, Legalism, and Daoism in his book *Knowledge and Action* (1995). Then he constructed another model on conflict resolution in Chinese society (Hwang, 1997) with a reference to his previous works, and reinterpreted findings of empirical research on moral reasoning which were unscorable by Kohlberg's scoring system (Hwang, 1998). His works may provide an example for establishing a research tradition of indigenous social psychology in Taiwan.

[*See also* China.]

Bibliography

Bond, M. H. (Ed.). (1986). *The psychology of the Chinese people.* Hong Kong: Oxford University Press.

Bond, M. H. (Ed.). (1996). *The handbook of Chinese psychology.* Hong Kong: Oxford University Press.

Cheng, C. M. (1993). *Cognitive psychology* [in Chinese]. Taipei: Gueiguan.

Hwang, K. K. (1987). Face and favor: The Chinese power game. *American Journal of Sociology, 92,* 945–974.

Hwang, K. K. (1995). *Knowledge and action: A social psychological interpretation of Chinese cultural tradition* [in Chinese]. Taipei: Xin-li Publisher.

Hwang, K. K. (1997). Guanxi and Mientze: Conflict resolution in Chinese society. *Intercultural Communication Studies, 7,* 17–42.

Hwang, K. K. (1998). Two moralities: Reinterpreting findings of empirical research on moral reasoning in Taiwan. *Asian Journal of Social Psychology, 1,* 211–238.

Kleinman, A., & Lin, T. Y. (Ed.). (1981). *Normal and abnormal behavior in Chinese culture.* Holland: D. Reidel.

Lin, T. Y., Tseng, W. S., & Yeh, E. K. (Eds.). (1995). *Chinese societies and mental health.* Hong Kong: Oxford University Press.

Kwang-Kuo Hwang

TALENT. Talent refers to an ability or skill, usually innate, which is valued in a particular culture. For example, in the United States, a person's ability to hit with a stick a small ball that travels at 90 miles per hour would be construed as talent in baseball, whereas in most of the world such a skill would pass unnoticed or unrewarded. The ability to write great verse or to make vast sums of money might be called a talent metaphorically, but because these skills depend on a great deal of complex learning, which is unlikely to be innate, they would not be considered a talent in the strictest sense. Some scholars have begun to cast doubt on the notion that talent is based on genetic differences and have suggested that early exposure, training, and practice are sufficient to explain superior performance (Ericsson & Charness, 1995; Howe, Davidson, & Sloboda, in press).

Other related concepts include that of *genius,* which is used to describe very rare individuals whose abilities are such that they astonish even experts in the field, and *creativity,* which denotes individuals who produce ideas or objects that are new and subsequently adopted by the culture. Talent is presumably a prerequisite for being a genius or for being creative, but a talented person is not necessarily either. Although people must show actual achievement to be recognized as geniuses or as creative, talent is often just a potential that may or may not be fulfilled. There is a cynical but realistic saying in the arts that "talent is cheap," meaning that very few people who show promise will actually be recognized in the long run. [*See* Genius; *and* Creativity.]

Varieties of Talent

Talent is thought to be based on genetically inherited neurological differences, although very little is known about what these are. Cerebral lateralization research suggests that children born with left-hemisphere dominance will have a greater facility with analytic tasks; by extension, other skills might similarly depend on the relative development of specific neural mechanisms. Howard Gardner's (1983) analysis of seven basic intelligences also supports the conclusion that talent in music, dance, literature, and other areas of human excellence might be, in part, genetically determined.

Despite the fact that talents manifest themselves in many forms, most research in the United States has been focused on general intelligence, or IQ, which has been considered a meta-skill underlying performance in all intellectual areas. Educational programs usually define as "gifted and talented" those children who perform in the upper 3 to 5% of the IQ score range. One of the earliest studies of talented children (as defined by IQ) was conducted by Lewis M. Terman (1947) and his collaborators, who tested a cohort of children born in Berkeley, California, and then followed a group of over 1,000 children with a mean IQ of 152 well into middle age. The findings generally support the conclusion that high-IQ children grow up as stable, reasonably successful adults, although the highest scoring individuals (with a mean IQ of 177) failed to achieve greater occupational success or fame than the rest. [*See the biography of Terman.*]

Despite the widespread idea that talented children must be intelligent and show high abilities across the board, the more typical situation is for them to show a high ability in one specific area, and not in others. In this respect, they seem to be on a continuum with those idiot savants who have a remarkable capacity for mental calculation, for instance, but otherwise are woefully weak intellectually. On the other hand, a few gifted children are able to perform at a high level in several domains, especially those domains that share similarities in their symbolic structure, such as chess, mathematics, and music (Winner, 1996).

Prodigies are children who show early signs of extraordinary talent. They tend to be recognized in domains where performance can be easily detected and measured. Some children show expert adult skills at such an early age that they cast doubt on accepted models of cognitive development (Feldman, 1986). For example, Feldman described boys proficient at calculus by age four, and composing concerti at age seven. Prodigies are, by definition, off the developmental scale and thus encounter many problems that are of no consequence to other children. Among other things, it is difficult to find tutors who are advanced enough to teach them, and often parents have to protect prodigies from the fawning and adulation heaped on such precocious children. Not surprisingly, prodigies often fail to develop their talent and end up as unremarkable adults. [*See* Prodigies.]

Talent in mathematics is probably the most widely studied and supported, inasmuch as quantitative skills are of increasing importance to society. Julian Stanley at Johns Hopkins University developed a mathematical talent identification program, which has grown into a national network, that offers testing and accelerated learning courses for able youngsters; this program is now continued under the direction of Stanley's former student and associate, Camille Benbow, at Vanderbilt University (Stanley, Keating, & Fox, 1974).

The Development of Talent: Motivation and Support

Talent might be based on innate sensory or intellectual superiority, but it only remains a promise unless it is cultivated throughout a lifetime. It is true that talented children tend to be driven to develop their gift, and find every opportunity to learn by themselves (Winner, 1996); nevertheless, a great deal of support is needed if they are to realize their potentialities. Benjamin Bloom (1985) described in great detail the sacrifice in time and money that parents have to make in order to find tutors, coaches, and mentors who will refine the potential into actuality.

Young people may give up on developing their talents for a variety of reasons: Lack of resources and opportunities is often the cause. In addition, families that are uninterested or unable to provide encouragement is another. Often, talented teenagers who feel emotionally neglected by parents turn to peers for support, and give up on the strenuous work required to cultivate their gifts further. The best conditions for talent development include two complementary attitudes: an enjoyment of the talent for its own sake, and a clear idea of how it could be parlayed into a lifelong career (Csikszentmihalyi, Rathunde, & Whalen, 1993). Young people talented in music and the arts typically love to play and draw, but they rarely see this as a future occupation. Teenagers who are good at math and science generally don't like to do math or run experiments, but see this as a good way to make a living. In either case, those who combine momentary enjoyment with long-term goals are the ones most likely to persevere.

Even so, the opportunities to use talent once it is developed might not be available in the culture. It has been observed that of the dozens of outstanding young pianists competing for the Van Cliburn prize, only a very few could find gainful employment. Similarly, many excellent young physicists are now out of jobs. There is a huge amount of wasted talent that only serious attention at the national level can correct.

[*See also* Giftedness.]

Bibliography

Bloom, B. (1985). *Developing talent in young people.* New York: Ballantine.

Csikszentmihalyi, M., Rathunde, K., & Whalen, S. (1993). *Talented teenagers: The roots of success and failure.* New York: Cambridge University Press.

Ericsson, K. A., & Charness, N. (1995). Expert performance: Its structure and acquisition. *American Psychologist, 49,* 725–747.

Feldman, D. (1986). *Nature's gambit.* New York: Basic Books.

Gardner, H. (1983). *Frames of mind: The theory of multiple intelligences.* New York: Basic Books.

Howe, M. J. A., Davidson, J. W., & Sloboda, J. A. (in press). Innate talent: Reality or myth? *Behavioral and Brain Sciences.*

Stanley, J. C., Keating, D. P., & Fox, L. H. (Eds.). (1974). *Mathematical talent: Discovery, description, and development.* Baltimore, MD: Johns Hopkins University Press.

Terman, L. M. (1947). Subjects of IQ 170 or above. *Genetic studies of genius* (Vol. 4). Stanford, CA: Stanford University Press.

Winner, E. (1996). *Gifted children: Myths and realities.* New York: Basic Books.

Mihaly Csikszentmihalyi

TASTE. [*This entry comprises two articles: an anatomical and physiological description of human taste buds (and other mechanisms involved); and a survey of the behavioral and functional aspects of taste buds. For a broad overview of the sensory systems (visual, auditory, tactile, and the chemical senses), see* Sensory Systems.]

Biological Organization

The peripheral sensory organs for taste are polarized neuroepithelial cells clustered into buds and distributed on the dorsal surface of the tongue, tongue cheek margin, base of the tongue near ducts of the sublingual glands, the soft palate, pharynx, larynx, epiglottis, uvula, and first one third of the esophagus (Norgren, 1990; Reutter and Witt, 1993; Schiffman, 1983; Scott, 1992). Taste receptor-like cells are also found in the mucosa of the stomach and intestine (Höfer et al., 1996). Taste buds are ovoid-shaped and consist of approximately 50 to 100 cells arranged like segments of an orange. Individual taste cells undergo continuous renewal with a life span of approximately 10 to 10½ days; this renewal process can be compromised by malnutrition (Schiffman, 1983).

Taste cells extend from the base of the bud to the taste pit where they terminate as microvillar taste hairs that project into the mucus of the pit. The apical margin of the pit extends to the epithelial surface to form the taste pore, which averages 4 to 10 microns in diameter. Anatomical studies have shown that individual cells in taste buds differ structurally but it is not known currently whether cells that differ in appearance have different taste functions. Anatomical classifications based on visual appearance of different cells types are as follows: (1) dark cells (type I cells), (2) light cells (type II cells), (3) type III cells, and (4) basal cells (type IV cells). Dark cells are slender cells with dark granules that line the taste pore and appear both at the margin and the center of the taste bud. Dark cells are the most predominant cells in the bud and stain relatively electron dense. Light cells cells are slender and stain less electron dense than type I cells. Type III cells are similar to light cells but have numerous dense-cored vesicles not found in light cells. Basal cells are situated at the base of the taste bud and lie directly on the basal lamina that separates the taste bud epithelium from the adjacent connective tissue (Reutter and Witt, 1993).

Taste buds on the tongue are located on specialized epithelial projections termed papillae. Four different kinds of papillae occur on the tongue: fungiform, foliate, and circumvallate (which contain taste buds) and filiform papillae (which do not contain taste buds). Approximately 200 fungiform papillae are located on the anterior two thirds of the tongue, with the highest concentration at the tip of the tongue. Fungiform papillae are shaped somewhat like mushrooms and bear 1 to 20 taste buds at their apex. Foliate papillae occur on the posterior-lateral sides of the tongue and consist of linear depressions or vertical folds. Taste receptor cells in foliate papillae tend to be especially sensitive to sour tastes. Circumvallate papillae contain the largest number of taste buds and are situated on the posterior tongue arranged in a chevron-shaped form pointing caudally. There are 8 to 12 circumvallate papillae with buds located in deep moats surrounding the papilla. The burrows and trenches of both foliate and circumvallate papillae contain seromucous secretions that derive from von Ebner's glands. These seromucous secretions are believed to circulate tastants so that they come in contact with receptors; in addition, these secretions remove waste from the crypts of the foliate and circumvallate papillae. Filiform papillae are the numerous conical projections of epithelium on the tongue that function to provide friction for movement of food; these do not bear taste buds.

Three cranial nerves transmit information from taste buds to the central nervous system (CNS) and ultimately to the brain. These three nerves are the chorda tympani nerve (seventh nerve), the glossopharyngeal nerve (ninth nerve), and the vagus nerve (tenth nerve) (Norgren, 1990; Pritchard, 1991). Taste buds on the anterior two thirds of the tongue are innervated by axons of the chorda tympani nerve. The chorda tympani not only transmits information from buds on fungiform papillae but also from buds located on the anterior walls of the foliate papillae. The greater superficial petrosal nerve (another branch of the seventh nerve) relays information from most taste buds of the soft palate although a few are innervated by the deep petrosal branch of the glossopharyngeal nerve. Taste buds in the circumvallate papillae as well as posterior walls of the foliate papillae are innervated by the glossopharyngeal nerve. The superior laryngeal branch of the vagus nerve innervates taste buds located on the far posterior tongue, the epiglottis, the larynx, and the esophagus.

These three cranial nerves project to the rostral portion of the nucleus of the solitary tract (NST) in the medulla in the brain stem (Norgren, 1990; Pritchard, 1991; Schiffman and Warwick, 1992; Scott, 1992). The solitary tract (NST) is a longitudinally organized column of neurons in the dorsal medulla that receives both taste information as well as visceral information from sensory fibers originating in the esophagus, stomach, intestines, and liver (Pritchard, 1991; Schiffman and Warwick, 1992). Visceral projections terminate in the caudal portion of the NST. The NST is the first neural projection center in which joint processing taste and visceral sensory information can occur. Visceral information from the NST is relayed directly to motor nuclei associated with ingestive and digestive behavior (Sawchenko, 1983 for a review) including the dorsal motor nucleus of the vagus nerve and the nucleus ambiguus. The dorsal motor nucleus of the vagus innervates the gastrointestinal tract, and activation of the motor fibers from the dorsal motor nucleus induces gastric, intestinal, and pancreatic secretion, increased gastrointestinal peristalsis and tone, and constriction of the gallbladder to expel bile. The nucleus ambiguus gives rise to parasympathetic preganglionic fibers of the vagus, glossopharyngeal, and accessory nerves, which terminate in striated muscles of the larynx and the pharynx. The NST also projects to motor nuclei of three cranial nerves (facial [VII], trigeminal [V], and hypoglossal [XII] nerves) that innervate muscles of the face and tongue. These motor nuclei receive projections from both the rostral (taste) and caudal (visceral) sections of the NST. Thus the anatomical arrangement of the NST permits taste signals to impact ingestive and digestive activity. The NST also receives information from the olfactory (first cranial) nerve (Van Buskirk and Erickson, 1977).

Neurons from the rostral portion of NST (those that predominantly relay taste information) project to the ventroposteromedial nucleus of the thalamus (Pritchard, 1991). Axons from the caudal division of NST (those that predominantly relay visceral information) branch to the parabrachial nucleus with subsequent projections to lateral hypothalamus, amygdala, and the bed nucleus of stria terminalis. Taste neurons in the ventroposteromedial nucleus of the thalamus then project to the primary gustatory cortex, which consists of two discontinuous areas, the insula-operculum as well as a spatially separate area on the lateral convexity. Neurons on the anterior insula finally project to secondary cortex that is located on the orbitofrontal surface. Electrophysiological studies in animal models have been performed to determine how taste information is coded in these pathways.

General afferent activity in the oral cavity is mediated by the trigeminal (fifth cranial) nerve as well as free nerve endings of the seventh, ninth, and tenth nerves (Green, 1996). The sensations that result from activation of these free nerve endings are currently called chemesthetic sensations and include touch, pain, and temperature. Fibers of the lingual branch of the trigeminal nerve terminate in fungiform and foliate papillae and transmit chemesthetic sensations from the anterior two thirds of the tongue. Pungent sensations such as those from chili peppers and nicotine are examples of chemesthetic qualities. Chemesthetic sensations are generally not considered tastes but rather a different sense related to nociception.

Taste sensations occur when chemicals from food and beverages stimulate a variety of structural components in taste cells during chewing and swallowing. These structural components include receptors associated with ion channels, second messenger systems, and transepithelial currents (Kinnamon and Margolskee, 1996; Spielman, Huque, Whitney, & Brand, 1992). Our present knowledge of taste transduction suggests that sodium channels, potassium channels, and several second messenger systems, the adenylate cyclase system, the phosphatidylinositol system, and the α-gustducin–phosphodiesterase pathway play a role in taste transduction (see Gilbertson, 1993; Kinnamon and Cummings, 1992; Margolskee, 1993 for reviews). The salty taste of sodium salts results from the influx of $Na+$ ions through sodium channels in the membranes of taste cells (Schiffman, Lockhead, & Maes, 1983). The salty taste can be modulated by the movement of the anion of the salt as it diffuses across tight junctions through paracellular pathways (Ye, Heck, & DeSimone, 1992). The taste of potassium salts, like sodium salts, involves conductance of the potassium cation through taste cell membranes (Kim and Mistretta, 1993). Some but not all sweet compounds bind to seven-membrane-spanning cell surface receptors that activate the adenylate cyclase second messenger cascade (Lindemann, 1996). In the 1990s, the thinking is that two pathways play the most important role in bitter taste transduction: (1) the phosphatidylinositol cascade second messenger cascade, and (2) the α-gustducin–phosphodiesterase pathway (Lindemann, 1996). Transduction mechanisms for tastes other than salty, sweet, and bitter (such as calcium salts, organic and fatty acids, amino acids, peptides, and astringent compounds) are not well understood.

Bibliography

Gilbertson, T. A. (1993). The physiology of vertebrate taste reception. *Current Opinions in Neurobiology, 3(4)*, 532–539.

Kim, M., & Mistretta, C. M. (1993). 4-aminopyridine reduces chorda tympani nerve taste responses to potassium and alkali salts in rat. *Brain Research, 612*, 96–103.

Kinnamon, S. C., & Cummings, T. A. (1992). Chemosensory transduction mechanisms in taste. *Annual Review of Physiology, 54*, 715–731.

Kinnamon, S. C., & Margolskee, R. F. (1996). Mechanisms

of taste transduction. *Current Opinions in Neurobiology, 6*, 506–513.
Lindemann, B. (1996). Chemoreception: tasting the sweet and the bitter. *Current Biology, 6*, 1234–1237.
Margolskee, R. F. (1993). The biochemistry and molecular biology of taste transduction. *Current Opinions in Neurobiology, 3*, 526–531.
Norgren, R. (1990). Gustatory system. In G. Paxinos (Ed.), *The human nervous system* (pp. 845–861). San Diego: Academic Press.
Pritchard, T. C. (1991). The primate gustatory system. In T. V. Getchell, R. L. Doty, L. M. Bartoshuk, & J. B. Snow (Eds.), *Smell and taste in health and disease* (pp. 109–125). New York: Raven Press.
Reutter, K., & Witt, M. (1993). Morphology of vertebrate taste organs and their nerve supply. In S. A. Simon, & S. D. Roper (Eds.), *Mechanisms of taste transduction*. Boca Raton, FL: CRC Press.
Sawchenko, P. E. (1983). Central connections of the sensory and motor nuclei of the vagus nerve. *Journal of the Autonomic Nervous System, 9*, 13–26.
Schiffman, S. S. (1983). Taste and smell in disease. *New England Journal of Medicine, 308*, 1275–1279, 1337–1343.
Schiffman, S. S., Lockhead, E., & Maes, F. W. (1983). Amiloride reduces the taste intensity of Na^+ and Li^+ salts and sweeteners. *Proceedings of the National Academy of Sciences USA*, 80, 6136–6140.
Scott, T. R. (1992). Taste: The neural basis of body wisdom. *World Review of Nutritionists and Dieticians, 67*, 1–39.
Spielmen, A. I., Huque, T., Whitney, G., & Brand, J. G. (1992). The diversity of bitter taste signal transduction mechanisms. *Soc. Gen. Physiol. Ser., 47*, 307–324.
Van Buskirk, R. L., & Erickson, R. P. (1977). Odorant responses in taste neurons of the rat NTS. *Brain Research, 135*, 287–303.
Ye, Q., Heck, G. L., & DeSimone, J. A. (1992). The anion paradox in sodium taste reception: Resolution by voltage-clamp studies. *Science, 254*, 724–726.

Susan Schiffman

Behavioral and Functional Aspects

The chemical senses, smell and taste, are the most primitive of the sensory systems, having evolved in coelenterates some 500 million years ago. Accordingly, they serve the most primitive biological functions: reproduction and feeding. Smell has become more specialized for the former, taste for the latter. The sense of taste lies at the beginning of a long chemosensory tube, extending from tongue to intestines, with receptors along the way having sensitivity to the molecules being liberated by the digestive process. Taste is privileged, however, for it is set at the threshold between the external and internal milieux, the point at which a final decision must be made to accept a chemical. Therefore, signals from the taste system serve not only to identify a stimulus in the mouth, but also to drive the reflexes of swallowing or of rejection, to initiate visceral reflexes that prepare the gut for digestion, and to activate sensations of pleasure or disgust. Through these various processes, taste largely manages dietary selection.

Development of the Taste System

Gustatory information is transduced by taste cells, which are gathered in groups of 50 to 150 in goblet-shaped taste buds. These, in turn, are concentrated in small mounds on the tongue (papillae), or in the epithelium of the soft palate, larynx, pharynx, and epiglottis.

Development proceeds from large to small structures: from papillae to buds to cells. Papillae are formed between 8 and 9 weeks of gestation, appearing as protuberances on the tongue that stand out in increasingly bold relief as the epithelium that surrounds them grows downward. Soon thereafter, buds inhabit the papillae. The cells within them are initially covered by epithelium, but gradually elongate to span this overlying tissue. At 12 weeks, a channel forms in the epithelium, opening a pore at the top of the bud through which developing taste cells may send microvilli to sample the chemical environment. Taste cells are formed and functional at 26 weeks. A fetus will increase its rate of sucking *in utero* when saccharin is injected into the amniotic fluid, indicating that sweet sensitivity is not only intact well before birth, but also offers reward and can motivate behavior.

Functional Architecture of Taste

A series of basic issues may be addressed to define the organization of the taste system.

The Stimulus Characteristics that Determine Taste Quality. There is no single feature of a molecule that confers the full range of taste qualities, as wavelength does for color, or frequency for pitch. Rather, taste stimuli appear to be organized along the physiological dimension of their effects on health. The more toxic a chemical, the more it is perceived as objectionable and is rejected; the more nutritious a substance is, the more appealing and acceptable it will be. This innate gustatory wisdom is not surprising, for those of our predecessors who made appropriate selections of the few nutrients from among the many toxins in their environments were more likely to survive to become our ancestors.

Primary Tastes. There is a wealth of evidence from studies of receptor processes and from human reports that four primary taste qualities—sweet, salty, sour, and bitter—define the gustatory domain. Others argue that these divisions simply reflect a dearth of descriptors for taste experiences, which are actually more complex and subtle than this scheme would imply. Indeed, when linguistic biases are reduced through use of semantic differential scales, the separation among the primary tastes becomes less obvious. Still, the existence of primary taste qualities is widely accepted, in part because it offers a useful organization for the taste system.

The number of primary taste qualities is not yet settled. Sweet, salty, sour, and bitter have always been recognized, while other candidates have come and gone. *Umami* (Japanese for "delicious"), represented by the taste of monosodium glutamate, is thought by many to be a fifth primary, the taste of complex carbohydrates may be a sixth, and fat a seventh.

Neuron Types. The question of primary taste qualities relates to the perceptual organization of tastes. A related issue is whether there is a small number of discrete types of taste cells—one for each primary quality—that impose that organization, or whether each taste cell has a unique range of sensitivity. Thus, the activity profiles of thousands of taste cells in rodents and primates in response to batteries of taste stimuli have been analyzed to determine whether they could be categorized into groups. They can. The number of categories is typically three or four, one of which, comprising about 40% of the cells in primates, is mainly responsive to sugars. A second category, with about 25% of the cells in primates is mainly responsive to sodium salts. A third group is more broadly responsive to a range of qualities, but particularly to acids and bitter compounds. If there is a fourth, it is more specifically responsive to bitter stimuli. Within each group, the neurons do not have identical profiles. However, they are significantly related to each other, and significantly different from the profiles of cells outside the group.

The implication of gustatory neuron types is reinforced by the results of using a taste modifier. Amiloride is a compound that, when placed on the tongue, largely blocks the sensation of saltiness. Recordings from rat taste cells revealed that those in the salt group had their responses to NaCl severely inhibited, while the smaller response to NaCl in the acid-bitter group of cells was unaffected. Thus, the activity in a particular channel of cells was parallel to the gustatory experience, implying that this discrete group is responsible for signaling saltiness. This is strong evidence for the existence of gustatory neuron types, and for their relevance in transmitting information on the primary taste qualities.

The Gustatory Neural Code. In the preceding section it was shown that taste cells could be categorized, and that those within each group bore primary responsibility for one taste of quality. Thus, it is possible that each group represents a labeled line for its associated quality. The persistent difficulty facing this *labeled-line theory* is that most taste cells are sensitive to a wide range of qualities. The more broadly responsive a cell is, the larger the portion of its activity that is devoted to stimuli outside the labeled line of which it is presumed to be a part. This portion must be ascribed to noise.

The competing *pattern theory* has no such problem. Here the notion is that all cells contribute equally to the signal for taste quality through their relative rates of response. A stimulus evokes a certain rate of discharge from each taste cell, generating a pattern of activity unique to itself, and that serves as its neural representation. The shape of the pattern carries the information on quality, while the total area under the pattern represents stimulus intensity. Since a neuron contributes one point to the pattern, each is theoretically of equal importance in conveying information on every stimulus. The more similar two patterns of response are, the closer the perceived qualities of the two stimuli that evoked them.

Pattern theory has appeal for several reasons. First, it incorporates the characteristic breadth of responsiveness among taste cells as its fundamental tenet. Second, it employs all cells for all qualities, a useful feature in a system with so few neurons. Finally, it has predictive power. Stimuli that elicit highly similar patterns are difficult to distinguish from one another, require more time for discrimination, and cross-adapt readily with one another.

Thus, there is strong evidence both for labeled lines, each responsible for coding a particular primary taste quality, and for patterns of activity whose shapes, read across all taste cells, convey the quality code. The primary reason why a resolution between these theories has been elusive is that both account for nearly all the data. Stimulus patterns become more highly correlated as more of the neural discharges share a common channel. While a patterning theorist may not recognize the existence of a channel, and a labeled-line theorist nothing *but* the channel, the fact is that the same cells, channel or not, are generating most of the activity.

In fact, the two systems may operate cooperatively, either in series or parallel. Bold distinctions among primary qualities may be made within channels, then subtle discriminations among stimuli within a primary quality (say glucose versus fructose) may be based on the patterns they evoke. The suggestion of parallel cooperation comes from studies of the catfish. This creature has one set of taste cells specifically and exquisitely tuned to l-arginine, and another broadly responsive to a range of other amino acids, salts, and acids. Thus, the catfish devotes a large portion of its neural resources to the identification of a particularly salient stimulus (a labeled line), while reserving the balance to survey the remainder of its chemical environment (patterns).

Taste and Hedonism

Nearly all gustatory experiences include a component of pleasure or disgust. The visual or auditory systems may survey the environment continuously and often without passion; taste, however, is called upon only infrequently to pass judgment on the acceptability of allowing a substance to enter the body. This evaluation drives brainstem reflexes for accepting or rejecting the chemical, along with an hedonic aspect that provides the motivation to extend a bite to a meal, a meal to a diet.

The anatomical connections of taste are appropriate for this role. Taste fibers project not only to the thalamus and primary gustatory cortex for an analysis of quality and intensity, but also to higher-order cortical areas and to hypothalamus and amygdala for hedonic coloring. Having discrete processing areas for analysis of quality and of hedonics means that these two components may be separated in experience. Offer a hungry person glucose and he will report that it is sweet, strong, and pleasant. Let him eat to satiety first, and he will describe the same glucose as sweet and strong, but not pleasant.

Disorders of Taste

The positive hedonics of eating are our most basic reward, providing pleasure so intense that it often overrides our most resolute intentions. Negative hedonics associated with toxins or spoiled foods offer us protection. Loss of these sensations diminishes our quality of life and exposes us to chemical dangers. Indeed, a recent survey of patients with chemosensory disorders revealed that 68% reported a diminished quality of life, 56% felt their psychological well-being had been compromised, and 46% said that the deficit had affected their appetite or weight.

The term *ageusia* refers to taste loss, and it may be general (no taste sensations) or partial (the loss of certain qualities). A pathological decline in taste sensitivity is termed *hypogeusia*, and it too may be general or partial. Distortions of taste perception are referred to as *dysgeusias* (or *parageusias*). They may involve the perversion of a normal taste, or a taste sensation that occurs in the absence of chemical stimulation (a gustatory hallucination). *Hypergeusia* refers to an unusually enhanced taste sensitivity, and it may be general to all qualities, or partial. Finally, *gustatory agnosia* refers to the inability to identify or categorize taste stimuli, despite the capacity to experience them. The primary causes of taste deficits are loss of access to the receptor, damage to or loss of receptor cells, and destruction of sensory nerves or central gustatory relays.

When access to receptors is compromised, it is typically because of abnormalities in saliva, the broth of water, electrolytes, proteins, and mucus that creates the chemical environment into which external stimuli are introduced. Saliva contains Na^+ and Ca^{++} to carry the depolarizing potentials of the taste signal. It has a protein, dubbed VEG, that presumably transports hydrophobic stimuli to receptor sites that would not otherwise be available to them. It has HCO_3^- to buffer acids, and enzymes to begin the digestive process. Variations from normal concentrations of any of these except the last affects taste sensitivity.

Taste receptors are in constant flux: the entire receptor population is renewed about every twelve days. Therefore, radiation, chemotherapy, or the use of antirheumatic or antibiotic drugs may destroy taste receptors, or slow their continuous replacement by interfering with cell division. In either case, ageusia or hypogeusia results. Receptor processes are also involved in taste loss associated with diabetes and hypothyroidism, though by unknown mechanisms. Severe hypogeusia results from a genetic abnormality called familial dysautonomia, in which no papillae or taste buds are produced. Neural growth into the tongue is attenuated, causing loss not only of taste, but of oral somatosensation as well.

Peripheral or central afferent fibers may be damaged in several ways. Upper respiratory tract infections can interfere with the function of the chorda tympani nerve as it courses through the middle ear. Bell's palsy, resulting from damage to the facial nerve, is often accompanied by taste loss. In the central nervous system, epilepsy is sometimes presaged by a gustatory aura, and 4% of epileptic patients report taste hallucinations. Psychiatric disorders, including anorexia nervosa, bulimia, and occasionally obesity, interfere with the hedonic responses to foods. Purging bulimics also damage taste receptor cells on the palate.

Conclusion

The sense of taste is situated at the interface between the external and internal environments. Its mission is to match the available chemical resources around it with the biochemical needs of the body; thus, it must monitor both. Taste has two faces, one of which is turned outward to detect and to orchestrate the rejection of toxins while recognizing and accepting nutrients; the other is turned inward to monitor the effects of accepted foods, and to remain current with bodily needs. The four known systems to which taste information is distributed—somatic reflexes for acceptance or rejection, autonomic reflexes to initiate digestion, cortical processing of quality and intensity, and cortical and limbic analysis of hedonic value—are the vehicles through which the ever-changing match is made.

If successful, stimuli with the greatest hedonic appeal should also be those that the body most needs at any time. The better a food tastes, the better it should be for us. Yet in industrialized societies, the reverse seems true. Indeed, the chemical environment in which our taste systems evolved for 500 million years has changed just in the past few centuries. The effort had been to consume sufficient carbohydrates, proteins, fats, and sodium to live long enough to reproduce, and it remains so in much of the world. With the technical advances that have provided these nutrients in abundance, however, the goal is to resist consuming so much as to invite pathologies that had not played into our evolutionary development: adult onset diabetes, cardiovascular disease, hypertension. The sense of taste, tuned exquisitely to the chemical environment in which we evolved, has clashed with the society that has learned to pander to it. Thus the biological pleasure of consumption is dulled by the social disgrace of gluttony and by deleterious effects on health that appear only at ages our ancestors never achieved.

Bibliography

Bartoshuk, L. M. (1978). History of taste research. In E. C. Carterette & M. P. Friedman (Eds.), *Handbook of perception* (Vol. 6A, New York: Academic Press, pp. 3–18).

Doty, R. L. (Ed.). (1995). *Handbook of olfaction and gustation.* New York: Marcel Dekker.

Getchell, T. V., Doty, R. L., Bartoshuk, L. M., & Snow, J. B. (Eds.). (1991). *Smell and taste in health and disease.* New York: Raven Press.

Norgren, R. (1984). Central neural mechanisms in taste. In I. Darien-Smith (Ed.), *Handbook of physiology—The nervous system: Vol. 3. Sensory processes 1* (pp. 1087–1128). Washington, DC: American Physiological Society.

Pfaffmann, C., Frank, M., Bartoshuk, L. M., & Snell, T. C. (1976). Coding gustatory information in the squirrel monkey chorda tympani. In J. M. Sprague & A. N. Epstein (Eds.), *Progress in psychobiology and physiological psychology* (Vol. 6, pp. 1–27). New York: Academic Press.

Rolls, E. T. (1997). Taste and olfactory processing in the brain and its relation to the control of eating. *Critical Reviews in Neurobiology, 11,* 263–287.

Schiffman, S. S., Erickson, R. P. (1971). A psychophysical model for gustatory quality. *Physiology and Behavior, 7,* 617–633.

Steiner, J. E. (1979). Human facial expressions in response to taste and smell stimulation. In H. W. Reese & L. P. Lipsitt (Eds.), *Advances in child development* (Vol. 13, pp. 257–295). New York: Academic Press.

Thomas R. Scott

TASTE AVERSION LEARNING is a form of classical conditioning in which animals or humans come to avoid a taste conditioned stimulus (CS) that has previously been paired with a treatment that produces transient illness (unconditioned stimulus; US). Simply put, animals learn to avoid foods that may have made them sick, and they do this with remarkable facility. Thus, taste aversion learning is unusually robust and has clear adaptive advantages, particularly in animal species that must select from a range of nutrients, some of which may be toxic.

Taste aversion learning is interesting when viewed in this adaptive context, but it is also interesting for other reasons. For one it is unusual because it occurs so rapidly and potently under conditions that could not support other types of learning. As such it provides a challenge to theorists who aim to develop general laws of learning that apply over the entire continuum of learning types. Likewise, it challenges neuroscientists who try to generate models for the types of neuronal events that can underlie learning or plasticity. Also, since humans, as well as other animals, readily display taste aversion learning there are a range of situations in which such aversions can affect people's choices of foods and beverages.

Taste aversion learning was first described in some detail in the 1960s and the original reports met with considerable skepticism because certain features of this learning did not conform to the general laws of learning accepted at that time. For example, while most conditioning protocols require a great many CS–US pairings or trials before a reliable conditioned response can be measured, strong conditioned taste aversions are frequently demonstrated after a single trial, that is only one pairing of CS (taste) and US (illness). Although one-trial learning is not unique in the conditioning literature it is quite unusual. Even more unusual is the fact that taste aversion learning can occur despite lengthy delays between exposure to the CS (taste) and US (illness). This means that a person or animal can eat something and become ill minutes or hours later and still develop a learned taste aversion, and they may do so after only one such experience. Since taste aversions were acquired so quickly, under what were viewed as particularly unfavorable conditions for learning, they seemed to some more like innate than learned behaviors. However, John Garcia's original studies, as well as the hundreds of experiments done since then, have amply controlled for other explanations of taste aversions and taste aversion learning has become widely accepted as a clear example of a type of learning shaped by its adaptive significance. That is, an effective learning mechanisms for toxin avoidance can not require multiple conditioning trials since multiple exposures to a toxin can lead to severe illness or death. Similarly, an effective learning mechanism cannot require nearly simultaneous exposure to taste and illness since the gastrointestinal system is slow and ingested toxins take time to cause illness.

In the laboratory, taste aversion learning has most often been studied in the rat. This is likely to have been a fortuitous choice since rats have proven to be good at taste aversion learning. This may be due to two characteristics of this species; one is that they are omnivores and opportunistic foragers, which means that in their natural environment they frequently sample new foods and are thus at risk for encountering toxins. Secondly, they are unable to vomit, which means that once they eat something toxic they can't dispose of it easily. For these reasons, this species may have been under particularly strong evolutionary pressure to develop a robust and efficient taste aversion conditioning mechanism as a means of toxin avoidance. But rats are certainly not unique in this ability. Taste aversion learning has been demonstrated in an enormous range of animal species, from the very simple, such as the garden slug, *limax*, to the very complex, such as humans.

In the laboratory, training generally consists of the presentation of a palatable taste solution, such as dilute saccharin, followed by the injection of a nonlethal toxin. In the untrained rat, saccharin is highly preferred and consumed with enthusiasm. This makes the behavior of the conditioned animals particularly striking, because they avoid the saccharin and appear to actually be disgusted by it. In this example it is the taste of the solution, and not its odor, that serves as the CS. Odors can also become effective CSs in taste aversion learning, but for the rat at least, they are not as effective as tastes. One feature of a taste stimulus that is particularly important in this learning is its novelty. Thus, robust, single-trial learning occurs when the CS taste is novel (e.g., the animal has not been exposed to it before) while learning is considerably less rapid and efficient when the CS taste is familiar.

People also acquire learned taste aversions, and these often arise when the consumption of a food or drink is followed by nausea or gastrointestinal malaise. Sometimes the illness is actually caused by the food or beverage consumed, but it is frequently the case that the food and illness are only coincidentally associated. Nonetheless, strong, durable aversions to specific tastes can develop even when people recognize that the offending food was not the actual cause of their illness. An example of the former type of aversion is the rather common occurrence of aversions to specific alcoholic beverages, such as bourbon or tequila that were consumed in excess and led to a bout of nausea and vomiting. Such aversions are particularly prominent in surveys done on populations of college students. Another situation in which food aversions develop is in patients receiving cancer chemotherapy. Drugs used to treat cancer, while frequently effective in halting the growth of tumor cells, can have severe side effects including nausea and vomiting. Cancer patients often develop aversions to specific foods they consume before these treatments, in spite of the fact that the patients generally recognize that their chemotherapy and not their lunch was the cause of their unpleasant symptoms. Recognition that cancer patients are at risk for the development of learned food aversions and that this can affect their appetite and nutritional status has led to interventions that can prevent the development of these aversions.

The rapid acquisition and robustness of learned taste aversions have made them an attractive tool in therapeutic efforts to modify problem behaviors such as alcoholism and smoking. It is interesting to note that a natural consequence of alcohol overconsumption is illness, often including severe nausea and vomiting. As noted above, these symptoms are effective in inducing aversions to specific alcoholic beverages in many college students. Do alcoholics fail to acquire such aversions? If they acquire such aversions, how do the aversions subsequently affect their drinking? A survey of alcoholics in a treatment facility indicated that alcoholics do acquire taste aversions to alcoholic beverages as a natural consequence of overconsumption. In general, when a taste aversion to a specific alcoholic beverage was acquired, the subjects did not drink that particular beverage again, choosing to drink other alcoholic beverages instead. Chemical aversion therapy involves the use of drugs, such as emetine, to induce nausea and vomiting after alcohol consumption. This form of therapy has been incorporated into a range of alcoholism treatment packages. Available outcome data from a number of these programs indicate that the effectiveness of their treatment packages in promoting abstinence is quite good. However, the contribution of chemical aversion therapy, per se, to the effectiveness of the entire treatment package has not been explicitly evaluated and therefore it remains unknown. Aversion therapy has also been used as an aid to smoking cessation. This involves a rapid smoking procedure that conforms to the taste aversion learning paradigm in that it involves pairing the flavor cues associated with smoking cigarettes with aversive symptoms such as nausea and headache. This procedure has been reported to be effective in producing aversions to the taste and smell of cigarettes and to improve abstinence rates in smoking cessation programs.

The discovery of taste aversion learning grew out of relatively esoteric studies in animal learning laboratories. The impact of these discoveries has been widespread, both in the way that learning theorists look at the learning process and in the practical applications of these findings to clinical problems such as food aversions in cancer patients and promoting abstinence in smokers and alcoholics. Promising directions for the future of taste aversion research are likely to be as varied. One area that is particularly challenging is the identification of the neural mechanisms that underlie this learning. The robustness and rapidity of the learning make it likely that dramatic changes in neuronal signaling accompany it. It remains to be seen whether these changes prove to be similar to those currently being uncovered for other learning paradigms, such as fear conditioning, or prove to be quite different, because of the unique demands of this learning.

[*See also* Learning.]

Bibliography

Bernstein, I. L. (1991). Flavor aversion. In T. V. Getchell, R. L. Doty, L. M. Bartoshuk, & J. B. Snow (Eds.), *Smell and taste in health and disease* (pp. 417–428). New York: Raven Press. A recent overview of research on taste aversion learning.

Braveman, N. S., & Bronstein, P. (Eds.). (1985). Experimental assessments and clinical applications of conditioned food aversions. *Annals of the New York Academy of Sciences, 443,* 1–441. A collection of chapters covering a broad range of research on conditioned food aversions.

Garcia, J., Hankins, W. G., & Rusiniak, K. W. (1974). Behavioral regulation of the *milieu interne* in man and rat. *Science, 185,* 824–831. A classic description of taste aversion learning in an adaptive context by John Garcia, the man who is responsible for the original work identifying and characterizing this learning.

Logue, A. W., Ophir, I., & Strauss, K. E. (1981). The acquisition of taste aversions in humans. *Behavioral Research and Therapy, 19,* 319–333.

Ilene L. Bernstein

TAT. *See* Thematic Apperception Test.

TAVISTOCK INSTITUTE is a well-established social science research and consulting organization located in London, England. A central theme underlying much of its work over the last 50 years has been the importance of systemic ways of thinking about social and organizational issues, leading to a speciality in dealing with the psychological and political dynamics of development and change. The Tavistock Institute enjoys an international reputation in the design of work organizations, the psychodynamics of groups and larger social systems, collective processes for development and change, and action research approaches to study and intervention.

In 1946, the Tavistock Clinic, which was about to join the National Health Service, received a grant from the Rockefeller Foundation to found a separate, independent organization that would address "wider problems not accepted in the area of mental health." The Tavistock Institute of Human Relations was incorporated as a not-for-profit organization in 1947, stating aims that remain operational today: "the study of human relations in conditions of well-being, conflict and change, in the community, the work group and the larger organization, and the promotion of the effectiveness of individuals and organisations." The founders—notably Wilfred Bion, a psychiatrist; Eric Trist, a clinical and social psychologist; and Jock Sutherland, a psychologist and psychoanalyst—wanted to foster peacetime applications of wartime advances in "social psychiatry," a phrase coined in reference to a philosophy for treating mental-health outpatients in a way that looked beyond the psychopathology of the individual to the pathology of the social setting that produced it.

During World War II, the institute's founders used social psychiatry to advise the army about underlying psychological factors related to morale and effectiveness. A significant change program, the War Office Selection Boards, concerned recruiting an enormous number of new officers in a way that cut through conventional socioeconomic barriers. Another program, the Civil Resettlement Units, established transitional communities that helped tens of thousands of returning prisoners of war readapt to civilian life. After the war, the success of these programs laid the groundwork for the newly formed institute to make a significant contribution to social reconstruction.

The first two decades at the institute brought scientific innovations that continue to be influential worldwide. "Sociotechnical systems," an approach to job and organizational design, considers the interdependencies between psychological, technical, economic, and other needs for flows of work, tasks, and roles. The "group relations" model applies the British "object relations" school and social-systems theory to the understanding of small group, intergroup, large group, and institutional dynamics. The internationally known Leicester Conference, operating since 1957, still provides an extensive opportunity to study authority, leadership, and organization. This work continues at the institute under the Group Relations Programme, directed by Eric Miller, a social anthropologist, who was also significantly involved with the development of sociotechnical systems theory.

Current staff build on these authoritative traditions while applying newly emerging theories and methodologies to contemporary organizational and social challenges. In 1990, a reorganization resulted in the creation of the units and programs that now carry out the institute's work under the phrase "social science in action." On average, 40 staff work at the Tavistock Institute. Its psychologists apply psychoanalysis, cognitive theory, social psychology and organizational psychology, while the institute's early commitment to interdisciplinary collaboration also resulted in scientific staff being recruited from social anthropology, sociology, economics, and political science.

In addition to the Group Relations Programme, the Organizational Change and Technological Innovation Programme, codirected by Richard Holti, an industrial sociologist, and Jean Neumann, an organizational behaviorist, focuses on organizational design, development, and "change agentry." Elliot Stern, a political scientist, directs the Evaluation, Development, and Review Unit, which specializes in participatory approaches to the evaluation of public policy. Frank Heller, a social and organizational psychologist, directs the Centre for Decision-Making Studies, which coordinates an international network of scientists concerned with management practices.

One constant throughout the institute's history has been its journal, *Human Relations: Towards the Integration of Social Sciences*, also founded in 1946. Interdisciplinary and international, this journal ushered in the beginning of several fields of psychology, notably social psychology, occupational and organizational psychology, and organizational behavior. Owned and edited by the Tavistock Institute, it remains in the top ten of the most cited journals.

Bibliography

Dicks, H. (1970). *Fifty years of the Tavistock Clinic*. London: Routledge. Provides a thorough history of the organization from which the Tavistock Institute founders emerged, with some reference to the institute's inception from the perspective of the clinic.

Everett, J. E. (1994). The journal relations of *Human Relations, Human Relations, 1*, 1–13. Summarizes research on the international use and influence of social science journals and indicates that *Human Relations* is in the top ten.

Heller, F. (Ed.). (1992). *Decision-making and leadership*. Cambridge, England: Cambridge University Press. Provides a collection of recent organizational psychology essays on the relationship between processes of decision-making and the development of organizational leaders.

Miller, E. J. (1993). *From dependency to autonomy: Studies in organization and change*. London: Free Association Books. Draws together action research and consultancy projects from two decades in which the combined perspectives of group relations and social-systems theory are applied.

Miller, E. J., & Rice, A. K. (1967). *Systems of organisation*. London: Tavistock. The influential book by two social anthropologists applying psychoanalysis, field theory, and systems thinking into the organizational theory that became known as sociotechnical systems.

Neumann, J. E., Holti, R., & Standing, H. (1995). *Change everything at once! The Tavistock Institute's guide to developing teamwork in manufacturing*. Didcot, England: Management Books 2000. Demonstrates a new generation of action research that combines classic sociotechnical systems thinking with other organizational theory and approaches to organizational development that use large-group planning and problem-solving.

Stern, E. (1995). Editorial. *Evaluation: The International Journal of Theory, Research, and Practice, 1*, 5–11. Introduces the inaugural issue of this new journal and summarizes a practical rationale and the theoretical values underlying participatory and developmental evaluation of public and social policy.

Trist, E., & Murray, H. (1990/1993). *The social engagement of social science: A Tavistock approach. Volume 1: The sociopsychological perspective. Volume 2: The sociotechnical perspective*. Philadelphia: University of Pennsylvania Press/London: Free Association Books. Brings together in one place many of the original articles that underpinned the application of psychoanalysis to groups and organizations and combines them with previously less available, relevant work.

Jean E. Neumann and Eric J. Miller

TEACHERS. [*This entry comprises two articles:* Assessment of Teacher Effectiveness *and* Teacher Relationships. *The first article provides a general survey of assessments of teacher effectiveness in various contexts. The second article describes the nature of the relationship between teachers and students and between teachers and other groups. For a general discussion of learning, see* Learning.]

Assessment of Teacher Effectiveness

Addressing teacher effectiveness and its measurement manifestation—teacher evaluation—is a complex task because teacher effectiveness is a determinant of complex, interacting factors, including legal, political, social, research, theory, and measurement factors. For example, within the legal context there are various constitutional, statutory, and case law considerations that must be utilized to balance the individual rights of teachers and those of society (Tucker & Kindred, 1997). Although legal issues are complex, teacher effectiveness (as defined in retention or dismissal of teachers) from a legal perspective deals essentially with determining that a teacher knows her or his subject matter, can motivate and engage students in learning, and can maintain discipline. Although states mandate general areas that need to be included in the evaluation process, the specific performance standards are typically left to the discretion of the local school board. For example, in California, the state deems the following areas a mandatory part of evaluation: student achievement, instructional strategies, ability to implement curriculum objectives, and the establishment of a suitable learning environment.

Legal Issues

Tucker and Kindred (1997) report that the use of student achievement data for teacher evaluation purposes is a relatively new and controversial development. Another controversial area in the selection of performance criteria for teacher evaluation is the use of standardized tests for assessing teachers' knowledge. The court in one case has upheld the use of the National Teacher Examination (NTE) as a basis for verifying minimal level of knowledge within a subject area. However, in another case the court noted that the examination does not measure teaching skill or effectiveness. Hence, tests such as the NTE may be used for assessing content-area knowledge, but they have not been accepted as an indicant of teacher performance per se.

Tucker and Kindred (1997) note that 10 legal principles need to be observed in any teacher evaluation. These include: (1) written policy (the criteria and procedures for evaluation must be explicit) (2) legal compatibility (written policy must satisfy state mandates and extant collective bargaining agreements), (3) prior notification (employees must have complete information before the evaluation process begins), (4) trained evaluators (evaluators must know job requirements and have explicit training in collecting data), (5) job-related criteria (criteria should be objective and reflect actual job requirements), (6) equitable treatment (everyone has the same process and criteria), (7) pattern of performance (a single event cannot be over-interpreted), (8) documentation (written communication about all aspects of teacher performance should be maintained), (9) opportunity to improve following unsatisfactory evaluation (there must be direction and time for improvement), and (10) substantiation for decisions (documentation should be provided to support the personnel decisions).

Measurement Issues

Independent of external factors such as legal requirements and political and social factors (for a discussion of political and social factors, see Good, 1996), determining teacher effectiveness involves difficult definitional problems and raises serious measurement difficulties (Millman, 1997). Teaching is a broad umbrella proxy that represents a myriad set of tasks including, according to Raths (1971), (1) explaining, (2) directing and administering, (3) unifying the group, (4) establishing security, (5) clarifying attitudes and problems, (6) identifying and responding to learning problems, (7) creating curriculum materials, (8) evaluating and reporting, (9) enriching community activities, (10) organizing and managing classrooms, (11) participating in school activities, and (12) participating in professional activities. We also know that teachers need to have adequate knowledge of subject matter and to be able to handle various special responsibilities (e.g., coaching, playground supervision, editing newsletters).

Further, many policy makers and educators argue that it is important to understand that students are more than learners of subject matter and must be seen as needing to develop self-evaluation, goal coordination, and social responsibilities. Students need to be seen and taught as social beings and future responsible citizens, not just passive learners (McCaslin & Good, 1996). Clearly, teachers can be exceptional in some areas (e.g., planning for instruction), average in other areas (e.g., delivering instruction), and poor in still other areas (e.g., evaluating student progress, reporting to parents). Thus, in addition to legal issues, researchers and practitioners must attend to definitional issues. To label a teacher as effective requires a specification of particular teaching tasks and documentation of the quality of performance in designated areas.

Foundations for Building Evaluation Systems

Wheeler and Scriben (1997) identify six distinct types of foundations on which a teacher evaluation system can be built: (1) what teachers are doing, or say they are doing, as part of their job; (2) what administrators or others would like teachers to be doing; (3) what research says effective teachers do; (4) what theories of teaching and learning say teachers should do; (5) what the outcomes of teaching are; and (6) what the roles and responsibilities of teachers are. They argue that as a general principle the more of these foundations that are used, the better (i.e., more comprehensive) the evaluation will be. Further, they suggest that the use of any single foundation (independent of how strong one feels that foundation is) is inadequate for a fair evaluation.

Biddle, Good, and Goodson (1997) note that there are traditional sources of knowledge about teachers and their effects on students, as well as new knowledge contributions in emerging areas, that demand serious attention by those who would describe or evaluate teaching. Classic views of teaching have generally assumed two positions. The first view is that teachers, in their official capacities, are employees in formal organizations charged with instructing young persons and providing associated services. The second perspective deals with the realities that confront teachers as they interact with students in a complex social setting. Here the focus is placed on professional training and concerns of teachers and the actual interactive processes involved in instruction. Biddle, Good, and Goodson (1997) note that many emergent issues are important to consider, including the feminization of teaching, teacher stress and professional burnout, teacher leadership in restructured schools, and recent research on the professional lives and careers of teachers—especially studies that try to increase the professional status of teachers and that give teachers a voice in public education decisions.

Research Knowledge and Teacher Evaluation

Good (1996) notes that the recent history of defining effective teaching can be organized into the following types of research: teacher personality, teacher behavior, teacher time allocations, teacher cognition, student mediation, and emerging constructivist perspectives such as teaching for understanding. Each of these research areas has useful information about teaching and learning that is helpful in defining effectiveness and in stimulating student learning and the continued self-development of teachers. The application value of this body of research has been extensively presented in *Looking in Classrooms* (Good & Brophy, 1997).

Still there are various problems with using research findings for evaluation purposes, especially if findings are narrowly applied. For example, Good and Power (1976) noted some time ago that different patterns of behavior are often functionally equivalent. Whether a comprehensive review is conducted by students, the teacher, or students working in pairs may be irrelevant in many contexts, as long as there is an active systematic attempt to integrate information. Further, existing findings on quantity of instruction are stronger and more consistent than the findings on quality, because so many findings have been derived from a naturalistic context in which there are major differences in how teachers allocate time to academic activities. Thus differences in student opportunity to learn created by time variations are most likely to mask the effects of whatever differences have occurred in the quality of instruction (Brophy & Good, 1986).

Although the distinction between form and quality may appear obvious, it is a point that has eluded reformers as the field of education has moved from fad to fad with little interest in defining the key qualitative aspects of the new *Zeitgeist*. As a case in point, in the span of a few years, we have seen the state of California first reject phonetics in favor of whole language approaches to reading instruction, only to reject whole language methods later. Presently, there is considerable advocacy for constructivist instruction (student centered) but with little specification of those qualities that differentiate effective and ineffective constructivist learning experiences.

Use of research to improve practice is often largely unsuccessful because knowledge about instructional behaviors is overgeneralized (used without regard to context) and equated with effective teaching *per se*. In too many cases, simply performing a behavior is seen as appropriate regardless of how well the behavior is performed. Good and Mulryan (1990) describe the problem this way:

> Overgeneralizing the utility of knowledge from process-product research on teaching is similar to equating a good physician with the ability to interpret an x-ray correctly, defining a successful mechanic as one who can tune a car, or reducing a competent basketball player to one who can hit a 15-foot jump shot. The skills and knowledge required to be successful in any vocation are numerous and diverse (a good physician must understand cell structure, bone structure, as well as principles of physiology and pharmacology, to name but a few; a good mechanic must know about carburetors, fuel-injection systems, principles of suspension, and how to identify the cause of engine malfunctions; or a basketball player must have skills of defense, rebounding, running the court, and passing, as well as court presence). (pp. 206–207)

Although research can provide a useful foundation, many evaluation experts contend that in the 1980s there was too much literal use of research (i.e., research was used independently of a particular context or the unique goals of particular teachers). In the 1990s it appears that there is an overemphasis or misemphasis on theory—only one of the many possible foundations for teacher evaluation. Current theory recommends the use of constructivist teaching and curricula as effective instruction. Those who use this theoretical orientation should be aware that the research basis relating student achievement to constructivist classroom teaching is quite limited. Other problems of using theory alone have been identified by Wheeler and Scriben (1997). They contend that theoretical foundations for teacher evaluation are typically based only on the preferences and beliefs of key leaders in subject matter areas rather than on an understanding of what works well for a given teacher and her or his students. Further, they note that the use of theory for evaluation (i.e., to say what teachers should do) "is based on a certain orientation or way of thinking about teaching and learning, such as constructivism or cognitive psychology, that may be inappropriate for the teacher in the school and that limits the ways of looking at teaching and learning" (p. 42).

Planning and Conducting Teacher Evaluation

Professionals acknowledge the difficulty of teacher evaluation, and they note that to do it adequately requires that many technical dimensions (e.g., reliability) be well addressed. A technically sound evaluation system cannot guarantee effective evaluation. However, as Stronge (1997) notes, the best way to guarantee a flawed evaluation is to use procedures or instruments that have technical difficulties.

Extensive detail has been provided about the technical criteria that must be present in any evaluation system. McConney, Schalock, and Schalock (1997) argue that decisions to use any type of student learning measure for evaluating teachers should take into account the following criteria: (1) freedom from bias (measures are not based on personal preference but result from objective, fair, and impartial scoring and observing rules, etc.); (2) usefulness for diagnosing the need to alter or improve instruction; (3) validity (scores measure schools' and teachers' effects on student learning and should be consistent with the curricula actually being taught); (4) reliability (consistency of measurement); (5) broadness (teachers are responsible for more than simply subject matter knowledge; hence, performances must cover a wide variety of student learning); (6) equitability (teachers are evaluated on the same common measure); and (7) comparability (teachers should not be evaluated until scores have been adjusted to take into account differences in context, such as students, classrooms, and so on).

Historically, the primary method of teacher evaluation has been for principals to observe classroom instruction. Although some outstanding principals do observational analysis exceedingly well, most do not. Evaluation experts agree that observational evaluation has been and continues to be done poorly. For example, Frase and Streshly (1994) note that some principals have been found to provide teachers with inflated evaluations. Accordingly, there is considerable advice about how principals can improve their skills for conducting classroom activities and conducting evaluative conferences (Good & Brophy, 1997).

Many who write in the area of evaluation effectiveness recommend that classroom observational reports be supplemented with student reports, parent reports, administrative reports, and documentation of professional activity. The use of parent and student reports in teacher evaluation is relatively new in elementary and secondary schools, and these procedures are used only in a minority of schools. Some evaluators are notably supportive of using such "consumer satisfaction" sources and present evidence that they can be used in ways that teachers find informative and helpful (Stronge & Ostrander, 1997). However, most evaluation specialists caution that if parent or student reports are used, they should be restricted to only those aspects of teaching that parents and students have directly observed.

Peterson (1995) identifies other problems that need attention if evaluation is to be improved: (1) teachers not choosing to support evaluation activity; (2) oversimplification of difficulties with teacher evaluation; (3) assessment of minimum competency but not of appropriate use of competency; (4) evaluation not addressing exceptional teacher cases; (5) many systems featuring overquantification; and (6) laypersons not being reassured by current teacher evaluation. We agree that too much effort is spent in dealing with ineffectiveness—more evaluation time focused on issues of effectiveness and exceptionality would help to convey to the public more information about the quality of teachers.

Everyone recognizes the importance of minimizing any surprises in the evaluation process. Helms (1997) suggests several things that principals and teachers can do to maximize the productivity of evaluative conferences: the principal should set a date with the teacher that is mutually convenient and be sure to confirm the date well in advance; provide the teacher with the evaluation report and encourage him or her to peruse it for self-appraisal; ask the teacher to organize, review, and submit any other performance documentation; and ask the teacher to be prepared to discuss successes, unmet challenges, and ways in which the principal or school can help the teacher in achieving goals. Similarly, the principal should review the teacher's job description and previous evaluations; complete a tentative evaluation and prepare notes summarizing the teacher's successes and concerns; plan a script to address concerns honestly but with sensitivity and provide opportunities for teachers to present meaningful analysis of their strengths and needed areas of improvement; organize any documentation relevant to teacher performance; and consider how the principal or school system can help the teacher achieve greater effectiveness.

The evaluation of teaching is a complex task. To conduct successful evaluations, evaluators must possess knowledge of alternative ways to assess classroom performance (e.g., observation, interview, work samples) and be aware of the technical issues involved in the use of any methodology. Further, evaluation experts are increasingly recommending the need for the evaluation process to include more data sources (i.e., parents, students, peers, principal, and self-evaluation).

Bibliography

Biddle, B., Good, T., & Goodson, I. (1997). The changing world of teachers. In B. Biddle, T. Good, & I. Goodson (Eds.), *International handbook of teachers and teaching* (Part 1, Vol. 1, pp. 1–9). Netherlands: Kluwer.

Brophy, J., & Good, T. (1986). Teacher behavior and student achievement. In M. Wittrock (Ed.), *Handbook of research on teaching* (3rd ed., pp. 328–375). New York: Macmillan.

Frase, L., & Streshly, W. (1994). Lack of accuracy, feedback, and commitment in teacher evaluation. *Journal of Personnel Evaluation in Education, 1*, 47–57.

Good, T. (1996). Teaching effects in teacher evaluation. In J. Sikula, T. Buttery, & E. Guyton (Eds.), *Handbook of research on teacher education* (2nd ed., pp. 617–665). New York: Macmillan.

Good, T., & Brophy, J. (1997). *Looking in classrooms* (7th ed.). New York: Longman.

Good, T., & Mulryan, C. (1990). Teacher ratings: A call for teacher control and self-evaluation. In J. Millman & L.

Darling-Hammond (Eds.), *The new handbook of teacher evaluation: Assessing elementary and secondary school teachers* (pp. 191–215). Newbury Park, CA: Sage.

Good, T., & Power, C. (1976). Designing successful classroom environments for different types of students. *Journal of Curriculum Studies, 8*, 1–16.

Helms, V. (1997). Conducting a successful evaluation conference. In J. Stronge (Ed.), *Evaluating teaching: A guide to current thinking and best practice* (pp. 152–169). Thousand Oaks, CA: Corwin Press.

McCaslin, M., & Good, T. (1996). *Listening in classrooms*. New York: HarperCollins.

Millian, J. (Ed.). (1997). *Grading teachers, grading schools: Is student achievement a valid evaluation measure?* Thousand Oaks, CA: Corwin Press.

Peterson, K. (1995). *Teacher evaluation: A comprehensive guide to new directions and practices*. Thousand Oaks, CA: Corwin Press.

Raths, L. (1971). What is a good teacher? In J. Raths, J. Pancella, & J. Van Ness (Eds.), *Studying teaching* (2nd ed., pp. 3–9). Englewood Cliffs, NJ: Prentice-Hall.

Stronge, J. (1997). Improving schools through teacher evaluation. In J. Stronge (Ed.), *Evaluating teaching: A guide to current thinking and best practice* (pp. 1–17). Thousand Oaks, CA: Corwin Press.

Stronge, J., & Ostrander, D. (1997). Client surveys in teacher evaluation. In J. Stronge (Ed.), *Evaluating teaching: A guide to current thinking and best practice* (pp. 129–157). Thousand Oaks, CA: Corwin Press.

Tucker, P., & Kindred, K. (1997). Legal considerations in designing teacher evaluation systems. In J. Stronge (Ed.), *Evaluating teaching: A guide to current thinking and best practice* (pp. 59–85). Thousand Oaks, CA: Corwin Press.

Wheeler, P., & Scriben, M. (1997). Building the foundation: Teacher roles and responsibilities. In J. Stronge (Ed.), *Evaluating teaching: A guide to current thinking and best practice* (pp. 27–54). Thousand Oaks, CA: Corwin Press.

Thomas L. Good and DeWayne A. Mason

Teacher Relationships

In their role in the classroom, teachers link students, other teachers, school administrators, families, and community members together to foster the learning success and healthy development of their students. The nature of these interactions with different involved individuals varies depending on the teachers' intent and the determined needs of their students. Students, particularly those at risk of school failure, can benefit from certain "protective supports provided by teachers" (Wang, Haertel, & Walberg, 1994, p. 59). The teacher's role in creating an environment and building relationships conducive to learning goes beyond the traditional academic duties to include the provision of additional support and care. By developing positive, nurturing relationships with their students, teachers can buffer the impact of certain basic factors that may have negative impact on a student's academic achievement. These relationships—their nature, quality, and effects—have been well researched and documented.

Teachers and Students

The relationship between the teacher and the student has been a focus of writing and inquiry for more than 2,000 years. Although the emphases of this study have changed and evolved over time, the centrality of the teacher's role in affecting student learning has remained constant.

Plato, Socrates, and Confucius established much of the philosophical guidelines for teaching. Emphasizing the acquisition of knowledge through dialogue, these philosophers stressed a commitment to the teacher-student relationship. Each of them as teachers questioned and pushed his pupils to look within themselves for answers. Plato served as a guide for his students, often speaking allegorically and thereby requiring his students to think independently and to question. Socrates made famous the method of teaching through direct questioning. And Confucius manifested his beliefs in teaching through his own pursuit of truth and harmony with the world. Central to each approach is the powerful connection between student and teacher and the effect of this relationship on a student's acquisition of knowledge, skills, and character. Centuries later, in the Age of Enlightenment, Jean-Jacques Rousseau posited the idea that children learn from their own explorations and that a child should be allowed to progress in accordance with his or her own nature.

In the twentieth century ideas about teacher-student relationships have proliferated. Echoing the sentiments of Rousseau, John Dewey and other progressive educators of the early twentieth century theorized that children flourish if allowed to grow freely in their own way and their own time without being forced or limited by too much teaching. Maria Montessori similarly argued that children should discover knowledge for themselves and learn by doing, with a clear emphasis on sensory perceptions.

In the 1900s, proponents of stimulus-response learning theory, such as E. L. Thorndike and B. F. Skinner, defined teachers as transmitters of knowledge and students as passive recipients. According to their respective theories of associationism and behaviorism, the classroom teacher presented content to children and conducted drill and review as children memorized the material.

The relationship between teacher and student was redefined with the advent of cognitive psychology. Following the principles of constructivism, teachers and students were said to construct knowledge jointly. Teachers and students were believed to constitute a community of learners that engages in social discourse and produces common understandings. Teachers were seen as facilitators who scaffold, guide, and enrich children's learning activities, with students serving as co-contributors to the learning process.

Correlational and descriptive studies of the classroom promoted a view of student-teacher relationships in terms of the nature, amount, and quality of interactions (Brophy & Good, 1986). These studies noted the positive effects of active instruction on student achievement: teachers should be engaged and work directly with their students rather than requiring students to learn on their own through seat work. Teacher-student interactions of particular salience included the questions teachers ask, the corrective feedback they provide, and the use of praise and reinforcement. Brophy and Good note that when soliciting information from the students, teachers must consider both the level of difficulty of the question and its cognitive level. Although teachers do not necessarily need to constantly praise students for performance, they should acknowledge correct answers and provide critical feedback to students. Information on the particulars of student and teacher interactions has led to new and more specific understandings about how teachers affect students' cognitive, affective, and behavioral outcomes.

Psychologists have recently addressed the psychosocial dimensions of teachers' relationships with students. Research on resilience indicates that caring teachers who express concern for students and act as confidants, role models, and mentors can contribute to children's capacity to overcome personal vulnerabilities and environmental adversities (Wang, Haertel, & Walberg, 1994). Werner (1989) showed that supportive teacher relationships greatly benefit students, particularly those at risk of school failure, over the long term. Focusing on the psychosocial aspects of teaching is especially important with older children. Close, caring relationships with teachers facilitate children's successful transition from elementary to junior high school. Unfortunately, although teachers are relatively well connected with elementary-aged children, as children get older, teachers have less close contact with them, and fewer resources are available to promote healthy development of the teacher-student relationships. Contrary to the traditional notion that adolescents are alienated and rebellious, recent work shows that they need and desire guidance from respected members of the community, specifically their teachers (Takanishi, 1993). The relationship of teachers with secondary school youth has been a neglected area of research.

Teachers and School Staff

Teachers' relationships with their peers, other school staff, and school administrators have been researched for decades. These studies reveal that teachers are often isolated from their peers and other school professionals (Goodlad, 1984; Lortie, 1975). Thus increasing teachers' opportunities for interaction and collegiality has been a goal of recent efforts to increase teacher professionalism.

Smylie (1994) reviewed studies of participative decision making, in which teachers worked with other teachers and school staff members on school management tasks, that reveal increased teacher commitment, satisfaction, and morale. Although teachers may participate in organizational level activities, curriculum and classroom practices are usually unaffected by their participation in indirect activities, such as modifying budgets and/or school policies. Smylie also reviewed research that indicates that when teachers and instructors take an active role in school-based management practices, their instructional effectiveness can actually worsen as their energy and efforts are divided and distracted from a classroom focus. Other research has found a positive relationship between participative decision making and classroom instruction, noting an increase in innovations adopted by schools, in professional development activities, in teacher exchange of ideas and knowledge, and in improved understanding of learning and classroom instruction (Lieberman, Darling-Hammond, & Zuckerman, 1991).

Research on teachers who play leadership roles (e.g., mentor teachers, liaisons with university teacher education departments) and on increased opportunities for professional relationships demonstrates that there are benefits for these teachers, but there is little evidence that they are able to provide much support or benefit to other teachers. This lack raises organizational and policy questions on the extent to which conferring upon teachers additional roles and responsibilities for professional development of peers can be effective in making specific changes in teacher practice at the organizational level.

Professional relationships among teachers adhere to norms that govern the ways teachers ask for and provide help. Research on professional development, especially mentoring programs and peer coaching, reveal that interactions among mentors and their paired teachers are often reserved, nonproblematic, and uncritical. These studies show that in the beginning of such supervisory relationships, the content of the interpersonal interactions is informational and focuses on district policies and procedures—not classroom practice. Relationships between mentor teachers and novices tend to be about maintaining harmony and support rather than developing competence (Hollingsworth, 1989). Further research suggests that increasing the quality of teachers' work relationships cannot be accomplished by individual job enrichment but requires professional and organizational change. One proposed solution to this problem is the establishment of professional communities, including professional development schools, in which teachers' work is collaborative, coordinated, and interdependent (Darling-Hammond, 1994).

Educating new teachers in the field should focus on strengthening interpersonal relationships among new teachers and their mentors. Professional development programs should stress collegiality and the creation of shared standards of practice in the hopes of building and sustaining communities of learners (Darling-Hammond, 1994). Sergiovanni (1994) argues that a community of learners, or the creation of an environment in which teachers learn from each other, from students, and from other participants, is fostered by an approach to shared inquiry. Inquiry encourages dialogues and reflection among and between teachers and administrators and brings individuals together through a commonly developed set of ideas.

Teachers and Parents

Teacher-parent relationships affect students' learning and well-being. Many teachers attempt to involve parents in school management or classroom activities. These parent-involvement efforts not only help establish and foster parent-teacher relationships but also function to include parents in educational interventions, which are significantly more effective when parents are involved than when they are not (Shartrand, Weiss, Kreider, & Lopez, 1997; Walberg & Paik, 1997).

Parent-involvement programs promote a number of desirable student outcomes, including decreased teen pregnancy and dropout rates, increased graduation rates, and improved achievement and school attendance. High expectations and parent tutoring also increase student performance (Peterson, 1989). Teachers can encourage and support parental involvement through home visits and parent-teacher conferences. Parents who participate in these programs are more likely to further their own educations by attending classes and are more able to provide increased support to their children and their learning needs.

Caring parents and teachers who act in concert can strengthen the effects of educational and social interventions. When there are positive relationships among parents and teachers, the resources of the home and school contexts are amplified, providing a greater likelihood of positive outcomes for children.

Teachers and the Community

In order to create rich, nurturing educational environments in the classroom, schools need to maximize the use of resources available in their communities. Teachers can incorporate parents (their skills and knowledge), organizations, and local programs into their curricula to offer students supplementary knowledge and information to complement their basic course work. Many teachers collaborate with local universities, museums, and community service organizations to expand the cultural resources available to students, enhancing their educational experience. Teachers can forge relationships with outside agencies and community members to provide children with the best possible learning environment. For example, one program in the Boston metropolitan area invites teachers to bring their students to a local museum to view exhibits, engage in discussions about the displays, and incorporate their experiences into their classroom curricula.

In an effort to meet the diverse needs of students in our public schools, community services and service providers often collaborate with schools. As organizations, schools have the advantage of having the most frequent contact with students and therefore the potential to truly benefit children by integrating school-linked services to meet the children's needs (Kirst & Kelly, 1995). Teachers may work with social workers, vocational trainers, family counselors, local health care providers, and others to address and fulfill the needs of their students. In order to create supportive learning environments, teachers can establish and build these relationships with the adults who play positive roles in the students' lives. According to Jonathan Kozol (1997), schools need to serve as bridges into the community. When students receive similar support and care from teachers, schools, and community members, they have a better chance of benefiting from their educational opportunities, as they receive consistent and clear messages about appropriate and desired norms of behavior.

Conclusions

The relationships forged by teachers with different members of the learning community promote students' learning success and healthy development. The relationships with parents, students, colleagues, and community members differ tremendously, drawing on different skills and responsibilities of the teacher. Ideas governing the structure of these relationships have changed dramatically across time. As new constructs for education and the school community are developed, the pivotal role of teachers as facilitators must be considered. The teacher often serves as the linchpin between the different groups involved. Teachers understand the daily life of students, can appreciate the innovations and support of fellow teachers and school staff, and can communicate children's different needs and strengths to parents. Teachers also serve as instrumental ties to the community, acting as spokespersons or advocates for their school or students. The study of teacher relationships with their students, fellow teachers, school administrators, parents, and community members yields a greater understanding of the daily tasks and challenges faced by all teachers. Support from the broader educational community of teachers' endeavors to develop strong connections with different groups provides teachers with a more solid foundation on which to build communication networks that aid all students.

Bibliography

Brophy, J., & Good, T. (1986). Teaching behavior and student achievement. In M. Wittrock (Ed.), *Handbook of research on teaching* (pp. 328–375). New York: Macmillan.

Darling-Hammond, L. (1994). Developing professional development schools: Early lessons, challenge and promise. In L. Darling-Hammond (Ed.), *Professional development schools: Schools for developing a profession* (pp. 1–27). New York: Teachers College Press.

Goodlad, J. (1984). *A place called school.* New York: McGraw-Hill.

Hollingsworth, S. (1989). Prior beliefs and cognitive change in learning to teach. *American Educational Research Journal, 26*, 160–190.

Kirst, M., & Kelly, C. (1995). Collaboration to improve education and children services: Politics and policy making. In L. Rigsby, M. C. Reynolds, & M. C. Wang (Eds.), *School-community connections: Exploring issues for research and practice* (pp. 21–43). San Francisco: Jossey-Bass.

Kozol, J. (1997, November). Reflections on resiliency. *Principal, 77* (2), 5–8.

Lieberman, A., Darling-Hammond, L., & Zuckerman, D. (1991). *Early lessons in restructuring schools.* New York: Columbia University, National Center for Restructuring Education, Schools, and Teaching.

Lortie, D. (1975). *Schoolteacher.* Chicago: University of Chicago Press.

Peterson, D. (1989). Parental involvement in the educational process. [ED 312 776]

Sergiovanni, T. (1994). *Building community in schools.* San Francisco: Jossey-Bass.

Shartrand, A. M., Weiss, B., Kreider, H. M., & Lopez, M. E. (1997). *New skills for new schools: Preparing teachers in family involvement.* Cambridge, MA: Harvard University Graduate School of Education.

Smylie, M. (1994). Redesigning teachers' work: Connections to the classroom. *Review of Research in Education, 20*, 129–177.

Takanishi, R. (1993). Changing views of adolescence in contemporary society. *Teachers College Record, 94* (3), 459–465.

Walberg, H. J., & Paik, S. J. (1997). Home environments for learning. In H. J. Walberg & G. D. Haertel (Eds.), *Psychology and educational practice* (pp. 356–368). Berkeley, CA: McCutchan.

Wang, M. C., Haertel, G. D., & Walberg, H. J. (1994). Educational resilience in inner cities. In M. C. Wang & E. Gordon (Eds.), *Educational resilience in inner-city America: Challenges and prospects* (pp. 45–72). Hillsdale, NJ: Erlbaum.

Werner, E. (1989, April). Children of the garden island. *Scientific American, 260* (4), 106–108.

Margaret C. Wang and Geneva D. Haertel

TEAM TRAINING is now more popular and important as groups arc explicitly being used as the basic building blocks of organizations. Many companies are experimenting with self-managing teams, quality circles, and other flexible work practices (Lawler, Mohrman, & Ledford, 1992). Cross-functional teams of diverse professionals are formed to develop new products, improve productivity, and solve a great array of complex problems (Iansiti & West, 1997). Virtual teams use technology to combine the expertise of people from around the world (Lipnack & Stamps, 1997). Superior customer service, total quality management, and supply chain management all posit teamwork as critical for successful organizational performance.

Social, work, and organizational psychology have explored the effectiveness, development, structure, climate, and innovation of groups as well as their relationship with each other and the organization. Training and educational psychologists have investigated how teams can be used to improve the declarative knowledge of information and ideas and the procedural skill learning of individuals and groups. Teams are "hot" for both researchers and practitioners.

The available psychological research supports the proposition that teams can contribute significantly to organizational innovation and productivity (Johnson, 1994). They can also effectively train individuals in a wide variety of organizational tasks as well as in the interpersonal capabilities needed to work in groups. However, evidence does not suggest that teams are panaceas. They are not useful for all organizational tasks, nor is any kind of team training more effective than individual training. Teams must be appropriately used and competently structured and managed before they yield significant value for organizations and training (Gruenfeld, Mannix, Williams, & Neale, 1996).

There remain gaps in the research that prevent making unqualified, firm conclusions about team training effectiveness. Team training research suffers from the shortcomings of training research more generally, namely, a lack of careful needs assessment, the failure to develop training programs based on this assessment, and ill-defined ways to evaluate the training's impact (Goldstein, 1991). However, considerable research from diverse psychological fields can be brought to bear to highlight the potential of team training and identify the mediators and conditions under which it is effective.

Distinctions

Groups are typically defined as a collection of interdependent persons who interact face-to-face. Practitioners have argued that teams are designed to accomplish specific purposes, whereas groups also include social and family collectives. Teams are also popularly used to refer to groups that perform effectively. However, effectiveness should not be included in the definition of a team;

it is confusing to define a variable by its outcomes. Psychologists, arguing that even families have goals, have used groups and teams interchangeably (Guzzo, 1996). In this context, teams will refer to groups that are formed and designed to accomplish specific goals whether they are successful or not.

Team effectiveness includes goal attainment. The quality and creativity of the solution, the efficiency of operations, and the satisfaction of the stakeholders and consumers have all been used to measure goal attainment (Pritchard, 1992). However, effectiveness also includes outcomes that impact future goal attainment. The quality of the relationship among team members can leave them prepared to share information, integrate their perspectives and efforts, and learn so that they can accomplish future tasks (Hackman, 1987). Psychological competence and well-being can help individuals be directed, energetic, and learn from their experience, which in turn enhances the group's task capabilities (Argyris, 1970).

Team training can be divided into training *in* teams and training *for* teams. Training in teams refers to instruction carried out in groups to develop procedural knowledge to accomplish organizational tasks; for example, technicians from the region discuss, observe, and give each other feedback to learn to repair a new X-ray machine. Training for teams is to help group members learn the communication, influence, and conflict management skills needed to make groups effective; employees who join quality teams learn to communicate nonevaluatively and supportively. Team building focuses on developing the appropriate norms and relationships for an intact team rather than training to learn general teamwork skills.

Training in teams emphasizes task work, the specific procedures and skills needed to get the job done. Training for teams emphasizes teamwork skills. Yet task work and teamwork are highly related. Few organizational tasks can be accomplished with complete independence. An operator can keep one machine working to make one part; teamwork skills are not very relevant. However, interpersonal skills are becoming more important as employees form quality, continuous improvement, and new product groups to help their organizations respond to the competitive marketplace. When required to improve productivity and innovate, machine operators must coordinate with people in upstream and downstream activities and discuss with their coworkers how to develop more effective ways of operating machines.

Employees who lack confidence in their teamwork skills may be unable to engage in appropriate task work. They may be self-conscious and withdraw from the task and be so overloaded with demands that their attention shrinks (Johnson, 1994). Training in and for teams, it can be speculated, will become more critical so that employees have the well-learned teamwork skills needed to concentrate on complex, demanding tasks as well as to work in team-based organizations.

Training in Teams

The purpose of training is to develop the procedural knowledge and skills needed to execute a job well. What is learned should be transferred and sustained in the workplace. Training is more than learning facts and information to answer examination questions; it requires learning to apply knowledge in an organization. Need assessment strategies can identify the specific knowledge, skills, and attitudes particularly relevant to accomplish a targeted job (Goldstein, 1991). Then the issue is to identify, from a wide range of possibilities, the most effective instructional strategies. Research to be reviewed questions the present high reliance on training that focuses on the individual and independent assignments, activities, and assessment. However, this research also indicates that training in teams must be well structured to help individuals learn procedural skills.

Educational psychologists have conducted considerable research on education and training in groups compared to individuals. In a recent meta-analysis of more than 120 studies on adults, teams were found to result in higher levels of procedural knowledge than individual learning structured competitively or individually (mean differences equal to 0.54 and 0.51 standard deviations, respectively). These results held for verbal, mathematical, and procedural tasks (Johnson, 1994). Some evidence suggests that individual training is as effective as team training for simple, rote tasks.

Organizational and industrial psychologists have documented several dynamics that suggest how teams contribute to procedural learning (Johnson, 1994). Behavioral modeling can facilitate training; employees in teams can model the targeted behaviors for each other. Team members can give each other appropriate feedback that stimulates learning. Team training can also promote a professional identity that aids learning and its transfer.

Team training, especially with intact groups, may well facilitate the transfer of learning to the organization. Team members continue to engage in the behavioral modeling, feedback, and professional identity processes of team training in the organizational setting. They remind each other of the new skill, provide social and task cues that encourage its use, hold each other accountable, reward each other for success, and solve the problems encountered as they implement new practices. With intact teams, team training also serves as team building. Team members develop the norms and procedures that support the use of the new skills on the job. Research is needed to investigate these potentials of team training for training transfer.

These facilitating dynamics do not occur in all groups. Having teams in training does not guarantee the interaction that facilitates learning. Educational psychologists have identified psychological conditions under which team training is effective (Johnson, 1994; Tjosvold & Tjosvold, 1995). Team members who believe that their goals are cooperative rather than competitive or independent are more likely to help each other practice and learn. In addition, holding individuals accountable for learning, fostering face-to-face supportive interaction, and encouraging teams to reflect on their dynamics complement cooperative goals to support learning in teams.

Training for Teams

Training for teams is to develop the interpersonal skills needed to work in groups to apply many procedural skills in organizations. In addition to needs assessment, theory and research are used to identify targeted teamwork skills. For example, research provides the rationale and identifies the particular skills needed for employees to learn to negotiate and manage conflict (Tjosvold & Tjosvold, 1995).

Shared mental model theory proposes that if team members have a shared understanding of a task, understand the roles and expertise of other group members, and understand the context in which they work, they can predict the information and assistance that each other needs (Tannenbaum, Salas, & Cannon-Bowers, 1996). Then they can coordinate effectively even without explicit coordination activities. Training then should insure that group members understand the steps to accomplish the tasks, the roles members play, and the processes by which the team should coordinate. Cross training, in which employees practice each other's tasks, is a particularly potent, practical way to facilitate learning of the common goal and the steps and abilities each person must perform to reach it.

Considerable research has developed general models of effective groups. These models tend to describe broad classes of inputs into groups (e.g., group size and composition) and processes (e.g., communication patterns) that have an impact on outcomes (e.g., cohesion), but they do not provide testable predictions that can develop and modify the models (West, 1996). These models seem too general to provide much specific guidance for training.

Pritchard and colleagues (1988) developed and tested a model that includes setting group goals, receiving feedback, and setting incentives to strengthen team motivation and productivity. The researchers helped army groups develop their goals, determine how their productivity could be measured, and identify incentives that the team would find attractive. Through systematic involvement in many discussions and meetings to develop the system, team members created reasonable goals, were aware of what they needed to do to accomplish them, and knew how they would be rewarded. They came to see themselves as a unit.

For the first 5 months, the researchers provided feedback to each group in terms of the percentage of their maximum output at the end of each month, and held meetings to review the feedback. In the next phase of the experiment, team members established aspiration levels, that is, how many of the goals they wanted to achieve in the next month. In the final phase, they added the incentive of time off from work for maintaining a high level of performance and additional incentives for exceeding that level.

The results indicate that the program was highly successful in motivating team members. Group involvement and feedback were particularly useful; adding the goal setting and incentives were not critical. This and other studies underscored the value of team members' participation aimed to develop and strengthen their ties. They understood their team goals and felt cooperatively interdependent, believing that they had the resources needed to reach their goals and to work together to solve problems.

Tjosvold (1991) developed an overall model of team effectiveness built upon Deutsch's (1973) theory of cooperation and competition, and the research that has tested and extended it. The Team Organization Model integrates the conditions and processes that contribute to effective teamwork: Envision, unite, empower, explore, and reflect are mutually reinforcing steps to an effective group. Specifically, a team vision provides a common direction for team members and helps them believe that their goals are cooperative rather than competitive or independent. Experimental and field studies indicate that group members with cooperative goals feel more confident and able to exchange each other's abilities and resources to accomplish their goals (Alper, Tjosvold, & Law, 1998). They are also prepared and able to express and integrate their divergent views to identify and solve problems. They use their experiences and conflicts to reflect, learn, and adjust so that they can continue to work together and move toward their vision. This model applies to a small group and to the organization as a whole.

A key advantage of this integrated model of team effectiveness is that all members can use it to develop a set of ideals for how they can develop their team and the common skills needed to work together productively. Group members are often frustrated because they have incompatible notions of the kind of team they should be; they want to develop a productive team but have opposing views of the means to do so. Some group members may assume that they must work harmoniously to be "cooperative"; others believe that they must confront conflict. Discussing and using the framework can help team members become co-oriented with common aspirations of how they should strive to work together. They can then reach agreement on when and how they are going to use conflict to be cooperative and productive. They can learn key skills together and use the model to develop their norms and the contexts that support the use of those skills. Preliminary tests have been successful, but systematic research is needed to develop this approach.

Challenges for Team Training

Research identifies considerable potential for team training but also major obstacles. Trainers who have relied on individualistic methods must learn the complex skills of structuring teams effectively for training in teams and training for teams. Teams are highly pressured to form and perform quickly, meet pressing deadlines, and reduce their costs. Team training will be expected to be efficient as well as effective.

Team training, especially for intact groups, has potential drawbacks as well as advantages. Groups trained together may become highly cohesive and antagonistic to other groups. A solution may be to train teams that must work together at the same time so that they do not develop their unity around seeing other groups as enemies. Trainers have found that team building for a whole organization can develop cohesive small groups that understand that they can be successful by helping other groups reach their goals (Jusela et al., 1986).

Recent workforce developments place additional demands. Because of immigration flows, differential birthrates, and organizational policy, the workforces of the United States and many other countries are becoming increasingly diverse. Teams are likely to encounter gender, racial, and cultural differences.

Research on team composition has developed our understanding of the impact of the homogeneity and heterogeneity of group members, but it does not provide simple, straightforward answers to how diversity can be managed (Jackson, May, & Whitney, 1995). Evidence indicates that diversity need not make teamwork less effective. Being similar neither insures nor undermines effective teamwork. Indeed, diverse composition often results in more divergent views and, if these views are discussed constructively and cooperatively, they can improve the quality of group work.

Organizations from different nations are joining forces to take advantage of the global marketplace. In these alliances, people with much different cultural backgrounds and living in different business and social climates are often asked to work together. Moreover, they must often do so under the constraint of little face-to-face interaction. Much more research is needed, given the importance and complexity of cross-cultural teamwork.

Research has documented that cultural values and nationalities affect ways of working in groups. However, these differences are not so straightforward. For example, people from collectivist cultures are not simply more cooperative; they can work cooperatively or competitively. However, it appears that they make a more defined distinction between in-group members with whom they work together and out-group members from whom they must protect themselves (Smith & Bond, 1993).

The most general conclusions from diversity and cross-cultural research is that these teams pose significant barriers to making teams effective. These teams members have to be particularly flexible, empathetic, and skillful conflict managers (Leung & Tjosvold, 1998).

Validated theory identifying the nature of team effectiveness and the major training requirements may be particularly useful for meeting the efficiency, diversity, and cross-cultural challenges of team training. A theory validated by research with various populations and nations can guide team training for diverse groups. For example, recent studies indicate that the theory of cooperation and competition can successfully analyze teamwork in Europe and Asia as well as North America (Tjosvold & De Dreu, 1997; Tjosvold, Hui, & Law, 1997). However, the particular operations of the theory, that is, the conditions that result in cooperative goals and the ways used to discuss diverse views open-mindedly, vary from one culture to another. But diverse people can agree to use this theory to guide their training in and for teams. Together they create the particular ways to develop a cooperative team relevant and appropriate for their cultures, for themselves as individuals, and for their situations.

Managers and psychologists can agree that teams have considerable potential to learn procedural competencies and to improve organizational performance as well as be psychologically fulfilling for people, and that realizing these potentials requires developing the appropriate facilitating conditions. Teams are not simple solutions; they can give more, but they require more. Appropriately used and skillfully structured, teams train people to acquire the procedural knowledge to perform many vital organizational tasks. Cooperative goals, individual accountability, skillful feedback, and discussion of how to use and sustain the skills are important contributors to effective training in teams.

Working as a team can be very challenging. Training for teams helps employees come to a common vision of how their team should be managed and shared norms and understanding of how they want to work together. Research indicates that when they understand that they are cooperatively interdependent and know how they can combine their abilities and discuss their opposing perspectives constructively, they are more prepared to grapple with adversities and overcome barriers so that they get the job done and strengthen their team and themselves.

[*See also* Training.]

Bibliography

Alper, S., Tjosvold, D., & Law, K. S. (1998). Interdependence and controversy in group decision-making: Antecedents to effective self-managing teams. *Organizational Behavior and Human Decision Processes, 74*, 33–52.

Argyris, C. (1970). *Intervention theory and method: A behavioral science view*. Reading, MA: Addison-Wesley.

Deutsch, M. (1973). *The resolution of conflict*. New Haven, CT: Yale University Press.

Goldstein, I. L. (1991). Training in work organizations. In M. D. Dunnette & L. M. Hough (Eds.), *Handbook of industrial and organizational psychology* (2nd ed., Vol. 2, pp. 507–619). Palo Alto, CA: Consulting Psychologists Press.

Guzzo, R. A. (1996). Fundamental consideration about work groups. In M. A. West (Ed.), *Handbook of work group psychology* (pp. 3–21). Chichester, England: Wiley.

Gruenfeld, D. H., Mannix, E. A., Williams, K. Y., & Neale, M. A. (1996). Group composition and decision-making: How member familiarity and information distribution affect process and performance. *Organizational Behavior and Human Decision Processes, 67*, 1–15.

Hackman, J. R. (1987). The design of work teams. In J. Lorsch (Ed.), *Handbook of organizational behavior* (pp. 315–342). Englewood Cliffs, NJ: Prentice Hall.

Iansiti, M., & West, J. (1997). Technology integration: Turning great research into great products. *Harvard Business Review*, 69–79.

Jackson, S. E., May, K. E., & Whitney, K. (1995). Dynamics of diversity in decision-making teams. In R. A. Guzzo & E. Salas (Eds.), *Team decision-making effectiveness in organizations* (pp. 204–261). San Francisco: Jossey-Bass.

Johnson, D. W. (1994). Training in teams. In D. Druckman & R. Bjork (Eds.), *Learning, remembering, believing: Enhancing human performance* (pp. 140–170). Washington, DC: National Academy Press.

Jusela, G. E. Chairman, P., Ball, R. A., Tyson, C. E., & Dannermiller, K. D. (1986). Work innovations at Ford Motor. In Y. K. Shetty & V. M. Buehler (Eds.), *Quality productivity and innovation: Strategies for gaining competitive advantage* (pp. 123–145). New York: Elsevier.

Lawler, E. E., Mohrman, S. A., & Ledford, G. E. (1992). *Employee involvement and total quality management: Practices and results in Fortune 1000 companies*. San Francisco: Jossey-Bass.

Leung, K., & Tjosvold, D. (1998). *Conflict management in the Asian Pacific: Assumptions and approaches in diverse cultures*. Singapore: Wiley.

Lipnack, J., & Stamps, J. (1997). *Virtual teams: Reaching across space, time, and organizations with technology*. New York: Wiley.

Pritchard, D. (1992). Organizational productivity. In M. D. Dunnette & L. M. Hough (Eds.), *Handbook of industrial and organizational psychology* (Vol. 3, pp. 443–471). Palo Alto, CA: Consulting Psychologists Press.

Pritchard, R. D., Jones, S. D., Roth. P. L., Stuebing, K. K., & Ekeberg, S. E. (1988). Effects of group feedback, goal setting, and incentives on organizational productivity. *Journal of Applied Psychology, 73*, 337–358.

Smith, P. B., & Bond, M. H. (1993). *Social psychology across cultures: Analysis and perspectives*. Hemel Hempstead, England: Prentice Hall/Harvester Wheatsheaf.

Tannenbaum, S. I., Salas, E., & Cannon-Bowers, J. A. (1996). Promoting team effectiveness. In M. A. West (Ed.), *Handbook of work group psychology* (pp. 503–529). Chichester, England: Wiley.

Tjosvold, D. (1991). *Team organization: An enduring competitive advantage*. New York: Wiley.

Tjosvold, D., & De Dreu, C. (1997). Managing conflict in Dutch organizations: A test of the relevance of Deutsch's cooperation theory. *Journal of Applied Social Psychology, 27*, 2213–2227.

Tjosvold, D., Hui, C., & Law, K. S. (1997). The leadership relationship in Hong Kong: Power, interdependence, and controversy. In K. Leung, U. Kim, S. Yamaguchi, & Y. Kashima (Eds.), *Progress in Asian social psychology* (Vol. 1, pp. 295–310). Singapore: Wiley.

Tjosvold, D., & Tjosvold, M. W. (1995). *Psychology for leaders: Using motivation, conflict and power to manage more effectively*. New York: Wiley.

West, M. A. (1996). *Handbook of work group psychology*. Chichester, England: Wiley.

Dean Tjosvold

TECHNICAL AND PROFESSIONAL EDUCATION. The common goal of vocational, professional, and technical education is to prepare individuals for work. For the purposes of this article, these terms will be considered synonymous, though distinctions have been made among them in the literature. For brevity, the term vocational education will be used to refer to these forms of education.

Historically, psychologists have always been interested in the relationship between psychology and work, and several eminent psychologists have written extensively about this relationship. Sigmund Freud considered love and work to be the two major areas of human endeavor, and proposed that an individual's self-worth was intimately related to work. Erikson proposed that work contributed to one's identity and believed that it was a particularly important contributor to development during adolescence. Bruner believed that neuroses among young people were more likely to involve choices about work and preparation for work than they were to involve sex. Carl Jung contended that individuals in their natural state would not work and that work was enculturated through civilization. Relatedly, eminent vocational psychologists like Super (1990) and

Holland (1985) have emphasized the relationship among work and self-concept, self-esteem, and personal/social adjustment.

An Overview of Vocational, Professional, and Technical Education

Unfortunately, schools have done an inadequate job in preparing young people for work. A 1993 Gallup Poll indicated that 60% of American adults believe that high schools devote enough attention to preparing students for college, but not enough attention to helping non-college-bound students get jobs. Schools direct most of their resources toward preparing students for college. Yet only about 15% of incoming ninth graders graduate from high school and then obtain a 4-year college degree within 6 years of their high school graduation (Morra, 1993). Relatedly, almost two thirds of the projected growth in jobs between 1996 and 2006 will be in occupations that require less than a college degree, and three of every four job openings will be in occupations that generally require less than a bachelor's degree (U.S. Department of Labor, 1998).

Stern, Finkelstein, Stone, Latting, and Dornsife (1995) noted that after leaving high school, most young people "spend a number of years 'floundering' from one job to another, often with occasional spells of unemployment" (p. 5). A report from the Government Accounting Office (1993) noted that "many youth are ill prepared for work when they leave high school, often with long term negative consequences. For example, about 30% of youth aged 16 to 24 lack the skills for entry level employment, and 50 percent of adults in their late twenties have not found a steady job" (p. 1).

For individuals with emotional and learning disabilities, the population psychologists most frequently work with, the situation is even more dismal. Unemployment and underemployment rates among individuals with disabilities are significantly higher than those of the general population and have been linked to the excessively high dropout rate for this population. Dropout rates of over 50% have been reported by some researchers (Gajar, Goodman, & McAfee, 1993), with students who have emotional or learning problems being at the greatest risk of dropping out. Given such statistics, the need for effective vocational education may never have been greater.

As stated at the outset, the purpose of vocational education is to prepare individuals for work. Often, curricula consist of hierarchically arranged occupational skills that are taught sequentially and that will prepare individuals for entry-level employment in a particular occupation. Often, this is combined with instruction in job-seeking and job-acquisition skills, such as resume preparation and interviewing. Although direct instruction in occupational social skills (those skills necessary to get along with others in the workplace) are less often included in vocational education programs, they may be the most important skills necessary for acquiring and maintaining a job, given research that suggests individuals lose jobs because of social, not technical, work skill deficits (Greenspan & Shoultz, 1981).

There are numerous methods by which individuals may be provided with vocational education. In addition to the vocational training and work experience programs offered by most public school districts, individuals may gain additional training after high school via apprenticeship programs, the military, trade and technical schools, vocational rehabilitation facilities, community colleges/junior colleges, and 4-year colleges and universities. In instances where public school programs overlap with the training offered by other institutions or programs, cooperative arrangements are sometimes developed that allow students who receive credit in high school for partial completion of a vocational program to transfer that credit to other institutions or programs when continuing for additional training in the same area. Tech-prep is such a program, and it was established as a separate item with the reauthorization of the Carl D. Perkins Vocational and Applied Technology Act Amendments of 1990. Tech-prep is an educational approach for merging academic preparation for continuing education with the teaching of technical skills and knowledge needed in the modern work force (Lewis, 1992). Tech-prep blends academic and advanced technological studies at the high school level with connections to community and technical colleges and high-tech career fields. It is a planned sequence of course work that begins at any point during the ninth through twelfth grade and continues through the attainment of either a 2- or 4-year postsecondary degree. Tech-prep integrates college academic preparatory course work with vocational/technical course work and allows students to move directly from high school to a postsecondary institution to continue their studies.

Roles for Psychologists

Among psychologists, school psychologists have been most closely associated with providing services that support vocational education. Although other types of psychologists are often employed in settings that offer vocational education, their focus is often on clinical or organizational rather than educational issues. While active in providing services to support vocational education in public schools, and to a lesser extent in vocational rehabilitation facilities, community college settings, and 4-year colleges, there is little evidence of extensive school psychologist involvement in other settings that provide vocational education.

In the last 15 years, much has been written about the school psychologist's involvement in vocational education, most commonly with regard to the provision of vocational assessment and the transition from school to work services (Levinson, 1993, 1998). The fact that five major publications of the National Association of School Psychologists (NASP) all include a chapter relevant to vocational/career development, vocational assessment, and/or transition from school to work attests to the significance of the topic for the profession of school psychology. Additionally, NASP has incorporated both vocational assessment and intervention practices into its *Standards for the Provision of School Psychological Services* (Thomas & Grimes, 1995). These standards, which encompass the areas of assessment, consultation, and direct services, specify that "psychological and psychoeducational assessments include evaluation, as appropriate, of the areas of . . . career and vocational development, aptitude, and interests"; that "school psychologists provide skill enhancement activities (such as . . . vocational development . . .) to school personnel, parents, and others in the community, regarding issues of human learning, development, and behavior"; and that "school psychologists design direct service programs to enhance cognitive, affective, social, and vocational development."

Despite these publications, data indicate that school psychologists are interested in, but not particularly involved in, vocational aspects of practice. Shepard and Hohenshil (1983) surveyed 218 practicing school psychologists and found that 75% of the respondents applied 3% or less of their time to vocational responsibilities, and that 91% felt unprepared to provide effective vocational services, despite perceiving these activities to be important. Levinson (1988), in a study of Pennsylvania school psychologists, found that 66% had no involvement in vocational assessment, 61% had no involvement in vocational counseling, 59% had not consulted with vocational instructors, and 87% had no involvement in vocational program development. Similarly, Carey (1995), in a national study of school psychologists, found that less than 1% of time was spent in vocational assessment. Staab (1996) surveyed a randomly selected sample of 602 school psychologists working at the secondary level and found that school psychologists were interested in school-to-work transition planning activities, perceived these activities to be important, but generally felt unprepared to perform the activities listed. Other than functions listed under the category of assessment, school psychologists did not describe the school-to-work transition activities listed by Staab as being "regularly" or "routinely" performed. Only two transition activities were described as activities that school psychologists "definitely should" perform: "explain test results to students so that they understand their strengths/needs, and modifications/adaptations needed for successful transition planning and programming," and "complete triennial evaluations to help meet transition planning needs." Approximately half of the school psychologists surveyed indicated that school psychology skills were "underutilized" in the school-to-work transition process.

Psychologists contribute to the vocational education process by providing services in the following domains: assessment, counseling, consultation, direct intervention, and research. From an assessment perspective, psychologists assist in the development and implementation of assessment programs designed to help individuals identify and select vocational education programs that are appropriate for them to pursue. Via counseling, psychologists assist individuals in choosing among the variety of programs that may be appropriate for them, given the unique combination of their personalities (interests, aptitudes, values, etc.) and the unique demands associated with each program. Psychologists use their knowledge of learning and behavior to consult with vocational instructors and assist them in developing and implementing vocational training objectives, and in creating conditions under which optimum learning and performance can occur. In particular, psychologists can assist in identifying necessary modifications or adaptations in instruction that may be necessary for an individual to achieve success. On a group or individual basis, psychologists also design and implement programs that teach occupational social skills or job readiness and acquisition skills. They also plan and conduct research designed to assess the effectiveness of vocational education programs. Lastly, the psychologists' understanding of learning and behavior, combined with their understanding of disabilities, renders them especially effective in assisting individuals with disabilities who may be pursuing vocational education. Given this population's disadvantage in acquiring and maintaining jobs, individuals with disabilities are often targeted for school-to-work transition services and may be most in need of effective vocational education services.

Bibliography

Carey, K. (1995, April). *A national study of the role and function of the school psychologist.* Paper presented at the annual meeting of the National Association of School Psychologists, Chicago, IL.

Gajar, A., Goodman, L., & McAfee, J. (1993). *Secondary schools and beyond: Transition of individuals with mild disabilities.* New York: Merrill.

Government Accounting Office. (1993, September). *Transition from school to work: States are developing new strategies to prepare students for jobs* (Report to Congressional Requesters by the General Accounting Office, GAO/HRD-93-139). Washington, DC: Author.

Greenspan, S., & Shoultz, B. (1981). Why mentally retarded adults lose their jobs: Social competence as a

factor in work adjustment. *Applied Research in Mental Retardation, 2*, 23–38.
Holland, J. L. (1985). *A theory of vocational personalities and work environments.* Englewood Cliffs, NJ: Prentice Hall.
Levinson, E. M. (1988). Correlates of vocational practice among school psychologists. *Psychology in the Schools, 25*(3), 297–305.
Levinson, E. M. (1993). *Transdisciplinary vocational assessment: Issues in school-based programs.* Brandon, VT: Clinical Psychology.
Levinson, E. M. (1998). *Transition: Facilitating the postschool adjustment of students with disabilities.* Boulder, CO: Westview Press.
Lewis, J. (1992, April). Interlinking technology education and Tech-Prep: One school system's approach. *Technology Teacher*, 26–28.
Morra, L. G. (1993). *Transition from school to work: H.R. 2884 addresses components of comprehensive strategy* (GAO/HRD-93-32) (Testimony before the Committee on Education and Labor, U.S. House of Representatives). Washington, DC: General Accounting Office.
Shepard, J. W., & Hohenshil, T. H. (1983). National survey of career development functions of practicing school psychologists. *Psychology in the Schools, 20*(4), 445–449.
Staab, M. J. (1996). The role of the school psychologist in transition planning (Doctoral dissertation, University of Kansas, Lawrence, 1996). *Dissertation Abstracts International, 58*, 281.
Stern, D., Finkelstein, N., Stone, J. R., Latting, J., & Dornsife, C. (1995). *School-to-work: Research on programs in the United States.* Bristol, PA: Falmer Press.
Super, D. (1990). A life-span, life-space approach to career development. In D. Brown & L. Brooks (Eds.), *Career choice and development: Applying contemporary theories to practice* (2nd ed., pp. 197–261). San Francisco: Jossey-Bass.
Thomas, A., & Grimes, J. (1995). *Best practices in school psychology-III.* Washington, DC: NASP.
United States Department of Labor (1998). *Occupational outlook handbook.* Washington, DC: Author.

Edward M. Levinson

TECHNOLOGY. [*This entry comprises two articles:* Technology and Communication *and* Technology and Disabilities. *The first article discusses the extensiveness of psychological research on human communication and on the use of various types of communication equipment in many contexts. The second article examines psychology's contribution to the design, development, and evaluation of technological devices intended to be used by people with some form of physical or mental disability.*]

Technology and Communication

There is little, if any, evidence of human ingenuity more compelling than the numerous methods that have been used to enable or facilitate human communication. Technological advances, which have increased the ease with which people can communicate at a distance, have had an immeasurable impact on the way we live. Many of those advances have occurred in the relatively recent past. Until late in the nineteenth century, the speed of long-distance communication was limited by methods of transportation. To transmit a message from Point A to distant Point B, one put the message on some physical medium, such as paper, and transported that medium from the one point to the other. The inventions of the telegraph, radio, and telephone made it possible to send messages over long distances rapidly.

Among the more significant events in the very recent history of long-distance communication have been the development of satellite communication systems, the connection of America and Europe by transatlantic fiber-optic cable, the development of cellular telephone technology, and the building of computer-based communication networks. The kind of global connectivity that computer networks are expected to provide in the future, coupled with the continuing development of associated technologies, means not only increased access to information and information resources, but also increased access to people, independent of their location.

The phenomenal growth in computer networks since the establishment of the first experimental one in the mid-1960s has brought with it many new tools and resources to facilitate interperson communication. These include electronic mail, electronic bulletin boards, forums, chat rooms, and the World Wide Web (WWW). From the earliest days of computer networks, a major, if not *the* major, use of them has been for communication between people (human-to-human contact; Denning, 1989), although this was not the primary reason for their development. Uses of computer networks for purposes of interperson communication include sending and receiving messages to and from individuals—the electronic analogue to the traditional postal service—posting and reading of messages on special interest bulletin boards, distribution of memos or draft reports to lists of recipients, participation in real-time conversations and teleconferencing sessions, and posting information for anyone who wishes to access it on a WWW home page.

During the first decade or so after computer networks began to be established, they were used primarily by people involved in the development of this technology in one way or another, and by professionals in a few industries that made heavy use of computing resources. As accessibility to networks increased, and more and more people acquired desktop or laptop computers for professional or personal use, the community of network users (especially those who used electronic mail and related communication tools) grew rapidly and became increasingly heterogeneous with respect to backgrounds, interests, and skills. Scientists and engineers, who initially were the predominant users, comprised an ever-smaller fraction of the total user community, which came to include salespeople, hotel clerks, airline reservation personnel, travel agents, librarians, farmers, bankers, pharmacists, homemakers, and students at all levels of education.

How many people are using this technology at the end of the twentieth century in a more-than-incidental way is impossible to tell. Judging from the annual doubling of the number of host computers on the Internet through 1996 and the reaching of an estimated 13 million in that year (Lynch, 1997), the user community must be expanding at a very great rate. A large and growing fraction of the workforce, representing a wide assortment of industries and occupations, uses computer networks for communication on a daily basis. More and more individuals are using this technology as a preferred mode of private communication as well.

Computer networks have already greatly increased the accessibility people have to other people and to information resources of many sorts. In all likelihood, the number of people who make regular use of such facilities will continue to increase rapidly during the foreseeable future. What the long-term effects of this technology on interperson communication will be remains to be seen. It seems safe to assume that they will be substantial and that there will be surprises. A few empirical studies have been done about how it has been used to date, but questions abound and there is room for a great deal of research.

Much applied psychological research has focused on the design of input-output devices (displays, keyboards, mice, and other pointing devices) and, more generally, what is usually referred to as the *person-computer interface*, which encompasses not only physical devices but languages, conventions, and other cognitive aspects of interaction (Nickerson, 1986). Interest in speech for both input and output has been keen for some time; the technology has been gradually improving and speech-production and speech-recognition capabilities have been incorporated into some systems, but this is still a very active area of development.

Some attention has been given to the question of how computer-mediated communication differs, psychologically, from face-to-face communication. One interesting finding is that it appears to be somewhat more egalitarian in some respects. Social status seems to be a less important determinant of behavior; for example, higher status individuals are less likely to dominate interactions, and characteristics that are sometimes impediments to easy participation in face-to-face-meetings (soft voice, physical unattractiveness) are not discernible in electronically mediated communication. On the other hand, most of the nonverbal cues that convey nuances of meaning and affect in face-to-face situations are missing from most computer-mediated forms of communication, and this can be an impediment to understanding (Kiesler, Siegel, & McGuire, 1984).

Electronic mail and related resources have not existed long enough for widely accepted rules of etiquette to have become well established, but there is at least suggestive evidence that when they do, they are likely to differ from those that pertain to face-to-face interactions. As well as being more egalitarian, communication by electronic mail tends to be somewhat more open (less inhibited) than face-to-face communication (Sproull & Kiesler, 1991). This can make for more effective communication in some instances, but it also may encourage venting of anger and incivility in others.

Inasmuch as interperson communication (face-to-face, by telephone, or in writing) is the most common form of office activity (Bair, 1987), it was inevitable that computer-mediated communication resources would have significant effects on the way office work gets done. Such resources, as they multiply and evolve, are likely to change office work even more in the future than they have in the past. Some observers expect the widespread use of computer-mediated communication to affect the way companies structure themselves; one prediction is a decrease in the layers of management and a general move away from steeply hierarchical to more horizontal types of structures (Long, 1987). This technology has already made it possible for many people to telecommute, or work from their homes. Whether it will materially increase office productivity remains to be seen; the general effect that the introduction of computer technology in the workplace has had on productivity is a matter of some debate (Landauer, 1995). An equally important, and unanswered, question is the effect that technology in the workplace will have on the quality of workers' lives.

Electronic bulletin boards, WWW home pages, and other forms of focused "broadcast" communication seem likely to have a large effect on the way people communicate with each other in the future. A common use of bulletin boards is the posting of "does anybody know" questions, which can be an effective way of getting information that otherwise might be hard to find. As more and more people acquire access to computer networks, they will also be acquiring access to widely distributed communities with common interests. Understanding what this will mean for people's daily lives and for the functioning of localized and spatially distributed communities is a challenge for research.

Some of the possibilities that computer-mediated communication capabilities represent are captured in ideas like that of "scholarly skywriting" (Harnad, 1990), which connotes the electronic distribution of research results and discussion of same; that of the whole community as a "learning environment" (Brown, 1982), which hints at the possibility of facilitating continuous learning on a grand scale; and that of "the globalization of intellectual circles" (Levinson, 1988), which suggests the facilitation of the formation of communities of discourse based on common interest, not on common locale. Levinson contrasted the intellectual circles to which he referred with Marshall McLuhan's "global village," whose inhabitants received common information from television, but usually were not able to create or exchange it.

> The computer conferencing network establishes on a geographically irrelevant basis the possibilities for reception and initiation and exchange of information that heretofore have existed only in in-person, localized situations. The result is that members of these electronic communities know each other much as a members of a real-life local intellectual community such as a university do, but as members of a global television audience do not. (p. 205)

These are very positive visions. Unfortunately, not all of the possibilities that the technology represents are desirable, and evidence of the ways in which it can be used for socially detrimental ends already abounds. Like the telephone, which provides invaluable access to people with whom one wishes to communicate, but also makes one accessible to people from whom one has no desire to hear, computer-mediated communication technology will bring much benefit but some grief as well. And because it is a powerful technology, its potential for both types is incalculably great. Helping to steer applications of the technology to socially desirable purposes is a challenge to many professions, psychology among them.

A promising potential that networks and allied technologies represent is that of opportunities of new types of collaborative work among geographically distributed teams. The coupling of very high-bandwidth computer networks with high-resolution graphics will make it increasingly feasible for people to collaborate at a distance in real time on problems that require their collective expertise. The prospects are foreshadowed by a "telepathology" system, set up to connect pathology departments of separate hospitals so that a robotically controlled microscope at one of the facilities can be manipulated by a pathologist viewing an image on a high-definition television display at the other (Erickson, 1990).

Two implications that information technology have already had for its users are greatly shortened turnaround time for written communication, and increasing the number of people with whom one can communicate. Its eventual effect on the quality of communication remains to be seen. Will people communicate effectively with a greater number of other people than they now do? Or will communication with more people be realized at the cost of less substantive communication with all? How satisfying will computer-mediated communication be? Will it replace certain other modes of communication or just supplement them? What abuses will be made of it? What effect, on balance, will it have on the ability of people to get along with each other? Will it increase understanding among people from different cultures or inhibit it? How will the integration of speech technology with electronic mail change the character of the medium? What needs will computer-mediated communication capabilities create for personal information management tools? These and numerous related questions represent opportunities for psychological research that can only increase in importance as the technology continues to advance, extending the communication capabilities it affords.

Bibliography

Bair, J. H. (1987). User needs for office systems solutions. In R. E. Kraut (Ed.), *Technology and the transformation of white collar work* (pp. 177–194). Hillsdale, NJ: Erlbaum.

Brown, G. E., Jr. (1982). A congressional view of the coming information age. In R. A. Kasschau, R. Lachman, & K. R., Laughery (Eds.), *Houston Symposium III: Information technology and psychology* (pp. 41–55). New York: Praeger.

Denning, P. J. (1989). The science of computing: Worldnet. *American Scientist, 77*, 432–434.

Erickson, D., (1990). Do you see what I see? *Scientific American, 263*(1), 88–89.

Harnad, S. (1990). Scholarly skywriting and the prepublication continuum of scientific inquiry. *Psychological Science, 1*, 342–344.

Kiesler, S., Siegel, J., & McGuire, T. (1984). Social psychological aspects of computer-mediated communication. *American Psychologist, 39*, 1123–1134.

Landauer, T. K. (1995). *The trouble with computers: Usefulness, usability and productivity.* Cambridge, MA: MIT Press.

Levinson, P. (1988). *Mind at large: Knowing in the technological age.* Greenwich, CT: JAI Press.

Long, R. J. (1987). *New office information technology: Human and managerial implications.* London: Croom Helm.

Lynch, C. (1997). Searching the Internet. *Scientific American, 276*(3), 52–56.

Nickerson, R. S. (1986). *Using computers: The human factors of information systems.* Cambridge, MA: MIT Press.

Sproull, L., & Kiesler, S. (1991). *Connections: New ways of working in the networked organization.* Cambridge, MA: MIT Press.

Raymond S. Nickerson

Technology and Disabilities

The disabled population is large. Approximately 30% of the U.S. population, about 75 million people, report

TECHNOLOGY: Technology and Disabilities. Table 1. Summary of disabilities in the United States (1990 estimates)

	Any Impairment	Severe Impairments	
Disability	Persons (000s)	Persons (000s)	Percentage of Population
Sensory			
Visual impairment	8,600	2,000	0.8
Hearing impairment	22,000	2,400	1.0
Motor, physical			
Orthopedic impairments	23,400	13,300	5.3
Cognitive			
Specific learning disabilities	18,700	6,200	2.5
Impaired speech	2,000	200	0.1
Mental retardation	3,000	3,000	1.2
Total	77,700	27,100	10.9

Data are derived from the 1987 and 1989 *Statistical Abstracts of the United States*, published by the U.S. Department of Commerce by extrapolation to 1990.

having some kind of sensory, physical, or cognitive disability. Approximately 25 million people have disabilities that are sufficiently severe to interfere with work, career aspirations, daily activities, and otherwise constitute a serious handicap. Table 1 shows the incidence of the different types of disability (Elkind, Nickerson, Van Cott, & Williges, 1995). The incidence of disability increases with age, and more than half of the elderly (over 65 years of age) report physical or activity limits.

People with disabilities are disadvantaged in work and other situations because they cannot easily use equipment and facilities principally designed for the able-bodied population and because their performance in common tasks and functions is not as good as that of their able-bodied peers. They are often slower and less accurate, and have less endurance, range of movement, and ability to automatize functions. They would benefit both from more accessible design of standard equipment and facilities and from assistive devices that enhance their performance.

Technology has been central both in providing better access and enhancing the performance of the disabled. The great advances in micro-electronics, personal computer, software, and communications technologies have been especially important. An enormous number and variety of assistive devices are available, many based on personal computers and associated software. Access to computers themselves has improved greatly in recent years. The prospects for future gains in both areas are very positive, as the cost and power of electronic systems continue to improve in accordance with Moore's law, which states that the number of components that can be put onto semiconductor devices will double every 18 months or so.

Providing good access to the disabled as well as to the able-bodied is becoming a common requirement of the design of new devices and systems. However, it is a requirement that is often difficult to achieve. There are many different types of disabilities; people do an almost innumerable variety of tasks at work, home, and recreation; the disabled have a wide range of sensory, motor, and cognitive capabilities and limitations; and these are often considerably different from those of the able-bodied population. The design of assistive devices and equipment is similarly complex.

To deal with this complexity, a well-structured human-centered design methodology is required. Human factors provides such a design process, which is illustrated schematically in Figure 1 (Salvendy, 1987; Elkind, Nickerson, Van Cott, & Williges, 1995). It is based on analyses of tasks that the human user is to perform, data and models that describe human performance capabilities and limitations, the synthesis of potential designs, and the evaluation of these designs. This process is applied iteratively until a satisfactory design is obtained.

Task Analyses

A variety of techniques are used to develop an understanding of the tasks that disabled people must perform in their daily activities, and of the perceptual, motor, and cognitive capabilities needed to perform them. These include observations, video analyses, taxonomies, scenario generation, time lines, workloads, and

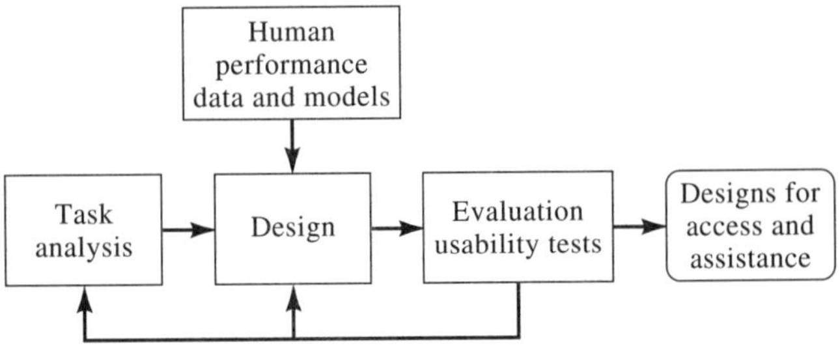

TECHNOLOGY: Technology and Disabilities. Figure 1. Human factors design methodology.

input/output analyses (Elkind, Nickerson, Van Cott, & Williges, 1995). In doing task analysis for disabled users, we need to take account of the fact that tasks take longer to accomplish and are performed less accurately and less automatically than would be the case for able-bodied users. Incomplete automatization means that tasks we would ordinarily consider to be unitary, like deciding the sequence of letters to use for a word when writing, might have to be divided into subtasks, each of which requires conscious cognitive processing.

Human Performance Data and Models

A large body of performance data and models about human capabilities, capacities, and limitations is available in databases, design guides, textbooks, and models to inform human factors design for able-bodied users (see, for example, Boff & Lincoln, 1988). However, few data are available for most disabled populations, especially data describing their motor and cognitive functioning. An interesting exception is the work of Kelley and Kroemer, who extended an anthropometric database to include the elderly (1990). Handbooks sometimes include a chapter on disability (Salvendy, 1987), and sometimes have data relevant to the elderly.

Most existing models of human performance were not developed with the disabled population specifically in mind, but they do provide a framework for characterization of their performance. Interesting models include anthropometric models (McDaniel & Askren, 1985; Paquette, 1990); workload models (Hartzell, Aiken, & Voorhees, 1984); models of vision (Larimer, Arditi, Bergen, & Badler, 1989; see also Elkind, Card, Hochberg, & Huey, 1990); and simple cognitive models such as the Model Human Processor and the GOMS model (Card, Moran, & Newell, 1983).

Researchers in psychology have become more interested in the problems of the disabled. Recent special issues of *Human Factors*, "Assisting People With Functional Impairments" and "Aging," and a recent book on disabilities and human-computer interaction (Edwards, 1995) are examples of the growing interest in this area.

There is an extensive literature from the medical, rehabilitation, occupational therapy, prosthesis, and other specialized communities on the characteristics of various disabled populations. Not much of this information has yet found its way into the human factors literature, in part because it is not well organized for use in human factors design. The information is often largely prescriptive and not quantitative.

Design for Accessibility

There are clearly difficulties in designing equipment and systems so that they are accessible for use by the disabled as well as the general population without imposing unacceptable cost or performance penalties. The disabled population, although large in total, is composed of many subgroups, many of which are small. Although it is impossible to design everything to be accessible to all subgroups, products can be designed so that they are accessible, or at least more accessible, to major segments of the disabled population. Because such designs pay attention to the capabilities of users who have sensory, motor, and cognitive limitations, they often turn out to be simpler and easier for the able-bodied to use (Newell, 1995).

There are many examples of successful accessible designs for computer systems, such as "sticky" keys, which substitute the sequential activation of keys for simultaneous activation for others with impaired hand control and zoom enlargement of displays for those with poor vision. The capabilities that computer systems need to be accessible to people with sensory and physical impairments are summarized by Scadden and Vanderheiden (1988). Different subgroups often require different presentations of information and different ways of exercising control, so a single interface for the entire user community, disabled as well as able bodied, is not possible. Specialized interfaces for different subgroups are required to provide different surface representations of underlying data and controls. To facilitate the design of these user interfaces, standard programmatic interfaces to underlying data and controls are being developed. Active Accessibility, the recently announced Microsoft accessibility standards, is an important step in this direction (Lowney, 1996).

Design of Assistive Devices

Literally thousands of assistive devices have been designed to enhance the performance of disabled people (see Casali & Williges, 1990, for a list of available databases). Examples are speech generation devices for those with severe speech impairments and eye tracking systems as a substitute for keyboard input for those with severe manipulatory impairments. Assistive devices for enhancing cognitive functions include computer readers that use speech synthesis to read text to dyslexic users, and speech recognition systems for those who have difficulty writing. Computer and communications technologies have made it possible to bring jobs to people who cannot easily take themselves to jobs (telecommuting) and have increased the disabled's access to other people and resources (Williges & Williges, 1995).

The large number of assistive devices and systems available for the disabled raises the problem of how to locate and select a particular device that matches the needs of an individual user. There have been several attempts to provide a systematic method for selecting assistive devices and systems. Casali reviews this literature and describes a comprehensive and quantitative approach that uses detailed information about particular types of devices, the residual capabilities of the disabled user, analysis of the requirements of the tasks to be performed, and tests to evaluate the devices (1995). This approach mirrors the design methodology depicted in Figure 1.

Evaluation

Evaluation of proposed designs with usability experiments is essential to the design process. It is important to conduct user experiments to determine how well a tentative design matches the need of the disabled individuals for whom it is intended. Only by careful examination of the shortcomings of one design is it possible to know where to place the effort on making improvements. Evaluation is facilitated by models of human performance such as those described above. For example, Elkind and Shrager applied GOMS models to the analysis of computer-supported composition by dyslexic individuals to evaluate existing designs for assistive devices and to propose modifications (1995).

General models tend to describe average performance. It is important to keep in mind that each person with a disability has specific impairments and must be understood individually. Assistive devices must be adjusted for these individual differences. To adapt general models so that they represent the characteristics of disabled populations and individuals within them will require new data from these populations and extensions to current models.

Bibliography

Boff, K. B., & Lincoln, J. E. (1988). *Engineering data compendium, human perception and performance.* Wright-Patterson Air Force Base, OH: Armstrong Aerospace Medical Research Laboratory.

Card, S. K., Moran, T. P., & Newell, A. (1983). *The psychology of human-computer interaction.* Hillsdale, NJ: Erlbaum.

Casali, S. P. (1995). A physical skills-based strategy for choosing an appropriate interface method. In A. D. N. Edwards (Ed.), *Extra-ordinary, human-computer interaction.* London, England: Cambridge University Press.

Casali, S. P., & Williges, R. C. (1990). Databases of accommodative aids for computer users with disabilities. *Human Factors, 32,* 407–422.

Edwards, A. D. N. (Ed.). (1995). *Extra-ordinary human-computer interaction.* London, England: Cambridge University Press.

Elkind, J. I., Card, S. K., Hochberg, J., & Huey, B. M. (Eds.). (1990). *Human performance models for computer-aided engineering.* San Diego: Academic Press.

Elkind, J. I., Nickerson R. S., Van Cott, H. P., & Williges, R. C. (1995). Employment and disabilities. In R. S. Nickerson (Ed.), *Emerging needs and opportunities for human-factors research.* Washington, DC: National Academy Press.

Elkind, J. I., & Shrager, J. (1995). Modeling and analysis of dyslexic writing using speech and other modalities. In A. D. N. Edwards (Ed.), *Extra-ordinary human-computer interaction.* London, England: Cambridge University Press.

Hartzell, E. J., Aiken, E. W., & Vorhees, J. W. (1984). *Aircrew-aircraft integration issues in future U.S. Army helicopters.* In AGARD Human Factors Considerations in High Performance Aircraft. Moffett Field, CA: National Aeronautics and Space Administration.

Kelley, P. L., & Kroemer, K. H. E. (1990). Anthropometry of the elderly: Status and recommendations. *Human Factors, 32,* 571–595.

Latimer, J., Arditi, A., Bergen, J., & Badler, N. (1989). *Visibility modeling project.* Moffett Field, CA: National Aeronautics and Space Administration.

Lowney, G. C. (1996). Removing barriers: Active Accessibility; Designing applications and objects communicate and automate. *Microsoft Developers Network News.*

McDaniel, J. W., & Askren, W. B. (1985). *Computer-aided design models to support ergonomics.* Wright-Patterson Air Force Base, OH: Harry G. Armstrong Aerospace Medical Research Laboratory.

Newell, A. F. (1995). Extra-ordinary human-computer interaction. In A. D. N. Edwards (Ed.), *Extra-ordinary human-computer interaction.* London, England: Cambridge University Press.

Paquette, S. P. (1990). *Human analogue models for computer-aided design and engineering applications.* Natick, MA: Army Natick Research and Engineering Center.

Salvendy, G. (Ed.). (1987). *Handbook of human factors.* New York: Wiley.

Scadden, L. A., & Vanderheiden, G. C. (1988). *Considerations in the design of computers and operating systems to increase their accessibility to persons with disabilities.* Trace Research and Development Center on Communication, Control, and Computer Access for Handicapped Individuals. Madison: University of Wisconsin.

Williges, R. C., & Williges, B. H. (1995). Travel alternatives for the mobility impaired: The surrogate electronic traveler (SET). In A. D. N. Edwards (Ed.), *Extra-ordinary human-computer interaction*. London, England: Cambridge University Press.

Jerome I. Elkind

TELEPATHY. *See* Parapsychology.

TEMPERAMENT. A temperamental quality is a relatively stable psychobiological profile, under some genetic control, that combines behavior, emotion, and physiology. At the present time the physiological features that are the presumed components of each of the many temperaments have not yet been discovered; hence, most scientists rely either on a person's behavior or patterns of responses to questionnaires to classify a person as a member of a particular temperamental category.

Two ancient physicians, Hippocrates and Galen, who are regarded as the founders of a temperamental theory (Siegel, 1968), suggested that temperament primarily referred to emotion and action profiles. Galen believed that the relative concentrations of 4 body humors—blood, phlegm, and yellow and black bile—created within each person a combination of the opposed dimensional qualities of warm versus cool and dry versus moist. The four basic temperamental types, called melancholic, sanguine, choleric, and phlegmatic, were the products of a particular combination of these two dimensions. Melancholics were high on the qualities of cool and dry because they possessed greater amounts of black bile. Sanguine persons were high on warm and moist qualities because of excess blood. The choleric was high on warm and dry because of an excess of yellow bile, and the phlegmatic was high on the qualities of cool and moist because of an excess in phlegm. Although each temperament had its roots in the person's constitution, this physiology was malleable, to some degree, to external events, especially to changes in climate and diet. For example, Galen believed that most adults became melancholic in the fall because the autumnal season led to a rise in black bile.

Although the Chinese view of human nature, two millennia before Galen, shared some features with the latter position, it was different in several important ways. The critical balance in Chinese speculative philosophy was among forces of energy rather than material substances like bile or blood. The energy of the universe, called *ch'i* and regulated by the complementary relation between the active force of yang and the passive force of yin, must be in balance for optimal human functioning. However, because the energy of *ch'i* is always changing, a person's moods and behaviors cannot be permanent. A person might be melancholic temporarily but not because he possessed the melancholic temperament.

Although temperamental ideas remained popular until the end of the nineteenth century, the biological signs used to diagnose the quality became more observable. Lombroso suggested an association between an individual's body type and criminal tendencies (1911). Kretschmer believed that schizophrenics and manic-depressives possessed different temperaments but each represented the extremes of two basic, inherited temperaments that could be seen in less extreme form in normal individuals (1925). Cyclothymes were relaxed, spontaneous extraverts, while schizothymes were timid, subdued introverts.

However, temperamental concepts lost their appeal during the first half of this century as behaviorism and psychoanalysis ascended in significance. Freud made important changes in nineteenth-century Galenic views. First, he awarded extraordinary power to early experience, minimized, but did not deny, the relevance of temperament, and substituted the energy of the libido for the four humors. Although his early writings acknowledged the influence of both temperamental differences as well as experience in the amount of libido, his later work awarded greater importance to childhood events and, accordingly, the contribution of temperament faded.

Two American psychiatrists, Alexander Thomas and Stella Chess, reintroduced the idea of temperament in the late 1950s to the psychiatric and psychological communities (1977). They defined a temperamental quality as a distinctive style of behavior and posited 9 temperamental dimensions in infants and young children based on interviews with a large number of parents. The dimensions were activity level, regularity, reaction to unfamiliarity, ease of adapting to new situations, responsiveness to stimuli, level of energy, dominant mood, distractibility, and attention span. Combinations of these dimensions produced, in their view, three more abstract categories. The most prevalent category, called the easy child and comprising about 40% of their sample, were children who were regular in their daily routine and typically approached unfamiliar people and situations with minimum fear. The slow-to-warm-up child, about 15% of the sample, typically reacted to unfamiliar events with withdrawal and signs of fear. The least frequent category was the difficult child, about 10% of the sample, who was irregular in routine, often irritable, and usually withdrew from unfamiliar situations. This last type was more likely than the first two to develop psychiatric symptoms in later childhood.

Most students of temperament agree that individuals who belong to a particular category can vary in their degree of membership. It is believed that the defining psychological and physiological features have moderate stability over time and situations, are under some genetic influence, and usually appear during the childhood years.

There is disagreement, however, as to which temperamental qualities should be given priority in theoretical discussions. Some scientists believe that the primary adult temperamental dimensions are avoidance of dangerous situations, seeking of novelty, and dependence on social rewards (Cloninger, 1987). Other theorists posit emotionality, activity, and sociability as the three major adult temperaments (Buss & Plomin, 1984).

The concepts of reactivity and self-regulation have been nominated as two fundamental temperaments in infants and young children (Rothbart, 1989). Reactivity refers to the ease with which some response—motor activity, crying, vocalization, smiling, or physiology—is provoked by an event. Thus, an infant who shows vigorous motor activity or loud vocalizations to the appearance of a familiar adult would be regarded as reactive. Regulation refers to the modulation of reactivity and includes patterns of attention, approach-withdrawal or attack to an event, or self-initiated soothing responses, like sucking the finger or twirling the hair.

Although these two concepts have a great deal of utility, they are insufficiently definitive in their specification of the age of the child—3 months or 2 years—as well as the incentive situation. Most 4-month-old infants become motorically active and show a rise in heart rate to many nonsocial, visual stimuli, but will vocalize and show a decrease in heart rate to most auditory events. They will cry to unpleasant tastes or smells but smile to human faces. Thus, the form that the reactivity assumes is dependent, in a major way, on the nature of the provocative event, suggesting that scientists should invent a construct that includes, in its referential meaning, the specific response displayed and the provoking event. The same principle holds for the idea of regulation. Some 1-year-olds approach an unfamiliar adult; others retreat; still others turn their gaze away from the stranger. The preference for one of these regulating responses over the others is often a stable trait and, therefore, it is useful to parse the term *regulation* into different types.

A final problem with the idea of regulation is that the observer cannot know whether absence of a regulatory reaction (for example, failure to retreat from a stranger) is due to an appropriate and efficient regulation of fear or failure to experience any change in emotion. If the child did not become fearful to the stranger, there would be no need for any regulation.

Although most scholars believe that each temperamental type has a unique set of physiological features, their nature remains undiscovered. The brain contains almost 200 different chemicals, each of which influences the excitability of particular ensembles of neurons and brain circuits. It is believed that children inherit different concentrations of these chemicals, as well as different densities of the relevant receptors on neuronal surfaces. These conditions are the bases for different temperaments. One example involves the neurotransmitter norepinephrine. An enzyme called dopamine-beta-hydroxylase, which is under some genetic control, is necessary for the final step of the synthesis of norepinephrine. Children with very low levels of this enzyme will have low levels of norepinephrine. Because brain norepinephrine increases the probability of a fear state, children with low levels of the enzyme should be less fearful. The evidence indicates that boys with conduct disorder, who seem to be unafraid of punishment, have very low levels of this enzyme (Rogeness et al., 1988).

Dopamine, another essential neurotransmitter, plays an important role in motor behavior and in the integrity of processes mediated by the frontal cortex (Carlson, 1998). Because the frontal lobes mediate the planning, inhibition, and control of impulsive decisions, it is possible that children who inherit low levels of dopamine in the frontal areas will be unusually impulsive. The rationale for administering the drug Ritalin to children who have been diagnosed as impulsive or hyperactive is that this drug increases the level of dopamine in frontal areas and helps children control inappropriate behavior (Carlson, 1998).

Although the degree of irritability, laughter, activity level, and attentional processes vary among infants, most research on temperament has involved the Chess and Thomas categories of "easy" and "slow to warm up." The latter individual is shy and timid in unfamiliar social situations while the former is sociable. These two qualities are among the most stable and heritable in human personality, with heritability coefficients ranging between 0.3 and 0.6 (Kagan, 1994).

The shy, timid, and wary child has also been called the inhibited child, while the sociable, bold, fearless child has been called uninhibited. These two temperamental groups possess different physiological characteristics. For example, inhibited children display greater than normal sympathetic reactivity to cognitive stress, while uninhibited children show smaller changes in heart rate and blood pressure in response to unfamiliarity and challenge. Furthermore, inhibited children are more likely to show activation of the right frontal lobe, as measured by suppression of alpha frequencies, while uninhibited children are more likely to show greater activation of the left frontal area. This fact is in accord with research indicating that the right hemisphere participates more fully in states of fear, anxiety, or depression, while the left hemisphere is a more significant participant in the emotions of happiness or joy (Davidson, 1995).

Children who were inhibited in the second year displayed very high levels of motor activity combined with crying when presented with visual, auditory, and olfactory stimuli at 16 weeks of age. This pattern, called high reactivity, is characteristic of about 15 to 20% of healthy infants (Kagan, 1994). The children who become uninhibited in the second year displayed, at 16 weeks of age, very low levels of motor activity and minimal distress to the same events. These infants are called low reactive and comprise about 35 to 40% of healthy infants. The differences between high and low reactive infants can be explained by assuming that the two groups differ in the excitability of the amygdala and its projections to the cortex, brain stem, and autonomic nervous system as a function of variation in inherited neurochemical profiles.

The inhibited child is at slightly greater risk than most children for developing some form of anxiety disorder in later childhood and adolescence. About 20% of 7-year-old children who had been highly reactive infants showed serious symptoms of anxiety or fear, compared with less than 5% of all other children. Uninhibited children, by contrast, are at slightly greater risk for conduct disorder, but only if they grow up in family environments that are permissive of aggression and in neighborhoods that are provocative of anger, frustration, and temptations to asocial behavior.

There is disagreement as to whether temperamental characteristics should be viewed as continuous dimensions or qualitative categories. Thomas and Chess regarded the easy, difficult, and slow-to-warm-up children as belonging to discrete categories. But other scientists regard the tendency to approach or to withdraw from unfamiliarity as a continuous dimension. The evidence in favor of categories comes from the fact that inhibited children tend to have a narrower facial skeleton and, if Caucasian, more often possess very light blue eyes. The inheritance of these features implies the influence of a set of genes that affects characteristics as diverse as the profile of the facial skeleton, production of melanin in the iris, ease of arousal in infancy, and timidity to unfamiliar events. Furthermore, only about 15% of 2-year-olds are consistently shy and timid in a variety of unfamiliar situations, while most children are shy and subdued in only one class of unfamiliar situations. This implies that this small group are qualitatively different from children who are subdued or shy in only one context.

Although genes may make a modest contribution to these temperamental profiles, biology always shares power with experience. Over one third of 4-month-old infants classified as highly reactive were not shy and fearful in the second year; a few were fearless. Furthermore, mothers who set firm limits for the highly reactive infants help them overcome their fearfulness. By contrast, mothers of highly reactive infants who are oversolicitous tend to exacerbate the child's tendency to be timid and shy.

Temperamental variation among ethnic groups is a delicate issue because of the ethnic strife that exists around the world. One group of scientists compared the frequencies of over 100 different alleles for geographically separate populations and regarded the average difference in allele frequency between two groups as an index of the genetic distance between that pair of populations. The average genetic distances were largest when Asians, Africans, and European Caucasians were compared with each other. But even within the group called European Caucasian, people from Scandinavia, England, and the rest of northern Europe were genetically different from Caucasians living in Spain, Italy, the Balkans, and the rest of southern Europe. It is not unreasonable to assume that some of the alleles in this analysis contribute to variation in temperament qualities.

The most consistent set of data on early infant temperament compared Asian with Caucasian infants and found that the former were less reactive than the latter (Kagan, 1994). These ethnic differences in ease of becoming aroused might have derivatives in childhood. Chinese mothers of school age children in Shanghai describe them as less active, less impulsive, and more controlled than mothers of Caucasian children living in the Pacific Northwest (Weisz et al., 1988). Moreover, Asian American psychiatric patients require a lower dose of psychotropic drugs than do European American patients with the same symptoms living in the same state. This fact implies that Asian populations may be at a lower level of limbic arousal.

It is also believed that vulnerability to the emotions of guilt and shame might be differentially associated with particular temperaments. Many boys with conduct disorder, who tend to be uninhibited, possess very low heart rates and blood pressures, implying that they have a higher threshold for becoming fearful (Raine, Venables, & Williams, 1990). It is possible that a very small group of criminals who commit violent crimes possess a rare temperament. A group of delinquents growing up in New Zealand were rated as possessing unusually low control of their behavior when they were 3 to 5 years old (Caspi et al., 1995).

The increased interest in temperament by scientists and the general community has generated discussion over the degree of responsibility each person has for his or her behavior. An observer's assumption regarding the degree of self-conscious control another person possesses will determine how the latter is evaluated when he or she violates community standards. Western society has been relatively Puritan in its commitment to the belief that each person has sufficient willpower to exert control over behavior. This philosophical view has been eroded over the last half century, as a growing number of citizens has become willing to excuse some criminal actions because they believed those acts were not always within the agent's sphere of control. Some adults are even willing to apply this principle to behaviors that have a partial origin in the individual's temperament. It is not obvious, however, that this permissiveness is more adaptive for our society than the traditional assumption that one of the significant products of human evolution is the capacity to select and monitor one's behavior. Most individuals begin each day with the twin assumptions that everyone has an obligation to be aware of the needs of the other and to be loyal to that imperative. For that reason, justifiable anger can be generated if someone fails those obligations. The concept of temperament has its most ambiguous implications in these everyday applications. An ethical conflict is posed if a temperamental bias can create psychological states that, on occasion, render a person's will temporarily impotent. Is a friend, colleague, or spouse obligated to accept frustrating behavior in another, or is the former justified in becoming irritated with a partner who violates an imperative that most members of a society accept? At the moment, we must live with ambiguity on that issue.

[*See also* Personality.]

Bibliography

Buss, A. H., & Plomin, R. (1984). *Temperament: Early developing traits*. Hillsdale, NJ: Erlbaum.

Carlson, N. R. (1998). *Physiology of behavior* (6th ed.). Boston: Allyn & Bacon.

Caspi, A., Henri, B., McGee, R. O., Moffitt, T., & Silva, P. A., (1995). Temperamental origins of child and adolescent behavior problems: From age 3 to 15. *Child Development, 66*, 55–68.

Cloninger, C. R. (1987). A systematic method for clinical description and classification of personality variants. *Archives of General Psychiatry, 44*, 573–588.

Davidson, R. J. (1995). Cerebral asymmetry, emotion, and affective style. In R. J. Davidson & K. Hugdhal (Eds.), *Brain Asymmetry* (pp. 361–388). Cambridge, MA: MIT Press.

Kagan, J. (1994). *Galen's prophecy*. New York: Basic Books.

Kagan, J., Arcus, D., Snidman, N., Yu-Feng, W., Hendler, J., & Greene, S. (1994). Reactivity in infancy. *Developmental Psychology, 30*, 342–345.

Kretchmer, E. (1925). *Physique and character* (2nd ed.). (W. J. H. Sprott, Trans.). New York: Harcourt Brace.

Lombroso, C. (1911). *Crime and its causes*. Boston: Little, Brown.

Raine, A., Venables, P. H., & Williams, M. (1990). Autonomic orienting responses in 15-year-old male subjects and criminal behavior at age 24. *American Journal of Psychiatry, 147*, 933–937.

Rogeness, G. A., Mass, J. W., Javors, M. A., Masedo, C. A., Harris, W. R., & Hoppe, S. K. (1988). Diagnoses, catecholamines, and plasma dopamine-beta-hydroxylase. *Journal of the American Academy of Child and Adolescent psychiatry, 27*, 121–125.

Rothbart, M. K. (1989). Temperament in childhood: A framework. In G. A. Kohnstamm, J. E. Bates, & M. K. Rothbart (Eds.), *Temperament in childhood* (pp. 59–76). New York: Wiley.

Siegel, R. E. (1968). *Galen's system of physiology and medicine*. Basel: Karger.

Thomas, A., & Chess, S. (1977). *Temperament and development*. New York: Brunner/Mazel.

Weisz, J. R., Suwanlert, S., Chaiyasit, W., Weiss, B., Walter, B. R., & Anderson, W. W. (1988). Thai and American perspectives on over- and undercontrolled child behavior problems. *Journal of Consulting and Clinical Psychology, 56*, 601–609.

Jerome Kagan

TERMAN, LEWIS MADISON (1877–1956), American psychologist. Terman was committed to applying psychology to the needs of society. In his own specialty of measuring individual and group differences, his objective was to foster the use of psychological assessment tools to meet the demands of an industrialized society that required an increasingly specialized labor force by the early twentieth century. In particular, he sought to demonstrate that measures of intellectual and personality differences could be used to sort individuals into the social roles they were best qualified to fulfill. The most intellectually and emotionally competent individuals would occupy the highest positions of responsibility and leadership. As a result of such a meritocratic structure, both individual and social efficiency would be maximized.

Terman was born and raised on a farm in central Indiana, the twelfth of 14 children. After several years as a schoolteacher and school principal, he decided on a career in psychology and obtained his master's degree at Indiana University in 1903 and his doctorate at Clark University in 1905. He taught child study and pedagogy at the Los Angeles State Normal School for four years and then received an appointment in the education department at Stanford University in 1910. He spent the rest of his career at Stanford, becoming head of the psychology department in 1922, a position he held until his retirement in 1942. At Stanford, he renewed his doctoral research on mental testing by working on a revision of Alfred Binet's scale of intelligence, which had first been published in France in 1905. Collaborating with graduate students, Terman's revision was published in 1916 as the "Stanford–Binet." An innovative feature of the Stanford–Binet was the inclusion of the "Intelligence Quotient" or IQ—that is, the ratio between mental and chronological ages—a concept first introduced by the German psychologist William Stern, but not previously used in mental tests. While there were several competitive versions, Terman's revision of the Binet utilized the largest standardized sample and, by the 1920s, became the most widely used individually administered intelligence scale. The scale has been revised several times and is still in use.

With the publication of the Stanford–Binet, Terman became a highly visible figure in the mental testing movement. He subsequently played a major role in the development of various measures of individual differences. During World War I, he worked with other testing psychologists to produce intelligence tests aimed at ferreting out the mentally unfit from the army. As a result, the first group-administered intelligence tests were constructed (the army Alpha and Beta examinations). The widespread use of these mental tests in the military led to the development of group-administered intelligence tests for schoolchildren in the early 1920s. Terman was involved in the construction of these tests and became a leading advocate for their use in sorting schoolchildren into homogeneous ability groups, that is, a "tracking system." This educational practice became well established in American schools by the 1930s. Terman was also a leader in the development of group achievement tests, which assessed school learning. He collaborated on the construction of the Stanford Achievement Test, the first test battery of its kind.

Terman viewed the widespread adoption of tests in the schools as a reflection of how testing could be of use to American society. It was to be the major means of achieving his vision of a meritocracy within the American democratic ideal—a social order based on ranked levels of native ability. Consistent with the views of other leading American mental testers, Terman believed that mental abilities were primarily a product of heredity. The highest purpose that testing could serve was the identification of intellectually gifted children—the potential leaders of society. To accomplish his meritocratic objectives, Terman launched a longitudinal study of gifted children in 1921. This was the first longitudinal study in psychology to use a large sample. Canvassing elementary and secondary schools in California, Terman and his research team came up with a sample of close to 1,500 gifted children. This sample was followed up as the participants moved through their adolescence, adulthood, and retirement years. When Terman died in 1956, his research associates carried on the project. Terman collaborated on the publication of the first five monographs reporting the results of the study.

In an attempt to dispel the popular notion that gifted children were underdeveloped in nonintellectual areas, Terman included medical and physical assessments, as well as measures of personality, character, and interests. Compared with a control group of California schoolchildren, Terman reported that gifted children excelled in measures of academic achievement. The composite portrait of the gifted children also revealed that they were emotionally as well as intellectually mature. At midlife, the intellectual level of the gifted group continued to be within the upper 1% of the general population, and their vocational achievement was well above the average of college graduates. Furthermore, as earlier reports had indicated, they showed few signs of such serious problems as insanity, delinquency, or alcoholism. The midlife report also included some striking gender differences. While the men as a group had attained a high level of career success, few women had comparable levels of career achievement. As the research team noted, career opportunities for women were restricted by gender-role conformity and job discrimination.

Terman's interest in the measurement of individual and group differences extended beyond mental abilities and achievement. As a consequence of his research on the gifted, he became interested in nonintellectual traits. By assessing emotional and motivational characteristics, he was able to demonstrate that the gifted had well-adjusted and well-rounded personalities. The approach he pursued in this area was to measure appropriate gender identification. In 1936, with his research associate Catharine Cox Miles, he produced the first questionnaire measure of masculinity-femininity, labeled the "Attitude-Interest Analysis Test" to disguise its purpose. The test was made up of about 450 multiple-choice items that assessed preferences for a variety of activities and interests, as well as reactions to emotionally laden situations. In an attempt to validate the masculinity-femininity test, Terman was able to collect test protocols from a group of male homosexuals in San Francisco. As he expected, the results revealed that male homosexuals had high feminine scores. He thus concluded that marked deviations from gender-appropriate behaviors and norms were psychologically unhealthy because such deviations could very likely lead to homosexuality. The results of his research on masculinity-femininity were reported in the 1936 book, *Sex and Personality*, coauthored with Miles.

Terman's interest in gender expanded to research on marital adjustment. He conducted a large-scale survey of several thousand married and divorced couples. According to Terman, the major finding was that the combination of personality and background factors was more influential in predicting marital happiness than sexual compatibility. This conclusion was contrary to previous marriage studies that argued that sexual compatibility was the key to marital happiness. Terman pointed out that this discrepancy was due to the fact that previous studies had neglected to consider psychological factors because physicians and social workers had carried them out. He thus indicated the importance of psychology in the study of marital relations and human sexuality. In his study, Terman stressed that the key to marital adjustment was the extent to which each spouse accepted the other's needs and feelings and did not fight to get his or her own way. Happily married women, therefore, were characterized as being cooperative and content with their subordinate status. Terman's conventional views on gender carried over from his masculinity-femininity study to his marital research.

Terman's seminal contributions to the development of psychological testing and the study of the intellectually gifted ensure his position as one of the pioneers of American psychology. Perhaps more than any of the other advocates of the testing movement, he was successful in devising a wide variety of methods assessing individual differences. His interest in the gifted led him to go far beyond the measurement of ability. He was thus in the forefront of developing indices of school achievement, gender identity, interests, marital adjustment, and sexual behavior. His hereditarian position on group differences in intelligence, however, became controversial by the 1940s—a time in which psychologists began to take environmentalist factors into account, especially with respect to racial differences. While he moved away from arguing that class and racial differences in intelligence were primarily explained by heredity, he was steadfast in his hereditarian view of individual differences in mental ability. He therefore continued to believe that intelligence tests given to schoolchildren were effective in making long-term predictions of intellectual and vocational achievement. With the impact of the civil rights movement in the 1960s, however, psychologists and educational specialists became more sensitive to the social inequities faced by ethnic minority children. Intelligence tests in the schools thus began to be used more as diagnostic rather than prognostic instruments. The changing social context of the 1960s brought about a more critical evaluation of the accomplishments of the American mental testing movement and its pioneer proponents, such as Terman.

Bibliography

Chapman, P. D. (1988). *Schools as sorters: Lewis M. Terman, applied psychology, and the intelligence testing movement, 1890–1930.* New York: New York University Press. Includes the role of Terman in the adoption of intelligence tests in American schools.

Fancher, R. R. (1985). *The intelligence men: Makers of the IQ controversy.* New York: Norton. Reviews the biographies and contributions of the leading figures in the mental testing movement.

Gould, S. J. (1981). *The mismeasure of man.* New York: Norton. A critique of the hereditarian view of intelligence, including coverage of craniometry, phrenology, and IQ tests.

Herrnstein, R. J., & Murray, C. (1994). *The bell curve: Intelligence and class structure in American life.* New York: Free Press. A controversial treatment of class and race differences that focuses on the hereditarian interpretation of intelligence.

Jacoby, R., & Glauberman, N. (Eds.). (1995). *The bell curve debate: History, documents, opinions.* New York: Random House. Includes reactions to the Herrnstein and Murray book as well as articles by significant figures in the history of mental testing.

Kimmel, M. (1996). *Manhood in America: A cultural history.* New York: Free Press. Includes a discussion of the influence and implications of Terman's work on gender.

Minton, H. L. (1988). *Lewis M. Terman: Pioneer in psychological testing.* New York: New York University Press. A biography of Terman's life and work.

Samelson, F. (1979). Putting psychology on the map: Ideology and intelligence testing. In A. R. Buss (Ed.), *Psychology in social context* (pp. 103–168). New York: Irvington. A critical analysis of the weaknesses of intelligence testing in World War I.

Seagoe, M. V. (1975). *Terman and the gifted.* Los Altos, CA: William Kaufmann. A biography by an admiring former student.

Sokal, M. M. (Ed.). (1987). *Psychological testing and American society 1890–1930.* New Brunswick, NJ: Rutgers University Press. Includes chapters about the leading figures in the early development of intelligence tests.

Henry L. Minton

TERMINAL DECLINE. The concept of terminal decline is initially attributed to Kleemeier (1962), who used the term as a possible interpretation for the longitudinal cognitive declines experienced by some older adults, but not others. In the subsequent empirical literature on psychological aging, there has been strong and consistent interest in understanding the psychological (especially cognitive) changes that may occur just prior to the onset of death. In more recent studies, a focus has been on using cognitive and other psychological variables as predictors of imminent mortality. Although a small number of studies has considered personality, self-evaluation, and social antecedents of mortality, the largest amount of research in this area (and consequently in this review) has focused on cognitive functioning. In recent decades, survival or mortality studies have become common in gerontological research (e.g., Crimmins, Hayward, & Saito, 1996), and psychological studies of terminal decline represent a special subclass of such studies.

As articulated by Berg (1996), the terminal decline hypothesis states that some intraindividual changes in functioning are linearly related to distance from death. A related hypothesis, *terminal drop*, postulates a quadratic or accelerated function, such that declines are of increasingly greater magnitudes with increased proximity to death (Palmore & Cleveland, 1976). Terminal drop is essentially a special form of the more general terminal decline hypothesis, and such accelerated premorbid psychological decline has not received strong empirical support.

Methodologically, there are generally two requirements for terminal decline studies. First, the studies must have a longitudinal component. That is, they must permit the examination of psychological functioning at some point in time, and collection of follow-up data on mortality (e.g., which participants have died) at some future measurement occasion. In the simplest design, survivors and nonsurvivors are compared in their psychological functioning at some earlier time of measurement. In more complex designs, changes in functioning over measurement occasions are related to the subsequent occurrence of mortality. Second, the population under study must include individuals at some reasonable risk of death. Consequently, most studies examining terminal decline have included individuals in the later decades of life (i.e., age 60 and older).

Historically, a large number of studies have reported that intellectual functioning is significantly associated with nearness to death (see Berg, 1996, for a review). Some debate has occurred around the question of whether *particular* abilities are especially related to mortality. One argument has been that verbal ability, which shows a less negative relationship with age than other intellectual abilities in many studies, should be most clearly related to mortality (colloquially speaking, when verbal ability "goes," the individual is truly at risk; White & Cunningham, 1988). There has not been consistent evidence for this position; the specific abilities best related to mortality or time to death have varied from study to study (Berg, 1996).

Another interesting finding emerging from the cognitive literature suggests that the predictive period for terminal decline may be quite short. White and Cunningham (1988) reported that only a time-to-death of 2 years or less could be predicted by cognitive functioning (but see Berg, 1996, for several exceptions). In addition, some investigators have suggested that systematic terminal decline phenomena may be specific to certain periods of old age. Deeg, Hofman, and van Zonneveld (1990) reported that the relationship between cognition and time to death was stronger for persons aged 70 and older than it was for persons aged 65 to 69. In contrast, White and Cunningham (1988) reported that the prediction of mortality is stronger in the young old than in the old old, perhaps because death in very old survivors is a more random event (Riegel & Riegel, 1972).

Several methodological factors constrain the ability to carefully examine terminal decline in most data sets, and limit the usefulness of many early studies. First, the wider the temporal gap between measurement and subsequent mortality, the less likely investigators are able to observe premorbid phenomena. Second, in studies with high rates of panel attrition (i.e., persons who drop out of the study), individuals most likely to be at risk for mortality are likely to be excluded. Third, given gender differences in life expectancy, studies that do not include sufficient representation of both males and females, such that terminal decline can be examined separately for both genders, are unlikely to yield meaningful results. Finally, studies examining predictors of mortality and time to death must control for chronological age, since age and time to death are related.

Recent research has attempted to address early limitations of the terminal drop literature by studying heterogeneous samples of older adults, and by drawing on more powerful statistical techniques. Through the use of survival analyses and related techniques, such as hazard analysis or Cox regression, researchers have examined the extent to which performance on various psychological measures, both cognitive and noncognitive, and both at a single occasion and in performance changes between multiple occasions, is related to subsequent mortality. This treatment of prior functioning as a predictor of subsequent mortality differs from the more prevalent earlier analytic approach, which utilized time to death as the predictor of prior functioning.

Recent investigations, which have adopted a multidisciplinary approach (including both psychological and other constructs), have begun to disentangle the possible unique and shared predictive components of cognitive and noncognitive markers of terminal decline (e.g., Bosworth & Schaie, 1999; Maier & Smith, 1999; Maxson, Berg, & McClearn, 1996). The remainder of this review highlights three exemplary studies that reflect state-of-the-art terminal decline research.

One study, using data from the ongoing Seattle Longitudinal Study (SLS; Bosworth & Schaie, in press), examined the extent to which level of, and longitudinal change in, performance on a battery of cognitive measures was related to mortality (Bosworth & Schaie, 1999). To do so, a group of decedents and a survivor control group matched on age, education, and gender were identified. Results indicated that not all cognitive measures were equally predictive of mortality. Specifically, performance at the last occasion of measurement prior to death on measures of crystallized or verbal ability and perceptual speed as well as the 7-year change in Verbal Meaning (a measure of crystallized ability) prior to this last occasion was a stronger predictor of death than performance on other ability measures. These results are consistent with the earlier White and Cunningham (1988) findings.

The SLS pattern of findings became more diffuse when the full sample was divided into younger (i.e., 74 years of age and below) and older adult (i.e., 75 years of age and above) groups. Performance on a measure of fluid ability, after controlling for age, education, and gender, was the only significant predictor of mortality in the younger group. For the older group, poor performance on a broader set of cognitive measures including crystallized ability, spatial ability, verbal memory, and perceptual and psychomotor speed was significantly related to subsequent mortality. A differential pattern of risk factors also emerged when males and females were examined separately. Low levels of perceptual speed put women at greater risk of death, while poor performance on measures of crystallized ability, verbal memory, and perceptual speed were significant risk factors for males.

Intriguing findings have also emerged from the Berlin Aging Study, one of the most comprehensive investigations of the old and very old. Maier and Smith (1999) examined the extent to which cognitive functioning predicted mortality 3 to 6 years later, in a sample of old and oldest-old adults (i.e., 70 to 103 years of age). These authors reported that, not unlike the research with older SLS participants, lower performance on both crystallized (i.e., verbal knowledge and verbal fluency) and fluid abilities (i.e., speed, reasoning, and memory) was significantly related to an increased risk of mortality, and the magnitude of these predictive relationships was roughly equivalent across cognitive measures. There was a suggestion, however, in some reduced models, that perceptual speed was slightly more predictive than crystallized ability (i.e., verbal knowledge). These relationships remained significant, although slightly attenuated, even after controlling for the effects of chronological age. Furthermore, the predictive strength of the cognitive measures extended over at least a 4-year period.

Examining the predictive salience separately in the old (70–84 years) and oldest-old (85–103 years), the authors reported that the relationships between the cognitive measures and mortality were relatively equivalent. However, it was noted that perceptual speed and verbal fluency were less predictive of mortality in the oldest-old group.

Berg and his colleagues have conducted a substantial number of terminal decline investigations in several Swedish studies (see Berg, 1996). In one study, Maxson, Berg, and McClearn (1996) examined survival rates in four groups of 70-year-olds. An interesting element of this study was that the participants were all the same age, effectively eliminating the potential confound of age-related variance in the results. These groups were identified on the basis of their scores in five areas using cluster analysis: functional capacity, well-being, social interaction, subjective health, and cognition. Results indicated that a group with severe deficits only in cognition had a similar survival expectancy as a group with low scores in three domains (i.e., well-being, social interaction, and subjective health), and a lower expectancy than a group with low scores in all domains. While this study also found that performance in noncognitive domains was related to survival, it clearly highlighted the central importance of cognition in accounting for subsequent mortality.

In conclusion, recent research has confirmed the importance of studying cognitive performance as a marker of terminal decline. Poor cognitive performance is a consistently strong indictor of subsequent mortality within older adult populations. Further research must continue to investigate whether the predictive salience of cognition is pervasive (e.g., Maier & Smith, 1999) or localized to specific abilities (e.g., Bosworth & Schaie, 1999). Furthermore, the differential predictive salience of cognitive abilities in younger and older groups is still unclear. One important emerging trend in mortality prediction research is the recognition that the investigation of cognitive terminal decline phenomena must be embedded in more fully specified multidisciplinary models of mortality risk.

Bibliography

Berg, S. (1996). Aging, behavior, and terminal decline. In J. E. Birren & K. W. Schaie (Eds.), *Handbook of the psychology of aging* (3rd ed., pp. 323–337). San Diego, CA: Academic Press.

Bosworth, H. B., & Schaie, K. W. (1999). Survival effects: Cognitive function, cognitive style, and sociodemographic variables in the Seattle Longitudinal Study. *Experimental Aging Research, 25*, 121–139.

Crimmins, E. M., Hayward, M. D., & Saito, Y. (1996). Differentials in active life expectancy in the older population of the United States. *Journal of Gerontology: Social Sciences, 51B*, S111–S120.

Deeg, J. H., Hofman, A., & van Zonneveld, R. J. (1990). The association between change in cognitive function and longevity in Dutch elderly. *American Journal of Epidemiology, 132*, 973–982.

Kleemeier, R. W. (1962). Intellectual changes in the senium. *Proceedings of the American Statistical Association, 1*, 290–295.

Maier, H., & Smith, J. (1999). Psychological predictors of mortality in old age. *Journal of Gerontology: Social Sciences, 54B*, S44–S54.

Maxson, P. J., Berg, S., & McClearn, G. (1996). Multidimensional patterns of aging in 70-year-olds. *Journal of Aging and Health*, *8*, 320–332.

Palmore, E., & Cleveland, W. (1976). Aging, terminal decline, and terminal drop. *Journal of Gerontology*, *31*, 76–81.

Riegel, K. F., & Riegel, R. M. (1972). Development, drop, and death. *Developmental Psychology*, *6*, 306–319.

White, N., & Cunningham, W. R. (1988). Is terminal drop pervasive or specific? *Journal of Gerontology: Psychological Sciences*, *43*, P141–P144.

Michael Marsiske and Jason C. Allaire

TERRITORIALITY involves using and controlling places and objects in ways that support and contribute to several psychological functions associated with ownership, personal and group identity, regulation of social systems, and control of sociability and seclusion.

Human territoriality involves psychosocial bonds between humans and places and objects. Territories are important in (1) the regulation of contact with others and the world and (2) the creation of affectively and symbolically valued extensions of self or group to places and objects. Territories may be marked with a variety of personalizations and markers; sometimes these places and objects are defended against intrusion or threat.

Types of Territories

Three different types of territories vary along a continuum of psychological centrality and function. Primary territories are the most psychologically important and are generally under the permanent or long-term control of the territory holders—for example, the home or places in a home. These territories allow individuals and groups to both cultivate and display their personal and social identities through physical personalizations or markers and use of the territory. The markers may guard claims to space and may be viewed by territory holders as personal expressions of taste or interests. Markers of primary territories can involve a wide range of physical objects that take on a variety of meanings, including personal or private meanings. Intrusions into primary territories evoke strong reactions from territory holders, with societal laws and cultural customs reinforcing their claims to territory.

On the other end of the continuum, public territories have little psychological centrality and are used for short periods of time. These territories, such as seats at a library table or bar, or sunning spots on a beach, or even one's place in line at a water cooler or game arcade, are often claimed for very temporary uses. Territory holders use a limited number of widely recognized territorial markers to guard the area from intrusion, such as placing books or coats at a library table. Public territory holders recognize the temporary nature of their claims, as they rarely mark the territories with permanent or valuable objects that could be stolen; they frequently retreat if the territory is violated.

Along the middle range of the continuum, secondary territories have a moderate degree of psychological centrality and are used regularly. These territories are often shared by a group, such as club members, neighbors, or coworkers. For example, residents' decorations of their home exteriors and yards have been linked to feelings of neighborliness and joint concern over the residential block. Regular territory users may also cooperate in the defense of territory or in creating and sharing territorial bonds to places.

Because territoriality is a function of the way humans use and perceive places, rather than an intrinsic quality of the place or object itself, use and control of territories may often be contested. Therefore, children who see all front yards on the block as their secondary territory may pose problems for homeowners who see their yards as private primary territories. Gangs' hostilities have been traced to conflicts over turf, marked by competing graffiti markings. Or conflict may arise from changing uses of territory over time. For instance, grown children may be dismayed to return home and find that their former primary territory, their bedroom, has been converted to a guest room. Another source of territorial conflict can involve cultural variations in territorial definition and use. Some societies believe that women should not venture into public areas alone, which may confuse visitors from other countries.

In other cases, complex territorial definitions operate quite smoothly, with changing use and control at different times. A mall may be used by older adults for walking exercise in the morning but may become a place for teens after school hours. Territories are also defined within a frame of reference. Neighbors typically do not walk into one's home without invitation. They treat the entire home as a primary territory of the homeowners. However, once inside the home, both visitors and guests recognize differential territorial claims across rooms. Guests comfortable in the kitchen may not consider going into a bedroom. Residents within the home may seldom share bedrooms or studies but may treat family rooms or kitchens as shared family secondary territories.

Social Regulation Function

Primary, secondary, and public territories all aid in regulating social systems. The use of classrooms or libraries becomes easier when other users respect territorial claims. The division of space in shared bedrooms may avoid conflict and ease day-to-day life when one's clothes, toothbrushes, and other possessions have regular locations in the territory. More central territories, such as bedrooms, are used as personal retreats that protect individuals from intrusion, provide solitude for reflection and planning, and offer emotional refuge.

The operation of status and dominance hierarchies is a social regulation system that has often been studied in relationship to territoriality. It has been noted that larger offices, better furniture, better locations, and other physical amenities may reveal the power hierarchy of an organization. The tangible manifestation of the organizational hierarchy provides incentives and rewards for organization members and clarifies and communicates the hierarchy to visitors. In children's group homes, more dominant individuals have been shown to control and have access to many areas, including the territories of less dominant children. In simulated office interactions, supervisors presume they can enter their subordinates' workspaces, yet subordinates seek special permission to visit superiors' offices. In interactions between students in residence halls, research reveals that the room resident is more often able to avoid persuasion than a visitor. Similarly, students are better able to withstand social pressure to sign a petition when approached in their primary bedroom territory than in more public territories. A home court advantage has also been found in college and professional sports competition. Perhaps the familiarity of the court, the absence of travel fatigue, and the support of the fans spur home teams to victory.

Early writings treated animal and human territoriality as a largely biologically determined instinct, linked to mating, child rearing, control of resources, and other functions and often involving aggressive defense. However, research has revealed that even among nonhuman animals, territoriality is expressed within a social system and fluctuates over time and circumstances, rather than being a simplistic biological reaction. Research also shows that territoriality may help prevent a great deal of aggression by providing clarity in the use and control of space rather than inevitably leading to aggressive encounters. In humans, territoriality may help provide distribution of humans across resources in ways that can preserve the viability of natural resource systems instead of depleting them through competition. In preindustrial nomadic groups, territories may preserve human groups, and negotiations over access to territories involve social and cultural systems of negotiation rather than biological marking. Thus human territories are more complicated than nonhuman territories because of the larger array of ways in which social and cultural variations are expressed in territories. A debate still continues over whether and to what degree human territoriality is biologically based.

Territory and Identity

Another function of territoriality is to develop and express personal and social identity to the self and to the world. Studies of the favorite objects of individuals show that certain possessions are kept, cherished, and displayed for their ability to remind the owner of important values and social relationships, as well as embodying handicraft skill or taste. Similarly, studies of places show that individuals and groups value their ties to places across the lifespan. Both territories and markers cultivate and communicate a sense of identity, which may include messages about the actual or desired image of the territory holder. The very act of personalizing a territory, such as gardening or decorating for a holiday such as Halloween or Christmas, strengthens territorial bonds. In addition to adding to a sense of community, personalizing creates a statement of personal identity and uniqueness. Territory holders avoid looking identical to their neighbors, as when people avoid painting their houses exactly the same color as that of their neighbors.

The visitor can also use territorial appearances to develop impressions of the territory holder. Studies have shown that visitors can accurately gauge the social class and personal qualities of individuals by looking at their home interiors and exteriors. In addition, the way the home and block are decorated can reflect the owners' social and cultural ties. For example, Slavic Americans and Mexican Americans have been shown to have distinctive ways of changing or maintaining their property through choices of fencing materials, upkeep practices, and the use of plantings.

Institutional environments often thwart the residents' desires to establish and express uniquely valued bonds with places and people. Institutional settings such as some offices and nursing homes may have rules against bringing in favorite reminders of home, such as wall decorations or furniture. Residence halls at universities may have restrictions on decoration, even though particular decorative displays have been associated with staying in the university.

Recent work on place attachment and place identity reveals how territoriality is central to the regulation and expression of cultural and social systems. Place attachment involves the long-term development of psychosocial bonds to people and places. These bonds evolve so naturally over time that they often become most noticeable in their absence. Studies of natural disasters, relocations, and homelessness indicate how bonds to places had been important in defining who belonged in a household, how ordinary routines of life involved managing access to places, and how human dignity and identity are often supported by customary uses of places for privacy and sociability.

Applications of Territoriality

One major application of the concept of territoriality involves crime prediction and prevention. Some places are more vulnerable to crime than others, and territoriality has been a useful concept in helping to understand the design and social qualities of places that underlie vulnerability to crime. Architect Oscar Newman found that public housing developments that allowed residents to develop effective territorial controls and that instilled residential pride in residents were less vulnerable to crime; these places were termed "defensible spaces." Today, the U.S. government has often stopped supporting the building of public housing without defensible space qualities. In many neighborhoods, both the absence of symbols of territorial personalization and the presence of negative features called incivilities, such as graffiti, litter, and dilapidated housing, have been related to both crime and fear of crime on residential blocks.

In suburban settings, burglarized homes have been found to differ from nonburglarized homes. Generally suburban houses that were less likely to be burglarized were more likely to look occupied, cared for, and clearly private but easily surveyed. There is conflicting evidence concerning whether burglars choose or avoid houses that appear to be valuable. Burglars in Canada claim that they favor expensive-looking homes, but crime data in the United States suggest that low-income homes are more likely to be burglarized. A U.S. study showed that burglars say they avoid a house if its appearance suggests that the neighbors would react to their presence in front of the house. A study of burglary victims revealed that such an intrusion into territory can be distressing, especially if the burglar violated the territory even further by ransacking, stealing from a large number of rooms, or stealing goods that had both monetary and sentimental value.

There are additional applied uses of the understanding of territoriality and place attachment. Territoriality concepts and research may enable greater sensitivity to human needs among family therapists, emergency aid officials, advocates for the homeless, lawyers interpreting Fourth Amendment search and seizure rights, gerontologists' efforts to provide places and services for the elderly, urban and neighborhood planners, housing designers, and workplace facility managers.

In sum, territoriality operates pervasively in all aspects of life. It varies over time and across cultures, but it is intrinsic to social relations with the world and to personal and social aspects of identity and well-being.

Bibliography

Altman, I. (1975). *Environment and social behavior: Privacy, personal space, territory, and crowding*. Monterey, CA: Brooks/Cole (reprinted by Irvington Press, New York, 1981). Provides the classic early description of human territoriality.

Brown, B. B. (1987). Territoriality. In D. Stokols & I. Altman (Eds.), *Handbook of environmental psychology* (Vol. 2, pp. 505–531). New York: Wiley. Updates and expands the Altman (1975) book in one chapter.

Brown, B. B., & Bentley, D. L. (1993). Residential burglars judge risk: The role of territoriality. *Journal of Environmental Psychology, 13*, 51–61.

Brown, B. B., & Harris, P. B. (1989). Residential burglary victimization: Reactions to the invasion of primary territory. *Journal of Environmental Psychology, 9*, 119–132.

Brown, B. B., & Perkins, D. D. (1992). Disruptions in place attachment. In I. Altman & S. Low (Eds.), *Place attachment* (pp. 279–304). New York: Plenum Press.

Harris, P. B., & Brown, B. B. (1996). The home and identity display: Interpreting resident territoriality from home exteriors. *Journal of Environmental Psychology, 16*, 187–203.

Harris, P. B., Brown, B. B., & Werner, C. W. (1996). Privacy regulation and place attachment: Predicting attachments to a student family housing facility. *Journal of Environmental Psychology, 16*, 287–301.

Taylor, R. B. (1988). *Human territorial functioning: An empirical, evolutionary perspective on individual and small group territorial cognitions, behaviors, and consequences* (pp. 136–165). New York: Cambridge University Press. Emphasizes crime and biological roots of territoriality.

Taylor, R. B., & Brower, S. (1985). Home and near home territories. In I. Altman & C. Werner (Eds.), *Home environments* (Vol. 8, pp. 183–212). New York: Plenum Press.

Taylor, R. B., & Stough, R. R. (1978). Territorial cognition: Assessing Altman's typology. *Journal of Personality and Social Psychology, 36*, 418–422.

Vinsel, A., Brown, B. B., Altman, I., & Foss, C. (1980). Privacy regulation, territorial displays, and effectiveness of individual functioning. *Journal of Personality and Social Psychology, 39*, 1104–1115.

Werner, C. M., & Altman, I. (1998). A dialectic/transactional framework of social relations: Children in secondary territories. In *Children, cities, and psychological theories: Developing relationship* (pp. 123–154). Berlin: de Gruyter.

Werner, C. M., Peterson-Lewis, S., & Brown, B. B. (1989). Inferences about homeowners' sociability: Impact of Christmas decorations and other cues. *Journal of Environmental Psychology, 9*, 279–296.

Barbara B. Brown, Carol M. Werner, and Irwin Altman

TERRORISM. Analysis of the psychology of terrorism is a relatively new field, emerging in reaction to the terrorist events of the 1970s and 1980s. It is a complicated field for research, due primarily to the difficulties of investigating the motivations for terrorist behavior. Confusion over how to define and identify terrorism has also obstructed inquiry. For the purposes of this article, terrorism is defined as a particular variant of the use or threat of violence to oppose the authority of governments. It is distinguished by clandestinity, small-group actors, and symbolic or demonstrative rather than purely destructive violence. *Terrorism* is a highly politicized concept, and the mere use of the term often arouses strong feelings. Yet the fact that so few of the people who are exposed to the same environment and presumably the same processes of social learning, who even agree on political objectives, resort to terrorism promotes the credibility of a psychological approach. Certainly the response to terrorism—a response that is out of proportion to the numbers of casualties or destruction caused, compared to other societal risks—requires a psychological explanation. Terrorism is intended to shock and horrify an audience that extends well beyond its immediate victims, and it often succeeds.

The Individual Terrorist

Terrorism is not typically the result of psychopathology nor is there a single "terrorist personality." Instead the individuals attracted to terrorism are diverse, linked by commitment to a shared ideology and membership in the group. It is important to analyze both cognitive and emotional determinants of terrorist behavior as well as to understand the historical context within which terrorism occurs. It would be a mistake to assume that terrorism is always the result of mental disturbance, lacking instrumental purpose.

Terrorism is a form of calculated, organized, and deliberate violence, not a spontaneous outburst. The individuals who might be classified as "terrorists" will occupy different roles in an organization; consequently their participation takes different forms. The distinction between leaders and followers is a significant role differentiation, for example. Terrorism is performed in the service of different doctrines (such as revolutionary, nationalist, right extremist, or religious). Organizations using terrorism have different relations with society. National separatists in divided societies, for example, are much more likely to have some local community support, which makes it unlikely that they feel alienated from society, whereas ideological groups usually lack this social rootedness. Important differences may exist between left revolutionary and right extremist terrorism; the "paranoid" quality of the American far right has frequently been noted. There are also multiple paths of entry or recruitment into underground organizations. Some individuals appear to join because of personal ties with members rather than because of ideological commitment.

Terrorist actions are also varied. Terrorism includes bombings (the most common form of violence), armed assaults, kidnappings, hijackings, "barricade" type events, and assassinations. Some acts cause mass casualties (the Oklahoma City bombing, for example), while others are bloodless. A hostagetaker or kidnapper has personal contact with his or her victims, while the person who conceals a bomb on an airliner (such as Pan Am 103) never sees the physical results. The psychology of the so-called suicide bombers in the Middle East has attracted specific attention (on this subject see Ariel Merari, "The readiness to kill and die: Suicidal terrorism in the Middle East," in W. Reich, Ed., 1990).

If there is a common emotional drive behind terrorism, it seems to be the desire for vengeance. This trait is linked to a tendency to dehumanize and demonize the enemy and to nurture a self-image of a valiant elite acting in the name of an oppressed and somewhat abstract "people," who are unable to help themselves. The delegitimization of governing structures is complete. Other possible common motivations include a desire for adventure and excitement, bonding and identification with the group, impatience and predilection for action, need for power and self-esteem, and prior exposure to violence. However, none of these traits is distinctive to participation in terrorism. It is the political interpretation given to grievances that probably turns these emotional and cognitive predispositions toward terrorism. However, for an argument emphasizing the premise that terrorism is the result of psychological compulsion, and that ideology is primarily a rationalization (see J. M. Post, "Terrorist psycho-logic: Terrorist behavior as a product of psychological forces," in W. Reich, Ed., 1990).

Ironically, however, the background of members of the organizations that practice terrorism—usually small, underground conspiracies—is not always identical to the community they aspire to represent and on whose behalf they claim to act. It is not uncommon in revolutionary movements to find that students and young professionals predominate, although they claim to be acting in the interests of the working classes or the peasantry. It is also the case that most participants in terrorist activity are young and male, although there is significant female participation in some groups. There is some disagreement over whether the motivations of men and women differ. Leaders of groups are typically men, somewhat older than the rank and file, while it is more likely that women will fill logistical or support roles.

It is probably not surprising to find little evidence of empathy for victims in the communications of such groups. Social psychologist Albert Bandura has analyzed the psychological mechanisms by which practitioners of terrorism overcome moral inhibitions ("Mechanisms of moral disengagement," in W. Reich, Ed., 1990). These mechanisms include moral justifications; euphemistic labeling; advantageous comparison; displacement of responsibility; misrepresentation of the consequences of actions; attribution of blame to the government or victims in order to exonerate oneself;

moral disengagement or brutalization through repeated acts of violence; or thinking of oneself as an agent or functionary rather than a responsible actor.

It is also unsurprising that participants in terrorist activities reject psychological explanations of their behavior. Even imprisoned terrorists are usually inaccessible to investigators for this reason, although it is also difficult to penetrate official barriers to empirical research. Opponents of governments also reject the label entirely, claiming that governments instead are the real "terrorists." State terrorism has been an enormously destructive historical force, and the violence of governments has inspired desires for revenge in numerous cases, but references to the misdeeds of governments as justification for terrorism are much less plausible when the governments in question are liberal democracies, as has frequently been the case.

Group Dynamics

Most analysts agree that the group is more important than the individual to the initiation and continuation of terrorist behavior. Identification with the group and its collective beliefs, the need for solidarity, and pressures toward conformity contribute significantly to individual commitment. Group cohesiveness is obviously important for practical reasons as well as psychological needs, since an underground group needs to maintain strict secrecy for security purposes. But most research shows that the comfort of belonging to a like-minded group of people and the psychological interdependencies that the group fosters are powerful attractions. We still know very little about the sources of authority in such organizations, but loyalty to the group is paramount.

The consequences of identification and solidarity with the group may include not only activists' unwillingness or inability to disagree, but also collective isolation from society and from sources of information that would discredit the group's ideology and perceptions, increased willingness to take risks, and desperation or panic if the group's existence is threatened. Some incidence of survivor guilt may occur when comrades are killed or arrested. It is possible that loyalty to or dependence on the group is a factor in hostage takings in which the demand is the release of imprisoned colleagues. Perceptual distortions and lack of objectivity are likely. Reliance on the group also facilitates the abandonment of reponsibility for one's actions, and the claim that one is acting merely as an agent and not an actor. Ego involvement in prior commitments is strong, and the emotional cost of abandoning a commitment for which one has killed and comrades have died may be intolerable. Furthermore, all the mechanisms that permit moral disengagement are reinforced by the group. Terrorism becomes ritualistic rather than purposeful in an objective sense.

It may seem paradoxical, given the pressures toward uniformity, that dissent within the group, dangerous both to security and to identity, is typically suppressed until it breaks out into internal conflict. Such conflicts often result in the fragmentation of the organization into factions, leading sometimes to internecine violence. For example, many examples of such splintering are found in the Palestinian resistance movements of the 1970s and 1980s.

Looking at the level of the group also draws our attention to the changing character of group interactions and relationship between the individual and the group and the group and society. The development of a campaign of terrorism is not static. Governments and their challengers react to each other. The users of terrorism may shift targets and even justifications. Such changes undoubtedly affect the commitment and outlook of members of the group.

Responses to Terrorism

Little is known about the psychology of government decision making with regard to terrorism. Often reactions to terrorism fall into the category of crisis responses, and many of the factors that encourage less than optimal decisions (time pressures, extremely consequential outcomes, lack of information, and concern for public image or reputation) are present.

Hostage takings in particular produce enormous stress, although in some cases decision making is drawn out over a long period of time rather than being sharply compressed. American presidents, at least, have tended to personalize such crises and to feel great empathy with the victims. One need think only of Jimmy Carter and the failed rescue mission in Iran and Reagan's role in the Iran–Contra scandal to recognize the emotional pressures that democratic leaders experience. Leaders are caught in a painful dilemma, facing a perceived value trade-off between humanitarian goals—saving the lives of the hostages—and deterrence of future terrorism. How can they avoid an appearance of either weakness or heartlessness? They are subject to pressure from the public, from Congress, and from the victims' families.

The response of the audience for terrorism, the general public, may also be highly emotional. Here one cannot ignore the role of the news media in sensationalizing and dramatizing terrorist incidents. The "social construction" of terrorism promotes exaggeration of the threat and consequently heightened fear. Tourism declines noticeably, for example, when there are bombings in major European capitals, although the likelihood of individual travelers being harmed by terrorism is less than the likelihood that they will have an automobile accident on the way to the airport.

Here a distinction should be introduced among different types of audiences. People who identify with the victims can be defined as direct audiences, while those who are merely observers are indirect audiences. The latter group may feel less emotional involvement because they feel less threatened or less indignant. However, terrorism does not always frighten or intimidate. Reactions are not always negative. Terrorism may elicit enthusiasm and unite populations who sympathize with the cause that inspires it. In the Gaza Strip, for example, some Palestinians reacted with jubilation to the news of bus bombings in Tel Aviv or Jerusalem.

Last, one should not forget the actual physical victims of terrorism. There is no doubt that the experience produces deep and long-lasting emotional trauma. Societies appear to be resilient in the face of terrorism, even violence of relatively high magnitude. However, individuals who survive and even the relatives of those killed often suffer severe psychological damage, ranging from immediate shock and grief to long-term mental disability. Coping with this psychological aftermath of terrorism has become an important public policy concern. In this respect, one should note the late-1990s fear concerning terrorism, namely the danger of nuclear, chemical, and especially biological terrorism. The potential number of casualties would be immense should such attacks occur, and the psychological reaction of survivors and audiences would be correspondingly acute. The reaction would be heightened not only by the number of victims but by horror at the violation of a long-standing taboo against the use of these weapons.

On the individual level, several kidnapping victims have written their memoirs, which are instructive for the study of emotional reactions to the experience of terrorism. Noteworthy are the compelling personal accounts of former hostages in Beirut: Terry Anderson (*Den of Lions*), Brian Keenan (*An Evil Cradling*), and Terry Waite (*Taken on Trust*).

[*See also* Enemy Image; Intergroup Relations; International Relations; Political Behavior; *and* Propaganda.]

Bibliography

Crenshaw, M. (1986). The psychology of political terrorism. In M. G. Hermann (Ed.), *Political psychology: Contemporary problems and issues* (pp. 379–413). San Francisco: Jossey-Bass. A comprehensive overview of psychological research on terrorism; assesses the state of the field in the mid-1980s.

Crenshaw, M. (1988). The subjective reality of the terrorist: Ideological and psychological factors in terrorism. In R. O. Slater & M. Stohl (Eds.), *Current perspectives on international terrorism* (pp. 12–46). London: Macmillan. Argues that terrorist behavior is based on perceptions of the environment that are filtered through identifiable belief systems, the content and structure of which are analyzed.

Crenshaw, M. (1992). Decisions to use terrorism: Psychological constraints on instrumental reasoning. In D. della Porta (Ed.), *Social movements and violence: Participation in underground organizations.* Greenwich, CT: JAI Press. Suggests that psychological factors constitute important barriers to instrumental logic in terrorist decision making.

Rabbie, J. M. (1991). A behavioral interaction model: Toward a social-psychological framework for studying terrorism. *Terrorism and Political Violence, 3,* 134–163. Suggests the application of a behavioral interaction model to the analysis of terrorism, to explain intra- and intergroup dynamics.

Reich, W. (Ed.). (1990). *Origins of terrorism: Psychologies, ideologies, theologies, states of mind.* Cambridge, UK: Woodrow Wilson International Center for Scholars and Cambridge University Press. A collection of original essays covering the origins of terrorist behavior, ideological and religous motivations for different varieties of terrorism, how terrorists think, decision making in response to terrorism, and the future of psychological research on terrorism.

Taylor, M. (1988). *The terrorist.* London: Brassey's. An overview of the psychology of the individual terrorist and terrorist behavior, with some attention to groups and processes of interaction and to the difficulties of defining terrorism.

Martha Crenshaw

TERTIARY INTERVENTION. *See* Intervention.

TEST CONSTRUCTION. *See* Scale Development; *and* Testing.

TESTING. Psychological testing deals with the development, validation, administration, scoring, and interpretation of psychological tests. Psychological tests are defined as standardized, repeatable procedures used to elicit and measure samples of human behavior. Testing thus differs from unstructured evaluative techniques such as interviews or behavioral observations, which do not present respondents with a uniform set of stimuli and instructions and do not prescribe the parameters within which responses can be made. Because testing involves measurement, tests have procedures for coding, scoring, or quantifying the behavior that is elicited so that it can be compared with normative data systematically collected on similar samples.

Testing is used to evaluate (1) human abilities, including intelligence, aptitudes, skills, and achievement in various areas; (2) personality characteristics, which include traits, attitudes, interests, and values; and (3) adjustment and mental health, which involves detecting signs and symptoms of psychological and neurological disorders and appraising the effectiveness of psychological functioning.

Types of Tests

Psychological tests are used in a broad range of settings. These include (1) academic settings, where tests are used to evaluate students' abilities, aptitudes, and educational progress and to screen applicants for admission to college and graduate school; (2) vocational settings, in which tests are used for personnel selection, advancement, and guidance; (3) clinical settings, in which tests are used for diagnosis of adjustment problems and psychopathology and to gauge clients' responses to psychological interventions; (4) medical settings, where they are used to assist in the diagnosis of neurological and psychogenic physical illnesses and to assess the effects of sickness on behavior; and (5) criminal justice and forensic settings, in which they are used for appraising legal competencies, evaluating impairment, and screening criminal offenders to determine the best management and treatment programs. Psychological tests are also widely used in research, especially for investigations of human cognition and personality functioning, and to a lesser extent, in social psychology to assess attitudes.

It would be difficult to overstate the importance of testing to applied psychology. From the early 1900s through the 1960s, testing was often the principal activity of clinical, counseling, school, and industrial psychologists. It was testing, along with research, that set psychologists apart from other professionals, and required courses in testing were a major part of an applied psychologist's graduate education. During the 1970s and 1980s, as opportunities for psychologists broadened, less emphasis was placed on testing, although expertise in testing and assessment was still required in most professional training programs and assessed in professional licensing examinations. In recent years, there has been renewed interest in testing as the widespread availability of computers has assisted the process of test construction and taken much of the drudgery out of test scoring and standardization. The 1990s witnessed the revision and restandardization of the major ability and structured personality tests and the development of a new generation of sophisticated tests for specialized applications in educational, medical, and forensic psychology as well as personality research.

History and Development

It appears that psychological tests were first developed in China around 2200 BCE for use in selecting civil service employees. Although written examinations were employed in European universities in the sixteenth century CE, the history of psychological tests as we know them began in the latter part of the nineteenth century when the German psychophysicists Ernst Weber, Gustav Fechner, and Wilhelm Wundt developed systematic, scientific methods of measuring human sensory abilities. The beginning of measurement also marks the beginning of psychology as a science because the scientific method requires that constructs and concepts be defined by the techniques used to measure them.

Ability and Achievement Testing

Ability and achievement tests appraise students' performance on the types of cognitive tasks that are employed in schools and other academic settings. Ability tests are designed to assess their capacity to learn material and profit from instruction, whereas achievement tests are used to assess how well they have mastered the subject matter in a course of instruction. However, the two constructs are closely related, and the content of ability and achievement tests is often similar.

The administration of ability and achievement tests is rigorously standardized, often involving timed performance on precisely defined tasks, and the scoring procedures are strictly delineated and often computerized. Considerable effort and expense go into the standardization of these measures to ensure that their norms are appropriate for the populations being tested.

History of Intelligence Testing

The first ability tests applied psychophysical techniques to the assessment of human performance. The eighteenth- and nineteenth-century British associationist philosophers such as John Locke, David Hume, and John Stuart Mill had argued that all human knowledge is obtained through the senses. In 1882, the British psychologist Sir Francis Galton proposed that measures of sensory discrimination and reaction time could be used to assess mental ability, and in 1890 an American psychologist, J. McKeen Cattell, devised 10 basic mental tests (a term he coined) to assess sensory and physiological abilities. Although Galton and Cattell had hoped that cognitive performance could be estimated on the basis of these basic faculties, Cattell's student, Clark Wissler, and others established that these tasks were not highly correlated with one another and were unrelated to school grades and similar criteria of academic achievement.

The French psychologist Alfred Binet felt that intellectual ability was more complex. To identify French schoolchildren who lacked the cognitive ability to profit from regular class instruction, he and Theodore Simon (1905) constructed an age-based scale to assess how each child's stage of mental development compared with the stages of other children of the same age. Revisions of the Binet Scale in 1908 and 1911 focused on tasks involving verbal ability, comprehension, and number concepts. Binet's approach was consistent with British scholar Charles Spearman's two-factor theory of intelligence, which stated that all intellectual tasks require general intelligence, (*g*), as well as specific factors(s) unique to each task. Binet's scales were aimed at assessing *g*.

In the United States, Lewis Terman revised Binet's scales and replaced Binet's "mental age" score with an "intelligence quotient" or "IQ," based on the ratio of mental age to chronological age. Terman's individually administered Stanford–Binet Intelligence Scale, which was published in 1916 and extensively revised in 1937, became the benchmark for early intelligence tests. An age scale, it rested on the assumption that general intellectual ability increases with age, at least in childhood and adolescence; its primary criterion for validity was the ability of its items to differentiate older from younger children.

A number of paper-and-pencil group IQ tests were also constructed, the most influential being the Army Alpha and Beta examinations, which were used to screen American recruits during World War I. Other group tests, such as the California Test of Mental Maturity, the Kuhlman–Anderson Tests of Mental Ability, the Otis–Lennon School Ability Test, and the Henmon–Nelson Tests of Mental Ability, were developed for use in schools. Their typical criteria for validity were Stanford–Binet IQs and school grades. In 1926, the Scholastic Aptitude Test (SAT) was developed to screen applicants for admission to college, and in 1936 the Graduate Records Examinations (GRE) were introduced.

Not all psychologists agreed on the overriding importance of *g*. In 1938, based on factor analyses of the Army Alpha Test, Leon Thurstone identified seven "primary mental abilities" that influenced different aspects of intellectual functioning, and in 1939 David Wechsler published an adult intelligence test, the Wechsler–Bellevue Intelligence Scale (W-B), that provided scores on 10 different subtests, with separate verbal and nonverbal ("performance") IQs in addition to an overall IQ. In place of Terman's ratio IQ, the W-B used "deviation IQs," standard scores with a mean of 100 and a standard deviation of 15. Over the years, all intelligence tests, including the Stanford–Binet, have adopted deviation IQs.

The W-B was extended to children with the publication of the Wechsler Intelligence Scale for Children (WISC) in 1949 and the Wechsler Preschool and Primary Scale of Intelligence (WPPSI) in 1968. Meanwhile, the Wechsler Adult Intelligence Scale (WAIS) replaced the W-B in 1955. All of these scales have since been updated and revised.

During the 1980s, tests measuring general intelligence were supplemented or supplanted in many educational settings by "psychoeducational test batteries," such as the Kaufman Assessment Battery for Children (K-ABC), the Differential Abilities Scales (DAS), and the Woodcock–Johnson Psycho-Educational Battery, all of which were designed to identify specific learning disabilities such as dyslexia. In response to this competition, and to court case rulings that some tests of general intelligence discriminated against minorities, in 1988 the venerable Stanford–Binet was revised to allow the assessment of specific abilities in various areas.

In addition to tests designed to assess general scholastic ability and achievement, a number of more specialized tests have been devised to screen applicants for employment in various occupations. Some are aimed at appraising the specific physical, mechanical, clerical, intellectual, or other skills demanded by various jobs, whereas others, such as the Strong–Campbell Interest Inventory and the Kuder Preference Survey, indicate the degree to which applicants' interest patterns resemble those of people who have achieved success in various occupations.

Personality Testing

Personality assessment rests on the assumption that people have stable dispositions to behave consistently across a range of different situations. Personality theorists call these dispositions "traits," social psychologists refer to them as "attitudes," and ethicists regard them as "values." Theorists regard attitudes and values as being acquired and amenable to change; traits are thought of as being more enduring and as possibly being influenced by heredity. Since many of these constructs are not directly observable, they are often defined operationally by the test scales used to measure them. Personality tests are also used by clinical psychologists to detect symptoms associated with various forms of psychopathology, such as depression or schizophrenia.

"Objective" or "structured" personality tests are typically paper-and-pencil instruments suitable for group administration. Respondents typically answer "true" or "false" to indicate if a list of characteristics describes their attitudes, feelings, or behavior or whether they agree or disagree with a series of statements. "Inventories" include a number of scales assessing a variety of traits or characteristics. Objective personality tests are not timed, but their administration is standardized and scoring can usually be done by computer.

Projective tests are less structured than objective tests, and respondents have a much broader array of response options available. They may be asked what they see in a series of inkblots, to tell stories suggested by pictures depicting various dramatic scenes, or to draw pictures of people or common objects. Projective tests are usually administered individually by specially trained psychologists. Their administration and scoring procedures are generally less standardized than those of objective tests, the interpretation of responses is more subjective, and most are less well standardized. Many psychologists consider projective tests to be more subtle and less subject to distortion than structured instruments, but the evidence for their reliability and validity is generally considered to be weaker.

History of Personality Testing

Sir Francis Galton pioneered the development of personality as well as ability tests, experimenting with both structured and projective techniques. In 1892 the German psychiatrist Emil Kraepelin used word association techniques to study schizophrenia, and in 1910 the Swiss psychiatrist Carl Jung developed a standardized list of word association stimuli and collected norms on the technique, which he published in 1918.

The most widely used early objective technique was Robert S. Woodworth's Personal Data Questionnaire, devised to screen American recruits in World War I. It consisted of 116 items cataloging a wide array of symptoms of maladjustment and neuroses that Woodworth had gleaned from psychiatric textbooks. Soldiers indicated which statements applied to them, and those scoring too high were referred for individual psychiatric evaluations. After the war, Woodworth's "logical content" approach was used to devise other structured personality tests such as the Bell Adjustment Inventory and the Bernreuter Personality Inventory. However, many psychologists questioned whether respondents could be trusted to answer truthfully, and Sigmund Freud's psychoanalytic studies caused others to doubt whether people were sufficiently aware of their problems to provide useful answers.

In 1921 Hermann Rorschach, a Swiss psychiatrist, published a psychodiagnostic technique based on inkblot perception. Rorschach's scoring and interpretation of the responses to his inkblots were based on his empirical observations of characteristic perceptual differences in the way different types of psychiatric patients dealt with the blot material. Since this task was so unfamiliar to respondents, many psychologists felt that it was less subject to distortion and better able to assess unconscious conflicts than self-report questionnaires. Unfortunately, Rorschach died in 1922, and competing schools emerged as various experts devised their own unique approaches to inkblot administration, scoring, and interpretation, thus hindering standardization of the Rorschach Test.

In the United States, Henry Murray devised the Thematic Apperception Test (TAT) in 1943. It consisted of a number of black-and-white drawings of ambiguous scenes. As with the Rorschach, different methods of administering, scoring, and interpreting the TAT emerged, and adequate norms for the TAT have never been collected. In the 1950s and 1960s, a number of other apperceptive techniques were developed using pictures and procedures specially designed for use with young children, adolescents, and minorities, as well as scenes focusing on particular settings such as the family or school.

Many individuals were trained in personality assessment in the military during World War II, and after the war personality assessment became a major activity of clinical and counseling psychologists. By the 1950s and early 1960s, projective tests such as the Rorschach and the TAT had became the most widely used and researched personality tests. However, validation of these instruments was made difficult by the lack of standardization, by disagreements as to whether they tapped conscious, preconscious, or unconscious levels of the personality, and by disputes over what constituted appropriate criterion measures. These difficulties led to the development of new validation techniques and more standardized approaches to projective test administration, scoring, and interpretation.

Many psychologists questioned the usefulness of the early rationally constructed personality questionnaires. The obvious content of the items and the authors' assumption that people would answer truthfully seemed to make them vulnerable to distortion, especially in settings where respondents might be motivated to dissimulate. In 1943, Starke Hathaway and J. C. McKinley used a new technique in constructing their Minnesota Multiphasic Personality Inventory (MMPI). After assembling a large pool of items typical of questions that might be asked during a psychiatric interview, they compared the response patterns of persons suffering from well-defined disorders with those of a nonclinical sample to determine empirically which items differentiated the two groups. This method treated the responses as a sample of behavior and made no assumptions regarding their truthfulness. Moreover, the MMPI provided special validity scales designed to identify clients who had misread the questions or who attempted to present an overly favorable or unfavorable picture of themselves. These innovations, which were widely adopted, rejuvenated objective personality testing, and by the 1970s and 1980s, objective personality tests had become more widely used and studied than projective instruments.

Today a broad array of structured instruments is available. Tests have been designed for adolescents and adults to assess behaviors ranging from superior adjustment to serious disturbance. Some tests assess traits based on psychological theory; for example the Myers-Briggs Type Indicator (MBTI) is designed to measure Jungian constructs, whereas the Edwards Personal Preference Inventory and the Jackson Personality Inventory assess "psychogenic needs" suggested by Henry Murray. Other instruments appraise constructs relevant to certain settings; the MMPI (now the MMPI-2) and the Millon Clinical Multiaxial Inventory II (MCMI–II) assess psychiatric disorders, whereas the scales of the Strong-Campbell Interest Inventory and the Kuder Preference Survey come from the world of work and occupations. The California Psychological Inventory (CPI) describes people on the basis of "folk culture" constructs used in everyday discourse, whereas the Sixteen Personality Factor Questionnaire (16 PF) and the NEO Personality Inventory were derived through factor analyses of descriptive adjectives.

In addition to "wide-band" inventories that have a broad array of scales, a number of "narrow-band" instruments assessing single dimensions such as anger, anxiety, or depression have been created. Some, such as the State-Trait Anxiety Inventory (STAI), provide separate scales for transitory emotional states and more enduring personality traits.

Testing Standards

Whether they are used for individual diagnosis, screening applicants for education or employment, or assessing whether criminal offenders should be released on probation or parole, psychological tests can have a profound influence on people's lives and on society as a whole. For this reason, the psychological associations and societies of various countries, including Britain, Canada, and the United States, have formulated detailed guidelines governing the construction, evaluation, and use of psychological tests and have incorporated these standards into their ethical codes. Similar regulations have also been adopted by many state and local licensing boards.

In testing, small but carefully chosen samples of behavior are used to estimate larger behavioral domains. Performance on the SAT, for example, is used to gauge how well high school seniors will perform over 4 or more years of college. Like any sampling procedure, testing necessarily involves error. It is the task of test authors, publishers, and users to minimize these errors. A number of standards govern test development and evaluation; chief among them are the following.

Validity. Validity refers to accuracy, the degree to which a test measures the behavior it is supposed to assess. Three broad types of validity have been defined.

Content validity is especially relevant to academic and achievement tests. It asks whether the items on a test sample the domain being assessed fairly. To have content validity, an achievement test should sample proportionately everything covered in the course of instruction and should exclude anything not covered in the course.

Criterion validity asks whether test scores systematically relate to independent, nontest measures of the behavior the test is supposed to assess. A test designed to appraise school performance might use grades as the criterion. In concurrent or diagnostic validity, the criterion data are collected at the same time that the test is administered. For example, test scores might be correlated with current grades. In predictive or prognostic validity, the forecasting ability of the test is assessed; in this case, test scores obtained at the beginning of the school year are correlated with grades obtained subsequently.

Construct validity assesses how well a test scale measures some abstract psychological attribute such as reasoning ability or dominance. Since hypothetical constructs are not directly observable, establishing the construct validity of a measure is a complex task, much like verifying a psychological theory. A conceptual framework is formed in which hypotheses are made about the observable behaviors the scale should relate to (convergent validity) as well as measures it should not relate to (discriminant validity). Although none of these independent measures is a completely adequate measure of the construct, as these propositions are tested empirically and evidence accumulates, the case for the construct validity of the measure is either strengthened or weakened. For example, a test purporting to assess intelligence should correlate positively with school grades, other intelligence tests, teacher ratings, and the like, but should not correlate highly with extraneous variables such as gender, popularity, or physical attractiveness.

Validation is a never-ending task. Each new application of a test should be validated, along with its usefulness in different settings and its appropriateness with various demographic groups.

Reliability. Reliability refers to consistency, the degree to which tests scores are free from random measurement errors. Temporal stability assesses whether test scores remain relatively constant over time. Barring practice effects or fatigue, when a test measures a relatively enduring attribute, such as intelligence, a person should obtain similar scores on repeated testings. Obviously, the shorter the time interval between test and retest, the higher the correlation should be. High test-retest reliability is not expected of scales designed to measure fluctuations in transitory emotional states.

Alternate forms reliability measures whether different versions of a test are equivalent. Not only should they correlate highly with one another, but their psychometric properties should be the same.

A third type of reliability, internal consistency, indicates whether all the items on a test measure the same thing. Although the validity of tests designed to predict complex criteria such as performance on a multifaceted job may benefit from heterogeneous content, homogeneous content is desirable on scales designed to assess unitary constructs. A number of statistical procedures have been developed to assess internal consistency.

Reliability coefficients can be used to compute the standard error of measurement, a statistic indicating the degree to which a scale is subject to random measurement errors and how close obtained scores are likely to be to the "true" scores that would have been obtained if the measurement process was free of such errors.

Standardization and Norms. It is essential that tests have standardized administration and scoring procedures so that everyone takes a test under the same conditions. Test scores have no meaning unless they can be compared with the scores obtained by well-defined samples of people who share the same basic demographic characteristics of those being tested. Obtaining representative test norms is a difficult and expensive task, especially if a test is to be used with males and females from different regions or countries reflecting a wide range of ages, ethnic backgrounds, social classes, and educational levels. Nevertheless, a test should not be used with a group until adequate norms have been collected on that group or it unless it has been demonstrated empirically that the national norms are applicable. Moreover, it is incumbent on test developers to revise and update their tests and norms at regular intervals so that they do not become outdated.

Standards Regarding Test Use

A number of standards also apply to how tests should be used. Psychological testing should be done only by or under the supervision of people who have the training and experience needed to use the tests appropriately. Test publishers do their best to limit the sale of tests to users who have licenses and credentials indicating that they are qualified to administer, score, and interpret them. Ethical standards require users to choose tests appropriate for the problem and the population being tested. The test user is responsible for the proper administration and scoring of the test, interpretation of the test scores, communication of the results, safeguarding the welfare of the test takers, and maintaining the confidentiality of their test records.

Test developers and publishers are responsible for making sure that the reliability and validity of the test for its intended use have been established and that current and appropriate normative data have been collected. They must prepare and make available a test manual that clearly sets forth the administration and scoring procedures and that fully reports the reliability, validity, and other relevant data concerning the test. The manual should also describe any special procedures or norms to be used with minorities, people with differing linguistic backgrounds, and those with handicapping conditions that may influence test performance. Moreover, the validity of the test when applied to such populations should be reported.

[*See also* Aptitude Tests; Assessment; Bender-Gestalt Visual Motor Test; Cross-Cultural Test Adaptation; Educational Testing Service; Hypothesis Testing; International Test Commission; Measures of Intelligence, *article on* Intelligence Tests; Peabody Picture Vocabulary Test; Rorschach Test; Scale Development; Self-Report; Standardized Tests; Thematic Apperception Test; *and* Wechsler Intelligence Tests.]

Bibliography

American Educational Research Association, American Psychological Association, and National Council on Research in Education. (1985). *Standards for educational and psychological testing.* Washington, DC: American Psychological Association. A detailed manual setting forth the standards governing the construction, distribution, and use of psychological tests.

Anastasi, A., & Urbina, S. (1997). *Psychological testing* (7th ed.). Upper Saddle River, NJ: Prentice Hall. A basic text on testing, which takes a topical rather than a historical approach.

Ben-Porath, Y. S., & Butcher, J. N. (1991). The historical development of personality assessment. In C. E. Walker (Ed.), *Clinical psychology: Historical and research foundations* (pp. 121–156). New York: Plenum Press. Traces the historical development and major themes in personality assessment, which is broader than testing, from biblical times to the present.

Kaplan, R. M., & Saccuzzo, D. P. (1997). *Psychological testing: Principles, applications, issues* (4th ed.). Pacific Grove, CA: Brooks/Cole. A basic text on testing that takes a topical rather than a historical approach.

Kaufman, A. S., & Harrison, P. L. (1991). Individual intellectual assessment. In C. E. Walker (Ed.), *Clinical psychology: Historical and research foundations* (pp. 91–119). New York: Plenum Press. Discusses the history of ability and intelligence testing.

Megargee, E. I, & Spielberger, C. D. (Eds.). (1992). *Personality assessment in America: A retrospective on the occasion of the fiftieth anniversary of the Society for Personality Assessment.* Hillsdale, NJ: Erlbaum. Presents major addresses concerning personality testing from 1938 to 1988. The closing chapter discusses personality assessment in the 1990s and projects future trends.

Rogers, T. B. (1995). *The psychological testing enterprise.* Pacific Grove, CA: Brooks/Cole. Presents a narrative, chronological discussion of the "psychological testing enterprise" from the nineteenth century to the present. Useful because it places developments in their historical context.

Edwin I. Megargee

TEST UTILITY. In the context of employment, utility refers to improvements in the quality of individuals hired or promoted over what would have been observed if a given test or other assessment procedure had not been used. Quality, in turn, may be expressed as: (1) the increase in the percentage of successful persons hired or promoted; (2) the increase in the average criterion score of those hired or promoted; or (3) the net economic payoff (gains minus costs) that results from use of the test to make employment decisions.

The term *test* is used in a broad sense to refer to any measure of behavior that is standardized in terms of content, administration, and scoring. *Utility* refers to usefulness, and it is the usefulness of a test as a measuring device that is the primary focus of utility analysis.

Alternative Models of Utility Analysis

The earliest systematic treatment of test utility was that of Taylor and Russell (1939). They showed that in practice, the usefulness of a test depends on more than criterion-related validity, which consists of a systematic statistical relationship (a correlation) between scores on a test and some measure of job performance (a criterion). Criteria may include measures of output, such as sales or units of production, or supervisory ratings of performance.

As their index of test utility, Taylor and Russell (1939) treated the percentage of individuals selected who are successful on the job. Based on the statistical properties of the normal curve, they showed that the percent successful depends on 3 parameters that characterize the situation in which a test is used: the criterion-related validity of the test, the selection ratio, and the base rate.

The selection ratio (SR) refers to the percentage of candidates selected. As the SR approaches 1.0 (all applicants must be selected), it becomes high or unfavorable from the organization's perspective. As it approaches zero, it becomes low or favorable, and the organization can afford to be selective by choosing only the "cream of the crop." Taylor and Russell showed that even tests with very low criterion-related validities can still be useful if the selection ratio is low (1939). Conversely, given high selection ratios, a test must demonstrate very high criterion-related validity in order to increase the percentage of success among those selected. The validity coefficient referred to by Taylor and Russell is based on present employees who have already been screened using methods other than the test. The SR is then applied to this population.

Taylor and Russell also showed that utility is affected by the base rate (BR), the proportion of applicants who would be successful without using the test. In order to be of any use in selection, a test must demonstrate incremental validity by improving on the BR, that is, the test must result in more correct decisions than could be made if it were not used.

While the Taylor–Russell model explicitly incorporates features that define the broader context in which tests are used (SR and BR), its major shortcoming is that it allows the usefulness of a test to be reflected only in terms of the success ratio and nothing else. Performance is viewed either as successful or unsuccessful, but not in relative terms that indicate how much more successful (or unsuccessful) one applicant is likely to be than another. A utility model that does provide such information is that of Naylor and Shine (1965).

The Naylor–Shine Utility Model (1965)

This index of utility is defined as the increase in the average criterion score to be expected from the use of a test (or other selection measure) with a given validity and selection ratio. Like Taylor and Russell, this model assumes that the test scores and measures of job performance are each distributed normally and linearly, and that the validity coefficient is based on present employees (that is, concurrent validity). However, the model does not require that employees be split into successful and unsuccessful groups based on an arbitrary cutoff on the measure of job performance. The basic equation underlying the model is:

$$\bar{Z}_{yi} = r_{xy}\,\frac{\lambda_i}{\phi_i}.$$

The average criterion (job performance) score of those selected equals the criterion-related validity coefficient (r_{xy}) times the ordinate (height) of the normal distribution at the cutoff on the test (λ_i) divided by the selection ratio (ϕ_i). Naylor and Shine developed a set of tables (reproduced in Cascio, 2000) that allow researchers to answer several important questions in the context of personnel selection:

1. Given a specified selection ratio, what will be the average performance level of those selected?
2. Given a desired SR, what will be the average performance level of those selected?
3. Given a desired improvement in the average criterion score of those selected, what SR or predictor cutoff value (in standard score units) should be used?

In general, the Naylor–Shine utility index is more applicable than the Taylor–Russell index because in most cases, given valid selection procedures, an organization could expect an increase in average performance as it becomes more selective in deciding whom to accept. However, neither model formally integrates the concept of cost of selection, or dollars gained or lost, into the utility index. The next model does.

The Brogden–Cronbach–Gleser Utility Model

Using the principles of linear regression, both Brogden (1946, 1949) and Cronbach and Gleser (1965) arrived at identical conclusions regarding the relationships of cost of selection, validity, and selection ratio to utility. They argued, as did Taylor–Russell and Naylor–Shine, that selection procedures should be judged on the basis of their contribution over and above the best available strategy that makes use of prior information. Hence, any new procedure must demonstrate incremental utility before it is put to use. They demonstrated that the net gain in utility from testing N persons is:

$$\Delta U = N(SD_y)(r_{xy})(\lambda_{y'}) - N(c_y).$$

Where c_y is the cost of testing one person, r_{xy} is the correlation of the selection procedure with the criterion expressed in dollars, SD_y is the standard deviation of this criterion, y' is the cutoff score on the test, and $\lambda_{y'}$ is the ordinate of the normal curve at that point.

In any given selection context, SD_y is constant and indicates both the magnitude and practical significance of individual differences in payoff. Thus, a test with a validity of .25 and an SD_y of $10,000 for one selection decision is just as useful as a procedure with a validity of .50 and an SD_y of $5,000 for some other decision (holding all other parameters constant). Thus, even a test with low validity can be very useful when SD_y is large.

Estimating SD_y

Several different methods have been developed to estimate the variability (standard deviation) of performance scores in dollars. The Schmidt–Hunter procedure (Schmidt, Hunter, McKenzie, & Muldrow, 1979) is based on the following reasoning: If job performance in dollar terms is normally distributed, then the difference between the value to the organization of the products and services produced by an employee at the eighty-fifth percentile of performance and that of an employee at the fiftieth percentile in performance is equal to SD_y. Likewise, the difference between the value to the organization of the products and services produced by an employee at the fiftieth percentile of performance and that of an employee at the fifteenth percentile in performance is also equal to SD_y. Averaging these two estimates across a large group of supervisors provides a fairly reliable estimate of the true value of SD_y. Later research has found that SD_y values typically vary from 40 to 70% of salary as job complexity increases from routine to medium to professional work (Hunter, Schmidt, & Judiesch, 1990).

A criticism of the Schmidt–Hunter procedure is that the components of each supervisor's estimates are unknown. A second procedure, called CREPID (Cascio & Ramos, 1986), avoids this problem. Its rationale is as follows. Assuming an organization's compensation program reflects current market rates for jobs, the economic value of each employee's labor is reflected in his or her annual wage or salary. CREPID breaks down each employee's job into principal activities, assigns a proportional amount of the annual salary to each principal activity based on supervisory ratings of frequency and importance, and then requires supervisors to rate each employee's job performance on each principal activity. A computer program then translates the resulting ratings into estimates of the dollar value for each principal activity. The sum of the dollar values assigned to each principal activity equals the economic value of each employee's job performance to an organization.

Boudreau conducted an exhaustive review of the literature on SD_y estimation (1991). He located 34 studies that computed more than 100 such estimates and concluded that differences in SD_y estimates using different methods are often less than 50%, and may be less than $5,000 in many cases. No matter which estimation method is used, the utility associated with valid human resource interventions is often substantial (see Cascio, 1991).

Bibliography

Boudreau, J. W. (1991). Utility analysis for decisions in human resource management. In M. D. Dunnette & L. M. Hough (Eds.), *Handbook of industrial and organizational psychology* (2nd ed., Vol. 2, pp. 621–745). Palo Alto, CA: Consulting Psychologists Press. This is a thorough review of the literature relevant to utility analysis.

Brogden, H. E. (1946). On the interpretation of the correlation coefficient as a measure of predictive efficiency. *Journal of Educational Psychology, 37*, 64–76.

Brogden, H. E. (1949). When testing pays off. *Personnel Psychology, 2*, 171–185.

Cascio, W. F. (2000). *Costing human resources: The financial impact of behavior in organizations* (4th ed.). Cincinnati, OH: Southwestern. Devotes four full chapters to issues relevant to test utility.

Cascio, W. F., & Ramos, R. A. (1986). Development and application of a new method for assessing job performance in behavioral/economic terms. *Journal of Applied Psychology, 71*, 20–28.

Cronbach, L. J., & Gleser, G. C. (1965). *Psychological tests and personnel decisions* (2nd ed.). Urbana, IL: University of Illinois Press. A classic, highly technical treatment of selection utility in both fixed and adaptive-treatments, second-stage and multistage selection, placement decisions, and classification decisions.

Hunter, J. E., Schmidt, F. L., & Judiesch, M. K. (1990). Individual differences in output variability as a function of job complexity. *Journal of Applied Psychology, 75*, 28–42.

Naylor, J. C., & Shine, L. C. (1965). A table for determining the increase in mean criterion score obtained by using a selection device. *Journal of Industrial Psychology, 3*, 33–42. This source is no longer in print. The tables have been reproduced in Cascio (2000).

Schmidt, F. L., Hunter, J. E., McKenzie, R. C., & Muldrow, T. W. (1979). Impact of valid selection procedures on work-force productivity. *Journal of Applied Psychology, 64*, 609–626.

Taylor, H. C., & Russell, J. T. (1939). The relationship of validity coefficients to the practical effectiveness of tests in selection. *Journal of Applied Psychology, 23*, 565–578.

Wayne Cascio

TEUBER, HANS-LUKAS (1916–1977), American psychologist, known worldwide as an authority on brain and behavior. Through systematic, controlled investigations of behavior changes following acute brain injuries, Teuber and his colleagues played a major role in establishing human neuropsychology as a rigorous experimental science (Gross, 1994; Hecan, 1979). Teuber's theoretical papers on behavior in relation to brain functioning were highly original syntheses of research from a wide range of disciplines. His theories of visual perception and of voluntary movement were particularly influential (Teuber, 1960, 1978; see Hurvich, Jameson, & Rosenblith, 1987).

As founder in 1963 of the department of psychology at the Massachusetts Institute of Technology, Teuber translated his (then very unorthodox) vision of psychology into a faculty, curriculum, and graduate training program. In retrospect, Teuber's vision of psychology, which he saw as the science bridging the gap between natural and social sciences, and the department's disciplinary scope (which included neuroanatomy, neurophysiology, and psycholinguistics, as well as experimental, comparative, and physiological psychology), looks like a forerunner of what today is called biological psychology or behavioral neuroscience or brain and cognitive sciences.

Hans-Lukas Teuber was born in Berlin, oldest son of Rose (Knopf) and Eugen Teuber. He was educated at the University of Basle, Switzerland (1935–1939), where he concentrated in philosophy, and at Harvard University, where he received his doctorate in psychology in 1947 with a dissertation under Gordon Allport. In 1941, he married Marianne Liepe, an art historian and fellow student at Basle; their two sons were Andreas, born in 1942, and Christopher, born in 1946.

From 1944 to 1946 Teuber served in the U.S. Navy, stationed at the San Diego Naval Hospital. There he and neurologist Morris Bender investigated changes in behavior following brain injuries sustained by men in combat. This work drew together important interdisciplinary influences from Teuber's earlier years: his father's interest in comparative animal behavior, Hans Spemann's lectures at Basle on embryology, and Karl Lashley's and Kurt Goldstein's Harvard lectures on brain and behavior.

In 1947, Teuber moved to New York City and embarked on a productive period of teaching and research at New York University, where he and his colleagues conducted their influential investigations of behavioral changes in brain-injured patients (Teuber, Battersby, & Bender, 1960; Semmes, Weinstein, Ghent, & Teuber, 1960). Theoretical papers synthesizing this research display not only Teuber's thoroughly developmental and comparative perspective but also some characteristic emphases: on organisms' voluntary behavior, global and specific effects of brain lesions, and the importance of control groups and control tasks for interpreting behavioral changes following brain injuries (Teuber, 1960, 1978).

In 1961, Teuber moved to the Massachusetts Institute of Technology, where he established and led the psychology department until his untimely death in 1977. An early faculty appointment was of Walle Nauta, a world famous neuroanatomist; others followed of scientists from a wide range of disciplines united by their common interest in behavior and brain functioning. From 1969 to 1976, the Sloan Foundation supported the department as a center of excellence in the neurosciences. Hans-Lukas Teuber received many awards and honors, including the Karl Spencer Lashley award (1966), election to the National Academy of Sciences, and two honorary doctorates.

Bibliography

Works by Teuber

Semmes, J., Weinstein, S., Ghent, L., & Teuber, H.-L. (1960). *Somatosensory changes after penetrating brain wounds in man.* Cambridge, MA: Harvard University Press.

Teuber, H.-L. (1955). Physiological psychology. *Annual Review of Psychology, 6*, 267–296. An influential review and synthesis of the field (see Gross, 1994).

Teuber, H.-L. (1960). Perception. In J. Field, H. W. Magoun, & V. E. Hall (Eds.), *Handbook of physiology, Section of Neurophysiology* (Vol. 3, pp. 1595–1688). Washington, DC: American Physiological Society. A major theoretical review and synthesis. Contains discussion of corollary discharge, a central and influential concept in Teuber's work.

Teuber, H.-L. (1978). The brain and human behavior. In R. Held, H. W. Leibowitz, & H.-L. Teuber (Eds.), *Handbook of sensory physiology, Vol. 8: Perception* (pp. 879–920). New York: Springer-Verlag. Posthumously published address delivered to the 21st International Psychology Congress in Paris. Gives a good overview of Teuber's research and theoretical perspective, with an emphasis on work conducted by Teuber and his colleagues at MIT and NYU. Gives a good sense of his engaging and elegant speaking style.

Teuber, H.-L., Battersby, W. S., & Bender, M. (1960). *Visual field defects after penetrating missile wounds of the brain.* Cambridge, MA: Harvard University Press.

Works about Teuber

Gross, C. G. (1994). Hans-Lukas Teuber: A tribute. *Cerebral Cortex, 5*, 451–454. An account of Teuber's life, career, and contributions by a former colleague. Less comprehensive than Hurvich, Jameson, and Rosenblith (1987) but more informative concerning Teuber's scientific impact.

Hecan, H. (1979). H. L. Teuber et la fondation de la neuropsychologie experimentale [H. L. Teuber and the founding of experimental neuropsychology]. *Neuropsychologia, 17*, 119 24. Discussion of Teuber's contributions by a major figure in research on the brain and human behavior. Calls Teuber "the founder and guiding spirit of contemporary neuropsychology."

Hurvich, L. M., Jameson, C., & Rosenblith, W. A. (1987). Hans-Lukas Teuber: A biographical memoir. National Academy of Sciences, *Biographical Memoirs, 57*, 461–490. The most complete account to date of Teuber's life, career, and scientific contributions.

Teuber, M. L. (1994). The founding of the Primate Station, Tenerife, Canary Islands. *American Journal of Psychology, 107*, 551–581. Detailed historical account by Marianne L. Teuber of Eugen Teuber's role as first director of the Primate Station on Tenerife Island, where Kohler's classic experiments on the intelligent behavior of apes were performed (1914–1920). Gives a good picture of E. Teuber's research style, which may have influenced his son's. Hans-Lukas Teuber makes a cameo appearance at the end of this account.

Mary Brown Parlee

THANATOLOGY. *See* Death and Dying.

THEMATIC APPERCEPTION TEST. Created by Christiana Morgan and Henry Murray (1935), the Thematic Apperception Test (TAT) is a storytelling procedure designed to explore the thoughts, wishes, motives and fantasies of persons without asking directly about these aspects of personality. The assumption is that, in the creation of a story, storytellers will express some of their own thoughts and feelings by attributing these to characters in the story.

The test consists of a set of 20 black and white pictures, for which storytellers are asked to describe the characters in the picture, tell what they are doing, thinking, and feeling, explain what has led up to the situation depicted, and provide the outcome. Stories may be told orally or may be written. A 5-minute time limit, per story, may be imposed. The pictorial content of the stimulus cards was selected to represent different potentially conflictual situations, some of which might be especially salient for different individuals. The pictures include realistic depictions of individuals and couples, males and females, adults and children, as well as more fantastic scenes. Frequently, a subset of 8 to 10 cards will be used, the selection based on the purpose and situation of the assessment. Thus, for children and adolescents, TAT cards depicting children alone or in combination with adults may be chosen, while the assessment of adults might include cards showing older people in relation to each other, or individually. For very young children, the Children's Apperception Test (Bellak, 1975) may be used.

TAT stories are narrative productions. As such, they share in the characteristic features of narratives: plot, intention, motives, causality. Because the test provides a group of narrative productions from the same individual, it is possible to discern repeated motives and intentions, and to note consistencies in cause-and-effect sequences.

This information provides a window into the psychic functioning of the individual; storytellers are often surprised to discover the personal relevance of the stories they tell, when this is pointed out to them. It is this aspect of the TAT that identifies it as a "projective test"; storytellers project their own thoughts, wishes and feelings, and their own construction of interpersonal causality into the story they tell.

Different TAT pictures tend to "pull" for different themes, based on the content of the picture. Psychologists who are experienced with this test will recognize the usual theme for each picture; these usual themes are also available in published sources (e.g., Holt, 1978). While the presence of common story themes is indicative of storytellers having shared a common human or cultural experience, variations on these themes express the uniqueness of each storyteller. Extreme uniqueness of stories may indicate great originality in the storyteller or may be suggestive of psychopathology, depending on other aspects of the storytelling.

Several systematic coding schemes, with demonstrated reliability and validity, have been developed to assess different aspects of personality functioning from TAT stories. These include the assessment of motives for achievement, power, affiliation, and intimacy, as well as gender identity, defense mechanisms, and object relations (the mental processes that influence individuals' functioning in intimate relationships). An extensive research literature exists in which these methods have been used to study personality. (For a summary of coding methods, see Cramer, 1996, and Smith, 1992.)

While some skepticism exists that personal motives, wishes or fears are actually expressed in these stories, experimental demonstrations of this thesis have been convincing. For example, experimentally depriving individuals of food for varying periods of time, thereby increasing the hunger drive, has been shown to increase the frequency of mention of food and food-getting activities in TAT stories. Other experiments have manipulated the strength of psychological motives. For example, situations in which the need to achieve was accentuated have produced TAT stories in which occurrence of the achievement motive increased; situations that intensified feelings of intimacy produced stories in which the expression of the intimacy motive increased; and situations in which the concern about power was salient produced stories in which themes of power were magnified. Further experiments have shown that the use of defense mechanisms, as assessed from TAT stories, increases under situations of stress, while clinical studies have demonstrated that TAT-based assessment of object relations will differentiate among diagnostic groups. (For a summary of this research, see Cramer, 1996.)

In addition to these experimental demonstrations, studies of individuals who are known to have strong achievement or power motives, such as successful entrepreneurs and politicians, have found that their narrative productions, when assessed by the TAT coding schemes, produced strong motive scores. The coding schemes have also been used to trace the development of these personality dispositions from childhood through adulthood (for a review, see Cramer, 1996).

The TAT is also used in clinical settings for purposes of diagnosis, personality description, and assessment of strengths and weaknesses in personality functioning; it is among the five most frequently used psychological tests for this purpose (e.g., Piotrowski, Sherry, & Keller, 1985). Significant deviations from the usual story, peculiar verbalizations, perceptual or verbal misrepresentations of the picture, and other anomalies such as non sequiturs, confusion of concrete and abstract, and blocking (the inability to think of or tell a story) are all used to construct a diagnostic picture or personality description of the individual. As with other projective tests, extensive training and experience are needed to be skillful in the use of the TAT for clinical purposes.

Because the basic structure of this assessment procedure differs from that of self-report questionnaires, care must be used, when studying reliability and validity, to select a method that is appropriate. For example, since the TAT cards (the test "items") have been chosen to represent different areas of psychosocial concern, one does not expect to find the same themes or personality dispositions portrayed in response to every TAT card. In turn, this means that measures of internal consistency are inappropriate for estimating reliability. Rather, the best estimate of measurement reliability will be found from the extent to which two individuals, using the same coding procedure, produce the same scores from the same story material, that is, from interrater reliability. In the assessment of validity, since measures derived from TAT stories reflect aspects of personality the storyteller may not be aware of, the use of self-report personality inventories as criteria for validity may be inappropriate, in that these latter measures generally require conscious awareness on the part of the test-taker regarding the personality dispositions being assessed. Better criteria for validity may be found by using observers' ratings as criteria, by demonstrating predicted differences between experimental or clinical groups, or by predicting external variables such as entrepreneurial success from the assessment of motives revealed in TAT stories.

[*See also* Projective Techniques; *and* Testing.]

Bibliography

Bellak, L. (1975). *The Thematic Apperception Test: The Children's Apperception Test and the Senior Apperception Technique in clinical use* (3rd ed.). New York: Grune & Stratton. Discusses versions of the TAT appropriate for young children and for older adults. Includes some review of the research literature.

Cramer, P. (1996). *Story-telling, narrative, and the Thematic Apperception Test.* New York: Guilford Press. A comprehensive review of the history and research findings pertaining to the TAT. Extensive examples of different methods used to code TAT stories, and numerous clinical and student case studies are provided. The relevance of narrative theory for TAT interpretation is discussed.

Holt, R. R. (1978). *Methods in clinical psychology.* New York: Plenum Press. Includes an extensive discussion of the thematic content characteristically found for each of the TAT pictures, integrating previous research on this topic. The most complete set of "norms" for the TAT.

Morgan, C. D., & Murray, H. A. (1935). A method for investigating fantasies: The Thematic Apperception Test. *Archives of Neurological Psychiatry, 34,* 289–306.

Murray, H. A. (1943). *Thematic Apperception Test manual.* Cambridge, MA: Harvard University Press. The manual contains the standard instructions for test administration and is accompanied by the complete set of 20 TAT pictures.

Piotrowski, C., Sherry, D., & Keller, J. W. (1985). Psychodiagnostic test usage: A survey of the Society for Personality Assessment. *Journal of Personality Assessment, 49,* 423–425.

Rossini, E. D., & Moretti, R. J. (1997). Thematic Apperception Test (TAT) interpretation: Practice recommendations from a survey of clinical psychology doctoral programs accredited by the American Psychological Association. *Professional Psychology, 28,* 393–398.

Smith, C. P. (Ed.). (1992). *Motivation and personality: Handbook of thematic content analysis.* New York: Cambridge University Press. Provides a detailed description of many TAT coding schemes, along with a set of expert coded stories. In addition, issues related to TAT use, such as the determination of reliability and validity, are examined critically.

Phebe Cramer

THEORETICAL AND PHILOSOPHICAL PSYCHOLOGY. As Karl Jaspers once observed, "There is no escape from philosophy. The question is only whether [a philosophy] is good or bad, muddled or clear" (*Way to Wisdom*, New Haven, 1954, p. 12). Even "scientific" disciplines such as psychology cannot escape from the theories and philosophies that underlie them. One of the purposes of theoretical psychology is to articulate, help evaluate, and generally make less "muddled" the theories and philosophies that are important to psychology (see B. Slife and R. Williams, *American Psychologist*, 1997, 52, pp. 117–129).

Impetus for Theoretical Psychology

Theoretical psychology is a new and emerging subdiscipline of psychology. Although psychology has long had a strong theoretical tradition, the impetus for a subdiscipline arises, in part, from a renewed awareness of the theoretical significance of scientific method. Modern psychology has often viewed theory as mere speculation or hypothesis to be tested with objective scientific methods. Recent work in the philosophy of science, however, clarifies the theoretical nature of these methods (e.g., I. Lakatos and A. Musgrave, *Criticism and the Growth of Knowledge*, Cambridge, 1970). Increasingly, psychologists are viewing the scientific method as itself a meta-theory—a theory for evaluating theories—rather than an objective or value-free tool for validating theories or disclosing facts.

This view has fostered significant theoretical issues that the field of theoretical psychology considers. If, for example, traditional scientific method is not value-free, how do its implicit values influence its use in assessing psychological theories and practices? Should other methods with other values (e.g., qualitative methods) be accorded an equal status with traditional scientific methods? As these questions illustrate, theoretical psychologists must now consider more than the content of psychological theories. They must also articulate, evaluate, and clarify the theories and philosophies that ground the methods used to investigate this content. Donald Polkinghorne's book, *Methodology for the Human Sciences* (Albany, 1983) is an example of this articulation and evaluation.

Another impetus for theoretical psychology is the increasing fragmentation of psychology. For example, biological psychologists are finding homes in centers for neuroscience, cognitive psychologists are moving into departments of cognitive science or artificial intelligence, and psychotherapists are shifting to professional schools. Fragmentation is also evident in the differing theoretical loyalties of the many professional societies in psychology. These societies often represent distinct theoretical communities, each with its own language, philosophy, and method.

Although many psychologists value diversity, this type of fragmentation seems so profound at times that communication among the various theoretical communities is jeopardized. Disputes about various methods (e.g., qualitative versus quantitative) serve to compound these problems because such disputes imply that there are no common grounds for evaluating theories. Without some communication, and some shared standard of evaluation, the coherence of the discipline is at stake. Fragmentation, then, is another example of the importance of distinctly theoretical questions to psychology: How serious is this fragmentation? How might disparate theoretical communities communicate with one another and arrive at some common criteria of evaluation? Arthur Staats's book *Psychology's Crisis of Disunity* (New York, 1983) exemplifies a thoughtful consideration of these questions.

The significance of such questions has provided an already strong theoretical tradition with new visibility and recognition. In the past, many psychologists seemed to assume that the scientific method would eventually address all the theoretical concerns of the discipline. However, as these questions illustrate, there are vital disciplinary issues that cannot be addressed through method. Moreover, the assumptions of the scientific method are often the bone of theoretical contention. Empirical research cannot address such issues alone; there is a bootstrap problem in a method that attempts to use its own validity procedures to validate itself. These procedures, and *any* research produced by them, must be at least supplemented with discerning theoretical and philosophical analyses.

The Emerging Role of a Theoretical Psychologist

The need for such analyses has helped shape the role of the theoretical psychologist. Theoretical psychologists not only consider all the relevant empirical information in generating new theories and hypotheses, but they also critically evaluate the assumptions of the theories and methods that produced this information. This critical evaluation includes an articulation of the implications of these assumptions as they affect important psychological issues. A recent book by Brent Slife and Richard Williams, *What's Behind the Research? Discovering Hidden Assumptions in the Behavioral Sciences* (Thousand Oaks, Calif., 1995), is an example of the attempt to articulate some of these assumptions and their implications.

At the disciplinary level, theoretical psychologists facilitate discussion about the foundational questions and issues of psychology. They do not preemptively decide these questions and issues for the whole of the discipline. Rather, their job is to keep fundamental questions in the forefront of disciplinary discourse, so that they can be addressed by all members of the discipline and all consumers of psychology.

At the local (college or department) level, theoretical psychologists function in essentially the same role as methodologists and statisticians—as consultants to other scholars in research and practice. Psychologists and other scholars can consult theoreticians about theories, explanations, and methods to see if they are coherent, hold hidden problems, or are appropriate to the assumptions being made. Theoretical psychologists bring to bear historical and philosophical perspectives as well as critical and analytical skills in these consultations. They also teach courses on these topics to both graduates and undergraduates, thus training future scholars and theoretical specialists.

Theoretical psychologists do not merely consider what the discipline is *currently* doing, they also reflect on the future of the discipline. Given psychology's history and present state, where will current trends likely lead us? Where *should* psychology be headed? As William James (1842–1910) and others have noted, no discipline, including the sciences, can ignore its moral grounding and consequences. Part of the task of theoretical psychology, therefore, is to clarify and submit for discussion this moral grounding. Daniel Robinson's edited volume, entitled *Social Discourse and Moral Judgment* (San Diego, 1992), is an example of this discussion.

Current Status of Theoretical Psychology

The past three decades in psychology have witnessed a remarkable and sustained growth in theoretical work. This growth is a testament to the accomplishments and vitality of the subdiscipline of theoretical psychology. Much of this work has been critical of mainstream psychology, but even the critical work has been constructive, laying out alternative approaches and methods. Important and influential early works include Amadeo Giorgi's book *Psychology as a Human Science* (New York, 1970), which contrasted the phenomenological approach with empirical psychology, and Joseph Rychlak's book *A Philosophy of Science for Personality Theory* (Boston, 1968), which analyzed the philosophical and scientific status of personality theories. Other scholars also contributed to the foundations of theoretical psychology, chiefly from the humanistic, existential, and postmodern perspectives (e.g., R. May, *Existential Psychology*, New York, 1969).

Recent critical contributions include the rich and impressive literature of social constructionism (e.g., K. Gergen, *The Saturated Self*, New York, 1991). Scholars who might be considered classicists, such as Daniel Robinson (*Philosophy of Psychology*, New York, 1985), have offered critiques and alternative formulations. Feminist scholars have challenged the traditional assumptions as well as the political implications of traditional social science (e.g., J. Morawski, *Practicing Feminisms, Reconstructing Psychology*, Ann Arbor, Mich., 1994). Several edited volumes, aimed at broadly articulating alternative theoretical perspectives, have appeared recently (e.g., J. Faulconer and R. Williams, *Reconsidering Psychology*, Pittsburgh, 1990).

Important theoretical work is also occurring within specific subdisciplines and topic areas. This work includes clinical psychology (e.g., R. Miller, *The Restoration of Dialogue*, Washington, D.C., 1992), social psychology (e.g., I. Parker and Shotter, *Deconstructing Social Psychology*, London, 1990), cognitive psychology and artificial intelligence (e.g., T. Winograd and F. Flores, *Understanding Computers and Cognition*, Reading, Pa., 1987), schizophrenia (e.g., L. Sass, *Madness and Modernism*, New York, 1992), the theory and practice of psychoanalysis (e.g., B. Barratt, *Psychoanalysis and the Postmodern Impulse*, Baltimore Md., 1993), the idea of time in psychological explanation (e.g., B. Slife, *Time and Psychological Explanation*, Albany N.Y., 1993), the psychology of minority groups (e.g., A. Jenkins, *Psychology and African Americans*, Boston, 1995), and human agency (e.g., R. Williams, 1992, *American Psychologist*, 47(6), pp. 752–760).

In the past 20 years, the number of journals devoted partly or entirely to theoretical work and alternative perspectives has increased dramatically. A partial list includes the *Journal of Theoretical and Philosophical Psychology, Theory and Psychology, New Ideas in Psychology, the Journal of Humanistic Psychology, Humanistic Psychology, Family Process, Studies in Linguistics and Philosophy, Consciousness and Cognition, Theoretical Issues in Cognitive Science, Behavior and Philosophy, American Psychologist, the International Journal of Personal Construct Psychology, the Annals of Theoretical Psychology, Psychological Inquiry, History and Philosophy of Psychology Bulletin, the Journal of Phenomenological Psychology, the Journal of Mind and Behavior*, and *Philosophical Psychology*. Moreover, many empirically oriented journals welcome theoretical contributions.

Several professional organizations provide forums for theoretical discussion, publication, and a scholarly critical mass. Examples include Theoretical and Philosophical Psychology (Division 24) and Humanistic Psychology (Division 32) of the American Psychological Association, the International Society for Theoretical Psychology, History and Philosophy of Psychology (Section 25) of the Canadian Psychological Society, the Section on History and Philosophy of Psychology of the British Psychological Society, the International Human Science conference, and the Society for Philosophy and Psychology.

Training and Employment

Training in theoretical psychology requires a perspective that would ordinarily be considered philosophical. However, theoretical psychology is not the same thing as philosophy. Professional philosophers concern themselves with many issues and questions that do not directly affect the theory or practice of psychology. The subdiscipline of theoretical psychology is applied philosophy, a field that takes from philosophy (as well as other sources) intellectual tools and ideas and brings them to bear on psychology in a way that is specifically relevant to its purposes and problems.

Theoretical psychology requires a broad education in areas both inside and outside the domain of psychology. Relations between psychology and other scholarly disciplines are part of the intellectual purview of this subdiscipline. Consequently, courses in the philosophy of social science, the intellectual history of psychology, epistemology, ontology, metaphysics, and ethics are crucial for training theoretical psychologists. Theoretical psychologists may also acquire an expertise in a traditional subdiscipline of psychology (e.g., clinical, cognitive, social). This permits them to focus their theoretical efforts on a more limited domain of interest.

Training in theoretical psychology can be found in a wide variety of programs, both within and outside other psychological subdisciplines. Duquesne University, the University of Dallas, Seattle University, and West Georgia have long had strong theoretical programs with a human science orientation. In Canada, the University of Calgary and the University of Alberta have been recognized as institutions where an emphasis in theoretical psychology and alternative perspectives could be pursued. York University in Toronto has, for a number of years, had a history of a psychology program with a significant theoretical/philosophical emphasis. More recently, Brigham Young University has established a theory/philosophy emphasis in their Ph.D. program, and the University of Notre Dame and Georgetown University have established programs in theory and philosophy.

Graduates of these programs work primarily in academic institutions. Some universities or colleges specifically advertise for theoretical psychologists. Others seek a specialist in another subdiscipline who has also acquired theoretical training. Many liberal arts colleges desire teachers who possess the broader perspective and training of theoretical psychology. Theoretical psychologists may specialize in the theoretical issues of a particular subdiscipline, but the nature of theoretical psychology calls them first to a more encompassing and thus more general standpoint.

Bibliography

Cushman, P. (1995). *Constructing the self, constructing America: A cultural history of psychotherapy*. Reading, MA: Addison-Wesley.

Denzin, N. K., & Lincoln, Y. S. (Eds.). (1994). *Handbook of qualitative research*. Thousand Oaks, CA: Sage.

Howard, G. S. (1986). *Dare we develop a human science?* Notre Dame, IN: Academic Publications.

(1993). Inescapable moralities: Psychology as public philosophy. [Special issue]. *Journal of Theoretical and Philosophical Psychology, 13*,(2), 87–153.

Koch, S., & Leary, D. E. (Eds.). (1985). *A century of psychology as science*. New York: McGraw-Hill. Contains many theoretically oriented articles by leading theoretical psychologists.

Messer, S. B., Sass, L. A., & Woolfolk, R. L. (Eds.). (1988). *Hermeneutics and psychological theory: Interpretive perspectives on personality, psychotherapy, and psychopathology*. New Brunswick, NJ: Rutgers University Press.

Miller, R. B. (Ed.). (1992). *The restoration of dialogue: Readings in the philosophy of clinical psychology*. Washington, DC: American Psychological Association.

Packer, M. J., & Addison, R. B. (Eds.). (1989). *Entering the circle: Hermeneutic investigation in psychology*. Albany: State University of New York Press.

Robinson, D. N. (1995). *An intellectual history of psychology*. New York: Macmillan.

Rychlak, J. F. (1997). *In defense of human consciousness*. Washington, DC: American Psychological Association.

Slife, B. D., & Williams, R. N. (1995). *What's behind the research? Discovering hidden assumptions in the behavioral sciences*. Thousand Oaks, CA: Sage Publications. An introduction to theoretical issues for the general reader.

Valle, R. S., & Halling, S. (Eds.). (1989). *Existential-phenomenological perspectives in psychology: Exploring the breadth of human experience*. New York: Plenum Press.

Brent D. Slife

THEORY OF MIND. The term *theory of mind* was coined by David Premack, an American psychologist who studies chimpanzees, to refer to our everyday propensity to explain and predict the behavior of social agents in terms of their mental states (Premack & Woodruff, 1978). We attribute a wide range of mental states, including intentions, hopes, fears, expectations, longings, imaginings, and so forth. However, three of these states are basic to how we interpret and predict people's behavior: desires (which identify the agent's goals), beliefs (which capture what an agent thinks is the true state of the world), and pretends (because people do not always mean what they do or say). Researchers have become interested in the early development of theory of mind.

Although the three basic theory of mind concepts are highly abstract, each develops during the preschool period. An American psychologist, Henry Wellman, showed that the concept of desire is understood by about two years of age (Wellman, 1990). Alan Leslie, a Scottish psychologist, showed that the concept of pretending is grasped between 18 months and 2 years (Leslie, 1987). There is still controversy surrounding the age at which the concept of belief is first employed.

It is generally accepted that to show a grasp of the concept of belief, the child must understand that what someone believes could be false. In a seminal paper, Heinz Wimmer and Josef Perner, working in Salzburg, Austria, tested children between 3 and 6 years of age on a task that required the child to predict an agent's behavior by attributing a false belief (Wimmer and Perner, 1983). Wimmer and Perner found that it was not until 6 years that a majority of their subjects passed their task.

Subsequently, Simon Baron-Cohen, Alan Leslie, and Uta Frith, working in London, England, simplified the Wimmer and Perner false-belief task and found that the vast majority of 4-year-olds could attribute a false belief (Baron-Cohen, Leslie, & Frith, 1985). The child is told a short story, with the aid of pictures or props, in which a character, Sally, has a marble that she places in a basket and covers. Sally then leaves and goes outside. While Sally is gone, naughty Ann enters the room, finds the marble in the basket, and moves it to a nearby box. The child is then asked two control questions to test basic comprehension: "Where did Sally put the marble in the beginning?" and "Where is the marble now?" Finally, the child is asked either directly about Sally's belief, "Where does Sally think the marble is?" or to predict Sally's behavior, "Where will Sally look for the marble?" In order to answer either of the latter questions, the child must attribute to Sally a belief that is false and therefore different from the child's own belief.

Baron-Cohen, Leslie, and Frith (1985) also found that older children with Down syndrome who had an average IQ of 64 (in the mildly retarded range) typically passed. However, the vast majority of a third group, composed of children with autism having an average IQ of 82 (in the low normal range), failed the false-belief task. Other versions of the false-belief task, involving deceptive appearances, are also passed by most normally developing 4-year-olds (Perner, Leekam, & Wimmer, 1987) but failed by most children with autism with mental ages in excess of 7 years (Perner, Frith, Leslie, & Leekam, 1989). This pattern of findings—that normally developing 4-year-olds and older moderate to mildly retarded children pass the false-belief task, and that most children with autism fail—have been widely replicated.

There are two main positions regarding how the abstract concepts underlying theory of mind are acquired. The first holds that the young child uses his or her general intellectual capacities to develop a commonsense theory of mental states, much as a scientist does, by examining evidence and testing hypotheses (Perner, 1991; Wellman, 1990). This position is called the theory-theory. The second position treats the term theory of mind as no more than a metaphor. It proposes that evolution has equipped the human brain with a special module, a theory of mind mechanism (ToMM), that helps normally developing children to attend to the invisible mental states of others (Leslie, 1987, 1994). This social instinct owes little to general reasoning powers and is selectively impaired in children with autism (Baron-Cohen, 1995; Leslie, 1992).

A continuing controversy surrounds the question of why normally developing 3-year-old children fail the false-belief tasks discussed above. The theory-theory claims that 3-year-olds have yet to discover a mature theory of belief. The ToMM position emphasizes 3-year-old success on simplified false-belief tasks. One way in which this question is being examined is by comparing 3-year-olds and older children with autism to see if they fail false-belief tasks for the same or for different reasons.

Bibliography

Baron-Cohen, S. (1995). *Mindblindness: An essay on autism and theory of mind.* Cambridge, MA: MIT Press.

Baron-Cohen, S., Leslie, A. M., & Frith, U. (1985). Does the autistic child have a "theory of mind"? *Cognition, 21,* 37–46.

Leslie, A. M. (1987). Pretense and representation: The origins of "theory of mind." *Psychological Review, 94,* 412–426.

Leslie, A. M. (1992). Autism and the "theory of mind" module. *Current Directions in Psychological Science, 1,* 18–21.

Leslie, A. M. (1994). *Pretending and believing*: Issues in the theory of ToMM. *Cognition, 50,* 211–238. Reprinted in J. Mehler and S. Franck (Eds.), *COGNITION on cognition,* pp. 193–220. (1995). Cambridge, MA: MIT Press.

Perner, J. (1991). *Understanding the representational mind.* Cambridge, MA: MIT Press.

Perner, J., Frith, U., Leslie, A. M., & Leekam, S. R. (1989). Exploration of the autistic child's theory of mind: Knowledge, belief and communication. *Child Development, 60,* 689–700.

Perner, J., Leekam, S. R., & Wimmer, H. (1987). Three-year-olds' difficulty with false belief: The case for a conceptual deficit. *British Journal of Developmental Psychology, 5,* 125–137.

Premack, D., & Woodruff, G. (1978). Does the chimpanzee have a theory of mind? *The Behavioral & Brain Sciences, 4,* 515–526.

Wellman, H. M. (1990). *The child's theory of mind.* Cambridge, MA: MIT Press.

Wimmer, H., & Perner, J. (1983). Beliefs about beliefs: Representation and constraining function of wrong beliefs in young children's understanding of deception. *Cognition, 13,* 103–128.

Alan M. Leslie

THEORY OF REASONED ACTION. Proposed by Martin Fishbein (1967) on the basis of Dulany's (1967) theory of propositional control, the *theory of reasoned action* (TRA) helped to clarify the relation between attitudes and behavior. Prior work by social psychologists had revealed that people often fail to act in accordance with their attitudes, and some theorists had called for abandoning the attitude construct. Responding to this crisis of confidence, Fishbein argued that broad measures of attitude cannot predict specific actions and proposed instead to focus on attitudes toward the specific behaviors of interest. In addition, he suggested that performance of a given behavior in a particular context is influenced not only by attitudes but also by behavior-specific social and personal norms. Subsequently, the model was developed and integrated with attitude theory (Fishbein & Ajzen, 1975), submitted to empirical tests (e.g., Ajzen & Fishbein, 1970), and put to use in a variety of applied domains (Ajzen & Fishbein, 1980).

In its present form, the TRA assumes that behavior is proximally determined by behavioral intention, and it postulates two conceptually independent determinants of intentions: attitudes toward the behavior and subjective norms. Attitudes represent personal evaluations of the behavior and are assumed to reflect the behavior's expected consequences. Expectations of mainly favorable outcomes produce a positive attitude whereas expectations of mainly unfavorable outcomes produce a negative attitude. Subjective norms refer to perceived social pressure to engage in the behavior, and they are assumed to derive from perceived behavioral expectations of important referent individuals and groups. As a general rule, the more favorable the attitude and subjective norm with respect to a behavior, the stronger the intention to perform the behavior. This model was named *theory of reasoned action* because it implies that human behavior, if not completely rational, at least follows from a reasonable set of considerations.

Successful application of the TRA is predicated on three conditions. First, the measures of attitude, subjective norm, and intention must be *compatible* with each other and with the measure of behavior in terms of the action involved, the target at which the action is directed, and the context in which it occurs (Ajzen & Fishbein, 1977). General attitudes are, in this sense, incompatible with specific actions, and thus have little predictive validity. Second, attitude, subjective norm, and intention must remain relatively *stable* prior to observation of the behavior. Any changes over time tend to impair their predictive validity. Long-range behavioral prediction is therefore more uncertain than short-range prediction. Third, the behavior of interest must be under *volitional control*, as implied by the assumption that behavior is determined by intentions. The presence of factors beyond a person's control weaken the intention-behavior relation.

The TRA is by far the best known and most popular attitude-behavior model. It has been used to predict and explain such varied behaviors as voting choice, use of safety helmets, energy conservation, drinking, smoking, drug use, exercising, tax evasion, dental care, fat consumption, breast self-examination, job search, condoms use, and a host of other activities related to health and safety, protection of the environment, crime, recreation, work, and virtually any imaginable area of human endeavor. The results of these investigations have, by and large, confirmed the theory's structure and predictive validity, especially when its constructs were properly operationalized (Eagly & Chaiken, 1993). Even without this caveat, the TRA has fared very well. In a meta-analysis of 150 data sets published between 1969 and 1989, the average correlation between intention and behavior was found to be 0.62; the average correlation of intention with attitude was 0.60 and with subjective norm 0.42 (Van den Putte, 1991).

Although popular and successful, the theory of reasoned action has not escaped criticism, some related to its structure, and some to its sufficiency. Structurally, the theory postulates causal links from attitudes and subjective norms to intentions, and from intentions to behavior. Some theorists have questioned the unidirectionality of the proposed links, arguing that these variables exert mutual effects on each other (Liska, 1984). Others have tried to show that attitudes not only influence intentions but also have a direct effect on behavior (Bentler & Speckart, 1979). Still others have argued that the distinction between attitudes and subjective norms is arbitrary and can perhaps be dispensed with (Miniard & Cohen, 1981). None of these possibilities, however, has received consistent empirical support, and the suggested modifications have not become an accepted part of the model.

A stronger case can be made for the claim that the constructs contained in the TRA may not be sufficient to account for all behaviors. The theory in fact leaves open the possibility that research may reveal the need for additional predictors (Ajzen & Fishbein, 1980). Over the years, investigators have proposed a number of additions to the model, including perceived moral obligation to perform the behavior (Gorsuch & Ortberg, 1983), a variable that has been found to explain additional variance for behaviors with moral connotations (Beck & Ajzen, 1991), and affective responses (Bagozzi, 1986) which can differ significantly from more cognitive evaluations (Ajzen & Driver, 1991). Another proposed addition is the frequency with which the behavior has been performed in the past, said to indicate habit strength (e.g., Bentler & Speckart, 1979; Fredricks & Dossett, 1983). A review of the literature offers support for the idea that frequently performed behavior may become automatic (Oullette & Wood, 1997), but the suggestion to add this variable to the model has met with resistance because not all frequently performed behaviors will necessarily habituate (Ajzen, 1991).

The only widely adopted extension to the TRA arose in an attempt to address the model's restriction to behaviors that are under complete volitional control. In his *theory of planned behavior*, Ajzen (1985, 1991) added perceived behavior control (PBC) as a predictor of intentions and behavior. PBC is similar to Bandura's (1977) concept of self-efficacy. It refers to the perceived ease or difficulty of performing a behavior and is assumed to reflect personal experience, modeling, self-knowledge, and anticipated support or obstacles. Like the TRA, the theory of planned behavior has been used in a great variety of contexts. Most applications have confirmed the proposed extension by showing that PBC improves prediction of intentions and behaviors beyond the level obtained by the original theory of reasoned action (Ajzen, 1991; Godin & Kok, 1996).

Bibliography

Ajzen, I. (1985). From intentions to actions: A theory of planned behavior. In J. Kuhl & J. Beckmann (Eds.), *Action-control: From cognition to behavior* (pp. 11–39). Heidelberg, Germany: Springer.

Ajzen, I. (1991). The theory of planned behavior. *Organizational Behavior and Human Decision Processes, 50*, 179–211.

Ajzen, I., & Driver, B. L. (1991). Prediction of leisure participation from behavioral, normative, and control beliefs: An application of the theory of planned behavior. *Leisure Sciences, 13*, 185–204.

Ajzen, I., & Fishbein, M. (1970). The prediction of behavior from attitudinal and normative variables. *Journal of Experimental Social Psychology, 6*, 466–487.

Ajzen, I., & Fishbein, M. (1980). *Understanding attitudes and predicting social behavior*. Englewood Cliffs, NJ: Prentice Hall.

Bagozzi, R. P. (1986). Attitude formation under the theory of reasoned action and a purposeful behavior reformulation. *British Journal of Social Psychology, 25*, 95–107.

Bandura, A. (1977). Self-efficacy: Toward a unifying theory of behavioral change. *Psychological Review, 84*, 191–215.

Beck, L., & Ajzen, I. (1991). Predicting dishonest actions using the theory of planned behavior. *Journal of Research in Personality, 25*, 285–301.

Bentler, P. M., & Speckart, G. (1979). Models of attitude-behavior relations. *Psychological Review, 86*, 452–464.

Dulany, D. E. (1967). Awareness, rules, and propositional control: A confrontation with S-R behavior theory. In D. Horton & T. Dixon (Eds.), *Verbal behavior and S-R behavior theory* (pp. 340–387). Englewood Cliffs, NJ: Prentice Hall.

Eagly, A. H., & Chaiken, S. (1993). *The psychology of attitudes*. Fort Worth, TX: Harcourt Brace Jovanovich.

Fishbein, M. (1967). Attitude and the prediction of behavior. In M. Fishbein (Ed.), *Readings in attitude theory and measurement* (pp. 477–492). New York: Wiley.

Fishbein, M., & Ajzen, I. (1975). *Belief, attitude, intention, and behavior: An introduction to theory and research*. Reading, MA: Addison-Wesley.

Fredricks, A. J., & Dossett, D. L. (1983). Attitude-behavior relations: A comparison of the Fishbein-Ajzen and the Bentler-Speckart models. *Journal of Personality and Social Psychology, 45*, 501–512.

Godin, G., & Kok, G. (1996). The theory of planned behavior: A review of its applications in the health domain. *American Journal of Health Promotion, 11*, 87–98.

Gorsuch, R. L., & Ortberg, J. (1983). Moral obligation and attitudes: Their relation to behavioral intentions. *Journal of Personality and Social Psychology, 44*, 1025–1028.

Liska, A. E. (1984). A critical examination of the causal structure of the Fishbein/Ajzen attitude-behavior model. *Social Psychology Quarterly, 47*, 61–74.

Miniard, P. W., & Cohen, J. B. (1981). An examination of the Fishbein behavioral intention model's concepts and measures. *Journal of Experimental Social Psychology, 17*, 309–329.

Oullette, J. A., & Wood, W. (1997). *Habit and intention in everyday life: The multiple processes by which past behavior predicts future behavior*. Unpublished manuscript. Texas A&M University.

Van den Putte, B. (1991). *20 years of the theory of reasoned action of Fishbein and Ajzen: A meta-analysis*. Unpublished manuscript. University of Amsterdam, The Netherlands.

Icek Ajzen

THERAPEUTIC ALLIANCE. *See* Working Alliance.

THERAPEUTIC COMMUNITIES have been treating substance abusers for four decades. Originating as an alternative to conventional medical and psychiatric approaches, the therapeutic community (TC) has become a major psychosocial treatment modality for thousands of chemically involved individuals. Today the term *therapeutic community* describes a variety of short- and long-term residential programs as well as day treatment and ambulatory programs serving a wide spectrum of drug and alcohol abusers. It is the traditional long-term residential prototype, however, which has documented effectiveness in rehabilitating substance abusers.

The Traditional Therapeutic Community

Traditional TCs are similar in planned duration of stay (15 to 24 months), structure, staffing pattern, perspective, and rehabilitative regime, although they differ in size (e.g., 30 to 600 beds) and client demography. Staff are composed of TC-trained clinicians and other human service professionals. Members of the primary clinical staff are usually former substance abusers who themselves were rehabilitated in TC programs. Other professionals provide medical, mental health, vocational, educational, family counseling, fiscal, administrative, and legal services.

The TC views drug abuse as a deviant behavior, reflecting impeded personality development or chronic deficits in social, educational, and economic skills. Thus, the principal aim of the therapeutic community is a global change in lifestyle: abstinence from illicit substances, elimination of antisocial activity, development of employability, and prosocial attitudes and values. The rehabilitative approach requires multidimensional influence and training, which for most can only occur in a 24-hour residential setting.

The traditional TC can be distinguished from other major drug treatment modalities in three broad ways. First, the TC coordinates multiple interventions and services in a single treatment setting. Second, the primary "therapist" and teacher in the TC is the community itself: peers and staff model successful personal change; staff serve as rational authorities and guides in the recovery process; and the community as a whole monitors and reinforces changes in conduct, attitudes, and emotions. Third, the TC approach to rehabilitation is based on an explicit perspective of the drug-abuse disorder, the client, the recovery process, and healthy living.

The Therapeutic Community Perspective. In the TC perspective, drug abuse is a disorder of the whole person, affecting many areas of functioning. Addiction is a symptom, not the essence of the disorder. Individuals in TCs have in common psychological dysfunction and social deficits; thus, they follow the same regime. Individual differences in social background and degree of dysfunction are recognized in specific treatment plans that modify the emphasis, not the course, of their experience.

Recovery involves a change in both lifestyle and personal identity. The primary psychological goal is to change the negative patterns of behavior, thinking, and feeling that predispose drug use; the main social goal is to develop the skills, attitudes, and values of a responsible drug-free lifestyle.

Client's motivation can arise from external or intrinsic factors but is critical to recovery. Changes in lifestyle are facilitated by a social context of self- and mutual help. Residency in the TC is a brief but intense period in an individual's life. The daily regime is demanding, and therapeutic confrontations unmoderated. TCs adhere to common views of healthy personal and social living. For example, TCs hold unambiguous moral positions regarding social and sexual conduct. Explicit right and wrong behaviors are identified and given appropriate rewards and sanctions. TCs also stress such values as personal honesty and truth as essential to social learning and personal growth. Although past behavior and circumstances are explored to illustrate current dysfunction, individuals are trained to assume personal responsibility for their present reality and destiny.

Therapeutic Community Clients

Clients in traditional programs are usually male (70–75%), but female admissions are increasing. Most community-based TCs are integrated across gender, race/ethnicity, and age, with most residents over 21. The majority of TC entries have histories of multiple drug use including marijuana, opiates, alcohol, pills, and crack cocaine as their primary drug of abuse. Clients manifest considerable psychosocial dysfunction in addition to their substance abuse. A third have current or continuing history of mental disorder. Typically, symptoms of depression and anxiety are high, socialization scores are poor, IQ is in the dull-normal range, and self-esteem is markedly low.

Traditional TCs maintain an "open-door" policy with respect to admission. Although the majority of entries to TCs are voluntary, various forms of perceived pressures from family/relationships, employment difficulties, or anticipated legal consequences are common. Among adolescents, 40 to 50% have been legally referred to treatment compared with 25 to 30% of adults. For some programs, legal referrals constitute considerably higher percentages of admissions. Specific exclusionary criteria that would exclude admission to TCs most often include histories of arson, suicide, and serious psychiatric disorder.

The Therapeutic Community Approach

The quintessential element of the TC approach may be termed *community as method*. What distinguishes the TC from other treatment approaches (and other communities) is the purposive use of the peer community to facilitate social and psychological change in individuals. Thus, in a therapeutic community all aspects of structure and process are designed to produce therapeutic and educational change in participants and all participants are mediators of these changes.

Therapeutic Community Structure. The TC is composed of relatively few staff and a stratified hierarchy of peers who constitute the community or family in the residence. This peer-to-community structure strengthens the individual's identification with an ordered network of others. More importantly, it arranges relationships of mutual responsibility to others at various levels in the program. The daily operation of the community itself, from cooking and cleaning, to running encounter groups, is the task of the residents, working together under staff supervision. Staff monitor and evaluate client status, supervise resident groups, assign and supervise jobs, and oversee house operations. Clinically, staff conduct therapeutic groups (other than peer encounters), provide individual counseling, organize social and recreational projects, and confer with significant others. They decide matters of resident status, discipline, promotion, transfers, discharges, furloughs, and treatments.

The new client enters a setting of upward mobility. Resident jobs are arranged in a hierarchy according to seniority, clinical progress, and productivity. Job assignments begin with menial tasks (e.g, mopping the floor) and lead vertically to levels of coordination and management. Indeed, clients come in as patients and can leave as staff. This social organization of the TC reflects the fundamental aspects of its rehabilitative approach, work as education and therapy, mutual self-help, peers as role models, and staff as rational authorities.

The Therapeutic Community Process. The typical day in a therapeutic community is highly structured, beginning at 7 A.M. and ending at 11 P.M. It includes a variety of meetings, job functions (work therapy), encounter and other therapeutic groups, individual counseling, and recreation. Activities may be grouped into three main elements: therapeutic-educative, community enhancement, and community management.

Therapeutic-Educative. There are four main forms of group activity in the TC: *encounters, probes, marathons*, and *tutorials*. All attempt to foster trust, personal disclosure, intimacy, and peer solidarity to facilitate therapeutic change. The encounter is the cornerstone of group process in the TC. It consists of a peer-led group of 12 to 20 residents, which utilizes a confrontational approach to directly modify negative behavior and attitudes. Probes have as their primary objective significant emotional change and psychological insight. Probes are staff-led group sessions composed of 10 to 15 residents, conducted to obtain in-depth clinical information on clients and explore psychological issues. Marathons are extended group sessions including larger groups of selected residents, the objective of which is to initiate resolution of life experiences that have impeded the individual's development. These groups meet for 18 to 36 hours and are conducted by all staff, assisted by senior residents with marathon experience. Tutorial groups are directed toward training or teaching. Tutorial groups, usually staff-led, consist of 10 to 20 residents, and address certain themes, including personal growth (e.g., self-reliance, maturity, relationships), job skills (e.g., managing the department or the reception desk), and clinical skills (e.g., use of encounter tools).

The four main groups are supplemented by a number of ad hoc groups that convene as needed. For example, gender, ethnic, or age-specific theme groups, or groups for residents with HIV may utilize encounter or tutorial formats. Dormitory, room, or departmental encounters may address issues of daily community living. One-to-one counseling, conducted as needed, balances the needs of the individual with those of the community. The staff counseling method in the TC is not traditional, as is evident in its main features: transpersonal sharing, direct support, minimal interpretation, didactic instructions, and concerned confrontation.

Community Enhancement and Management. Four main meetings both enhance and facilitate the management of the community by assembling the entire membership several times a day to address relevant community issues. Morning meetings, seminars, and house meetings occur daily; the general meeting is called when needed. A system of privileges, disciplinary sanctions, and surveillance (house monitoring and urine testing) ensures that resident life is orderly and productive. Additionally, various informal activities enhance the perception of community, such as the communitywide meals and celebrations (e.g., birthdays, national/ethnic holidays, program graduations).

Program Stages and Profiles. Clients pass through three major program stages: induction, primary treatment, and reentry. The main goals of the induction-orientation phase (the first 60 days) are assessment and orientation or assimilation of the individual into the community through involvement in all of its activities. Rapid assimilation is crucial at this point when clients are most ambivalent about the long tenure of residency. Socialization and psychological change are the goals of the primary treatment phase (2 to 12 months). The daily therapeutic-educational regimen, meetings, groups, job functions, and peer and staff counseling remain the same throughout the year of primary treatment. However, client progress on the interrelated dimensions of community-status, development-maturity, and overall psychological adjustment is reflected at the end of different phases.

The main goal of the early reentry phase (13 to 18 months), during which clients continue to live in the facility, is preparation for healthy separation from the community. Emphasis on rational authority decreases under the assumption that the client has acquired a sufficient degree of self-management. There is more individual decision making about privileges, social plans, and life design. A treatment focus is on skills training for life outside the of community (e.g., on budgeting, job seeking, use of alcohol, sexuality, parenting, use of leisure time). Individual plans and goal attainment schedules are developed for long-term psychological, educational, and vocational goals, including interpersonal and family relationships, and social and sexual behavior. Clients may attend school or hold full-time jobs (within or outside the TC) while assuming some community responsibilities (e.g., facility coverage at night).

In the later reentry phase (18 to 24 months), clients

work toward successful separation from residency. They are on "live-out" status, participate in full-time jobs or education, and maintain their own households, usually with live-out peers. They may attend such aftercare services as Alcoholics Anonymous or Narcotics Anonymous, or take part in family or individual therapy. Contact is gradually reduced to weekly telephone calls and monthly visits with a primary counselor.

Completion marks the end of active program involvement. The annual graduation is conducted in the facility for completees at usually a year beyond their residency. Completion or graduation is not an end but a beginning. Many contemporary TCs now offer explicit aftercare components within their systems or through linkages with outside agencies.

Research and Evaluation

A substantial evaluation literature documents the effectiveness of the TC approach in rehabilitating chemical abusers. Dropout is the rule for all drug treatment modalities, including TCs. For example, 30 to 40% of all admissions complete long-term therapeutic communities. However, the outcome studies indicate positive effects in relation to time in treatment; treatment completions show the best outcomes, while long-term dropouts show better outcomes than short-term dropouts. The relationship between time spent in treatment and successful outcome has been shown in large-scale field evaluations of several thousand admissions to TCs followed 1 to 12 years posttreatment and is confirmed in recently completed smaller studies utilizing randomized designs.

There are no reliable client characteristics that predict retention, except that severe criminality and/or severe psychopathology are correlated with earlier dropout. However, recent studies point to the importance of perceived legal pressure, motivation, and readiness as positive predictors of retention. While a legitimate concern, retention should not be confused with treatment effectiveness. Therapeutic communities are effective for those who remain long enough for treatment influences to occur. Obviously, however, a critical issue for TCs is maximizing holding power to benefit more clients.

Evolution of the Therapeutic Community

Today, TCs include a wide range of programs serving diverse clients who use a variety of drugs and present complex social-psychological problems. Client differences, clinical requirements, and funding realities have all encouraged the development of modified residential TCs with shorter stays of 3, 6, and 12 months, as well as TC-oriented day treatment and outpatient models. Correctional, medical, and mental hospitals, community residence and shelter settings, overwhelmed with alcohol and drug abuse problems, have implemented TC programs within their institutional boundaries.

Most traditional TCs have expanded their social services or incorporated new interventions to address the needs of special populations such as adolescents, mothers and children, homeless, mentally ill chemical abusers, and prison inmates. In these modifications the cross-fertilization of personnel and methods from the traditional TC, mental health, and human services portends the evolution of a new therapeutic community.

Bibliography

Anglin, M. D., & Hser, Y-I. (1990). Treatment of drug abuse. In M. Tonry & J. Q. Wilson (Eds.), *Drugs and crime: Crime and justice: A review of research* (Vol. 13, pp. 393–460). Chicago: University of Chicago Press.

Condelli, W. S. (1989). External pressure and retention in a therapeutic community. *International Journal of Therapeutic Communities, 10*, 21–33.

De Leon, G. (1989). Psychopathology and substance abuse: What we are learning from research in therapeutic communities. *Journal of Psychoactive Drugs, 21*, 177–188.

De Leon, G. (1994). Therapeutic communities. In M. Galanter & H. D. Kleber (Eds.), *Textbook of substance abuse treatment* (pp. 391–414). Washington, DC: American Psychiatric Press.

De Leon, G. (Ed.). (1997). *Community as method: Therapeutic communities for special populations in special settings.* Westport, CT: Greenwood.

De Leon, G., Melnick, G., Kressel, D., & Jainchill, N. (1994). Circumstances, motivation, readiness and suitability (the CMRS scales): Predicting retention in therapeutic community treatment. *American Journal of Drug and Alcohol Abuse, 20*, 495–515.

Leukefeld, C. G., & Tims, F. M. (Eds.). (1988). *Compulsory treatment of drug abuse: Research and clinical practice.* National Institute on Drug Abuse Research Monograph Number 86. DHHS Publication No. ADM 88–1578. Rockville, MD: National Institute in Drug Abuse.

Simpson, D. D. (1979). The relation of time spent in drug abuse treatment to posttreatment outcome. *American Journal of Psychiatry, 136*, 1449–1453.

Tims, F. M., De Leon, G., & Jainchill, N. (Eds). (1994). *Therapeutic community: Advances in research and application.* National Institute on Drug Abuse Research Monograph Number 144. NIH Publication No. 94–3633. Rockville, MD: National Institute on Drug Abuse.

George De Leon

THERAPEUTIC JURISPRUDENCE. *See* Mental Health Law.

THIBAUT, JOHN W. (1917–1986), American social psychologist. Born in Marion, Ohio, Thibaut showed an early interest in books and, after reading Plato in high school, decided to become a philosopher. Partially supporting himself by periods of work on blue collar jobs, he enrolled in the University of North Carolina, graduated in 3 years, and began graduate studies. His emerging interests in moral and theological philosophy were interrupted by military service that fortuitously landed him in a small unit of the Aviation Psychology Program. In informal seminars there, Thibaut got his first intensive exposure to psychology.

In 1946, after the war, he changed his career goals to psychology and, on the advice of a trusted professor at the University of North Carolina, enrolled in Kurt Lewin's new Research Center for Group Dynamics at the Massachusetts Institute of Technology. After Lewin's death, Thibaut completed his Ph.D. in 1949 with John R. P. French and worked with Leon Festinger at the University of Michigan. He went on to positions, successively, at Boston University, Harvard University, and finally, in 1953, back to North Carolina. There, he founded the program in social psychology, served as department chair, and in 1962 became Alumni Distinguished Professor. He founded the *Journal of Experimental Social Psychology* in 1965 and was its editor until 1970.

The centerpieces of Thibaut's career were two books with Harold Kelley: *The Social Psychology of Groups* (New York, 1958, reprinted in 1986) and *Interpersonal Relations: A Theory of Interdependence* (New York, 1979). The first of these, along with writings by George Homans and Peter Blau, defined what came to be known as social exchange theory. The Thibaut and Kelley writings, now referred to as interdependence theory, analyze interrelations among persons in terms of how their actions affect each other's rewards and costs and identify the standards of comparison by which they evaluate those outcomes. Outcome matrices, adapted from game theory, are used to specify patterns of interdependence and power, conflicts of interests, and exchange and coordination problems. Those patterns are shown to be at the basis of interaction and social norms, and, in the second book, to provide a theory that, reflecting Thibaut's sensitivity to moral questions, analyzes the processes through which social concerns emerge from individual concerns. The benefits derived from taking account of the broader context of one's actions are postulated to underlie the existence of the values uniquely relevant to social relations, such as altruism, competitiveness, dominance, and fairness.

Not surprisingly, in view of his early intellectual interests, the inspirations for Thibaut's thought often came from philosophy and social-political theory. This is most apparent in his work *Procedural Justice: A Psychological Analysis* (Hillsdale, N.J., 1975), written with a law school colleague, Laurens Walker. Starting from the philosopher John Rawls's concept of the "veil of ignorance," Thibaut and Walker's analysis delved deeply into the interplay between cognitive conflict and conflict of interest. Their studies continue to stimulate research on the procedural bases of perceived justice.

Thibaut's many empirical contributions were largely through laboratory experiments. Partly a personal predilection, this also reflected the dominant view of social psychologists in the 1950s and 1960s—a view that one cannot really understand a phenomenon until one can experimentally produce and control it. Given the typical sources of inspiration for Thibaut's work, it is accurate to describe it as an experimental social philosophy. Examples are provided by his dissertation research that concerned the cohesiveness of underprivileged groups in intergroup settings, studies with Claude Faucheux on interdependence factors promoting the development of norms of loyalty and fairness, and a series of studies with Chester Insko on trading among groups and the evolution of norms to ensure the orderly succession of leaders. An especially influential early study with Henry Riecken examined how the perception of the causes for behavior is affected by status and power relations among persons. Inspired by Fritz Heider and Albert Michotte, this study itself planted the seeds for work by other researchers (among them, Edward Jones and Harold Kelley) on self-presentation and attribution.

In developing and teaching interdependence theory, Thibaut conveyed a sense of being at the frontier of social psychology while also being in touch with the most basic phenomena of social life. His profound ideas and broad scholarship earned the respect of wide audiences within social science. This is shown in his election to the American Academy of Arts and Sciences (1978), and receipt of the Distinguished Senior Scientist Award from the Society for Experimental Social Psychology (1981) and the Distinguished Scientific Contribution Award from the American Psychological Association (1983).

[*Many of the people mentioned in this article are the subjects of independent biographical entries.*]

Bibliography

Works by Thibaut

Insko, C. A., Thibaut, J. W., Moehle, D., Wilson, M., Diamond, W., Gilmore, R., Solomon, M., & Lipsitz, A. (1980). Social evolution and the emergence of leadership. *Journal of Personality and Social Psychology, 39,* 431–448.

Thibaut, J. W. (1950). An experimental study of the cohesiveness of underprivileged groups. *Human Relations,* 3 251–278.

Thibaut, J. W., & Riecken, H. (1955). Some determinants and consequences of the perception of social causality. *Journal of Personality, 23,* 113–133.

Thibaut, J. W., & Faucheux, C. (1965). The development of contractual norms in a bargaining situation under two types of stress. *Journal of Experimental Social Psychology, 1*, 89–102.

Thibaut, J. W., Ross, M., & Evenbeck, S. (1971). Some determinants of the intensity of social protest. *Journal of Experimental Social Psychology, 7*, 401–418.

Works about Thibaut

Anonymous. (1984). Citation. *American Psychologist, 39*, 262–265. Includes biographical information and bibliography.

Jones, E., Kelley, H., & Schopler, J. (1987). John Walter Thibaut (1917–1986). *American Psychologist, 42*, 874–875.

Patnoe, S. (1988). *A narrative history of experimental social psychology: The Lewin tradition*. New York: Springer-Verlag. Pages 48–60 are based on an interview with Thibaut.

Harold H. Kelley

THINKING. [*This entry comprises three articles. The first article provides a brief overview of the thinking process, surveying the types and providing a general history of study. The second article describes the process of problem solving, including physiological and behavioral manifestations. The third article examines the process of reasoning, including physiological and behavioral manifestations. For independent entries related to thinking, see* Cognitive Psychology; Concepts; Conflict Resolution; Decision Making; Information Processing Theories; Language; Learning; Memory; Mental Imagery; *and* Mental Models.]

An Overview

Thinking involves the mental representation and processing of information, as well as their interaction. It is sometimes divided into categories. For example, a distinction may be made between analytical thinking, in which wholes are broken down into components, and synthetic thinking, in which components are integrated into wholes; or between divergent thinking, which involves the generation of many, diverse ideas, and convergent thinking, which involves focusing on a single idea, often to find a single correct answer to a problem. However thinking is divided, both mental representation and process, as well as their interaction, are key.

Because thinking involves so many different kinds of mental processes, its study is sometimes divided into major categories of one kind or another. Although there is no one categorical taxonomy that everyone would accept, a typical division into categories would include concept formation, problem solving, judgment and decision making, and reasoning. That is the taxonomy used in this article.

Concept Formation

Concept formation involves learning and thinking about the meanings underlying words or other symbols. It is sometimes studied under the rubric of learning, memory, or language.

At one time it was believed that people think about concepts in componential terms (Katz, 1972; Katz & Fodor, 1963), meaning that they disassemble words or other symbols into sets of meaning components. Each component is an essential element of the concept; together, the properties would uniquely define the concept.

But do people really think about concepts in this way? An alternative view, suggested by Eleanor Rosch (Rosch & Mervis, 1975), is that meaning is derived not from the defining features of a word, but from characteristic features that describe the prototypical model of the concept. A characteristic feature need not be possessed by all instances of a concept, but may be possessed only by some of them (see Smith, Shoben, & Rips, 1974). Thus, the ability to fly is typical of birds, but it is not a defining feature of a bird. An ostrich seems less birdlike than a robin, in part because an ostrich cannot fly. According to the prototype view, an object or idea will be thought of as an instance of a category if it is sufficiently similar to the prototype.

When we think of birds, we might not really think of any one prototype of a bird, say, one that is small, flies, builds nests, sings, and so on; rather, we may think of various exemplars of birds, including typical small harmless birds building nests in the eaves of our house, and also birds of prey and medium-sized waterfowl. According to some theorists (e.g., Medin, 1989; Ross & Spalding, 1994), we do not think in terms of prototypes of concepts, but rather in terms of exemplars—several alternative typical representatives of the class. Ross and Spalding suggest that if we have multiple exemplars, when we see an instance of a bird we can more flexibly match this instance to an appropriate exemplar than to a single prototype.

Not all our thinking is about concepts, however. Sometimes we need to think about how to solve problems that present themselves to us in the course of daily living.

Problem Solving

Problem solving involves moving from a problem situation to a solution, overcoming obstacles along the way.

Cognitive psychologists who study problem solving often distinguish between well-structured and ill-structured problems. Well-structured problems have a clear path to solution (e.g., How much is 24×185?), whereas ill-structured problems do not have such a clear path (e.g., How could a pastor marry 25 different women without getting into trouble with the law?).

Ill-structured problems are sometimes called insight

problems. There are many different theories of how people solve insight problems (see Sternberg & Davidson, 1995). However, it appears that for noninsight problems, people are aware when they are getting closer and closer to a solution. For insight problems, they are not aware that they are close to a solution until they have just about reached it (Metcalfe & Wiebe, 1987).

People seeking to solve problems can rely on either algorithms or heuristics. Algorithms are paths to a solution that, if followed, guarantee an accurate solution to the problem for which they are being used. Algorithms generally involve successive, somewhat mechanical iterations of a particular strategy until the correct solution is reached. For example, an algorithm for solving a crytogram—a puzzle involving secret writing—would be to try to substitute each letter of the alphabet for each cryptic letter until sense was made of the cryptogram. A heuristic is an informal, intuitive, speculative strategy, which sometimes works and sometimes does not. For example, you might try several different routes to work in the hope of finding the shortest one, but there would be no guarantee that there might not be some shorter one that you just didn't think to try.

Problem solvers apply algorithms and heuristics in a problem space (the universe of all possible actions that can be applied) to solve a problem (Newell & Simon, 1972). Various kinds of heuristics can be applied in this space. For example, in means-ends analysis, the problem solver analyzes the problem by viewing the end—the goal being sought—and then trying to decrease the distance between the current position in the problem space and the end goal in that space. In working forward, the problem solver starts at the beginning and tries to solve the problem from start to finish. In working backward, the problem solver starts at the end and tries to work backward from there. In generate and test, the problem solver simply generates alternative courses of action, not necessarily in a systematic way, and then notices in turn whether each course of action works.

Experts solve problems in ways that are different from those used by novices (Chi, Glaser, & Farr, 1988; Lesgold, 1988). For example, experts differ from novices in having large, rich schemas containing a great deal of declarative knowledge about a domain; in having well-organizing, highly interconnected units of knowledge in schemas; and in developing sophisticated representations of problems based on structural similarities among problems (see Sternberg, 1996, p. 374). In general, Chase and Simon showed that experts differ from novices more in the amount and organization of knowledge they possess than in the processes they use for problem solution (1973).

Often, both experts and novices have to make decisions on the basis of the problems they solve. How do they, or anyone, make these decisions?

Judgment and Decision Making

In judgment and decision making, we select from among choices or evaluate opportunities. Economic theories of decision making assume that decision makers have unlimited rationality and use it in making their decisions.

These rational theories include utility maximization theory, according to which the goal of human action is to seek pleasure and avoid pain. In making decisions, people thus maximize their positive utilities and minimize their negative ones. Some theorists have pointed out that there is no one set of utilities that would fit everyone, so they instead proposed subjective-utility theory, which allows everyone to have his or her own set of utilities to maximize.

In recent times, psychological theorists have tended to view decision makers as showing only bounded rather than full rationality. For example, people may satisfice—consider options one by one—and then select an option as soon as they find one that is satisfactory (Simon, 1957).

A related notion is that people may make many judgments by using a set of decisional heuristics (e.g., Kahneman & Tversky, 1971; Tversky & Kahneman, 1973). What are some examples of such heuristics?

One such heuristic is the representativeness heuristic, by which people judge the probability of an uncertain event according to: (a) how obviously it is similar to or representative of the population from which it is derived; and (b) the degree to which it reflects the salient features of the process by which it is generated (such as randomness). For example, people believe that tosses of a coin are more likely to yield H T H H T H than H H H H T H, because the first sequence appears to be more representative of a random process than the second, even though the two sequences are equally likely.

Availability, another heuristic, states that people make judgments on the basis of how easily they are able to call to mind what they perceive as relevant instances of a phenomenon. Newspapers, for example, give much more play to plane crashes than to car crashes, and it is thus usually easier to call to mind grim instances of plane crashes than of car crashes; this fact may lead people to fear planes more than cars, even though car crashes are far more common than plane crashes.

Yet another heuristic, overconfidence, leads to our believing we are more likely to be correct in our beliefs than we actually are (Fischhoff, Slovic, & Lichtenstein, 1977). We thus overestimate our likelihood of being correct in judgment tasks in which there are correct and incorrect answers. Clearly, our judgments are often faulty. At times, such faulty judgments are due to errors in our reasoning processes.

Reasoning

Reasoning involves drawing conclusions from evidence. There are two main types of reasoning: deductive and inductive. Deductive reasoning is the process of reasoning from one or more general premises to reach a logically certain, specific conclusion. Inductive reasoning is the process of reasoning from specific facts or observations to reach a general conclusion that may explain the facts; in inductive reasoning, it is not possible to reach a logically certain conclusion, only a more or less well-founded and more or less probable conclusion.

Deductive reasoning can take various forms. For example, syllogisms are deductive arguments that involve drawing conclusions from two premises. In categorical syllogisms, the two premises are about categories, such as: All psychologists are tennis players; all tennis players are politicians. We could then conclude that all psychologists are politicians. Note that the conclusion to a syllogism can be logically valid but factually incorrect. Categorical syllogisms comprise four main different kinds of statements: universal affirmatives (e.g., All A are B), universal negatives (e.g., No A are B), particular affirmatives (e.g., Some A are B), and particular negatives (e.g., Some A are not B).

In conditional syllogisms, the first major premise is in the form of an "if-then" statement, such as: If it is raining, I will bring an umbrella. The second, minor premise is in the form of an assertion, such as: It is raining. The conclusion may then either follow from the premises (e.g., I will bring an umbrella) or not follow (e.g., I will not bring an umbrella).

There are various theories of how people think in deductive reasoning in general, and syllogisms in particular. For example, some theorists believe that we use propositional rules (Rips, 1994), whereas others believe that we simulate possible configurations, or mental models of situations that might confirm or disconfirm our conclusions (Johnson-Laird & Steedman, 1978). Another theory is that we use pragmatic reasoning schemas, or general organizing principles related to particular kinds of goals, such as permissions, obligations, or causations (Cheng & Holyoak, 1985), whereas still other investigators believe that evolutionary principles—such as sensitivity to when we are cheated—may account for some of the kinds of errors we make or do not make (Cosmides, 1989).

In inductive reasoning, there are no certain conclusions to be had. Although it is possible to simulate inductive thinking (e.g., Holland, Holyoak, Nisbett, & Thagard, 1986), it is not possible to reach any certain answers with it. For this reason, perhaps, psychologists who study reasoning have tended to focus more on models of deductive than of inductive reasoning, although a growing literature on inductive reasoning, and particularly reasoning by analogy, can be found (e.g., Gentner, 1983). According to Gentner, analogies between problems involve mapping relationships between problems; the actual content attributes of the problems are irrelevant. In other words, what matters in analogies is not the similarity of the content, but how closely their structural systems of relationships match.

In conclusion, researchers studying thinking have investigated a variety of topics, such as concept formation, problem solving, judgment and decision making, and reasoning. Through their work, they have helped us understand how we represent and process information. Although there are few models of thinking that try to incorporate thinking in all its different aspects (see Anderson, 1983; Newell, 1990), it ultimately may be possible to understand thinking in all its aspects through a single model.

Bibliography

Anderson, J. R. (1982). *The architecture of cognition.* Cambridge, MA: Harvard University Press.

Chase, W. G., & Simon, H. A. (1973). The mind's eye in chess. In W. G. Chase (Ed.), *Visual information processing* (pp. 215–281). New York: Academic Press.

Cheng, P. W., & Holyoak, K. J. (1985). Pragmatic reasoning schemas. *Cognitive Psychology, 17,* 391–416.

Chi, M. T. H., Glaser, R., & Farr, M. J. (Eds.). (1988). *The nature of expertise.* Hillsdale, NJ: Erlbaum.

Cosmides, L. (1989). The logic of social exchange: Has natural selection shaped how humans reason? Studies with the Wason selection task. *Cognition, 31,* 187–276.

Fischhoff, B., Slovic, P., & Lichtenstein, S. (1977). Knowing with certainty: The appropriateness of extreme confidence. *Journal of Experimental Psychology: Human Perception and Performance, 3,* 552–564.

Gentner, D. (1983). Structure-mapping: A theoretical framework for analogy. *Cognitive Science, 7,* 155–170.

Holland, J. H., Holyoak, K. J., Nisbett, R. E., & Thagard, P. R. (1986). *Induction: Processes of inference learning, and discovery.* Cambridge, MA: MIT Press.

Johnson-Laird, P. N., & Steedman, M. (1978). The psychology of syllogisms. *Cognitive Psychology, 10,* 64–99.

Kahneman, D., & Tversky, A. (1972). Subjective probability: A judgment of representativeness. *Cognitive Psychology 3,* 430–454.

Katz, J. J. (1972). *Semantic theory.* New York: Harper & Row.

Katz, J. J., & Fodor, J. A. (1963). The structure of semantic theory. *Language, 39,* 170–210.

Lesgold, A. (1988). Problem-solving. In R. J. Sternberg & E. E. Smith (Eds.), *The psychology of human thought* (pp. 188–213). New York: Cambridge University Press.

Medin, D. L. (1989). Concepts and conceptual structure. *American Psychologist, 44,* 1469–1481.

Metcalfe, J., & Weibe, D. (1987). Intuition in insight and noninsight problem-solving. *Memory and Cognition, 15,* 238–246.

Newell, A. (1990). *Unified theories of cognition.* Cambridge, MA: Harvard University Press.

Newell, A., & Simon, H. A. (1972). *Human problem-solving.* Englewood Cliffs, NJ: Prentice Hall.
Rips, L. J. (1989). Similarity, typicality, and categorization. In S. Vosniadou & A. Ortony (Eds.), *Similarity and analogical reasoning* (pp. 179–195). New York: Cambridge University Press.
Rosch, E., & Mervis, C. B. (1975). Family resemblance studies in the internal structure of categories. *Cognitive Psychology, 3,* 573–605.
Ross, R. H., & Spalding, T. L. (1994). Concepts and categories. In R. J. Sternberg (Ed.), *Thinking and problem-solving* (pp. 119–148). San Diego, CA: Academic Press.
Simon, H. A. (1957). *Administrative behavior* (2nd ed.). Totowa, NJ: Littlefield, Adams.
Smith, E. E., Shoben, E. J., & Rips, L. J. (1974). Structure and process in semantic memory: A featural model for semantic decisions. *Psychological Review, 81,* 214–241.
Smith, E. E., & Medin, D. L. (1981). *Categories and concepts.* Cambridge, MA: Harvard University Press.
Sternberg, R. J. (1996). *Cognitive psychology.* Orlando, FL: Harcourt Brace.
Sternberg, R. J., & Davidson, J. E. (Eds.). (1995). *The nature of insight.* Cambridge, MA: MIT Press.
Tversky, A., & Kahneman, D. (1973). Availability: A heuristic for judging frequency and probability. *Cognitive Psychology, 5,* 207–232.

Robert J. Sternberg

Problem Solving

The famous mathematician George Polya made the following comment in his book *Mathematical Discovery* (1962):

> Solving a problem means finding a way out of a difficulty, a way around an obstacle, attaining an aim that was not immediately understandable. Solving problems is the specific achievement of intelligence, and intelligence is the specific gift of mankind: Solving problems can be regarded as the most characteristically human activity.

Most of us share the high esteem that Polya placed on people's ability to solve problems. Although solving problems is as old as civilization, the scientific study of problem solving has been going on for only a century.

Early Experimental Studies

In his book *Thinking, Problem-Solving, Cognition,* Richard Mayer lists some of the important movements in the experimental study of thinking (1992). Wilhelm Wundt started the first psychology laboratory at the University of Leipzig in 1879, but believed it was only the simple psychological processes such as sensation and perception that could be studied in the laboratory. It wasn't until the beginning of the twentieth century that a group of German psychologists in the city of Wurzburg began to study thinking by using the method of introspection. However, this method was soon challenged as being too subjective, and the introspections did not lead to a theory of thinking.

A theory of thinking had to wait until 1913, when Otto Selz proposed that thoughts were organized into structural relations (Selz, 1982). Thoughts were more than a string of associations. For instance, the famous example of Benjamin Franklin's kite involved an organized structure of ideas in which a kite was a means of connecting the storm clouds to the earth.

The importance of structural understanding was later emphasized in the writing of Gestalt psychologists. They began by examining the structural organization of perceptual patterns but later extended their ideas to solving problems. A well-known example is the problem described by Wolfgang Köhler in his book *The Mentality of Apes* (1925). Köhler hung some fruit from the top of a cage to investigate whether a chimpanzee could discover how to reach it. The cage contained several sticks and crates. The solution required that the chimp stand on the crate and use a stick to knock down the fruit. According to the Gestalt psychologists, solving a problem such as this one requires rearranging the parts of the problem (crate, chimp, stick) into a new structure.

One factor that can make it difficult to discover a correct arrangement of parts is functional fixedness—the tendency to perceive an object only in terms of its most common use. Subjects in an experiment by Karl Duncker were shown three small boxes that contained tacks, candles, and matches (1945). The goal was to find a way to place the three candles at eye level on the door. The solution required using the boxes as platforms to support the candles, but people's tendency to perceive boxes as containers rather than as platforms hindered finding the solution. When empty boxes were placed beside the other objects, more subjects solved the problem because the boxes were no longer used as containers.

Gestalt psychologists believed that the correct organization of the parts usually occurred as a flash of insight. Insight is the sudden discovery of the correct solution following a period of incorrect attempts, often based on trial and error. An experiment by Janet Metcalf produced evidence for insight on an anagram task (1986). Anagrams are strings of letters (such as *ssoia, pmuoi,* and *ttnua*) that can be rearranged to create words. Every 10 seconds subjects had to rate on a 10-point scale how close they were to solving the problem. Ratings of their progress remained very low until they suddenly discovered the correct answer.

For very difficult problems, insight might occur only after the problem solver has set the problem aside. In his book *The Art of Thought* (1926), Graham Wallas argued that problem solving involves four stages:

1. Preparation—preliminary attempts are made to solve the problem.

2. Incubation—the problem solver works on other activities or sleeps.
3. Illumination—the solution occurs.
4. Verification—the solution is checked to see whether it works.

Experimental evidence on the usefulness of the incubation period has been mixed. When obtained, the two most frequent explanations are that incubation occurs either because of unconscious thinking about the problem or because of the forgetting of misleading ideas (Gilhooly, 1988).

One limitation of the Gestalt contribution to problem solving is that Gestalt psychologists were only interested in a particular type of problem, which James Greeno calls an arrangement problem (1978). But Greeno identified other kinds of problems, such as inducing structure and transformation problems, that require skills different from rearranging parts. In inducing structure problems, the parts are fixed and the objective is to figure out the structure. For instance, which number comes next in the series completion problem 12834656? In transformation problems, there is a particular goal that requires a sequence of moves to reach. An example is the missionaries and cannibals problem in which the missionaries and cannibals have to be moved from one side of the river to the other. Determining how people solve such problems requires detailed models of their thinking. The cognitive revolution that began in the mid- to late 1950s provided the tools to construct such models.

Cognitive Revolution

The cognitive revolution was in part stimulated by increasing interest in using computers as a tool and as a metaphor for how people process information. The implications of this approach for studying problem-solving were demonstrated in the work of Allan Newell and Herbert Simon at Carnegie Mellon University. Their paper, "Elements of a Theory of Human Problem Solving" (1958), described the first 2 years of a project that involved programming a digital computer to solve problems. This work helped launch the new field of artificial intelligence—programming computers to perform intelligent tasks efficiently. But Newell and Simon were more interested in using their programs to build detailed models of how people solve problems, which they described in their 1972 book *Human Problem-Solving*.

An important component of Newell and Simon's theory was the identification of the basic characteristics of human information-processing that influence problem solving. For example, the limited capacity of working memory places a constraint on the number of operations that can be carried out mentally. Although most people can multiply 16 × 7 without using paper and pencil, multiplying 16 × 78 is difficult because there is too much information to keep active in working memory. Long-term memory does not have the capacity limitations of working memory, but it takes time to learn information so it can be stored in long-term memory.

The construction of detailed models of problem solving also requires discovering the details of how people think. Newell and Simon therefore collected verbal protocols by asking their subjects to report everything they thought about as they worked on the problem (1972). To avoid some of the criticisms that were directed toward the early introspection methods, Anders Ericsson and Herbert Simon later wrote a book about how to collect and validate accurate protocols (1993).

Most of the problems studied by cognitive psychologists during the 1970s were puzzle problems, such as the Tower of Hanoi (move a stack of rings from one peg to another without placing a larger ring over a smaller one) and the missionaries and cannibals problem (move missionaries and cannibals across a river without cannibals outnumbering missionaries). Because these transformation problems specify a particular goal, such as having all the missionaries and cannibals cross the river, a problem solver can use a strategy called means-end analysis to try to reach the goal (Newell & Simon, 1972; Greeno, 1978). The objective of means-end analysis is to make moves that reduce differences between the current problem state and the goal state. For instance, when moving missionaries and cannibals across the river, try to bring only one person back with the boat so you can leave as many people as possible across the river. The means-end analysis strategy results in the gradual elimination of differences, so problem solvers feel that they are making progress as they solve the problem (Metcalf, 1986).

A strategy such as means-end analysis is called a heuristic because although such general strategies are often effective, they do not guarantee a solution. At one point in solving the missionaries and cannibals problem it is necessary to bring more than one person back in the boat, which violates the means-end strategy. Other examples of heuristics are to formulate a subgoal and use the solution of an analogous problem. In contrast, algorithms consist of procedures for solving problems that guarantee a correct solution. Our knowledge of the rules of multiplication provide an algorithm for doing multiplication; we will calculate a correct answer if we follow the procedures correctly.

Domain-Specific Knowledge

During the 1980s, psychologists became interested in studying problems that students encounter in school, such as physics problems and algebra word problems. Although general strategies can be helpful, students also need to know specific subject-matter knowledge in order to solve these kinds of problems. Influenced by the work of George Polya on heuristics for solving mathematical problems (1945). Alan Schoenfeld taught his students five general strategies, such as draw a diagram, consider a problem with fewer variables, and try to establish subgoals (1985). The strategies were helpful, but knowledge of mathematics influenced how successful students were in implementing the strategies.

Other investigators questioned whether the application of strategies such as means-end analysis would result in learning the solutions. For example, a student might successfully apply this strategy to reach a solution but not remember the steps that got her there. John Sweller, R. F. Mawer, and M. R. Ward (1983) studied how students combined the information from several equations to solve physics problems. They found that students were more successful in learning solutions when asked to solve for as many variables as they could rather than for a particular variable. Solving for as many variables as possible discouraged the use of means-end analysis because using this strategy requires reducing differences to a particular goal. Sweller and his colleagues argued that the mental effort required to use means-end analysis distracts from learning the solution.

According to John Anderson, learning complex skills such as programming in LISP or proving geometry problems requires learning hundreds of rules. These rules, called production rules, have the structure: if (condition), then (action). The first part of the rule specifies when a particular action should be carried out. For example, if (your car doesn't start), then (check its battery). The details of Anderson's theory were initially specified in his book *The Architecture of Cognition* (1983). A key theoretical assumption is that knowledge about solving problems begins as declarative knowledge—knowledge about factual information. Forming production rules occurs through practice in applying this knowledge to solve problems. This type of knowledge is called procedural knowledge and relates actions to specific goals. Anderson's theory, ACT, has continued to evolve (Anderson, 1993) and now forms the most extensive theory of skill acquisition ever created.

But in order to use rules efficiently we need our factual knowledge to be well organized. For instance, expert chess players organize the pieces on the board into groups that help them plan moves and that help them reproduce a chess board from memory (de Groot, 1965). Another example is solving algebra word problems. People typically solve algebra word problems by categorizing the problem as a particular type, such as a distance problem, a mixture problem, or a cost problem. These categories suggest which rules are appropriate for solving the problem (Hinsley, Hayes, & Simon, 1977). Therefore, successful problem solving depends on the effective use of general heuristics, well-organized factual knowledge, and the timely application of specific rules.

Transfer

A goal of education is that learning will transfer to situations beyond the specific problems solved in the classroom. Much of the research on problem solving has therefore focused on transfer—how well students can use the solution of a problem to solve a related problem. Let's consider three different ways in which a problem can be related.

The first way is that two situations share the same structure but have different objects. An example is an atom and the solar system. Although the objects differ, there are identical relations among the objects that create a similar structure. Electrons revolve around the nucleus of the atom and planets revolve around the sun. Dedre Gentner (1983) has proposed a structure-mapping theory in which our ability to use one situation as an analogy for the other depends on how well we can find corresponding objects and relationships in the two situations.

In this case, the obstacle that limits transfer is that people often fail to notice the structural similarity because the objects in the two circumstances are different. If students are told the two situations are analogous they are often successful in solving a problem by using the solution of the analogous problem. Mary Gick and Keith Holyoak (1983) were successful in increasing students' ability to notice the similarity of analogous problems by encouraging them to think about the solutions on a more abstract level. They helped students discover the solution to Duncker's radiation problem (rays converge to destroy a tumor without destroying the surrounding healthy tissue) by telling them a story in which an army converges to capture a fortress. However, students noticed the similarity of the two problems only when they thought about the fortress problem on a more abstract level in which a force converges on a central target.

A second way in which two problems are related occurs when the objects are the same but the solutions are slightly different. Imagine that you learned how to solve a work problem in which two workers labored together to complete a task. You now have to solve a problem in which one worker labors more hours than the other. The obstacle here is not in noticing the similarity of the two problems but adapting the solution of one to fit the other. Research has focused on how best to instruct students to successfully adapt solutions (Reed, 1993).

A third way in which two problems are related is that they are both solved by using the same general method of solution. For example, constructing a Venn diagram may be helpful in solving both problems. Laura Novick labels this "representational transfer" to distinguish it from analogical transfer, in which a specific solution is transferred. Very little research has been done on representational transfer, but its success, as for analogical transfer, depends on both noticing and then correctly applying the same method of solution (Novick & Hmelo, 1994).

A word of caution: Transfer can occasionally have negative consequences, as demonstrated in a classic study by Abraham Luchins (1942). His problems required using three differently sized jars to obtain a specific amount of water. After solving a series of problems that required filling and pouring from the jars in the same sequence of steps, participants were given a problem that could be solved in fewer steps. However, most of the subjects showed an *einstellung* effect, that is, they continued to use the longer solution that had worked on the previous problems.

Instruction

The study of problem solving should help us design instruction to make people better problem solvers. The success of the instruction can then be used to evaluate and modify the theory behind the instruction. A good example of this interplay between theory and instruction has been the development of Anderson's ACT theory. Anderson has used the theory to design entire courses at Carnegie Mellon University, such as a LISP programming course. Students have typically completed these computer-based courses in less time and with higher grades than students in the standard courses (Anderson, Corbett, Koedinger, & Pelletier, 1995). In addition, the occasional discrepancies between theoretical predictions and actual performance has helped Anderson modify his theory.

The ACT theory is a theory of skill (procedural) learning, and some psychologists and educators have questioned whether this restriction will limit its usefulness in situations in which conceptual understanding is important (Ohlsson, 1990). An increased emphasis on the development of conceptual understanding has been the cornerstone in many curriculum reform efforts, such as those based on the recommendations of the National Council of Teachers of Mathematics (1989). It has also been a topic of investigation by cognitive psychologists who want to learn how the ability to explain solutions is related to success in solving problems (Chi & Van Lehn, 1991).

Another NCTM recommendation is that mathematics courses should include more problem-solving. Although the suggestions for enhancing conceptual understanding and problem-solving skills may seem uncontroversial, the recommendations have been hotly debated, as opponents are concerned that the new curriculum will diminish the learning of basic computational skills. Therefore, an applied challenge for psychologists interested in problem solving is to help educators utilize research on problem solving to improve instruction while building on a solid foundation of basic skills (Reed, 1999).

Bibliography

Anderson, J. R. (1983). *The architecture of cognition.* Cambridge, MA: Harvard University Press.

Anderson, J. R. (1993). *Rules of the mind.* Hillsdale, NJ: Erlbaum.

Anderson, J. R., Corbett, A. T., Koedinger, K. R., & Pelletier, R. (1995). Cognitive tutors: Lessons learned. *Journal of the Learning Sciences, 4,* 167–207. Reviews the 10-year history of tutor development based on ACT models of how students solve problems in LISP, geometry, and algebra.

Chi, M. T. H., & Van Lehn, K. A. (1991). The content of physics self-explanations. *Journal of the Learning Sciences, 1,* 69–105.

de Groot, A. D. (1965). *Thought and choice in chess.* The Hague: Mouton. A psychological study of how experts differ from novices in their chess strategies.

Duncker, K. (1945). On problem-solving. *Psychological Monographs, 58*(Whole No. 270). A good example of the Gestalt approach to studying problem-solving.

Ericsson, K. A., & Simon, H. A. (1993). *Protocol analysis: Verbal reports as data* (Rev. ed.). Cambridge, MA: MIT Press. A critical analysis of the proper use of protocol analysis and its relation to information-processing theories.

Gentner, D. (1983). Structure-mapping: A theoretical framework for analogy. *Cognitive Science, 7,* 155–170.

Gick, M., & Holyoak, K. (1983). Schema induction and transfer. *Cognitive Psychology, 15,* 1–38.

Gilhooly, K. J. (1988). *Thinking: Directed, undirected, and creative* (2nd ed.). London: Academic Press.

Greeno, J. (1978). Natures of problem-solving abilities. In W. K. Estes (Ed.), *Handbook of learning and cognitive processes* (Vol. 5). Hillsdale, NJ: Erlbaum. A classification of problems (arrangement, inducing structure, and transformation) based on the skills required to solve them.

Hinsley, D. A., Hayes, J. R., & Simon, H. A. (1977). From words to equations: Meaning and representation in algebra word problems. In P. A. Carpenter & M. A. Just (Eds.), *Cognitive processes in comprehension.* Hillsdale, NJ: Erlbaum.

Luchins, A. S. (1942). Mechanization in problem solving. *Psychological Monographs, 54* (Whole No. 248).

Mayer, R. (1992). *Thinking, problem-solving, cognition* (2nd ed.). New York: Freeman. A very readable and comprehensible textbook for readers who want an introduction to the psychological study of thinking and problem-solving.

Metcalf, J. (1986). Feelings of knowing in memory and problem-solving. *Journal of Experimental Psychology: Human Perception and Performance, 6,* 58–66.

National Council of Teachers of Mathematics. (1989). *Curriculum and evaluation standards for school mathematics.* Reston, VA: Author.

Newell, A., & Simon, H. A. (1958). Elements of a theory of human problem-solving. *Psychological Review, 65,* 151–166.

Newell, A., & Simon, H. A. (1972). *Human problem-solving.* Englewood Cliffs, NJ: Prentice Hall. A thorough presentation of Newell's and Simon's information-processing theory of problem-solving.

Novick, L. R., & Hmelo, C. E. (1994). Transferring symbolic representations across nonisomorphic problems. *Journal of Experimental Psychology: Learning, Memory, and Cognition, 20,* 1296–1321.

Ohlsson, S. (1990). Cognitive science and instruction: Why the revolution is not here yet. In H. Mandl, E. De Corte, N. Bennett, & H. F. Friedrich (Eds.), *Learning and instruction: European research in an international context.* New York: Pergamon Press.

Polya, G. (1945). *How to solve it.* Princeton, NJ: Princeton University Press.

Polya, G. (1962). *Mathematical discovery* (Vol. 1). New York: Wiley.

Reed, S. K. (1993). A schema-based theory of transfer. In D. K. Detterman & R. J. Sternberg (Eds.), *Transfer of trial: Intelligence, cognition, and instruction.* Norwood, NJ: Ablex.

Reed, S. K. (1999). *Word problems: Research and curriculum reform.* Mahwah, NJ: Erlbaum. An integration of research by cognitive psychologists and mathematics educators that considers its implications for curriculum reform.

Schoenfeld, A. H. (1985). *Mathematical problem-solving.* Orlando, FL: Academic Press. Discussion of research on mathematical problem-solving, emphasizing the role of resources, control, heuristics, and beliefs.

Selz, O. (1982). On the laws of ordered thinking. In N. H. Frida & A. D. de Groot (Eds.), *Otto Selz: His contributions to psychology.* The Hague: Mouton.

Sweller, J., Mawer, R. F., & Ward, M. R. (1983). Development of expertise in mathematical problem-solving. *Journal of Experimental Psychology: General, 112,* 639–661.

Wallas, G. (1926). *The art of thought.* New York: Harcourt.

Stephen K. Reed

Reasoning

Reasoning is the mental process of deriving consequences from given information. Its premises may be perceptions, descriptions, or memories. Its conclusion may be a statement, a thought, or a decision implicit in an action. The process itself may be one of which reasoners are painfully aware, or of which they are almost unconscious. But some systematic relation in content or form must govern the derivation of the conclusion from the premises if the process is reasoning, as opposed to an association of ideas. One such relation is that the conclusion must be true given that the premises are true, in which case the inference is a valid deduction. A weaker relation is that the conclusion is at least plausible given that the premises are true, in which case the inference is an induction. Without deduction there would be no logic or mathematics, and no human intelligence—at least as measured by intelligence tests.

The Psychology of Deduction

The nature of deduction is highly controversial. Psychologists have proposed that it depends on a memory for previous inferences, conditional rules that capture general knowledge, "neural nets" representing concepts, or specialized innate modules for matters that were important to our hunter-gatherer ancestors. But none of these accounts readily explains the ability to reason about the unknown:

If the piece is atonal then it is nondeterministic.
It is atonal.
∴ It is nondeterministic.

Even if you know nothing about atonality, you can grasp that the deduction is valid. Theories of this abstract reasoning ability are of two main sorts.

The first sort of theory postulates that the mind tacitly uses formal rules of inference. Such theories have many defenders, notably Lance Rips and the late Martin Braine and David O'Brien. According to these theories, the deduction about atonality depends on a formal rule known as *modus ponens*:

If A then B.
A.
∴ B.

Other deductions call for a chain of inferential steps. Consider, for example, these premises:

If the test is to continue, then the turbine should be producing emergency electricity.
The turbine is not producing emergency electricity.

The engineers at Chernobyl knew these facts, but they went ahead with the test anyway. Tragically, they failed to draw the valid deduction that the experiment should not continue. Formal rule theories account for this failure, and its replications in the psychological laboratory, by postulating that there is no mental rule for an inference of the form:

If A then B
Not B
∴ Not A.

The deduction depends instead on a chain in which each step is sanctioned by a mental rule of inference:

A (a supposition made for the sake of argument)
∴ B (using the rule: if A then B; A; therefore B)
∴ B and not B (using a rule for forming a conjunction, i.e., from a premise and the previous conclusion)
∴ Not A (using a rule that negates suppositions leading to contradictions)

Formal rule theories predict that the greater the number of steps in a chain, the harder the inference should be, although other factors cause difficulty, such as the availability and complexity of the rules. Investigators have corroborated their theories by using large batteries of deductions. The data are then fitted by estimating post hoc the correct use of each postulated rule of inference.

The second sort of psychological theory of reasoning assumes that logically untrained reasoners construct mental models of the premises (Johnson-Laird & Byrne, 1991). They imagine the relevant states of affairs based on their understanding of the premises and on their general knowledge. In these models they can formulate a conclusion that is true, and they can establish its validity by ensuring that no models of the premises refute it. A mental model is a representation of a possibility that may occur in many ways, and so the structure and content of the model capture what is common to these many ways. Given an assertion about some shapes on a blackboard:

> There is a circle or there is a triangle, but not both

reasoners construct two alternative models to represent the two possibilities:

○
  △

where each row denotes a separate model of a separate possibility. These models do not represent the size, color, or other unknown properties of the shapes, which yield the different ways in which the possibilities may occur. A conditional, such as:

> If there is a circle, then there is a triangle

calls for one explicit model of the salient possibility (the presence of the circle and triangle) and an implicit model that merely allows for other possibilities (in which it is false that there is a circle) without making them explicit, where the ellipsis represents the implicit model.

○ △
. . .

The model theory rests on a principle of truth:

> Individuals tend to minimize the load on working memory by constructing mental models that represent what is true but not what is false.

This accounts for the difficulty of the Chernobyl inference. Given premises of the form:

> If A, then B
> Not B

reasoners construct models of the conditional premise:

A B
. . .

The second premise, not B, is not consistent with the first of these models, which it therefore eliminates. Only the implicit model is left, and because it has no content it seems that nothing follows. In order to draw the correct conclusion, it is necessary to flesh out the implicit model to represent explicitly what happens when A is false:

$A \quad B$
$\neg A \quad B$
$\neg A \; \neg B$

where "¬" denotes negation. The premise, not B, eliminates the first two models, and so the conclusion, not A, follows from the remaining model. Other phenomena support the theory of mental models, for instance, inferences depending on one model are easier than inferences depending on multiple models. The theory extends to reasoning about what is possible and what is probable. But the controversy between rules and models can be resolved only by a crucial phenomenon. Consider this problem:

> Only one of the following premises is true about a particular hand of cards:
> There is a king in the hand or there is an ace, or both.
> There is a queen in the hand or there is an ace, or both.
> There is a jack in the hand or there is a 10, or both.
> Is it possible that there is an ace in the hand?

The model theory postulates that individuals consider the possibilities for each of the three premises. For the first premise, they consider three models, each of which correspond to a possibility:

king
    ace
king ace

These models suggest that an ace is possible. The second premise also suggests that an ace is possible. Hence, reasoners should respond yes. Logically untrained individuals draw this conclusion (Johnson-Laird & Goldvarg, 1997). Yet it is a fallacy, because with an ace, two of the premises would be true, contrary to the rubric that only one of them is true.

As the principle of truth predicts, individuals do indeed commit a wide variety of systematic fallacies. A compelling example is based on a disjunction, such as:

> If Viv is here, then Pat is here,
> or else if Viv isn't here, then Pat is here.
> Viv is here.
> What follows?

Nearly everyone, experts and novices alike, infers that Pat is here. But this is a fallacy. Granted a disjunction between the two conditionals, one or the other could be false. That is the force of "or else" between the two assertions. If the first conditional were false, for instance, then even though Viv is here, Pat may not be. Such illusory inferences are not easily explained by current theories based on formal rules, because these theories rely solely on valid rules of inference.

The difficulty of coping with falsity explains other phenomena. In the 'selection' task invented by the English psychologist Peter Wason (see Wason & Johnson-Laird, 1972), the experimenter lays down four cards:

A B 2 3

Each card has a number on one side and a letter on the other. The participants have to choose which cards to turn over to determine whether the following conditional is true or false: If a card has an *A* on one side, then it has a *2* on the other side. Most people correctly choose the A card, but some choose the innocuous 2 card too. However, few realize the need to choose the 3 card, though if it has an *A* on its other side, then the conditional is false.

When the selection task concerns what is permissible or impermissible, such as cheating or breaking a contract, then reasoners tend to make the correct selections. Evolutionary psychologists argue that such topics mattered to our hunter-gatherer ancestors, and so an innate module evolved for reasoning about them. The model theory, however, suggests an alternative explanation. People construct models of what is true, not of what is false, and so anything that makes the false cases more salient should improve performance. Recent studies have corroborated this explanation in selection tasks that do not depend on cheaters.

The theory of mental models rests on simple principles, but it led to the unexpected discovery that people commit systematic fallacies. It extends in a natural way to inferring probabilities, decision-making, and the informal inferences of daily life, whereas logic is notoriously of little help in analyzing them. But the theory is radically incomplete, and its critics have accused it of many shortcomings, from blatant falsehood to untestability. It implies that people can see the force of counterexamples, and it may well be overturned by counterexamples predicted by a superior theory, in which case it will at least account for its own demise.

The Psychology of Induction

Inductive reasoning, by definition, yields conclusions that go beyond the premises and that therefore may be false. Reasoners first understand some facts from perception or description. They generate a hypothesis, usually dependent on background knowledge, to account for these facts. And, if they are prudent, they try to check their hypothesis. Inductions in daily life often yield generalizations. After just one unfortunate experience, you are likely to infer:

> If you park your car illegally in London, its wheels will be clamped.

A special case of induction is an explanation of some phenomenon. Human reasoners are amazingly good at inventing putative explanations. Given two sentences selected at random from different stories, such as:

> Celia made her way to a shop that sold TV sets.
> She had recently had her ears pierced.

they readily offer explanations such as Celia was getting reception in her ears and wanted the TV shop to investigate. This propensity to generate explanations underlies both science and superstition.

There is no normative theory of induction and no comprehensive psychological theory of it, either. What does exist are a number of well-established heuristics, many of which were identified by two pioneering psychologists, the late Amos Tversky and Daniel Kahneman. Inductions depend on the availability of relevant knowledge. Most people, for example, judge that words beginning with the letter *r* are more frequent than words in which *r* occurs as the third letter. They are wrong, but it is easier to think of words beginning with *r* than of the other sort of words.

In judging probabilities, people rely on the representativeness of the evidence. Suppose, for instance, you are told that Bill is intelligent but unimaginative and lifeless. You may then judge that he is quite likely to be an accountant who plays jazz for a hobby. And the proposition seems more likely than that he merely plays jazz for a hobby. This judgment violates the principle of the probability calculus that a conjunction (being an accountant and playing jazz) cannot be more probable than one of its components (playing jazz). The description of Bill, however, is more representative of an accountant than of a jazz musician. Representativeness can override the laws of probability, granted that they apply to unique events.

Suppose a certain town has two hospitals: One is large and has about 45 births per day; the other is small and has about 15 births per day. Assuming that boys are born equally as often as girls, is there any difference between the hospitals in the number of days on which 60% or more of the newborns are boys? Most people say no. In fact, the outcome is likely to happen about twice as often in the small hospital: A smaller sample is more affected by chance fluctuations, and so it departs more often from the overall proportion of male births. As Socrates might have said: You knew *that* all along. It just seemed that the two hospitals were equally representative of the population.

One special form of induction is reasoning by analogy. In science, theories have been inspired by analogies between the heart and the pump, the moon and falling objects, and the atom and the solar system. An analogy is thus the mapping of a relation, or system of relations, from one domain of knowledge to another. If people are told a story about the capture of a fortress by troops attacking simultaneously from different directions, then they seldom realize that it is a helpful analogy for how to use X rays to destroy a tumor without damaging the surrounding healthy flesh (see Holyoak & Thagard, 1995). Unfortunately, similarity in meaning triggers analogies, whereas the useful information is often more abstract. Thus, what is carried over from the fortress story to the X-ray problem is the idea of splitting a force into separate components and applying them from different directions.

Several theories have been developed to explain the analogical transfer of information. Dedre Gentner (1989) proposes that reasoners tend to transfer higher-order relations, such as causation, rather than simple properties. Likewise, Holyoak and Thagard (1995) describe a program that establishes mappings between two domains, such as:

army ↔ X rays
fortress ↔ tumor
capture ↔ destroy

The program links hypotheses in a network so that they can excite or inhibit one another. The activation in the network settles down to a stable state that establishes the mappings. Mark Keane and his colleagues (1994) have also implemented a program that discovers such mappings in an incremental way using the structure of the target problem to aid the process. In the search for a useful analogy, there is a vast space of potentially relevant knowledge—so vast that an unconstrained search based on links among concepts takes exponentially longer as the number of relevant domains increases. How scientists find fruitful analogies is thus a problem that has yet to be solved.

What makes some inductions stronger than others? Dan Osherson and his colleagues (1986) have laid out seven possible answers, but they boil down into three main principles. An induction is strong if given some background knowledge, it is a valid deduction; it is a valid deduction in reverse, such as an argument from specific facts to a generalization that implies them; and the premises and conclusion concern similar subjects. As an example of this last principle, consider the argument:

Robins use serotonin as a neurotransmitter.
Bluejays use serotonin as a neurotransmitter.
∴ Sparrows use serotonin as a neurotransmitter.

This induction is stronger than one in which the subject of the conclusion refers to geese, which are less similar than sparrows to the birds in the premises. The investigators extended their theory to deal with predicates, which can override similarity of subjects (1993). Thus the inference:

Poodles can bite through wire.
∴ German shepards can bite through wire.

is stronger than one with one more similar dogs:

Dobermans can bite through wire.
∴ German shepards can bite through wire.

The predicate (can bite through wire) calls to mind attributes of the subject (its strength). If the subject does not have the required attributes (poodles aren't strong enough), then they are scaled down (it isn't necessary to be so strong). And so the subject of the conclusion is more likely to satisfy them, and the inference will seem stronger.

When you have formulated an inductive hypothesis, a sensible policy is to test it. Here, once again, laboratory studies of people testing hypotheses show that they often fail to seek falsifying evidence. The price of tractable induction includes the fads of pseudo-science and the superstitions and wishful thinking of daily life, which have their origin in the human inferential mechanism. The limits of working memory create a focus on what is explicitly represented in mental models, that is, on what is held to be true. Induction should come with a government warning because it can damage your health.

The Essence of Human Reasoning

In both deduction and induction, human beings tend to focus on truth. This focus is a sensible way to deal with limited working memory, but it does lead to systematic fallacies. It does not imply, however, that people are irredeemably irrational. The fallacies can be alleviated with preventative methods, and the discipline of logic provides a still more powerful safeguard. But without these methods, reasoners remain at risk to errors in reasoning.

Bibliography

Braine, M., & O'Brien, D. (1998). *Mental logic*. Mahwah, NJ: Erlbaum.

Cosmides, L. (1989). The logic of social change: Has natural selection shaped how humans reason? Studies with the Wason selection task. *Cognition, 31*, 187–276. A pioneering study of evolutionary psychology.

Evans, J. St. B. T., Newstead, S. E., & Byrne, R. M. J. (1993). *Human reasoning: The psychology of deduction*. Hillsdale, NJ: Erlbaum. A scholarly review of the field.

Gentner, D. (1989). The mechanisms of analogical learning. In S. Vosniadou & A. Ortony (Eds.), *Similarity and analogical reasoning* (pp. 199–241). New York: Cambridge University Press.

Holland, J. H., Holyoak, K. J., Nisbett, R. E., & Thagard, P. (1986). *Induction: Processes of inference, learning, and discovery*. Cambridge, MA: MIT Press. An advanced account of induction in terms of "genetic" algorithms.
Holyoak, K., & Thagard, P. (1995). *Mental leaps*. Cambridge, MA: MIT Press.
Jeffrey, R. (1981). *Formal logic: Its scope and limits* (2nd ed.). New York: McGraw-Hill. A highly readable account of the most intuitive way to do logic.
Johnson-Laird, P. N. (1993). *Human and machine thinking*. Hillsdale, NJ: Erlbaum. Describes the role of mental models in deduction, induction, and creativity.
Johnson-Laird, P. N., & Byrne, R. M. J. (1991). *Deduction*. Hillsdale, NJ: Erlbaum.
Johnson-Laird, P. N., & Goldvarg, Y. (1997). *Proceedings of the nineteenth annual conference of the Cognitive Science Society*. Mahwah, NJ: Erlbaum.
Johnson-Laird, P. N., & Savary, F. (1996). Illusory influences about probabilities. *Acta Psychologica, 93*, 69–90. Studies showing that the failure to represent falsity yields fallacies in probabilistic reasoning.
Kahneman, D., Slovic, P., & Tversky, A. (Eds.). (1982). *Judgment under uncertainty: Heuristics and biases*. New York: Cambridge University Press. A collection of classic papers.
Keane, M. T., Ledgeway, T., & Duff, S. (1994). Constraints on analogical mapping: A comparison of three models. *Cognitive Science, 18*, 387–438.
Langley, P., Simon, H. A., Bradshaw, G. L., & Zytkow, J. M. (1987). *Scientific discovery: Computational explorations of the creative processes*. Cambridge, MA: MIT Press. Includes an account of BACON, a suite of programs for making inductions in science.
Osherson, D. N., Smith, E. E., & Shafir, E. (1986). Some origins of belief. *Cognition, 24*, 197–224.
Posner, M. I. (Ed.). (1997). Neuroimaging of cognitive processes [Special issue]. *Cognitive Psychology, 33*(1). Includes a study of brain imaging during reasoning.
Rips, L. (1994). *The psychology of proof*. Cambridge, MA: MIT Press.
Shafir, E., & Tversky, A. (1992). Thinking through uncertainty: Nonconsequential reasoning and choice. *Cognitive Psychology, 24*, 449–474. Disjunctions cause difficulties in choosing options.
Shastri, L., & Ajjanagadde, V. (1993). From simple associations to systematic reasoning: A connectionist representation of rules, variables, and dynamic bindings using temporal synchrony. *Behavioral and Brain Sciences, 16*, 417–494. A neural-net model of reasoning.
Smith, E. E., Shafir, E., & Osherson, D. N. (1993). Similarity, plausibility, and judgments of probability. *Cognition, 49*, 67–96.
Sperber, D., Cara, F., & Girotto, V. (1995). Relevance theory explains the selection task. *Cognition, 52*, 3–39. Reports a series of studies that suggest that the relevance of false instances determines performance in the selection task.
Wason, P., & Johnson-Laird, P. N. (1972). *Psychology of reasoning*. Cambridge, MA: Harvard University Press.

Philip N. Johnson-Laird

THOMSON, GODFREY HILTON (1881–1955), British psychologist. Although he received little formal training in psychology, Godfrey H. Thomson became a leading authority on educational tests and psychometric methods. At 13, Thomson won a scholarship to Rutherford College, Newcastle. After distinguishing himself on his examinations, he entered what is now known as King's College in Newcastle upon Tyne. There, he studied the sciences with an emphasis on mathematics and physics, and he earned his bachelor's of science degree in 1903. Thomson then received a fellowship from King's College to pursue doctoral training in physics at Strasbourg University, Germany. During that time, his course of study was a conventional physics curriculum.

His introduction to psychology began when he returned to England as an assistant lecturer in education at King's College. Having no background in educational psychology, Thomson began a program of self-education. During the summer of 1911, Thomson met Charles Myers, who introduced him to psychology and served as a tutor during an extended vacation. As a part of his study, Thomson read William Brown's *The Essentials of Mental Measurement*. The book had a profound effect on Thomson as he spent the rest of his professional career applying his talents in mathematics to the problems of psychological measurement and statistical analysis. After 2 additional years of self-training, Thomson received a doctorate of science in psychology on the basis of an oral exam administered by Myers and another member of the faculty.

Thomson's first contribution to psychology was his critique of Charles Spearman's single factor model of intelligence, *g*. In a series of articles, Thomson used mathematical analysis and Monte Carlo simulations to demonstrate that Spearman's methods did not provide definitive proof for the existence of a single factor. In one article, Thomson reported the analysis of test scores generated by throws of dice. Although the data were randomly generated, analysis of the correlations among the tests yielded a hierarchy that met Spearman's criteria for the two-factor hypothesis (the general factor, *g*, and specific factor, *s*).

Thomson continued his guarded appraisal of factorial methods throughout his career. In 1939 he published the first edition of *The Factorial Analysis of Human Ability*. The book was one of the first comprehensive reviews of the mathematical foundations of factor analysis. Thomson revised the book in five editions, the last being published in 1951. Perhaps one of the more innovative contributions was the chapter on sampling theory. L. L. Thurstone praised Thomson's work in the preface of his text on factor analysis, *Multiple-Factor Analysis* (Chicago, 1947).

Thomson's second general contribution to psychology was the development of the Northumberland Tests used to evaluate students in the British school system.

Because an early scholarship allowed Thomson to obtain an education his parents could not afford, he strove to create assessment tools that gave talented students access to free secondary education. In a selfless act, Thomson used the money earned from these tests to create Moray House Tests, a nonprofit trust that supported research on and development of educational tests. The Moray House Tests soon become a standard measure of academic achievement and aptitude in England.

Bibliography

Drever, J. (1955). Godfrey Hilton Thomson: 1881–1955. *American Journal of Psychology, 68,* 494–496.

Thomson, G. (1952). Godfrey Thomson. In E. G. Boring et al. (Eds.), *A history of psychology in autobiography.* (Vol. 4, pp. 279–294). Worcester, MA: Clark University.

Thurstone, L. L. (1955). Sir Godfrey Thomson. *Psychometrika, 20,* 171–172.

David J. Pittenger

THORNDIKE, EDWARD LEE (1874–1949), American educational and comparative psychologist. The son of a Methodist minister, Thorndike was born in Williamsburg, Massachusetts. He was raised in an environment marked by sternness and religious exhortation, but as a young adult chose to eschew religion and pursue a personal code derived from his commitment to inductivism. The code is evident in his autobiography of 1936, which modestly characterizes his career as an aggregate of responses to contingencies, opportunities, and demands. Inductivism suffused connectionism, his main contribution to psychology, which emerged as early as his dissertation, in 1898. It became formalized in his three-volume magnum opus, *Educational Psychology* (1913–1914), as the Laws of Learning and remained substantially unchanged throughout his career.

Connectionism distills the process of learning into three factors, S (for situation), R (for response), and the bonding of the two. S entails inherited influences, and R experience with environment. Their bonding produces mental organization, as habits of thought and behavior. The Laws of Learning—readiness, exercise, and effect (Thorndike, 1913–1914)—also represent the forces of nature, nurture, and the effective integration of the two. The theory of connectionism, which rejects rationalist views of the immaterial origins of mind, is notable for its placement of the learning process within the framework of Charles Darwin's theory of natural selection by demonstrating the interaction of heredity and environment.

The forerunner of connectionism was William James's *Principles of Psychology*, which Thorndike discovered at Wesleyan University (B.A. degree, 1895). James's vivid writing appealed to the undergraduate, who was considering a career in literature and had just encountered the new discipline of psychology. Enrolling at Harvard University, where he received a second B.A. degree in 1896, Thorndike began studying with James. Although James supported the student's (then unusual) interest in testing animals—chickens, cats, and dogs—through the controlled use of puzzle boxes, others at Harvard did not. After completing his M.A. degree in 1897, Thorndike studied with James McKeen Cattell at Columbia University, where he was able to conduct this new research and write his doctoral dissertation. The published version, *Animal Intelligence* (1898), rapidly became a classic in American psychology. Rigorously empirical, self-consciously "radical," and wryly contemptuous, it attacked preprofessional conventions of armchair speculation and anecdotes about animal rationality.

The dissertation is remarkable not only for the methodological standards it set for comparative research and apparatus construction, but also as a sign that the skepticism associated with the Age of Enlightenment would now be directed at the process of enlightenment itself. Scientific, repeatable testing demonstrated animal stupidity, not intelligence; the cats did not solve (exit) their puzzle boxes by imitation, directed example, or even immediate reward. Instead, learning, like evolution itself, proceeded randomly. While flailing their paws in an irrational frenzy, the chance of striking a latch (or string, or button) initiated, but by no means ensured, learning. (Unsuccessful cats received no food for extended periods.) Only a succession of random strikings (originating in heredity), followed by the pleasures of release and food (environment), would "stamp in" the action useful to know (through interaction of heredity and environment). The controlled test also allowed for the measurement of learning speed (the learning curve), as the amount of time spent in the cage steadily decreased over the series of trials: Infrequent accidental hits became immediate knowing pounces. As an evolutionary process, learning could now be seen as an externally directed experience, at least for animals. As Darwin was reluctant to apply the theory of natural selection to humans in *The Origin of the Species* (1859), Thorndike claimed in 1898 that human learning ability was qualitatively different from, if related to, that of other animals.

After a year's employment at the College for Women of Western Reserve University, Thorndike joined the faculty of Columbia University Teachers College in 1899, where he became a professor in 1904 and remained one until his retirement in 1940. Although the new expert in learning theory took positions in institutions that emphasized pedagogy, he lacked interest in teaching and was skeptical about what most classroom instruction could accomplish. Thorndike's first book, *The Human Nature Club* (1900), was a literary rendering of his early lectures in introductory psychology. It shows both his belief that human learning was best advanced in small groups of reasonable people enjoying Socratic dialogues and his hope to succeed James as the moral authority of American education. The popular style did not suit him, however, and he did not continue in this genre. Moreover, his students were more likely to encounter large classrooms than drawing room conversation.

Thorndike's preference for research over teaching led to criticism of his using the classroom as an opportunity to conduct research. Although he promoted the addition of research skill training in the elementary school curriculum, he increasingly facilitated the division of labor—between research and teaching—that has come to mark modern higher education. As his dean, James E. Russell, initiated the first curriculum for educational administration, Thorndike increasingly conceived of the mass classroom environment as a place to sort children—largely on the basis of inherited differences—to help students adapt to the demands of school and society.

Thorndike's skepticism about human learning potential became clear in two articles of 1901. "The Evolution of Human Intellect" linked his conclusions about animal (trial and error) learning to humans and reduced the activities of imitation and directed learning to the "stamping in" process; and his critique (with Robert S. Woodworth) of the traditional "mental discipline" theory of transfer, which had held that learning one subject (say, Latin) readily improved a person's efficiency in learning another subject (say, the law). The critique of transfer legitimated the ongoing transition in the leadership of American higher education from the moral purpose and mental disciplinary pedagogy of the old-time college to the research mission and curricular freedom of the university. The hardheaded message of both articles extended his dissertation's attack on armchair assumptions about learning to the realm of human learning.

Thorndike's drive to reduce human learning to the animal level slowed during the next few years, as he sought James's moral mantle. Although in "Evolution of Human Intellect" he brashly suggested that James was a "false prophet" for concluding that a study of "psychogenesis" (linking animal and human mentality) was futile, he detoured from reductionism in 1905, when he published *The Elements of Psychology* (1913) with a preface by James. The latter returned the "false prophet" compliment, revealing his fear that Thorndike had been laboring on behalf of the new textbook Moloch (see Leviticus 18:21) that was devouring children's minds. Perhaps to assuage James's fears, Thorndike asserted the causal power of "ideational and moral life" and, in 1909, left open the possibility of human volition (Thorndike, 1949).

After James's death, Thorndike resumed the ardent positivism he had announced in 1901. His 1912 presidential address to the American Psychological Association (Thorndike, 1949) confirmed his break with James's moralism, as he repudiated the theory of ideomotor action outright. Although he dedicated *Educational Psychology* (1913–1914) to James, Thorndike affirmed his determinism by promulgating laws of (human) learning. These were, first, the inherited individual readiness of the individual; second, the exercise of particular responses; and third, the effect of the interaction of the environment and the individual. The laws showed the functionality of learning for humans, as James had stressed, but without recourse to unempirical abstractions such as "will."

Further intensifying Thorndike's positivism was the new science of statistics, a subject which he taught himself and on which he published one of the first major handbooks for social scientists (1904/1922). Convinced that all academic performance could be measured, Thorndike innovated numerous classroom assessments to objectify the subjective. One example, a rating scale of handwriting, allowed "competent judges" to quantify evaluations of skill and the aesthetic sense, if not the moral quality of an individual student. Thorndike published a prolific amount of research on methods for teaching and testing achievement in basic arithmetic skills and vocabulary. In order to advance the scientific means to make mass education a training ground for industrial employment, he began expanding psychology's applications to the workplace, developing tests for Metropolitan Life Insurance after 1913.

Thorndike's concern to make the school an environment in which students might begin to adapt to job environments deterred him from testing for "general intelligence," also known as "*g*." In 1904, Charles Spearman had developed *g* testing in part to protect the liberal arts curriculum from utilitarian purposes, and he singled out Thorndike's and Woodworth's critique of transfer as a "vigorous onslaught" against *g*. In 1909, Thorndike, Lay, and Dean published one of the first major criticisms of this new unitary theory of intelligence. Thorndike also resisted the reduction of intelligence to a unitary factor because, as a theoretical matter, he appreciated the multifold interaction of heredity with environment in natural selection, and, as a practical matter, he was more concerned with helping schools fit average students into useful careers than with the extremes of intelligence, which dominated the interests of the early *g* testers. Although Thorndike also traced the origins of "individual differences" to inheritance, the *g* testers had reverted to preprofessional idealization—in his view—disregarding the individual as a product of heredity, environment, and the fortuitous interplay of both. Thorndike resisted this tendency in psychological testing, just as he resisted the opposite extreme of behaviorism, which aspects of his learning theory had influenced.

Because he tested for environmentally relevant "intelligence in general," instead of "general intelligence," Thorndike was able to make a key contribution to one of the most celebrated experiences in the history of psychology. During World War I, when U.S. Army leaders were contemplating various offers of scientific assistance, rival psychological leaders (Robert Yerkes and Walter D. Scott) depended upon Thorndike, as chairperson of the Committee on the Classification of Personnel in the Army, to oversee the entire wartime project. Although he remained at Columbia during the war, it was his timely intervention that allowed the first group test of intelligence to become validated through corroboration with the results of a rating scale. Thus the testing of intelligence—notorious for its hereditarian origins—only became widely utilized as it addressed the (employment) environment. Amidst the flurry of postwar publicity that the army testing experience received, Thorndike helped write the National Intelligence Test.

Thorndike oversaw the creation of the Institute of Educational Research at Teachers College in 1921, funded by the Carnegie Corporation, the General Education Board, and the Commonwealth Fund. Assisted by Edward Strayer, Arthur Gates, and others, he developed a series of manuals for classroom instruction that set standards for content expectations in arithmetic and vocabulary by grade. During the 1930s, when he served as president of the American Association for the Advancement of Science (1934), he led a study funded by the Carnegie Corporation to combine psychological research with data from other social sciences. In *Your City* (1939) and *Human Nature and the Social Order* (1940), Thorndike attempted to expand the utility of connectionism to human relations, government, and the economy. Both books continued to balance factors of environment and inheritance, although in their macrocosmic, transdisciplinary scope they were laden with sweeping and racist generalizations.

Thorndike suffered one major failure in his career: not receiving James's mantle as moral leader of American education in the secular era. This privilege went to Columbia colleague John Dewey. If Dewey became the visionary architect of modern universal education, however, Thorndike became its practical contractor, crafting the managerial infrastructure of the mass classroom, an achievement as influential as it is overlooked.

Thorndike married Elizabeth Moulton, with whom he had five children. Their son, Robert Ladd, became a distinguished psychologist. Thorndike died at his home in Montrose, New York, in 1949.

Bibliography

Burnham, J. C. (1972). Thorndike's puzzle boxes. *Journal of the History of the Behavioral Sciences, 8*, 159–167. Classic historical description of apparatus design.

Jonçich, G. (1968). *The sane positivist: A biography of Edward L. Thorndike*. Middletown, CT: Wesleyan University Press. The standard, comprehensive biography; very thorough, if apologetic.

Karier, C. J. (1986). *Scientists of the mind: Intellectual founders of modern psychology*. Urbana, IL: University of Illinois Press. A biographical essay that is critical, yet not unfair.

Spearman, C. E. (1904). General intelligence objectively determined and measured. *American Journal of Psychology, 15*, 201–293.

Thorndike, E. L. (1898). Animal intelligence: An experimental study of the associative processes in animals. *Psychological Review, Monograph Supplements, 2* (Whole No. 8). Also published in 1911 as *Animal Intelligence* (New York: Macmillan).

Thorndike, E. L. (1900). *The human nature club: An introduction to the study of mental life*. Chautauqua, NY: Chautauqua Press.

Thorndike, E. L. (1901). The evolution of the human intellect. *Popular Science Monthly, 60*, 58–65. Established continuity between animal and human learning.

Thorndike, E. L. (1910). Handwriting. *Teachers College Record, 11*, 1–81. Exemplifies the positivist quest to quantify the qualitative or objectify the subjective.

Thorndike, E. L. (1913; reprint of 2nd ed., 1907). *The elements of psychology*. New York: A. G. Seiler.

Thorndike, E. L. (1913–1914). *Educational psychology*. New York: Teachers College Press. Thorndike's magnum opus, which articulated the Laws of Learning.

Thorndike, E. L. (1922). *An introduction to the theory of mental and social measurements* (2nd ed.). New York: Teachers College Press. (Original work published 1904)

Thorndike, E. L. (1936). Edward Lee Thorndike. In C. Murchison (Ed.), *A history of psychology in autobiography* (Vol. 3, pp. 263–270). Worcester, MA: Clark University Press.

Thorndike, E. L. (1939). *Your city*. New York: Harcourt, Brace.

Thorndike, E. L. (1940). *Human nature and the social order*. New York: Macmillan. Late career effort to apply connectionism to political, economic, and social reform.

Thorndike, E. L. (1949). *Selected writings from a connectionist's psychology*. New York: Appleton-Century-Crofts. A collection of several key essays, including "Darwin's Contribution to Psychology" (1909) and the American Psychological Association Presidential Address on "Ideo-Motor Action" (1912).

Thorndike, E. L., Lay, W., & Dean, P. R. (1909). The relation of accuracy in sensory discrimination to general intelligence. *American Journal of Psychology, 20*, 364–369. Rejected Spearman's "general intelligence" theory.

Thorndike, E. L., & Woodworth, R. S. (1901). The influence of improvement in one mental function upon the efficiency of other functions. *Psychological Review, 8*, 247–261, 384–395, 553–564. Highly influential attack on "mental discipline" pedagogy.

Richard T. von Mayrhauser

THURSTONE, LOUIS LEON (1887–1955), American psychologist. Thurstone was born in Chicago. At age 8, he moved to Sweden with his family. They returned 6 years later to Jamestown, New York, where Thurstone practiced diligently to improve his spoken English. Throughout adulthood, he remained sensitive about speaking English with a Swedish accent.

Thurstone completed high school and entered Cornell University as an engineering major. His interests were in machine design and in how operators master the visual-motor coordination skills required to operate machines. Those interests prompted his first contact with psychology, attending lectures of Madison Bentley and Edward Bradford Titchener.

While an undergraduate, Thurstone designed, constructed, and patented a motion picture camera and projector that eliminated flicker. He demonstrated his machine for Thomas A. Edison in West Orange, New Jersey. After earning a master of engineering degree from Cornell in 1912, he then spent a brief period as Edison's assistant.

From 1912 to 1914, Thurstone was instructor of geometry and drafting in the engineering college at the University of Minnesota. He also enrolled in psychology courses offered by Herbert Woodrow and James B. Miner. In 1914, he began graduate study at the University of Chicago, where his mentor was James Rowland Angell. In his autobiography, Thurstone wrote, "My first degree was M. E., and I was never flattered when it was interpreted at Chicago as a Master's degree in Education!" (Thurstone, 1952, p. 300).

In 1915, he became an assistant to Walter Van Dyke Bingham in the division of applied psychology at the Carnegie Institute of Technology where, in 1917, he completed his dissertation on the learning curve equation, earning a doctorate from the University of Chicago. By 1920, Thurstone had become full professor and chairman of the psychology department at Carnegie Tech.

In 1923–1924, Thurstone worked in Washington, D.C., at the Institute for Government Research on the redesign of civil service examinations. His assistant was Thelma Gwinn, who also had earned a master's degree in psychology at Carnegie Tech. In 1924, the two were married; that fall they moved to the psychology department at the University of Chicago—she as a graduate student, he as an associate professor.

His first published article on psychological testing set forth a method for scaling test scores that, by assuming a normal distribution of scores within age groups, depended simply on estimating a mean and a variance of scores at each age. In the following 4 years, he published 20 related papers in major psychological journals, establishing not only what then became the standard theory for psychological testing, but also a basis for the measurement of human attitudes and opinions.

Thurstone's office in Washington had been on Dupont Circle, in the building that also housed offices of the American Council on Education (ACE). Having become acquainted with the Thurstones there, personnel at ACE provided funds in 1924 (and continuing to 1947) to support the Thurstones' development and maintenance of annual editions of the ACE Psychological Examination for High School Graduates and College Freshmen. In 1947, these were converted to the Scholastic Aptitude Tests, administered by the Educational Testing Service, founded in Princeton, New Jersey, primarily for that purpose.

An innovation established by Robert Hutchins, president of the University of Chicago, in the early 1930s allowed students to earn credit by examination. Thurstone became chief examiner, responsible for creating the exams and for their administration and scoring.

To develop better tests and to generate underlying theory for them, Thurstone created new factor-analysis procedures, using communalities as diagonal entries in an intercorrelation matrix and employing factor rotation to "simple structure" to discover psychologically meaningful dimensions (Thurstone, 1931, 1935, 1947). He then derived a conceptual scheme for the structure of primary mental abilities (PMA) and developed the PMA tests (Thurstone, 1938a, 1938b). In 1938, Science Research Associates was founded in Chicago by Thurstone's associates Robert Burns and Lyle Spencer to publish and distribute PMA tests.

Thurstone was a pioneer of American psychometrics, that branch of quantitative psychology concerned with tests and measurements. With encouragement (and financial support) from current and recent graduate students, in 1936 he launched the Psychometric Society as its charter president and established the society's journal, *Psychometrika*, dedicated to "the development of psychology as a quantitative rational science." Many of his doctoral students later initiated psychometric graduate programs at other universities. Postdoctoral scholars from the United States and abroad also studied with Thurstone, and they, too, promulgated his contributions upon return to their home institutions.

Thurstone displayed his deep commitment to science through his research and teaching, and in other ways as well. Almost daily when in Chicago, Thurstone lunched at the Faculty Club, usually with colleagues from other departments, discussing his current work and inviting suggestions from mathematicians and social scientists about how to improve and make more useful his new quantitative methods. And at his home in Hyde Park, near the University of Chicago, he hosted regular Wednesday evening seminars, typically inviting 20 to 30 guests to discuss work in progress presented by a guest lecturer.

Thurstone was president of the Midwestern Psychological Association in 1930–1931 and president of the American Psychological Association, 1932–1933. In 1938, he was elected to the National Academy of Sciences. He was an elected Fellow, American Academy of Arts and Sciences, Fellow (and member of the Board of Directors), American Statistical Association, and Honorary Fellow, British Psychological Society, Spanish Psychological Society, and Swedish Psychological Society. He was awarded an honorary doctorate by the University of Göteborg in 1954.

When faced in 1952 with mandatory retirement from the University of Chicago at age 65, Thurstone became professor of psychology at the University of North Carolina, where he established a new psychometric laboratory. That laboratory continues to be a site for research and education of doctoral students in quantitative psychology.

[*See also* American Psychological Association; British Psychological Society; Educational Testing Service; Factor Analysis; Machine Design; Midwestern Psychological Association; National Academy of Sciences; Psychometrics; Psychometric Society; *and the biographies of Angell, Bentley, Bingham, and Tichener.*]

Bibliography

Works by Thurstone

Thurstone, L. L. (1919). The learning curve equation. *Psychological Monographs, 26*, no. 114.

Thurstone, L. L. (1925). A method of scaling psychological and educational tests. *Journal of Educational Psychology, 16*, 433–448.

Thurstone, L. L. (1931). Multiple factor analysis. *Psychological Review, 38*, 406–427.

Thurstone, L. L. (1935). *The vectors of mind.* Chicago: University of Chicago Press.

Thurstone, L. L. (1938a). Primary mental abilities. *Psychometric Monograph No. 1.* Chicago: University of Chicago Press.

Thurstone, L. L. (1938b). *Tests for primary mental abilities, experimental edition.* Washington, DC: American Council on Education.

Thurstone, L. L. (1947). *Multiple-factor analysis.* Chicago: University of Chicago Press.

Thurstone, L. L. (1952). L. L. Thurstone. In E. G. Boring, H. S. Langfeld, H. Werner, & R. M. Yerkes, (Eds.), *A history of psychology in autobiography* (Vol. 4, pp. 295–321). Worcester, MA: Clark University Press. Thurstone's frank and carefully crafted autobiography.

Works about Thurstone

Adkins Wood, D. (1962). *Louis Leon Thurstone, creative thinker, dedicated teacher, eminent psychologist.* Princeton, NJ: Educational Testing Service. Dorothy Adkins Wood had assisted Thurstone as an examiner at the University of Chicago. Later, she chaired the psychology department at the University of North Carolina, where she recruited Thurstone as professor in 1952. This 65-page monograph includes a warmly personal biography, several photographs, and a complete bibliography of published works, tests, research reports, and microfilms.

Guilford, J. P. (1957). Louis Leon Thurstone, 1887–1955. *National Academy of Sciences Biographical Memoirs, 30*, 349–382. An extensive professional biography, including a bibliography.

Jones, L. V. (1998). L. L. Thurstone: A vision of psychology as a quantitative rational science. In G. A. Kimble & M. Werthemier (Eds.), *Portraits of pioneers in psychology* (Vol. 3). Mahwah, NJ, and Washington, DC: Erlbaum and American Psychological Association. While following the outline of the present entry, this is a somewhat more comprehensive biography and includes a section of personal reminiscences.

Lyle V. Jones

TIME PERCEPTION is a distinct area of study with its own psychophysical methods (such as estimation, reproduction, and production) designed for assessing the perceived duration of a temporal interval. In both estimation and reproduction, the temporal interval to be judged (e.g., a 1-second tone) is presented to the subject. In estimation, the subject is required to provide a verbal estimate (either in clock or arbitrary units) of the perceived duration of the interval, whereas in reproduction, the subject is required to reproduce the temporal interval—for example, by holding down a button. Production differs from reproduction in that the temporal interval is stated rather than presented. Other psychophysical procedures have been developed for determining sensitivity to temporal differences. In the method of comparison, for example, two temporal intervals are presented and the subject is required to indicate which one is longer. The method of comparison provides for the assessment of the smallest difference between two temporal intervals that can be discriminated.

Until recently, time perception was almost exclusively a human-based research area. There was not one reference to animal studies in Lorraine Allan's (1979) review of the time perception literature. Since then, however, the perception of time (as distinct from schedules of reinforcement and temporal variables in classical conditioning) has become an important area of research among animal learning psychologists. These researchers have developed new and powerful procedures for the study of time perception in nonhumans. There is now considerable collaboration and interaction between researchers interested in human timing and those interested in animal timing, with many investigators engaged in both. This interaction has resulted in the appearance of human analogs of the timing tasks designed originally for animal timing research. Methodology in timing research has been influenced by other developments as well. For example, many current psychophysical procedures derive directly from the application of Signal Detection Theory to issues in time perception.

Today, time perception is being studied not only by time psychophysicists but also by researchers working within other areas of psychology such as memory, attention, and animal behavior. Because time perception is a broad and diverse research area, any overview has to be selective. The present overview focuses on prospective timing, in contrast to retrospective timing. In a prospective timing task, the subject is aware before the temporal interval is presented that a temporal judgment will be required, whereas in a retrospective timing task, the subject in not aware until after the temporal interval has been presented that a temporal judgment is required. Richard Block and Dan Zakay compared prospective and retrospective timing (*Psychonomic Bulletin and Review*, 1997, 4, 184–197), and concluded that the two are fundamentally different. Within prospective timing, there is evidence that the perception of brief intervals (milliseconds and seconds) differs from the perception of longer intervals (minutes and hours). This overview is restricted to brief temporal intervals.

Perceived time is variable; a constant physical duration does not produce an invariant temporal judgment. Rather, a constant physical duration results in a distribution of temporal judgments. It is generally agreed that variability in perceived time increases with mean perceived time and that the best description of this relationship, for both human and animal timing, is provided by Weber's law. Weber's law takes different forms for different tasks, but for our purposes it may be thought of as a linear relationship between the standard deviation of perceived time (σ) and mean perceived time (μ)—that is, a constant coefficient of variation (σ/μ). Strict adherence to Weber's law sometimes deteriorates at the shortest and longest duration values of the range of values being presented. Data inconsistent with Weber's law are generated by well-practiced subjects, who sometimes show constant variability over a range of duration values. Between ranges, however, Weber's law applies.

Although perceived time is variable, mean perceived time is systematically related to physical time. The relationship between mean perceived time and physical time is referred to as the "Psychophysical Law" for time. There is general agreement that the psychophysical law for time is monotonic with physical time, and there are data from many timing tasks, from both humans and animals, indicating that the psychophysical law is a power function rather than a logarithmic function. The controversy has been over the value of the power exponent. Some have argued for an exponent of less than 1.0 (about 0.9), but others have concluded that the exponent is 1.0 and therefore that perceived time is linear with physical time.

Temporal judgments are influenced not only by physical duration but also by such nontemporal variables as the characteristics of the duration marker, prior experience with the duration values (aftereffects), and the presentation order of the duration values to be judged (the time-order error). Most of the research concerned with these nontemporal variables has been conducted with human subjects. Although the effects of nontemporal variables are well documented, their source is not fully understood. Nontemporal variables could produce their effects through the introduction of a constant error in perceived time, through increased variability in perceived time, through increased variability in remembered time, and/or through the introduction of response biases.

A temporal interval must be delineated, and the characteristics of the marker affect the judged duration. A temporal interval can be marked throughout its extent (filled), or only at the beginning and at the end (empty). A filled interval usually is judged longer than an empty interval (the filled-duration illusion), and an empty interval that is partially filled is judged longer than a completely empty interval. Duration markers can be presented in any modality. Most research has used the auditory and visual modalities, and typically a filled auditory interval is judged longer than a filled visual interval. Modality effects are present even with empty intervals. For example, variability in perceived time is less when the empty interval is marked in the same modality (e.g., a tone at the beginning and a tone at the end) then when it is marked in two modalities (e.g., a tone at the beginning and a light at the end).

Physical dimensions of markers such as amplitude (loudness), frequency (pitch), luminance (brightness), size, complexity, and familiarity also influence the judged duration. A temporal interval marked by the high end of the nontemporal dimension typically is judged longer than a temporal interval marked by the low end of the nontemporal dimension. For example, the kappa effect refers to the finding that the judged duration of an empty interval marked by two separated locations in visual or tactile space increases with the spatial separation between the two markers. This interaction between temporal extent and spatial extent is bidirectional. The tau effect refers to the finding that the judged spatial extent between the two markers increases with the temporal interval between the markers. Both kappa and tau effects have been demonstrated in the auditory modality as well, with pitch replacing space.

Repeated exposure (adaptation) to a value of constant duration influences the judged duration of post-adaptation probe values. For example, a probe duration is judged as relatively short after adaptation to a duration longer than the probe and as relatively long after adaptation to a duration shorter than the probe. This duration aftereffect of prior adaptation is negative in that the judged duration of the probe moves away from the adaptation duration. The duration aftereffect can be made contingent on a nontemporal characteristic of the duration maker. For example, after adaptation to a long-duration, high-pitched tone alternating with a short-duration, low-pitched tone, a high-pitched tone is perceived as short (relative to preadaptation) and a low-pitched tone as long (relative to preadaptation). In contrast, after adaptation to a short-duration, high-pitched tone alternating with a long-duration, low-pitched tone, a high-pitched tone is perceived as relatively long and a low-pitched tone as relatively short. That is, adaptation results in a negative duration aftereffect contingent on pitch: a tone is perceived as relatively short if its pitch had been paired with the long duration, and it is perceived as relatively long if its pitch had been paired with the short duration.

Some time perception tasks involve the sequential presentation of two or more duration values. In such tasks, judgments are often influenced by the order of presentation of the temporal intervals. For example, in a forced-choice discrimination task involving two duration values, there are two presentation orders, long followed by short (LS) and short followed by long (SL), resulting in two correct responses, (R_{LS}ILS) and (R_{SL}ISL). The two correct response probabilities are often different, and the difference between these probabilities [P(R_{LS}ILS) − P(R_{SL}ISL)] is referred to as the time-order error (TOE). The TOE usually is positive for very brief durations and negative for longer durations, and the size of the TOE decreases as the interval between the two durations increases.

There is now an extensive database to guide the development of models of time perception. Most timing models are psychophysical in nature and are firmly rooted in an internal clock. Internal-clock models postulate a timing-specific mechanism that produces perceived temporal values that bear orderly relations to real time. This timing-specific mechanism, or internal clock, is an interval timer rather than a periodic or oscillatory mechanism. A periodic clock, like the kind responsible for circadian rhythms, is continuously running and self-sustaining. In contrast, interval clocks need to be initiated with a signal. Once started, the system goes to completion, comes to an end on its own, and must be restarted.

Various internal-clock models of timing have been developed. Some models, like the one originally proposed by Douglas Creelman in 1962, derive from signal detection theory. Others, like the parallel-clock model of Hannes Eisler, are more closely related to the psychophysical methodology and theorizing associated with S. S. Stevens. Michel Treisman in 1962 introduced an information-processing model, and this tradition was continued in the attentional models of Ewart Thomas and Nancy Cantor and in the scalar timing model proposed by John Gibbon in collaboration with Warren Meck and Russell Church. Scalar timing has been reformulated as a connectionist model by Russell Church and Hillary Broadbent. In direct contrast to the information-processing models is the behavioral theory of timing (BeT) formulated by Peter Killeen and Gregor Fetterman.

Scalar timing is now the most prominent of the models, both in animal and in human timing. There are three stages in the scalar timing information-processing model: the clock stage, consisting of a pacemaker, a mode switch, and an accumulator; the memory stage, consisting of working memory and reference memory; and the decision stage, consisting of a comparator. During the clock stage, objective time is transformed into subjective time; pulses from the pacemaker are gated into the accumulator (a temporal integrating mechanism) through the mode switch, which closes when a timing signal is present. During the memory stage, the clock information is stored; working memory is loaded from the accumulator and stores temporal information from the current trial, whereas reference memory stores critical temporal information from past trials. During the decision stage, a comparison is made between current time and remembered time; the comparator determines a response on the basis of a decision rule that involves a comparison between a value in working memory with values in reference memory.

For some theorists, the internal clock is no more than a heuristic. Others have been interested in establishing a biological link. Experiments concerned with identifying the neural substrate of timing behaviors are being conducted with both animal and human subjects. The animal research is based mainly on lesion and drug manipulations, whereas the human research relies largely on the study of special populations such as individuals afflicted with Parkinson's disease and the application of position emission tomography and functional magnetic resonance imaging to normal adults. The research focused on establishing a biological link between the conceptual internal clock and the brain is still in its infancy, but recent evidence suggests that two subcortical structures, the cerebellum and the basal ganglia, play a critical role in short-duration timing.

Psychophysicists have found that the concept of an internal clock provides a convenient metaphor to guide thinking and research. Some cognitive psychologists, however, have raised doubts about the value of internal-clock models and have even questioned the study of time as a distinct area of investigation. These cognitive psychologists have been supporters of "timing without a timer" models (i.e., models that do not rely on an internal clock) and have been harsh critics of internal-clock models. Some critics, however, such as Richard Block and Dan Zakay, have come to see the value of internal-clock models and have incorporated the clock into their cognitive models of time perception.

Bibliography

Review Articles and Books

Allan, L. G. (1979). The perception of time. *Perception and Psychophysics, 26*, 340–354. Reviews human time perception research concerned with the psychophysical law, Weber's Law, the time-order error, and the role of nontemporal information on temporal judgments, and also presents a summary of the quantitative models available at that time. Even though the article was published 20 years ago and much more is now known about time perception, it remains a valuable source of information.

Fraisse, P. (1963). *The psychology of time*. New York, Harper & Row. (Original work published in 1957 as *Psychologie du temps.*) This book, although not recent, is an excellent source of information concerning the perception of relatively long temporal intervals.

Meck, W. H. (1996). Neuropharmacology of timing and time perception. *Cognitive Brain Research, 3*, 227–242. This article provides an excellent review of the literature on psychophysical and neuropharmacological timing data, and the relationship of these data to the Scalar Timing Model of time perception.

Wearden, J. H. (1994). Prescriptions for models of biopsychological time. In M. Oaksford & G. Brown (Eds.), *Neurodynamics and psychology* (pp. 215–236). London: Academic Press. This article provides an excellent summary of current quantitative models of time perception including data on both humans and animals.

Conference Proceedings

Gibbon, J., & Allan, L. (1984). *Timing and time perception* (Vol. 423). New York: New York Academy of Sciences.

Macar, F., Pouthas, V., & Friedman, W. J. (1992). *Time, action and cognition: Towards bridging the gap*. Dordrecht, Netherlands: Kluwer.

Richelle, M., Keyser, V. D., d'Ydewalle, G., & Vandierendonck, A. (1995). *Time and the dynamic control of behavior*. Liège: Université de Liège.

Edited Volumes

Block, R. A. (Ed.). (1990). *Cognitive models of psychological time*. Hillsdale, NJ: Erlbaum.

Lejeune, H., & Macar, F. (Eds.). (1993). *Psychologica Belgica: Temporal processes* (Vol. 33). Leuven, Belgium: Belgium Psychological Society.

Maier, S. F., & Church, R. M. (Eds.). (1991). *Learning and motivation: Special issue on animal timing* (Vol. 22). New York: Academic Press.

Lorraine G. Allan

TIMESHARING. *See* Multi-Task Performance.

TINBERGEN, NIKOLAAS (1907–1988), Dutch ethologist. The defining event in the scientific career of Niko Tinbergen was his 1973 receipt of the Nobel Prize in Physiology or Medicine, shared with Konrad Lorenz and Karl von Frisch. Remarkably, his older brother Jan received a Nobel Prize in Economics 4 years before Niko received his. Overemphasis on the Nobel Prize, however, will miss the essence of this modest man as a dedicated naturalist, skilled scientist, and concerned environmentalist. Together with Lorenz, Tinbergen established European ethology as the study of the natural behavioral patterns of animals in the context of the natural environments in which they had evolved.

Tinbergen was born in The Hague, Netherlands, the third of five children in a happy family. Camping, birdwatching, and hockey kept him from being a serious student in his youth. He found the lure of the beautiful Dutch coast irresistible and was aided in its appreciation by some of the leading Dutch naturalists. The young Tinbergen found academic biology unattractive, but his love of nature and a taste of ornithological research won out, and he read biology at Leiden University. He received his Ph.D. degree in 1932 with a 32-page dissertation, the shortest on record there.

Tinbergen married Elisabeth Rutten, and the couple spent a 14-month interval in Greenland studying a variety of organisms including phalaropes, Eskimo dogs, and Eskimo hunters. He then taught at the University of Leiden and began some of his classic research on gulls and stickleback fish. The Tinbergens spent the spring of 1937 with Lorenz in Austria, and their names have been linked ever since. In the same year Tinbergen visited American laboratories, though he never warmed to the more behavioristic approaches they represented.

During World War II Tinbergen spent 2 years imprisoned in a German hostage camp because he supported Jewish faculty colleagues. He returned to Leiden after the war, becoming a full professor in 1947. Wanting to bring the ethological perspective to English-speaking audiences, Tinbergen resigned his position and moved to the University of Oxford in 1949. He lived in Oxford for the rest of his life.

Tinbergen was always the curious naturalist, seeking to understand the world around him. He systematized such understanding with respect to four sets of questions that provide the framework of ethology: immediate causation, development, adaptive function, and evolution. This schema, adopted by animal behaviorists around the world, serves to help keep different questions about nature separate and to ensure that the information provided in answers is indeed appropriate to the question under consideration.

Where Lorenz was a bold theorist, Tinbergen was a careful observer and experimenter with a genius for devising simple, yet insightful, experiments in the natural habitat. Typically, he would construct a blind and make careful observations of the animals under study. These observations would lead to experiments that could clarify what he had observed. His research on the behavior of gulls is classic, especially the role of various stimuli acting at key points. For example, he observed that shortly after their young hatch, the parents remove the egg shells from the vicinity of the nest. He then conducted a series of experiments demonstrating that the function of this seemingly trivial behavior lay in keeping the young hidden from predators. His work with orientation in insects and numerous other species in nature was in the same spirit. Beyond this, Tinbergen conducted important laboratory research on the courtship and mating of stickleback fish. Among his last research projects was a study of early childhood autism in humans.

Despite his distrust of behaviorism, Tinbergen was a pivotal player in helping to bring European ethologists and comparative psychologists together. More accommodating than Lorenz, he and his students developed a variety of ethology more sensitive to the concerns of North American workers regarding such issues as the complexity inherent in the development of behavior.

As much as he enjoyed his zoological work, Tinbergen was deeply concerned with the state of the world around him and struggled with his career as a researcher, wanting to do more to help humanity and the surrounding environment. His modesty was linked, in part, to his feelings that he had not done enough in this sphere.

As befits a Nobel Prize winner, Tinbergen received many other honors. These included the Swammerdam medal and honorary degrees from the Universities of Edinburgh and Leicester. He was a Fellow of the Royal Society, a foreign member of the U.S. National Academy of Sciences, and the recipient of a Distinguished Scientific Contribution Award from the American Psychological Association. Among his books were *The Study of Instinct* (1951), *Curious Naturalists* (1958), and his collected papers, *The Animal in Its World* (1972, 1973).

Bibliography

Works by Tinbergen

Tinbergen, N. (1951). *The study of instinct.* Oxford: Clarendon.

Tinbergen, N. (1953). *The herring gull's world.* London: Collins.

Tinbergen, N. (1953). *Social behaviour of animals.* London: Methuen.

Tinbergen, N. (1958). *Curious naturalists.* London: Country Life.

Tinbergen, N. (1963). On aims and methods of ethology. *Zeitschrift für Tierpsychologie, 20,* 410–433.

Tinbergen, N. (1972). *The animal in its world* (Vol. 1). London: Allen & Unwin.

Tinbergen, N. (1973). *The animal in its world* (Vol. 2). London: Allen & Unwin.

Works about Tinbergen

Dewsbury, D. A. (1990). Nikolaas Tinbergen (1907–1988). *American Psychologist, 45,* 67–68.

Hinde, R. A. (1990). Nikolaas Tinbergen, 15 April 1907–21 December 1988. In *Biographical Memoirs of Fellows of the Royal Society* (Vol. 36, pp. 549–565) London: Royal Society.

Tinbergen, N. (1985). Watching and wondering. In D. A. Dewsbury (Ed.), *Leaders in the study of animal behavior* (pp. 430–463). Lewisburg, PA: Bucknell University Press.

Donald A. Dewsbury

TITCHENER, EDWARD BRADFORD (1867–1927), American experimental psychologist. Titchener was born and raised in Chichester, England, and attended Oxford University, staying an extra year to work with the eminent physiologist John Scott Burdon-Sanderson (1828–1905). He received his B. A. degree in 1890. Becoming acquainted with Wundt's work through Burdon-Sanderson, Titchener went to Leipzig and received his Ph.D. in 1892 for a study of the binocular effects of monocular stimulation. After a short stay at Oxford, Titchener took over the newly founded laboratory of experimental psychology at Cornell University, building Cornell's lab into a major outpost of brass-and-glass psychology. He remained at Cornell until his unexpected death in 1927.

Although his system of psychology is often mistakenly regarded as similar to Wundt's, in fact Titchener was a Machian positivist who developed a unique structuralist view of psychology. According to Titchener, the purpose of psychology was to determine the elements of mind; only after these were fully described could the functional relations among the elements be determined. Initially accepting sensations and affects as the basic elements, he later argued that even affects could be reduced to sensations. A major goal of his programmatic research was to determine the exact attributes of these elements; for Titchener, it was an empirical finding that all sensations possessed the attributes of intensity, clearness, duration, and quality. Attributes of quality are what characterize a sensation's type. In the auditory domain, for example, tones are characterized by the qualities of pitch and volume, whereas visual sensations are characterized by the qualities of hue, tint, and saturation, representable in the familiar color pyramid.

Adopting a rigorously experimental approach, and thereby rejecting the armchair introspection of earlier psychologists, Titchener and his students used systematic introspection as an analytic tool. Given a precisely controlled stimulus, experimental observers were trained to report on the sensory and emotional elements and attributes of the resulting experience. In a typical Titchenerian study, the experimenter manipulated stimulus variables in a precisely controlled fashion (much as in current experimentation), recording observer reports for analysis. Such reports were valuable to Titchener provided the observer avoided stimulus error, that is, reporting on the nature or meaning of the object producing the sensation, rather than the sensations and their attributes themselves. For example, the touch of a needle against the arm might be reported as, "It felt sharp, like a needle, but seemed to pass quickly"; this would be an unsatisfactory report, one reflecting a judgment or inference about the nature of the stimulus. Instead, a proper report would be, "Bright pressure, changing in duration, an unpleasant affect which seemed to blur the experience, a fading clearness"; in this form, the report avoids such inferences and concentrates upon the elemental aspects of the experience. Note that this form of systematic introspection differs from modern studies of verbal protocols, first in the insistence upon experimental manipulation and second in the goal of the procedure. Furthermore, Titchener's insistence upon the training of observers can be understood in this context; naive or untrained observers must necessarily commit the stimulus error.

Gathered across a large variety of experimental conditions, such reports were often highly regular, often varied lawfully with changes in experimental conditions, and permitted Titchener to investigate most domains of experience. His programmatic approach led him to study all of the sensory modalities, as well as such nonsensory domains as attention, which, Titchener argued, could be reduced in all cases to the sensory attribute of clearness. Because of this, Titchener argued against those who regarded attention as either a functional category or as a basic cognitive process. Thus, in common with the behaviorists, he preferred parsimonious accounts, although, unlike the behaviorists, he insisted upon the centrality of experience as the subject matter of psychology. Interestingly, his response to Watson's manifesto, "Psychology as the behaviorist views it" (*Psychological Review*, 1913, *20*, 158–177) was surprisingly mild; in a paper in the *Proceedings of the American Philosophical Society* (1914, *53*, 1–17) he rejected behaviorism as a basis for psychology, but he nevertheless accepted its potential value as a psychotechnology.

Beginning in 1907, Titchener was forced to deal directly with the claims of the Würzburg School (especially the works of Karl Bühler) that imageless thought elements were detectable in certain introspective accounts. Titchener and his students subsequently engaged in an 8-year program of research, attempting to show that all such reports, when gathered appropriately, in fact did involve transient sensations, not a new thought element. The issue was especially important to Titchener because it could undermine his central theoretical claim (that all conscious experience could be resolved into sensations and affects) and because it challenged the possibility of avoiding stimulus error. Thus, much of his response to the Würzburgers amounted to a claim that insufficient care had been taken in their research, particularly in their use of poorly trained observers. He further claimed that the thought elements could not be true elements, insofar as they were reported only under certain circumstances, whereas sensations were always detectable. In retrospect, as William Book noted in 1910 (*Psychological Review*, *17*, 381–398), imageless thoughts seemed to occur only with well-learned, or automated, skills, whereas Titchener was correct—there were detectable sensory elements—only for relatively novel skills. Book's point turns on a functional distinction, however, since degree of learning is a functional category, relegated by Titchener to the realm of applied concerns, and thus irrelevant to basic issues in theoretical psychology. In the end, Titchener's claim is compelling: If the goal is to identify the elements of all experience, then elemental status cannot be given to entities that are sometimes present and sometimes not present. In recent decades, of course, most psychologists have rejected such goals, or, if they do seek to identify elements, do so in the realm of behavior, not experience.

After 1915, Titchener worked on a systematic psychology, a comprehensive statement of his theory. During this time, his students engaged in extensive laboratory work designed to show the range of problems that his approach could handle. His early death in 1927 left his theoretical book unfinished, however, and only the first several chapters were published posthumously (*Prolegomena to a Systematic Psychology*, New York, 1929). There has been speculation about what he might have written, but it now seems clear only that he would have reduced affects (previously elements in their own right) to sensations. In the end, all psychological experience was therefore reduced to sensation elements.

Like his mentor Wundt, Titchener regarded applications of psychology with extreme suspicion; psychology was to be a pure science. And, like Wundt, Titchener sought to establish himself as an authority in the new science. His prolific writing thus included textbooks at various levels, as well as translations of important German works by Külpe and Wundt. A widely read man, Titchener was able to range widely over the sciences and humanities in defense of his positions; even so, his work never attempted to solve the range of problems that Wundt saw as part of psychology.

An early supporter of the American Psychological Association (APA), Titchener resigned in 1897 over what he saw as its soft attitude in a case of supposed plagiarism. In 1904 he founded The Experimentalists, an exclusively male club that later became the Society of Experimental Psychologists. Titchener was prolific as a teacher and mentor, supervising 56 Ph.D.s, including such notable psychologists as E. G. Boring and Karl Dallenbach. In spite of his imperious attitude toward women (reflected clearly in his correspondence), nearly half of his students were women, including his first student, the distinguished Margaret Floy Washburn, who was elected president of the APA in 1921. In an ironic note, Titchener was one of only a few psychologists to defend the behaviorist John B. Watson following the divorce scandal that resulted in Watson's leaving psychology. He and Watson remained friends for years.

Titchener's system is often caricatured in textbooks today (and sometimes mistakenly attributed to Wundt). In part, this stems from E. G. Boring's presentation of Wundt as if he were a structuralist (*A History of Experimental Psychology*, New York, 1929). Perhaps Boring was too steeped in the Titchenerian worldview to appreciate the profound differences between the two. At least in North America, however, a kind of mythical Titchener/Wundt is often held out as an example of how introspectionist structuralisms failed in the early part of psychology's history. Such views do little justice to either thinker.

While there are no remaining structuralists in Titchener's sense of the word, his enduring legacy of experimental and theoretical work contributed to the early definition of psychology as founded upon a rigorous scientific approach and upon continuous critical analysis. In his words (in a letter to Adolf Meyer): "I am not sure that the clearest thinking will ever be adequate to the universe, but I am very sure that muddy thinking cannot be."

Bibliography

Boring, E. G. (1927). Edward Bradford Titchener, 1867–1927. *American Journal of Psychology, 38*, 489–506. Respectful obituary by one of Titchener's favorite students.

Danziger, K. (1990). *Constructing the subject: Historical origins of psychological research*. Cambridge: Cambridge University Press. Essential for understanding the context of Titchener's use of observers, rather than subjects, Danziger uncovers the surprising origins of many of the unstated assumptions of American psychology.

Evans, R. B. (1972). E. B. Titchener and his lost system. *Journal of the History of the Behavioral Sciences, 8*, 168–180. Evans provides an overview of Titchener's theoretical ideas.

Leys, R., & Evans, R. B. (Eds.). (1990). *Defining American psychology: The correspondence between Adolf Meyer and Edward Bradford Titchener*. Baltimore, MD: Johns Hopkins University Press. Titchener's correspondence with the functional psychiatrist Meyer reveals two sharp and incisive thinkers attempting to clarify differences and find common ground. Few other sources so clearly reveal the tensions and concerns of the new science of psychology.

Titchener, E. B. (1901–1905). *Experimental psychology: A manual of laboratory practice: Vol. I. Qualitative experiments, Part I, Student's manual; Part II, Instructor's manual. Vol. II. Quantitative experiments, Part I, Student's manual; Part II, Instructor's manual*. New York: Macmillan. This massive survey is the definitive account of the methods and major findings of experimental psychology at the beginning of the twentieth century. A book that repays browsing even today, it influenced generations of American psychologists.

Titchener, E. B. (1909). *Lectures on the experimental psychology of the thought-processes*. New York: Macmillan. Probably the most widely read of Titchener's books today; an important account of the nature of thinking and his major statement against the Würzburg claim of imageless thought.

Tweney, R. D. (1987). Programmatic research in experimental psychology: E. B. Titchener's laboratory investigations, 1891–1927. In M. G. Ash & W. R. Woodward (Eds.), *Psychology in twentieth-century psychology* (pp. 35–57). Cambridge: Cambridge University Press. An overview of Titchener's experimental research.

Ryan D. Tweney

TOKEN ECONOMY. The token economy is a psychosocial intervention designed to develop positive prosocial behaviors and to decrease maladaptive behaviors through positive reinforcement. A token economy includes three components: the tokens, or medium of exchange; the rewards, referred to as backup reinforcers, that can be purchased with the tokens; and a set of rules that specify what behaviors earn tokens, how many tokens are earned, and the cost of the backup reinforcers. Typically, tickets, stars, coins, points, poker chips, or check marks serve as tokens. These are not valuable in themselves but become valuable because they can be traded or exchanged for other rewards, such as privileges, activities, money, and food, depending on the population and setting. Thus tokens operate very much like money in a national economy.

Research has repeatedly demonstrated that positive reinforcement, such as the delivery of praise, privileges, attention, and feedback immediately after behavior, is effective in developing that behavior. Token reinforcement has several advantages because tokens can develop and maintain behavior at a high level, are less subject to satiation or the temporary loss of value of a reward because they can be used to purchase many different rewards, and permit implementation of a large-scale incentive program using a single system of reinforcements. All persons in the setting, such as children at home with their families, in a classroom, or in an entire school, can receive a common reinforcer (tokens) and exert their individual preferences by exchanging these for backup rewards.

The effectiveness of a token economy depends on providing tokens only when the desired behavior is performed, immediately after the behavior, and on all or most occasions on which the behavior occurs. Departure from these conditions can attenuate or negate the impact of the intervention. Careful specification of the behaviors is important as well to ensure that the tokens are administered consistently. Although emphasis is placed on positive reinforcement, punishment may be included as well. Tokens can be withdrawn when undesired behaviors occur, a procedure referred to as response cost.

History

The use of tokens to promote behavior has many historical examples antedating contemporary work. For example, in the early 1800s, some schools in England provided students with tickets for making progress in academic subjects. Tickets were exchanged for prizes and also earned special recognition and the opportunity to progress to higher levels within the class. The program was intended to help manage large classes, often with hundreds of students. The reported success of this system led to its widespread adoption in Europe, Africa, Asia, and North and South America.

Contemporary token economies can be traced directly to the development of operant conditioning and the work of B. F. Skinner (*The Behavior of Organisms: An Experimental Analysis*, New York, 1938). Extensive animal and human laboratory research elaborated the effects of positive reinforcement, punishment, and extinction on behavior. This research provided the experimental underpinnings of contemporary token economies and other applications of reinforcement principles.

Token economies developed in the early 1960s as part of a larger movement of applying operant conditioning principles and procedures to applied problems, an area known more generally as applied behavior analysis. Early applications of token reinforcement with hospitalized psychiatric patients and mentally retarded children in special education classrooms demonstrated marked changes in behavior. For example, in a seminal book, Theodore Ayllon and Nathan Azrin (*The Token Economy: A Motivational System for Therapy and Rehabilitation*, New York, 1968) reported controlled experiments showing that token reinforcement could alter a variety of behaviors among psychiatric patients. Prior to this work, Allyon had shown that positive reinforcement in the form of food or attention could change behaviors among individual psychiatric patients. The token economy represented an innovative way to implement reinforcement on a larger scale. Many behaviors, patients, and backup rewards could be integrated into a single system.

Applications and Effectiveness

The token economy has been applied to an enormous range of clients, settings, and behaviors. For example, in the contexts of treatment, education, and rehabilitation, token economies have been used with persons diagnosed with psychiatric disorders or mental retardation; with children, adolescents, and college students in school settings; with delinquents and prisoners in group homes and institutional settings; with geriatric patients and nursing-home residents; and many others. The token economy has been extended to behaviors in everyday life, such as training parents to provide basic care for their children or to promote prosocial behavior at home and at school and encouraging people to conserve energy, use mass transportation, wear seat belts while driving, recycle trash, diet, and exercise. Token economies in business and industry are used to improve employee performance and foster practices that reduce accidents and injury. Research has consistently attested to the effectiveness of token economies in changing behavior. In fact, there probably is no other psychological intervention that has been applied so broadly among populations and settings and that at the same time has been so well investigated as has the token economy.

Key Issues

Behavior changes achieved in token economies are not automatically maintained and may not carry over to new settings after the program is discontinued. Special procedures are usually required after behaviors have been developed so that the changes are maintained and extend to other settings. Gradually withdrawing token reinforcement after the desired behaviors have been developed and shifting from tokens to other reinforcers, such as praise and attention, are among the many procedures that can sustain performance.

Occasionally, parents and teachers object to the use of token reinforcement as a way of changing behavior. The objections are based on the view that many behaviors of interest ought to be completed without such inducements or that such inducements may hamper performance in the long run. Yet the token economy is extremely useful in developing behaviors that otherwise are not occurring or are occurring infrequently or inconsistently. Also, if deviant or maladaptive behaviors are occurring, the token economy can decrease these behaviors. The token economy can develop the desired behaviors in a systematic way and at a high level, after which tokens can be withdrawn. Although token reinforcement is very effective, other reinforcers such as attention, praise, and feedback, when delivered immediately for specific behaviors, can be very effective as well in developing and promoting behavior.

Bibliography

Ayllon, T., & Azrin, N. H. (1965). The measurement and reinforcement of behavior of psychotics. *Journal of the Experimental Analysis of Behavior, 8*, 356–383.

Ayllon, T., & Michael, J. (1959). The psychiatric nurse as a behavioral engineer. *Journal of the Experimental Analysis of Behavior, 2*, 323–334. This is one of the early applications of reinforcement to changing the behavior of hospitalized psychiatric patients. The report was significant in showing how changes in reinforcement could alter behaviors outside of the laboratory setting in which operant conditioning principles were developed.

Glenn, S. M. (1990). Token economy approaches for psychiatric patients. *Behavior Modification, 14*, 383–407.

Kazdin, A. E. (1977). *The token economy: A review and evaluation*. New York: Plenum Press. This book traces the history of the token economy, the range of applications across settings and populations, and the evidence in support of the technique.

Kazdin, A. E. (1982). The token economy: A decade later. *Journal of Applied Behavior Analysis, 15*, 431–445.

Phillips, E. L., Phillips, E. A., Fixsen, D. L., & Wolf, M. M. (1971). Achievement Place: Modification of the behaviors of predelinquent boys within a token economy. *Journal of Applied Behavior Analysis, 4*, 45–59. This article describes a token economy for delinquent youths in a community-based setting. This program has had an impact on the development of token economies. Many articles have appeared on this community-based program.

Skinner, B. F. (1953). *Science and human behavior*. New York: Free Press. This book discusses how principles of operant conditioning apply to everyday life.

Alan E. Kazdin

TOLMAN, EDWARD CHACE (1886–1959), American psychologist. The emergence of the field of comparative cognition has once again brought attention to the ideas of learning theorist Edward C. Tolman. Tolman, who advanced his theory—purposive behaviorism—during the 1930s, was a contemporary of Clark Hull and B. F. Skinner. All three men were behaviorists, influenced by John B. Watson's popularization of this reaction to mentalism. Although Tolman's version of behaviorism was well-known and highly regarded, it was less popular than Hull's in the 1940s and Skinner's in the 1950s. Tolman's ideas were ahead of their time. He anticipated a cybernetic approach to the study of behavior and the emphasis on cognitive processes that now predominates in psychology. Although Tolman did not directly influence these developments, the relevance of his ideas to modern approaches to the study of human and animal behavior is undeniable.

Tolman was born in West Newton, Massachusetts. His choice of a career in psychology was at least in part determined by rivalry with an elder brother. Richard Tolman was already becoming a well-known physical chemist when Edward received his bachelor's degree in electrochemistry from the Massachusetts Institute of Technology in 1911. Edward also wanted to be a scientist but did not want to compete directly with Richard. The new science of psychology was the perfect solution. Edward received his doctorate from Harvard University in 1915, for studies of human memory supervised by Hugo Münsterberg. Tolman spent 3 years on the faculty at Northwestern University and then, in 1918, accepted an appointment at the University of California at Berkeley, where he remained for the rest of his career. California provided a congenial atmosphere for Tolman, both personally and academically. Before the move west, he was timid and reserved; in California, he revealed an outgoing, fun-loving nature. His research interests also changed, and he began to study the behavior of rats rather than humans. Tolman would later claim that "everything important in psychology . . . can be investigated in essence through the continued experimental and theoretical analysis of the determiners of rat behavior at a choice point in a maze" (*Psychological Review*, 1938, 45, p. 34).

In *Purposive Behavior in Animals and Men* (New York, 1932), Tolman presented in detail the theory he had developed in a series of articles in the *Psychological Review* during the 1920s. In the book, Tolman set out to show that "mental processes are most usefully to be conceived as but dynamic aspects, or determinants, of behavior. . . . functional variables which intermediate in the causal equation between environmental stimuli and initiating physiological states or excitements, on the one side, and final overt behavior, on the other" (p. 2). Cognitions were expectations about the relationship between environmental support stimuli, referred to as signs, and the goals, or significates, that they indicated. The purposive nature of behavior was defined by its persistence until the goal was achieved. These motivational and cognitive determinants of behavior, defined objectively by means of operational definitions, were later labeled intervening variables. Introduction of the intervening variable concept is one of Tolman's most important contributions to psychology.

For Tolman, there were two types of intervening variables: those related to the past and those that were present on a particular trial of an experiment. The first, the means-end-readinesses or beliefs, referred to continuing dispositions that the animal had concerning what-leads-to-what in its environment. They were innate or acquired as a result of past associative learning. However, on any particular trial, depending on the animal's motivational state and the stimulus situation, particular perceptions, expectations, representations, and valences (values attached to the goal) were available. These he called sign-gestalt expectations.

Performance has both strength and direction, and Tolman, influenced by the ideas of Gestalt psychologist Kurt Lewin, talked about performance vectors. He even used vector mathematics in a mechanistic model, introduced to account for the function relating intervening variables to behavior, that came to be known as the schematic sowbug. The model came into being when Tolman decided to animate Lewin's oval representation of the psychological lifespace by adding appendages and a sensory surface. The result resembled a sowbug, and the label stuck. The schematic sowbug moved tropistically toward a goal in the environment, characterizing both the purposive and behavioristic nature of Tolman's theory. The evolutionary biologist Donald Campbell (in "A tribal model of the social system vehicle carrying scientific knowledge," *Knowledge: Creation, Diffusion, Utilization*, 1979, 1, 181–201) suggested that this model, introduced in the 1930s, was a precursor to the approach later taken by "cybernetics, servosystem engineering, automaton theory, and artificial intelligence" (p. 187).

The importance of vectors in Tolman's approach relates to his penchant for considering all performance in spatial terms; he even declared that the "spatial concepts of distance and direction [were] the very warp and woof of all our thinking about performances" (Tolman, 1959). There are spatial metaphors throughout Tolman's work, the best known of which is the cognitive map, an analogy for the way in which rats, and humans too, represent their worlds. Tolman suggested that rather than the formation of simple stimulus–response connections, "in the course of learning something like a field map of the environment gets established in the rat's brain" (Tolman, 1948, p. 192). This idea of a cognitive map, introduced by Tolman in the late 1940s, has received widespread attention recently from psychologists studying comparative cognition and with this has come a renewed interested in Tolman's theoretical perspective in general.

Tolman described broad and narrow (restrictive) cognitive maps; his own was a broad map. Tolman's approach to psychology was eclectic; by exploring diverse paths, he hoped to find the road to understanding why people behave as they do. Tolman's intellectual breadth and tolerance extended to his own laboratory—he encouraged students not converts. His graduate learning seminar was a forum for discussion and argument, a lively exchange of ideas, not the recitation of a scientific litany. Many of his students became distinguished psychologists in their own right in a number of different fields of psychology, yet Edward Tolman remained their hero, a role model for whom they set aside singular words of gratitude.

Tolman was concerned with using psychology to help humanity. He was a founding member of the Society for the Psychological Study of Social Issues, and he played an active role in the American Psychological Association's attempts to find positions for émigré psychologists forced to leave Europe following the rise of Adolph Hitler. He also felt compelled to apply his expertise as a psychologist to the issues of war and peace and, in 1942, published a slim volume titled *Drives Toward War*. The book, which began as a motivation textbook, had one major underlying theme: how to change society so that war between nations was no longer inevitable. Although he was a pacifist, during World War II, Tolman spent time in the Office of Strategic Services, helping to select individuals for the secret service. As a result of his involvement in these testing sessions, his interest in personality and social psychology was stimulated, and late in his career he would claim that, if he were a young man just starting out, this was the area of psychology that he would enter.

Tolman was fired from the University of California in 1950 for refusing to sign an anti-Communist loyalty oath imposed on the faculty by the regents of the university. Although not a Communist, Tolman opposed the oath because he believed that such political tests for employment were a violation of academic freedom and tenure. Tolman and a few other nonsigners, the Group for Academic Freedom, successfully challenged the oath in the courts. Tolman returned to his position at Berkeley in 1953 and retired the following year. He died in 1959.

Tolman received many honors during his career. In 1937, he was elected to the prestigious National Academy of Sciences, where he joined his brother, Richard Tolman, then an eminent professor of physical chemistry at the California Institute of Technology, becoming one of only a few pairs of brothers to be so honored. In that same year, he was elected president of the American Psychological Association. The APA also awarded him its Distinguished Scientific Contribution Award in 1957.

Tolman's attempts to bring the objective study of animal behavior and concepts like purpose and cognition into a harmonious relationship set him apart from other behaviorists of his day, as did his personal approach to science and theory development. Toward the end of his life, after summarizing and evaluating his theoretic system, Tolman concluded that in science—particularly in a relatively undeveloped science such as psychology—the best approach is for the scientist to "follow his own gleam and his own bent" and above all "to have fun."

Bibliography

Works by Tolman

Tolman, E. C. (1936). Operational behaviorism and current trends in psychology. *Proceedings of the 25th Anniversary Celebration of the Inauguration of Graduate Studies at the University of Southern California* (pp. 89–103). Los Angeles: University of Southern California Press. Outlines an operational approach involving intervening variables.

Tolman, E. C. (1938). The determiners of behavior at a choice point. *Psychological Review, 45*, 1–41. Tolman's presidential address to the American Psychological Association.

Tolman, E. C. (1939). Prediction of vicarious trial and error by means of the schematic sowbug. *Psychological Review, 48*, 318–336.

Tolman, E. C. (1942). *Drives toward war.* New York: Appleton-Century.

Tolman, E. C. (1948). Cognitive map in rats and men. *Psychological Review, 55*, 189–210.

Tolman, E. C. (1951). *Behavior and Psychological Man.* Berkeley: University of California Press. A collection of Tolman's major journal articles (1922–1948), along with a forward by former students assessing his contributions.

Tolman, E. C. (1952). Edward Chace Tolman. In E. G. Boring, H. S. Langfeld, H. Werner, & R. M. Yerkes (Eds.), *A history of psychology in autobiography* (Vol. 4, pp. 323–339). Worcester, MA: Clark University Press. Tolman's autobiography.

Tolman, E. C. (1959). Principles of purposive behavior. In S. Koch (Ed.), *Psychology: A study of a science* (Vol. 2, pp. 92–157). New York: McGraw-Hill. Tolman's final version of his theory.

Works about Tolman

Innis, N. K. (1992). Lessons from the controversy over the loyalty oath at the University of California. *Minerva, 30*, 337–365.

Innis, N. K. (1998). Edward C. Tolman's purposive behaviorism. In W. O'Donohue & R. Kitchener (Eds.), *Handbook of behaviorism* (pp. 97–117). New York: Academic Press.

Ritchie, B. F. (1963). Edward Chace Tolman. *National Academy of Sciences Biographical Memoirs, 37*, 292–317.

Smith, L. D. (1986). *Behaviorism and logical positivism: A reassessment of the alliance.* Stanford, CA: Stanford University Press. Excellent assessment of the theories of Tolman, Hull, and Skinner.

Smith, L. D. (1990). Metaphors of knowledge and behavior in the behaviorist tradition. In D. E. Leary (Ed.), *Metaphors in the history of psychology* (pp. 239–266). New York: Cambridge University Press. Discussion of Tolman's spatial metaphors, including the cognitive map.

Nancy K. Innis

TOUCH. [*This entry comprises two articles: an anatomical and physiological description of the skin senses; and a survey of the behavioral and functional aspects of the skin senses. For a discussion on the physiological mechanisms of pain and pain management, see* Pain. *For a broad overview of the sensory systems (visual, auditory, tactile, and the chemical senses), see* Sensory Systems.]

Biological Organization

The sense of touch allows us to identify and use objects and surfaces that contact, indent, or vibrate the skin and deeper tissue. Whereas shapes and textures can be perceived passively when pressed against the skin, larger objects and surfaces are often actively explored. Thus, the processing of tactile information depends not only on the activation of sensitive mechanoreceptors in the skin but also on deeper receptors in muscles, joints, and skin that indicate finger and mouth positions, as well as a complex central system of interconnected nuclei and cortical areas that can integrate and use the inputs from different receptor classes over time and stimulus conditions. Here we consider the major features of the somatosensory system of humans and other primates that mediate the sense of touch. Most studies have involved the parts of the system related to receptors of the glabrous skin of the hand, a very important tactile surface.

The basic parts of the somatosensory system are outlined in Figure 1. Afferents from tactile receptors in the skin of the hand course via peripheral nerves and

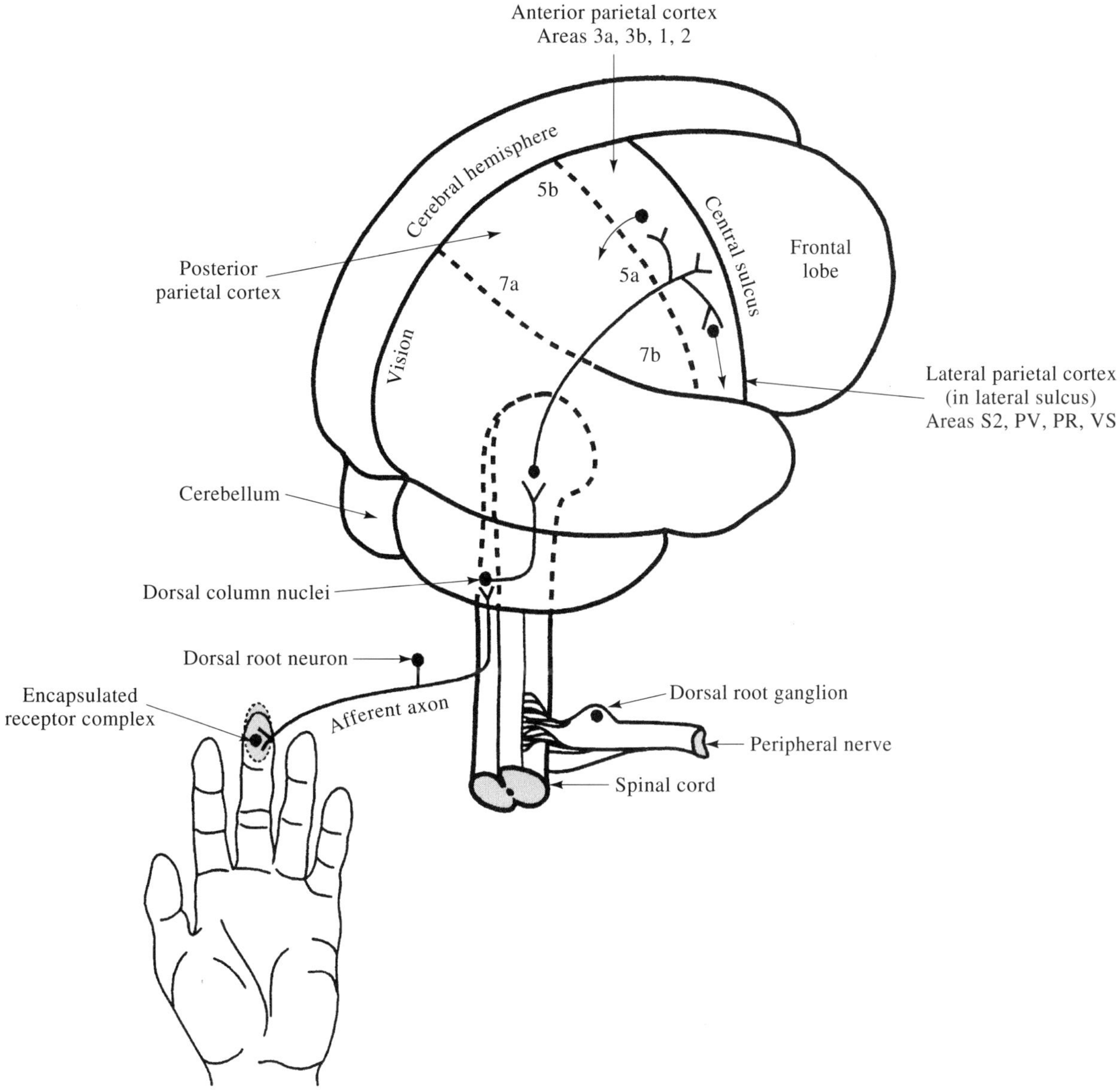

TOUCH: Biological Organization. Figure 1. The major divisions and pathways of the somatosensory system outlined on a posterolateral view of a human brain. Tactile afferents enter the dorsal spinal cord and rise to the lower brain stem, where a second set of neurons send axons to the opposite thalamus. Thalamic neurons project to the anterior parietal coretx, where processing is distributed to the anterior and lateral parietal cortices.

the dorsal roots into the dorsal spinal cord, where they activate spinal cord neurons and send major branches rostrally through the dorsal columns of the spinal cord to terminate in the dorsal column nuclei of the lower brain stem. Other spinal cord pathways exist, but those in the dorsal columns are predominant for touch. Neurons in the dorsal column nuclei send axons to the opposite side of the brain stem, where they ascend to the ventroposterior nuclear complex of the thalamus. Neurons in the ventroposterior complex relay to four subdivisions of the anterior parietal cortex traditionally numbered 3a, 3b, 1, and 2. These four interconnected areas project to additional somatosensory areas in the posterior parietal cortex and lateral parietal cortex on the banks of the lateral sulcus, and to motor and premotor fields of the frontal lobe. Thus, an extensive network of processing structures is involved with touch perception.

Receptors and Afferents

Afferents from four types of receptors mediate tactile sensations from the glabrous skin of the hand. The terminations of afferents in the skin contact specialized receptor cells, so that each afferent type is especially sensitive to particular tactile stimuli. Thus, receptors are sometimes described as filters, and each afferent type can be considered as contributing most to certain aspects of perception. Nevertheless, most stimuli activate all four classes of receptors, and they often contribute jointly to perception. Finally, receptors in muscles contribute to a sense of position that is important in interpretations of information obtained as digits change position during tactile exploration.

A major afferent in the skin of the digits is the rapidly adapting type I or RA-I. These afferents have disklike terminations encapsulated by other cells to form the receptor complex, the Meissner corpuscle. Because fibrils link the corpuscles to adjacent epidermal cells, skin deformations stretch the corpuscle and initiate action potentials. Each afferent innervates a small, tight group of corpuscles, resulting in a small receptive field. Meissner corpuscles are concentrated in the fingertips and are numerous enough to be used in precise localization. As rapidly adapting afferents, they provide accurate information about when stimuli change. Electrical stimulation of single RA-I afferents in humans produces a sensation of a series of punctate taps at low frequencies that merge at higher frequencies into a fluttering sensation.

The other major afferent of the glabrous skin is the slowly adapting type I or SA-I. These afferents branch to terminate in several closely spaced, specialized skin cells, the Merkel disks. The SA-I afferents are numerous and concentrated in the tips of the fingers, and they have small receptive fields. They respond throughout short periods of skin indentation, and they are quite responsive when the edge of an object indents skin within the receptive field. Electrical stimulation of the afferents in humans leads to a sensation of light pressure at a skin location corresponding to the receptive fields. SA-I afferents appear to provide the only high-resolution neural image that is isomorphic with the forms of small objects. Thus, they seem to be the primary receptor for the discrimination of the details of surfaces such as braille patterns. Because they signal levels of pressure, they also probably encode softness (compliance).

A third type of afferent, the rapidly adapting type II, RA-II, terminates in Pacinian corpuscles (also known as PC afferents). The corpuscle consists of a nerve fiber termination wrapped in 50 to 60 layers of lamellar cells, which effectively damp low-frequency components of skin indentations while preserving high-frequency components. They are especially sensitive to transient indentations of the skin. Sensitivity to a stimulus decreases only gradually with distance from the receptor, and receptors are sparsely distributed. Thus, receptive fields are large and spatial resolution is poor. The RA-II afferents appear to be the only afferents capable of signaling high-frequency vibrations, and their major role seems to be in detecting and approximately locating sudden skin deformations produced by ground and air vibrations and skin contacts. Electrical stimulation of these afferents can produce a sensation of vibration.

The slowly adapting type II afferents (SA-II) terminate in Ruffini corpuscles, consisting of a complex of several layers of cells and collagen fibrils that deform the corpuscle when surrounding skin is stretched. Thus, the afferents are extremely sensitive to skin stretch and often to the direction of skin stretch. Each afferent usually innervates several corpuscles, resulting in a fairly large receptive field, often located around the nail bed or near folds in the skin. These afferents are relatively sparse, and they are not concentrated in the fingertips. They poorly represent the form or location of punctate stimuli, and they appear to produce a buzz-like sensation at high rates of stimulation. As they signal skin movement and displacement, they may have an important role in limb and finger position sense. Both SA-II and RA afferents on the back of the hand are often located near joints, where they are stimulated by skin movement to help signal finger positions. Other useful position information comes from muscle spindle afferents.

Afferent Targets on the Spinal Cord and Brain Stem

The four major classes of afferents from the glabrous hand enter the spinal cord via the dorsal roots of peripheral nerves, where they terminate on neurons in the dorsal horn of the spinal cord or ascend in the dorsal column fiber pathway of the dorsal spinal cord to reach the dorsal column nuclei in the lower brain stem. The spinal cord terminations activate spinal neurons that project in the contralateral spinothalamic tract, as well as in other pathways, as additional sources of tactile information for higher centers. Thus, simple tactile abilities remain after section of the dorsal columns, although dorsal column damage produces major defects in tactile abilities.

Inputs from the skin terminate in an ordered pattern to represent the body systematically in the dorsal column nuclei. Most likely, each type of afferent terminates on separate groups of cells. Neurons in the nuclei send axons to the opposite half of the brain stem, where they form a fiber pathway known as the medial lemniscus, which ascends to the ventroposterior complex of the dorsal thalamus.

Somatosensory Thalamus

The somatosensory thalamus includes three major nuclei: the ventroposterior nucleus (VP), the ventroposterior superior nucleus (VPS), and the ventroposterior inferior nucleus (VPI). VP includes the medial ventroposterior subnucleus (VPM) representing the face and the lateral ventroposterior subnucleus (VPL) representing the body. VPI, VP, and VPS all receive somatotopically ordered inputs, so that they each represent the body from foot to hand to face to tongue in a lateromedial sequence. VP receives the inputs from the four classes of skin mechanoreceptors, where they terminate, at least in part, on separate clusters of neurons. VPS receives inputs relayed predominantly from muscle spindle receptors, whereas VPI largely receives spinothalamic terminations related to touch, pain, and temperature. VP and VPS project almost exclusively to the anterior parietal cortex. VPI projects most densely to areas in the lateral parietal cortex, with sparser projections terminating in the superficial layers of the fields of the anterior parietal cortex. The adjacent anterior pulvinar connects broadly with subdivisions of the somatosensory cortex to receive and distribute somatosensory information. The VP and VPS projections are thought to be powerful sources of activation for cortical neurons, and the VPI and anterior pulvinar inputs apparently modulate ongoing activity.

Anterior Parietal Cortex

The anterior parietal cortex consists of four striplike areas, each representing the body from tail (or foot) to tongue in a mediolateral cortical sequence. Area 3b or S-1 proper can be considered to be the first stage of cortical processing of tactile information. Neurons in area 3b have small receptive fields and simple response properties, reflecting the relay from VP of largely SA-I or RA-I classes of information. Area 3b, in turn, provides the major activating input to area 1, although this area also receives VP projections. Area 1 neurons have larger receptive fields and more complex response properties. Area 2 neurons receive tactile information from area 1 and limb and digit position information from VPS. Area 2 neurons have large receptive fields, and they are highly active when objects are being explored. Area 3a resembles area 2 in that it receives tactile information from area 3b and proprioceptive information from VPS. However, the major outputs of area 3a to the motor cortex suggest an early role for this field in guiding motor behavior rather than a major role in sensory perception. Lesions in area 3b produce severe deficits in most tactile discriminations, area 1 lesions especially degrade discriminations of texture, and area 2 lesions degrade object discriminations. Thus, the three areas have different roles in tactile perception.

Posterior and Lateral Somatosensory Cortex

The posterior parietal cortex guides motor behavior, such as hand movements to reach and grasp objects, whereas the lateral cortex has critical functions in object identification. The posterior parietal cortex has been somewhat arbitrarily divided into areas 5 and 7, after Brodmann's numbering scheme. Major inputs are from area 2, and outputs are distributed to the lateral somatosensory cortex, premotor cortex, and limbic cortex of the medial wall of the cerebral hemisphere. Area 5 processes somatosensory information, and rostral area 7 appears to be involved in higher-order somatosensory processing related especially to guiding hand movements. More caudally, area 7 is related to visual and visuomotor activities. Lesions of the posterior parietal cortex in humans and monkeys cause errors in reaching for and localizing objects, as well as neglect of touches on the contralateral body and of objects in the contralateral visual hemifield. Many functions of the posterior parietal cortex appear to depend greatly on their outputs to motor and premotor areas of the frontal cortex. The connections of the posterior parietal cortex with the cingulate limbic cortex could relate to motivational and attentional aspects of tactile perceptions.

The cortex of the upper bank of the lateral fissure contains four or more systematic representations of the contralateral body surface. The second somatosensory area, S-2, has inputs from all four subdivisions of the anterior parietal cortex and outputs to other parts of the lateral somatosensory cortex and to motor and premotor areas. Important regional connections are with the adjoining ventral parietal area (PV), a more rostral parietal field (PR), and a ventral somatosensory area (VS). These adjoining areas provide inputs to the perirhinal cortex and the amygdala, and then indirectly to the hippocampus, structures essential for the formation of long-term memories and thus object identification. Consistent with the theory that these lateral areas are highly involved in the identification of objects by touch, the learning of shape discriminations is severely impaired by lesions of the S-2 region.

Summary

The process of exploring and identifying objects by touch involves four major touch channels, especially the SA-I afferents, as well as afferents that signal finger and joint positions during the exploration period. The extraction of useful information from these inputs involves preprocessing in lower brain stem and thalamic structures and the concurrent activation of local processing circuits in an array of cortical areas, each interconnected with several other fields in the same hemisphere, two or three areas in the opposite hemisphere, and a number of subcortical structures. Although serial aspects of processing exist, feedback and parallel distributions of information are important. Somatosensory areas at all levels are involved in the control of motor behavior, but the posterior parietal cortex has an enhanced role. The lateral parietal cortex is especially involved in object recognition and memory.

Bibliography

Carlson, M. (1990). The role of somatic sensory cortex in tactile discrimination in primates. In E. G. Jones & A. Petus (Eds.), *Cerebral cortex* (Vol. 3b, pp. 451–486). New York: Plenum Press.

Jain, N., Catania, K. C., and Kaas, J. H. (1997). Deactivation and reactivation of somatosensory cortex after dorsal spinal cord injury. *Nature, 386*, 495–498.

Johnson, K. O., Hsiao, S. S., & Twombly, I. A. (1995). Neural mechanisms of tactile form recognition. In M. S. Gazzaniga (Ed.), *The cognitive neurosciences*, (pp. 253–267). MA: Cambridge, MIT Press.

Kaas, J. H. (1990). The somatosensory system. In G. Paxinos (Ed.), *The human nervous system* (pp. 813–844). New York: Academic Press.

Kaas, J. H. (1993). The functional organization of somatosensory cortex in primates. *Annals of Anatomy, 175*, 509–518.

Kaas, J. H., & Pons, T. P. (1988). The somatosensory system of primates. In H. P. Steklis (Ed.), *Comparative primate biology: Vol. 4. Neurosciences* (pp. 421–468). New York: Alan R. Liss.

Krubitzer, L., Clarey, J., Tweedale, R., Elston, G., & Calford, M. (1995). A redefinition of somatosensory areas in the lateral sulcus of macaque monkeys. *Journal of Neuroscience, 15*, 3921–3939.

Mishkin, M. (1979). Analogous neural models for tactual and visual learning. *Neuropsychologia, 17*, 139–151.

Vallbo, A. B. (1995). Single-afferent neurons and somatic sensation in humans. In M. S. Gazzaniga (Ed.), *The cognitive neurosciences* (pp. 237–252). Cambridge, MA: MIT Press.

Jon H. Kaas

Behavioral and Functional Aspects

The hand is the main instrument by which we gain information about the environment through touch and with which we handle objects. This perceptual and manipulative capacity of the hand, referred to as haptics, combines touch and kinesthetic information coming from the muscles and joints. By means of haptic exploration alone, we are able to identify a large number of everyday objects relatively rapidly. It can also be shown that different haptic strategies are used for different purposes. If asked to identify the texture of an object, a person will lightly rub his or her fingertips, the most sensitive area of the hand, across the surface of the object. If asked to identify the form of an object, the person will try to envelop the object with the hand or run the hand around its outer edge.

Regional Differences in Touch

Although much of what we know about touch comes from studies conducted on the glabrous (hairless) skin of the hand, tactual perception is possible across the entire skin surface. When one considers the entire skin as the sense organ for touch, there are two observations that stand out. First, there is a lot of it, approximately 1.8 square meters for an adult human. Second, it is not uniformly sensitive. The variations in sensitivity depend to a large extent on how sensitivity is measured. For tactile stimuli, *sensitivity* generally refers to either absolute sensitivity or spatial sensitivity. With absolute sensitivity, one is concerned with the minimum stimulus intensity required to detect a stimulus reliably. How do different parts of the body compare in terms of the ability to detect weak tactile stimuli? The answer depends on the kinds of stimuli used to probe the skin. If a pressure stimulus is used, it is often generated by what are called von Frey hairs. The hair, nowadays more commonly a nylon bristle, is applied to the skin with sufficient force to bend the bristle. Beyond this point, additional force simply causes additional bending of the bristle without exerting more force on the skin. A set of calibrated stimuli is created by using bristles of different lengths and thicknesses. Sensitivity measured in this way reveals regional differences, but these differences are not always in agreement with our everyday observations. The lip and facial regions are very sensitive and the soles of the feet are relatively insensitive, as might be expected; however, by this same measure, the fingertips are no more sensitive than the chest. Absolute sensitivity can also be measured by using vibration, a repetitive, mechanical stimulus. When a 200-hertz vibratory stimulus is used, the fingertips are clearly the most sensitive area of the body and can detect displacements of less than 0.1 micron; however, with this type of stimulation, the facial region now ranks below the forearm and foot in sensitivity.

Measures of spatial sensitivity (spatial acuity) produce striking variations in sensitivity across the body surface, and these variations in sensitivity are in closer accord with our everyday observations. The traditional measure of spatial acuity is the two-point limen, also known as the two-point threshold. This is the distance between two points of stimulation on the skin that can be clearly identified as two points rather than as a single point. By this measure, the most sensitive regions are the lips and fingertips. The fingertip may be as much as 30 times more sensitive than the shoulder. It is instructive to hold a pair of toothpicks so that the tips are about 1 centimeter apart and lightly draw the tips down the arm across the wrist and the palm and on to the index fingerpad. Most people report that the apparent distance between the two points of stimulation widens as the points move from a region of less sensitivity, the arm, to a region of more sensitivity, the fingerpad.

As a reliable, and ultimately valid, measure of spatial acuity, the two-point limen has a number of flaws. Chief among these is the problem of maintaining a fixed criterion for subjects to respond "two." As the distance between two points is increased, a number of perceptual responses can be elicited, ranging from "an elongated single point" to a "dumbbell shape" to "two points touching one another" and so forth. It is difficult for observers, particularly when tested repeatedly, to select and maintain a particular point along this perceptual continuum. Fortunately, several new measures of spatial acuity have been proposed and tested that overcome these difficulties. These include detecting a gap in an otherwise solid edge or identifying the orientation of a grating consisting of alternating grooves and ridges. In the latter case, the subject must choose between two orientations of the grating, one of which is presented at right angles to the other. Because it is a forced-choice measure in which subjects must choose one of the two orientations, this type of task avoids the problem of the subject's criterion for responding "one point" or "two points." The gap-detection task shows the fingertips and lips to be very sensitive.

The variations in both absolute and spatial sensitivity are due to a number of factors, including the structure of the skin, the nature of the underlying receptors, and the number of receptors in a particular area of skin. The density of innervation is particularly important in determining spatial acuity, the rule being that the greater the density of innervation, the better the acuity.

Neural Basis of Touch

The joint study of psychophysical (perceptual) responses and neurophysiological recordings in touch has a long and fruitful history. Investigators have recorded neurophysiological responses of both peripheral and central neurons to tactile stimulation. Studies have been done with anesthetized monkeys and with awake, behaving monkeys. The same stimulus conditions used with the monkeys can then be used with human observers, and the human's ability to identify or discriminate the tactile stimulation can be measured. For example, spatial gratings, such as those described above, have been placed on a monkey's fingerpad, and the neural responses from peripheral neurons have been recorded. The same gratings have then been presented to human subjects to determine the minimum width of the grating that is resolvable by the subjects. Such studies have demonstrated how spatial information is encoded by the nervous system.

An even more direct method of determining how neural responses are related to perceptual experience is to measure single-unit neural responses in awake human subjects. The subjects report on their perceptual experiences while their neurophysiological responses are being recorded. That this step has been taken is remarkable. Volunteers have had microelectrodes inserted into the backs of their hands or forearms. No anesthesia is used, so the subject can help the experimenter determine when the microelectrode has penetrated a sensory nerve. Stimuli are then applied to the fingerpads, and the subject's responses, both verbal and neurophysiological, are recorded. The recording electrode can also be used as a stimulating electrode to determine what perceptual responses can be elicited by direct stimulation of the neuron.

The human and nonhuman studies have produced a reasonably coherent picture of the encoding of mechanical stimuli, at least in the peripheral nervous system. In the glabrous skin of humans, there appear to be four kinds of neurons sensitive to tactile stimuli. These neurons can be distinguished from one another on the basis of their responses to sustained mechanical stimuli—specifically, how rapidly they adapt to such stimuli (rapidly vs. slowly adapting) and the size of their receptive fields (large vs. small). Most touch-sensitive neurons respond vigorously when a mechanical stimulus is first applied to the skin. The rates of firing of some neurons decline rapidly; that is, they adapt rapidly to a sustained mechanical stimulus. Other neurons continue to respond to the sustained stimulus and are referred to as slowly adapting. Neurons with small receptive fields may respond when mechanical stimuli are presented to only a small area of skin, such as a few square millimeters on the fingerpad. Neurons with large receptive fields may respond to a stimulus presented anywhere on the hand. The major difference between the innervation of the glabrous skin of humans and that of monkeys is that one of the four types of neurons, the slowly adapting receptor with large receptive fields, is lacking in monkeys.

There appears to be some division of labor and some overlap of labor among the four types of neurons. As one might expect, the neurons with the small receptive fields convey information about spatial patterns such as the finer gratings, braille patterns, or raised letters. The sensitivity of the slowly adapting neurons with small receptive fields (SA-Is) matches closely the limits of sensitivity determined by psychophysical studies. These neurons are particularly sensitive to edges. In addition to conveying some spatial information, the rapidly adapting neurons with small receptive fields (RA-Is) respond vigorously to movement across the skin. The remaining two types of neurons have large receptive fields. The slowly adapting neurons with large receptive fields (SA-IIs) respond to a stretching of the skin, and the rapidly adapting neurons respond to vibratory stimuli. The rapidly adapting neuron has been closely linked with a particular receptor, the Pacinian corpuscle (PC), which is very sensitive to small vibratory movements of the skin.

A complex tactile stimulus such as might be produced by a person gripping a baseball is likely to produce neural activity in all four types of neurons. Information from the neurons is sent to particular areas of the brain, where the processes involved in identifying the object are carried out.

Sensory Substitution

One of the ways that touch reveals some of its capabilities and some of its limitations is when it is used to substitute for another sense. The most widely used sensory substitution system involving touch is braille. The braille system communicates print to blind people. Each braille cell consists of a series of one to six raised dots arranged in a 2-column by 3-row matrix. There are 2^6 (64) possible cells. In Grade I braille, 26 of the cells are assigned to letters of the alphabet. In Grade II braille, the remaining cells are assigned to short words and contractions. Blind users run their fingers, often the index fingers of the left and right hands, lightly over the braille cells. Although considerably slower than visual reading rates, braille reading rates can exceed 80 to 90 words per minute. Such rates indicate that the sense of touch is capable of rapid processing of spatial patterns. A person reading Grade I braille at a rate of 60 words per minute is processing a spatial pattern every 180 milliseconds.

There have been numerous attempts to use the skin as a speech aid for the profoundly deaf. Many of the devices that have been developed use small wearable vibrators. The vibrators can be worn on the wrist, arm, or fingertips. Speech information is converted to electrical signals that can be imposed on one or more vibrators. The result is a complex spatiotemporal tactile signal that can be used by a deaf person as an aid to lipreading. In one of the most remarkable uses of touch as a sensory aid, some deaf-blind individuals are able to understand speech by placing their hands on the face of a talker. The hand is placed so that the thumb rests lightly on the talker's lips and the remaining fingers are spread along the jaw and neck. The receiver feels the articulatory gestures of the talker, that is, the movement of the jaw, the air stream and movement of the lips, and the vibrations of the neck. Using this method, called "Tadoma," some deaf-blind individuals are able to understand somewhat slower than normal rates of speech.

Functional Significance of Thermal Sensitivity

Many of the properties of warm and cold sensitivity can be understood by considering their functional significance. Thermal sensations play an important role in several types of behavior, such as object identification, object avoidance, and thermal regulation. In identifying objects by means of touch, thermal cues work in conjunction with mechanical and kinesthetic cues to tell us what the object is made of, such as wood or plastic or metal. The thermal sensations are generated by contact between the skin and the object. The sensations are generally perceived as being part of the object. Thermal sensations tell us when objects are so hot or so cold that they can cause tissue damage and therefore should be avoided.

Thermal sensations are an important part of thermoregulation. Thermoregulation can take place either by autonomic means, such as sweating and vasoconstriction, or by behavioral means, such as putting on a coat, turning down the thermostat, or finding shade. For successful thermoregulation, it is important to have a measure of the overall warming or cooling of the body. A mechanism to respond to overall energy changes ought to integrate (summate) stimulus energy over both space and time. The threshold for detecting thermal stimuli should decrease as larger areas of skin are stimulated or as the duration of stimulation is increased. For example, with warm stimuli, spatial summation is nearly perfect up to areas as large as 60 square centimeters. That is, for every doubling in area, the intensity of the thermal stimulus can be halved and warmth can still be detected. Similarly, as the duration of a thermal stimulus is increased up to approximately 1 second, temporal summation is nearly perfect. If the duration is doubled from 100 to 200 milliseconds, the intensity required to detect a stimulus can be halved.

The ability to summate energy over large surfaces comes at a price: the inability to localize thermal stimuli accurately. In fact, the inaccuracy of localization of warmth is so great that subjects make a significant number of errors in deciding whether a warm stimulus has been presented to the chest or to the back. This observation may seem hard to believe and quite at odds with the first function of thermal regulation noted earlier: detecting the temperature of objects. We seem perfectly capable of telling whether the glass we are holding is cold or not because there is simultaneous tactile stimulation. Localization is poor when thermal stimulation occurs without tactile stimulation. When subjects erred in localizing a warm stimulus presented to the chest or back, the stimulation was provided by an infrared source that was not touching the skin. Localizing warm stimuli on the skin improves with higher levels of stimulation. In fact, localization is fairly accurate at temperatures that may produce pain. The adaptive significance is clear: at levels that may produce tissue damage, we can tell where that damage is likely to occur, even without corresponding tactile stimulation.

Thermal Adaptation

One of the most striking and revealing capacities of the thermal sense is the way it adapts to constant stimulation. Within a range of temperatures above and below normal skin temperature, the thermal sense shows complete adaptation. Suppose the skin temperature of your hand is 32°C and you place your hand in water that is 35°C. Initially the water will feel warm. Then the sensation of warmth will fade, and finally it will cease altogether. Adaptation is complete. (All sense modalities show adaptation, but few to the extent that the sensation ceases altogether.) What is particularly remarkable is that if a thermal stimulus of 34°C is presented to the adapted area of skin, the person will report that this temperature now feels cool, even though prior to adaptation, the same temperature feels warm. Physiological zero, the temperature to which the skin is adapted, has shifted. Stimuli above this temperature will feel warm; those below it, cool. This capacity is the basis for a well-known demonstration, the three-bowl experiment, attributed to the philosopher John Locke. In this demonstration three bowls are filled with water, one with water that feels warm, one with water that feels cool, and a third with tepid water that evokes neither warm nor cool sensations. A person places the left hand in the bowl of warm water, and the right hand in the bowl of cool water, and waits several minutes until the sensations of warmth and coolness disappear. Then both hands are placed in the tepid water. The left hand feels cool and the right hand feels warm. The philosopher's point: a demonstration of the difference between objective and subjective reality. The sensory psychologist's point: the thermal sense makes a poor thermometer. The skin can detect small changes in temperature, less than 0.01°C, but it is inaccurate in reporting absolute temperature.

Bibliography

Boring, E. G. (1942). *Sensation and perception in the history of experimental psychology* (pp. 463–522). New York: Appleton-Century-Crofts. The chapter on touch in this book provides a good historical background for understanding touch and thermal sensitivity.

Cole, J. O. (1995). *Pride and a daily marathon.* Cambridge, MA: MIT Press. This case history account describes the situation faced by a man who loses all sensation of light touch and kinesthesis below the neck. The book provides a vivid example of the importance of touch.

Franzén, O., Johansson, R., & Terenious, L. (Eds.). (1996). *Somesthesis and the neurobiology of the somatosensory cortex.* Basel: Birkhäuser Verlag. This volume consists of a series of papers covering recent work on touch, with an emphasis on neurophysiological studies.

Greenspan, J. D., & Bolanowski, S. J. (1996). The psychophysics of tactile perception and its peripheral physiological basis. In L. Kreuger (Ed.), *Handbook of perception and cognition: Vol. 7. Pain and touch* (pp. 25–103). San Diego, CA: Academic Press. Provides a good review of recent work in tactile perception, including an extensive list of references.

Heller, M. A., & Schiff, W. (1991). *The psychology of touch.* Hillsdale, NJ: Erlbaum. The best single source for an overview of touch and the skin senses. Chapters are grouped into sections covering sensory phenomena, development and intermodal relations, tactile pattern perception, and tactile perception and the visually impaired.

Johnson, K. O., & Hsiao, S. S. (1992). Neural mechanisms of tactual form and texture perception. *Annual Review of Neuroscience, 15,* 227–250. This review shows the close relationship between psychophysics and neurophysiology in understanding the encoding of spatial information.

Katz, D. (1989). *The world of touch.* (L. E. Kreuger, Trans.). Hillsdale, NJ: Erlbaum. (Original work published 1925.) A classic; describes much of the phenomenology of touch.

Loomis, J. M., & Lederman, S. J. (1986). Tactile perception. In K. Boff, L. Kaufman, & J. Thomas (Eds.), *Handbook of perception and human performance* (pp. 31-1–31-41). New York: Wiley. This chapter covers tactile and haptic pattern perception and kinesthetic perception.

Schiffman, H. R. (1996). *Sensation and perception: An integrated approach* (pp. 413–448). New York: Wiley. The chapter on the skin senses in this textbook provides a brief, clear overview of touch and thermal sensitivity.

Sherrick, C. E., & Cholewiak, R. W. (1986). Cutaneous sensitivity. In K. R. Boff, L. Kaufman, & J. P. Thomas (Eds.), *Handbook of perception and human performance: Sensory processes and perception* (pp. 12-1–12-58). New York: Wiley. This chapter covers touch, thermal sensitivity, and pain and provides summaries of the important psychophysical results in these areas.

Stevens, J. C., & Green, B. G. (1978). History of research on feeling. In E. C. Caterell & M. P. Friedman (Eds.), *Handbook of perception* (pp. 3–25). New York: Academic Press. This chapter provides a historical account of several theories of cutaneous sensitivity and a context for understanding contemporary work.

Summers, I. R. (Ed.). (1992). *Tactile aids for the hearing-impaired.* London: Whurr. The chapters cover topics ranging from basic sensory processes to the design of transducers to the effectiveness of various tactile aids for the hearing impaired.

James C. Craig

TRAINING. [*This entry comprises two articles. The first article provides a broad survey of the current training needs in psychology in general and across subdisciplines, with comparative reference to past requirements. The second article discusses unique training requirements in specific subdisciplines of psychology. See also* Team Training.]

An Overview

Preparation for a career in the practice of psychology requires graduate education in pertinent theories, methods, and facts of scientific psychology, integrated with training in the skills and values of professional service. Training is accomplished by many means, but the central feature of most training is supervised experience in the performance of professional activities. Trainees "learn by doing" under the guidance of qualified supervisors across a sample of settings in which professional work is done.

Efforts to train psychologists as practitioners began early in American psychology. In 1896, Lightner Witmer established a psychoeducational clinic at the University of Pennsylvania that provided services for children with learning disabilities, "defects of character," and other problems. At the same time, the clinic provided a situation in which students could learn the "clinical method" of child study. During the early twentieth century, similar clinics were established in other locations. Courses in clinical psychology, industrial psychology, educational psychology, vocational guidance, and other forms of applied psychology appeared increasingly in the curricula of psychology departments, and doctoral programs in clinical psychology, consulting psychology, and applied psychology were advertised by several universities.

Throughout this period, however, and indeed throughout the first half-century of psychology's existence, training for practice was limited and unsystematic. Until the 1940s, the clear and common goal of doctoral education in psychology was to prepare people for careers of scholarly research. Nowhere was preparation for practice conceived as a major aim of graduate study, and the scattered forms of supervised experience available to students interested in practice varied widely from one institution to another.

World War II and the Scientist-Practitioner Model

To an even greater extent than World War I, World War II accelerated the development of applied psychology. In the assessment and selection of personnel, design of equipment, treatment of psychiatric casualties, and other ways, psychology convincingly demonstrated its usefulness, and the groundwork was laid for fundamental change in the training of professional psychologists.

The changes were immediate, extensive, and profound. In 1946, the constitutional purpose of the American Psychological Association (APA) was extended from advancement of psychology "as a science" to advancement of psychology "as a science, as a profession, and as a means of promoting human welfare." The following year, 18 APA divisions were created, including several in various forms of professional and applied psychology. The need to assist 16 million war veterans in their return to civilian life led to the development of training programs in clinical and counseling psychology administered by the Veterans Administration (VA). These provided financial support and training facilities for students and required contractual partnerships between academic departments and the VA hospitals and clinics where much of the training took place. Further financial support for students and faculty was provided by training grants awarded through the National Institute of Mental Health. Within a short time, fully half of the graduate students in many psychology departments were in clinical programs. A request from VA officials for a list of programs qualified to provide clinical training led the APA to establish a system of program accreditation. The demand to specify curricula, the kinds and amounts of supervised experience, and other aspects of training required integration around a set of guiding principles. The principles that came to dominate doctoral training in clinical and counseling psychology immediately following World War II, and school psychology not long after, were articulated in the scientist-practitioner model of education.

During the war, a committee on clinical training chaired by David Shakow had proposed a standard program that began with basic education in scientific psychology, proceeded through practicum training and a mandatory internship, and concluded with a dissertation in empirical research. Emphasis on research was to be sustained in graduate education. The new clinicians would be scientist-practitioners, competent to practice the profession of the time but ever mindful of the need to test and improve their procedures and prepared to meet the need through scientific research.

National Training Conferences

In 1949, a conference on training in clinical psychology was convened in Boulder, Colorado. Leaders in American psychology endorsed and amplified the principles proposed by the Shakow committee. Since 1949, many other conferences, as listed in Table 1, have addressed issues in the training of professional psychologists.

The basic principles that guide the training of scientist-practitioners in clinical psychology were reaffirmed at the Chicago conference on clinical training in 1965 and reemphasized in the Gainesville conference on the scientist-practitioner model in 1990. The Thayer conference of 1954 has been described as school psychology's Boulder conference. In school psychology too, doctoral education was designed to produce scientist-practitioners, though the school rather than the clinic, hospital, counseling center, or practitioner's office was to be the main setting for practice and research. A distinctive role, with preparation at the master's degree

TRAINING: An Overview. Table 1. National training conferences

Date	Name	Scope
1949	Boulder	Clinical psychology
1951	Northwestern	Counseling psychology
1954	Thayer	School psychology
1955	Stanford	Psychology in mental health
1958	Miami	Graduate education in psychology
1964	Peabody	Internships in school psychology
1964	Greyston	Counseling psychology
1965	Chicago	Clinical psychology
1973	Vail	Professional psychology
1980	Spring Hill	School psychology
1981	Olympia	School psychology
1987	Utah	Graduate education in psychology
1987	Georgia	Counseling psychology
1987	Gainesville	Internships in professional psychology
1990	Gainesville	Scientist-practitioner model
1995	Villanova	Law and psychology

level, was defined for school psychological examiners. The distinction was maintained 25 years later at the Spring Hill symposium and the Olympia conference on the future of psychology in the schools.

The scientist-practitioner model has also prevailed in defining the identity of doctoral-level counseling psychologists, from the founding conference at Northwestern University in 1951 through the Greyston conference of 1964 to the Georgia conference in 1987. All the conferences in counseling psychology have been concerned with distinctions between counseling and clinical psychology, with general consensus that counseling psychology places greater emphasis on career development and positive mental health in people who are functioning relatively well, as against the more severe psychopathologies of major concern to clinical psychologists. The distinction between doctoral-level counseling psychologists and master's degree–level practitioners in marriage and family counseling, educational counseling, and other specialties has also concerned conference participants.

Psychologists who practice in the workplace have participated in nearly all the national conferences, but leaders in industrial/organizational psychology have elected to address issues in education and training through their own committees and task forces rather than through conferences with broader representation. Terminal master's degree programs for the practice of applied psychology in business and industry have been established in many universities, generally following guidelines approved by the Society of Industrial and Organizational Psychology. At the doctoral level, the dominant emphasis on applied research has been vigorously sustained.

Requirements for internship training have posed several dilemmas for educators of professional psychologists. The first internships in clinical psychology were in medical settings, and most still are. Resulting authority and identity problems have been resolved in various ways, with varying degrees of success. The need to develop school-based internship opportunities for school psychologists was a major topic of the Peabody conference of 1964. Many issues in internship training across the entire field of professional psychology were addressed in the national conference of 1987, though the most frequently noted resolution of that conference—to extend internship requirements from 1 year to 2—has not been widely accepted.

Two conferences, in Miami, Florida, in 1958 and Salt Lake City, Utah, in 1987, were devoted to the entire field of graduate education in psychology. At the Utah conference, a compromise between the conflicting needs for academic autonomy in training for research and more closely controlled specificity in training for practice was attained. The conference endorsed an APA-specified core curriculum in preparation for licensable practice, but freed departments to define their own curricula for students not preparing for careers of professional service. Between the time of the Miami and Utah conferences, a considerable number of professional schools had been established. Many were free-standing schools, unaffiliated with universities. Concern over the quality of education in the free-standing schools was widespread. In the resolutions of the Utah conference, the concept of direct education for practice was approved, but closer liaison between free-standing schools and universities was encouraged, with the expectation that many free-standing schools would eventually affiliate with universities.

The conferences in Chicago in 1965 and Vail, Colorado, in 1973 were more contentious than the others. In both the Chicago and Vail conferences, the most controversial issue was that of complementing scientist-practitioner programs with others expressly designed to prepare psychologists for careers of practice. In Chicago, a proposal for programs in professional psychology leading to the doctor of psychology (Psy.D.) degree was not endorsed by the majority of participants, though some "recognition" of the concept was offered, and a Psy.D. program was subsequently developed at the University of Illinois. In Vail, resolutions recognizing professional schools and the Psy.D. degree, along with resolutions affirming continued support for scientist-practitioner programs leading to the Ph.D. degree, were approved.

The Practitioner Model

Before 1973, only three Psy.D. programs and a small number of professional schools were in operation. In 1997, the National Council of Schools and Programs of Professional Psychology (NCSPP) listed 45 member institutions, all devoted to direct education for the practice of psychology and nearly all awarding the Psy.D. degree.

Soon after it was founded in 1976, the NCSPP began its own series of conferences to examine the broad issues as well as the particulars of education and training in professional psychology. By 1997, 11 conferences had taken place. These began with the definition of basic issues and a collaborative self-study of all the member schools and programs in the organization. Later conferences defined a generic core of competencies required for the effective practice of psychology, the curricular requirements for each form of competence, elements of clinical training, and cultural changes required for the advance of ethnic and gender diversity in psychology. Two "meta-conferences" were designed to synthesize and disseminate the myriad issues considered and resolutions adopted in the previous conferences. These resulted in a journal article defining the NCSPP's practitioner model of education and a book defining the standards for the education of professional psychologists. The second meta-conference also initiated a self-study of member organizations comparable with the study done some 15 years before but advantaged by the larger size and ensuing experience of the constituency. Conferences continue on an annual basis.

Organizations Concerned with Professional Training

Besides the NCSPP, many other organizations have a stake in training for practice in psychology. The Council of University Directors of Clinical Psychology is primarily concerned with the education of scientist-practitioners in the clinical specialty. Comparable councils of directors monitor doctoral training in counseling and school psychology. Heads of psychology departments in the Council of Graduate Departments of Psychology are also concerned with professional training, especially in relation to training for research and the linkage between clinical programs and research programs in personality, social psychology, human development, and other areas of graduate study.

The practice and education directorates of the APA serve the interests of practitioners and educators in psychology, and the boards of professional and educational affairs guide policy in their respective areas. The APA Committee on Accreditation reviews all doctoral programs and internships in professional psychology, annually publishes a list of approved programs, and periodically reexamines policies and procedures of program accreditation. The APA divisions of clinical, counseling, school, and industrial/organizational psychology are strongly concerned with policies of education and training in their respective fields, as are divisions of such newer specialties as health psychology and clinical neuropsychology.

Beyond the APA, the American Association of Psychology Internship Centers is especially devoted to the development of national standards for internship training, and the American Association of State Psychology Boards is concerned with the promulgation of national standards for licensure and certification to practice psychology, including training requirements.

Further Perspectives

Focus on American psychology in this account does not mean that training for practice in psychology does not occur elsewhere. Doctoral-level training in professional psychology is active in Norway, for instance, and is advancing in several other European countries. However, in countries other than Canada and the United States, most training for professional service in psychology takes place at the master's degree level, and preparation for careers of research is not expected of practitioners, as it is for American scientist-practitioners.

Whatever happens internationally, the systematic examination of training is likely to continue in America, where new roles for psychologists are continually forming and patterns of training are changing apace. For example, the advent of managed health care in the United States, with attendant demands for cost containment and accountability, has spurred the development of brief forms of clinical treatment and improved documentation of the effectiveness of clinical procedures of all kinds. Increasing recognition of the importance of behavioral factors in heart disease, cancer, and other ailments has led psychologists to form partnerships with cardiologists, oncologists, and other medical specialists in the prevention and treatment of various forms of illness. The move beyond mental health to more broadly conceived health care requires different emphases in training from those that have traditionally prevailed.

Moves to secure legal privileges for psychologists to prescribe psychotropic drugs have already led to model training programs for "prescribing psychologists," and further actions along these lines seem likely. Advances in forensic psychology have encouraged partnerships with the legal profession and the increasing availability of joint programs in psychology and law. A national conference was held at Villanova University's law school in 1995 to evaluate and improve training models in law and psychology. From the start, school psychologists have worked with teachers and other school personnel. Closer engagement with special education was one of the major themes of the Olympia conference on the future of psychology in the schools. Some training in business and management has long been involved in the preparation of industrial/organizational psychologists, and psychologists are increasingly employed on the faculties of business schools. As society changes and psychology develops, the training of psychologists continues to evolve.

To a mythical observer unbounded by time and place, however, the constancies might seem more impressive than the changes, and similarities more striking than differences. Educators in all the specialties of professional psychology agree that comprehensive preparation for practice requires education at the doctoral level. Despite the variations in setting, client population, and specific technique, all professional psychologists base their practices on a common core of psychological knowledge and learn comparable strategies of assessment and change. All the major specialties now claim to prepare practitioners to perform their inquiries and offer their ministrations at the individual, group, and organizational levels. In practitioner models and scientist-practitioner models alike, the core of professional service is conceived as disciplined inquiry. As professional psychology evolves, differentiation into further specialties will inevitably occur, new roles will form, and special training for each will be required, but the common core that has developed throughout the past century seems likely to remain.

Bibliography

Freedheim, D. K. (1992). *History of psychotherapy: A century of change.* Washington, DC: American Psychological Association. Extensive coverage of education and training, as well as theory, practice, and research in psychotherapy.

French, J. L. (1990). History of school psychology. In T. B. Gutkin & C. R. Reynolds (Eds.), *The handbook of school psychology* (2nd ed., pp. 3–20). New York: Wiley.

Gelso, C. J., & Fretz, B. R. (1992). *Counseling psychology.* New York: Holt, Rinehart, & Winston. A college text on counseling psychology with thorough coverage of training issues.

Katzell, R. A., & Austin, J. T. (1992). From then to now: The development of industrial-organizational psychology in the United States. *Journal of Applied Psychology, 77,* 803–835.

Peterson, D. R. (1997). *Educating professional psychologists: History and guiding conception.* Washington, DC: American Psychological Association. Conceptual statements and historical accounts by the founder of the first doctor of psychology program in the United States.

Peterson, R. L., Peterson, D. R. & Abrams, J. C. (in press). *Standards for the education of professional psychologists.* Washington, DC: American Psychological Association. A comprehensive statement of training standards as endorsed by the National Council of Schools and Programs of Professional Psychology.

Peterson, R. L., Peterson, D. R., Abrams, J. C., & Stricker, G. (1997). The National Council of Schools and Programs of Professional Psychology educational model. *Professional Psychology: Research and Practice, 28,* 373–386.

Phillips, B. N. (1990). *School psychology at a turning point: Ensuring a bright future for the profession.* San Francisco: Jossey-Bass. A college text in school psychology with thorough coverage of training issues.

Reisman, J. M. (1991). *A history of clinical psychology* (2nd ed.). New York: Hemisphere.

Donald R. Peterson

Special Training Issues

Psychology is a science, an academic discipline, and a learned profession. As a result, advanced education is necessary to participate in the field at any level. Courses in psychology are offered on the undergraduate level leading to a bachelor's degree and on the graduate level leading to a master's or doctoral degree. Bachelor's degrees offered in psychology are generally the bachelor of arts (B.A.) or bachelor of science (B.S.) degree. Likewise, the master's degree is typically a master of arts (M.A.) or master of science (M.S.), though in some universities training in psychology may also be offered through a master of education (M.Ed.) degree program. Doctoral degrees in psychology include the doctor of philosophy (Ph.D.), doctor of psychology (Psy. D.), or in some universities, doctor of education (Ed.D.).

The use of the doctor of philosophy degree for psychology is based on historical custom dating back to times when philosophy was the generic discipline for all knowledge. It does not imply that psychology is a branch of philosophy any longer, since the field has been recognized as a science for over 100 years. Psychology is the science that studies human behavior. The Psy.D. degree was created because there was a desire by some to have a degree that prepared recipients for *applied* professional careers. The Ph.D. degree is an academic degree in most fields, indicating that the person holding the degree has been trained as a scholar-researcher rather than a practitioner. The use of education degrees (M.Ed. and Ed.D.) for psychology training occurs because there is much overlap between the fields and it is sometimes more convenient or efficient at a particular university to offer the training in the education department, particularly if it is related to the field of educational psychology (e.g., school or counseling psychology). In reality, the degrees are largely interchangeable. Many applied practitioners earn a Ph.D degree, many Psy.D. holders find careers in academic research work, and people with Ed.D. degrees may be found in a wide range of positions beyond traditional school or educational settings.

The vast range of inquiry encompassed by psychology makes it possible for individuals with widely different interests and backgrounds to participate in various ways (Woods & Wilkinson, 1987). Psychologists are involved in basic as well as applied research; teaching from high school through graduate university programs; provision of services including school, counseling, community, and clinical; employment and consultation in business-industrial-governmental settings; and social action programs, to name but a few (National Science Foundation, 1986).

Some psychologists developed their interest in psychology early on as a result of various personal experiences or through a course in psychology at the high-school or college level. Others, however, developed their interest much later. Many psychologists entered the field after successful careers in other fields, because they became interested in knowing more about human behavior.

Graduate Training

Different areas of psychology require different programs of study. The basic academic areas of psychology emphasize research skills. Students in these areas have extensive training in research methods and statistics as well as in related courses from other scientific areas such as math, chemistry, physiology, and so forth. They also generally spend a considerable amount of time working with faculty on projects in research laboratories.

Students specializing in professional areas of psychology first complete basic core courses in academic and experimental areas of psychology, after which they take a number of specialized courses to prepare them for their later professional work.

There are four major areas of professional psychology: clinical, counseling, school, and organizational-industrial. All four require practical experience along with the basic classroom work (Matthews & Walker, 1997). For example, students in clinical psychology complete intensive courses in psychopathology, psychotherapy, personality assessment, medical psychology, neuropsychology, and related areas to prepare them to work with patients who have significant emotional disturbance. Their course work is then supplemented by clerkships or practicum experiences working under supervision in hospitals and clinics to give them real-life experiences in their chosen specialty as they progress in their training.

Often, students in counseling and clinical psychology undergo very similar programs of study, and there is much overlap in the employment opportunities when they graduate. However, it is customary to think of counseling psychologists as working with less disturbed clients and placing more emphasis on maximizing personal functioning in individuals rather than dealing with clinical populations. Thus, counseling psychology students often take additional course work in vocational testing, educational assessment, career guidance, and short-term interventions. Their pattern of practical experience is similar to that described for clinical psychology students, except that the settings for their work are more likely to be in outpatient clinics and in school or college counseling centers rather than in hospitals.

School psychologists work primarily in elementary and secondary schools. Students in these programs take considerably more course work in education than other psychology students. They must be familiar with educational theory, classroom management, all areas of intellectual–academic assessment, learning disabilities, brief counseling, and consultation. In many states they are required to teach in an actual classroom for a specified number of years to qualify as a school psychologist. Thus, they often must take sufficient courses in their undergraduate years to become certified as teachers. Their practicum experiences are obtained in school counseling and guidance centers.

Students in organizational and industrial psychology receive extensive training in research methods since they are often involved in research to improve functioning and performance for the company they are employed by or in basic market research on products or customers. They also take courses in group dynamics, leadership, management business decision making, consultation, and related areas since their work is often related to management. While they do not have as many practical experiences as other professional psychology students, they generally have some on-the-job experiences in industry as part of their preparation.

The practical experiences for students in training for professional fields of psychology generally follow a pattern of increasing complexity and responsibility as one moves through the program. Their first experiences might include observing an experienced person doing an assessment or some form of therapy. They might then administer some simple assessment instruments or do an interview under close supervision. This would take place in their first year of graduate school. In the succeeding years they learn to administer more complicated assessment procedures, conduct more intensive interviews, and see patients or clients for brief treatment. All of this is under careful supervision. When possible, they would sit in as an observer or cotherapist during assessment and treatment before they attempted it on their own. A common practice is to use advanced students to help train beginning students by allowing the beginning students to observe the advanced students and by having the advanced students sit in with them on their first experiences. Faculty members and experienced professionals in the community are often involved as well. A common way to accomplish this is to have teams that work together, with the team composed of one or two beginning students, one or two advanced students, and a faculty or community supervisor.

In contrast to many of the other health-care professions, training in professional psychology involves a much higher emphasis on research, scholarship, and development of academic skills. In addition to the large number of courses dealing with research that students complete, typically they are also involved in numerous practical research experiences. Many of their courses require them to complete scholarly projects involving laboratory and/or library research. In addition, many students find employment during their training as laboratory research assistants for faculty who are engaged in ongoing research programs. Beyond that, completion of degree programs in psychology typically requires completion of one or more original research projects that form the basis for a thesis or dissertation. A thesis is written for completion of the master's degree and a dissertation for a doctoral degree. The thesis is generally equivalent to an extensive scholarly article or a short book. The dissertation generally is the length of a book. The research and writing of the thesis and the dissertation are carefully supervised by a faculty member known as the major professor for the student. This work is also supervised by a committee, chaired by the major professor, composed of other faculty in the student's department and from other departments in the university. Upon completion of each of these projects, the student presents his or her work to the faculty committee and is required to the defend the methods employed and conclusions drawn in the work.

It is also quite common, as a part of the training in psychology, for the student to have teaching and supervision experience. Students may begin by performing duties as a teaching assistant to a faculty member. Their duties might involve grading papers, tutoring students who need extra help, leading a group discussion with a small group of students from the class, and giving an occasional lecture. Later on, they may be given responsibility for teaching a course on their own to undergraduate students. With respect to supervision, advanced students, depending on their specialty, are frequently employed as supervisors for beginning students who are conducting research, teaching, or providing clinical services. This supervision is under the guidance of senior faculty.

Students in psychology are carefully evaluated at every stage of their training. These evaluations include regular classroom exams; ratings of their performance in practicum experiences and/or research work; oral examinations on their thesis and dissertation; and comprehensive written examinations over all of their work followed by an in-depth oral examination generally halfway through their program, in connection with receipt of their master's degree, and again at the end of their training program prior to being awarded the doctoral degree.

Internship

At the conclusion of the on-campus training, which generally takes between 3 and 5 years, students in most professional areas of psychology do a 1-year supervised internship off campus where they work full time in an applied setting. There they perform professional duties, attend advanced seminars, and receive additional supervision in development of their skills. For professional psychologists who wish to be licensed to offer therapeutic services to the public, an additional year of supervised practice is required in most states.

Since professional psychologists offer services directly to the public, they must adhere to the highest standards of ethics and practice. All professional training programs are required to cover ethical principles and behavior as part of the training. In addition, the extensive supervised experiences described above are used to teach ethical practices and to evaluate the suitability of the student to perform as an independent professional. Many students decide or are advised that such a career is not suitable for them and opt to pursue other career options. However, it is even more common for students in academic research areas to decide that they wish to become licensed as professional psychologists. To do this, they must return to university training and complete all courses needed to be licensed as a professional in whatever area they have chosen.

Postdoctoral Training

There has been a significant increase in postdoctoral training in all areas of psychology. Individuals with research interests are able to avail themselves of a wide variety of opportunities to serve as research associates to more senior investigators. The senior investigator generally is able to support one or more recent graduates by employing them on grants held by the senior investigator. Graduates in professional areas are able to locate a large number of opportunities to do research, to increase their clinical skills, or to develop skill in a specialty area while employed as staff in clinical service settings. For the academically inclined psychologist postdoctoral research experience prepares them for the competition for employment in universities by enabling them to increase their research skills and publish some of their research, which is generally required to obtain a university faculty position. They also develop additional skills in such areas as grant writing and research administration.

With respect to psychologists headed for a professional career, since most states require a year of supervision beyond receipt of the doctoral degree and internship in order to be licensed, postdoctoral training is often an attractive way to complete this year in preparation for licensure. There is discussion among educators and directors of graduate training programs about the possibility of making a 2-year residency program a requirement for completion of the doctoral degree as opposed to the one year of internship that is currently required.

Continuing Education

There is increased emphasis on continuing education for psychologists after they have completed their university training. Most states currently require a specified number of hours of continuing education each year in order for a professional psychologist to remain licensed. Increasingly, requirements for this training specify that a certain number of the hours be in specific areas such as child abuse or ethics. This and additional training is intended to ensure that psychologists continually update their skills and are able to offer the highest quality of care for those they serve.

Currently there is a movement in professional psychology to obtain the necessary training and legal status to prescribe medication for patients treated by the psychologist. This movement is in response to the fact that research has indicated that optimal care for patients with certain disorders must include a combination of medication as well as psychotherapy. Obtaining prescription privileges will require intensive training either as a part of a doctoral training program or as a postdoctoral specialty. It will also require changes in the laws governing the practice of psychology. Several psychologists trained and practicing in military settings have already been granted prescription writing privileges.

Psychology is a broad field involving research, practice, education, administration, and social advocacy. It has been a dynamic and rapidly expanding field for over 100 years. Most projections regarding the future indicate that it will continue to be a field with extensive career opportunities (Sternberg, 1997). New and exciting innovations will be necessary and can be anticipated in training for psychology. Psychologists' understanding of human behavior and the learning process uniquely suits them to lead in educational innovation.

In 1993, 3,651 psychology doctoral degrees were awarded (2,236 to women and 1,415 to men). The largest number of doctoral degrees each year are in clinical psychology. Starting salaries for new doctoral-level psychologists in 1995 averaged from around $35,000 to $61,000. The higher salaries were generally in applied service provision positions (business, industry, hospitals, clinics, etc.), whereas the lower salaries were generally in academic and educational areas (Wicherski & Kohout, 1997).

Bibliography

Matthews, J. R., & Walker, C. E. (1997). *Basic skills and professional issues in clinical psychology*. Boston: Allyn & Bacon.

National Science Foundation. (1986). *Characteristics of recent science/engineering graduates: 1984*. Washington, DC: Author.

Sternberg, R. J. (Ed.). (1997). *Career paths in psychology: Where your degree can take you*. Washington, DC: American Psychological Association.

Wicherski, M., & Kohout, J. (1997). *1995 doctorate employment survey*. Washington, DC: American Psychological Association.

Woods, P. J., & Wilkinson, C. S. (1987). *Is psychology the major for you?* Washington, DC: American Psychological Association.

C. Eugene Walker

TRAITS. *See* Personality Traits.

TRANCE. *See* Hypnosis; *and* Non-Western Therapies.

TRANSFERENCE is a central construct in psychoanalytic theory. Over time, its multiple revisions of meaning reflect the history of psychoanalytic thought. This history begins with Freud. Closely related to his discovery of the unconscious and his development of the first versions of psychoanalytic theory and practice was his identification of the phenomenon of transference (Freud, 1912/1959). In the effort to probe the unconscious mind, Freud found that his patients' responses to him were, in many cases, distortions based on their earliest experiences with significant others, usually parents. While initially these distortions were viewed as disruptive of the analysis, they came to be seen as invaluable tools and avenues for understanding the unconscious residues of early experience. More importantly, these transferences, defined as distortions of unconscious feelings, thoughts, and behaviors from the past that are projected onto the present figure of the analyst, became central to psychoanalytic cure. Interpretation of transference was the means by which patients were enabled to relinquish the pathological past that was embedded in their unconscious minds. Similarly, interpretation and resolution of these transferences, when they deepened, intensified, and became concentrated on the analyst, in what is referred to as the transference neurosis, became the ultimate aim of a psychoanalysis (Greenson, 1967).

The meaning of transference in what is frequently referred to as classical or structural theory is closely entwined with the vicissitudes of instinctual development elaborated in the metapsychology of this theory. Vicissitudes of instinctual or drive development refer to the many possible pathways and complications that can arise as the instincts, especially the sexual instinct, evolve in the course of personality development. A range of transferences have been described, both positive and negative, based on diverse early object figures, not only parents, and deriving from different stages of psychosexual development, such as an Oedipal paternal transference.

However, as classical theory developed, so, too, did an understanding of the significance of object relationships (early significant interpersonal relationships) in development, thus ushering in a second phase of psychoanalytic theory, what might be called the object relational phase, and the deepening and transformation of the meaning of transference. In object relational theory, broadly construed to span many different theoretical systems, from Klein to Fairbairn and Winnicott (Greenberg & Mitchell, 1983), transference is defined as a distortion of an early object relationship projected onto the analyst, with the early object ties of greater significance than early instinctual drive-based development. Thus, the tendency of a patient to experience the analyst as a cold and distant figure from an object relational perspective could be a transference indicative of that patient's early experience with a cold and distant parental figure.

The object relational phase is particularly important for the development of the meaning of transference in that the role of interpersonal experience in the shaping of the human mind, rather than the vicissitudes of drive development, is central. Once the importance of interpersonal experience in early development is acknowledged, a consideration of its importance at later stages of development becomes possible. In this phase, the meaning of transference was modified to reflect a response of the patient to the analyst that includes both a distortion from the past and a response to the personality of the analyst in the present. Thus, the analyst who is perceived by the patient as cold and distant might have had cold and distant parents or other early object figures, and also might be responding to cold and distant elements in the analyst's personality. This shift in contemporary psychoanalytic theory is referred to as a shift from a one-person psychology (in which the analyst can be an objective observer and interpreter of the patient's transferences from the past) to a two-person psychology, in which the patient's responses to the analyst are always some mixture of a distortion from the past and a response to the present relationship with the analyst (Gill, 1994).

Gill (1994) emphasized that attention needs to be paid to the intrapsychic components of both aspects of the transference, that is, the innate and the experiential. While the patient may, in fact, be experiencing the analyst as cold and distant due to aspects of the personality that she or he brings into the analytic situation, the experience of the analyst as cold and distant is rooted in the patient's intrapsychic modes of experiencing.

The development of self psychology by Kohut (1984) marks a third phase in psychoanalytic theory with significant implications for the meaning of transference. Similar to the discovery by Freud of the classical meaning of transference in his exploration of the unconscious mind, Kohut, using the empathic mode of inquiry, identified a constellation of transferences in his explorations of the self-experience of patients. These transferences, typically referred to as selfobject transferences, reflect deprivations in the early selfobject ties between the child and early objects. These ties refer to early needs in the development of the self to be mirrored, to idealize, and to be together with the object, hence the descriptors of merging, idealizing, and twinship selfobject transferences. Rather than viewing these transferences as distortions from the past, the selfobject transferences indicate the unfulfilled needs of patients, due to their pasts, that become active in the present relationship with the analyst. In the selfobject transferences the past emerges in the present. In self psychology, the empathic mode of inquiry shifts the meaning of transference from a distortion of the present by the past to the past as present in the analytic encounter. The presence of these transferences provides an opportunity for the patient to experience and develop the kinds of empathic selfobject ties necessary for the maintenance, coherence, and stability of the self. Rather than resolving these transferences, the goal is to experience them, understand them, and develop the capacity for increasingly mature selfobject relationships with both the analyst and other figures in patients' lives (Ornstein & Ornstein, 1996).

The meanings of transference are further clarified by distinguishing it from two other major constructs describing the dimensions of the therapeutic relationship, the real relationship and the working, or therapeutic, alliance. The real relationship refers to that between the therapist and patient, based on the constellation of personality characteristics and attributes that each brings to the therapeutic encounter (Gelso & Hayes, 1998). In the early classical epoch, the real relationship had little to do with the therapeutic action of analysis. The analyst was considered a blank screen in the analytic situation upon which the patient projected his or her transferences. The real relationship stood apart from this process.

In its clear separation of transference from the real relationship, the idea of the analyst as a blank screen bears some resemblance to the selfobject transferences of self psychology. To the extent that the analyst fulfills the early selfobject needs of the patient, the real relationship between analyst and patient is separate and irrelevant to the therapeutic action. That is, the analyst's ability to fulfill the selfobject needs of the patient is critical to the therapeutic action in self psychology. The real relationship between patient and analyst is distinct from this process. However, most contemporary self psychologists are similar to the object relational theorists in emphasizing that the selfobject transferences are codetermined by the patient and the analyst, thereby implicating the real relationship in the transference. Since many contemporary classical or structural theorists also subscribe more or less to a two-person psychology, for most contemporary analysts of diverse theoretical persuasions the real relationship is intertwined with the transference.

At the extreme, the real relationship and the transference are merged or become indistinguishable by those who emphasize the interactional, relational, and intersubjective nature of the psychoanalytic encounter in the present (Stolorow, Bradshaft, & Atwood, 1987). Instead of transference, such theorists tend to refer to the patient's organizing activity in assimilating the present to the past, or emphasize the significance of the therapeutic interaction in the present with less attention to the transference.

While the meaning of the real relationship and transference are intertwined in contemporary analytic theory, the meaning of the working or therapeutic alliance is more stable, more distinguishable from transference, and has gradually attracted more attention, particularly from researchers (Gelso & Hays, 1998). Based on the distinction between an observing and experiencing self, or ego, the working alliance refers to the motivation to engage in the analytic relationship, with adherence to and belief in its goals, methods, and techniques, and the development of an emotional bond between the analyst and patient (Gelso & Hays, 1998). While this aspect of the relationship between the analyst and patient has been referred to as both the working and the therapeutic alliance, use of the term *working* best captures the fact that it is this aspect of the relationship that has most to do with the commitment by both parties to the work of the analysis.

Finally, while the meanings of transference have arisen predominantly in the literature on psychoanalysis and psychoanalytic psychotherapy, the meanings of transference have had an impact far beyond these narrow confines. Transference is acknowledged as ubiquitous in human interactions. Its meanings have provided a basis for a life-span developmental psychology of the self (Galatzer-Levy & Cohler, 1993) and have been identified as critical in a theoretical consideration of the adaptive design of the human psyche (Slavin & Kriegman, 1992). The role of transference in counseling and short-term dynamic psychotherapy is recognized. Attempts to study the role of transference in a range of therapeutic encounters promises to further expand and elucidate its meanings (Gelso & Hayes, 1998).

[*See also* Countertransference; Psychoanalysis, *article on* Psychoanalytic Psychotherapies; *and* Psychotherapy, *article on* Research.]

Bibliography

Freud, S. (1959). The dynamics of transference. In E. Jones (Ed.) & J. Riviere (Trans.), *Collected papers* (Vol. 2, pp. 312–322). New York: Basic Books. (Original work published 1912.) Describes the early foundational understanding of transference.

Galatzer-Levy, R. M., & Cohler, B. J. (1993). *The essential other: A developmental psychology of the self.* New York: Basic Books. Bases a life-span developmental psychology on an expanded understanding of the self-object transferences.

Gelso, C. J., & Hayes, J. E. (1998). *The psychotherapy relationship: Theory, research, and practice.* New York: Wiley. Presents a current understanding of the dimensions of the psychotherapy relationship, including transference with emphasis on empirical support for these dimensions.

Gill, M. (1994). *Psychoanalysis in transition: A personal view.* Hillsdale, NJ: Analytic Press. Provides a comprehensive discussion of the complexities of the intrapsychic and interpersonal components of transference.

Greenberg, J. R., & Mitchell, S. A. (1983). *Object relations in psychoanalytic theory.* Cambridge, MA: Harvard University Press. Reviews contemporary theoretical perspectives in psychoanalysis in light of the tension between object relational and instinctual drive-related theories.

Greenson, R. R. (1967). *The technique and practice of psychoanalysis* (Vol. 1). New York: International Universities Press. Considered to be a standard text that presents the principles of psychoanalytic practice according to classical theory.

Kohut, H. (1984). *How does analysis cure?* (A. Goldberg, Ed.). Chicago: University of Chicago Press. The last and most significant formulation of self-psychology by Kohut, the founder of self-psychology.

Ornstein, A., & Ornstein, P. H. (1996). Some general principles of psychoanalytic psychotherapy: A self-psychological perspective. In L. E. Lifson (Ed.), *Understanding therapeutic action: Psychodynamic concepts of cure* (pp. 87–102). Hillsdale, NJ: Analytic Press. Explains the therapeutic role of the self-object transferences.

Slavin, M. O., & Kriegman, D. (1990). *The adaptive design of the human psyche: Psychoanalysis, evolutionary biology, and the therapeutic process.* New York: Guilford Press. Presents a theory of the evolutionary and adaptive nature of human functioning in which transference plays a central role.

Stolorow, R., Brandshaft, B., & Atwood, G. (1987). *Psychoanalytic treatment: An intersubjective approach.* Hillsdale,

NJ: Analytic Press. Describes an intersubjective position that negates or blurs the distinction between the intrapsychic and the interpersonal.

Mary Sue Richardson

TRANSPERSONAL PSYCHOLOGY emerged in the late 1960s because of a growing concern that Western psychology and culture seemed to be overlooking some of the most crucial and meaningful dimensions of human experience. Psychoanalysis and behaviorism had focused primarily on pathology and behavior, thereby omitting the study of subjectivity, health and well-being, values, and meaning. Furthermore, there was a tendency to pathologize certain dimensions of experience such as spirituality.

Transpersonal psychology emerged as a separate discipline with the founding of the *Journal of Transpersonal Psychology* in 1969. This journal was launched by a group of psychologists who had been part of the humanistic psychology movement, including Abraham Maslow and Anthony Sutich. They felt that the humanistic approach did not adequately address the farther reaches of human nature. Maslow's work proved catalytic because of his finding that exceptionally psychologically healthy, self-actualizing individuals tended to have what he called peak experiences. These were spontaneous, ecstatic, unitive experiences, and those who experienced them were found to score significantly above average on a variety of measures of psychological well-being. These experiences were akin to the mystical experiences that have been highly valued across cultures and suggested that psychological health and development may include possibilities unknown to mainstream psychology. Transpersonal psychology expanded the field of psychological inquiry to investigate these possibilities.

Initially it was assumed that peak experiences were necessarily spontaneous and brief. However, when researchers turned their attention to contemplative practices and traditions, especially Asian ones, they found maps of a wide variety of such experiences, as well as psychologies and philosophies based on them. They also learned of techniques, such as meditation and yoga, designed to induce and sustain these experiences. Beyond self-actualization lay the potential of self-transcendence. The word *transpersonal* implied that it was possible to transcend and include personal concerns.

Gradually it became apparent that Western culture and psychology are what anthropologists call monophasic. That is, we value, and derive our wordview almost exclusively from, a single state of consciousness: our usual waking state. By contrast, *polyphasic* cultures and psychologies derive their worldview from multiple states, including waking, dreaming, and various contemplative states. One of the goals of transpersonal psychology was to expand the scope of Western psychology to encompass a polyphasic perspective.

Transpersonal experiences can be defined as experiences in which the sense of identity or self extends beyond (trans) the individual or personal to encompass wider and deeper aspects of humankind, life, psyche, and cosmos.

Transpersonal psychology is the psychological study of transpersonal experiences and their correlates, including the nature, varieties, causes, and effects of transpersonal experiences.

Developmental Perspective

An important organizing perspective, championed largely by the theorist Ken Wilber, is a developmental view. There is now broad agreement among psychologists that development proceeds through three major stages: preconventional, conventional, and postconventional, or prepersonal, personal, and transpersonal. We are born unsocialized and without a coherent sense of self and are then gradually acculturated to the conventional or personal stage. However, it is now clear that development can proceed beyond the conventional to transconventional or transpersonal stages. Examples include Maslow's metamotives, Lawrence Kohlberg's postconventional morality, Jane Loevinger's integrated self-sense, postformal operational cognition, and Fowler's universalizing faith. Based on his extensive cross-cultural survey of contemplative disciplines, Wilber argues that these psychologists are beginning to map transpersonal stages originally discovered by contemplatives and described in some of their philosophies. That is, contemporary Western psychology and ancient contemplative disciplines from around the world are beginning to intersect in their mapping of transpersonal development. Although transpersonal experiences can break through at any stage, they are more common and can be better integrated at higher developmental stages.

This developmental perspective has several important implications. First, it suggests that what has been called normality reflects an arbitrary, culturally determined form of developmental arrest. As Maslow (1968) summarized it, "What we call 'normal' in psychology is really a psychopathology of the average, so undramatic and so widely spread that we don't even recognize it ordinarily" (p. 16). Second, it suggests that transpersonal development is available to all of us and can be fostered.

Third, a developmental perspective reduces the risk of what Ken Wilber, a major transpersonal theorist, calls the pre/trans fallacy. This is the error of confusing prepersonal and transpersonal experiences. This error can take two forms. The first is reductionistic and involves pathologizing transpersonal experiences and regarding them as prepersonal. Freud, for example, made this error when he interpreted transpersonal experiences as expressions of infantile regression. The second type of pre/trans error occurs when prepersonal experiences are elevated and confused with transpersonal ones.

A transpersonal orientation does not commit anyone to specific interpretations of transpersonal experiences or to any particular metaphysics, doctrine, or philosophy. Rather, its investigation of subjective experiences allows them to be interpreted in different ways according to the context in which they may occur. In contrast to religion, which offers a particular creed, community, and code of ethics to the faithful, subjective spirituality and transpersonal experiences can be explored both within and outside of religious traditions.

Epistemology

A crucial factor determining the scope and subject matter of any psychology is its epistemology, that is, its methods for acquiring and assessing knowledge. Transpersonal researchers advocate an epistemological pluralism that includes scientific empiricism, intellectual analysis—especially philosophy and hermeneutics (the art of interpretation)—introspection, and contemplation. This is in contrast to many schools that focus on a single epistemology. For example, psychoanalysis emphasizes introspection, behaviorism focuses on empirical science, and yogic psychologies emphasize contemplation. Transpersonal psychology is thus empirical and scientific in the broad sense of acquiring knowledge based on experience and being open to verification and falsifiability.

To date the transpersonal disciplines stand alone in advocating an eclectic epistemology that includes both Eastern and Western science, philosophy, introspection, and contemplation and in seeking to integrate them into a comprehensive approach adequate for the full range of human experiences and possibilities. One result of this inclusive perspective is the suggestion that apparently conflicting psychological schools may address different perspectives, dimensions, and stages of experience and may therefore be partly complementary rather than mutually exclusive.

Areas of Interest

A wide range of topics is of interest to transpersonal psychologists. These include the nature of consciousness, alternate states such as dreams, lucid dreaming, and near-death experiences, as well as psychedelic, yogic, and meditative states. Transpersonal experiences, including emotions such as love and compassion and motivations such as altruism and service, are a focus, as are the contemplative practices that foster them. Spirituality and mysticism are regarded as important human dimensions to be studied, and there is considerable interest in applying transpersonal insights to clinical and social concerns.

Clinical Applications

Transpersonal perspectives have been applied in three main areas: psychotherapy, transpersonal developmental crises, and the understanding of psychopathology.

The goals of transpersonal therapy include traditional ones such as relieving symptoms of illness and addressing basic ego needs such as self-esteem and intimacy. However, in acknowledging a larger potential for psychological well-being and development, a transpersonal perspective offers individuals who are ready to do so the opportunity of working in an expanded context. By recognizing the value of transpersonal and spiritual experiences and yearnings, the individual can treat them appropriately as valuable opportunities for growth, rather than overlooking or pathologizing them, as sometimes happens with other approaches.

Clients who seek out transpersonal psychotherapy are often on a spiritual path. Work with such clients may involve a wide range of issues from unresolved Oedipal conflicts to understanding and integrating deep spiritual experiences. Existential issues, such as the confrontation with death, freedom, isolation, and authenticity, are a common focus.

Although transpersonal therapists are expected to be well grounded in traditional clinical skills, transpersonal therapy is oriented toward a growth model rather than a medical model of curing disease. As such, practitioners may employ the full range of traditional techniques as well as, where appropriate, a variety of intuitive, meditative, and yogic practices.

The second area of clinical application is developmental crises. Developmental crises may occur at any stage, and at transpersonal stages they are particularly common in people engaged in intensive spiritual practice. These crises have been called by many names, including *transpersonal crises* and *spiritual emergencies*.

Such crises may take a variety of forms, including the sudden upwelling of primitive psychodynamic conflicts, confrontation with existential issues of meaning and death, intense energetic experiences akin to those described in kundalini yoga, and powerful archetypal imagery. A distinguishing feature is that these experiences usually have significant spiritual elements. Clinical studies suggest that such crises may resolve best if the client is given an explanation of the condition as part of a developmental process and is supported in viewing it as an opportunity for learning.

Finally, transpersonal perspectives are now being applied to the understanding of psychopathology. Maslow (1968) was one of the first to suggest that we may sicken if our transpersonal potentials are not actualized. This sickness may take subtle forms, such as existential inauthenticity and Maslow's "metapathologies," such as meaninglessness, cynicism, and alienation. Other pathologies, such as addiction, may also have transpersonal and spiritual roots. This element is specifically addressed in Alcoholics Anonymous and other comparable groups. Carl Jung also pointed out that numinous spiritual experiences are instrumental in curing pathology.

Current Status

Transpersonal psychology has become an international, interdisciplinary movement with organizations in many countries and with related fields of transpersonal psychiatry, anthropology, sociology, social work, and ecology. In the United States, major resources for the field include the Association for Transpersonal Psychology and the *Journal of Transpersonal Psychology*, both located in Palo Alto, California. The Association for Transpersonal Psychology was formed in 1971 and continues to provide a forum for interdisciplinary discussion of transpersonal ideas. The Institute of Transpersonal Psychology, founded in 1975, also in Palo Alto, offers graduate programs in transpersonal psychology.

For a description of transpersonally oriented colleges and training programs, see *The Common Boundary Graduate Education Guide* (Bethesda, 1994). The Association for Transpersonal Psychology publishes an annual unscreened listing of schools and programs of variable quality.

Major theorists include Charles Tart, an American psychologist who has provided valuable models of states of consciousness, and Stanislav Grof and Christina Grof, who have pioneered a number of clinical applications. Stanislav Grof is a psychiatrist who was trained as a psychoanalyst in Czechoslovakia. Ken Wilber, an American scholar of wide-ranging inerests, has created a vast interdisciplinary synthesis of unprecedented scope. His book on transpersonal development, *The Atman Project* (Wheaton, Illinois, 1980), traces development from infancy through adulthood into transpersonal stages. Wilber has published numerous books in the field, and his theoretical work continues to expand. In a major scholarly work, *Sex, Ecology, and Spirituality: The Spirit of Evolution* (Boston, 1995), he provides a foundational map for interdisciplinary transpersonal studies.

Future work must include more extensive experimental investigation of transpersonal phenomena, better understanding of disciplines such as meditation and yoga, further integration with mainstream psychology, and more extensive training programs for transpersonal psychologists that foster traditional scientific and analytic skills along with contemplative disciplines.

Bibliography

Boorstein, S. (Ed.). (1997). *Transpersonal psychotherapy* (2nd ed. rev.). Albany: State University of New York Press. An anthology of widely diverse perspectives on clinical applications of transpersonal psychology.

Grof, S. (1988). *The adventure of self-discovery*. Albany: State University of New York Press. A far-reaching account and theoretical exploration of transpersonal experiences.

Maslow, A. (1968). *Toward a psychology of being*. New York: Van Nostrand. A classic text for both humanistic and transpersonal psychology.

Murphy, M., & Donovan, S. (1997). *The physical and psychological effects of meditation* (2nd ed.). Sausalito, CA: Institute of Noetic Sciences. A review of contemporary research from 1931 to 1996, with a comprehensive bibliography.

Scotton, B. W., Chinen, A. B., & Battista, J. R. (Eds.). (1996). *Textbook of transpersonal psychiatry and psychology*. New York: Basic Books. A wide range of contributors describe cases, practical techniques, outcomes, and risks of various interventions in the fields of transpersonal psychiatry and psychology.

Tart, C. (1983). *States of consciousness* (2nd ed.). El Cerrito, CA: Psychological Processes. This book describes one of the most comprehensive theories of states of consciousness.

Tart, C. (Ed.). (1992). *Transpersonal psychologies* (3rd ed.). New York: HarperCollins. An examination of spiritual traditions as applied to transpersonal psychologies.

Vaughan, F. (1995). *The inward arc: Healing in psychotherapy and spirituality* (2nd ed., rev.). Nevada City, CA: Blue Dolphin. An overview of transpersonal development and its facilitation that draws on both psychological and spiritual perspectives.

Walsh, R., & Vaughan, F. (Eds.). (1993). *Paths beyond ego: The transpersonal vision*. Los Angeles: Tarcher/Putnam. Fifty essays apply transpersonal thinking to individual growth, psychotherapy, meditation, dreams, science, ethics, philosophy, ecology, and service.

Wilber, K. (1996). *A brief history of everything*. Boston: Shambhala. A popular, easy-to-read synthesis of the major themes in *Sex, Ecology, Spirituality*, grounded in the physical, biological and human sciences, cosmology, anthropology, sociology, psychology, philosophy, ecology, and religious studies.

Wilber, K. (1996). *Eye to eye: The quest for the new paradigm* (3rd ed., rev.). Boston: Shambhala. Contains important discussion of the epistemological foundation of transpersonal disciplines, as well as essays on a variety of other topics.

Wilber, K. (1998). *The marriage of sense and soul: The integration of science and religion*. New York: Random House. An original and lucid perspective on the challenge of integrating science and religion.

Wilber, K., Engler, J., & Brown, D. (Eds.). (1986). *Transformations of consciousness: Conventional and contemplative perspectives on development*. Boston: New Science Library/Shambhala. A collection of theoretical and research papers on transpersonal development and its stages, pathologies, and therapies.

Frances Vaughan and Roger Walsh

TRANSPORTATION SYSTEMS DESIGN. The movement of people and freight is a global activity that has been increasing over the last 20 years. Some representative numbers for domestic passenger travel in 1991 (billions of kilometers) and domestic freight in 1994 (metric ton kilometers per capita) reveal the staggering amount of world transportation: United States (6,135; 19,683), Western Europe (4,250; 4,271), Japan (1,331; 4,491), and China (618; 1,752) (U.S. Department of Transportation, 1997). The United States spends over $1 trillion on transportation services each year, amounting to nearly 17% of the gross domestic product. The transportation industry employs almost 20% of American workers. The public has made a $2.4 trillion investment in transportation infrastructure, such as highways, airports, and waterways. These substantial expenses (Transportation Research Board [TRB], 1995) are necessary to support a safe, efficient, and environmentally sustainable transportation system that allows people to exercise the freedom to travel easily to work and leisure and to obtain a wide variety of goods from diverse locations at reasonable prices.

Behavioral science plays a key and expanding role in improving human performance in transportation systems, as recognized in the National Science and Technology Council's Strategic Implementation Plan. Reasons offered to illustrate why human-factors research should play a prominent role in transportation research and development efforts include:

- *To put people first.* Human factors is a discipline that stresses the importance of people in ensuring transportation usability and efficiency.
- *To improve inadequate products and procedures.* The need for human factors input is evident when one considers existing products with poor human-factors design that make it difficult and sometimes unsafe to operate vehicles and move freight.
- *To ensure safety.* This is the traditional justification for most human-factors work. The long-established recognition in aviation of the value of considering human-factors principles has spread to all other modes of transportation.
- *To improve the quality of life.* Designs that incorporate good human-factors practices are easy, safe, and efficient to use (TRB, 1995, pp. 81–82).

Intelligent Transportation Systems

Intelligent Transportation Systems (ITS) refer to a multitude of new technologies that increase the usability of highways, including in-vehicle information systems, automated highways where drivers do not control vehicles, and improved traffic management centers (IVHS America, 1992). From 1990 to 1995, the total amount of highway and street mileage has increased only 17%, much less than concomitant increases in the numbers of licensed drivers, registered motor vehicles, and vehicle miles traveled (National Highway Traffic Safety Administration, 1996). Many areas of the United States cannot afford, financially and/or environmentally, to build sufficient roads to solve congestion problems. The Intermodal Surface and Transportation Efficiency Act of 1991 (ISTEA) and its successor legislation now being written (NEXTEA) direct the Department of Transportation to solve this problem using "advances in human-factors engineering, micro-electronics, computer technology, and new materials." This is a once in a lifetime opportunity for psychologists to make a substantial contribution to ground transportation systems, especially since the legislation provided millions of dollars for behavioral research.

The human-factors profession has accepted this challenge, and ITS research is ongoing in many countries, including the United States, Western Europe (where it is termed Advanced Transport Telematics), Japan, and Australia. Two important European research programs, Dedicated Road Infrastructure for Vehicle Safety in Europe (DRIVE) and PROMETHEUS have already improved road safety (Parkes & Franzen, 1993). These are cooperative programs between industry and government; for example, government provides only about one third of the 90 million ECU annual budget of PROMETHEUS.

Probably the most prolific research area focuses on in-vehicle devices such as navigation and route-guidance systems, as well as safety and warning systems. Japan has been a world leader in deploying such systems. The Vehicle Information and Communication System (VICS) is an in-vehicle navigation system that provides continuous traffic and parking information to drivers free of charge, although users must purchase a unit for their vehicle from one of several industry suppliers. The development of VICS required the participation of 45 companies; 21 companies sell units, and 2,600,000 navigation units have been sold as of early 1998. The emphasis is on designing driver interfaces to these new subsystems so that overall driving performance is enhanced rather than degraded (Noy, 1997).

Improper design of in-vehicle information systems (IVIS) can lead to safety problems; the best example of this is the cellular phone, which human-factors experts have long recognized as a dangerous device if used when the vehicle is in motion (Goodman, Tijerina, Wierwille, & Bents, 1999). When attention is diverted away from the highway to focus on some IVIS, safety can be compromised. Human-factors experts are also producing ITS human-factors design guidelines, both in the United States (e.g., Campbell, Carney, & Kantowitz, 1997) and in Europe (1995), to assist manufacturers in producing and integrating new IVIS devices. While such guidelines are the most visible human factors products in the transportation industry, it is important to realize that advances in driver information systems are based on (1) programs of systematic research using analytic techniques to identify system objectives and describe system functions, (2) task analysis and comparable systems analysis, (3) identifying user characteristics and requirements, (4) evaluating display formats, and (5) conducting empirical research studies in driving simulators and instrumented vehicles (Kantowitz, Granda, & Moyer, 1997).

Aviation

In 1992, the approximately 7,300 commercial air carrier aircraft registered in the United States flew for 16.6 million hours to expedite 473 million passenger boardings (Billings, 1997). The global aviation marketplace has a cash flow of $3.5 trillion per year, making the world travel and tourism industry the largest on earth (Davis, 1993). Boeing estimates that 14,000 new aircraft needed to meet industry demand will cost $980 billion.

Aviation was the cradle of the human factors profession, probably because human error in aviation has immediate, dramatic, and expensive consequences. The earliest studies on pilot error demonstrated that such error did not occur randomly but could be systematically related to the display-control interface built into the airplane. Thus, so-called pilot error, which is the single greatest cause of aircraft accidents, can be substantially reduced by following good human factors practices.

The two most important human factors problems in aviation are automation (Billings, 1997) and pilot workload (Kantowitz & Campbell, 1996); the literature on each of these topics is immense (Parasuraman & Mouloua, 1996). These topics are studied in simulators and in the air. An example of a field study is an analysis of incident reports from the NASA Aviation Safety Reporting System (see Kantowitz & Campbell, 1996, pp. 121–123). A major Japanese airline wanted to know if the latest model of wide-body highly automated aircraft (called glass cockpit aircraft due to the large number of video displays) was more likely to be involved in certain kinds of incidents. The study did a statistical analysis of 140 incident reports involving glass and nonglass airplanes. Three factors, crew coordination, instrument scan, and procedure following, distinguished between glass and nonglass flight decks. Furthermore, incidents occurring in glass cockpit aircraft tended to be more severe, causing greater disruption of pilot workload. These results allowed the airline to modify its training procedures to anticipate and avoid these new sources of error absent in older aircraft. The relationship between automation and pilot workload is fascinating and complex; the important lesson is that automation must anticipate the expectations and limitations of the human pilots who use it.

Maritime

Maritime shipping is encountering many of the same issues involving automation and technology that are found in the aviation industry. As competition and the desire to lower costs forces drastic reductions in crew size—crews of 30 to 40 were common in the 1960s and 1970s, versus crews of 20 to 30 today in the United States and even smaller crews of 9 to 14 in western Europe, Scandinavia, and Japan (National Research Council, 1994)—the need for effective crew-system interfaces becomes increasingly critical. Furthermore, maritime culture and practices that in some cases go back to the days of sail are often inappropriate for human interactions with advanced technology. For example, a crew member called the helmsman is responsible for entering control inputs to steer the ship under the direction of the officer in command. In the chain of events that starts with the determination of what course should be steered until the ship's rudder is placed in the correct position in a timely manner, all of which interact with the local environment, which consists of wind, waves, navigation hazards, and other shipping, there are many possibilities for human error. In other transportation modes, the control inputs are usually made either by a single person or by automation. Imagine how cumbersome a manual system to steer a car or an airplane through a sequence of turns would be if we added a helmsman inside the control loop. Now imagine what would happen to such an awkward system when automation is added when both the helmsman and the officer in command have to decide jointly what the automation is really doing. There is a long time lag in ship control, yet it takes miles and minutes to stop or turn a vessel, so errors may not be detected rapidly.

It is only recently that maritime shipping has benefited from the same kinds of systems analyses that are routine in aviation (National Research Council, 1994). Such analyses often reveal contradictions. For example, the desire to use double-bottom ships to increase environmental safety necessarily implies either larger ships to carry the same amount of cargo or more smaller ships. Both these outcomes can decrease system safety. There are many interesting and vital human factors issues in the maritime industry, and research plans are being developed to address critical problems. But it is not yet clear how much improvement this nascent research will accomplish given economic and sociological forces that determine current practices in the shipping industry (National Research Council, 1994).

Rail

High-speed rail service in Japan (*shinkansen*) and Western Europe (TGV in France and ICE in Germany) is an established technology serving travelers and commuters every day. It seems most likely that future improvements in surface rail transport will be incremental developments of such established technology, perhaps with some newer technology, such as magnetic levitation, so that current speeds of 200–320 kilometers per hour (km/h) will increase to 450–500 km/h (Luedeke, 1995). Human factors issues in high-speed ground transportation are similar to those in aviation because human perceptual limitations force increasing automation.

At speeds of 360 km/h, human operators cannot detect wayside signals. Thus, in-cab display of all system information is required. Similarly, operators will be unable to detect objects on the tracks with unaided vision. Even an oncoming train with a bright headlight cannot be detected by the unaided human eye in time to initiate safe manual braking. Thus, a variety of computer-assisted displays are required. This includes predictor displays, which contain an internal model of the system that executes in real time to display system states, such as predicted train position under emergency braking, before they occur.

As is the case with aviation and maritime transportation, the necessary automation for train control carries with it the potential for new types of error. Although it is commonly believed that automation reduces the importance of the human operator, in an ironic way this is often untrue because the functions that are too difficult to automate get assigned to the human being. This increases the possibility that human error will have a drastic consequence. Furthermore, a human operator who is supervising automation, rather than controlling a system manually, may often have trouble remaining alert, vigilant, and aware of the true current state of the automation. Thus, the operator may be less than fully prepared should the need to take over from the automation occur suddenly.

Bibliography

Billings, C. E. (1997). *Aviation automation: The search for a human-centered approach*. Mahwah, NJ: Erlbaum.

Bureau of Transportation Statistics (USDOT). (1997). *Global trends: Passenger mobility and freight activity* (Transportation Statistics Annual Report). Washington, DC: Author.

Campbell, J. L., Carney, C., & Kantowitz, B. H. (1997). *Human-factors design guidelines for advanced traveler information systems (ATIS) and commercial vehicle operations (CVO)* (FHWA-RD-98-057). Washington, DC: Federal Highway Administration.

Davis, R. (1993, October). *Human factors in the global marketplace*. Keynote address to the Human Factors and Ergonomics Society, Seattle, WA.

European Conference of Ministers of Transport (ECMT). (1995). *New information technologies in the road transport sector: Policy issues, ergonomics, and safety*. Paris: Author.

Goodman, M., Tijerina, L., Wierwille, W., & Bents, F. (1999). An investigation of the safety implications of wireless communication in vehicles. *Transportation Human Factors Journal, 1*, 3–42.

IVHS America. (1992). *Intelligent vehicle-highway systems (IVHS) safety and human-factors considerations* (Publication No IVHS-AMER-ATMS-92-1). Washington, DC: Author.

Kantowitz, B. H., & Campbell, J. L. (1996). Pilot workload and flight deck automation. In R. Parasuraman (Ed.), *Human performance in automated systems* (pp. 117–136). Mahwah, NJ: Erlbaum.

Kantowitz, B. H., Granda, T. M., & Moyer, M. J. (1997). Human-factors advances in driver information systems. *Proceedings of ASEAN Ergonomics 97–5th SEAES Conference*. Kuala Lumpur: SEAES.

Luedeke, J. F. (1995). *Safety of high speed ground transportation systems: Analytical methodology for safety validation of computer controlled subsystems: Volume II. Development of a safety validation methodology* (Report No. DOT/FRA/ORD-95/10.2). Washington, DC: Federal Railroad Administration.

National Highway Traffic Safety Administration. (1996). *Traffic facts 1995: A compilation of motor vehicle crash data from the fatal accident reporting system and the general estimates system*. Washington, DC: U.S. Department of Transportation.

National Research Council. (1994). *Minding the helm: Marine navigation and piloting*. Washington, DC: National Academy Press.

Noy, Y. I. (Ed.). (1997). *Ergonomics and safety of intelligent driver interfaces*. Mahwah, NJ: Erlbaum.

Parasuraman, R., & Mouloua, M. (Eds.). (1996). *Automation and human performance*. Mahwah, NJ: Erlbaum.

Parkes, A. M., & Franzen, S. (Eds.). (1993). *Driving future vehicles*. London: Taylor & Francis.

Transportation Research Board. (1995). *Proceedings of the forum on future directions in transportation R&D*. Washington, DC: National Academy Press.

Barry H. Kantowitz

TRANSSEXUALISM. The term *transsexualism* denotes strong and persistent feelings of discontent with one's biological sex, the desire to possess the body of the opposite sex, and to be regarded by others as a member of the opposite sex. The broader term *gender dysphoria* encompasses transsexualism as well as milder forms of the same condition.

The word *transsexualism* is usually attributed to an American physician, David O. Cauldwell, who labeled the phenomenon in a 1949 article as "psychopathia transsexualis." Until about 1960, mental-health professionals sometimes referred to transsexuals as transvestites.

There are two distinct types of transsexualism, each of which probably has different causes. These types differ in their age and type of onset, clinical course, associated features, and—to some extent—response to treatment.

The defining feature of homosexual transsexualism is erotic attraction to members of the individual's own biological sex. Homosexual transsexuals typically do not consider themselves homosexual because they believe that inside they are really members of the opposite sex and that this makes their sexual and romantic desires heterosexual. Homosexual transsexualism occurs in both biological males and females.

The other main type of transsexualism—nonhomosexual—occurs almost exclusively in biological males. Nonhomosexual transsexuals comprise men erotically attracted to women, to both sexes, and to neither sex. It is likely that those individuals attracted to women constitute the prototype and that bisexual and asexual individuals represent secondary variations. Because nonhomosexual transsexual men, like homosexual transsexuals, believe that inside they are really members of the opposite sex (i.e., women), they may—paradoxically—label their erotic feelings for women as homosexual and view themselves as lesbians trapped in a man's body.

Homosexual transsexuals show signs of clear cross-gender identity in early childhood. The boys prefer girls' games and toys and female playmates and the company of adult women rather than adult men. They often or always take female roles in fantasy play (e.g., princess, ballerina), and they identify with female characters in television stories or other media. Future homosexual transsexual girls show the corresponding picture but, unlike ordinary tomboys, they do not merely enjoy some activities stereotyped as male, but they systematically and vehemently reject all activities, clothes, and so on, that would identify them to the world as female. Nonhomosexual transsexual men, in contrast, are not conspicuously cross-gendered in childhood. They are rarely labeled sissies by their peers; and their cross-gender behavior is typically restricted to secret, solitary cross-dressing, in garments surreptitiously borrowed from females in their households.

Whereas homosexual transsexuals are not sexually aroused by cross-dressing, nonhomosexual transsexuals are typically aroused by cross-dressing in puberty and early adolescence.

Homosexual transsexualism reaches its fullest intensity in childhood or adolescence, and homosexual transsexuals (both male and female) typically seek clinical help for their condition when they are in their mid-20s. Nonhomosexual transsexualism, on the other hand, tends to develop more slowly and often has the character of a progressive disorder. Nonhomosexual transsexuals usually present to clinicians in their mid-30s, and it is not rare for a nonhomosexual transsexual to seek professional help for the first time when he is over 50 or 60 years of age. By the time the condition is completely established, most transsexuals of all types are dressing and living as much as possible in the cross-gender role, and the desire to alter their bodies to resemble those of the opposite sex has become a major preoccupation.

The prevalence of transsexualism is difficult to estimate, but it is rare—perhaps 1 case per 40,000 or 50,000 adults. The sex ratio is between two and four males for each female. The main reason for the male bias in the sex ratio is that the females consist almost entirely of one type—homosexual transsexuals—whereas the males include homosexual transsexuals and nonhomosexual transsexuals.

The causes of transsexualism are not known. Most of the available theories are psychodynamic in nature and they are not, in general, readily amenable to formal quantitative testing.

Psychological treatments are generally ineffective in eliminating transsexualism. Sex reassignment surgery—essentially a palliative treatment rather than a cure—does, however, allow transsexuals to feel more comfortable with themselves and to function better in society. All reputable gender identity clinics require transsexuals to live full-time in the desired gender role for an extended trial period, usually one or two years, before approving them for surgical sex reassignment. Surgery can create a cosmetically convincing and sometimes functional vagina in biological males. The surgical creation of a penis in biological females is considerably less satisfactory, and most female-to-male transsexuals undergo no further surgery after hysterectomy, ovariectomy, and construction of a male chest contour.

[*See also* Sexual Disorders.]

Bibliography

Blanchard, R. (1989). The classification and labeling of nonhomosexual gender dysphorias. *Archives of Sexual Behavior, 18*, 315–334.

Blanchard, R., Clemmensen, L. H., & Steiner, B. W. (1987). Heterosexual and homosexual gender dysphoria. *Archives of Sexual Behavior, 16*, 139–152.

Blanchard, R., & Freund, K. (1983). Measuring masculine gender identity in females. *Journal of Consulting and Clinical Psychology, 51*, 205–214. Presents a self-administered, paper-and-pencil questionnaire for the assessment of cross-gender identity in women, primarily intended for research purposes.

Blanchard, R., & Steiner, B. W. (Eds.). (1990). *Clinical man-*

agement of gender identity disorders in children and adults. Washington, DC: American Psychiatric Press. A clinical handbook on practical aspects of assessment and treatment, with particular emphasis on the hormonal and surgical treatment of adult patients.

Freund, K., Langevin, R., Satterberg, J., & Steiner, B. (1977). Extension of the gender identity scale for males. *Archives of Sexual Behavior, 6,* 507–519. Presents a self-administered, paper-and-pencil questionnaire for the assessment of cross-gender identity in men, primarily intended for research purposes.

Mate-Kole, C., Freschi, M., & Robin, A. (1990). A controlled study of psychological and social change after surgical gender reassignment in selected male transsexuals. *British Journal of Psychiatry, 157,* 261–264.

Petersen, M. E., & Dickey, R. (1995). Surgical sex reassignment: A comparative survey of international centers. *Archives of Sexual Behavior, 24,* 135–156. Summarizes the policies and procedures employed at major gender identity clinics in screening patients for sex-hormone treatment and sex reassignment surgery.

Zucker, K. J., & Bradley, S. J. (1995). *Gender identity disorder and psychosexual problems in children and adolescents.* New York: Guilford Press. Includes in-depth, comprehensive reviews of biological and psychosocial theories of sexual orientation and gender identity development as well as sections on assessment and treatment.

Ray Blanchard

TRANSVESTISM. The term *transvestism* denotes habitual cross-dressing in a heterosexual male that, at least in puberty or adolescence, is accompanied by sexual arousal. Until about 1960, the label transvestite was sometimes applied by professionals to other types of cross-dressers, including individuals who today would be called transsexuals, and it is still commonly used by the lay public to refer to homosexual cross-dressers (colloquially, drag queens). This inconsistent usage can make earlier books and articles on the subject confusing to unwary readers.

The word transvestism was coined in 1910 by the eminent German sexologist Magnus Hirschfeld. He named the syndrome after its most salient observable feature (Latin *trans* = across, *vestire* = to dress), but he believed that the essence of transvestism is the symbolic or psychological meaning of women's garments, not their objective properties as physical objects. With the exception of terminological refinements, the concept of transvestism has undergone little development since it was introduced by Hirschfeld. It has recently been proposed that transvestism is merely one of a larger class of sexual behaviors, whose common feature is a man's erotic arousal at the thought or image of himself as a woman (autogynephilia). Other autogynephilic phenomena, which often occur in association with transvestism but sometimes independently of it, include masturbatory fantasies, sometimes aided by appropriate props, of having women's breasts or genitals, of being pregnant, lactating, or menstruating, or of engaging in stereotypically feminine activities such as knitting.

Transvestites are not conspicuously effeminate in boyhood or adulthood. Transvestite boys begin secret cross-dressing in childhood or puberty, rarely later than midadolescence. Articles of clothing—often, but not always, underwear—are usually borrowed without permission from a mother, sister, or other female in the household.

Prior to puberty, cross-dressing produces generalized feelings of pleasurable excitement. With the arrival of puberty, dressing in women's clothes begins to elicit penile erection, and, in some cases, leads directly to the boy's first ejaculation. In many cases, cross-dressing elicits less and less sexual excitement as the transvestite grows older; eventually it may produce no discernable penile response at all. The desire to cross-dress, at the same time, remains the same or grows even stronger. Such individuals typically say that the sexual excitement of cross-dressing has been replaced by feelings of comfort or well-being.

Transvestism generally competes and interferes with heterosexual attraction to some degree; however, a majority of transvestites marry and father children. It is quite common for transvestites to lose interest in cross-dressing when they first fall in love with a woman and begin a relationship, but such abatement usually proves temporary.

Some transvestites, who regard their cross-dressing as a harmless and pleasurable pastime, join clubs and organizations for heterosexual cross-dressers; whereas others, who feel guilt and shame over their behavior, cross-dress secretly and privately their entire lives. Men with the latter reaction are prone to repeated and usually vain efforts to overcome their orientation. Vowing to renounce cross-dressing, they periodically destroy all their feminine clothes, only to begin the process of acquiring new ones a few months later.

Transvestism appears to have a greater than chance association with masochism. One common masochistic fantasy of transvestitic men is that they are forced to cross-dress or to put on make-up by a dominant woman. Others are bondage or whipping at the hands of a dominant woman, serving as the maid of a severe and demanding mistress, and coercion to perform cunnilingus or anilingus on a controlling and sadistic female. Strong masochistic trends, however, are found in only a minority of individuals. A rare but particularly pernicious form of masochism that has a very strong association with transvestism is autoerotic asphyxia. This is the practice of inducing cerebral hypoxia, usually by means of self-devised ligatures, while the individual masturbates to orgasm. Roughly one fourth of men who die accidentally while engaging in this are found partially or completely cross-dressed.

Some men, who appear indistinguishable from other transvestites in adolescence or early adulthood, gradually develop desires to remain in the female role for longer periods and to feminize their anatomy. In some men, this is limited to a desire for estrogenic hormones to produce a more feminine chest contour; in others, it culminates in full-blown transsexualism, including the desire for sex reassignment surgery to create female genitals. Because transvestism often follows a somewhat progressive course—for example, short cross-dressing sessions in adolescence may progress, in adulthood, to hours or days in feminine attire outside the home—it is difficult to predict, from an individual's early behavior, precisely where he will stabilize.

The percentage of adult men who could be described as transvestites cannot be stated with precision but is certainly very small. It is likely that a larger percentage of males engage, during puberty, in occasional episodes of cross-dressing with masturbation, which are not desired or repeated in later life.

The causes of transvestism are not known. The most common theoretical explanations are simply specific applications of more general theories. Thus, for example, behavior theorists have hypothesized that transvestism results from accidental conditioning of sexual arousal to women's garments, whereas psychoanalytic theorists have asserted that transvestism is a defense against castration anxiety.

For research purposes, transvestism may be assessed with either phallometric testing or with self-administered questionnaires. For clinical purposes, it is usually diagnosed in interview.

Transvestism is generally a chronic condition. The amount of distress, if any, that it causes to the individual depends on many cofactors. A realistic goal of therapy is to help the individual live with transvestism rather than cure him of it. Psychological treatments may help the individual—or the transvestite and his wife—either to accept the man's transvestism without guilt or to minimize the interpersonal problems it is producing. Pharmacological treatments may attempt to lower either the sexual motivation fueling the cross-dressing or obsessional preoccupations associated with it.

[*See also* Sexual Disorders.]

Bibliography

Blanchard, R. (1985). Research methods for the typological study of gender disorders in males. In B. W. Steiner (Ed.), *Gender dysphoria: Development, research, management* (pp. 227–257). New York: Plenum Press. Includes a self-administered, paper-and-pencil questionnaire for assessing sexual arousal associated with cross-dressing, primarily intended for research purposes.

Blanchard, R. (1991). Clinical observations and systematic studies of autogynephilia. *Journal of Sex & Marital Therapy, 17,* 235–251. A theoretical analysis of transvestism and other sexual behaviors closely related to it.

Blanchard, R. (1993). The she-male phenomenon and the concept of partial autogynephilia. *Journal of Sex & Marital Therapy, 19,* 69–76.

Blanchard, R., & Collins, P. I. (1993). Men with sexual interest in transvestites, transsexuals, and she-males. *Journal of Nervous and Mental Disease, 181,* 570–575. A study of men who advertised for male sexual partners by means of a voice mail system, including transvestites who sought other cross-dressers for sexual encounters or romantic liaisons.

Blanchard, R., Racansky, I. G., & Steiner, B. W. (1986). Phallometric detection of fetishistic arousal in heterosexual male cross-dressers. *Journal of Sex Research, 22,* 452–462. Describes the assessment of transvestitic sexual arousal by means of phallometry, a laboratory procedure in which a man's penile blood volume is monitored during and after the presentation of potentially erotic test stimuli.

Buhrich, N. (1976). A heterosexual transvestite club: Psychiatric aspects. *Australian and New Zealand Journal of Psychiatry, 10,* 331–335.

Buhrich, N., & Beaumont, T. (1981). Comparison of transvestism in Australia and America. *Archives of Sexual Behavior, 10,* 269–279.

Buhrich, N., & McConaghy, N. (1976). Transvestite fiction. *Journal of Nervous and Mental Disease, 163,* 420–427. A content analysis of fantasy stories about cross-dressing written by and for transvestites.

Ovesey, L., & Person, E. (1976). Transvestism: A disorder of the sense of self. *International Journal of Psychoanalytic Psychotherapy, 5,* 219–235.

Person, E., & Ovesey, L. (1978). Transvestism: New perspectives. *Journal of the American Academy of Psychoanalysis, 6,* 301–323.

Ray Blanchard

TREATMENT. Psychological treatments have been given a variety of names, including psychotherapy, clinical interventions, behavior change procedures, and behavior modification. Specific forms of treatment differ with respect to many dimensions, including their stated goals, the mechanisms by which behavior change occurs, the role of the therapist, the type and duration of treatment contact, and the anticipated effects of intervention. However, a number of features are common to all forms of psychological treatment.

It is important to define the boundaries of the term *treatment*. Although a number of behavior change agents exist in our culture (e.g., advertisers and clergy), psychological treatments are the exclusive purview of trained mental-health professionals. As such, treatment involves methods of producing change in an individual's actions, thoughts, and feelings, as conducted by a trained professional. The typical focus of treatment is to increase or decrease a particular set of behaviors, symptoms, or patterns, through learning.

Who and What Is Involved in Treatment

Treatment involves the client and the therapist. The client is often an individual who is distressed or disturbed by some aspect of their own behavior. Although many people feel stressed occasionally, individuals who seek psychological treatment typically have become so disturbed that their usual coping methods no longer alleviate this discomfort. The goal in seeking treatment is to obtain professional advice and direction with the aim of reducing distress. Alternatively, the client may be an individual whose behavior, moods, or attitudes are disturbing to others. An example of this situation might involve a 9-year-old boy brought to treatment by his parents, owing to frequent temper tantrums.

The therapist is an individual who by training and experience is uniquely equipped to help the client. Therapists may possess a number of different educational degrees (e.g., a doctorate in clinical psychology, a master's degree in social work). The training requirements for determining who may call themselves a psychologist may differ by country or state. Although training philosophies vary across doctoral programs in clinical psychology, each psychologist has completed courses in psychopathology, assessment, and treatment approaches. This background allows the psychologist to evaluate the client with respect to the nature of the presenting problem, the diagnosis, and the strengths and weaknesses that the client brings to treatment, all information that is essential for formulating a treatment plan. The treatment plan is the blueprint by which the psychologist outlines the approach to intervention.

In addition to specialized training, the therapist should have personal characteristics that facilitate the conduct of treatment. Irrespective of the specific form of treatment that the therapist is trained to conduct, it is important that he or she is able to listen effectively to the client in a manner that is both understanding and nonjudgmental. Equally important is the ability to help the client to take responsibility for initiating and maintaining behavior change. Although the specific skills involved may vary, depending on the theoretical approach of the therapist, all types of treatment strive to help the client obtain the necessary skills to manage their moods, attitudes, and behavior. The fact that personal characteristics are relevant for the conduct of treatment has led some experts in the field to speculate that advanced training is not necessary for psychologists. At present, this issue has not been resolved, although nonprofessional helpers can clearly be effective in some cases, as noted by the existence of organizations such as Alcoholics Anonymous.

Recognizing that there are a number of approaches to psychological treatment, it is important to highlight the types of problems that are not appropriate for this type of intervention. Problems involving legal disputes, for example, are not the purview of treatment, although the stress created by legal problems may exceed the individual's ability to cope, thus prompting the need for treatment. Because psychologists currently cannot prescribe psychotropic medication, this is not a focus of treatment. However, referral to a physician for medication management is common. Additionally, difficulties with public assistance or transportation do not fall within the scope of treatment. Although organizations sometimes seek help in resolving negative group dynamics, this type of intervention is called organizational behavior management, and thus is not included under the scope of psychological treatment. Treatment, therefore, tends to focus on individuals' thoughts, feelings, and behavior. However, this does not mean that only individuals are seen in treatment. Depending on the nature of the problem, treatment can involve both members of a couple or the members of a family. Typically, the psychologist provides input concerning who should attend treatment sessions. Finally, psychological treatment is sometimes administered to small groups.

Goals of Treatment

Many authors have devised classification schemes for the various forms of treatment. Irrespective of the particular goals of treatment, the ultimate intention is to change the client's behavior, thought processes, or feelings and to allow the individual to function with less distress and greater competency. Depending on the theoretical orientation of the therapist, the goals of treatment may focus on restructuring the individual's personality, providing a supportive environment for the individual to express negative emotions, or teaching new coping skills. Older, traditional forms of treatment were based on the notion that the client's problems were a result of unconscious processes, such as conflicts pertaining to unresolved sexual issues. These unconscious processes required the client to gain insight, specifically defined as increased awareness of the impact of childhood experiences, particularly those involving the client's relationship with their parents. Some authors have referred to these forms of treatment as focusing on "depth" issues, reflecting the purported goal of resolving deep conflicts that stem from childhood. Obviously, these forms of treatment tend to be long-term and time intensive.

More recently, newer forms of treatment have been developed that are centered around behavior change.

These forms of therapy are typically time limited and involve specific techniques that teach the patient new ways to think and act, with the aim of developing new habits, modifying long-standing patterns of maladaptive behavior, and changing thought patterns that lead to negative feelings. Given the increased emphasis on shorter-term therapies, these types of treatment have enjoyed considerable popularity recently. Other types of treatment focus on providing support during a period of crisis (e.g., a patient seeks an evaluation in the local emergency room, owing to feeling suicidal). Clearly, the goals of treatment should be discussed by the therapist and the client and a consensus reached regarding the focus of treatment.

Treatment Modalities

In many respects, the diverse range of available treatment modalities can be grouped according to the target for change. Recognizing that each form of therapy is based on a particular theoretical framework, there is commonality across various modalities of treatment that unite these approaches. Some treatments focus heavily on promoting changes in behavior. Examples of these treatments include behavior modification (where deliberate application of positive and negative consequences follow behavior, with the goal of changing the future probability of those behaviors) and some forms of couples therapy (where members of the dyad are instructed to behave in positive, rewarding ways in order to bring about more pleasant actions from their spouse). In these forms of treatment, the unifying principle of change rests on the notion that once an individual begins to act in a different fashion, a host of other changes will occur, such that their thoughts and feelings will change, as will their relationships with other people.

Another modality of treatment places emphasis on promoting changes in thoughts, specifically helping the client to deliberately change the specific thoughts that they have during problem situations. Examples of these treatments include some of the interventions used in stress management training (e.g., teaching the client to reattribute responsibility in nonhostile ways) and cognitive therapy (which involves helping the client identify distortions in the logic of their thinking). The underlying principle of these modalities of treatment involves the belief that people can direct and control their thoughts, and that through these efforts they will feel differently and behave in more adaptive ways.

Yet another modality of treatment focuses on promoting changes in feelings. Despite the common belief that people cannot control their feelings, these modalities of treatment rest on the notion that through a variety of corrective emotional experiences the client will come to experience a change in emotional reactions to difficult situations. Examples of these types of therapies include psychoanalytic therapies (where the therapist serves as the "good" authority figure, thus allowing the client to understand their negative emotional patterns involving their parents) and play therapy (where children are allowed to act out negative feelings using dolls in order to facilitate emotional expression and correct misperceptions involving adults). Additionally, certain forms of behavior therapy fit under this rubric. In these therapies, the unifying idea rests on the notion that once the individual has expressed maladaptive feelings in a safe environment, she or he will come to understand that these feelings no longer need to be a driving force in their actions, thoughts, and interactions with others.

A fourth modality of treatment focuses on the client's interactions with others. Examples of these types of treatment include milieu therapy (a form of treatment wherein a warm, accepting environment is created within an inpatient psychiatric ward, with the intent of facilitating adaptive interactions between the hospital staff and the patients) and Rogerian therapy (which is based on the notion that positive, unconditional regard from the therapist is the essential ingredient for positive change). As with other therapeutic modalities, these forms of therapy rest on the belief that once the individual has experienced a warm, accepting relationship with the therapist, positive changes will occur.

To date, there is controversy over which of these therapeutic modalities is the most effective. Specifically, it is not clear whether behavior change is necessary for changes in thoughts and feelings, or conversely, if changing a client's thoughts will lead to radiating changes in their actions and emotions. Given the complexity that most human problems present, this issue most likely is not one that will receive a clear answer. Rather than focus on this issue, research on the various forms of treatment has attended to identifying specific forms of treatment that have scientific support for alleviating specific problems. To date, a growing number of treatments have been identified that have scientifically been shown to reduce panic attacks, depression, persistent reactions following a traumatic event, sexual dysfunction, bed-wetting, and a host of other specific problems.

Elements of Treatment

A number of specific elements are involved in many forms of treatment. First, it is typical to begin treatment with a thorough initial evaluation. This includes an assessment of the client's current level of functioning, a detailed examination of the problem that has brought the individual to therapy, a review of the individual's educational, social, and family background, assessment of whether medical conditions are present, history of therapy, and sometimes, an evaluation of whether or not the client meets the criteria for any psychiatric diagnoses. This initial evaluation forms the basis for the determination of treatment goals, which should be explicitly discussed with the client prior to the onset of treatment.

Second, therapists often provide new information as a fundamental aspect of treatment, which is termed psychoeducation. For example, information about the expected course of bereavement can facilitate an individual's expectations concerning the gains anticipated from therapy. Likewise, information concerning normal developmental processes may be an important feature of therapy involving parents of an adolescent. Some forms of therapy rely almost exclusively on psychoeducation as a central element of treatment, although this typically represents only one element of treatment. Third, it is not unusual for many forms of treatment to involve "homework," tasks that the client performs in the context of their everyday life that are designed to facilitate positive transfer of the increased awareness and new skills that the client has gained through treatment. Depending on the therapist's theoretical orientation, homework can include tasks such as practice in approaching feared objects, initiating a family discussion about a previously taboo topic, or writing in a diary in order to express feelings.

Fourth, irrespective of the theoretical orientation of the therapist, at some point during treatment compliance may become an issue. This sometimes takes the form of the client failing to complete homework. At other times, this is reflected in the client arriving late to a therapy appointment, or precluding the examination of an emotional topic owing to time constraints. There are many diverse methods for handling problems with compliance. Behaviorally oriented therapists, for example, will try to find out the reasons for noncompliance: Is the client not completing the recommended homework because it exceeds his current level of skill for handling the problem? Or is the client receiving positive gains from others in her life for maintaining the problem behavior? Other theoretical orientations, such as the psychodynamic approach, will provide an interpretation of the client's poor compliance in an effort to foster insight. Regardless of the theoretical orientation of the therapist, poor compliance needs to be addressed in order for treatment to be effective.

Fifth, some schools of therapy emphasize the "stage" or phase of the therapeutic process, specifically, whether therapy is in the beginning, middle, or final stages. According to some theoretical schools, each of these phases is associated with unique types of interpersonal dynamics, which are viewed as the active ingredient of the change process. Irrespective of whether a particular therapist adheres to these theoretical orientations, all forms of treatment pay some attention to the steps involved in ending treatment, which is referred to as termination. Typically, once the therapist and client agree that treatment should end, regular meetings are spaced at progressively longer intervals to allow the client to take control over maintaining the gains that were made in treatment. If the client were seeking help for a problem that involved an addiction process (such as alcohol dependence) or a long-standing habit, it is common for attention to be paid to relapse prevention. Relapse prevention refers to a collection of treatment techniques designed to help the client to regain control if they experience a "lapse" and engage in their problem behavior again. Originally derived from clinical research on heavy alcohol use, relapse prevention approaches have been applied to a diverse set of target problems, including trichotillomania (habitual hair-pulling), excessive sexual behavior, and cigarette smoking.

Ethical Issues Involved in Treatment

The ethical principles of the American Psychological Association provide a set of guidelines that are available to all psychologists concerning the ethical boundaries involved in treatment. For example, according to these principles, the psychologist has the obligation to inform the client concerning the procedures involved in treatment at the start of therapy. This ethical boundary is designed to ensure that the client understands what is involved in treatment and is willing to undergo the procedures that the therapist suggests. Additionally, psychologists should protect the confidentiality of the client by safeguarding all information pertaining to treatment. This includes information gathered during the initial evaluation, detailed notes pertaining to each treatment session, and summaries that are written upon treatment termination. Clearly, the provision of confidentiality helps the client be assured of the protected and private nature of the therapy setting, which is particularly important given the focus of treatment. Additional ethical boundaries involve guidelines concerning how psychologists describe their services in advertising efforts, proscriptions concerning sexual and romantic relationships with current or former therapy patients, regulations concerning fee-setting and collection, and guidelines concerning the use and interpretation of assessment techniques. Although the details of the ethical principles of the American Psychological Association are outside of the scope of this entry, it is significant to note that these guidelines are an important feature of treatment, as they specify the ethical parameters of psychotherapy provided by psychologists within the United States.

Efficacy of Treatment

For many years, psychologists have argued among themselves over which form of treatment is the most effective. Initially, this argument was driven by theoretical allegiances, although most recently the emphasis has shifted to examination of specific interventions. Many years of research have clearly established that no one form of treatment is effective for 100% of the people with whom it is tried. For this reason, it is important that the therapist use some form of assessment to determine if a specific form of treatment is effective with an individual client. This can range from simple frequency counts (e.g., how many panic attacks did the client have in the past week) to more involved psychological testing (e.g., did a child's score on an aptitude test improve, reflecting his improved ability to concentrate?). Ideally, measurements of treatment effectiveness need to be administered at regular intervals, particularly at the beginning of treatment. One reason for this recommendation is that it can be demoralizing to the client to be treated with an approach that is not effective. Additionally, this is an era of increasing accountability for psychologists, indicating the need to document treatment efficacy.

Maintaining Gains Following Treatment

Many forms of treatment include some provisions for the maintenance of gains following treatment. Examples include teaching the client to identify "early warning signs" that their troubles are returning so that they can either resume therapy or increase the use of the coping strategies that were acquired during treatment. Additionally, sometimes the therapist will schedule booster sessions following termination of treatment. Booster sessions typically occur 1 to 3 months following termination and serve to remind the client of specific skills that are useful for coping with problem behaviors. The intent of these provisions is to prevent the client from relapsing following termination of treatment. Different problems have markedly different rates of relapse, with some difficulties showing considerable resistance to change (e.g., smoking cessation). For these types of problems, therapists will often include relapse prevention strategies, discussed earlier.

Bibliography

Neitzel, M. T., Bernstein, D. A., & Milich, R. (1994). *Introduction to clinical psychology* (4th ed.). Englewood Cliffs, NJ: Prentice Hall.

Phares, E. J. (1992). *Clinical psychology: Concepts, methods, and profession* (4th ed.). Pacific Grove, CA: Brooks/Cole.

J. Gayle Beck

TRICHOTILLOMANIA (TM) is a disorder characterized by repetitive hair pulling that results in noticeable hair loss. Other diagnostic criteria include increasing tension immediately before pulling or when attempting to resist the behavior, feelings of pleasure or relief during pulling, and significant distress or impairment in life function resulting from the behavior (American Psychiatric Association, 1994). The pulling of scalp hair is most common, although eyelash and eyebrow pulling are also common, and any body hair can be affected (Christenson & Crow, 1996). Most patients pull from more than one site, and resultant hair loss can range from visible thinning to nearly total baldness at the site(s). Psychosocial and medical complications of TM can be severe. In the psychosocial domain, patients report extensive amounts of time consumed by pulling and associated attempts to conceal hair loss, avoidance of activities and interpersonal relationships wherein hair loss might be obvious, and distressing emotional consequences, including guilt, humiliation, and lowered self-esteem (Mansueto, Stemberger, Thomas, & Golomb, 1997). Medical sequelae include skin irritations, infections, or lesions, as well as muscle strain and gastrointestinal difficulties secondary to hair ingestion (O'Sullivan et al., 1997).

The majority of chronic hair pullers do not maintain continued, focused awareness of the behavior while it is occurring, and pulling often occurs during sedentary activities such as reading, watching television, driving, or talking on the phone (Christenson, Mackenzie, & Mitchell, 1991). Other precipitants for pulling include sensory stimuli (e.g., itching or burning sensations and the texture of certain hairs), cognitive activity (e.g., ideas that hair growth should be symmetrical), and negative affect (e.g., boredom and tension; Mansueto, Stemberger, Thomas, & Golomb, 1997). TM often is associated with high rates of coexistent disorders, most frequently major depression or generalized anxiety disorder.

No large-scale epidemiological investigations have as yet estimated the prevalence of TM, although preliminary data suggest a lifetime rate of 0.6% in a college population (Christenson & Crow, 1996). Gender ratios in clinic and community settings suggest higher rates of the disorder among women, although gender distribution in young patients may be more equal (Christenson & Crow, 1996). Symptoms occur cross-culturally, and age of onset is generally in early adolescence (Stanley & Mouton, 1996). The course of the disorder appears to be chronic, although there is significant variability in symptom severity both across and within patients. Furthermore, there is some suggestion that very early onset (i.e., before age 2) is associated with remission before school age (O'Sullivan et al., 1997).

TM is currently classified in the psychiatric nomenclature as an impulse control disorder (American Psychiatric Association, 1994), although the syndrome actually has been conceptualized from a wide range of perspectives. Most notably, it has been suggested that

TM may be a variant of obsessive-compulsive disorder (OCD), given that both disorders are characterized by repetitive, maladaptive behaviors over which the patient perceives no control. However, important phenomenological variables actually preclude this classification, in particular, the peripheral role of cognition in TM, the feelings of pleasure associated with hair pulling, and the precipitating sensory stimuli reported by patients with TM (Stanley & Cohen, 1999). A related view considers TM and OCD to be distinct disorders, both of which are members of a larger class of obsessive-compulsive spectrum disorders (OCSDs), which share features with OCD, including phenomenology, neurobiological correlates, family history, clinical course, and treatment response. Empirical data in this domain are mixed, and it has also been suggested that any apparent overlap between TM and OCD may result from the heightened negative affect states associated with both disorders (Stanley & Cohen, 1999).

Another conceptualization of TM is based on behavioral learning principles. This perspective posits that hair pulling begins as a normal reaction to stress but then becomes strongly established as a habit disorder when the behavior is conditioned through classical and operant mechanisms to occur in response to a variety of environmental, sensory, cognitive, and affective cues (Azrin & Nunn, 1973; Mansueto, Stemberger, Thomas, & Golomb, 1997). This model has served as the basis for the development of behavioral treatments for TM, the goals of which are to break the conditioned sequences of behaviors that define the disorder.

Conceptualizations of TM have led to two primary treatment modalities. First, characterization of the disorder as a variant of OCD has suggested the potential utility of serotonergic reuptake inhibitors (SSRIs), the pharmacological treatment of choice for OCD. Three controlled clinical trials of SSRIs for TM have been conducted, and the results have been mixed (O'Sullivan et al., 1997). Second, behavioral conceptualizations of TM have led to the use of a behavioral approach known as habit reversal training (HRT; Azrin & Nunn, 1973). The goal of HRT is to increase awareness of the behavioral sequences and to teach coping skills that interrupt these. One controlled clinical trial of HRT for TM has been conducted, with results documenting the efficacy of this intervention in reducing hair pulling by 97%.

Bibliography

American Psychiatric Association. (1994). *Diagnostic and statistical manual of mental disorders* (4th ed.). Washington, DC: Author.

Azrin, N. H., & Nunn, R. (1973). Habit-reversal: A method of eliminating nervous habit and tics. *Behaviour Research and Therapy, 11*, 619–628.

Christenson, G. A., & Crow, S. J. (1996). The characterization and treatment of trichotillomania. *Journal of Clinical Psychiatry, 57*, 42–49.

Christenson, G. A., Mackenzie, T. B., & Mitchell, J. E. (1991). Characteristics of 60 adult chronic hair pullers. *American Journal of Psychiatry, 148*, 365–370.

Mansueto, C. S., Stemberger, R. M. T., Thomas, A. M., & Golomb, R. G. (1997). Trichotillomania: A comprehensive behavioral model. *Clinical Psychology Review, 17*, 567–577.

O'Sullivan, R. L., Keuthen, N. J., Christenson, G. A., Mansueto, C. S., Stein, D. J., & Swedo, S. E. (1997). Trichotillomania: Behavioral symptom or clinical syndrome? *American Journal of Psychiatry, 154*, 1442–1449.

Stanley, M. A., & Cohen, L. J. (1999). Trichotillomania and OCD. In D. Stein, G. Christenson, & E. Hollander (Eds.), *Trichotillomania: New developments* (pp. 511–525). Washington, DC: American Psychiatric Association Press.

Stanley, M. A., & Mouton, S. G. (1996). Trichotillomania treatment manual. In V. B. Van Hasselt & M. Hersen (Eds.), *Sourcebook of psychological treatment manuals for adult disorders* (pp. 657–687). New York: Plenum Press.

Melinda A. Stanley

TROLAND, LEONARD THOMPSON (1889–1932), American psychologist. Leonard Troland was a contemporary of those psychologists—Walter Hunter, Clark Hull, E. C. Tolman, and Leonard Carmichael among them—who established psychology as a respected scientific field in the United States. Troland was trained in physical science before embarking on his psychological career, obtaining his B.S. degree from The Massachusetts Institute of Technology in 1912 and winning the Bowdoin prize in chemistry at Harvard in 1914 for work on enzyme action. He received a Ph.D. degree from Harvard under Hugo Münsterberg and E. B. Holt in 1915 for a thesis on visual psychophysics, and returned there in 1916 after a year at the Nela Laboratory in Cleveland, serving on the faculty for 15 years. During World War I he assisted the Navy with the development of underwater listening devices and was a member of a subcommittee of the National Research Council on vision and aviation psychology. He became one of the most respected visual scientists in America, authoring a significant monograph on visual science early in his career for the National Research Council (*The Present Status of Visual Science*, Washington, D.C., 1922). A unit of retinal illumination, the *troland*, was named after him. His aspirations, however, were toward a comprehensive motivational psychology. Throughout the 1920s, Troland carried on a campaign, in books aimed at both general audiences (*The Mystery of Mind*, New York, 1926) and specialists (*Fundamentals of Human Motivation*, New York, 1928, and the multivolume *Principles of Psychophysiology*, New York, 1929–1932), for two ideas: hedonism and "complete technology." Troland's hedonism, in contrast to contemporary theories which allowed feelings no causal role in behavior, considered pleasant feelings to be causes as well as effects. At the time, this view was considered outdated—E. C. Tolman's argument against Troland's hedonism was a key component of his purposive behaviorism (*Purposive Behavior in Animals and Men*, New York, 1932). Today, however, it appears that Troland anticipated the importance of cognitive emotional factors in the regulation of behavior. Troland's hedonism was interconnected with the philosophical system he termed *paraphysical monism* in which psychophysics—his specialty—would bridge the gap between objectivity and subjectivity (*Philosophical Review*, 1918, *27*, 39–62). A consequence of his attempt to reconcile science and philosophy was his adoption of a panpsychic view of a universe governed by hedonistic laws. Troland's ethical views led him to propose a utopian vision of a society under the efficient and benign control of what he termed *complete technology*. This he contrasted with current technologies which, he believed, were incomplete because they did not start from the premise of assuring the greatest possible happiness for those affected by them. Troland's ethical theory can be traced to his attraction to the work of the American Fabian socialist James MacKaye (1872–1935), who, in 1906, described a process by which engineers would produce a maximum of happiness through a totalistic system of social regulation called *pantocracy* (*The Economy of Happiness*, Boston, 1906). But perhaps Troland's commitment to the idea of psychology as technology can best be explained by noting that he was himself a technological innovator, coinventing the Technicolor process for motion picture film and serving, from 1918 onward, in increasingly demanding roles in the nascent Technicolor Corporation. His career was cut short by an accidental fall while being photographed on Mount Wilson in Los Angeles in May 1932, where he had gone as a consultant for Technicolor. In many ways, psychology has evolved into the sophisticated technology Troland envisioned.

[*Many of the people mentioned in this article are the subjects of independent biographical entries.*]

Bibliography

MacKaye, J. (1906). *The economy of happiness*. Boston: Little, Brown.

Tolman, E. C. (1932). *Purposive behavior in animals and men*. New York: Century.

Troland, L. T. (1918). Paraphysical monism. *Philosophical Review*, *27*, 39–62.

Troland, L. T. (1922). *The present status of visual science*. Washington, DC: National Academy of Sciences.

Troland, L. T. (1926). *The mystery of mind*. New York: D. Van Nostrand.

Troland, L. T. (1928). *Fundamentals of human motivation*. New York: D. Van Nostrand.

Troland, L. T. (1929–1932). *Principles of psychophysiology* (Vols. 1–3). New York: D. Van Nostrand.

David C. Devonis

TRUANCY. *See* School Refusal.

TURKEY. The year 1915 marks the beginning of psychology as a scientific discipline in Turkey. This is when an invited German professor, Anschutz, started the first experimental psychology course at Istanbul University. During that year, psychology was also introduced in teacher training institutes. At the same time, the first psychology book, in child psychology, was published, and the Binet–Simon Test of Intelligence was translated into Turkish, a year before its American adaptation. These early beginnings were not followed by a smooth and continuous advancement of the field due to tumultuous times in the country and the world, including the First World War, the collapse of the Ottoman Empire, the War for Independence, the establishment of the Turkish Republic, and the introduction of the Atatürk reforms in all walks of life followed by secularization, urbanization, and industrialization.

Both before and during the Second World War, the European, especially German, influence in psychology was apparent. In 1937, the first experimental psychology laboratory was founded by Peters, who was among the second wave of invited German professors. S. Tunc was the first Turkish academic with a doctorate in psychology from Geneva, who brought in a Swiss influence. In the 1930s, another pioneering Turkish psychologist, M. Turhan, who studied in Germany and England, introduced the Gestalt tradition and wrote about social issues.

The first empirical work on social/technological change and its psychological concomitants, however, was that of Muzafer Sherif in rural villages. Sherif studied in the United States and taught in Ankara between 1936 and 1945. His work covered broad ground, from laboratory experiments in social psychology to the translation and the standardization of the Terman and Merrill and Army Beta tests, from the study of the impact of technological change on cognitions, to political attacks on racist ideology (Acar & Sahin, 1990; Basaran & Sahin, 1990). The void created by Sherif's departure for the United States in 1945 was never filled. Later on his students M. Kiray and F. Basaran pursued significant field work in social change and its psychological ramifications.

The 1960s marked the beginning of the impact of American psychology in Turkey. It was also a period when psychologists started collaborating with other social scientists in the study of the human issues involved in societal transformations. During the 1970s, a number of psychology departments were established in universities, and young faculty with American doctorates started to teach there. While previously psychology had been seen as a discipline relevant mainly to teacher training, starting in this period its scope and applications progressively expanded.

Psychological research greatly increased in the 1980s and 1990s. Most areas of scientific psychology have been represented in research (for reviews see Acar & Sahin, 1990; Basaran & Sahin, 1990; Kagitcibasi, 1994; Sahin, 1997). Nevertheless, some patterns of research orientation are discernable. In particular, the interest in the psychological ramifications of modernization have paved the way toward the development of a cultural and cross-cultural perspective in psychology. With the recognition that psychological phenomena may be influenced by cultural context and contextual change, some Turkish psychologists are less willing to adopt Western (mainly American) theory at face value. Instead, they are more likely to do research to test the theory and modify it if needed. There is also new theory development, for example in family dynamics and change, gender, human development, the self, and values (e.g., Fisek, 1991; Imamoglu, 1998; Kagitcibasi, 1996a,b).

Current work in psychology shows much topical and methodological diversity. Almost all the known fields of psychology and related disciplines are represented in current research. Experimental research is conducted in such areas as human development, learning, memory, perception, psycholinguistics, and biopsychology, all with international outlets (e.g., Aksu-Koc, 1994; Hortacsu, 1997; Koksal, Domjan, & Weisman, 1994; Talasli, 1993). This kind of work involves significant scientific contributions and reflects a notable progress in scientific psychology in Turkey. However, basic research tends to get done in individual projects and is not known sufficiently well by colleagues outside the specialization field in question, let alone the general public.

In contrast, there are applied projects of greater relevance to societal development issues. Some of this work tends to get done more in collaborative interdisciplinary team work and is better known, at times even influencing social policy. Examples are projects in health, education, gender issues, and early childhood care (e.g., Kagitcibasi, 1996a). New applied areas are emerging such as industrial-organizational psychology, traffic psychology, and health psychology, in addition to the older fields such as counseling and clinical psychology. The main challenge faced by "pure" research is to establish its importance and relevance in a developing country with pressing human problems that require solutions. The main challenge faced by "applied" research is to achieve theoretical sophistication and to avoid turning into quick and ready remedies or empirical shots in the dark.

A recent overview of the field (Sahin, 1997) notes that currently some 158 psychology faculty, 114 of whom have at least a Ph.D. degree, are active in research and teaching in Turkish universities. Half of the Ph.D.'s have been earned abroad (mostly in the United States and secondly in the United Kingdom). This enables many Turkish psychologists to have international contacts and access to international publications. Most of the psychology faculty teach in psychology departments, but many are employed at university hospitals and education and business schools. The greatest numbers are in clinical psychology, 20% in psychology departments and 27% in hospitals or private practice; 16% are in social psychology; 10% are in experimental psychology; 9% are in psychometrics; and 8% are in developmental psychology.

Of the 65 textbooks published to date (Sahin, 1997), most are translations of foreign texts. Original scientific publications are limited in number, and most are in Turkish, though publications in international journals are on the increase, and books are beginning to appear in the international scene (Kagitcibasi, 1996a). An important periodical is *Turk Psikoloji Dergisi* (Turkish Journal of Psychology). First published in 1978, it brings out two regular and two special issues a year and since 1995 has been indexed in the Social Science Citation Index.

Psychological assessment has always been at the forefront of the field. Some notable examples of work in this area are the Turkish standardization of the WISC-R by I. Savasir and N. Sahin and devising a developmental screening inventory for ages 0 to 6 by N. Erol, I. Savasir, and N. Sezgin. It is estimated that some 400 assessment tools have been used in one form or another. Of the 179 tests reviewed (Oner, 1994), only 27% are found to be original; the rest are translated or adapted from foreign instruments. There is ongoing work toward developing standards for test use and forming a test bank.

The Turkish Psychological Association is the scientific/professional organization of psychologists in Turkey. It is a member of IUPsyS and EFPPA. Under the auspices of the TPA, biennial national psychology congresses are held regularly, hosted by psychology departments. TPA oversees the growing professional needs of some 2,000 psychologists working in diverse employment contexts, including hospitals, universities, schools, the military, prisons, the police, labor unions, research institutes, NGOs, the media, advertisement firms, industries and other business, traffic administration, and private practice/consultancy. In 1990, most psychologists were employed by the health sector (46%), followed by academia (16%) and early child care and education (15%) (Basaran & Sahin, 1990).

Despite rather early beginnings, it may be said that psychology did not fall on fertile ground in Turkey and had only a marginal status for decades. As an imported discipline, it remained "foreign" despite the rich cultural heritage in this part of the world, which contains a myriad of clues to the human psyche. Integrative approaches involving anthropological insight into this heritage may disclose the themes of indigenous psychological knowledge and culture-sensitive theorizing, which could enrich contemporary psychology.

The topical and methodological diversity is a sign of expanding scope and may signal the healthy development of the field. It is incumbent on the psychologists themselves, however, to make their work known better and to make a niche for themselves among the socially relevant sciences. The beginnings of such an orientation may be apparent in an emerging search for a more "appropriate" and "relevant" psychology. This would lead to a better recognition of the field and increase the limited resources presently allocated to psychological research.

The current situation in Turkey gives us reason for a tentative optimism. There is much potential for growth and progress in the field today, given the increasing demand for psychological services in a rapidly changing society. This potential can be realized with a better recognition of and support for psychology as a science and as a profession. Of particular significance would be more favorable science policies and professional legal structures. Such supportive policies and legislation could, in turn, be facilitated by psychologists themselves, as they get better organized and establish the scientific and societal significance of their discipline.

Bibliography

Acar, G., & Sahin, D. (1990). Psychology in Turkey. *Psychology in Developing Societies, 2,* 241–256.

Aksu-Koc, A. (1994). Development of linguistic forms. In R. Berman & D. Slobin (Eds.), *Relating events in narrative: Cross-linguistic developmental study.* Mahwah, NJ: Erlbaum.

Basaran, F., & Sahin, N. (1990). Psychology in Turkey: Status report on teaching and research. In G. Shouksmith & E. Shouksmith (Eds.), *Psychology in Asia and the Pacific.* Bangkok: UNESCO, RUSHSAP Series, 34.

Fisek, G. O. (1991). A cross-cultural examination of proximity and hierarchy as dimensions of family structure. *Family Process 30,* 121–133.

Hortacsu, N. (1997). The cross-cultural comparison of need importance and need satisfaction during adolescence: Turkey and USA. *Journal of Genetic Psychology, 158,* 287–296.

Imamoglu, E. O. (1998). Individualism and collectivism in a model and scale of balanced differentiation and integration. *Journal of Psychology, 132,* 95–105.

Kagitcibasi, C. (1994). Psychology in Turkey. *International Journal of Psychology, 29,* 729–738.

Kagitcibasi, C. (1996). *Family and human development across cultures: A view from the other side.* Mahwah, NJ: Erlbaum.

Kagitcibasi, C. (1996). The autonomous-relational self: A new synthesis. *European Psychologist, 1,* 3, 180–186.

Koksal, F., Domjan M., & Weisman, G. (1994). Blocking of the sexual conditioning of differentially effective conditioned stimulus objects. *Animal Learning and Behavior, 22,* 103–111.

Oner, N. (1994). *Turkiye'de kullanilan psikolojik testler: Bir basvuru kaynagi* [Psychological tests used in Turkey: A resource book]. Istanbul: Bogazici University Press.

Sahin, N. (1997). Psychology. In *Cumhuriyet doneminde Turkiye'de bilim* [Science in Turkey during the republican period]. Ankara: TUBA 1997.

Talasli, U. (1993). On the possibility of intermittence during fixations: A conceptual assessment. *Perceptual and Motor Skills, 77,* 323–329.

Cigdem Kagitcibasi

TVERSKY, AMOS (1937–1996), Israeli American psychologist. Tversky was born in Haifa, Israel, where his father was a veterinarian and his mother was a social worker and member of the Israeli parliament. He majored in philosophy and psychology at Hebrew University in Jerusalem, receiving a B.A. degree in 1961. He then began graduate work at the University of Michigan's mathematical psychology program headed by Clyde H. Coombs and was greatly influenced by Ward Edwards. After completing the program in 1965 with an award-winning dissertation under Coombs, he worked on the anomaly of intransitive choice, developing a mathematical model of dimensional processing that specified when to expect such intransitivity. He soon constructed another dimensionally based mathematical model of choice, called elimination by aspects, according to which people often choose among multidimensional alternatives by considering each dimension in succession and eliminating alternatives failing some minimal criterion on it before considering the next.

Moving to judgments of similarity, Tversky developed a model that incorporated some asymmetries of such judgments (e.g., that North Korea is judged to be more similar to Communist China than vice versa). Tversky constructed mathematical models of his choice and judgment theories, including fundamental measurement conditions, and together with other such models, they culminated in a collaboration with his colleagues David Krantz, Duncan Luce, and Patrick Suppes on the classic and monumental three-volume work on *Foundations of Measurement* (1971, 1989, 1990).

But the most influential collaboration in Tversky's life, lasting from the late 1960s until Tversky's death, was with Daniel Kahneman. They developed the "heuristics and biases" approach to behavioral decision making. This approach accounts for intuitive judgment and choice in terms of a few very simple psychological principles. For example, the representativeness heuristic involves judging the probability of a sample on the basis of the similarity of its basic features with those of the source population, while the availability heuristic involves judging the probability (or extent) of a class by the ease with which instances of it come to mind. Although such heuristics and principles of intuitive choice are often satisfactory, they can lead to systematic error, much as visual illusions result from processes that generally lead to veridical perception. For example, representativeness combined with availability to the imagination yields the "conjunction fallacy," whereby a likely constituent of a compound class or event is judged to be more probable than the entire class or event.

A keystone of Tversky's work was a paper with Kahneman on prospect theory, which was published in *Econometrica* in 1979 and became its most cited paper ever. Prospect theory is a descriptive counterpart of normative utility theory and accounts in a formal manner for some well-known anomalies of choice in terms of simple psychological principles, such as loss aversion, the certainty effect, the reflection effect, and framing effects—particularly those that result from framing the same choice in terms of gains versus in terms of losses.

At the time of his death, Tversky was working on what he termed *support theory*, a theory based on the observation that when an event (e.g., a car's failure to start) is unpacked into its constituents (e.g., weak battery, empty gas tank, broken starter), the judged probabilities of the separate constituents usually add up to much more than the judged probability of that event. His development—as always—was based on three scientific principles: (1) Judgments of probability are as important as (and no different in kind from) judgments about what to choose. ("A person bets on team A rather than on team B because he believes that team A is more likely to win; he does not infer this belief from his betting preferences. Thus, in reality, subjective probabilities determine preferences among bets and are not derived from them"—Tversky & Kahneman, 1974, p. 1130.) (2) Systematic deviation from standard rationality is an inevitable characteristic of human intuition. (3) The psychological processes involved are best understood by developing a precise mathematical description (theory).

Tversky began as a professor at the Hebrew University (1966–1978) and then became the first Davis-Brack Professor at Stanford University (1978–1996). He was also (1992–1996) a senior professor and permanent fellow of the Sackler Institute of Advanced Studies at Tel Aviv University. He won the Distinguished Scientific Contribution Award of the American Psychological Association in 1982 and a MacArthur Prize in 1984 and was elected as a foreign member of the United States National Academy of Sciences from 1985. He was awarded honorary doctorates by the University of Göteberg (Sweden), the State University of New York at Buffalo, the University of Chicago, and Yale University, and he held a citation for bravery from Israel. His work was extremely influential, not only within cognitive and social psychology, but also in economics, statistics, philosophy, and law.

Bibliography

Kahneman, D., & Shafir, E. (1998). Amos Tversky (1937–1996). *American Psychologist, 33*, 793–794.

Kahneman, D., & Tversky, A. (1979). Prospect theory: An analysis of decision under risk. *Econometrica, 47*, 263–291.

Tversky, A., & Kahneman, D. (1974). Judgment under uncertainty: Heuristics and biases. *Science, 185*, 1124–1131.

Tversky, A., & Kahneman, D. (1981). The framing of decisions and the psychology of choice. *Science, 211*, 453–458.

Tversky, A., Krantz, D. H., Luce, R. D., & Suppes, P. *Foundations of Measurement* (Vol. 1, 1971; Vol. 2, 1989; Vol. 3, 1990). New York: Academic Press.

Robyn Dawes

TWELVE-STEP PROGRAMS are the most common type of self-help group. Members of 12-step self-help groups meet regularly with others who have the same illness or problem. To use their own terminology, 12-step self-help groups offer members both "fellowship" and a "program." The fellowship is the support and encouragement of peers who have a problem in common (e.g., alcoholism, obsessive-compulsive disorder), including individuals who can serve as role models because they are recovering from the problem successfully. The 12 steps themselves comprise the program (see Table 1), which is a structured set of tasks intended to help resolve members' problems and promote spiritual growth. Although 12-step self-help groups bear some similarities to group psychotherapy, they are dis-

TWELVE-STEP PROGRAMS. Table 1. The 12 steps as used in Alcoholics Anonymous (AA, 1952)

1. We admitted we were powerless over **alcohol**—that our lives had become unmanageable.
2. Came to believe that a power greater than ourselves could restore us to sanity.
3. Made a decision to turn our will and our lives over to the care of God as we understand Him.
4. Made a searching and fearless moral inventory of ourselves.
5. Admitted to God, to ourselves, and to another human being the exact nature of our wrongs.
6. Were entirely ready to have God remove all these defects of character.
7. Humbly asked Him to remove our shortcomings.
8. Made a list of all persons we had harmed, and became willing to make amends to them all.
9. Made direct amends to such people wherever possible, except when to do so would injure them or others.
10. Continued to take personal inventory and when we were wrong promptly admitted it.
11. Sought through prayer and meditation to improve our conscious contact with God as we understood Him, praying only for knowledge of His will for us and the power to carry that out.
12. Having had a spiritual awakening as a result of these steps, we tried to carry this message to **alcoholics**, and to practice these principles in all our affairs.

Note: Words in boldface are modified by other 12-step groups to be appropriate to the particular problem on which they focus (e.g., gambling, drugs, food, etc.).

tinct in at least three respects: (1) 12-step groups are operated and facilitated by members themselves rather than helping professionals; (2) 12-step groups charge no fee other than "passing the hat" for small voluntary contributions; (3) 12-step groups are supportive of lifetime membership and friendship building, and, expect members both to give and to receive help. In other words, 12-step self-help organizations are in many regards more like churches, clubs, or other community-based organizations than they are like professionally administered psychotherapeutic interventions.

Individual 12-step groups are usually joined in a loose federation under a larger umbrella organization. For example, Narcotics Anonymous (NA) has a World Services Board, which maintains a registry of all individual NA groups and arranges NA's national and international conferences. The central office or service board of 12-step organizations also typically publishes literature that explains the 12-step philosophy and how it may be applied to various problems. Despite serving these important functions, by design organizational service boards have very little control over how individual 12-step groups operate. Rather, each group is considered the ultimate authority in matters affecting it. This decentralization of authority is mirrored at the group level, where the leadership of group meetings rotates between members. These organizational rules promote a sense of responsibility for the organization in all members rather than only in a select few, and also prevent a single charismatic leader from being able to dominate the organization. Absence of charismatic leadership, along with the fact that 12-step groups do not recruit new members or prevent current members from leaving at any time, distinguishes 12-step organizations from cults.

The origin of 12-step self-help groups can be traced to the 1930s and the founding of Alcoholics Anonymous (AA). In developing the 12 steps, early AA members drew upon their hard-won experiential wisdom, as well as philosophical and psychological writings (e.g., the works of the American psychologist William James; the teachings of the Oxford Group, a 1920s spiritual movement). AA's 12 steps and self-help group format were soon adopted by other organizations. In the 1940s, spouses of AA members formed groups for families of alcoholics, and in 1951 these became a separate organization, Al-Anon. Concurrently, individuals with problems with drugs other than alcohol organized the first meetings of NA. In the ensuing decades, more and more 12-step organizations were founded, and the scope of problems addressed by them came to include gambling, overeating, incest, debt, smoking, chronic mental illness, and relationship problems, among many others. Following AA, most 12-step organizations adopted the name "Anonymous" in their title (e.g., Overeaters Anonymous).

The Twelve Steps

AA's version of the 12 steps is presented in Table 1. Most subsequent 12-step organizations adopted the 12-steps of AA verbatim, with the exception of modifying steps 1 and 12 to refer to problems other than alcoholism. A few groups modified the language of the steps to make references to God gender-neutral (e.g., "Made a decision to turn our will and our lives over to the care of God as we understand *God*"). GROW, a 12-step organization for chronic mental patients, reworded the steps more extensively to make them simpler and less focused on God or a higher power (e.g., step 2 became "We cooperated with help," step 12, "We carried the GROW message to others in need").

Regardless of the specific wording employed, certain themes appear in all known versions of the 12 steps. Twelve-step philosophy holds that suffering individuals do not wish to admit their role in their own problem because this would be a blow to their sense of personal power and control. Hence, the first component of any 12-step program is to admit that one has a problem that one cannot solve on one's own (step one). Because the 12 steps locate the source of the problem inside the individual rather than in the environment, this admission implies that intrapersonal change will be required for the person to resolve his or her difficulty.

The second key component of the 12 steps—"surrender to a Higher Power"—is probably the aspect of these groups most misunderstood by outsiders, including psychologists. In 12-step programs, surrender is not an abdication of responsibility. Rather, surrender involves recognizing realistic limits on personal control over one's problems. To 12-step group members, this recognition is not a cause for despair because more powerful forces are available in the environment that can aid the member (steps two and three). For many members, surrender to a "Higher Power" involves coming to believe in God or a spiritual force that members define as they wish. For other members, it means admitting that one needs help from particular group members or from the fellowship as a whole.

Steps four through nine comprise an organized review of members' current and past behavior. Originally, these steps were intended to lead members who had caused suffering (e.g., alcoholics who had abandoned their families, addicts who had robbed others) to make restitution and in the process to relieve their shame and guilt about past transgressions. As the 12 steps began to be used by groups composed of individuals who more often had been victimized than they had victimized others (e.g., incest survivors), some groups modified their use of steps four through nine to be an even-handed review both of wrongs committed by and wrongs done to the member, allowing expression of resentment and anger, as well as relief of shame.

The 12 steps are designed based on the assumption that recovery is a lifelong process, and therefore that members never "complete the 12 steps." This viewpoint is reflected in steps 10 to 12, which are designed to maintain the personal and spiritual changes that members have undergone in their practice of earlier steps. The twelfth step embodies the altruistic spirit of the program by emphasizing that those who have been helped have an obligation to help others who are still suffering. Twelve-step programs assume that this helping of others will also benefit the helper. By continually attempting to incorporate the 12-step program into their daily lives, members are intended to experience not only resolution of the problem that brought them to the group, but also a sense of spiritual peace or "serenity." Hence, members who experience remission of their immediate problem (e.g., an NA member who abstains from drugs) are not considered recovered until they also undergo basic changes in character and worldview that bring them serenity.

From a philosophical point of view, the concepts embodied in the 12 steps have a long history. Many religious and spiritual traditions emphasize that selfish defects such as grandiosity, greed, and arrogant pride (the "hubris" of many of the Greek tragedies) cause suffering and block spiritual growth. In these traditions, admission of the limited nature of the self is the door to spiritual redemption and serenity. Twelve-step programs, beginning with AA, translated this ancient wisdom and set of healing rituals into modern language and applied it to modern problems. This may be why 12-step programs are so popular in countries with a Judeo-Christian tradition, for they resonate with spiritual themes already embedded in these cultures.

In practical terms, the 12 steps are not treated as a mandate. Group members are not required to take the steps or even to know them well. AA's cofounder wrote that "our 12 steps of recovery are suggestions" (1952). Many members of 12-step organizations do not make working the steps, spiritual change, or worldview transformation a central focus of their participation. Just as in any other organization that has a developed worldview (e.g., churches, political movements), individuals attend 12-step groups for diverse reasons, including the fellowship and support of other people.

Prevalence and Effects of 12-Step Self-Help Organizations

In 1990, Robin Room and Thomas Greenfield conducted a national survey of 12-step group involvement using a representative sample of 2,058 persons (1993). United States attendance rates in the past year for 12-step organizations were 3.6% for AA, 1.7% for Al-Anon, 0.8% for Adult Children of Alcoholics, and 1.6% for all other 12-step groups combined (e.g., Gamblers Anonymous, Narcotics Anonymous). These prevalence rates indicate that 12-step programs are the most widely diffused form of group help seeking in the United States, substantially outstripping group psychotherapy and professionally facilitated support groups in popularity. Because the sum of these attendance rates for individual organizations (7.7%) is greater than the proportion of the U.S. population reporting attendance at any 12-step self-help group in the prior year (5.3%), a significant proportion of 12-step group members must attend more than one type of 12-step group.

Most studies of the effects of participating in 12-step organizations have been conducted with AA members, and are therefore discussed elsewhere in this volume. A variety of methods have been employed to study other 12-step groups. Kennedy and Humphreys (1994) conducted qualitative, participant observation studies of GROW and Adult Children of Alcoholics and found that experienced members reported significant changes in their worldview congruent with the philosophy embodied in the 12 steps. Specifically, highly involved members come to be more accepting of their problem and of themselves, have a more positive view of other people, and experience a closer connection to God. Such ethnographic studies of experienced members show that 12-step group involvement can be a positive and extremely meaningful experience but do not allow evaluation of how common this experience is among members or whether such changes in worldview necessarily produces the behavioral changes that most members are seeking.

Quantitative studies of 12-step group members have also been conducted. In one such study, Kenneth Maton (1989) found that active members of Overeaters Anonymous report a greater sense of connection with God than do members of non-12-step self-help organizations. The research of Christo and Franey has shown that long-term NA members have similar self-esteem and anxiety levels as never addicted college students, and that attending NA after substance abuse treatment is linked to lower likelihood of relapse (1995).

These and other studies of 12-step self-help groups point to positive effects of participation. However, several cautions are warranted. First, although the effectiveness of AA has been supported in several studies, the research base on other 12-step groups is very small. Second, many of the evaluations that have been conducted of 12-step groups were cross-sectional and did not include a comparison group, making any inferences about cause and effect difficult. Hence, although initial results are promising, a sustained and sophisticated research effort will be necessary to acquire definitive information on the effects of participating in community-based 12-step self-help groups.

In addition to influencing members, 12-step groups have also had an impact on the professional treatment system. Although professional treatment is different from community-based, indigenously controlled 12-step groups, many treatment programs (particularly those for substance dependent patients) attempt to adopt some 12-step principles. A controlled study of 1,726 alcohol dependent patients found that a professionally administered "12 step facilitation therapy" that attempted to convey 12-step concepts and encourage attendance at AA was just as effective as cognitive-behavioral and motivational enhancement psychotherapies (1997). Hence, despite some underlying value differences between 12-step groups and professional psychotherapists (e.g., on whether it is appropriate to charge money for help) it may be possible for certain techniques used in 12-step groups to be successfully employed in professional service contexts.

Twelve-step groups are an important cultural phenomenon and represent both an asset and a challenge to people interested in human psychology. They are an asset for what they teach us about how to help individuals with diverse problems in living. They are a challenge in that they are a free, widely available, popular source of nonprofessional help, and therefore raise questions of whether clinical training is actually a prerequisite for helping people who have severe problems. Twelve-step groups have occasional "open" meetings which interested nonmembers are welcome to attend. Individuals who wish to learn more about 12-step groups should take advantage of this opportunity in their community. Contact information for all 12-step organizations is available from the sourcebook of the American Self-Help Clearinghouse, a non-profit organization located in Denville, N.J.

[*See also* Alcoholics Anonymous.]

Acknowledgments. The author acknowledges the support of the Rotterdam Addiction Research Institute and the Veterans Affairs Mental Health Strategic Health Group.

Bibliography

Alcoholics Anonymous. (1952). *Twelve steps and twelve traditions.* New York: AA World Services. The founders of AA explain the development and rationale of the 12-step approach.

Christo, G., & Franey, C. (1995). Drug users' spiritual beliefs, locus of control and the disease concept in relation to Narcotics Anonymous attendance and six-month outcomes. *Drug and Alcohol Dependence, 38*, 51–56.

Humphreys, K. (1993). Psychotherapy and the twelve step approach for substance abusers: The limits of integration. *Psychotherapy, 30*, 207–213. An essay reviewing the differences between 12-step self-help groups and professional psychotherapy.

Kennedy, M., & Humphreys, K. (1994). Understanding worldview transformation in mutual help groups. *Prevention in Human Services, 11*, 181–198.

Kurtz, E., & Ketcham, K. (1992). *The spirituality of imperfection: Modern wisdom from classic stories.* New York: Bantam. Intended for a popular audience, this book explores how the philosophy inherent in the 12 steps has developed in various religious and cultural traditions through history.

Kurtz, L. F. (1997). *Self-help and support groups: A handbook for practitioners.* Thousand Oaks, CA: Sage.

Maton, K. I. (1989). Towards an ecological understanding of mutual-help groups: The social ecology of "fit." *American Journal of Community Psychology, 17*, 729–753.

Nowinski, J., & Baker, S. (1992). *The 12-step facilitation handbook: A systematic approach to early recovery from alcoholism and addiction.* New York: Lexington Books. Describes an effort to integrate aspects of 12-step groups in professional counseling.

Project Match Research Group. (1997). *Journal of Studies on Alcohol, 58*, 7–29.

Room, R., & Greenfield, T. (1993). Alcoholics anonymous, other 12-step movements and psychotherapy in the US population, 1990. *Addiction, 88*, 555–562.

White, B. J., & Madara, E. J. (1998). *The self-help sourcebook* (6th ed.). Denville, NJ: American Self-Help Clearinghouse. Accessible and comprehensive listing of self-help organizations in the United States.

Keith Humphreys

TWINS. The use of twins in research on the causes of individual differences in mental and physical characteristics was introduced by Sir Francis Galton (1876, 1883), who was the first to note that the existence of two types of twins, identical and fraternal. He afforded a method by which it was possible to assess the relative effects of "nature and nurture" in the development of individual differences. His insight later became known as the classical twin method. Galton himself never applied it in any precise, quantitative way because he lacked the objective, quantitative measures of behavioral traits on which correlation analysis depends and also the essential statistical tools. Karl Pearson did not invent the product-moment correlation until 1896, and Sir Ronald Fisher had not yet invented the analysis of variance, yet these statistical methods are required for the classical twin method to yield a quantitative interpretation when applied to a metric trait. Galton, however, collected many anecdotal examples of the high degree of behavioral resemblance between identical twins as compared with the lesser resemblance between fraternal twins and pairs of singleton siblings. He observed that when sets of identical twins are compared alongside sets of fraternal twins, the relative influences of nature and nurture on many types of behavior appeared to be of nearly comparable magnitude to their generally obvious effects on visible physical characteristics. He asserted, "There is no escape from the conclusion that nature prevails enormously over nurture when the differences of nurture do not exceed what is commonly to be found among persons of the same rank of society and in the same country" (Galton, 1876, p. 576). [*See the biographies of Fisher, Galton, and Pearson.*]

Galton's essential method has been applied in modern times, but with greater psychometric and statistical sophistication, to the study of the relative effects of heredity and environment on many types of behavior, particularly mental abilities and personality traits (Bouchard & Propping, 1992; Eaves et al., 1989). The twin method has proved so valuable in the genetic study of physical and mental afflictions that many countries now maintain national twin registries to provide subjects for genetical research.

Types of Twins

Identical, or monozygotic (MZ), twins result from a single fertilized ovum, or zygote, which splits in the early stages of mitosis to produce two individuals who carry exactly the same complement of genes; that is, they are clones, with identical DNA. Conjoined twins are the rare occurrence of an incomplete separation of the zygote (about 1 in 200 MZ twin births). MZ twins are, of course, always the same sex.

Fraternal, or dizygotic (DZ), twins result from two separate ova that have been fertilized by separate sperm. Hence DZ twins are genetically as much alike as ordinary full siblings born as singletons, with each individual inheriting a random half of each parent's genes. Like a pair of ordinary siblings, DZ twins can be of the same or opposite sex. In general, DZ twins are, on average, approximately half as genetically similar to one another as MZ twins. Because of the random assortment of the parental genes in the formation of ova and sperm, the degree of genetic resemblance in a specific trait between the members of a given pair of DZ twins can vary widely among different pairs. The two members of the pair of DZ twins can be nearly as much alike as MZ twins on a particular trait, especially if it is controlled by very few genes, or they can be much more dissimilar than most DZ twins or single-born siblings. It is only on average that DZ twins, theoretically, are half as similar genetically as MZ twins.

Frequency of Twinning

Approximately 1 pregnancy in 89 produces twins, although this figure varies in different populations. More specifically, in every 1,000 pregnancies there are, on average, 3 to 4 MZ twins and, in the United States, 7 to 12 DZ twins. Unlike MZ twinning, which occurs at random and with the same relative frequency in every population, the frequency of DZ twinning varies according to the age of the mother (increasing with maternal age), parity (increasing with the number of previous pregnancies), and race: The frequency range per 1,000 births is 2 to 7 for Asians, 7 to 13 for Europeans, and 45 to 50 for sub-Saharan Africans. A woman's probability of giving birth to DZ twins is hereditary or familial, but a hereditary tendency for MZ twinning has not been clearly established.

Zygosity Diagnosis

When using twin data for genetical research, it is important to obtain an accurate diagnosis of the twins' zygosity (whether MZ or DZ). There are several methods of zygosity diagnosis, which differ much less in accuracy than in cost or convenience (Bulmer, 1970). The choice of method depends on the size of the twin sample, the cost, the personal accessibility of the subjects for examination, and the importance of minimizing error for the purpose of the particular study. The various methods have misclassification rates ranging from zero to about 10%. When samples are large and there is a good estimate of the error rate for a particular method of zygosity diagnosis, it is possible to apply a statistical correction in the data analysis that estimates the MZ and DZ correlations as if they were free of classification errors. The less reliable methods can be used in combination to decrease the overall error rate. Although MZ twins are generally born with one placenta and DZ twins with two, this and other obstetrical information, which is not always available or may be unreliably reported, is nowadays seldom used to ascertain zygosity.

The simplest and least expensive method is a self-report questionnaire, given to the twins or their parents, asking questions about eye color, hair color, hair whorls, degree of facial resemblance, height, weight, and other visible features. Such questionnaires are about 95% accurate. Monozygosity can be ruled out through a simple test for the twins' ability to taste the synthetic chemical phenylthiocarbamide (PTC), which is a single-gene trait. The fingerprints of MZ twins are as much alike as the fingerprints from the two hands of one individual, whereas DZ twins have distinctly different fingerprints. The number of matching blood types for a pair of twins establishes zygosity with an error rate inversely related to the number of different blood groups and their population frequencies. A skin graft between any two individuals except MZ twins is rejected and is a definitive test of zygosity. Today, however, when 100% accuracy is required, the method of choice is to use DNA markers, but this method, though noninvasive, is still costly and time-consuming.

Misclassifying twins' zygosity attenuates the estimate of genetic variance yielded by the classic twin method, because the MZ correlation is decreased by including misdiagnosed DZ twins in the MZ twin sample, while the DZ correlation is increased by including misdiagnosed MZ twins in the DZ twin sample.

Twin Correlations

The degree of resemblance between twins cannot be measured properly by the simple Pearson product-moment coefficient of correlation, *r*, which can yield many different values depending on the order in which members of each twin pair are assigned to each of the correlated variables in the bivariate distribution. To overcome this shortcoming of *r* for research on twins, Pearson proposed the double-entry method for calculating the correlation coefficient, whereby each pair of twins (say, twins A1 and A2) is entered twice, in the orders A1, A2 and A2, A1, before calculating the Pearson *r*. This method, however, has now been replaced by the intraclass correlation, r_i, invented by R. A. Fisher expressly for representing the correlation between two (or more) variables when their means and standard deviations in the population are assumed not to differ. This assumption statistically allows the sample value of r_i to have one more degree of freedom and hence a smaller standard error than the double-entry Pearson *r*. The intraclass correlation is defined in terms of the analysis of variance. Its theoretical population value is $\rho = \sigma_B^2/(\sigma_B^2 + \sigma_w^2)$, where σ_B^2 is the population variance *between* twin pairs and σ_w^2 is the population variance *within* twin pairs. The estimated value of ρ calculated from a sample of twins is $r_i = (V_B - V_w)/(V_B + V_w)$, where V_B is the sample variance *between* twin pairs and V_w is the sample variance *within* twin pairs. Because of the common practice of squaring the correlation coefficient to determine the proportion of variance in one variable that can be predicted by another variable, it is important to note that the correlation between twins (either MZ or DZ, or any other kinship), whether Pearson's double-entry *r* or Fisher's intraclass r_i, represents a proportion of the phenotypic variance and therefore should not be squared. (Henceforth, for simplicity of notation, the intraclass correlation, which will be used exclusively throughout, is symbolized simply as *r*.)

Monozygotic Twins Reared Apart

MZ twins separated in infancy and reared apart (MZA) are extremely rare; fewer than 170 such MZ pairs are reported in research literature, not counting the 53 MZ pairs reported by Burt, which are now conventionally excluded because their authenticity has been questioned (Mackintosh, 1995). Horatio H. Newman, Frank N. Freeman, and Karl J. Holzinger (1937) published the first important study using MZA to estimate the heritability of intelligence. MZA are particularly valuable for this purpose, because theoretically the intraclass correlation coefficient (r_{MZA}) between MZ twins reared apart in random or uncorrelated environments provides a direct estimate of the proportion of total genetic variance for the measured trait, which is also termed its *broad heritability*, or h_B^2 (i.e., the proportion of the total phenotypic variance attributable to all genetic influences—additive, dominant, and epistatic). In other words, theoretically $r_{MZA} = h_B^2$. (The square root of the broad heritability, or h_B is equal to the correlation between the genotypic and phenotypic values of the characteristic in question.) The degree of accuracy with which an observed correlation based on a sample of MZ twins actually estimates the population value of h_B^2 can only be answered empirically, by determining whether the MZ sample meets the assumption that they were reared in uncorrelated environments that also represent the range of environmental variation in the population to which the value of $r_{MZA} = h_B^2$ is to be generalized. Also, like any correlation, r_{MZA} has a standard error, which is inversely related to the number of twin pairs in the sample. Twin correlations are also attenuated by measurements that have imperfect reliability; the correlations can be statistically disattenuated if the reliability coefficient of the measurements in known.

If there is a significant correlation between separated twins for certain features of the environments in which they were reared, it is then necessary to determine the degree to which the correlated environmental variables are trait relevant (i.e., correlated with the trait in question). For example, if it is found that r_{MZA} for IQ is .75 in a given sample, and it is found that some aspect (X), of the twins' environments is positively correlated between twins, then we must ask whether variable X is relevant to IQ by determining its correlation with IQ. If the twin correlation for trait-relevant environmental variables is statistically significant, it can be taken into account in a path model for estimating the twin correlation for the trait of interest independent of the environmental effect (Bouchard, 1997, pp. 144–145). In doing this, one has to guard against the risk of statistically controlling the effects of certain environmental variables that have a substantial genetic component themselves, such as the education and socioeconomic status of the probands' biological parents. Other personal attributes, such as physical appearance, should also be examined as possible trait-relevant variables. It has been argued, for example, that MZ twins are highly similar in IQ because they look so much alike and therefore presumably are treated alike by others. This conjecture has been invalidated empirically by finding that "looks" are negligibly correlated with IQ (Bouchard, 1997).

The Classical Twin Method

This is based on the correlations of a particular metric trait between monozygotic twins reared together (MZT) and dizygotic twins reared together (DZT). Researchers usually obtain the DZT correlations separately for sets of same-sex and opposite-sex twins and combine these groups only if there is a nonsignificant difference between the correlations. The logic of the twin method is that the phenotypic correlation between MZT pairs (r_{MZT}) comprises the proportion of genetic variance shared in common by the twins (V_{GC}), which for MZ twins is the total genetic variance, or 1 V_{GC}, plus the environmental variance they have in common (V_{EC}). The DZT correlation (r_{DZT}) comprises one-half of the genetic variance ($V_{GC}/2$) plus the shared or common environmental variance (V_{EC}). The genetic and environmental components of the DZT correlation are subtracted from the corresponding components of the MZT correlation:

$$\begin{aligned} r_{MZT} &= 1\ V_{GC} + V_{EC} \\ r_{DZT} &= \tfrac{1}{2}\ V_{GC} + V_{EC} \\ \hline r_{MZT} - r_{DZT} &= \tfrac{1}{2}\ V_{GC} + 0 \end{aligned}$$

Hence the formula $2(r_{MZT} - r_{DZT})$ estimates the proportion of the total variance of the trait measurements that is attributable to genetic variance (V_G), which is an estimate of the heritability (h^2) of that trait. The proportion of environmental variance, e^2, is $1 - h^2/r_{XX}$, where r_{XX} is the reliability coefficient for the measurements. The component attributable to the shared, or common, environment is estimated by $e_c^2 = r_{MZT} - r_{MZA}$. The component attributable to the unshared, or unique, environment is estimated by $e_u^2 = 1 - r_{MZT}/r_{XX}$. In the case of IQ, the source of the unique environmental variance, e_u^2, which is better termed nongenetic variance, seems to be a host of virtually random prenatal and postnatal microenvironmental conditions with largely biological effects (Jensen, 1997).

This simple formulation may provide only a rough estimate of h^2, because all of its assumptions are usually not met. The model assumes entirely additive genetic variance and random mating of the twins' parents. These assumptions, however, are open to empirical investigation, the results of which can be used in more complex analytic models to obtain a more accurate estimate of h^2 (Neale & Cardon, 1992). For traits that have dominance variance, as does IQ for example, r_{DZ} is decreased, thereby inflating the estimate of h^2. Assortative mating (implying a genetic correlation between the twins' parents for the trait in question) increases r_{DZ}; assortative mating, however, does not affect r_{MZ}. (Jensen, 1978). The decrease in r_{DZ} caused by dominance may or may not balance out the increase in r_{DZ} caused by assortative mating. More complex models, therefore, take genetic dominance and assortative mating into account to derive a more accurate estimate of h^2 from the twin data. Another assumption is that the similarity of the twin's common environment, V_{EC}, is the same for the MZ and DZ twins. But it can be argued that MZT twins are more alike in a given trait because they are treated more alike by parents and peers than are DZT twins. Whether this is true and what effect it may have on the estimate of h^2 as calculated from the twin method is wholly an empirical question. In the case of IQ, it has been answered by obtaining the correlations for MZ twins whose parents mistook them for DZ, and for DZ twins who were mistaken for MZ, and treated them accordingly. In these specially selected samples, the MZ and DZ correlations were not significantly different, on average, from the typical MZ and DZ correlations in all other studies.

Typical Twin Correlations

Correlations reported in the literature for both MZ and DZ twins vary over a considerable range depending on many conditions, such as sample size, the population sampled, the particular trait, the age of the subjects, restriction of variance on the measured trait, differences in the reliability of the trait measurements, and statistical sampling error. The average correlations for IQ based on nearly all of the MZ and DZ correlations reported in the world literature (excluding Burt's data) have been determined as follows: MZA = 0.75, MZT = 0.86, DZT = 0.60 (Bouchard et al., 1990). For various personality traits, twin correlations range widely and, with a few exceptions, are generally lower than for IQ (Eaves et al., 1989).

Bibliography

Bouchard, T. J., Jr. (1997). IQ similarity in twins reared apart: Findings and responses to critics. In R. J. Sternberg & E. L. Grigorenko (Eds.), *Intelligence, heredity and environment* (pp. 126–160). Cambridge, England: Cambridge University Press.

Bouchard, T. J., Jr., Lykken, D. T., McGue, M., Segal, N. L., & Tellegen, A. (1990). Sources of human psychological difference: The Minnesota study of twins reared apart. *Science, 250*, 223–228; *Differences, 13*, 869–882.

Bouchard, T. J., Jr., & Propping, P. (Eds.). (1992). *Twins as a tool of behavioral genetics*. Chichester, England: Wiley.

Bulmer, M. G. (1970). *The biology of twinning in man*. Oxford, England: Clarendon.

Eaves, L., Eysenck, H. J., & Martin, N. (1989). *Genes, culture and personality: An empirical approach*. New York: Academic Press.

Galton, F. (1876). The history of twins, as a criterion of the relative powers of nature and nurture. *Journal of the Anthropoloigical Institute of Great Britain and Ireland, 5*, 391–406.

Galton, F. (1993). *Inquiries into human faculty and its development*. London: Macmillan.

Jensen, A. R. (1978). Genetic and behavioral effects of nonrandom mating. In R. T. Osborne, C. E. Noble, & N. Weyl (Eds.), *Human variation: The biopsychology of age, race, and sex* (pp. 51–105). New York: Academic Press.

Jensen, A. R. (1997). The puzzle of nongenetic variance. In R. J. Sternberg & E. L. Grigorenko (Eds.), *Intelligence, heredity and environment* (pp. 42–88). Cambridge, England: Cambridge University Press.

Mackintosh, N. J. (Ed.). (1995). *Cyril Burt: Fraud or framed?* New York: Oxford University Press.

Neale, M. C., & Cardon, L. R. (1992). *Methodology for genetic studies of twins and families*. Boston: Kluwer.

Newman, H. H., Freeman, F. N., & Holzinger, K. J. (1937). *Twins: A study of heredity and environment*. Chicago: University of Chicago Press.

Arthur R. Jensen

TYLER, LEONA E. (1906–1993), American counseling psychologist. Leona E. Tyler's psychological legacy covers research, theory, well-organized textbooks, and significant service to the profession. Her specialties were individual differences, interest measurement, human development, and counseling psychology. She consistently pursued research and theory to support professional practice aimed at bettering the human condition, including the peace movement. Her work as a counselor, researcher, writer, teacher, and graduate school dean mutually informed and influenced her research and writing. With astounding clarity, she integrated ideas and communicated the complexities of human multipotentiality.

Tyler gained a background in individual differences from her graduate work at the University of Minnesota. Her Ph.D. was granted in 1941, the year after she had joined the psychology faculty at the University of Oregon. She published one of the first books on individual differences, *The Psychology of Human Differences* (New York, 1947) and later published *Tests and Measurements* (New Jersey, 1963). She challenged traditional assessment practice by suggesting that tests be used to increase client self-awareness as well as for diagnosis or selection. She shifted the field's focus away from psychometrics for classification and directed inquiry toward the developmental and learning processes that influence how people develop differences.

Founding one of the first university counseling centers at the University of Oregon, Tyler provided direction to counseling as a specialty as it was emerging from the influences of other fields. With her early research in career development, she encouraged counseling psychology to stay focused on vocational development and the real-life problems of ordinary people. Her book *The Work of the Counselor* (New York, 1953) was the leading textbook for several generations of professionals, addressing personality theory and lifespan development. *Clinical Psychology* (with Sundberg & Taplin, New York, 1962) was also a leading textbook. She was a pioneer in considering cross-cultural and gender differences and highlighting the importance of both environmental and individual influences on development.

Tyler developed a card-sort method, the Choice Pattern Technique, to examine people's cognitive structures for organizing choices. Her "theory of possibilities" proposed that in most life situations choices are required, that opportunities are made by the individual as well as offered by the environment, and that individuals can actualize only a fraction of their possibilities. In later writings (e.g., *Individuality*, San Francisco, 1978), she strove to shift psychologists' concerns from individual differences to individuality and from trait psychology to inclusion of the whole person in the life history. Tyler suggested that counselors assist clients with making choices when they feel confused by all the possibilities in a complex world. She later utilized this theory to investigate how scientists become limited in what they choose to study. In *Thinking Creatively* (San Francisco, 1983) she suggested that science would be enriched if different paradigms could coexist and inform each other.

An active leader in both her local and professional communities, Tyler was respected and trusted for her intelligence, fairness, warmth, and decisiveness in both conflict and agreement. She made significant contributions to the University of Oregon, where she served in multiple roles for 33 years. Many years of leadership in professional organizations led to her serving as the eighty-first president of the American Psychological Association (1972–1973), only the fourth woman to be elected to that office. Her publications include 11 books, 14 book chapters, and more than 50 articles. She was the recipient of many awards, culminating in the prestigious American Psychological Foundation's Gold Medal for Lifetime Achievement in the Public Interest. Overall, an optimism about human development and human behavior underlies her work, which has provided a vital humanistic foundation for psychology.

Bibliography

Sundberg, N. D. (1991). Award citation. *American Psychologist, 46,* 330–332.

Sundberg, N. D., & Gilmore S. K. (1994). In memoriam: Leona E. Tyler, counseling pioneer. *Counseling Psychologist, 22,* 179–182.

Tyler, L. E. (1973). Design for a hopeful psychology. *American Psychologist, 28,* 1021–1029.

Tyler, L. E. (1988). Leona E. Tyler. In A. N. O'Connell & N. F. Russo (Eds.), *Models of achievement: Reflections of eminent women in psychology* (pp. 44–55). Hillsdale, NJ: Erlbaum.

Tyler, L. E., Sundberg, N., Rohila, P. K., & Greene, M. M. (1968). Patterns of choices in Dutch, American, and Indian adolescents. *Journal of Counseling Psychology, 15,* 522–529.

Zilber, S. M., & Osipow, S. H. (1990). Leona E. Tyler. In A. N. O'Connell & N. F. Russo (Eds.), *Women in psychology: A biobibliographic sourcebook* (pp. 335–341). Westport, CT: Greenwood.

Suzanne Mann Zilber and Norman Sundberg

TYPE A PERSONALITY. *See* Coronary Heart Disease; *and* Personality.

U

UNCONSCIOUSNESS. *See* Consciousness and Unconsciousness.

UNDERWOOD, BENTON J. (1915–1994), American psychologist, methodologist, and theoretician. During his 42 years (1941–1982) at Northwestern University, Underwood had 193 publications in the area of verbal learning and memory, including 174 journal articles (47 as sole author, 127 with coauthors), 10 book chapters, and 9 books. His importance as a methodologist can be seen in his books, which included *Experimental Psychology* (New York, 1949; 1966) *Psychological Research* (New York, 1957), and *Experimentation in Psychology* (New York, 1975). His importance as a theoretician is evident in his journal articles, including "Attributes of memory" (*Psychological Review*, 1969, *76*, 559–573) and "Individual differences as a crucible in theory construction" (*American Psychologist*, 1975, *30*, 128–134).

A prototypical functionalist, Underwood embodied the finest attributes of that tradition: integrity and a genuine priority of data. In addition, he was an "incurable associationist," an orientation enhanced by his mentors Arthur W. Melton, James A. McGeoch, and Kenneth W. Spence. As one of the foremost methodologists and theoreticians in the field, Underwood's contributions included the development or demonstration of (a) stage analysis of paired-associate learning; (b) the existence of implicit associative responses; (c) a frequency theory to explain verbal-discrimination learning and recognition memory; (d) the research area examining the ability of subjects to discriminate among words based on different laboratory-induced frequencies; (e) the importance of retroactive and proactive interference in long-term and short-term forgetting; and (f) the effect of distribution of practice on learning and memory. These contributions are briefly summarized.

In paired-associate learning, the task is to produce a particular response word when presented with a specific stimulus word. Underwood's basic conception of this paradigm as involving a response learning stage during which the response terms become available as units and an associative stage during which these units are hooked-up with the stimuli is still useful today. After demonstrating the existence of implicit associative responses, Underwood established their importance for theoretical accounts of paired-associate learning, free-recall learning, and recognition memory.

When learning a verbal-discrimination list, a subject's task is to learn which unit in a pair of verbal units has been arbitrarily designated as the correct unit. In 1966, Bruce Ekstrand, William Wallace, and Underwood (*Psychological Review, 73*, 566–678) proposed a theory to explain how subjects learn such a list. This line of research was expanded to investigate the ability of students to make recognition decisions and to discriminate among words presented for varying frequencies. Research in these areas continues to this day.

Prior to publication in 1957 of his oft-cited paper on interference and forgetting, (*Psychological Review, 64*, 49–60), the primary explanation for the forgetting observed in laboratory situations was retroactive interference. (Material learned after a critical list interfered with recall of that list.) Underwood's analysis indicated that the massive forgetting obtained over a 24-hour retention interval by Hermann Ebbinghaus (*Memory*, New York, 1885/1964) and others was more a result of proactive interference produced by associations acquired in earlier lists than it was retroactive interference. [*See the biography of Ebbinghaus.*] The importance of proactive interference in short-term memory was demonstrated in 1962 by Geoffrey Keppel and Underwood (*Journal of Verbal Learning and Verbal Behavior, 1,* 153–161).

Underwood's 16-year quest for an empirical and theoretical description of the effects of massed and distributed practice, while leading to several important methodological techniques, did not produce the hoped for supportable empirical generalizations.

Bibliography

Freund, J. S. (1998). Benton J. Underwood: A tribute of memories. In G. A. Kimble & M. Wertheimer (Eds.). *Portraits of pioneers in psychology* (Vol. 3, pp. 309–326). Mahwah, NJ: Erlbaum. Biographical material and reminiscences from his students about Underwood as man and teacher.

Postman, L. (1972). The experimental analysis of verbal learning and memory: Evolution and innovation. In C. P. Duncan, L. Sechrest, & A. W. Melton (Eds.), *Human memory: Festschrift in honor of Benton J. Underwood.* New York: Appleton-Century-Crofts. An analysis of Underwood's contributions up to that time, with papers by his students.

Underwood, B. J. (1982). *Studies in learning and memory: Selected papers.* New York: Praeger. Includes a biographical sketch, historical perspective, and reprints of 15 selected papers.

Joel S. Freund

UNEMPLOYMENT. *See* Job Loss and Unemployment.

UNION OF SOVIET SOCIALIST REPUBLICS. *See* Russia and the Former Soviet Republics.

UNIONS have enjoyed a controversial place in American society throughout the twentieth century. The decline in union membership in the United States and elsewhere (e.g., Britain) has led to questions about the future viability and even necessity of unions. However, coming at the same time as fundamental changes in the nature of work (Tetrick & Barling, 1995) and a new political perspective by the AFL-CIO under President John Sweeney that emphasizes mass organizing in place of political action, the demise of unions is by no means assured. Given that unions exert some role on individual behavior in organizations and organizational functioning (Barling, Fullagar, & Kelloway, 1992; Freeman & Medoff, 1984), the contribution of psychology to an understanding of these issues is of considerable theoretical and practical importance.

An examination of the research conducted by psychologists on unions reveals two interesting trends. First, there would appear to be three separate streams of research, namely voting behavior in union elections, union commitment and participation, and conflict and its associated activities (e.g., conflict, conflict resolution, grievances, and negotiation). The first two streams focus on the individual, while the third focuses on group behavior.

Second, this research focus has been intermittent. Considerable research was conducted during the 1950s. Following this, however, much less research took place for the next 15 years, a period characterized by mutual distrust between union officials and psychologists. Several factors account for this: among others, organizational psychologists' tendency to (a) be affiliated with management, (b) often subscribe to the "unitary perspective" of industrial conflict, and (c) prefer to refrain from studying value-laden issues such as union membership (Barling, Fullagar, & Kelloway, 1992; Gordon & Nurick, 1981).

Union Commitment and Participation

Since 1980, psychologists have again turned their focus to understanding unions and their members. Clearly, the major impetus for this was the work of Michael Gordon. Not only was Gordon legitimizing the study of unions and exhorting his colleagues to again direct their attention to unions (e.g., Gordon & Nurick, 1981), his landmark study of union commitment set the research agenda for at least the next decade (Gordon, Philpot, Burt, Thompson, & Spiller, 1980). Gordon and his colleagues identified four factors of union commitment, namely loyalty to the union, willingness to work for the union, responsibility to the union, and belief in unionism (1980). The factor structure of union commitment then attracted some attention in the United States, South Africa, the Netherlands, and Canada. Irrespective of whether a two-, three-, or four-factor structure emerged, union commitment and its components were invariably associated with union participation in these cross-sectional studies.

Toward the end of the 1980s, attention also focused on the antecedents and outcomes of union commitment (Fullagar & Barling, 1987). Studies from different perspectives confirmed the utility of union commitment. Union commitment consistently predicted participation in union activities (Fullagar & Barling, 1987; Kelloway & Barling, 1993), and also predicted the propensity to strike (see Barling, Fullagar, & Kelloway, 1992). In an intriguing twist, a study in the Netherlands showed that when union members can leave the union voluntarily, union commitment was negatively associated with intent to leave the union. Thus, research has consistently demonstrated that union commitment is a statistically significant predictor of outcomes of considerable relevance to unions, in cross-sectional and longitudinal studies, in the United States and many other countries.

It should be noted, however, that the earliest research on union commitment focused exclusively on the question of "dual commitment" or dual allegiance, namely, whether individuals could be loyal to their organizations and their unions simultaneously. Interestingly, the impetus for this line of research derived from a larger social issue: In the early 1950s, considerable interest centered around the issue of whether American citizens could be loyal to two disparate political systems simultaneously, namely the United States and the Soviet Union. As Gordon and Ladd suggest (1990), interest in dual commitment was initially sustained by the assumption of industrial harmony that underlies this concept. More recently, the provision of a reliable and valid measurement of both union commitment and organizational commitment render this research question more accessible.

Literally scores of studies have now been conducted on dual commitment between a union and a company, and the results can be readily consolidated. When union-management relations are favorable, positive correlations emerge between union and organizational commitment. For example, in a situation in which management and the union agreed to a no-layoff provision in exchange for greater union cooperation, the relationship between union and company loyalty was +.27. In contrast, where union-management relations are strained, the correlation between union and company commitment is invariably significant and negative; this correlation was −.25 in a sample of community teachers 2 months after striking employees had been legislated back to work without a settlement. In a similar vein, a study in South Africa revealed that the relationship between union and company commitment is negative (−.26) in "aggressive" unions but significant and positive in "protective" unions (+.43), which see their aim as maintaining the status quo. Dual commitment is therefore an outcome variable, serving as a proxy for the nature of union-management relations (see Barling, Fullagar, & Kelloway, 1992).

Despite the ease with which these findings on dual commitment can be categorized, it is unlikely that much research will focus on this concept in the future. First, it is questionable whether our conceptual or practical understanding of unions and their members is advanced by such findings. Second, and perhaps more ominously, Gordon and Ladd advise against further research on dual commitment (1990). One possible factor underlying the research on dual commitment has been interest in developing a profile of the "union activist," that is, someone who is unilaterally committed to the union. It behooves psychologists to avoid falling into this trap: First, from a scientific perspective, the amount of variance accounted for in any of these studies is probably insufficient on which to base any selection (or exclusion) decisions. Second, using these data to exclude union activists from the organization may well violate the ethical principle of ensuring that data derived from people cannot be used to harm them. Third, any such use of these data would invariably set back the hard-won relationship between psychologists and union officials and members.

Voting for Unions in Certification Elections

The separate question of why people would vote for unions in certification elections has attracted more empirical attention, and for a longer time period, than union commitment and union participation (see Barling, Fullagar, & Kelloway, 1992, for a review). For example, early research in the 1930s pointed to the role of social factors in the decision to join a union. By the 1940s it was clear that economic benefits are not the only goal of unions and that focusing entirely on them would underrate the importance of unions. The potential role of early family experiences was recognized, and subsequent research replicated these early findings (see Barling, Fullagar, & Kelloway, 1992). However, these findings identified single predictors in isolation. More recent research has diverged from this early focus inasmuch as omnibus models explicating the individual decision-making process have now been proposed.

Perhaps the most important study, and also the most hotly debated, is that of Getman, Goldberg, and Herman, who analyzed data from 31 union representation elections (1976). Based on these data, Brett generated arguably the first psychological model of union voting behavior (1980). Within this model, initial interest in unionization is stimulated by current job dissatisfaction, typically dissatisfaction with extrinsic factors such as wages and supervision. Dissatisfaction by itself, however, would not be sufficient. Individuals would also need to see that the union is instrumental in overcoming the specific dissatisfactions. The attitudes of other employees and other salient individuals (e.g., family members and friends) would also be important. Lastly, the individuals' own attitudes toward unions in general would either exacerbate the likelihood of a prounion vote if the attitudes to unions were positive or decrease the likelihood of a prounion vote if attitudes were not favorable. This model obtained some support from a subsequent meta-analysis.

Two recent developments in the study of individual voting behavior in union elections, one practical and one conceptual, have the potential for advancing the field as well as changing its direction somewhat. From a practical perspective, whether the union wins the election or not, union elections are invariably decided by a small margin. What is more important from a practical perspective is that the number of people who choose not to vote is usually sufficient to change the outcome of the election. This raises the question of why people would choose not to vote. For example, Hepburn, Loughlin, and Barling showed that abstainers differ from voters (irrespective of the direction of their vote) in that they perceived their vote as significantly less likely to make a difference in the outcome of the election and expressed less interest in its outcome (1997).

Consistent with the long-held idea that early family experiences would affect an individual's willingness to vote for a union, Barling, Kelloway, and Bremermann (1991) argued against the notion of assessing whether parents' union status (i.e., members or not) would exert any effect on children's attitudes toward unions. Instead, because parents could be members of a union but actively opposed to it or not be members of a union but strongly in favor of one, they argued that children's perceptions of their parents' union participation and attitudes would be more salient in influencing their own union attitudes, which in turn would predict union voting behaviors. Their model was supported and has since been replicated.

What this means is that potential influences on individuals' decisions to vote for or against a union begin well before individuals encounter the workplace. This has two important implications. From a conceptual perspective, it means that the unionization process, which was previously regarded as only comprising the organizing campaign and the actual vote, now begins well beforehand. Taking voting for a union as the first indication of prounion participation, the unionization process also extends well beyond the initial vote. From a research perspective, the fact that young children's union attitudes are being shaped by early family socialization suggests a possible wider role for psychologists in understanding the unionization process.

Conclusion

The research that has been conducted thus far has provided a framework for understanding psychological aspects involved in the broad unionization process. Given changes within the external environment that affect workers, such as the move toward a new employment relationship (Tetrick & Barling, 1995), new directions in this research are now needed. Arguably, psychological research on unions and their members will be enhanced to the extent to which psychologists broaden their focus to understand how unions can be more effective in serving their members' needs.

[*See also* Conflict Resolution; *and* Negotiation.]

Bibliography

Barling, J., Fullagar, C., & Kelloway, E. K. (1992). *The union and its members: A psychological approach.* New York: Oxford University Press.

Barling, J., Kelloway, E. K., & Bremermann, E. H. (1991). Preemployment predictors of union attitudes: The role of family socialization and work beliefs. *Journal of Applied Psychology, 76,* 725–731.

Brett, J. M. (1980). Why employees want unions. *Organizational Dynamics, 8,* 47–59.

Freeman, R. B., & Medoff, J. L. (1984). *What do unions do?* New York: Basic Books.

Fullagar, C., & Barling, J. (1987). Toward a model of union commitment. In D. Lewin, D. B. Lipsky, & D. Sockell (Ed.), *Advances in industrial and labor relations* (pp. 43–78). Greenwich, CT: JAI Press.

Getman, J. G., Goldberg, S. B., & Herman, J. B. (1976). *Union representation elections: Law and reality.* New York: Russell Sage Foundation.

Gordon, M. E., & Ladd, R. T. (1990). Dual allegiance: Renewal, reconsideration, and recantation. *Personnel Psychology, 43,* 37–69.

Gordon, M. E., & Nurick, A. J. (1981). Psychological approaches to the study of unions and union-management relations. *Psychological Bulletin, 90,* 293–306.

Gordon, M. E., Philpot, J. W., Burt, R. E., Thompson, C. A., & Spiller, W. E. (1980). Commitment to the union: Development of a measure and an examination of its correlates. *Journal of Applied Psychology, 65,* 474–499.

Hepburn, C. G., Loughlin, C., & Barling, J. (1997). Abstaining from voting in union certification elections. In M. Sverke (Ed.), *The future of trade unionism: International perspectives on emerging union structures* (pp. 249–262). London: Ashgate.

Kelloway, E. K., & Barling, J. (1993). Members' participation in local union activities: Measurement, prediction, and replication. *Journal of Applied Psychology, 78,* 262–279.

Tetrick, L. E., & Barling, J. (1995). *Changing employment relations: Behavioral and social perspectives.* Washington, DC: American Psychological Association.

Julian Barling

UNITED KINGDOM. *See* England; Northern Ireland; Scotland; *and* Wales.

UNITED STATES DEPARTMENT OF VETERANS AFFAIRS. The Veterans Administration (VA) was established in 1930 to consolidate federal government activities affecting war veterans. Prior to 1930, three agencies administered benefits for veterans: the Veterans Bureau, the Bureau of Pensions, and the National Homes for Disabled Volunteer Soldiers. Brig. Gen. Frank T. Hines, who had headed the Veterans Bureau for 7 years, was named the first administrator of Veterans Affairs. With the executive order that established the VA, 54 VA hospitals were created from preexisting Veterans Bureau Homes and National Homes for Disabled

Volunteer Soldiers. Many of the new VA hospitals were designated as facilities for the treatment of tuberculosis or had large tuberculosis treatment services.

The end of World War II increased the veteran beneficiary population by nearly 16 million. In 1944, the G.I. Bill of Rights authorized vocational, educational, and mental-health assistance for veterans, and the VA was given the responsibility of providing these rehabilitation services. In the 1940s, many new VA hospitals were constructed or acquired from the military to respond to this additional workload.

In 1946, the Department of Medicine and Surgery was established as a separate organizational unit within the VA Central Office (VACO) to be responsible for providing medical care to veterans. Also initiated was a system of affiliations with medical schools and universities to help train the many professionals needed to work in VA hospitals. Vocational counseling became a separate service in VA hospitals, with clinical psychology a division or section under psychiatry service, which, in some hospitals, was a division under medical service.

James Grier Miller was appointed the first chief clinical psychologist for the VACO in 1946. Prior to this time, doctoral psychologists were very scarce, and the VA had hired master's degree–level clinical and counseling psychologists to provide the rehabilitation and counseling benefits mandated by Congress. Miller was instrumental in having the doctoral degree and internship adopted as the minimum qualification standards for the employment of VA clinical psychologists in 1946.

Succeeding Miller as VA chief clinical psychologist were Harold M. Hildreth in 1948, Max Houtchens in 1956, and Cecil Peck in 1962. These individuals continued to develop a vision and standard of excellence for psychological services and programs in the VA. By 1982, appointment as a psychologist in the VA required a doctoral degree in clinical or counseling psychology from a graduate school approved by the American Psychological Association (APA). An APA-approved internship was also required, as was state licensure or certification.

Psychology Programs and Research in the Veterans Administration

With the establishment of psychology sections in VA hospitals in 1946, VA psychologists were instrumental in developing and directing token economy programs, behavioral medicine clinics for treatment of phobias and addictions, and partial hospitalization programs for psychiatric patients, such as day treatment centers and day hospitals. The Psychiatric Evaluation Program (PEP), headed by psychologist Lee Gurel in VACO, documented the important role of long-term treatment for psychiatric patients. The PEP both institutionalized evaluation research in the VA and served as a model for the subsequent VA Cooperative Study research program, which involved psychologists and other researchers and research populations from multiple hospitals in studying many important health issues for veterans.

VA psychologists also assumed critical consultant roles for hospital management in program development and training programs. The TIGER program (Training in Individual and Group Effectiveness and Resourcefulness) was one major training program headed by Philip Hanson and a group of other psychologists at the VA hospital in Houston in the early 1970s. TIGER provided leadership and interpersonal training to over 40,000 employees.

Following the Vietnam War, Congress authorized the establishment of small treatment teams of mental-health professionals and paraprofessionals in Vet Centers to provide readjustment counseling to veterans of that war. This program was initially assigned to the Mental Health and Behavioral Sciences Service in VACO in 1979 and was headed by psychologist Donald Crawford.

The Veterans Administration Psychology Training Program

Seeing the need for well-trained and qualified psychologists, the VA started a field training program in clinical psychology in 1946. This program introduced a number of significant features that guided the training of psychologists in this country. A decision was made to train and recruit doctoral psychologists with both academic and clinical training. This scientist-practitioner model preceded the Boulder Conference, which promoted this model for other training programs. The VA asked the APA to identify schools that could provide this training. This request led the APA to begin the development of an accreditation process for graduate programs in clinical and counseling psychology.

By the late 1960s, the VA was providing practicum and internship training to over half of the clinical and counseling psychologists receiving such training in this country. The administration of the VA psychology internship training program in use today gives training funds to APA-approved VA psychology services to select and train students from APA-approved graduate school programs in clinical or counseling psychology.

Veterans Administration Psychology Today

In 1989, Congress designated the Veterans Administration a cabinet-level department, and the agency was renamed the Department of Veterans Affairs. In 1996, there were 1,408 full-time psychologists and 658 psychology technicians and vocational rehabilitation specialists employed in 171 VA hospitals and 232 outpatient clinics. In 1991, the VA established its first funded psychology postdoctoral training positions in substance abuse. Funding for postdoctoral fellowships in gero-psychology followed in 1992. For the 1996 to 1997 training year, the VA funded 393 predoctoral psychology internship positions in 90 APA-approved VA training sites.

VA psychologists are involved in consultation and research, in addition to treatment, assessment, and training activities. Staff psychologists provide services to patients in both general and specialized psychiatric, medical, and surgical programs, such as substance abuse, posttraumatic shock disorder, and spinal cord injury treatment programs. VA psychologists also hold faculty appointments in affiliated medical schools and universities.

The Association of VA Chief Psychologists was founded in 1977 to address organizational and clinical issues affecting psychology in the VA. In 1982, the National Organization of VA Psychologists was formed as a companion group to focus on professional and clinical concerns of VA staff psychologists. Both groups established working relationships with the APA to promote the independent practice of psychologists in the VA and to enhance the patient care, training, and research activities of VA psychologists.

Bibliography

Baker, R. R. (1992). *VA Psychology: 1946–1992*. (Available from Rodney R. Baker, Chief of Psychology, South Texas Veterans Health Care System, San Antonio, Texas.)

Moore, D. L. (1992). The Veterans Administration and the training of psychology. In D. K. Freedheim (Ed.), *History of psychotherapy* (pp. 776–800). Washington, DC: American Psychological Association.

Rodney R. Baker

UNOBTRUSIVE MEASURES. Unobtrusive was the label given to a large class of diverse measures that had the common aim of dealing with problems of bias in measurement in the social sciences arising from the fact that most measures result in biased estimates of the phenomenon of interest. A frequent source of that bias is that measures are reactive: The act of measurement changes the phenomenon being measured. For example, tell a person, "Stand up against this wall. I want to see how tall you are," and almost everyone will pull himself or herself up to maximum height, which may be contrasted with "walking around height." Or, let a person know, intentionally or inadvertently, that a questionnaire is a measure of attitudes toward minorities, and the person's inclination to endorse diverse statements will change. The assumption underlying unobtrusive measures is that if a person or group is unaware of the measurement process, reactivity will be averted.

The problem of central interest is reactivity of measurement; unobtrusiveness is simply a tactic for reducing reactivity. A whole range of methods for reducing reactivity of measurement exists, ranging from promising anonymity and assurances that responses will be used only for "scientific" purposes, to the use of special instrumentation, obscuring the purpose of the measurement, and obscuring the fact of measurement. The term *unobtrusive* has come to serve as a generic term for those methods.

Every measurement procedure carries with it characteristic sources of bias, that is, consistent direction in error of measurement. Accuracy of measurement (reduced bias) can be improved by using multiple measures not sharing the same sources of bias. Unobtrusive measures are not assumed to be without their own sources of error, but they may often be assumed not to reflect the same type or degree of reactivity as other measures. Questionnaires and interviews are particularly likely to reflect tendencies on the part of respondents to want to make some particular impression. In addition, both are dependent upon consensual understanding of conventions concerning the meanings of words and the circumstance of being "measured." Because they reflect different approaches to measurement, unobtrusive measures can often get around the limitations of self-report measures.

Unobtrusive measures may be derived in many different ways: simple observation, archives, physical traces, episodic public and private records, and contrived observation and hidden hardware. The possibilities are almost unlimited. Unobtrusive measures are not the exclusive domain of social science researchers. A recent news story reflected an observation that military dictators who begin to detect resistance and desire to establish their legitimacy tend to abandon their military uniforms and don civilian attire (simple observation), with recent appearances of Saddam Hussein of Iraq in regular business suits cited as an interesting prospect. Detectives rely on physical traces (erosion and accretion) of responses they have never seen; real estate companies are tested for racially discriminatory practices by persons pretending to be clients (contrived observation); video cameras (hidden hardware) are ubiquitous; and archived data are regularly used to track behaviors that might otherwise not be detectable save by self-report. Episodic personal and private records are in heavy use in hearings involving activities in the White House to check on the veracity of self-reports by those whose actions are in question. Even though unobtrusive measures are not used as often as would be desirable in social science, their legitimation is reflected in the fact that the term is no longer capitalized, italicized, or given any specific literature citation.

It is important that unobtrusive measures not be regarded as substitutes for other kinds of measures; that would be the antithesis of their rationale. They are properly thought of as complementary to other measures, such as self-reports. Unobtrusive measures may at times be used as measures in their own right, for example, as when archived records of the U.S. Congress are used to track some tendency in its behavior, such as lapses of courtesy and manners. Unobtrusive measures can also be used to good effect in parallel with other measures to provide sources of information complementary to surveys or questionnaires. Unobtrusive measures are particularly useful as probes to accompany other measures in order to provide indicators of the other measures' trustworthiness.

Unobtrusive measures are often neither simple nor cheap to collect, and at least some uses of them may raise ethical issues by the very fact of their unobtrusiveness. Also, their psychometric properties are little studied. Regrettably, the lack of systematic study makes hazardous the formation of scales and indicators based on unobtrusive observations. Nonetheless, their use can be strongly recommended, and their increased use will inexorably lead to their improved understanding and the ultimate refinement of the methods by which they are assembled and employed.

Bibliography

Webb, E, Campbell, D. T., Schwartz, R. D., & Sechrest, L. (1966). *Unobtrusive measures: Nonreactive measures in the social sciences.* Chicago: Rand McNally.

Webb, E., Campbell, D. T., Schwartz, R. D., Sechrest, L., & Grove, J. B. (1981). *Nonreactive measures in the social sciences* (2nd ed.). Boston: Houghton Mifflin.

Lee Sechrest

UPHAM, THOMAS COGSWELL (1799–1872), American mental philosopher. Regarded as the author of the first American textbook in psychology, Upham was born in Rochester, New Hampshire, and graduated from Dartmouth College in 1818 and Andover Theological Seminary in 1821. In 1824, while serving as pastor of the Congregational church in Rochester, he was appointed professor at Bowdoin College in Brunswick, Maine. He retired in 1868 as professor of mental and moral philosophy.

Upham published *Elements of Intellectual Philosophy* in 1827 (Portland, Me.). A second edition appeared in 1828 and a third, under the title of *Elements of Mental Philosophy*, was published in 1832 (Boston). Upham's text was widely used in American colleges long before others appeared. His pioneering work included the diversity of topics that now represent the discipline. For example, he included chapters on abnormal mental functioning and published an expanded treatment in 1840 as *Outlines of Imperfect and Disordered Mental Action* (New York), the first book on the subject in America written from a psychological, rather than a medical, point of view.

Upham's 1832 text organized mental processes under the rubrics of the intellect and the sensibilities; the former represented cognitive functions of the mind whereas the latter encompassed emotion, motivation, and instinctual activities. In 1834, Upham added a third component, the will, and within the sensibilities distinguished between the natural (emotional, motivational, and instinctual) sensibilities and the moral sensibilities (conscience) to describe the choice involved in voluntary action. Upham's philosophy was published in three volumes, covering the intellect, the sensibilities, and the will under the title *Elements of Mental Philosophy* (New York, 1840); abridged single volumes were printed throughout the nineteenth century, the last in 1886.

Upham approached mental philosophy as mental science; like the other scientists of his era, he proceeded in good Baconian fashion to gather facts from his own and others' observations and from medical and other written accounts of behavior (including literature and the Bible) and tested his accounts of mind against the evidence of his own experience and consciousness (and invited his readers to do the same). His account of mind was developed within the English philosophical tradition begun by John Locke and the Scottish tradition of Thomas Reid, Dugald Stewart, and Thomas Brown. His tripartite division of the mind represented a classification scheme, not independently functioning faculties, and his philosophy was an attempt to describe the way in which the cognitive processes of the intellect interact with those of the sensibilities to produce action through the operation of the will. Upham's mental philosophy helped to provide the topics and concerns to which subsequent generations applied the experimental procedures of the laboratory to produce the "new psychology" that developed rapidly in the twentieth century.

[*Many of the people mentioned in this article are the subjects of independent biographical entries.*]

Bibliography

Evans, R. (1984). The origins of American academic psychology. In J. Brozek (Ed.), *Explorations in the history of psychology in the United States* (pp. 17–60). Lewisburg, PA: Bucknell University Press, Evans credits Upham with publishing the first textbook in psychology and describes the topics covered to demonstrate the continuity between Upham's text and topics in contemporary texts.

Fay, J. W. (1939). *American psychology before William James.* New Brunswick, NJ: Rutgers University Press. Fay's classic study of psychology in America from the colonial period to the advent of experimental psychology describes the development of Upham's philosophy; see especially pages 91–109.

Roback, A. A. (1952). *History of American psychology.* New York: Library. Roback, like Fay, describes Upham's pioneering work as part of the development of psychology in America.

Alfred H. Fuchs

URBAN COMMUNITIES are different from rural areas and small towns because of the size and density of their populations. Cities are also known for their cultural and intellectual innovations, including the study of psychology. Whether it was Wundt's Leipzig or Freud's Vienna, the discipline and practice of psychology first arose and flourished in urban communities. Psychology of the city and psychology in the city have evolved together.

The scale and nature of urban communities have changed greatly over the course of human history. The earliest cities scarcely reached 30,000, whereas today some cities like São Paulo in Brazil exceed 15 million. Not only has city size increased, but the proportion of the world's population residing in urban communities has vastly expanded. In any living population, diversity increases with size. The historical role of cities as magnets for people from different regions and cultures increases that diversity. Social scientists have attributed distinct forms of psychological and social life to population size and diversity.

Theories of Urban Life

Claude Fischer's book *The Urban Experience* (1976) provides a good review of theories of urbanism throughout the first three-quarters of the twentieth century. The urban theories he described provide the guiding concepts for much social and psychological research.

In 1903, Georg Simmel set out many of the themes that will mark the psychological and social study of urban life in his famous essay "The Metropolis and Mental Life." He identified the experience of "difference" as the signature state of urban dwellers. The perceptual world appeared as constantly shifting, thus threatening the urban dweller with emotional upheaval. In response to this threat, Simmel believed urban dwellers cultivated an intellectual rather than emotional or habitual way of responding to the world. The prominence of the money economy further contributed to the intellectual organization of mental life because transactions based on money were abstracted from particular social relationships. Thus Simmel saw urbanites as having a calculating attitude, with numerous psychological and social consequences: the threat of a sense of personal worthlessness, a lack of regard for or aversion toward others, weak group solidarity, and a resultant freedom for individual expression. Simmel identified this convergence of the money economy and the exposure to stimulation and difference cities afforded as producing a form of mental life departing from that of ancient civilizations, although amplified by the historical tendency of cities to support a more highly developed division of labor. Simmel's theory of urban life is considered deterministic because it states that the environment will always have a particular effect on people.

These themes were echoed and elaborated by his students Park, Burgess, and especially Wirth, who became known as the Chicago School. Wirth built Simmel's idea that cities strained the psychological capacity of urbanites into a sociological theory of urban life that identified decreased adherence to a common moral order, the weakening of primary social bonds, loss of a sense of community, and, in addition, greater reliance on formal organizations and regulatory structures as consequences of population size and density. Much research on urban crime and violence, child development in cities, homelessness, and urban social behavior is still organized around such concepts as social support, sense of community, social cohesion, and social disorganization.

Psychologists contributed to the development of the Chicago School by studying the implications of urban life for mental health and social norms. Some of their more dramatic findings have since been refuted. For example, Faris and Dunham's (1939) study claimed to show that the social disorganization of inner-city neighborhoods increased mental illness rates. Later studies replicated the association between inner-city residence and higher rates of mental illness but found that mentally ill people tended to drift into pockets of social disorganization within cities, rather than becoming mentally ill as a result of living in the inner city. Angell's (1951) book, *The Moral Integration of American Cities*, exemplifies psychology's contribution to research on the connection of urban life to social disorganization, emphasizing particularly the negative effects of racial heterogeneity on social solidarity.

Psychologists have investigated the consequences of large numbers of people in close proximity and the stimulation they produce. Crowding, density, noise, pollution, and interference with behavior associated with large numbers of people have been related to peculiarly urban behavior and psychological states. Social psychologist Stanley Milgram provided a more recent formulation of the problem of excess stimulation when he attributed aloof behavior, lack of interpersonal involvement, the rapid pace of city life, and inattention to others to information overload in the urban environment. Other psychologists have retained the original idea of overstimulation by emphasizing physiological arousal and focusing on outcomes related to health, psychological well-being, and coping strategies. A third perspective attributes the psychological effects of urban phenomena to the difficulty an individual has in controlling the environment, or to *learned helplessness*, the internalization of the expectation that efforts to affect the environment will be ineffectual.

Many psychological, physical, and behavioral consequences of the major dimensions of urban life have been studied. Researchers have related the speed of walking, talking, and performing transactions to the size of populations in towns and cities. Studies of environmental stress have attempted to link physiological arousal, the secretion of stress hormones, cognitive limitations, and aggression or social withdrawal to exposure to crowding and noise. Psychologists have investigated the idea that when large numbers of people witness a crime or an accident, they will be less likely to help because they feel little individual responsibility.

Many of these studies, especially those related to stress, have moved away from a concern with the nature of urban life to a more limited analysis of specific variables in smaller, more controlled settings. Psychological research has become less environmentally deterministic because psychological and social processes are thought of as mediators. Psychological research rarely tries to capture the effects of the variety of environmental conditions and social relationships that make up urban life.

Simmel's other students, Park and Burgess, initiated a series of descriptive studies of the varied lifestyles, subcultures, and "types" of people to be found in the city. They also defined a theory of the ecology of cities, known as natural area analysis, that described how different districts within a city developed. This approach to understanding urban life suggests that people are not so much influenced by the size and diversity of urban populations as by the characteristics of the small social worlds they live in. The city simply provides the setting and the population to support the existence of more different kinds of groups, jobs, and personalities.

Two kinds of urban theory emerge from this tradition. Compositional theorists assert that behavior is most influenced by characteristics of people and families such as ethnicity, social class, age, marital status, etc. For compositional theorists, any differences between urbanites and others are due to differences in these traits. Subcultural theorists see the large and diverse populations of urban areas as providing the opportunity for distinct subcultures to develop and flourish, thus intensifying the social bonds of urbanites. Both of these perspectives contradict the idea that urban life in and of itself leads to social disorganization. For example, higher levels of crime could arise either because more residents of cities are members of groups who are more likely to commit crimes or because the subcultural and organizational supports for criminal behavior are more highly developed in urban communities.

When research on the effects of community size and density has taken into account the composition of the population, many of the negative effects of living in dense urban areas tend to disappear. However, some studies still find a relationship between physical and mental health and size or density. When studies on the effects of city size are compared across countries and topics, it becomes clear that the specific social, cultural, and physical environments in different cities, regions, and societies very often determine how population size affects well-being. For example, researchers in some countries find that death rates from diseases related to stress are higher in larger communities, even after controlling for population characteristics. However, in other countries with very good health care and public health education systems, residents of larger cities are healthier, presumably because the most advanced health education and care programs are found in these cities.

Urban Diversity

The popular image of urban communities in the United States is one of disintegration, violence, unemployment, and disadvantage, contributed to in part by the large amount of social science research documenting the combined poverty and racial segregation of specific cities, especially Chicago. Poverty and relative deprivation, that is the gap between the income and living conditions of the best- and the worst-off residents of a community, are well known to have bad consequences, including worse physical and mental health and lower educational achievement. The equation of these problems with urban life neglects the dynamic, multiethnic, multiclass reality of cities like Los Angeles and New York, as well as the entrenched poverty and racial segregation of places like the rural South. Corporate headquarters, great cultural institutions, mansions, and gated communities are as integral to the fabric of urban communities as public housing projects, failing inner-city schools, and abandoned lots.

In the last quarter of the twentieth century, urban theorists focused on the place of different cities in the changing world economy and the internal divisions and differences in urban life. Cities are seen not as natural objects but as the result of human actions, the exercise of power, the requirements of a competitive global economy, and contested cultural ideals. In her 1991 book *Changing Cities*, sociologist Janet Abu-Lughod suggested that the study of urban communities must ask how the city is produced, and how it is consumed. Urban space includes the objective but variable physical and social world of urban communities and the more idiosyncratic spaces of awareness, access, action, and social participation. Urban space is constructed not just with stone and concrete but also by media images and cultural myths. The reality of urban communities depends on the specific historical and social formation of the place and on the race, class, gender, and biographies of the individuals and groups living there.

Psychological Research and Practice in Urban Communities

Psychologists explicitly concerned with urban life still often address problems of poverty and race in their work. However, psychological research and practice in urban communities reflect a more differentiated view of urban life by examining the different lived realities of residents within the same communities, the social, political, and economic forces that affect them, the interpretations they give to their lives, and the personal and public actions they take. For example, Michelle Fine and Louis Weis's book, *The Unknown City*, analyzes how class, gender, and race affect perceptions of violence, opportunity, and racial and gender stereotypes.

Many studies of the impact of poverty, race, and family structure on child development involve the study of inner-city populations. The urban focus of this research was stimulated in part by William Julius Wilson's book *The Truly Disadvantaged: The Inner City, the Underclass, and Public Policy* (1987) and a series of other books and articles that called attention to the concentration of poverty in racially segregated inner-city neighborhoods. Wilson and others pointed out that a combination of public policies, racial discrimination, and loss of low-skilled jobs in the economy has led to the desertion of some inner-city neighborhoods by Whites and middle class Blacks. Poor, minority, female-headed households have been left behind. They argued that the result has been the development of an "urban underclass" in which generations of children grow up without being exposed to norms and behaviors associated with steady employment and economic advancement.

Much urban underclass research has examined the relationship of concentrated poverty to outcomes like juvenile delinquency, teen pregnancy, dropping out of school, receiving welfare or unemployment, and violence, where both poverty and outcomes are measured at the census tract level. One problem with this kind of argument is that it can confuse the negative effects of being poor with the effects of living in a poor urban community. Many researchers also assume that psychological and social processes like copying neighbors' behavior, social norm formation, lack of working role models, absence of supervision of youth, and so on, lead to poor life outcomes for residents of poor neighborhoods. However, the research does not measure these processes. Psychologists, and a small number of sociologists, have contributed to the study of the effects of impoverished urban neighborhoods by measuring poverty, parent and child behavior, social relationships, and various outcomes at the individual and household level. Then the effects of concentrated poverty at the neighborhood level can be analyzed separately from the effects of individual and household level variables.

Developmental psychologists who study child development in poor inner-city neighborhoods often use the theoretical perspective of Urie Bronfenbrenner. His approach is termed "ecological" because it looks at the development of individual children as occurring within a nested set of relationships. Children develop in relationship to the face-to-face interactions with their parents, siblings, and others around them. The kind of interactions they have depends to some extent on what happens in the variety of places that growing children and their parents experience in daily life. The kinds of settings that make up these everyday experiences depend on what kind of environments and institutions the society produces, for example, schools, day-care centers, grocery stores, markets, or subsistence farms. Even larger social forces of culture, economy, politics, and history are reflected in the way the society produces these environments and distributes resources. It is not surprising then that psychologists studying urban communities and child development often examine the effect of schools, child care arrangements, parental employment, social services, homelessness, and income support programs. They use their research to evaluate existing public policies and recommend ones that would be more supportive for children and parents. They also design and evaluate interventions that they think will lead to better developmental outcomes for children, for example, programs for schools and parents to reduce the risk of aggressive behavior among at-risk children.

Community psychology and environmental psychology take an ecological perspective on the relationship between the individual and the physical and social community. While much of the research and practice in these fields are concerned with the specific problems of poor and minority residents in urban communities, working- and middle-class urban and suburban dwellers of different races are also often included in this research. As in the earlier intellectual traditions of studying urban life, problems of social isolation and loss of community are central concerns. But they are not seen as natural accompaniments of urban life. Rather, many community and environmental psychologists have been interested in social and psychological processes that reverse these tendencies. They have generated a body of research and theory on the sense of community and group processes that promote perceptions of individual and group efficacy. Participation in small groups and taking action to change problematic urban conditions are seen as routes to personal and collective empowerment. Churches, block associations, tenant associations, support groups, and other voluntary associations form important links between individuals and the urban community. They provide opportunities for collective action, social solidarity, and skill development that can lead to better mental health, a more democratic and socially integrated community, and better quality of life.

Empowerment-oriented psychological research and practice also provide a bridge to a more political analysis of urban communities that characterizes the interdisciplinary social science of urban studies. Some psychologists, sociologists, and political scientists examine the relationships among resident characteristics, community conditions, community cohesion, participation in voluntary associations, and political participation. Action research uses the process of social science inquiry to affect social decision making. Action researchers work with members of a community to define the issues that should be studied and the interpretation and use of data, sometimes involving them in the actual data gathering. Action research can be used to design a program, for example, a support system for people suffering from AIDS, or to provide an information base for policy advocacy. Action research is also used to involve people who are going to use a particular setting, neighborhood, or city in its planning and design. This approach, called participatory design and planning, has been developed through collaboration among social scientists, architects, planners, and policy makers. Psychologists have worked on the design and planning of urban environments in other ways too. Many studies have examined the physical characteristics of urban communities that are associated with fear of crime and actual criminal behavior. Research on cognitive maps and way finding has been used in urban planning. Psychologists have evaluated the way specific environmental qualities affect users' experience of many urban facilities such as museums, workplaces, parks, multifamily housing, and schools. Studies have documented the contribution of green spaces, trees, and even small amounts of vegetation in urban environments to physical health, children's play experiences, property values, and residential satisfaction. Resource conservation and recycling have also been examined in urban contexts.

Beyond the Urban-Rural Continuum

The differences within cities and among urban communities have raised questions about the value of identifying communities as urban, suburban, or rural. In addition, some of the social and psychological consequences of urban life are not necessarily confined to urban communities. Urbanization (or the invention and application of technologies and social forms that support larger population aggregations) is a term that has also implied industrialization and modernization. In a meaningful sense, postmodern, postindustrial life offers some of the psychological and social experience of large and diverse populations even to, for example, the computerized office in the Connecticut woods or the factory compound in rural Indonesia. Increasingly, societies are organized economically and socially in complex, interdependent processes that require, and are affected by, the actions of huge numbers of others not just in an urban community, or even a particular nation, but throughout the world. These changes call for new typologies of communities and different kinds of research on their relationship to human life.

Bibliography

Abu-Lughod, J. L. (1991). *Changing cities*. New York: HarperCollins.

Angell, R. C. (1951). *The moral integration of American cities*. Chicago: University of Chicago Press.

Bronfenbrenner, U. (1979). *The ecology of human development*. Cambridge, MA: Harvard University Press.

Faris, R. E., & Dunham, H. W. (1939). *Mental disorders in urban areas*. Chicago: University of Chicago Press.

Fine M., & Weis, L. (1998). *The unknown city: Lives of poor and working class young adults*. Boston: Beacon Press.

Fischer, C. S. (1976). *The urban experience*. Chicago: Harcourt Brace.

Milgram, S. (1970). The experience of living in cities. *Science, 167*, 1461–1468.

Park, R. E., & Burgess, E. W. (1925). *The city*. Chicago: University of Chicago Press.

Simmel, G. (1971). The metropolis and mental life. In D. N. Levine (Ed.), *Georg Simmel: On individuality and social forms* (pp. 324–339). Chicago: University of Chicago Press. (Original work published 1903)

Wilson, W. J. (1987). *The truly disadvantaged: The inner city, the underclass, and public policy*. Chicago: University of Chicago Press.

Wirth, L. (1938). Urbanism as a way of life. *American Journal of Sociology, 44*, 3–24.

Susan Saegert

U.S. VETERANS ADMINISTRATION. *See* United States Department of Veterans Affairs.

V

VAIL CONFERENCE. *See* Training.

VALIDITY describes the extent to which a psychological instrument measures what it is supposed to measure. The term comes from the Latin word *valere*: to be strong. Thus, valid measures are "strong" measures, upholding their promise to measure the psychological qualities we have entrusted them to measure.

Although apparently straightforward, the concept of validity has been the topic of much scholarship. This is because, as psychology developed, ideas about validity developed in parallel. The validity of early psychological tests was evaluated in terms of *content*. To the extent that a test covered the right material, it was considered a valid measure of that material. Obviously, this perspective has limitations. Even if a test appears content valid, is it useful? Hence, psychologists next became concerned with the ability of tests to *predict* outcomes. This reflected the applied nature of early psychological testing. For example, the first intelligence tests (e.g., the Binet–Simon) were tools designed primarily to predict which children were unlikely to keep up in school. Similarly, the first personality questionnaire (Woodworth's Personal Data Sheet) was created with an explicit applied purpose in mind: to screen out psychologically disturbed men who were unfit for military service.

These early concerns with content and prediction persist to this day and are covered in more detail below. Nevertheless, they are both types of *construct validity*, a concept that can be traced back to the publication of the American Psychological Association's 1954 *Technical Recommendations for Psychological Tests and Diagnostic Techniques* (*Psychological Bulletin, 51*, supplement), and the classic exposition by Cronbach and Meehl (1955) that followed. Historically speaking, the Cronbach and Meehl paper was nearly unparalleled in its importance to thinking about validity. (Hence, a separate entry in the *Encyclopedia of Psychology* is devoted to construct validity and should be consulted for a complete description.) [*See* Construct Validity.] For our purposes, we note that construct validity refers to the extent to which a psychological instrument measures the theoretical entity (the "construct") that it was designed to measure. In this way, the construct validity of a test refers to the theoretical meaning of the test scores. Thus, with the publication of the Cronbach and Meehl paper, psychologists were given a sound theoretical edifice on which to build their applied investigations. That is, psychological instruments—whether used in basic or applied research—are measures of scientific constructs. To the extent that they have the content accorded them by a relevant theory and predict outcomes in the manner described by that theory, they measure the construct they are designed to measure.

Although we feel that construct validity subsumes other types of validity, these other types of validity are worthy of exposition in their own right. This is because each "subtype" of validity describes a procedure for documenting the construct validity of a psychological instrument. Our review of these subtypes is far from exhaustive because psychologists have invented a host of "different" validities to describe almost any sort of construct validation enterprise one might undertake. Thus, we focus on what we feel are the most essential "types" of validity, as they relate to the overall psychological assessment enterprise. We conclude by considering the applicability of ideas about validity in experimental contexts.

Content Validity

Content validity refers to the extent to which a psychological instrument accurately reflects the investigator's conception of the construct being assessed. Content validation is a multifaceted enterprise and involves evaluation of all elements of the instrument (e.g., questions, responses, stimuli). Consider five basic steps taken to create a content-valid measure. First, the investigator carefully defines the construct to be measured. This involves describing both what the construct is and what it is not, as well as delineating different facets of the construct, if any. Ruthless attention to detailed, explicit description at this stage is crucial; the key is to compose a clear and succinct description of the construct. This stage is vital because it provides the foundation for the second step, generation of an initial item pool. This is a "brainstorming" phase, in which it is useful to be overinclusive of items to ensure that all aspects of the construct are well represented. Once initial items are written, a third stage commences, in which decisions regarding response formats and the length of the inventory are made. At this stage, one must carefully consider the purpose of the instrument. For example, a brief inventory of mental status to be administered during hospital rounds requires straightforward response formats and rapid administration time, given the pressures of the situation in which the instrument will be used. Fourth, the initial pool of items should be reviewed by both experts in the field and members of the target population to gauge their assessment of whether the items reflect the target construct. If needed, items can be refined at this point. Obviously, the appropriateness of using various expert or target population samples will depend on the nature of the construct. For example, various experts might not agree with the investigator's definition of the construct if it is particularly novel, and various target populations (e.g., very young children) may not be capable of offering much useful feedback. Finally, once the items for the final version of the test have been selected, these items should be compared to the original description of the construct, to ensure that all aspects of the construct remain equally well represented. If these steps have been followed, then the measure is likely to have high content validity.

Face Validity. Face validity is a subtype of content validity. Face validity refers to the extent to which respondents and/or professional users regard the items of an assessment instrument as appropriate for the construct being assessed. Decisions about face validity are decisions about the *apparent* validity of the instrument. The issue here is primarily one of public relations. If a test does not appear to be valid "on the face of it," respondents may be resistant and uncooperative, and, hence, test users may be uncomfortable with the test. For example, if adults were presented with a test of mathematical ability that consisted of simple addition problems, they might feel that the test is beneath their ability and not expend any effort on the individual items.

Criterion Validity

Criterion validity refers to the ability of a psychological instrument to predict a criterion—an extra-test variable that, in theory, the instrument should be capable of predicting. The criterion could be an important outcome, such as success in a scholastic endeavor, a physician's diagnosis, a level of performance on another test, or even some combination of these individual possibilities. Any extra-test variable that a test should predict is, potentially, a relevant criterion.

When estimating the criterion validity of a measure, one must always be wary of the possibility of *criterion contamination*. Consider, for example, using teachers' ratings of scholastic performance as a criterion to validate a test of scholastic aptitude. In general, such a design would be sound and logical. However, if teachers are provided with information about students' scholastic aptitude scores *prior* to making their ratings, this information may bias the rating process. That is, the criterion—teachers' ratings—may be contaminated by the aptitude test information, thereby potentially creating a spurious correlation between aptitude test scores and teachers' ratings. To eliminate criterion contamination, one must always ensure that criterion scores are assigned independently of test scores.

Criterion validity can be broken down into two basic subtypes depending on the temporal relations between the test itself and the outcome being predicted. *Concurrent validity* refers to the extent to which an assessment instrument is capable of predicting criteria that have been measured at the same point in time that the instrument was administered. Consider, for example, an assessment of vocational interests. If such an assessment is valid, then test scores should differ among persons who are happily employed in various professions. For example, our vocational assessment may be targeted at identifying persons who might like police work. To establish the concurrent validity of our measure, it could be given to a sample of police officers, a sample of postal workers, and a sample of accountants. If the police officers score highest on our measure, we could claim that concurrent validity has been established. Persons who were concurrently employed in various professions at the time the test was administered received different scores, with the target group, police officers, receiving the highest scores.

Predictive validity refers to the extent to which an assessment instrument predicts criteria that are measured after the instrument was administered. Predictive validity is often of cardinal importance in psychological assessment. For example, the utility of tests of scholastic aptitude is primarily judged in terms of predictive validity, as the primary goal of scholastic aptitude testing is to predict future academic performance. The value of psychological testing in clinical situations is also often judged in terms of predictive validity. Does a test provide information that is useful in predicting important clinical variables, such as length of treatment? To the extent that a test can predict important clinical outcomes, it may be said to possess predictive validity in clinical situations.

In assessing predictive validity, one perennial issue is whether the criterion measure that has been chosen is optimal. Many relevant criteria are simply too far in the future or too amorphous to be useful. For example, tests of aptitude would ideally predict success in a given profession. Indeed, one might say that a worthy goal of aptitude testing would be to determine which potential students are likely to make novel contributions to the field. Although it is possible to measure such a construct (e.g., via a poll of persons working in the field), the time lag between aptitude testing and contributing to the field may be prohibitively long. Thus, we are often left with a useful, but less-than-ideal criterion to predict. For example, tests of scholastic aptitude are often validated using measures that are more tractable than "ultimate contribution to the field."

Attenuation and Restriction of Range. To evaluate the validity of a measure, researchers correlate their measure with other criterion measures. One very important issue needs to be considered when evaluating such correlation coefficients. This issue is known as *attenuation.* Attenuation results from a very simple fact: Assessment instruments are never perfectly reliable. That is, the scores people obtain when they are assessed typically vary for reasons other than those intended. Unreliability is random noise (or "error variance"), and it attenuates (reduces) the maximum possible strength of the relationship between measures and their criteria. Consider all of the reasons why an assessment may reflect things other than peoples' "true" scores on that assessment. Some people may be distracted by other worries or concerns, some people might have a headache, others might simply be having an unusually good day. Because such factors can never be completely eliminated, tests are never perfectly reliable. Hence, criterion validity coefficients are often *underestimates* of the "true" relationships between measures and criteria—the relationships that would be obtained if only "perfect," errorless measurement was possible.

Criterion validity coefficients can also be attenuated for reasons other than the influence of error variance. One important way in which such coefficients are often attenuated is *restriction of range.* Essentially, the maximum possible criterion validity of a test is limited by the extent to which people vary on both the test and the criterion. If either distribution is limited to a restricted range, then the "variance" available for prediction will be a fraction of what it would be if the range of scores were unrestricted. Consider the predictive validity of tests of scholastic aptitude. When schools use an aptitude test as a screening device, they admit only those students who have high scores. This restricts the range of scores on the aptitude test, which compromises the ability of the test to predict later performance—there is less variance in the aptitude test scores available to discriminate between students on later measures of performance. On the other hand, if schools simply admitted all applicants, the range of scores on the aptitude test would be maximized, and the estimated criterion validity of tests of scholastic aptitude would increase. In sum, when evaluating the criterion validity of a psychological test, one should always be cognizant of the ways in which attenuation and restriction of range can reduce the magnitude of criterion validity coefficients.

Convergent and Discriminant Validity and the Multitrait-Multimethod Matrix

The terms *convergent validity, discriminant validity,* and *multitrait-multimethod matrix* were introduced into the psychological literature by Campbell and Fiske (1959). These concepts represent ways of investigating the construct validity of a psychological test—that is, ways of documenting the meaning of the test scores. To illustrate these concepts, imagine that you were interested in a specific personality trait, extroversion—the tendency to be outgoing and sociable. Theoretically, this kind of trait should be manifested in various ways. For example, it should show up in people's answers to questions about their personality (extroverted people should rate items such as "I like to go to parties" as true of themselves). It should show up in other people's ratings (the partners of extroverted people should describe them as enjoying parties and being gregarious). Finally, it should show up in their actual behavior (if you observe extroverted people, say, in a waiting room, they should more readily make conversation with strangers). These are three different methods for measuring extroversion (known, respectively, as self-report, other-report, and behavioral observation). *Convergent validity* is established when measures of extroversion that were made using different methods are shown to correlate highly. Now imagine that you had measured the same people in the extroversion study on two other, different traits (for example, vocabulary and interest in a military career), using the same three methods. The measures that are supposed to measure different traits should not be highly correlated, even if they were measured using the same method. That is, they should have *discriminant validity.*

The correlations among these three traits measured in these three different ways can be arranged in a square multitrait-multimethod matrix (MTMM), where the columns and the rows of the matrix represent each trait, measured by each method. For our example, there would be nine rows and nine columns in the MTMM (three traits times three measures = nine different variables). The MTMM is a convenient way of displaying the correlations among these nine variables. By examining the values in the MTMM, one can determine the convergent and discriminant validity of the measures.

Consequential Validity

Recent contributors to the literature on validity (most notably Samuel Messick) have noted that validity encompasses more than simply the technical features emphasized so far in this entry. Psychological tests affect nearly all members of western, industrialized societies, in forms such as tests of scholastic aptitude, or tests that are used for preemployment screening purposes. Thus, the psychological testing enterprise has extensive social consequences that, inevitably, intertwine with the ethical values of societies that place a great emphasis on results from psychological tests. The sum of the social and ethical implications of using a test has been referred to as that test's *consequential validity*.

Although an emphasis on the ethical implications of testing and the impact of testing on society has been welcomed, commentators on these issues have also noted that such concerns may be better addressed elsewhere, rather than via the validity concept. The complex nature of ethical and social concerns suggest that they may be better handled on their own terms, rather than lumped together with other "validities." That is, such concerns are so important that they deserve consideration separate from validity per se; a test can measure what it claims to measure and still have egregious consequences for society. Hence, social and ethical concerns that arise from psychological testing and assessment are regarded by some as equally fundamental, yet separate from concerns about validity.

Validity in Psychological Experiments

Although our review has focused on validity in psychological testing and assessment, ideas about validity are also applicable to psychological experiments. Specifically, the validity of experimental designs is often evaluated along two dimensions: internal and external validity. *Internal validity* refers to the extent to which an experimental design can be trusted to reveal the impact of the independent variable(s) (manipulated by the investigator) on the dependent variable(s) (measurements that reflect the outcome of the experiment). An internally valid experiment is one in which *only* the independent variable can account for the outcome of the experiment. Common examples of threats to internal validity include nonrandom assignment of participants to experimental conditions or the failure of experimental manipulations.

External validity refers to the extent to which the results from the experiment generalize beyond the experiment itself, to other situations that the experiment is designed to resemble. Various factors can unintentionally affect the outcome of an experiment. For example, experimenters may have certain expectations about the outcome of the experiment that they indirectly convey to the participants. Consider an experimenter who is very enthusiastic about a new drug and conveys this enthusiasm to experimental participants treated with the drug. Factors such as this threaten external validity because the experimental results cannot be generalized to the range of situations that the experiment is intended to represent. In our example, improvement may be seen in the participants not because the drug works, but because the drug was administered along with high hopes for its success. Hence, the experimental results will not generalize to other situations in which the drug is used—the results were externally invalid, as they were due to the experimenter's enthusiasm, not to the drug itself.

[*See also* Reliability.]

Bibliography

Anastasi, A., & Urbina, S. (1997). *Psychological testing* (7th ed.). Upper Saddle River, NJ: Prentice Hall. The most recent revision of a well-regarded textbook on psychological testing and assessment; notable for its detailed coverage of validity.

Angoff, W. H. (1988). Validity: An evolving concept. In H. Wainer, & H. I. Braun (Eds.), *Test validity* (pp. 19–32). Hillsdale, NJ: Erlbaum. Provides a review of the history of validity as a concept in psychological science.

Campbell, D. T., & Fiske, D. W. (1959). Convergent and discriminant validation by the multitrait-multimethod matrix. *Psychological Bulletin, 56*, 81–105. The original description of convergent and discriminant validity and the multitrait-multimethod matrix as a means of estimating these quantities.

Cronbach, L. J. (1989). Construct validation after thirty years. In R. L. Linn (Ed.), *Intelligence: Measurement, theory, and public policy. Proceedings of a symposium in honor of Lloyd G. Humphreys* (pp. 147–171). Champaign, IL: University of Illinois Press. Provides an update and an overview of developments in thinking about validity in the decades since the publication of the Cronbach and Meehl (1955) paper.

Cronbach, L. J., & Meehl, P. E. (1955). Construct validity in psychological tests. *Psychological Bulletin, 52*, 281–302. The classic paper in which the construct validity concept was introduced to psychology.

Meier, S. T. (1994). *The chronic crisis in psychological measurement and assessment: A historical survey*. San Diego, CA: Academic Press. Provides an overview and empirical critique of validity in psychological testing and assessment.

Messick, S. (1995). Validity of psychological assessment: Validation of inferences from persons' responses and performances as scientific inquiry into score meaning.

American Psychologist, 50, 741–749. Reconceptualizes the validity concept by asserting that psychological testing inherently involves both social values and consequences.

Robert F. Krueger and Kristen C. Kling

VALUES are beliefs about which outcomes and courses of action are desirable or good. They are one of a family of psychological constructs that are presumed to regulate a person's adjustment to his or her social world. Other members of this family include attitudes, needs, traits, norms, and interests, all of which overlap, to some extent, with values. However, values are meaningfully distinct from these other constructs. For example, values, like attitudes, are evaluative beliefs, but they differ from attitudes in that, for each individual, they are fewer in number and more central and self-defining, they apply broadly across specific objects and situations, they are more normative (involving an assessment of what should be, rather than simply what one would like to be), and they have a stronger motivational component. Values, like needs, are motivationally based, but they differ from needs in that they have a stronger cognitive component and derive from social and societal, as well as intrapsychic, demands. Values, like traits, are self-defining, but they differ from traits in that they are less characterological and more amenable to modification. Values, like norms, have a strong prescriptive component, but they differ from norms in that they transcend specific situations and are personal and internal, rather than consensual. Finally, values, like interests, guide evaluations, choices, and actions, but they differ from interests in that they are broader and more enduring and have a stronger normative component. In more formal terms, psychologists define values as follows: They are beliefs pertaining to desirable end states or modes of conduct that transcend specific situations, are organized into coherent systems, and guide selection and evaluation of people, behaviors, and events.

Values have been an important topic of theory and research in the social sciences; by contrast, psychologists have devoted little research attention to values, especially relative to traits and attitudes. This comparative neglect derives, in large part, from the way researchers in relevant areas of psychology have defined their domains of inquiry. Personality psychologists, on the one hand, have devoted most of their energies to describing and predicting individual differences in behavior. They have found traits, with their descriptive focus and close links to behavior, to be more useful than values in this regard. Indeed, with the exception of Adorno, Frenkel-Brunswik, Levinson, and Sanford's work on *The Authoritarian Personality* (New York, 1950), theories and research in personality have not encompassed individual differences in views of what is desirable or good. Social psychologists, on the other hand, have devoted most of their energies to investigating those psychological states that can be produced or modified by changes in situational contingencies. They have focused much of their attention on attitudes and have produced an impressive literature on the conditions and processes of attitude change. Values have stimulated much less interest among social psychologists, primarily because they are explicitly defined as being invariant across situations. Thus, values have not been well positioned to become a central concern of either personality or social psychologists. Add to this the fact that values, like traits, attitudes, and most other individual difference constructs, have not proven to be strong predictors of behavior, and it is easier to understand why they have received comparatively little research attention.

Measures of Values

Most research on values has employed one of two measures: The Study of Values (SOV) and the Rokeach Values Survey (RVS). These measures were developed out of very different theoretical conceptions of values. In 1960, Gordon Allport, Philip Vernon, and Gardner Lindzey (*A Study of Values*, Boston) developed the SOV to measure the relative prominence of six basic interests or motives in personality: the theoretical, economic, aesthetic, social, political, and religious. The measure was predicated on two general assumptions: that an individual's personality is revealed through his or her values and that individuals can express their values directly in a self-report instrument. The six values themselves were defined in terms of ideal types: the theoretical person values the discovery of truth; the economic person values that which is useful; the aesthetic person values form and harmony; the social person values love of others; the political person values power; and the religious person values unity and transcendence.

The SOV asks respondents to express preferences among pairs or sets of options that involve tradeoffs among these six basic values. For example, one question asks, "Which of the following men do you think should be judged as contributing more to the progress of mankind? (a) Aristotle; (b) Abraham Lincoln." Respondents distribute three points between these two options (which reflect theoretical and social values, respectively) depending on the degree to which they favor one over the other. Another question asks, "At an evening discussion with intimate friends of your own sex, are you more interested when you talk about (a) the meaning of life, (b) developments in science, (c) literature, (d) socialism and social amelioration?" Respondents rank order these four options (which reflect religious, theoretical, aesthetic, and social values, respectively). The SOV yields six scores for each respondent, which index the relative importance of the six basic values. Psychometric studies have shown these six scores to be reliable and to distinguish in predictable ways between gender and occupational categories. The SOV was developed for use with college students or with adults who have had some college education, although it has been used with high school students as well.

In 1973, Milton Rokeach (*The Nature of Human Values*, New York) developed the RVS with the goal of creating an all-purpose, objective, easy-to-administer measure of values and systems of values. The RVS was based on belief system theory, which offers a far-reaching account of relations among values, attitudes, self-conceptions, and behaviors. According to belief system theory, a value system is a hierarchically organized set of beliefs that certain modes of conduct are preferable to other modes of conduct and that certain end states of existence are preferable to other end states of existence. These preferences derive, in part, from individual needs and desires and, in part, from societal demands. Thus, values are individual needs represented in a socially acceptable form. Because values map onto biological and social needs, they are limited in number (the RVS includes 18 modes of conduct and 18 end states of existence). In addition, because values are central beliefs, changes in values lead to widespread changes in functionally related values, attitudes, and behaviors. Of course, value systems are fairly stable, but they can and do undergo change. In particular, because values are organized into hierarchies, they are continually in conflict. Acting to promote one value often means sacrificing another. Thus, a person is routinely forced to choose among values when expressing attitudes or behaviors, and this process can lead values to be reorganized or reordered.

The RVS presents respondents with two lists of 18 values each and asks them to rank the items on each list "in order of importance to YOU, as guiding principles in YOUR life." One list contains terminal values (desired end states of existence). This list includes a comfortable life, an exciting life, a sense of accomplishment, a world at peace, a world of beauty, equality, family security, freedom, happiness, inner harmony, mature love, national security, pleasure, salvation, self-respect, social recognition, true friendship, and wisdom. The other list contains instrumental values (desirable modes of conduct). This list includes ambitious, broad-minded, capable, cheerful, clean, courageous, forgiving, helpful, honest, imaginative, independent, intellectual, logical, loving, obedient, polite, responsible, and self-controlled. Like the SOV, the RVS meets acceptable standards of reliability and distinguishes sensibly between demographic groups. At the same time, it is a more flexible and versatile instrument than the SOV and therefore may have more general utility.

Structure of Values

Psychological researchers have proposed a number of distinctions between different types of values. For example, Rokeach divided terminal values into personal values (e.g., salvation, a sense of accomplishment) and social values (e.g, a world at peace, true friendship), a distinction that has been maintained in much of the literature. He divided instrumental values into moral values (e.g., honest, helpful) and competence values (e.g., imaginative, logical). Other researchers have distinguished between individualistic and collectivistic values; cultural, family and personal values; liberal and conservative values; materialist and postmaterialist values; and many others. In addition, a number of investigations have examined domain-specific values—for example, environmental values, consumption values, and eating values. These domain-specific values have often proven to be strong predictors of relevant behaviors, though it is not clear that they are values in the sense of being central, self-defining, and broadly applicable.

The most ambitious investigation of the structure of values comes from Shalom Schwartz (see his chapter "Universals in the content and structure of values: Theoretical advances and empirical tests in 20 countries," in M. Zanna, Ed., *Advances in Experimental Social Psychology*, 1992, 25). Relying heavily on the theorizing of Rokeach and earlier works by Kluckhohn (see "Values and value-orientations in the theory of action: An exploration in definition and classification," in T. Parsons and E. Shils, Eds., *Toward a General Theory of Action*, Cambridge, Mass.), Schwartz developed a taxonomy of 10 types of values that differ in the motivational goal they express. These 10 types of values (with examples of each) are: power (e.g., authority, wealth), achievement (e.g., successful, ambitious), hedonism (e.g., pleasure, enjoying life), stimulation (e.g., daring, an exciting life), self-direction (e.g., creativity, freedom), universalism (e.g., broadminded, social justice), benevolence (e.g., helpful, forgiving), tradition (e.g., humble, devout), conformity (e.g., politeness, self-discipline), and security (e.g., family security, social order). (Early versions of the theory postulated an eleventh type—spirituality—which has received uneven support in empirical investigations.) Schwartz derived this typology by reasoning that values represent three universal requirements of human existence: biological needs, requisites of coordinated social interaction, and demands of group survival and functioning. People represent these requirements cognitively in the form of specific values, which they use to explain and coordinate behavior.

The central claim of Schwartz's theory is that these

10 types of values are interrelated in a structure that is invariant across cultures. The basis for this claim is as follows: The actions people take in pursuit of their values have psychological, practical, and social consequences; these consequences may either conflict or be compatible with the pursuit of other values. For example, power and achievement are quite compatible, in that they both emphasize social superiority and esteem. Similarly, universalism and benevolence are compatible, in that they both entail concern for enhancement of others and transcendence of selfish interests. But power and universalism, achievement and benevolence conflict with each other and cannot easily be pursued at the same time. As a result, there is an natural organization to value systems, which can be represented as a two-dimensional structure. One dimension contrasts Openness to Change (the self-direction and stimulation value types) with Conservation (the security, conformity, and tradition value types). The other dimension contrasts Self-Transcendence (the benevolence and universalism value types) with Self-Enhancement (the power and achievement value types). The 10 types of values can be represented as a circular structure defined by these two dimensions, with competing value types on opposing sides of the center and complementary types adjacent or in close proximity. Schwartz maintains that this organization should characterize the value systems of all groups in all cultures.

To test for this universal structure of human values, Schwartz developed a modified version of the RVS that is more suitable for use in cross-cultural research. He replaced Rokeach's lists of 18 terminal and 18 instrumental values with a master list of 56 values (21 of which overlap the RVS lists) and replaced the rank-ordering procedure with a rating task. The new survey asks respondents to rate each of the 56 values "AS A GUIDING PRINCIPLE IN MY LIFE," using a scale from 7 (*of supreme importance*) to −1 (*opposed to my values*), with 6 labeled *very important*, 3 labeled *important*, and 0 labeled *not important*. These modifications were intended to allow respondents to consider a wider range of values, to rate multiple values as equally important, and to reject values, considerations that are likely to be especially important in cross-cultural studies.

The empirical evidence to date has supported Schwartz's claims for a universal structure. Schwartz and his collaborators have administered his values scale to multiple samples of participants in 41 countries and have analyzed the structure underlying their responses using smallest space analysis. The results have provided evidence for his two proposed dimensions of organization in 95% of these samples.

Values, Attitudes, and Behaviors

The primary goal of most research on values—indeed, the litmus test for the utility of any construct in psychology—is the successful prediction of behavior. Hundreds of studies have tested the straightforward hypothesis that people use their values to guide their more specific attitudes and behaviors. The results of these studies have been equivocal: Although many have demonstrated sensible and reliable relations among values, attitudes, and behaviors, an equal number have found no relation among these constructs. Moreover, when significant correlations between values and attitudes or values and behaviors have emerged, they have been weak, with values typically accounting for less than 5% of the variance in attitudes or behaviors.

More encouraging evidence that values do, in fact, guide attitudes and behaviors has come from experimental studies of value self-confrontation. Pioneered by Rokeach, value self-confrontation is a strategy for inducing change in values. It involves presenting individuals with feedback and interpretations concerning their own and significant others' values, attitudes, and behaviors. The theory is that for some, this information will induce a state of self-dissatisfaction by making them aware that they hold beliefs and engage in behaviors that violate their sense of themselves as moral and competent. As one means of reducing this dissatisfaction, these individuals will change their values, attitudes, and behaviors to become more consistent with their self-conceptions. For others, this information will induce a state of self-satisfaction that will lead them to continue or increase their expression of these beliefs and behaviors in the future.

Research on value self-confrontation has provided consistent support for these predictions. In the most impressive demonstration, the critical feedback was delivered in a specially produced television program that targeted the values of freedom, equality, a comfortable life, and a world of beauty. Compared with a control community who did not see the program, those who saw it uninterrupted showed significant increases in the value they attached to freedom and equality, became more favorable in their attitudes toward Blacks, women, and the environment, and responded more favorably to solicitations for money and support for antiracist, antisexist, and proenvironmental causes (see Sandra Ball-Rokeach, Milton Rokeach, and Joel Grube, *The Great American Values Test: Influencing Behavior and Belief Through Television*, New York, 1984). Still, it is important to note that exposure to the program accounted for less than 1% of the variance in these values, attitudes, and behaviors.

The weak relations of values to attitudes and to behaviors raise questions about their validity and utility in psychological research. Proponents of the values construct have offered two different responses to these questions. First, some researchers have traced low value-attitude and value-behavior correlations to problems with the measurement and conceptualization of values.

For example, Schwartz has argued that both attitudinal and behavioral prediction can be enhanced considerably by using his 10 value types, rather than individual values, as predictors. Such a strategy enables the researcher to obtain more reliable measures of values, to take into account known relations among values, and to include the full range of values in their analyses.

A second response has been to search for variables that moderate relations among values, attitudes, and behaviors. Researchers have identified a number of such variables, including moral reasoning, moral orientation, self-conceptions, self-evaluations, and various dimensions of personality. But a more successful use of the moderating-variable strategy has relied on an analysis of the functions, or psychological needs, that attitudes and behaviors serve. The functional approach is predicated on the assumption that attitudes and behaviors can serve a variety of psychological functions for their holders, only one of which involves the expression of values. For some people, value-expression will be an important need, and most attitudes and behaviors will serve this function; for others, value-expression will be relatively unimportant, and few attitudes and behaviors will serve this function. Similarly, some circumstances will make the value-expressive function salient, and others will not. The best way to demonstrate strong value-attitude and value-behavior relations, therefore, is to identify value-expressive individuals or circumstances under which this function will be salient. Researchers working in this tradition have done precisely that. Studies have shown that individuals low in self-monitoring—that is, individuals who are guided by internal as opposed to external social cues—show stronger relations of values to attitudes and to behaviors than individuals high in self-monitoring. When individuals claim that their attitudes and behaviors express their values, strong value-attitude and value-behavior relations emerge. And when values are primed or challenged, correlations with attitudes and behaviors are enhanced.

Finally, although research that has focused on the consequences of values for individuals' attitudes and behaviors has produced mixed results and uncertain conclusions, values have played an important role in theories of cultural differences, prejudice, political reasoning, and justice. Taken together, these theories have highlighted the extent to which relations among individuals and groups in society are influenced by conflicts among values, both those that actually exist and those that are erroneously assumed to exist. For example, recent work in cultural psychology has emphasized the importance of teaching people to understand and respect culture-based value differences to promote positive intergroup relations. By contrast, work on racism and prejudice has emphasized that conflicts between racial and ethnic groups are exacerbated by the (often erroneous) perception that outgroup members violate cherished values. Extending and reconciling these theories of the social and societal consequences of values are important topics for future research.

[*See also* Moral Development; *and* Religious Values and Mental Health.]

Bibliography

Adorno, T. W., Frenkel-Brunswik, E., Levinson, D. J., & Sanford, R. N. (1950). *The authoritarian personality*. New York: Harper & Row.

Allport, G. W., Vernon, P., & Lindzey, G. (1960). *A study of values* (3rd ed.). Boston: Houghton Mifflin.

Ball-Rokeach, S. J., Rokeach, M., & Grube, J. W. (1984). *The great American values test*. New York: Free Press.

Feather, N. T. (1975). *Values in education and society*. New York: Free Press. Develops a psychological theory of values and actions using an expectancy-value approach.

Kluckhohn, C. (1951). Values and value-orientations in the theory of action. In T. Parsons & E. A. Shils (Eds.), *Toward a general theory of action* (pp. 388–433). Cambridge, MA: Harvard University Press.

Maio, G. R., & Olson, J. M. (in press). Value-expressive attitudes and value associations. In G. R. Maio & J. M. Olson (Eds.), *Why we evaluate: Functions of attitudes*. Mahwah, NJ: Erlbaum. Provides an introduction to the functional approach with a focus on its implications for the relation of values and attitudes.

Mayton, D. M., Loges, W. E., Ball-Rokeach, S. J., & Grube, J. W. (Eds.). (1994). Human values and social issues: Current understanding and implications for the future. *Journal of Social Issues, 50*. Includes a set of articles that review contemporary research on values in light of the seminal contributions of Milton Rokeach.

Rokeach, M. (1968). *Beliefs, attitudes, and values*. San Francisco, CA: Jossey-Bass.

Rokeach, M. (1973). *The nature of human values*. New York: Free Press.

Rokeach, M. (Ed.). (1979). *Understanding human values*. New York: Free Press.

Schwartz, S. H. (1992). Universals in the content and structure of values: Theoretical advances and empirical tests in 20 countries. In M. P. Zanna (Ed.), *Advances in experimental social psychology* (Vol. 25, pp. 1–65). San Diego, CA: Academic Press.

Seligman, C., Olson, J. M., & Zanna, M. P. (Eds.). (1996). *The psychology of values: The Ontario Symposium, Volume 8*. Mahwah, NJ: Erlbaum. Consists of expanded versions of papers presented initially at a conference on the psychology of values, held at the University of Western Ontario in 1993.

Deborah A. Prentice

VANDALISM. *See* Antisocial Behavior; *and* Delinquency.

VARIABILITY. *See* Data Analysis.

VARONA Y PERA, ENRIQUE JOSÉ (1849–1937), Cuban psychologist, philosopher, educator, and politician. Varona was born in Puerto Principe, Camaguey, Cuba, on 13 April 1849 and was shot and killed on 19 November 1937 in Moron, Cuba. He was a successful politician, philosopher, and academician. Through his ample writings, institutional positions, and social activism, he is considered one of Cuba's greatest intellectual leaders.

After obtaining one of the first doctorates from the University of Havana, Varona fought in the Ten-Year War (1868–1878) and later in the Spanish-American War. After the death of Jose Marti, the ideological founder of an independent Cuba and an accomplished man of letters, Varona assumed the leadership of the nationalist movement left vacant by Marti's untimely death. He eventually became professor of psychology, sociology, and moral philosophy at the University of Havana. In 1900, he was promoted to the position of secretary of public (educational) institutions. During his tenure as secretary, he overhauled the University of Havana by suspending all professors, opening up existing positions through the process of competition, decreasing tuition, and modernizing the curriculum. Soon afterward, he was elected vice president of Cuba (1913–1916).

His publications include works in psychology, philosophy, political science, literature, and poetry. Besides being the founding editor of *Revista Cuba*, he was also editor of *La Patria* during his brief exile in New York. Varona is credited with over 2,000 published works, which are abridged in the four-volume *Obras* (1936–1938). In contrast to his political writings (e.g., *Cuba Contra Espana*, 1885) are the works interfacing literature and philosophy (*Estudios Literarios y Filosoficos*, 1882).

Varona's goals were the foundation of an independent Cuba, an honest and efficient government, and a vibrant and modern intellectual and educational climate for the new country. In his academic pursuits, Varona introduced novel thinking in psychology, philosophy, and pedagogy. In psychology, he proposed that mental acts occur in stages. First, a person acted; this was followed by thinking about that act, and finally the person acted again based on that thought. He also believed that intelligence was a complex mental activity that involved the understanding of how consequences affect purposeful behavior. Varona held psychology and physiology to be inseparable, possibly reflecting the contemporary views of Wilhelm Wundt. [*See the biography of Wundt.*]

In social philosophy, Varona believed that the individual was dependent on the group. Furthermore, morality was broadly defined as conformity with social solidarity. Thus, morality occurs as a function of socialization. As a positivist and an empiricist, Varona believed logic to be the foundation for pedagogy. In his later years, his interest shifted to the application of these principles to the social and political life of Cuba. He founded the Partido Nacionalista as well as the Federacion de Obreros de la Habana. His critique of both the colonial imperialist government of Spain and the inept fledgling new country of Cuba resulted in the development of one of the twentieth century's most unusual countries as well as his own death.

Bibliography

Fitzgibbon, R. H. (1964). *Cuba and the United States (1900–1935)*. New York: Russell & Russell.

Perez, L. A. (1988). *Cuba*. New York: Oxford University Press.

Santovenia, E. S., & Shelton, R. M. (1966). *Cuba y su historia*. Miami, FL: Cuba.

Antonio E. Puente and Krista L. Puente

VENEZUELA. The first psychologists in Venezuela were either emigrés from the Spanish Civil War, psychiatrists interested in psychology, or local young professionals who had been trained in the United States, Britain, or France. In 1950 the Institute of Psychology of the Universidad Central de Venezuela (UCV) was established in Caracas, and psychological courses were formally instituted there in 1956 at the school of psychology. Shortly afterward the Universidad Católica Andrés Bello (UCAB) began offering similar courses. The discipline developed under varied theoretical influences. Radical behaviorism obtained a strong foothold, particularly among clinical psychologists. Social psychologists started using cognitive-behavioral orientations for their research. Later, some opted for social representations, while others chose community social psychology. The developmental psychologists started with a strong Piagetian orientation, but more recently have turned to ecological frameworks, with a dominant interest in child development in the contexts of poverty.

An outstanding event in Venezuelan psychology was the creation during the 1979 to 1984 presidency of an *ad hoc* Ministry for the Development of Intelligence. Its aim was to promote a series of projects directed at stimulating cognitive development nationwide. After the government changed in 1984, most of these projects were discontinued, but some were incorporated into the Ministry of Education, and others were taken over by private organizations, although with a less ambitious scope.

Current Status of the Profession

At the moment there are approximately 7,000 psychologists in the country. A degree in the discipline can only be obtained in three universities: the two mentioned above and the Universidad Rafael Urdaneta (URU) in Maracaibo, the second largest city in the country.

A high-school graduate requires 5 years of university training to become a psychologist. Psychology is a very popular subject, and the ratio of applicants to available places is one of the highest among university options.

It is also possible to obtain master's and specialist's degrees in several fields of psychology in the three universities mentioned above, at the Universidad Simon Bolivar (USB), and in some training hospitals. At the UCV there is also a doctoral program in psychology, which was created in 1989.

Psychologists have attained high positions in Venezuela. Three psychologists have become ministers in national cabinets, several have been or are members of the National Congress, ambassadors, presidents, and vice presidents of national universities and deans of faculties.

There are approximately three times more women than men in the profession. The largest number of psychologists work in the clinical field, either in institutions or in private practice. They work either individually or in mental health teams, both in assessment and in treatment.

The second largest number of psychologists work in industry in personnel recruitment and selection, industrial relations, and personnel evaluation and training. Some have set up their own consulting firms.

Schools, both public and private, employ psychologists for psychological assessment, treatment of learning disabilities, teacher training, course evaluation, and so forth. Counseling (in secondary schools and at universities and college student services) also draws a certain number of psychologists.

Psychologists in Venezuela also work within the penal system, either in prisons or as parole officers, and in therapeutic communities. Some work in advertising and in the mass media, and some do community work. Finally, a number are engaged in teaching in secondary schools and universities.

Research Traditions

At present there are five research centers in universities corresponding to the four universities mentioned above where facilities exist for training in psychology at postgraduate levels. In addition, at the Universidad de los Andes (ULA), there is a very active research center that was founded in 1978.

One of the earliest lines of research was on child development, particularly within the contexts of poverty and deprivation. The work of Recagno (1982) and Manrique, Contasti, Alvarado, Cos, and Zypman (1991) must be mentioned in this context.

The team of researchers at the Laboratory of Experimental Analysis of Behavior at the Institute of Psychology at the UCV has produced both basic and applied research, particularly on learning in young children. Among the psychologists working in this group are Dembo and Guevara (1996).

Research on nationalism, national identity, and political psychology has had a strong tradition since the 1970s. Montero (1987), Banchs, Cadenas, Dominguez, and Montero (1993), and Salazar and Salazar (1998) represent examples of the sustained interest in these related topic areas. The research center at the ULA has developed a line of research on sociopsychological factors affecting academic achievement (locus of control, motivation, language, etc.). The leader of this group is Romero-Garcia (1994). There have also been important developments in instructional psychology and in cognitive development.

Environmental and later community psychology have become important. Names associated with these developments are Sánchez, Wiesenfeld, & Cronick (1983) and Montero (1997).

Great interest has also been taking shape in health psychology with an emphasis on the problems of drugs, hypertension, and psychosomatic ailments (Sánchez & Parada, 1993).

Psychological Societies and Associations

After a law governing psychological practice was passed in 1978, a federation of psychologists was established. Psychologists must hold membership in it in order to practice. The federation has as its main objective the defense of the profession.

As a parallel organizational structure there are 14 scientific societies that maintain a loose relationship with the federation (Rodriguez & Sánchez, 1996). The most successful, taking into account the number of scientific meetings that have being organized under their aegis, are those of social psychology and school psychology.

Journals

Four journals related to psychology are currently published in Venezuela: *Niños*, published by the National Institute of Child Psychiatry; *Psicologia*, published by the UCV School of Psychology, *Revista de Avepso*, published by the Social Psychology Association, and *Comportamiento*, published by USB. The Center for Psychological Studies at ULA publishes research reports under the series title *Monografias*, and AVEPSO publishes *Fasciculos*.

Future Directions

Both psychologists and financing institutions are aware of the need to carry out research aimed at solving or ameliorating the multiple social problems in Venezuela. There is also a move away from classical experimentation, and inroads have been made in constructivism and nonexperimental, nonquantitative research. How these two trends will become integrated is difficult to foresee.

Bibliography

Banchs, M. A., Cadenas, J. M., Dominguez, D., & Montero, M. (1993). Identidad nacional: Permanencia y cambio. *Revista Interamericana de Psicología/Interamerican Journal of Psychology, 27*, 107–114. A synthesis of four empirical studies related to national identity, elaborated by researchers of the Department of Social Psychology of the UCV.

Dembo, M., & Guevara, M. T. (1996). *Aportes a la psicología del comportamiento infantil y la educación pre-escolar.* Caracas: Facultad de Humanidades y Educacion, UCV. Presents the results of a series of studies carried out with young children attending an experimental kindergarten.

Manrique, B., Contasti, M., Alvarado, M. A., Cos, C., & Zypman, M. (1991). Aplicación de un modelo educativo multifactorial a familias de los barrios pobres de Caracas: Primeros resultados. *Revista Interamericana de Psicología/Interamerican Journal of Psychology, 25*, 171–184. Preliminary results are presented of a stimulation program originally developed within the Ministry for the Development of Intelligence.

Montero, M. (Ed.). (1987). *Psicología política Latinoamericana.* Caracas: Panapo. A compilation of studies, theoretical and empirical, on diverse aspects of political psychology by Latin American psychologists.

Montero, M. (Ed). (1997). *Psicología y comunidad.* Caracas: UCV. A compilation of recent studies on community psychology, carried out by psychologists working in different countries in the continent, originally presented as symposia at the 1995 Interamerican Congress of Psychology.

Recagno, I. (1982). *Hábitos de crianza y marginalidad.* Caracas: UCV. A complete presentation of an early study of socialization in a poor sector of Caracas.

Rodríguez, P., & Sánchez, L. (1996). La Psicología en Venezuela. *Papeles del Psicólogo,* Epoca III, No. 66, 45–50. A historical account of the development of psychology as a discipline and as a profession in Venezuela, and of its current status; included in one of the periodical publications of the Colegio Oficial de Psicologos of Spain.

Romero-García, O. (1994). Crecimiento psicológico y motivaciones sociales. In M. Montero (Ed.), *Construcción y crítica de la psicología social.* Barcelona: Anthropos. A synthesis of theoretical developments, based on many empirical studies, by the leader of an important research group.

Salazar, J. M., & Salazar M. A. (1998). Permanence and modification in national identities. In J. G. Adair, D. Belanger, & K. L. Dion (Eds.), *Advances in psychological science. Vol. 1: Social, personal and cultural aspects.* Hove, UK: Psychology Press. An analysis of studies on national identity published over a 10-year period, with emphases on those carried out in Latin America and Venezuela.

Sánchez, E., Wiesenfeld, E., & Cronick, K. (1983). Environmental psychology in Venezuela. *Journal of Environmental Psychology, 3*, 161–172. A synthesis of studies carried out in diverse communities in Venezuela, particularly in marginal areas of Caracas.

Sánchez, L., & Parada, M. I. (1993). La intervención del psicólogo en el campo de la salud. *Revista Interamericana de Psicología/Interamerican Journal of Psychology, 27*, 23–36. An analytic study of the contributions of psychologists in the area of health in Venezuela.

José Miguel Salazar

VETERANS. Understanding of the psychological and social adjustment associated with military service has changed dramatically over the last century in concert with evolving social, medical, and political trends. Nowhere is this more evident than in our recognition and treatment of soldiers' psychological responses to the stress of war. Psychological stress after combat, once viewed as a manifestation of personal weakness, has received growing attention in recent decades. One of the most important developments has been our increased appreciation of the role of the stressful experience itself (i.e., military service) in influencing soldiers' outcomes. Today, although science views individual characteristics as playing some role in reactions to wartime service, many war-related symptoms are better understood as "normal responses" to otherwise "abnormal" and brutal conditions. In this article, we review major developments of the war stress construct. We suggest that numerous developments over the past few decades have influenced recognition of the effects of wartime service, enhancing public awareness and improving treatment for service-related conditions, for example, posttraumatic stress disorder (PTSD).

World War I

War-related mental illness has been traced back to the Russo-Japanese, Serbo-Turkish, and Boer wars. Similar references are also found in the history of the U.S. Civil

War (cf. Feudtner, 1993; Mangelsdorff, 1985). However, it was the large-scale deployment of troops during World War I (WWI), combined with the brutality of trench warfare, that first brought the issue of soldiers' adjustment to public attention.

The trench warfare of WWI involved "massive and sustained artillery firepower against fixed human targets" (Neill, 1993). Not surprisingly, many soldiers experienced extreme emotional and behavioral reactions such as mutism, amnesia, hysterical paralysis, depression, agitation, and nightmares (Mangelsdorff, 1985; Neill, 1993). Early explanations for these severe disturbances focused on the problems of the individual soldier rather than the war itself. For example, disturbances in functioning were thought to stem from undetected neurological injury secondary to artillery-induced carbon monoxide or changes in atmospheric pressure (Mott, 1919, cited in Trimble, 1985). An alternative view, articulated by the British, attributed such disturbances to "constitutionally determined" individual vulnerabilities brought out by the stress of the war (Hausman & Rioch, 1967; Neill, 1993). This belief led to rapid evacuations from front lines to general and psychiatric hospitals, resulting in greatly reduced military manpower and often permanent disability in many soldiers. In contrast, the French viewed these disturbances as secondary to basic cowardice, reflecting soldiers' attempts at removal from battle. This perspective was associated with aversive treatments such as painful electrical stimulation, loss of privileges, and confinement. However, it also produced significantly higher rates of return to duty and less permanent disability (Hausman & Rioch, 1967; Mangelsdorff, 1985).

Benefiting from the experiences of their European counterparts, the United States entered WWI with a plan for treating psychiatric casualties and minimizing loss of manpower that involved assigning a psychiatrist to each military division. Also, "neurological hospitals" were erected close to front lines so soldiers could be treated in therapeutic settings, but with the expectation that they would return to duty (Hausman & Rioch, 1967). The principles inherent in this treatment were those of *proximity* (treating psychiatric casualties close to front lines), *immediacy* (as events arose), and *expectancy* (with the understanding that they would return to duty). From a military perspective these principles served American forces well: Between 40 and 70% of psychiatric casualties were eventually returned to some type of duty after receiving forward area treatment (cf. Mangelsdorff, 1985). Still, the long-term impact of this approach on the well-being of the individual remains unclear.

World War II

By the start of the Second World War, the field of American psychiatry had expanded, reflecting the popularity of psychoanalytic thinkers (e.g., Freud). Accordingly, stress-related reactions were described using new terms like *anxiety neurosis*. Novel treatments involving the use of barbiturates, hypnosis, and the "talking cure" emerged to facilitate the discharge of suppressed feelings. Unfortunately, this model advocated the evacuation of soldiers from front-line service, an action that, once again, had costly national and personal consequences.

As the war progressed, terms like *combat exhaustion* and *combat fatigue* appeared. These terms highlighted the role of external factors in adjustment to war. They were also more acceptable to military commanders because they seemed to emphasize that "the stress of combat could overwhelm anyone" (Joy, 1996). Ironically, this "newer" model invoked the reinstatement of the WWI principles of proximity, immediacy, and expectancy. Psychiatric service areas were eventually set up within the battle zones where soldiers were treated with the expectation that they would return to duty. Once in place, this program resulted in a significant improvement in the return of psychiatric casualties to duty (Hausman & Rioch, 1967).

Interestingly, ensuing research on WWII war-related stress reactions showed that, while preexisting conditions *could* increase vulnerability, the largest predictors of "war neurosis" were in fact elements of the war itself, such as type of duty and time in the war zone (Brill & Beebe, 1955). Fueled by a growing appreciation of the causes of war stress and a high rate of casualties, the U.S. Congress enacted several benefits for veterans during and after WWII including the GI Bill of 1944, which provided educational and occupational resources. These benefits were administered by the Department of Veterans Affairs (VA), which, since 1930, has coordinated many government activities affecting veterans. Such efforts emphasize the community's role in helping veterans readjust to postmilitary life. The VA plays a major role today in providing even broader services to veterans, including education and occupational training, disability compensation, cemetery administration, and health care. Of the approximately 26 million U.S. veterans, a substantial minority utilizes some form of benefits.

The Korean War Era

In 1950, with lessons from WWII still fresh in mind, the U.S. military entered Korea with an organized preventive psychiatry program. Divisional psychiatric services were implemented and psychiatric treatment centers were erected close behind divisions early in the first campaign. As a result, 65 to 75% of men diagnosed with "combat exhaustion" returned to some form of duty (Hausman & Rioch, 1967).

During the Korean War in 1952, the American psychiatric community formally identified "gross stress reactions" in its first official diagnostic publication (American Psychiatric Association, 1952). Yet, when the second manual was published in 1968 (APA), the concept of military stress reactions was submerged under the general category of "adjustment reaction." This classification was so broad that it essentially curtailed any scientific or clinical focus on traumatic stress. As a result, no further conceptual or treatment innovations were made until the Vietnam War when an unusual confluence of social and political factors radically changed the approach to war stress.

The Vietnam War

The Vietnam War appears to have done more to advance the understanding and treatment of war stress than any other event to date. Marked by grueling fighting conditions as in prior wars but with less social support, veterans returned to the United States in the late 1960s and early 1970s to find surprisingly few resources to help with their readjustment. Using their common experiences as soldiers, Vietnam veterans began to organize among themselves, often criticizing a government that had sent them to battle but provided little assistance on return (Williams, 1987). For perhaps the first time, veterans of all political leanings responded to their isolation by demanding that war stress be recognized and that appropriate resources be developed. One result of this combined movement was the listing of traumatic war stress as a distinct diagnostic category in American psychiatry's third diagnostic manual under the label *posttraumatic stress disorder* (PTSD; APA, 1980). Another important outcome was the Carter Administration's creation of VA's Readjustment Counseling Service in the late 1970s. This service established community vet centers across the country to provide veterans with easily accessible psychosocial services and support.

The movement described above was eventually supported by scientific evidence from many sources. Research confirmed that wartime participation could inflict long-lasting psychological, physical, and social problems. In 1983, Congress passed legislation instructing the VA to conduct a national study of rates of PTSD and related problems in the Vietnam generation. The National Vietnam Veterans Readjustment Study (NVVRS; Kulka et al., 1990) systematically interviewed 1,632 men and women who had served in the Vietnam theater, plus 736 Vietnam-era veterans who had served elsewhere, and 667 civilians of comparable age. The study confirmed that most Vietnam veterans had successfully reentered civilian life. However, more than 10 years after the war's end, a staggering 15.2% of male and 8.5% of female Vietnam theater veterans still suffered from PTSD. These rates were much higher than those found in either Vietnam-era veterans (2.5% for males, 1.1% for females) or civilians (1.2% of males, 0.3% of females). Moreover, over one half of Vietnam veterans reported significant stress symptoms at some point since their service. In fact, intensity of war service was directly associated with the development of PTSD and other adjustment problems.

Scientists and clinicians working in this area soon realized that effective treatments would require new approaches including: (1) a focus on the whole person, not just symptoms; (2) validation of the stressful experience; (3) attention to specific problems (e.g., substance abuse); and (4) use of combined therapies (e.g., behavioral, cognitive, psychoeducation, and medication). Based on research and treatment efforts, many gains were made during this time that advanced the recognition and treatment of war stress reactions and associated problems.

Post-Vietnam and the Persian Gulf War

Recent research suggests that rates of war-related stress disorders may be on the decline (Wolfe et al., 1998). For example, studies show rates of PTSD in Gulf War veterans ranging from 2 to 15% (Iowa Persian Gulf Study Group, 1997; Perconte, Wilson, Pontius, Dietrick, & Spiro, 1993). However, research on American veterans from Somalia shows that approximately 25% of soldiers still report significant distress (Litz, 1996). Information from these experiences highlight new issues associated with military service. These include the special needs and experiences of women in the military (now about 11% of the active duty force), effects of rapid, brief deployments (e.g., Panama, Lebanon, Bosnia), closer contact with civilians in the host nation, threat of biochemical warfare, increased use of reserve troops (including married couples and single parents), and, perhaps most importantly, the emerging dual role of the soldier as "warrior peacekeeper." With regard to the latter, new research suggests that one of the most difficult aspects of participation in peacekeeping is the role conflict associated with being a trained soldier who is restrained from use of offensive responses to threat (Litz, 1996). Together, these new experiences bring a series of challenges for the soldier, the family, the command structure, and the agencies responsible for soldiers' well-being. Finally, as the U.S. decreases its military manpower, soldiers may return from conflicts to find that a promotion or military career is no longer a possibility. These changes potentially impact soldiers in a number of ways (Ursano & Norwood, 1996).

The Future

Despite its risks, service in the military has offered generations of men and women the chance to improve their lives while providing service to their country (Schnurr & Aldwin, 1993). For many individuals, military service continues to offer the opportunity for strong vocational and leadership training, stable friendships, and readily accessible medical care. As a result many veterans credit military service with having changed their lives for the better. Many WWII and Vietnam veterans found their military experiences worthwhile even while experiencing initial delays in educational or occupational pursuits (cf. Gade, Lakhani, & Kimmel, 1991). A recent study of newly separated Army enlistees reported that 85% of those surveyed found their military service valuable and 75% said they would rejoin (Gade et al., 1991). Military service might be especially helpful to minorities and women as it provides opportunities not otherwise available. As a leader, the U.S. Armed Forces has been credited with breakthroughs in a number of areas, for example, racial integration and sexual equality. Although military service is likely to be redefined as national priorities and international alliances evolve over the years, the happiness and well-being of the individual soldier will constitute the foundation for these changes.

[*See also* Military Service.]

Bibliography

American Psychiatric Association. (1952). *Diagnostic and statistical manual of mental disorders*. Washington, DC: Author.

American Psychiatric Association. (1968). *Diagnostic and statistical manual of mental disorders* (2nd ed.). Washington, DC: Author.

American Psychiatric Association. (1980). *Diagnostic and statistical manual of mental disorders* (3rd ed.). Washington, DC: Author.

Brill, N. Q., & Beebe, G. W. (1955). A follow-up study of war neurosis. *VA Medical Monograph Series*. Washington, DC: USGPO.

Feudtner, C. (1993). "Minds the dead have ravished": Shell shock, history, and the ecology of disease-systems. *History of Science, 31*, 377–420.

Gade, P. A., Lakhani, H., & Kimmel, M. (1991). Military service: A good place to start? *Military Psychology, 3*, 251–267.

Hausman, W., & Rioch, D. M. (1967). Military psychiatry: A prototype of social and preventive psychiatry in the United States. *Archives of General Psychiatry, 16*, 727–739.

Iowa Persian Gulf Study Group. (1997). Self-reported illness and health status among Gulf War veterans. *Journal of the American Medical Association, 277*, 238–245.

Joy, R. T. (1996). Foreword. In J. A. Martin, L. R. Sparacino, & G. Belenky (Eds.), *The Gulf War and mental health: A comprehensive guide* (pp. ix–xvii). Westport, CT: Praeger.

Kulka, R. A., Schlenger, W. E., Fairbank, J. A., Hough, R. L., Jordan, B. K., Marmar, C. R., & Weiss, D. S. (1990). *Trauma and the Vietnam War generation: Report of findings from the National Vietnam Veterans Readjustment Study*. New York: Brunner/Mazel.

Litz, B. T. (1996). The psychological demands of peacekeeping for military personnel. *NCP Clinical Quarterly, 6*, 1–8.

Mangelsdorff, A. D. (1985). Lessons learned and forgotten: The need for prevention and mental health interventions in disaster preparedness. *Journal of Community Psychology, 13*, 239–257.

Neill, J. R. (1993). How psychiatric symptoms varied in World Wars I and II. *Military Medicine, 159*, 149–151.

Perconte, S. T., Wilson, A. T., Pontius, E. B., Dietrick, A. L., & Spiro, K. J. (1993). Psychological and war stress symptoms among deployed and non-deployed reservists following the Persian Gulf War. *Military Medicine, 158*, 516–521.

Schnurr, P. P., & Aldwin, C. M. (1993). Military service: Long-term effects on adult development. In R. Kastenbaum (Ed.), *Encyclopedia of adult development* (pp. 351–356). Phoenix, AZ: Oryx.

Trimble, M. R. (1985). Post-traumatic stress disorder: History of a concept. In C. R. Figley (Ed.), *Trauma and its wake: The study and treatment of post-traumatic stress disorder* (pp. 5–14). New York: Brunner/Mazel.

Ursano, R. J., & Norwood, A. E. (Eds.). (1996). *Those left behind: Psychological responses to war in families, children and soldiers*. Washington, DC: American Psychiatric Press.

Williams, T. (Ed.). (1987). *Post-traumatic stress disorders: A handbook for clinicians*. Cincinnati, OH: Disabled American Veterans.

Wolfe, J., Proctor, S. P., Davis, J. D., Borgos, M. S., & Friedman, M. J. (1998). Health symptoms reported by Persian Gulf War veterans two years after return. *American Journal of Industrial Medicine, 33*, 104–113.

Jessica Wolfe and Kathleen R. Melia

VIOLENCE AND AGGRESSION. According to the U.S. Federal Bureau of Investigation's 1996 *Uniform Crime Reports*, in 1995 a murder occurred every 24 minutes, a rape every 5 minutes, a robbery every 54 seconds, and an aggravated assault every 29 seconds. The corresponding rates per 100,000 people were 8.2 murders, 37.1 rapes, 221 robberies, and 418 assaults, totaling 684 violent crimes per 100,000 population. Violent crime has dropped somewhat in recent years. The 1995 rate was 6% lower than the 1990 rate. Even so, the 1995 rate was 142% of the 1975 rate, and 638% of the 1955 rate. These statistics underestimate the actual frequencies because of underreporting, especially of rape and domestic violence. Furthermore, these rates do not include the high rates of severe violence against children by their caregivers, which some estimate at 10%. Violent crime rates in other industrialized societies are lower, but are still unacceptable. Solutions require a thorough understanding of aggression and violence in general.

What Are Aggression and Violence?

Definitions have varied widely over time and across research domains. However, a consensus has emerged among psychologists studying human aggression and violence.

Aggression and Violence. Human aggression is behavior performed by one person (the aggressor) with the intent of harming another person (the victim) who is believed by the aggressor to be motivated to avoid that harm. "Harm" includes direct physical harm (e.g., a punch to the jaw), direct psychological harm (e.g., verbal insults), and indirect harm (e.g., destroying the victim's property).

Accidental harm is not "aggressive" because harm is not intended. Harm sought out by the target is also excluded from "aggression" because the harm-doer's intent in such cases is to help the person achieve other superordinate goals. For example, pain delivered during a dental procedure is not "aggressive."

Aggressiveness is not synonymous with "assertiveness," though the general public frequently uses them interchangeably. An "aggressive" salesperson is actually "assertive," unless of course the salesperson intentionally tries to harm customers. Similarly, coaches exhorting players to "be more aggressive" seldom mean that players should try to harm their opponents; rather, coaches want players to be more assertive or active.

Violence is a subtype of aggression, generally used to denote extreme forms of aggression such as murder, rape, and assault. All violence is aggression, but many forms of aggression are not violent.

Affective Versus Instrumental. Affective aggression has the primary motive of harming the target, and is thought to be based on anger. It is sometimes labeled *hostile, impulsive,* or *reactive* aggression, though these labels often carry additional meaning. When aggression is merely a tool to achieve another goal of the aggressor, it is labeled *instrumental* aggression. Most robberies are primarily instrumental, whereas most murders and assaults are affective. Similarly, Jack may hit Jim merely to obtain a desirable toy, a case of instrumental aggression. Jim may get angry and respond by hitting Jack in order to hurt him, a case of affective aggression.

Proactive Versus Reactive. Proactive aggression occurs in the absence of provocation. It is usually instrumental, as when Jack hit Jim to get the toy. Reactive aggression is a response to a prior provocation, such as when Jim retaliated. There is an asymmetrical relation between proactive and reactive aggression. Children who are high on proactive aggression usually are high on reactive aggression as well, but many children who are high on reactive aggression engage in little proactive aggression.

Distinguishing among types of aggression is difficult because motives must be inferred. Is Jim's angry attack on Jack purely anger-based, solely intended to harm Jack, or is there also some instrumental component? Some argue that all aggression is instrumental, serving goals such as social control, public image management, private image management (i.e., self-esteem), and social justice. Nonetheless, most aggression scholars find the affective-instrumental and the proactive-reactive distinctions helpful even though they recognize that anger-based aggression often serves multiple motives.

Thoughtful Versus Thoughtless. A final distinction concerns whether the aggressive act resulted from thoughtful or thoughtless (impulsive) psychological processes. Instrumental aggression is usually seen as being thoughtful, involving the careful weighing of potential costs and benefits. But frequent use of aggression to obtain valued goals can become so automatized that it becomes thoughtless. Affective aggression is usually seen as being thoughtless, but people sometimes consider various possible courses of action and decide that an angry outburst is the best way to achieve those goals. The thoughtful-thoughtless distinction has important implications for the development of and intervention in aggression.

What Causes Aggression?

We can analyze the causes of aggression and violence at two different levels—the proximate causes (in the immediate situation) and the more distal causes that set the stage for the emergence and operation of proximate causes.

Proximate Causes: Individual Differences. People differ widely in readiness to be aggressive. These differences show considerable cross-situational consistency.

Hostility Biases. These biases have been identified in aggressive adults and children, some as young as 6 years. The *hostile perception bias* is the tendency of aggression-prone people to perceive social behaviors as more aggressive than normal people. The *hostile expectation bias* is the tendency of aggression-prone people to expect and predict aggressive behavior in others. The *hostile attribution bias* is the tendency of aggression-prone people to attribute more hostile intent to others' accidentally harmful behaviors. For example, Kenneth Dodge had aggressive and nonaggressive children listen to a story about a boy who hurt another boy by hitting him with a ball. When asked, aggressive children attributed more hostile intent to the boy who threw the ball than did nonaggressive children (*Child Development*, 51, 162–170).

Attitudes and Beliefs. Aggression-prone people hold favorable attitudes toward aggression, believing that aggressive solutions to problems are effective and appropriate. Aggressive thoughts and aggressive solutions come to mind quickly and easily. However, creating nonaggressive alternatives is particularly difficult for the aggressive person.

For example, a longitudinal study by Malamuth, Linz, Heavey, Barnes, and Acker (1995) found that sexually aggressive males hold relatively positive attitudes toward the use of aggression against women, believe in numerous rape myths, engage in more impersonal sex, and are likely to aggress against women in nonsexual contexts as well.

Sex. Males and females differ in aggressive tendencies, especially in the most violent behaviors of homicide and aggravated assault. The ratio of male to female murderers in the United States is almost 10:1.

Laboratory studies show the same type of sex effect, but provocation has a greater effect on aggression than does sex. In a 1996 meta-analysis article, Ann Bettencourt and Norman Miller showed that sex differences in aggression practically disappear under high provocation.

Provocations that elicit aggressive responses also differ for males and females. Bettencourt and Miller showed that males are particularly sensitive to negative intelligence provocations whereas females were particularly sensitive to other types of insults. Males have been shown to be more upset by sexual infidelity of their mates than by emotional infidelity, whereas the opposite pattern occurs for females. Similar sex differences also have been demonstrated in mate retention tactics, including violence.

Biology. Other biological differences also contribute to aggression. Hormones (e.g., testosterone), neurochemicals (e.g., serotonin), attention-deficit/hyperactivity disorder, and general levels of arousal have all been linked to aggression. For example, Eysenck and Gudjonsson (1989) proposed that individuals whose nervous systems are relatively insensitive to low levels of environmental stimulation seek out high-risk activities, including criminal ones, to increase their arousal.

Many biological effects on aggression are neither as strong nor as consistent as the general public believes. For example, testosterone is frequently cited as the explanation for male-female differences in violence rates, but the human literature on testosterone effects is unclear.

Proximate Causes: Situational Factors. Most aggressive incidents can be directly linked to such factors as provocation, frustration incentives, aversive, stimulation and stress, alcohol and drugs, and so on.

Provocation. Some provocations are direct and obvious, such as verbal insults and physical attacks. Some are less direct, as when an expected pay raise fails to materialize. Most murders and assaults are the result of provocations of one kind or another, usually in a series of escalatory charges, threats, and counterthreats. FBI data reveal that most murders occur during arguments among family, friends, or acquaintances. Very often the provocations involve sexual or emotional infidelity or perceived insults to one's honor.

Frustration. When something blocks the attainment or threatens the continued possession of a valued goal objective, frustration occurs. For example, a supervisor's bad report may prevent a promotion, or a flood may destroy one's home. When the frustrating agent is another person, the frustrating event is also a provocation.

The original form of the frustration-aggression hypothesis was introduced by John Dollard and colleagues (*Frustration and Aggression*, New Haven, Conn., 1939). It stated that (1) all acts of aggression are the result of previous frustration; (2) all frustration leads to aggression. But some frustrations do not yield aggression, and some aggression is not the result of a prior frustration. One key set of studies focused on the mitigating consequences of justification, which frequently takes the form of claiming that a frustrating action was unintentional or uncontrollable. Apologies often take this form of justification, and are used to prevent aggressive responses. Many scholars believed that if a frustrating event was fully justified, the frustrated person would show no residual inclination to aggress.

However, one researcher claimed that even fully justified frustration can produce aggressive tendencies. It does so by automatically priming aggression-related thoughts and negative affect before the justification occurs. This modified frustration-aggression hypothesis has been shown to be correct (*Aggressive Behavior, 21*, 359–369). Although apologies and other justifications for frustrating behavior dramatically reduce aggression, they do not fully eliminate the instigated aggression tendencies.

Incentives. Many situations in politics, the business world, and sports encourage aggression by their incentives. Many expect their chances of winning an election, getting a contract, or defeating an opponent to be enhanced by harming their competitor. TV violence research has shown that seeing a character rewarded (or not punished) for aggressing increases subsequent aggression by the viewer more so than does unrewarded (or punished) TV violence.

The prototypical incentive-based example of aggression is the contract killer, who murders purely for the money. Such murders account for only a small percentage of the U.S. total, but they nicely illustrate the concept of anger-free instrumental aggression.

Aversive Stimulation and Stress. Almost any form of aversive stimulation increases the likelihood of aggression—noise, pain, crowding, cigarette smoke, heat, daily hassles, interpersonal problems. Sometimes the cause of an aversive stimulus is an identifiable person, such as a smoker. In such cases these factors are also provocations. As such, they can increase aggression directed at the person identified as the provocateur.

In other cases there is no identifiable human agent causing the aversive stimulation. In these cases the effects on aggression are often less noticeable, but much research demonstrates their reality. The most studied of these effects, with relevant data gathered for over 100 years, is the heat effect. Craig and Kathryn Anderson (in R. Geen & E. Donnerstein, Eds., New York, 1998) showed that a wide array of studies across time, culture, and method converge on the conclusion that hot temperatures increase aggressive tendencies. People who live in hotter cities have higher violent crime rates than those in cooler cities. This effect persists even when controlling for poverty, education, and culture. Violent crime rates are higher during hotter years, seasons, months, and days. When people are hot, they think more aggressive thoughts and feel more hostile.

Alcohol and Drugs. In a 1993 article, Brad Bushman (*Current Directions in Psychological Science, 2*, 148–152) showed that central nervous system depressants increase aggression. Interestingly, neither alcohol nor the belief that one has consumed alcohol were individually sufficient to produce reliable increases in aggression, but when research participants believed they had consumed alcohol *and* had actually consumed alcohol, aggression increased. The exact mechanisms underlying drug effects are not yet fully understood. One explanation of the alcohol effect is that *alcohol myopia* impairs key perceptual processes necessary to normal inhibitions against extreme and risky behavior.

Aggression Cues. Any object or event associated with aggression in semantic memory can cue or "prime" aggression-related thoughts, affects, and behavior programs also stored in memory. For instance, most people associate guns with human aggression. Therefore, seeing a gun can prime aggressive thoughts and increase aggressive behavior. Leonard Berkowitz and Anthony LePage (1967) first reported this "weapons effect." Research participants who had been provoked after seeing some weapons behaved more aggressively than similarly provoked people who had not seen weapons. This effect has been found in field and laboratory studies, in several different countries, with pictures of weapons and with real weapons. Recent research has confirmed that the mere sight of a weapon or of a weapon word automatically increases aggressive thoughts.

One prevalent source of aggressive cues in modern society is the mass media. Television shows, movies, and video games are filled with violence. Over 1,000 empirical comparisons, reviewed by Paik and Comstock (1994), have conclusively demonstrated that exposure to media violence increases aggression. There is some evidence that the immediate impact of viewing violent media is more pronounced for people with strong aggressive tendencies, as shown by Brad Bushman (*Journal of Personality and Social Psychology*, 1995, 69, 950–960). Generally aggressive people also are the most likely to seek out violent media.

Other more idiosyncratic aggression cues can also increase aggression. For instance, if you are repeatedly angered by a kid named Jack during childhood, your adult encounters with other people named Jack will tend to elicit aggressive thoughts. These thoughts can color interactions with and behavior toward these "Jacks" without your being aware that your childhood nemesis still disturbs your world.

Opportunity. Some situations restrict opportunities to aggress, whereas others provide "good" opportunities. For example, a normal church service is a situation with many impediments to aggression. There are witnesses, strong social norms against aggression, and specific nonaggressive behavioral roles for everyone in attendance.

Country and Western bars on Saturday nights present much better opportunities for aggression; some are noted for their fights. Many factors previously discussed as aggression facilitators are present: alcohol, aggression cues, aggression-prone individuals, males competing for the attention of females. Furthermore, there may be considerable anonymity both because of the relatively large number of strangers as well as the dim lighting. Arnold Goldstein (1994) explores many issues of aggression opportunity as they relate to both physical and social ecology.

Removal of Self-Regulatory Inhibitions. One often-neglected facet of human aggression concerns aggression inhibitions that normally operate in most people. In their article on moral agency, Bandura, Barbaranelli, Caprara, and Pastorelli discussed how these inhibitions are sometimes overridden (*Journal of Personality and Social Psychology*, 1996, *71*, 364–374).

People generally regulate their own behavior to a great extent. Most people could "get away with" considerable aggression without suffering negative consequences from society, simply because it would be undiscovered. However, people cannot so easily escape the consequences that they apply to themselves. Self-image, self-standards, and sense of self-worth—in other words moral standards—are used in normal self-regulation of behavior.

But sometimes people with apparently normal moral standards behave reprehensibly toward others, including such actions as murder, torture, even genocide. How can self-regulatory mechanisms fail so miserably? Bandura and colleagues proposed several "mechanisms of moral disengagement" to account for these failures. These mechanisms short-circuit normal moral self-regulatory processes by making them seem irrelevant. The two main mechanisms involve moral justification and dehumanizing the victim.

Individuals (or their social leaders) sometimes create moral justifications for violence. Common justifications include "it is for the person's own good," or the good of the society, or that personal honor demands the violent action. Such justifications can be applied at multiple levels, from a parent's abuse of a child to genocidal war.

By dehumanizing the victim, one's moral standards no longer apply. War propaganda obviously fits this mechanism. But people can also use this mechanism at an individual level. People create the ultimate outgroup—one that has no human qualities—and psychologically place the intended victims in that group.

The Escalation Cycle. Many proximate causal factors seem too trivial or weak to contribute to violence. How can seeing a weapon or being uncomfortably hot increase murder rates? The answer lies in the process that leads to violence—the escalation cycle. Deadly assaults do not typically result from one brief encounter or provocation. More typically, the people involved know each other and have had a series of unpleasant exchanges. The final encounter that leads to violence may well begin as a relatively minor one, but one person begins escalating the level of aggression. The other person, in turn, becomes even more angry because he or she perceives the other person's behavior as unjust, and subsequently increases the aggressiveness of the next response. Thus, a shouting match can quickly become a shoving match, which can lead to fists, guns, and death. Seemingly trivial factors can increase the likelihood of violence by increasing the accessibility of aggressive thoughts and hostile affect at each turn of the escalation cycle. In the early stages, an insult that normally would be a minor annoyance can instead be perceived as moderately provocative. This can produce a more aggressive response than normal, which then is interpreted by the other person as unjust, leading to another overreaction. In this way, any of the identified causal factors can increase the likelihood of truly violent behavior.

Distal Causes: Biological Factors. Distal causes of aggression and violence are those that make the human organism ready and capable of aggression. Some are structural, meaning that they are built into the human species. Others are developmental, and result in individual differences in preparedness to aggress.

Genetics. In the broadest sense aggression is a species characteristic. That is, the species has physical and emotional systems capable of intentionally inflicting harm on other humans. The specific genetic basis of aggression is easier to identify in nonhuman species, in which fighting behaviors can be produced by stimulating certain regions of the limbic system.

In the more usual sense, genetic influences refer to individual differences in aggressiveness that are linked to genetic differences. Human twin studies have yielded mixed results in estimates of the genetic contribution to human aggression. Donna Miles and Gregory Carey reported the results of a meta-analysis on 24 "genetically informative" studies (*Journal of Personality and Social Psychology*, 1997, *72*, 207–217). Two important conclusions were: (1) Up to 50% of variation in self- or parent-reported aggression was attributable to genetic effects; (2) When aggressiveness was measured by careful observation of laboratory behaviors the genetic effect disappeared and a strong family environment effect emerged. These contradictory findings highlight the importance of additional studies.

Mechanisms. Several biological mechanisms appear plausible. The most biological of these mirror many of the proximate biological factors discussed earlier: hormones, neurochemical transmitters, and general level of arousal. Some psychological variables with links to aggression also appear to have some genetic basis. Empathy, behavioral inhibition, negative affectivity, extraversion, neuroticism, and psychoticism all have yielded evidence of some heritability, and have obvious links to aggression. General intelligence may also link biological variation to aggressiveness; low intelligence increases the occurrence of frustrating failures and aversive conditions, which might increase the likelihood of aggressive personality development.

Distal Causes: Psychological Factors. Numerous psychological factors contribute to the development of habitual aggressiveness. Learning stands out as the most important factor of all.

Learning. Albert Bandura's *social learning theory* of aggression (1973) has been most influential. More recently, Patterson, Le Baryshe, and Ramsey presented a detailed look at the maladaptive social learning processes found in families of aggressive children. Among the problems are parental use of poor disciplinary measures and inadequate monitoring of their children's activities (*American Psychologist*, 1989, *44*, 329–335).

Cognitive psychology has also been crucial in the present understanding of the aggressive personality, as can be seen in books by Leonard Berkowitz (1993) and Russell Geen (1990), and in Rowell Huesmann's information processing theory of aggressive personality development (in Geen & Donnerstein, Eds., New York, 1998).

Learning processes determine how people perceive, interpret, judge, and respond to events in their lives. People learn perceptual schemata that help them decide what to look for and what is "seen." We learn rules for how the social world works. We learn behavioral scripts to guide our interpretations of events we observe and our behavioral responses to those events. These various knowledge structures develop over time, beginning in early childhood. They are based on the day-to-day observations of and interactions with other people, real (as in the family) and imagined (as in the mass media).

As knowledge structures develop, they become more complex, interconnected, and difficult to change. Child development is like slowly hardening clay. Changes in shape are relatively easy to make at first, but later changes are almost impossible. Longitudinal studies suggest that aggression-related knowledge structures begin to solidify around ages 8 or 9, and become more perseverant with increasing age. Children learn specific aggressive behaviors, the likely outcome of such behaviors, how and when to apply these behaviors. They learn hostile perception, attribution, and expectation biases. They learn callous attitudes and how to disengage normal empathic reactions.

The pervasiveness and thoroughness of any learned knowledge structure is largely determined by the frequency with which it is encountered, imagined, and used. With great frequency even complex perception-judgment-behavior knowledge structures can become *automatized*—so overlearned that they are applied automatically with little effort or awareness. Frequent exposure to aggressive models is particularly effective in creating habitually aggressive people, whether those models are in the home, neighborhood, or mass media.

Social Processes. Several social processes contribute to disproportionate exposure to and learning of aggression-related knowledge structures. Low intellect (social or academic) creates excessive failures and frustration in a variety of contexts. This leads to higher than normal levels of aggression, which in turn leads to further frustrating encounters with parents, teachers, and peers. Social ostracism resulting from excessive aggression forces children to spend more time with other social misfits who also have highly aggressive behavior patterns. This "gang" impedes further intellectual development and rewards antisocial tendencies. These processes can occur regardless of the cause of the initial aggression problem.

Environments. Many social environments foster development of aggressive personality. Such factors include poverty; violent neighborhoods; deviant peers; lack of safe, supervised child recreational areas; exposure to media violence; bad parenting; and lack of social support.

Poverty is associated with more frustrations, bad role models, and lack of good role models. Bad parenting includes several particularly common and damaging factors. These include lack of parental attention, inconsistent discipline, harsh and abusive discipline, and inattention to nonaggressive efforts at problem solving by the child.

Child Abuse. A self-perpetuating problem, child abuse is likely to lead abused children to becoming abusing parents and violent offenders. Abused children learn maladaptive beliefs, attitudes, and values from their abusing parents. Azar and Rohrbeck (*Journal of Consulting and Clinical Psychology*, 1986, 54, 867–868) reported that abusive parents hold unrealistic beliefs about children. For instance, abusing mothers were more likely to agree with the statement "A 5-year-old can be expected to help by feeding, dressing, and changing diapers for an infant" than nonabusive mothers.

Intervention: Prevention and Treatment

The knowledge structure approach explains the difficulty of rehabilitating adults who repeatedly commit violent crimes. A lifetime of developing aggressive behavior scripts and automatized hostile perception, expectation, and attribution biases cannot be unlearned easily. However, this approach says that preventing the development of aggressive personality is a reasonable goal if appropriate steps are taken prior to full maturation.

Preventing and Treating Aggressive Personality. There are three main loci for preventing a child from developing into an aggressive adult. First, one can reduce exposure to events that teach aggressive behaviors or scripts. This would include direct modeling (e.g., by abusive or violent parents) as well as indirect modeling (e.g., exposure to media violence). Second, one can reduce exposure to events that teach that aggression is rewarding. Third, one can reduce exposure to events that teach hostile perception, expectation, and attribution biases.

Treating people who have already developed a strong and stable aggressive personality is much more difficult. They must learn new nonhostile knowledge structures ranging from perceptual schemata through attributional ones to behavioral scripts. The knowledge structure approach explains why it is easiest to intervene successfully in younger children, whose personalities are still malleable, harder to succeed with violent juvenile offenders and young abusive parents, and hardest of all to succeed with habitually violent adult criminals.

Child Abuse: Treatment and Prevention. Early intervention attempts relied primarily on intensive dynamic psychotherapy with the abuser. Deborah Daro (*Confronting Child Abuse Research in Effective Program Design*, New York, 1988) showed that this approach is ineffective. More recently, a chapter by David Wolfe (in Melton & Barry, *Protecting Children from Abuse and Neglect*, New York, 1994) described a number of successful cognitive-behavioral interventions. This learning approach succeeds by teaching abusive caregivers nonaggressive child compliance techniques, personal anger control, and developmentally appropriate beliefs about childhood abilities. Peterson, Gable, Doyle, and Ewugman describe their Mom-Kid Trial project (*Cognitive and*

Behavioral Practice, 1997, *4*, 53–74) as an attempt to make these behavioral techniques easier to teach and longer lasting. By reducing caregiver aggression and substituting nonaggressive techniques, these interventions prevent the development of aggressive personality in children, while simultaneously treating the aggressiveness of the caregiver.

Reducing Exposure to Aggressive Social Models. At a broader level, reducing children's exposure to aggressive social models would reduce the percentage who grow up believing in and using aggressive tactics. Eron and Huesmann's work on the long-term effects of exposure to violent TV is especially important (*American Psychologist*, 1972, *27*, 253–263), as is Huesmann and Miller's chapter on television effects (in *Aggressive Behavior: Current Perspectives*, Huesmann, Ed., New York, 1994). They conclusively demonstrated that early and repeated exposure to violent TV causes children to become more aggressive as adults.

Reducing other types of exposure to violent social models would also help, such as in the Mom-Kid project described earlier or by reducing the frequency and visibility of violence in children's neighborhoods.

Treating Violent Juvenile Offenders. Many approaches have been tried with violent juvenile offenders, including such things as "boot camps," individual therapy, and group therapy; there is little evidence of sustained success for these approaches. One problem with these and many standard approaches is that they do not address the wide range of factors that contribute to the development and maintenance of violent behavior. Tate, Reppucci, and Mulvey (*American Psychologist*, 1995, *50*, 777–781) pointed out these problems and drew attention to one approach with impressive results—*multisystemic therapy* developed by Henggeler and Borduin. Borduin describes this approach (*Journal of the American Academy of Child and Adolescent Psychiatry*, 1999, *38*, 242–249). Briefly, multisystemic therapy is a family-based approach that first identifies the major factors contributing to the delinquent and violent behaviors. Biological, school, work, peers, and neighborhood factors are examined as well as the family itself. The intervention is then tailored to fit the individual constellation of contributing factors. Opportunities to observe and commit further violent and criminal offenses are severely restricted, whereas prosocial behavior opportunities (including studying school subjects) are greatly enhanced. The long-term success rate and cost-benefit ratio have exceeded other attempts at treating this population.

Adults. Treatment of violent adults is usually done in the context of prison programs, and is usually thought of as "rehabilitation." General consensus among social scientists and prison policy makers is that habitual violent offenders cannot be rehabilitated. However, Marnie Rice (*American Psychologist*, 1997, *52*, 414–423) reported the effects of an intensive program for violent offenders (up to 80 hours a week for at least 2 years). Recidivism rates were cut in half for nonpsychopathic offenders. However, the recidivism rate for psychopathic offenders was significantly increased by the treatment program. So there is some hope for a portion of this difficult population, but careful evaluation research is needed to be sure that the right program is used with the right kind of offender.

Making Society Less Aggressive

A number of controversial suggestions for social change emerge from the past 40 years of research on human aggression. Rather than concentrating on treating already violent people, or on intervening with at-risk populations, this approach focuses on society in general. The controversies that arise from these suggestions are political rather than scientific; data and theory clearly support them. (1) Reduce exposure to media violence and other aggressive role models, especially for children and adolescents. (2) Replace the use of corporal punishment with more positive child control techniques. (3) Reduce social rewards for aggressive activities, including those previously thought to be cathartic. (4) Increase social rewards and social support for nonaggressive prosocial activities (e.g., learning in school) while making success at such activities possible (e.g., by reducing class sizes). (5) Increase the quality of pre- and postnatal care, to decrease the proportion of the population suffering from developmental difficulties that interfere with normal learning and socialization processes. (6) Fully fund the Head Start program, which attacks several of the nutrition and early learning difficulties. [*See* Head Start.] (7) Increase the quality of parenting, by providing instruction, social support, and economic support.

[*See also* Child Abuse and Neglect; Domestic Violence; Family Violence; Impulsivity; Media Effects; Rape; Terrorism; *and* Violence Risk Assessment.]

Bibliography

Bandura, A. (1973). *Aggression: A social learning analysis.* Englewood Cliffs, NJ: Prentice Hall.

Baron, R. A., & Richardson, D. R. (1994). *Human aggression* (2nd ed.). New York: Plenum.

Berkowitz, L. (1993). *Aggression: Its causes, consequences, and control.* New York: McGraw-Hill.

Berkowitz, L., & LePage, A. (1967). Weapons as aggression-eliciting stimuli. *Journal of Personality and Social Psychology, 7*, 202–207.

Bettencourt, B. A., & Miller, N. (1996). Gender differences in aggression as a function of provocation: A meta-analysis. *Journal of Personality and Social Psychology, 119*, 422–447.

Geen, R. G. (1990). *Human aggression.* Pacific Grove, CA: Brooks/Cole.

Geen, R., & Donnerstein, E. (Eds.). (1998). *Human aggression: Theories, research and implications for policy.* New York: Academic Press.

Goldstein, A. P. (1994). *The ecology of aggression.* New York: Plenum Press.

Huesmann, L. R. (Ed.). (1994). *Aggressive behavior: Current perspectives.* New York: Plenum Press.

Malamuth, N. M., Linz, D., Heavey, C. L., Barnes, G., & Acker, M. (1995). Using the confluence model of sexual aggression to predict men's conflict with women: A 10-year follow-up study. *Journal of Personality and Social Psychology, 69,* 353–369.

Paik, H., & Comstock, G. (1994). The effects of television violence on antisocial behavior: A meta-analysis. *Communication Research, 21,* 516–546.

Rubin, J. Z., Pruitt, D. G., & Kim, S. H. (1994). *Social conflict: Escalation, stalemate, and settlement* (2nd ed.). New York: McGraw-Hill.

Strasburger, V. C. (1995). *Adolescents and the media: Medical and psychological impact.* Thousand Oaks, CA: Sage.

Straus, M. A., & Gelles, R. J. (1990). *Physical violence in American families: Risk factors and adaptations to violence in 8,145 families.* New Brunswick, NJ: Transaction.

Tedeschi, J. T. (1983). Social influence theory and aggression. In R. Geen & E. I. Donnerstein (Eds.), *Aggression: Theoretical and empirical reviews* (Vol. 1, pp. 135–162). New York: Academic Press.

Craig A. Anderson

VIOLENCE RISK ASSESSMENT. Over the past 40 years, the concept of dangerousness—the attribution that one individual is likely to physically harm another—has assumed center stage in mental health law. Since the 1960s, virtually every American state has transformed its standard for involuntary inpatient mental hospitalization from "need for treatment" to "dangerous to others" (or dangerous to self). Since the 1970s, most states have adopted the California Supreme Court's holding in *Tarasoff v. Regents* [551 P. 2d 334 (1976)] that mental health professionals could be found liable in tort for the foreseeable violent acts of their patients. Since the 1980s, most states have enacted statutes allowing the involuntary outpatient commitment of persons diagnosed as disordered and predicted to be violent. In the 1990s, the Americans with Disabilities Act was passed to protect the employment rights of persons with mental as well as physical disabilities, unless the persons with mental disabilities were predicted to be a "direct threat" of physical harm to others. In addition, in the 1990s, the United States Supreme Court, in *Kansas v. Hendricks* [117 S.Ct. 2072 (1997)], held that prisoners, on the completion of their sentences, could be transferred to civil mental hospitals if they could be diagnosed with a personality disorder (rather than with a major mental disorder) and were perceived to be "likely to engage in predatory acts of sexual violence" if released to the community.

Research has only recently managed to keep pace with these developments in law. A review of studies through the 1970s on the accuracy of clinical judgments of the likelihood of violent behavior toward others concluded somberly that "psychiatrists and psychologists are accurate in no more than one out of three predictions of violent behavior" (Monahan, 1981, p. 47). Very little work on violence prediction was published in the 1980s, but in the 1990s, researchers showed greatly renewed interest in this topic. For example, in the most sophisticated study of the clinical prediction of violence, Lidz, Mulvey, and Gardner (1993) took as their subjects male and female patients being examined in the acute psychiatric emergency room of a large civil hospital. Patients who elicited professional concern regarding future violence were found to be significantly more likely to be violent after discharge (53%) than were patients who had not elicited such concern (36%).

The field, now referred to as *violence risk assessment,* has seen a dramatic shift away from studies attempting to validate the accuracy of unstructured clinical predictions of violence and toward studies attempting to isolate specific risk factors that are actuarially (meaning statistically) associated with violence. For example, Steadman et al. (1998) found diagnosis and the presence of a co-occurring substance abuse disorder to be important risk factors for violence. The 1-year prevalence rates of violence to others by persons discharged from acute mental health facilities were: 17.9% for patients with an Axis I mental disorder (i.e., schizophrenia, major depression, or bipolar disorder) without a substance abuse diagnosis; 31.1% for patients with an Axis I mental disorder and a substance abuse diagnosis; and 43.0% for patients with some other form of mental disorder (primarily Axis II diagnoses of personality or adjustment disorder) and a substance abuse diagnosis.

Three actuarial tools combining a number of different risk factors are now being studied. A well-established instrument, which has been used to assess violence in many studies, is the Hare Psychopathy Checklist–Revised (Hare PCL–R). Hare (1998) argued that "psychopathy is the single most important clinical construct in the criminal justice system, with particularly strong implications for the assessment of risk for recidivism and violence" (p. 99). Another instrument that a comprehensive program of research is continuing to validate is the Violence Risk Appraisal Guide (Webster, Harris, Rice, Cormier, & Quinsey, 1994), an actuarial device that incorporates the Hare PCL–R as one of its predictor variables. Finally, the newest actuarial instrument to assess risk of violence, the HCR–20 (Webster, Douglas, Eaves, & Hart, 1995), consists of 20 ratings addressing *h*istorical, *c*linical, or *r*isk management variables, and is the subject of much ongoing research.

It is important to note that a wide range of procedures can be subsumed under the rubric of "actuarial" prediction, and that the actuarial versus clinical debate of previous decades may have been overplayed. Now, actuarial approaches are more likely to be promoted as adjuncts to clinical judgment than as replacements for it. Actuarial predictions are seen by many as anchoring or structuring clinical judgment, with clinicians free to override actuarially derived risk estimates to the limited extent that individualized considerations (not studied in the actuarial research) can plausibly be theorized to affect the likelihood of violence. As Webster et al. (1994) among the strongest advocates of actuarial prediction, noted:

> It should be clear from work that we have published over the years . . . that we have a profound distrust of *unbridled* clinical opinion. Saying this is not to mean that we see no place for trained clinicians in the assessment process. Quite to the contrary. It is only that such participation must be disciplined and checked and it is crucial that the process start with an actuarial estimate of risk. (p. 64)

The use of empirically derived actuarial instruments to support clinical judgment, along with improved strategies for communicating risk estimates to decision makers, is the most exciting development in this pivotal area of mental health law at the dawn of the twenty-first century, and the one most likely to improve the validity of violence risk assessment.

[*See also* Assessment.]

Bibliography

Bonta, J., Law, M., & Hanson, K. (1998). The prediction of criminal and violent recidivism among mentally disordered offenders: A meta-analysis. *Psychological Bulletin, 123*, 123–142.

Hare, R. (1998). The Hare PCL–R: Some issues concerning its use and misuse. *Legal and Criminal Psychology, 3*, 99–119.

Lidz, C., Mulvey, E., & Gardner, W. (1993). The accuracy of predictions of violence to others. *Journal of the American Medical Association, 269*, 1007–1011.

Link, B., & Stueve, A. (1994). Psychotic symptoms and the violent/illegal behavior of mental patients compared to community controls. In J. Monahan & H. Steadman (Eds.), *Violence and mental disorder: Developments in risk assessment* (pp. 137–159). Chicago: University of Chicago Press.

McNiel, D., & Binder, R. (1994). Screening for risk of inpatient violence: Validation of an actuarial tool. *Law and Human Behavior, 18*, 579–586.

Monahan, J. (1981). *The clinical prediction of violent behavior*. Washington, DC: U.S. Government Printing Office.

Monahan, J. (1997). Clinical and actuarial predictions of violence. In D. Faigman, D. Kaye, M. Saks, & J. Sanders (Eds.), *Modern scientific evidence: The law and science of expert testimony* (pp. 300–318). St. Paul, MN: West.

Monahan, J., & Steadman, H. (1996). Violent storms and violent people: How meteorology can inform risk communication in mental health law. *American Psychologist, 51*, 931–938.

Quinsey, V., Harris, G., Rice, M., & Cormier, C. (1998). *Violent offenders: Appraising and managing risk*. Washington, DC: American Psychological Association.

Steadman, H., Mulvey, E., Monahan, J., Robbins, P., Appelbaum, P., Grisso, T., Roth, L., & Silver, E. (1998). Violence by people discharged from acute psychiatric inpatient facilities and by others in the same neighborhoods. *Archives of General Psychiatry, 55*, 1–9.

Swanson, J., Estroff, S., Swartz, M., Borum, R., Lachicotte, W., Zimmer, C., & Wagner, R. (1997). Violence and severe mental disorder in clinical and community populations: The effects of psychotic symptoms, comorbidity, and lack of treatment. *Psychiatry, 60*, 1–22.

Webster, C., Douglas, K., Eaves, D., & Hart, S. (1995). *HCR–20: Assessing risk for violence* (Version 2). Vancouver: Simon Fraser University Press.

Webster, C., Harris, G., Rice, M., Cormier, C., & Quinsey, V. (1994). *The violence prediction scheme: Assessing dangerousness in high-risk men*. Toronto: University of Toronto Press.

John Monahan

VIRTUAL COMMUNITIES. When computer networks connect people and organizations, they are social networks. Unlike traditional communities based on face-to-face interaction, electronic (or "virtual") communities are based on computer-mediated communication. They connect friends and relatives, workmates and collaborators. Members of such communities can exchange interpersonal resources from the comfort and safety of their homes, offices, or while traveling. Like all communities, electronic communities are interpersonal social networks that provide members with companionship, information, emotional aid, material aid, and a sense of belonging. Unlike traditional communities based primarily on living or working in the same areas or shared social characteristics (such as kinship, ethnicity, or socioeconomic status), electronic communities are based primarily on shared interests.

Although electronic communities have been online since the early 1970s, they proliferated in the 1990s with the development of the Internet. Computer-mediated communication is a major form of interaction for most academics and white-collar corporate workers in the developed world, and it is spreading rapidly through the rest of the population as well as among professional and managerial segments of the less-developed world. Communication in electronic communities takes place heavily through electronic mail (e-mail) on the Internet or specialized computer networks. Although there may be some lag between the time when people receive messages and they answer, the asynchronous nature of electronic-mail aids communication between people in different time zones, allows messages to be received and responded to when most convenient, and enables people to attach additional documents to their messages. Each message can easily go to one or many recipients, and replies can go to the individual sender or all the other recipients. Messages that have been received can also be forwarded. Thus, e-mail supports both personal communities and group communities.

Several media principally support group communication in electronic communities: local "bulletin board systems" (BBSs), "newsgroups" open to all on the Internet, moderated and unmoderated discussion groups on the Internet (often called "listservs"), and proprietary services such as America Online. In all of these media, participants electronically post a message that can be read and responded to by other members whenever they log on. Because such messages contain the senders' e-mail addresses, participants can also continue their conversations through private e-mail.

By contrast to asynchronous means of computer-mediated communication, synchronous forms of electronic community allow two or many people to send messages to each other and read or respond to them while all participants are simultaneously online. Popular synchronous electronic communities include conversational "chat" groups with closed or open memberships (such as Internet Relay Chat, or IRC), Web chat groups, game-playing sites, and role-playing sites (such as multiuser dungeons, or MUDs). Although such real-time communication provides spontaneity and instant feedback, it requires all to participate at the same time. It does not facilitate sober second thoughts or forwarding messages to others.

Relationships in Electronic Communities

Some scholars have feared that the limited "media richness" and "social presence" of text-based computer-mediated communication would be suitable only for impersonal, task-oriented messages and be unable to convey the emotions and nuances necessary for community. Moreover, there are few social context cues online that convey information about the participants' roles, statuses, and institutional affiliations. Yet a wide range of relationships do flourish in text-based electronic communities. Indeed, limited social presence and social context cues can encourage people to communicate more freely and creatively than they do in person, at times "flaming" others by using extreme, aggressive language.

Social-information-processing theory suggests that people using any medium experience similar needs for reducing uncertainty and increasing affinity. To meet these needs online, communicators solicit and present socially revealing behavior, and they change into text what would ordinarily be nonverbal messages in face-to-face interactions. The anticipation of future interaction prompts people to seek more information about one another, to be more friendly and cooperative in negotiations, to value self-disclosure, and to use explicit text and typological "emoticons" to convey emotional information. Moreover, the current development of richer means of communication—such as videophones, video conferencing among groups, and animated avatars—may provide more channels for interaction as bandwidth becomes less constrained and computers more powerful.

If the Internet and other forms of computer-mediated communication were solely a means of information exchange, then electronic communities would contain only narrow, specialized relationships. Yet information is just one of many social resources exchanged on the Net. As social beings, those who use the Net also seek companionship, social support, and a sense of belonging. Members of electronic communities can obtain a variety of social support because computer-mediated communication is a relatively efficient way of maintaining ties with people of different social characteristics who participate in diverse social circles. People often obtain support in electronic communities from persons whom they have never met and know little about. Because the lack of social and physical cues online makes it more difficult to discover participants' social and physical characteristics, attention is focused more on the request for aid itself than the nature of the person requesting it. Electronic-community members observe and often reward those who provide support in the community, thereby fostering a norm of generalized reciprocity and mutual aid in it.

The ties people develop online are much like their real-life ties: intermittent, specialized, and varying in strength. Strong online ties engage in frequent, companionable, and supportive contact. They are voluntary, except in work situations. The few keystrokes needed to start replying facilitates reciprocal support. Moreover, the placelessness of contact through computer-mediated communication aids long-term contact without the loss of tie strength that often happens when community members move elsewhere.

Computer-mediated communication can support strong ties even when participants have never met face to face. Participants may idealize the impressions they have of each other, making over attributions based on the minimal social cues conveyed online. People can take advantage of computer-mediated communication's limited social presence to control their presentation of self and use the ability to edit messages to strengthen the intensity of interactions. The reciprocal interactions of selectively self-presented messages and idealized perceptions can provide behavioral confirmation, with people communicating with each other based on their mutual perceptions and their behavior converging with those expectations.

Implications of Electronic Communities

Although some electronic communities are so immersive that they resemble densely knit, tightly bounded villages, people rarely spend most of their nonworking time online. "Electronic life" and "real life" are not separate realities. To speak of computer-mediated ties as being solely online is to ignore those ties that also operate offline, but ties formed in one can easily be nurtured and extended in the other. Although time spent online may take away from the time spent in face-to-face interactions, this does not suggest that electronic communities are any less significant for participants. Indeed, computer-mediated communication may sustain community ties where time and circumstances make it difficult for people to meet face to face.

Even before the development of electronic communities, people usually cycled between multiple communities. Just as modern neighborhood ties do not fulfill all of a person's community needs, membership in a single electronic community does not meet all of a person's needs for information, support, and companionship. Electronic communities are usually communities of interest that expand the number and kind of persons known and open up new opportunities. They are only a part of a person's multiple communities of interest, kinship, friendship, work, and locality. People bring to their electronic communities such baggage as their gender, stage in the life cycle, cultural milieu, socioeconomic status, and off-line connections with others. Hence, electronic interactions are not isolated social phenomena but intersect with other aspects of people's lives.

The architecture of the Internet can encourage significant alterations in the size, composition, and structure of communities because it supports the maintenance of many ties unconstrained by distance or time zones. Although the Internet fosters membership in multiple communities, it weakens the solidarity that comes from membership in densely knit, bounded groups. Its asynchronousness, ease of group response, and message forwarding make it easy to maintain community ties with many people, put friends of friends in contact with each other, and fold participants into broader communities. Yet the ease of forming new groups online also supports splitting into specialized communities.

The worldwide proliferation of the Internet may produce a "glocalizing" countertrend to the contemporary privatization of community, as people shift their lives from public spaces to private homes. Yet much of people's on-line interaction is in electronic groups. Such public interaction can build social capital and integrate social systems by supporting ties that cut across groups, localities, organizations, and states.

Acknowledgments. This research was supported by grants from the Social Science and Humanities Research Council of Canada to the University of Toronto.

Bibliography

Agre, P., & Schuler, D. (Eds.). (1997). *Reinventing technology, rediscovering community.* Greenwich, CT: Ablex. A recent compilation of key articles.

Garton, L., Haythornthwaite, C., & Wellman, B. (1997). Studying on-line social networks. *Journal of Computer-Mediated Communication, 3*(1) [On-line]. http://www.usc.edu/dept/annenberg/vol3/issue1/garton.html. A guide to studying social relationships online. Available only from the Web site.

Hiltz, S. R., & Turoff, M. (1993). *The network nation* (2nd ed.). Cambridge, MA: MIT Press. The most important early book in the field, trendsetting and now updated.

Kiesler, S. (Ed.). (1997). *Culture of the Internet.* Mahweh, NJ: Erlbaum. A collection of key recent articles; most have been written for this book.

Kling, R. (Ed.). (1996). *Computerization and controversy* (2nd ed.). San Diego: Academic Press. A mammoth collection of important articles. The book to start with.

Kollock, P., & Smith, M. (Eds.). (1999). *Communities in cyberspace.* London: Routledge. A collection of key original articles directly relevant to electronic communities.

Rheingold, H. (1993). *The virtual community.* Reading, MA: Addison-Wesley. Sound and popularly written. Focuses on "the Well," a pioneering electronic community.

Sproull, L., & Kiesler, S. (1991). *Connections.* Cambridge, MA: MIT Press. An important synthesis of research into how people work and play together online.

Turkle, S. (1995). *Life on the screen.* New York: Simon & Schuster. Finding identity online. A widely known book.

Walther, J., Anderson, J., & Park, D. (1994). Interpersonal effects in computer-mediated interaction: A meta-analysis of social and antisocial communication. *Communication Research, 21,* 460–487. A statistically informed review of knowledge.

Wellman, B., Salaff, J., Dimitrova, D., Garton, L., Gulia, M., & Haythornthwaite, C. (1996). Computer networks as social networks. *Annual Review of Sociology, 22,* 213–238. A comprehensive guide to research about on-line relationships.

Barry Wellman, Keith Hampton, and Emmanuel Koku

VIRTUAL REALITY (VR) is an outgrowth of two kinds of human machine systems: (1) simulation, exemplified by flight trainers and video games; and (2) teleoperation, exemplified by remotely controlled lunar exploration and toxic waste disposal. Both simulation and teleoperation involve a human user and a human-machine interface that contains displays and controls. In simulation, the interface connects the human to a computer and the objective is to influence the state of the user (e.g., train the user). In teleoperation, the interface connects the human to a telerobot and the objective is to sense and manipulate the real world. In both cases, electromechanical mediation is used to create a new world with which the human interacts. In simulation, it is a computer-generated world; in teleoperation, it is the real world, but the human interacts with it through an effectively transformed sensorimotor system.

Many VR systems include both simulation and teleoperation. For example, simulation is often used in predictive modeling that is incorporated into teleoperator systems. Similarly, signals generated by computer and signals derived from the real world are integrated for presentation to the human in "augmented-reality" systems.

A VR system in which the world is computer generated (a "virtual-environment" system) differs from a classical simulation system by the extent to which

- it can be reconfigured by changing software rather than hardware;
- it can be used to create unnatural as well as natural environments;
- it is interactive and adaptive;
- it engages a wide variety of human sensorimotor systems (multimodal);
- it is immersive and causes the human user to experience a sense of presence in the artificial environment;
- it virtualizes the near field (the field within arm's reach of the human user) as well as the far field;
- it makes use of wearable interface devices (head mounted displays, gloves, body suits, etc.).

VR applications include (1) entertainment, (2) national defense, (3) design, manufacturing and marketing, (4) medicine and health care, (5) hazardous operations, (6) training, (7) education, (8) information visualization, and (9) telecommunication and teletravel. The main economic driving forces behind VR are entertainment and national defense.

The relation of VR to psychology is complex and reciprocal. The development of cost-effective VR systems requires extensive input from the field of psychology; and the availability of such systems facilitates research and applications in psychology.

Realism, Fidelity, and Cost-Effectiveness Trade-offs

The assumption is often made that VR should immerse the user in a synthetic environment that is indistinguishable from reality. This assumption, combined with technological obstacles and the desire to maximize cost-effectiveness, has led to studies of how performance and experience in virtual environments degrade as representational fidelity is reduced.

Knowledge of human performance limitations in sensing and control are used to determine upper limits on VR-system requirements. Additional consideration is then given to the degrading effects of cost-saving simplifications of the system. Often, reductions in fidelity are introduced to reduce costs, but efforts are made to preserve "cognitive fidelity."

Unfortunately, the results of studies that have examined such trade-offs seem to be task dependent, and, apart from generalizations derived from limits on human sensitivity, useful generalizations are difficult to demonstrate.

In the visual channel, attention has focused on head-mounted displays (HMDs) that present separate images to each eye determined by information on head orientation provided by a head tracking device. Apart from mass, inertia, and fit of HMDs, important parameters include resolution, contrast, and color; field of view and binocular overlap; time delay between head movement and image change; and frame rate. Of particular interest is the perception of distance, depth, and object size. Also considered is how subjective impressions and task performance are modified when the HMD is replaced by an off-head display and/or head tracking is eliminated.

In the auditory domain, work aimed at realism has focused on spatial perception when earphones are used. Perfect realism requires reproducing at the eardrums the same signals that would occur in the corresponding real environment. This requires not only head tracking, but also simulation of all acoustic effects that would occur as each sound wave propagates from sound source to eardrums, including those due to interaction of the sound wave with the physical environment and with the listener's body, head, and pinnae. Again, the main issues of interest, given the aim of realism, concern how the simulation can be simplified without too much loss of realism.

In the haptics domain (manual exploration and manipulation), realistic simulation is difficult; motor as well as sensory functions are involved; the sensing involves both tactile and kinesthetic information; and interface technology is still quite limited. Realistic simulation requires an interface that includes a means for sensing the position of the user's fingers, software for computing the appropriate forces to be applied based on position data and the characteristics of the virtual objects, and mechanical devices to generate and apply these forces.

Conventional devices, such as keyboards, mice, and trackballs, convey restricted motor actions to the computer, but do not provide information-carrying force feedback. Instrumented gloves, although allowing rich control via sensing of hand posture, again do not provide information-carrying force feedback. Vibratory arrays provide useful tactile information, but are far removed from object manipulation. Instrumented gloves that include vibrators or pneumatic bladders convey some force information, but are not able to provide realistic haptic images.

The most realistic haptic simulations mimic sensing and manipulating objects via a rigid tool. Independent of the complexity of the object and of the interactions of the working end of the tool with this object, only the net (resultant) forces and torques that would be sensed through the handle of the tool need to be computed and displayed. With appropriate hardware and "computer-haptic" software, one can simulate a wide variety of object shapes, textures, compliances, and dynamics as felt through a wide variety of tools (e.g., a scalpel).

Additional work related to providing the user with sensorimotor connections to the virtual world has focused on olfactory and thermal sensations, control modes derived from neurophysiological activity, and methods for moving through virtual environments.

Unless the user is driving a virtual vehicle through the virtual environment, an interface must be provided that facilitates simulation of walking, running, and so forth. Although conventional linear treadmills have been used for this purpose, and other ingenious mechanical devices have been developed, most VR systems make use of simpler and less realistic methods for achieving movement, such as gloved-hand gestures, or hand-controlled joysticks. The differential effects of different movement methods on perception and performance in virtual environments is one of the many topics now being investigated.

The VR application most concerned with realism is training. Furthermore, it is in this domain that one finds the most serious psychological studies. In addition to training transfer, issues related to cognitive task analysis, mental models, and comparative evaluations are all taken seriously here. It should also be noted that although many functions have been considered for VR training, including piloting, maintenance of equipment, and firefighting, the most highly studied functions relate to acquisition of spatial knowledge.

Spatial knowledge acquisition and multimodal interactions provide prime examples of the bidirectional relationship between VR and psychology: both topics are being studied to aid in the development of effective VR systems, and knowledge about both is being advanced through the use of VR systems as research tools.

Beyond Realism: Unnatural, Supernormal Systems

Realism has many advantages, including elimination of the need for users to adapt to new situations, construct new mental models, and learn new behaviors. However, in many cases the achievement of realism is not only impossible, it is not even desirable; unrealistic or unnatural systems, once adapted to, can lead to vastly improved performance.

This theme is evident in the use of nonanthropomorphic telerobots. Although properly matching human users to nonanthropomorphic telerobots is a challenging task, and considerable training may be required for users to become proficient at "driving" such systems, the results can far surpass those that would be achieved using anthropomorphic systems. At the most general level, this approach represents nothing more than a modern, high-tech example of human tool use.

In the area of computer-generated virtual environments, there are many efforts to improve performance by capitalizing on special advantages afforded by VR in ways that go well beyond realistic simulation. And in each case, there is a need to examine adaptation phenomenon, learning rates, and asymptotic performance.

One set of such efforts is concerned with creating supernormal sensory abilities in virtual environments. For example, studies have measured the extent to which auditory localization and visual depth perception can be improved by simulating an enlarged head. Similarly, although it may have been initially motivated by equipment constraints, unnatural methods used for moving through virtual environments (e.g., pointing a gloved finger) can, under certain conditions, provide superior performance.

A second set of such efforts relates to VR-assisted training. Performance in the real world subsequent to training may be superior if the training focuses in an unrealistic manner on the skills required for the task. This is especially true in VR-assisted training because of the extraordinarily large palette of training aids that can be realized in VR.

A third set of examples concerns the reception, manipulation, and understanding of large amounts of information. Clearly, in order to overcome the "information overload" problem, it is necessary to invent new ways of presenting and manipulating data. (The ability to present tables of numbers in the form of graphs made possible by the invention of analytical geometry was the last truly great advance in this area.) It is believed that VR has an important role to play here as a consequence of the multimodal sensorimotor interaction and immersion in 3D space available in VR.

Less concerned with achieving supernormal performance than with maintaining reasonable performance in unfamiliar settings is the effort to aid navigation in unrealistic, often abstract, virtual environments, such as information spaces. Aids useful for navigating through virtual environments that approximate realistic spaces may be different from those useful for navigating through unrealistic virtual spaces.

Further examples in the supernormal area concern augmented reality and the integration of stimuli arising from the real world (either directly or via a telerobot) with synthetic stimuli that are either computer generated or derived from stored representations of real-world scenes. To date, most work on augmented reality has focused on the visual channel and on applications in design/manufacturing and medicine. In applications such as surgery, the issue of properly aligning images is exceedingly important. Moreover, even when registration problems are minimal, it is likely that integrative problems will arise because of differences in perceptual responses to the two types of information (e.g., in the perception of size and distance).

Presence

The user's sense of being "present" in synthetic environments is regarded as a distinguishing characteristic of VR. In addition to possible connections between sense of presence and task performance, interest in presence results in part from the role it plays in entertainment and in part from its philosophical nature.

Measurement of presence can be achieved by questionnaires and subjective judgments of various types, as well as by direct behavioral responses such as reflex actions or by responses to contradictory information from real and virtual surroundings.

Generation of presence is facilitated by excluding real-world sensory stimuli; providing an immersive high-fidelity system with stimulus fields that surround the user and engage a wide variety of sensorimotor systems; and enabling interactions between the user and the virtual environment that are varied and predictable. Emotional and higher-level cognitive factors, such as those that play a strong role in literature or theater, must also be considered.

The relation between presence and task performance remains unclear. Although performance is often assumed to improve as presence increases, this is not necessarily correct. Not only do some studies show no correlation, but the correlation can be negative (e.g., when noxious or interfering stimuli present in the real world are excluded from the virtual world).

An often ignored but important characteristic of presence is its tendency to increase as familiarity with the environment increases. Also not yet studied is the relation between the sense of presence in synthetic environments and the sense of absence in real environments.

Virtual People

The greatest challenge to psychology raised by VR concerns the design of autonomous synthetic people. Independent of whether the synthetic people are robotic or computer-generated, the extent to which one can successfully design and construct a synthetic person constitutes a measure not only of our technological prowess, but also of our knowledge of human behavior. Currently, all of the behaving creatures found in synthetic environments are either extremely crude and oversimplified or are high-tech puppets (sometimes referred to as guided agents, or avatars) whose behavior is guided directly by real human beings. Most work on autonomous virtual people has focused on general visual appearance, on physically and biologically based models of body postures and movements, and facial expressions. Attempts are now being made, however, to create virtual people with richer and more realistic perceptual abilities, stimulus-response patterns, and behavioral repertoires.

Virtual Reality Sickness

Under certain conditions, people may become sick when using VR. Symptoms include eyestrain, headache, nausea, sweating, pallor, disorientation, postural instability, dizziness, drowsiness (sopite syndrome), fatigue, and apathy. Many symptoms are similar to those discussed for years in connection with simulator or motion sickness. Symptom incidence varies as a function of the equipment used, the virtual environment created, the task performed in this environment, and the individual. Although many factors have been suggested as contributing to VR sickness, no adequate theory is available to predict the occurrence of sickness during the VR experience or the occurrence of aftereffects of various types (e.g., increased sensitivity or visual flashbacks). One causative factor that has been proposed is the conflict between visual and vestibular information that arises when the visual input produces the illusion of self-motion (vection) while the body is at rest. However, this conflict is neither necessary nor sufficient to cause sickness.

Likelihood of sickness tends to increase when HMDs are used and when motion occurs (either the visually induced illusion of self-motion or actual head motion). Also, there is evidence that sickness increases as user control is reduced, analogous to the increased likelihood of car sickness when one is a passenger rather than a driver. When an HMD is used, the probability of sickness associated with head movements tends to decrease as the field of view is decreased, as the lag between head movement and scene change in the visual display is reduced, and as the mass of the HMD is decreased.

Applications of Virtual Reality to Psychology

There are many ways in which VR can be used to advance the field of psychology. One of the most obvious consists of using VR technology to conduct basic research in experimental psychology. Because an advanced VR system enables an investigator to present a wide variety of carefully controlled stimuli, elicit and measure a wide variety of responses, and manipulate software to easily change experimental paradigms, it constitutes an ideal laboratory facility for conducting experiments on human participants. Although VR systems are still primitive, they are already being used in this fashion. In fact, in much of the work currently being done by experimental psychologists in which VR systems are used, it is often difficult to determine the extent to which the goal is to make use of psychological knowledge and experimental techniques to improve VR, or to use VR to learn more about human perception, cognition, and performance.

Areas in which such "bidirectional motivation" is clearly evident include acquisition of spatial knowledge; perception of distance, depth and size; and the integrated perception of events involving stimulation in various modalities. In the third area, much work is focused on the interaction of visual and/or auditory stimulation with haptic actions made possible by development of haptic interfaces for VR.

VR is also beginning to play an important role in the area of neuropsychology and brain imaging. A good VR system is ideal for controlling and manipulating the stimulus field that produces the brain activity being imaged. In general, it is clear that the use of VR systems for basic research in psychology will continue to increase as more psychologists have access to and become familiar with VR and as VR systems are further developed.

In addition to applications in basic research, applications are being developed for assessment of cognitive function and clinical treatment of mental-health problems. Initial work in psychotherapy has focused on VR-assisted behavioral therapy for treatment of phobias. Now, however, other types of applications are being considered. In general, the domain of effectiveness will increase as (1) the development of virtual people advances so that virtual environments are better able to provide appropriate social situations, and (2) VR systems are designed specifically for therapeutic applications and include proper and well-integrated physiological monitoring systems, as well as appropriately designed and networked substations for patients and therapists.

Concluding Remarks

Almost all branches of psychology are challenged by the task of designing VR systems and evaluating the performance of these systems. Such areas as motivation, personality, and individual differences, although not discussed above, must be added to those considered in order to predict experience and behavior in VR. Furthermore, because many of the goals toward which the use of VR is directed, like training or information visualization, constitute challenges to psychology in their own right, there is often a complex intertwining between challenges generally associated with these goals and challenges that are specific to VR. Also, because of the rapid development VR is experiencing in technology and in various application domains, most results related to VR-specific challenges tend to be tied to specific facilities and specific tasks; generalizations that are both correct and meaningful are hard to make.

Finally, it seems clear that the debt to psychology being accrued in the effort to develop effective VR systems will be well repaid by applications of effective VR systems to both basic research problems and to clinical or therapeutic problems in the field of psychology.

[*See also* Human-Computer Interface Design.]

Acknowledgments. This work was supported by the Office of Naval Research, Grant N00014-97-1-0635.

Bibliography

Barfield, W., & Furness, T. H. (Eds). (1995). *Virtual environments and advanced interface design.* New York: Oxford University Press.

Durlach, N. I., & Mavor, A. S. (Eds.). (1995). *Virtual reality: Scientific and technological challenges.* Washington, DC: National Academy Press.

Kalawsky, R. S. (1993). *The science of virtual reality and virtual environments* Reading MA: Addison-Wesley.

Pew, R. W., & Mavor, A. S. (Eds.). (1998). *Modeling human and organizational behavior: Applications to military simulations.* Washington, DC: National Academy Press.

Seidel, R. J., & Chatelier, P. R. (Eds.). (1997). *Virtual reality, training's future? Perspectives on virtual reality and related emerging technologies.* New York: Plenum Press.

Stanney, K. M. (Ed.). (1999). *Handbook of virtual environments.* Mahwah, NJ: Erlbaum.

Journals of Interest

CyberPsychology & Behavior (Published by Mary Ann Liebert, Inc.).

International Journal of Virtual Reality (Published by IPI Press).

PRESENCE: Teleoperators and Virtual Environments (Published by MIT Press).

Virtual Reality: Research, Development, and Applications (Published by Springer-Verlag.)

Nathaniel Durlach

VISION AND SIGHT. [*This entry provides anatomical and physiological descriptions of the human eye, a survey of the behavioral and functional aspects of sight, and the effects of normal and pathological aging on vision. It comprises three articles:*

Structure and Function

Behavioral and Functional Aspects
Age-Related Changes, Optical Factors, and Neural Processes

For independent discussions dealing with color vision and spatial vision, see Color Vision *and* Spatial Vision. *For a broad overview of the sensory systems (auditory, tactile, visual, and the chemical senses), see* Sensory Systems.]

Structure and Function

The human eye, one of nature's crowning achievements, is a spherically shaped organ just a little smaller than a Ping-Pong ball. Befitting the predatory nature of our primate ancestors, our two eyes are located in the front of the head, providing a large degree of binocular overlap and, hence, stereoscopic vision.

Eyes vary greatly in structure and function among species. Nocturnal animals possess eyes specialized for dim-light conditions that leave humans in the dark, while some diurnal animals have eyes that afford color vision and acuity superior to anything we enjoy. Human vision is said to be *arhythmic*, meaning that our eyes can operate effectively, if not exceptionally, over a broad range of light levels, from dim starlight to bright sunlight. Underwriting this broad range of visual sensitivity is the duplex retina, in essence two visual systems packaged into one. The scotopic system, based on rod photoreceptors, operates under dim-light conditions, while the photopic system, based on cone photoreceptors, is specialized for high acuity, daylight vision.

Seeing starts with light reflected from objects in the environment. Those patterns of reflected light convey important information about the surface properties, and hence the identity, of those objects. The human eye is exquisitely designed to register the spatial distribution of light, including edges, contours, and colors that define objects. In overview, the eye consists of optical components, neural components, and neuromuscular components. In the properly functioning eye, these components work together to inaugurate what can rightly be characterized as a near-miracle: human vision.

Optics

The eye's optical components maintain a sharp, focused image of the world on the back of the eye. The cornea (the clear, front surface of the eye) bends light rays and redirects them through the pupil, the small, dark hole centered within the colored iris. Pupil size varies inversely with prevailing light level, ranging from about 1 to 8 millimeters in diameter. Like the diaphragm of a camera, the variable-sized pupil regulates the overall amount of light entering the eye.

Light passing through the pupil is further focused by the clear, oval-shaped lens onto the back of the eye, where the light-sensitive receptors are located. The lens' degree of focus depends on its shape, which can be varied under the control of the ciliary muscles that suspend the lens within the eye. Because the lens can vary its focal power—the process called *accommodation*—we are able to see objects clearly at different distances. With age the lens loses much of its elasticity, and consequently, older adults have trouble focusing on nearby objects such as printed words on a page. Called *presbyopia*, this condition can be corrected by spectacle lenses that magnify image size.

The interior of the eye is filled with vitreous, a clear, gelatinous fluid that maintains the eye's globular shape. Excessive buildup of vitreous within the eye raises intraocular pressure which can damage the eye's neural tissues and cause the potentially blinding condition known as glaucoma.

Retina

Lining the inside of the back of the eye is the retina, a sheet of neural tissue about the thickness of a postage stamp. The retina comprises a complex neural circuit consisting of millions of specialized cells. In overview, the retina converts light energy into neural signals and recodes those neural signals to convey useful information about the spatial distribution and the wavelengths of light forming the retinal image. The retina is an outgrowth of the brain and, as such, it is the only place where one person can visualize brain tissue within another living person's body, using an optical device called an opthalmoscope.

Light imaged on the back of the eye passes through several layers of neural tissue, ultimately reaching specialized cells containing light-absorbing photopigment. Within these photoreceptor cells light energy is captured and converted into tiny electrical signals. The human eye contains roughly 105 million photoreceptors divisible into different categories. The rod-shaped photoreceptors number about 100 million, and all contain the same kind of light-absorbing photopigment. Rod photoreceptors operate best under dim-light conditions, and they are unable to convey information about the colors of objects.

The remaining 5 million photoreceptors comprise cone-shaped cells that operate under daylight conditions. Each cone receptor contains one of three types of photopigment distinguishable in terms of the range of light wavelengths captured by that photopigment. Roughly 60% of cones contain pigment that is maximally responsive to longer wavelengths of light (a region of the spectrum associated with the color red), 30% of cones have pigment maximally responsive to medium wavelengths (green) and 10% to short wavelengths (blue). These three cone types are critically involved in our perception of color. Hereditary abnormalities in these three cone types produce predictable deficits in color vision, a condition called *color blindness* (something of a misnomer since colors can be experienced, albeit differently from normal).

Cone photoreceptors are highly concentrated at the very back of the eye, in the region called the *fovea*, and their density falls off rapidly in peripheral parts of the retina where rods predominate. Because high visual acuity is possible only within the cone-rich fovea, we must constantly reorient our eyes and heads to stare at objects of interest. Movements that redirect the foveae of the eyes to different objects within the visual field (such as the words on this page) are called *saccades*. These abrupt, high-velocity movements shift the eyes very rapidly from location to location. Slower, smooth eye movements that allow us to fixate and follow an object of interest (such as a person walking past us) are called tracking eye movements, or pursuit movements, and they too are designed to maintain the image of interest on the high-acuity fovea.

Light absorbed by the photoreceptor cells generates an electrical signal whose strength depends on the amount of light stimulating those cells. Photoreceptors are in contact with one another by way of cells with laterally spreading processes. Called horizontal cells, these lateral connections allow neighboring photoreceptors to influence one another's responses, thereby accentuating spatial differences in light levels across the receptor array. The photoreceptors transmit their graded electrical signals to bipolar cells, which come in two complementary types. "On" bipolar cells are activated by an *increase* in incident light while "off" bipolar cells are activated by a *decrease* in incident light. Bipolar cells are also richly interconnected with one another by laterally spreading processes, called amacrine cells. These cells enable bipolar cells to adjust their signal strength in response to the overall level of light.

The last links in this retinal chain are the ganglion cells, which number approximately 1 million per eye. When appropriately stimulated, ganglion cells generate action potentials, spikelike electrical discharges transmitted from the eye to the brain over the axons of the ganglion cells. Ganglion cells are distributed throughout the retina, but their axons are collected into a single "bundle" termed the *optic nerve*. This bundle exits the eye through the optic disk, otherwise known as the blindspot owing to the absence of photoreceptors—and hence visual sensation—within this limited region of the retina. Each ganglion cell receives input from a cluster of neighboring photoreceptors (a region termed the cell's *receptive field*), with the size of this input cluster varying from ganglion cell to ganglion cell. Some ganglion cells respond best to small regions of light seen against a dark background ("On" cells) while others register small regions of darkness seen against a light background ("Off" cells). Ganglion cells differ greatly in terms of their shapes, sizes, and response properties. By virtue of these differences, distinct subpopulations of ganglion cells form the initial stages of neural pathways specialized for perception of form, color, and motion.

Bibliography

Dawkins, R. (1987). *The blind watchmaker*. New York: Norton. An account of how evolution could have produced an organ so intricate as the human eye, without preconceived design.

Hubel, D. H. (1988). *Eye, brain and vision*. New York: Scientific American Library. Entry-level description of the visual pathways by a Nobel prize–winning physiologist.

Polyak, S. (1941). *The retina*. Chicago: University of Chicago Press. Classic description of the retina by one of the field's historically significant figures.

Rodieck, R. W. (1988). *The first steps in seeing*. Sunderland, MA: Sinauer. Richly illustrated, up-to-date account of the structure and function of the human eye.

Randolph Blake

Behavioral and Functional Aspects

Our sense of sight is at once the most obvious and the most intriguing of all the senses. What makes sight so compelling for the casual observer, the philosopher, and the scientist? In 1862, David Brewster, a physicist, wrote:

> Of all the organs by which we acquire a knowledge of external nature the eye is the most remarkable and the most important. By our other senses the information we obtain is comparatively limited. The touch and the taste extend no further than the surface of our own bodies. The sense of smell is exercised within a very narrow sphere, and that of recognizing sounds is limited to the distance at which we hear the bursting of a meteor or the crash of a thunderbolt. But the eye enjoys a boundless range of observation. It takes cognizance not only of worlds belonging to the solar system, but of other systems of worlds infinitely removed into the immensity of space; and when aided by the telescope, the invention of human wisdom, it is able to discover the forms, the phenomena, and the movements of bodies whose distance is as inexpressible in language as it is inconceivable in thought. (From *Letters on Natural Magic*, 1862; cited by Polyak, 1943)

Optics of the Eye

Our ability to see begins with the structure and function of the end organ, the eye. The front of the eye is an optical device that collects and focuses light onto a sheet of central nervous system cells called the retina, which lines the back of the eye. The vast majority of the focusing power of the eye is provided by the cornea, a convex transparent sheet of tissue that covers the front of the eye. However, the curvature of the cornea is fixed, and it cannot change its shape to provide focus for objects at different distances. Instead, a second structure in the eye, the lens, provides the fine focus that is needed. This dynamic and apparently effortless adjustment of the shape of the lens is called accommodation. To bring distant objects into focus the lens must flatten, while the opposite is required for near objects. The lens is most flexible in young individuals, and it becomes progressively stiffer with age. This means that the closest distance at which one can accommodate (bring an object into focus) increases with age. By the fourth or fifth decade of life the lens has become so stiff that significant accommodation is no longer possible, and corrective lenses are often required for both near and distance vision. This normal age-related deficit in accommodation is called presbyopia (*presby* = "elder," *op* = "eye").

The shape of the eyeball and the shape of the cornea also have significant effects on the sharpness of the image that is transmitted to the retina. If the distance between the lens and the retina is too great, an object at a given distance will be focused in front of the retina (resulting in myopia, or nearsightedness), while the opposite is true if the distance between the lens and retina is too short (resulting in hyperopia, or farsightedness). If the cornea is elliptical rather than spherical, then only part of a visual stimulus will be in correct focus at any one time, even though the entire stimulus is located at a single distance from the retina. The visual problem this creates is called astigmatism. Myopia, hyperopia, and astigmatism can all be corrected by artificial lenses (eyeglasses or contact lenses) placed in front of the cornea.

From Light to Signal

Specialized neurons within the retina, the photoreceptors, convert the energy in photons of light to electrical signals that propagate through the retina and optic nerve to reach visual centers elsewhere in the brain. The retina contains two classes of photoreceptors, the rods and cones. Rods contain a photopigment (rhodopsin) that is sensitive to very low light levels (a single photon can produce a signal that can be detected under optimal conditions). Cones have pigments that require more photons. They function when light is too bright for the rods. In rods or cones, photons interact with the photopigment to change the shape of the molecule. This initiates a cascade of biochemical events, including cleavage of part of the photopigment (the chromophore) from the rest of the molecule (the opsin). The cascade culminates in a change in the electrical signal transmitted by the photoreceptor to the next cell in the retina. In the absence of continued stimulation, the chromophore reassociates with the opsin to produce a new photopigment molecule, ready to respond to a new photon. Sensitivity to light depends on the proportion of photopigment molecules that are ready to interact with photons. The longer the retina has been kept in the dark, the more molecules will be ready to interact with photons. This means that the chance that any one photon will initiate a signal is increased. The gradual increase in functional photopigment in the dark, and the resulting increase in perceptual sensitivity to photons, is called dark adaptation.

Cones have many structural and functional similarities to rods, but there are important differences as well. Whereas all rods contain the same photopigment, rhodopsin, normal human retinae contain a mosaic of cones comprised of three populations, each with a different photopigment. The cone photopigments differ in their sensitivity to the wavelength of light. One population is maximally sensitive to short wavelength light (what we perceive as blues and greens); another population is maximally sensitive to middle wavelength light (what we perceive as greens and yellows), and the third population is maximally sensitive to long wavelength light (what we perceive as yellows and reds). Our perception of color depends on the relative excitation of these different cone populations by a visual stimulus. In very dim light, when only rods are active, we do not perceive color because all rods contain the same photopigment, rhodopsin. The relative sensitivity of rods to different wavelengths of light is different than the relative sensitivity of the cones. Rod sensitivity is biased toward middle and low wavelengths, compared to cone sensitivity. As a consequence, a red rose that might look brighter than other flowers in bright light will appear darker in dim light when rods dominate. This shift in spectral sensitivity with light level is known as the Purkinje effect, after the Czech scientist Jan Purkinje (1787–1869).

Visual Processing

The rods and cones of the retina are connected to bipolar cells, which in turn are connected to retinal ganglion cells. Information about light passes through this chain of cells and leaves the retina by way of the axons of the retinal ganglion cells. These axons (about 1 million in humans) comprise the optic nerve, which connects the retina with visual centers in the brain. However, visual information is modified as it passes through this system so that certain aspects are enhanced, and this has profound effects on what we see. For example, retinal cells are connected so that differences between the light and dark parts of a visual scene (visual contrast) produce a larger signal than homogeneous areas. Cells in the retina that make lateral connections (horizontal and amacrine cells) provide this enhancement through a process called lateral inhibition. Thus, the signal sent by a retinal ganglion cell to the brain is greatest when the cells connected to it detect a light area surrounded by a dark area, or vice versa. [*See* Spatial Vision.] One perceptual phenomenon that results from lateral inhibition is called simultaneous contrast. The same grey square appears darker on a light background and lighter on a dark background because lateral inhibition modifies the signal transmitted by the retinal ganglion cells that detect the square.

Another characteristic of visual processing that begins in the retina is the analysis of distinct attributes of a visual scene by distinct groups of cells. The chain of cells that processes a particular attribute has been described as a "channel" of visual information processing. Color is an example of a visual attribute that is first signalled by specific receptors in the retina. Many other attributes (e.g., motion, orientation, and so on) are not explicitly represented in the retina but are extracted from the brain from input sent from the retina. In humans (and nonhuman primates) many of these simple attributes are analyzed by specialized groups of cells in the parts of the brain that make up the visual cortex. Brain lesions provide one source of evidence for this specialization of function. A lesion is damage to brain tissue. Lesions can produce specific impairments in the perception of one attribute but not others.

Afterimages, Aftereffects, and Illusions

Afterimages and aftereffects also provide compelling evidence of some of these channels. Aftereffects are changes in our perception of a visual stimulus after exposure to that stimulus or to related stimuli. For example, if you look at a moving stimulus, such as a waterfall, and then switch your gaze to the stationary rocks on the side of the waterfall, the rocks will appear to be moving up, in the opposite direction from the original direction of motion. One simplified explanation is that the cells that respond to the original direction of motion become fatigued from the prolonged stimulation, leaving them unable to counteract baseline activity in a corresponding group of cells that would be excited by movement in the opposite direction. The brain has no choice but to interpret this unopposed low level of excitation as motion. There are aftereffects for all of the basic features of visual perception (orientation, size, color, and so forth). The negative image of a stimulus, seen after the stimulus is removed, is known as an afterimage. The black spot produced by the bright flash of a camera is an example. [*See* Visual Adaptation.]

When our perception of a stimulus is altered from physical reality because of the structure or functional state of our sensory system, we call this an illusion. Physically equal lines can be made to appear of different lengths, straight lines can appear curved, and so forth. The phenomena of simultaneous contrast and the motion aftereffect described above are examples of visual illusions. [*See* Visual Illusions.]

Putting Together a Visual World

Basic features like size, color, and orientation are pieces of a puzzle. The truly difficult work of vision creates perception of the external world out of these pieces. Many problems need to be solved. The two-dimensional images on the retina need to be related to the three-dimensional structure of the world. Local features need to be appropriately grouped into objects. Those objects need to be seen to be of stable color, shape, and size, even if there are changes in the illumination and/or the observer's viewpoint. The observer must understand the motion of objects and the perceptual effects of the motion of the observer. Also, objects must be recognized and integrated into scenes. As processing becomes more complex, it becomes impossible to process everything at once (Try reading two articles at the same time, for instance.) As a consequence, it becomes necessary to be able to select some objects for more intensive processing. Finally, the observer is not merely a passive consumer of perceptual experience. The processes of perception must be linked to the mechanisms of action because, in the end, we want to be able to pick the apple off the tree, not merely see it.

[*See also* Agnosias; Depth Perception; Motion Perception; Pattern Recognition; Perceptual Constancies; Perceptual Organization; Scene Perception; Sensory Systems; *and* Visual Search.]

Julie Sandell

Age-Related Changes, Optical Factors, and Neural Processes

Seeing begins with information contained in the light reflected from objects in the environment (Sekuler & Blake, 1994). The visual system's subsequent capture, transduction, and analysis of this light-borne information depend on a variety of optical factors and neural processes, all of which are subject to change with age.

Changes in the Eye

The eye makes two different but equally important contributions to vision: optical and neural. In the first contribution, various surfaces and structures admit light into the eye and focus it on the retina's specialized photosensitive elements (rods and cones). In the second contribution, a complex, organized network of neurons processes signals generated by photoreceptor transduction of light, extracting biologically significant information that is transmitted via the optic nerve to the brain.

Over the course of the human life span, no component of the eye is immune to change. During the latter portion of the life span, the most common and consequential optical changes are senile miosis, presbyopia, and cataract. The amount of light entering the eye depends on the area of the pupillary opening, which tends to shrink with age (senile miosis). Although there is considerable variation among individuals, as a rule the average 75- or 80-year-old dark-adapted eye admits only one half as much light as its teenage counterpart. Under light-adapted conditions, the age-dependent gap is somewhat smaller and less significant as a limiting factor in visual function.

Presbyopia refers to a loss of the eye's ability to focus ("accommodate") at different distances. An individual is said to be presbyopic when accommodation no longer provides clear vision at the customary reading distance. On average, this state is achieved at about age 45 years, when the accommodative reserve has been depleted to 3 diopters from 10 or more in childhood. Presbyopia's impact varies with the light level, the effort, and the demands of the visual task. The most likely causes include diminished elasticity of several related tissues, including the lens, lens capsule, and extralenticular fibers (Gilmartin, 1995).

The crystalline lens of a normal young eye is exceedingly transparent, which is highly beneficial for vision. Over time this transparency decreases, particularly for short-wavelength light. For example, at 420 nanometers ("blue") an 80-year-old lens absorbs about 10 times more incident light than a 20-year-old lens does. Light absorbed is light not transmitted and is therefore unavailable for vision. Age also brings increased lenticular scattering or opacification, which constitutes a cataract. The visual impact of any cataract depends on the position of the opacity in the lens; harm is greatest when the transparency of the lens's posterior surface is compromised.

Retinal Changes

Receptor topography in retinas from healthy donor eyes suggests that the spatial density of perifoveal rod photoreceptors decreases by 30% from the second to the ninth decade. In the same eyes, the population of cone photoreceptors is essentially unchanged with age. Because visual acuity depends on the cones, stability of the cone population suggests that some postreceptoral processes must play a role in visual acuity's well-documented decline with age. One candidate is the decreasing number of cells in the retina's ganglion cell layer.

Perceptual Consequences

Age-related changes in ocular structures tell only part of the story of aging and visual function. Connections between vision and aging have real and important consequences both for individuals and for society. Along with other senses, vision makes a central contribution to a wide variety of cognitive abilities, including reasoning and memory. Surveys reveal that older observers have particular difficulties with visual tasks involving rapid processing, high light sensitivity, dynamic vision, near vision, and visual search. Many of these difficulties go undetected on standard clinical examinations.

Pattern Vision

Starting at about 50 years of age, visual acuity diminishes year by year. (Acuity is indexed by the ability to resolve fine detail.) At low spatial frequencies, contrast sensitivity does not vary with age. However, at intermediate and high spatial frequencies (e.g., greater than 4 cycles per degree of visual angle), contrast sensitivity declines steadily with age, beginning as early as 30 years.

Optical factors (e.g., intraocular light scatter, reduced retinal illumination) contribute to the age-related decline in contrast sensitivity. Changes in photoreceptor properties play a role as well; although the number of cone photoreceptors remains fairly constant throughout life, degradation in the regularity and spacing of the receptor mosaic and morphological changes reduce the area of each receptor's effective aperture. Other factors include neural changes (decreased efficiency and reduced selectivity in low-level visual mechanisms). Age-related limitations on attention are also important.

Linking Low- and High-Level Vision

To enable us to perceive objects, the visual system must encode information not only about the size and contrast of visual elements, but also about the elements' positions relative to one another. This positional information is referred to as "spatial phase." The ability to encode spatial phase information decreases with age (Sekuler, Bennett, & Placenza, 1995). Because spatial phase contributes to the perception of shape or form, older observers' deficits in processing spatial phase information probably impair both perception and recognition of objects. Unfortunately, no research has addressed this important issue. In fact, aside from older observers' self-reports, almost nothing is known about how object perception changes with age.

Despite this obvious gap in knowledge, there has been some success in linking performance on lower and higher level tasks. For example, visual acuity accounts for a large proportion of age-related variance on many measures of cognitive functioning, including working memory, associative learning, and concept identification (Salthouse, 1996). Of course, this association does not guarantee that declining visual acuity causes declining cognitive functioning; some third common factor could mediate the association.

To examine the link between low- and high-level functions, Spinks, Gilmore, and Thomas (1996) constructed a digital filter that simulated the vision experienced by the average healthy 80-year-old person.

Then young participants looked through this filter while they performed several tests of intelligence and cognitive function. The filter's degradation of vision, including reduced contrast sensitivity, caused substantial drops in young participants' performance. Remarkably, young participants with artificially degraded vision performed as though they were 50 to 55 years old.

In addition, contrast sensitivity is a good predictor of visual complaints, particularly complaints of difficulty seeing at night, and is a major limiting factor in reading (Legge, Kiltz, & Tjan, 1997). Contrast sensitivity also shows promise as a predictor of age-associated diminished perception of faces, road signs, and objects.

Binocular Vision

Neural interactions between signals originating in the two eyes can significantly enhance visual function. Such an enhancement constitutes an emergent property, which originates in the visual cortex of the brain, where inputs from the two eyes are combined. The best known product of binocular integration is stereopsis, an important source of depth information. Stereopsis arises from the fact that objects at different depths are imaged on different parts of the two eyes (binocular disparity). With age, individuals require ever larger disparities in order to perceive depth from this particular cue (Bell, Wolf, & Bernholtz, 1974).

In addition to making stereopsis possible, the combination of signals from the two eyes produces binocular summation, which improves performance on a wide range of visual tasks. Binocular summation is measured by the ratio of binocular sensitivity to sensitivity measured with the better single eye. Although binocular summation ratios tend to decline with age, especially with targets of higher spatial frequency, not all binocular tasks show equivalent age-related changes. For example, appreciable age-related elevation of binocular depth thresholds can coexist with other measures of binocular function that show no change with age (Speranza, Moraglia, & Schneider, 1995). These differences between the impact of age on various tasks probably reflect differences in the underlying neural computational requirements of the tasks.

Perception of Dynamic Displays

Arguably, the most prominent functional decline with age is in the visual system's ability to detect temporal change. Age-related reduction in temporal resolution shows up in the altered temporal extent of visual masking, increased duration of visual afterimages, and reduced critical flicker fusion (the fastest rate at which an observer is able to perceive flicker). Little is known about age-related changes in the principal responses to a moving object: judgments of speed or direction. On the basis of limited data, it appears that speed discrimination is unimpaired by age but that discrimination of direction is impaired. One of the most common stimuli used in studying motion perception is the random dot cinematogram, in which neither form nor motion is apparent in a single frame but emerges across frames. With stimuli that contain a wide range of different, spatially intermingled direction vectors, observers must integrate direction information across space and time to perceive global flow in the cinematogram's mean direction. When they were asked to judge the direction of flow in such cinematograms, older observers made much larger errors than younger observers; the age difference was exacerbated by short stimulus duration (Dengis, Sekuler, Bennett, & Sekuler, 1998). In addition, confirming earlier results, cinematograms' motion signals were less detectable by older observers. This age effect was especially pronounced in the oldest observers.

Color Vision

Advancing age brings diminished ability to discriminate subtle differences of hue in the blue-green range, a deficit that is particularly noticeable under conditions of reduced illumination. Changed color vision probably reflects changes in the density of the ocular media and changes in sensitivity to all three types of cone photoreceptors. Despite the cone pathways' diminished sensitivity, the relative responses of the three different types of cone photoreceptors remain constant. Because perception of color depends on the relative responses within different types of cones, color vision remains stable across the life span, particularly when stimuli are well above threshold levels. For example, older and younger observers have similar color naming functions, loci of achromatic points, and loci of unique hues for yellow and blue. Thus, the visual system somehow continuously recalibrates the strength of color signals, maintaining color constancy throughout the life span (Werner & Schefrin, 1993).

Visual Attention: Useful Field of View

Many older people report difficulty in finding objects in visually cluttered scenes. These anecdotal reports are confirmed by empirical studies measuring the useful field of view, a laboratory analog to a cluttered visual environment (Ball & Sekuler, 1986). The useful field of view is that region of the visual field to which an observer can attend at any one time. There is virtually no relation between the size of an observer's useful field of view and the size of the observer's visual fields measured by clinical perimetry. However, the size of the useful field of view seems to be a particularly important measure because it correlates strongly with drivers' accident rates. The cause of the age-related decline in the useful field of view seems to be older observers' decreasing ability to process task-relevant information.

Visual Memory

Vision in complex environments requires observers not only to detect and discriminate stimuli presented simultaneously, but also to integrate information appropriately over space and time. One index of this ability is short-term memory for visual attributes, such as spatial frequency, that resist semantic encoding. Although older observers typically perform poorly on tasks that involve verbal memory, this age-related loss seems to spare memory for visual attributes. Nevertheless, brain imaging (positron emission tomography) studies reveal that different neural systems are responsible for spatial frequency memory in younger and older observers (McIntosh et al., 1997). These differences may reflect compensatory neural reorganization within the aging brain.

Bibliography

Ball, K., & Sekuler, R. (1986). Improving visual perception in older observers. *Journal of Gerontology, 41*, 176–182.

Bell, B., Wolf, E., & Bernholtz, C. D. (1974). Depth perception as a function of age. *Aging and Human Development, 3*, 77–81.

Dengis, C., Sekuler, A. B., Bennett, P. J., & Sekuler, R. (1998). Aging affects perceived direction of motion and detection of global flow in random dot cinematograms. *Investigative Ophthalmology and Visual Science Supplement, 39*, S1090.

Gilmartin, B. (1995). The aetiology of presbyopia: A summary of the role of lenticular and extralenticular structures. *Ophthalmic and Physiological Optics, 15*, 431–437.

Legge, G. E., Kiltz, T. S., & Tjan, B. (1997). Mr. Chips: An ideal-observer model of reading. *Psychological Review, 104*, 524–553.

McIntosh, A. R., Sekuler, A. B., Penpeci, C., Rajah, M. N., Grady, C. L., & Sekuler, R. (1997). Effects of aging on neural systems supporting visual perceptual memory. *Society for Neuroscience Supplement, 23*, 1402.

Salthouse, T. A. (1996). Interrelations of age, visual acuity, and cognitive functioning. *Journal of Gerontology: Psychological Sciences, 51B*, P317–P330.

Sekuler, A. B., Bennett, P. J., & Placenza, F. M. (1995). Spatial phase discrimination in older observers. *Investigative Ophthalmology and Visual Science Supplement, 36*, S912.

Sekuler, R., & Blake, R. (1994). *Perception* (3rd ed.). New York: McGraw-Hill.

Speranza, F., Moraglia, G., & Schneider, B. A. (1995). Age-related changes in binocular vision: Detection of noise-masked targets in young and old observers. *Journal of Gerontology B, Psychological Science and Social Science, 50*, P114–P123.

Spinks, R., Gilmore, G., & Thomas, C. (1996). *Age simulation of a sensory deficit does impair cognitive test performance.* Paper presented at the Cognition and Aging Conference, Atlanta, GA.

Werner, J. S., & Schefrin, B. E. (1993). Loci of achromatic points throughout the life span. *Journal of the Optical Society of America A, 10*, 1509–1516.

Robert Sekuler and Allison B. Sekuler

VISUAL ADAPTATION refers to reversible changes in perception caused by visual experience. For example, after staring at the downward motion of a waterfall, a vivid sensation of upward motion will be perceived when looking at a stationary object. Adaptation serves a functional role in the visual system by calibrating it to prevailing conditions and thus increasing the efficiency of visual coding. Insofar as the visual system is adapted to "normal" conditions, the visual system can be more sensitive to deviations from normality. Visual adaptation can be used as a scientific tool to study the visual system. For example, after staring at a patch of green light, the afterimage you see on a white surface will be red. This fact (which has nothing to do with physics) tells us about the color-opponency system in human vision. There are a variety of visual adaptations. This article will discuss four major classes of adaptation: *dark and light adaptation, visual aftereffects, contingent aftereffects*, and *visuomotor adaptations*.

Light and Dark Adaptation

Dark adaptation is the gradual adjustment to darkness that one experiences upon entering a darkened room; its converse is *light adaptation*. The process of dark adaptation is fairly slow. Thus a well-lit room with moonlight coming through the window may seem extremely dark upon first turning out the lights, but after 5 minutes may seem satisfactorily lit for safe navigation by moonlight alone. Full dark adaptation from a very bright environment to a very dark one takes about 30 minutes. Light adaptation, such as occurs when exiting a dark theater into a sunny parking lot, is complete within about 10 minutes for extreme cases; normal transitions take less time.

Light and dark adaptation allow the visual system to operate effectively under a large range of light levels. The absolute intensity of light reflected by white paper in sunlight is 1 million times greater than that reflected by the same paper in moonlight. However, within any given environment, the whitest white reflects no more than about 30 times the light reflected from the blackest black. Since the visual system cannot and needs not represent more than about a 100:1 variation, it uses dark and light adaptation to adjust its sensitivity to the prevailing conditions. (You may have thought this task was performed by the pupil of the eye, but the pupil can only change the quantity of light entering the eye by about a factor of 10.)

There are two receptor types in the human retina.

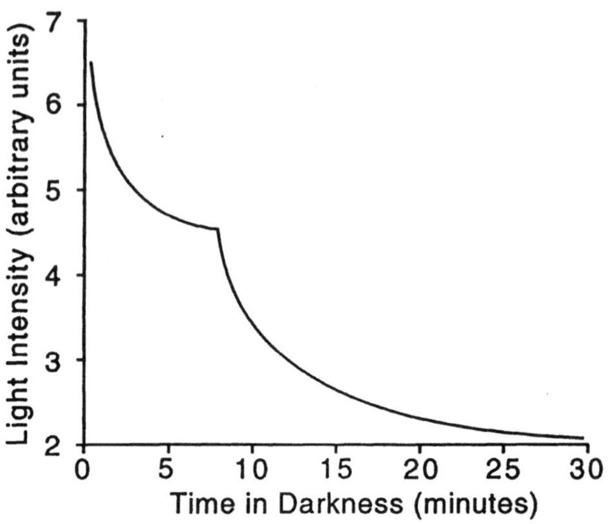

VISUAL ADAPTATION. Figure 1. Time course of dark adaptation is depicted as minimum intensity required to detect a point of light after prior exposure to a high-intensity light source for several minutes.

Cones are specialized for daytime (photopic) vision and only operate under relatively high light levels. Three different cone types, with different spectral sensitivities, provide access to color information as well as high-acuity vision near the center of gaze. *Rods*, on the other hand, are specialized for night (scotopic) vision. Both systems show adaptation within the range of intensities for which they are suited. Light and dark adaptation occur primarily by intrinsic modulation of receptor photopigment levels (caused by the "bleaching" of the photopigment in response to light), but also by other retinal and cortical compensations. The time course of dark adaptation is usually measured by determining the minimum light needed for contrast detection as a function of time. A graph of the change in threshold is shown in Figure 1. The "knee" in the graph shows the transition point between detection via cones and the more sensitive rod system.

Visual Aftereffects

Whereas dark and light adaptation represent a functional adjustment to ambient light energy, visual aftereffects, such as the waterfall illusion described above, represent an adaptation to the visual *information* provided by means of light. They typically occur for such simple visual properties as size, orientation, color, and motion, for which neural encoding mechanisms have been identified. They also occur in the perception of position, depth, texture density, and curvature. A number of simple *aftereffects of spatial vision* may be experienced with the aid of Figure 2. Most of these effects can be described as demonstrating *successive contrast*: the test figure is distorted as if by contrast with the adaptation figure.

Visual aftereffects can be measured both by distortions of subsequent perceptual experience (e.g., illusory upward motion of a static object following adaptation to downward motion) and by a reduced sensitivity to similar information. This reduced sensitivity is called *threshold elevation* because higher amounts of some specific stimulation than normal are required for the stimulation to reach the "threshold" of detection. Adapting to an oriented grating, for example, will mean that detecting a dim grating of similar orientation later will require that the grating be brighter than it would normally need to be to be visible.

It is possible to make inferences about the extent to which separate channels of information operate in vision by examining the specificity of such threshold elevation effects. For example, if I adapt to a grating of a particular orientation and then measure my thresholds for gratings of different orientations, I will find no evidence of threshold elevation for orientations distant from the adapted one. From this I would conclude that the process used to detect these distinct orientations was not the process adapted. In fact, only "near neighbors" of the adapted orientation will be affected. Careful analysis of threshold elevations associated with orientation and size adaptation have been used to make sophisticated inferences about the characteristics of cortical cells tuned for size and orientation.

The *perceptual* aftereffect associated with adaptation to orientation is that "near neighbors" of the adapting stimulus will appear to be shifted in orientation away from the adapting stimulus. For example, after adaptation to a grating tilted 15 degrees from vertical, a vertical line might appear to be tilted 3 degrees away from vertical in the other direction (see Figure 2a). Such effects can be understood in terms of *population*

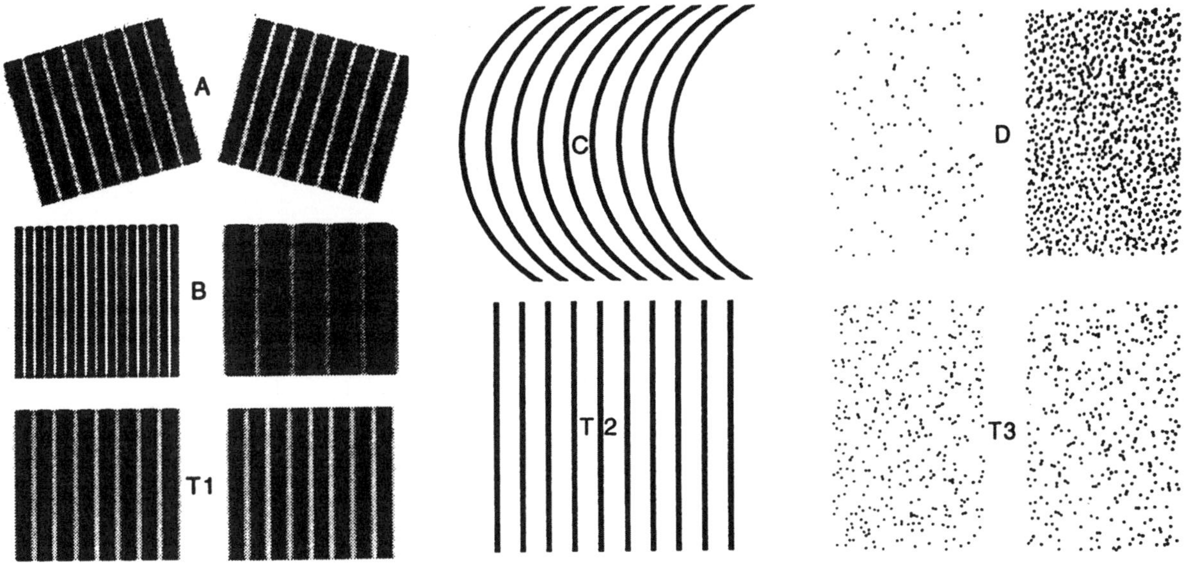

VISUAL ADAPTATION. Figure 2. Several aftereffects. A: A negative tilt aftereffect can be produced by gazing at the "A" in the top left panel for about 30 seconds. The gratings of the bottom left panel will appear to be tilted inwards at the top when gazing at "T1." B: Negative aftereffects of size may be produced by gazing at "B" for 30 seconds and subsequently inspecting T1: the bars on the left side will appear larger than those on the right. C: Adaptation to the curved lines while gazing at the "C" will produce opposite curvature in the straight lines while gazing at "T2," resulting from a combination of a true curvature aftereffect and a spatial displacement aftereffect. Adaptation to "D" produces a negative aftereffect of texture spacing (density) upon examination of the "T3."

coding, in which percepts are mediated by activation patterns across many neural units. In the case of orientation, banks of units sensitive to differently oriented patterns exist in the cortex for each local region of the retinal input. These detectors are *broadly tuned* so that they also respond to orientations within several degrees of their preferred orientation. Adaptation to a particular orientation, such as 15 degrees, reduces responsiveness of detectors in proportion to their activity during adaptation. As illustrated in Figure 3, the resulting population signal will be skewed away from the adapted orientation when a near orientation, such as vertical, is presented to the same retinal region. Population coding accounts are favored for tilt, size, depth (binocular disparity), and motion aftereffects, for which tuned detector systems exist. Similarly, certain figural aftereffects that produce shape distortions can be understood as resulting from aftereffects in the population coding of spatial location.

Aftereffects have proven to be a valuable tool for investigating the visual system's underlying "dimensions" of analysis. Chromatic aftereffects, for example, played an important role in developing Hering's opponent process theory of color vision: The opposition of green and red in color space is visually demonstrated by the pink afterimage obtained when looking at a white surface after staring at a green light or object.

The functional significance of color adaptation may be to "white-balance" visual input (remove artifactual color imbalances). A biological system of information transduction must be continually calibrated so it reads the world aright. In the very short term, a preponderance of a particular signal at a particular location is damped by adaptation processes, resulting in a short-term negative aftereffect. In the longer term, adaptation can help correct for accidental imbalances in color sensitivity across the retina.

Related functional accounts have been put forward for other forms of adaptation. Because the eyes typically change fixation several times each second, the average value of any signal over time at any retinal location should be the same. If one part of my visual field is constantly signaling higher texture densities than the rest of my visual field, for example, it is likely that my perceptual system needs to be adjusted. In order that things appear the same size, orientation, and color across the visual field, active calibration of each portion of the visual system must occur.

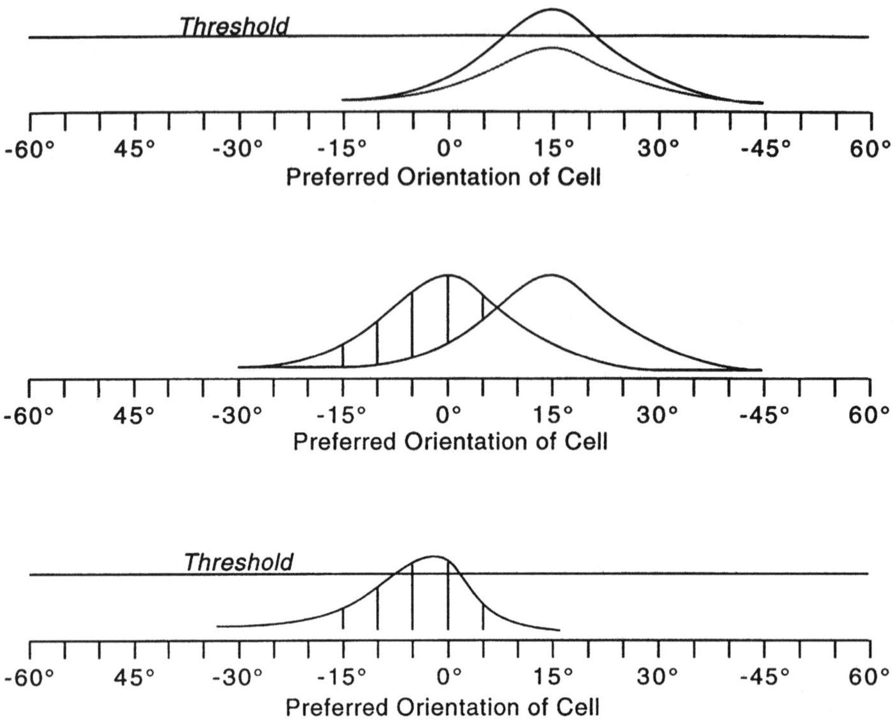

VISUAL ADAPTATION. Figure 3. Many aftereffects can be understood in terms of population coding, here illustrated for orientation. Each graph represents cell activation as a function of preferred orientation. In the top panel, the reponse to a dim 15° grating is illustrated both before (top line) and after (bottom line) adaptation to a 15° grating. In this case the response has dropped below a hypothetical detection threshold (the horizontal line). The middle panel shows the normal response to a vertical (0°) grating and indicates how the adapted response may be subtracted out. The result, depicted in the bottom panel, shows that the population code now signals an orientation that is shifted to the left of vertical by a few degrees.

Contingent Aftereffects

Some aftereffects, known as *contingent aftereffects*, arise in response to the local visual pairing of two different kinds of visual information. The classic example was that identified by Celeste McCollough in 1965. She found that adapting to colored edges in which a particular color was paired with a particular orientation could produce orientation-specific color aftereffects. Thus, for example, after staring at a grating composed of black and green vertical edges presented in alternation with one composed of black and red horizontal edges, a grating of black and gray edges will thereafter appear pinkish when oriented vertically and greenish when oriented horizontally. It is difficult to explain contingent aftereffects in terms of channel adaptation. Rather, these aftereffects appear to be by-products of recalibration or learning in the visual system.

Recalibration accounts take several forms. Fundamentally, they tend to propose that, in the case of the McCollough effect, the visual system assumes that vertical things should not, in general, be green, and corrects for any correlations it finds. In general, contingent aftereffects between other dimensions, such as color-contingent motion aftereffects, and size-contingent color aftereffects, can be treated as cases in which the visual system actively reduces correlated signals. An important alternative formulation suggests that contingent aftereffects may arise as an adaptation to actually existing correlations between sensory features so that vision can more efficiently code departures from normal correlations. This would explain why a large box that weighs 10 pounds feels less heavy than a 10-pound lead ball. In the case of contingent color aftereffects, this calibratory system could correct for chromatic aberrations in the optics of the eye (which would normally produce color fringes at luminance boundaries). However, such systems might also affect the integration of sensory information, as when information about self-motion will be correlated with image transformations due to the three-dimensional structure of the surrounding environment.

Contingent aftereffects are not the product of conscious experience, because they can be induced under various conditions in which the adapting information is not perceived including binocular rivalry and certain kinds of cortical form blindness. Contingent aftereffects are thought by many to be limited to simple visual features, like those susceptible to aftereffects, though conflicting reports exist. Contingent aftereffects tend to be more long-lasting than simple aftereffects, with durations of days and weeks rather than seconds or minutes. Varieties of both kinds of aftereffect have been shown to be preserved in strength during periods of visual inactivity, suggesting that they are due to active visual processes rather than neural fatigue.

Visuomotor Adaptations

These adaptations serve the functional role of calibrating perceptual space and motor space (or simply proprioceptive space). The act of reaching for a cup can be done rapidly and without thought, although it involves coordinating visual knowledge of the cup's location with motor knowledge concerning the commands necessary to move the appropriate hand to that location in space. If the perceived position of the cup in space is displaced by introducing a wedge prism in front of the eye, the hand will initially reach out to the wrong location and a visceral sense of surprise will result when the hand comes into view unexpectedly displaced. The novel relationship between action and vision is rapidly and completely adapted to. This adjustment results in a compensatory reaching error when the prism is first removed.

A variety of optical rearrangements have been studied, including left-right and up-down mirror reversals. In all cases, there is a gradual learning process (which can be quite rapid in the simple displacement case). Although sometimes described as a visual compensation for the optical transformation, such learning is actually specific to the motor systems involved. If correct reaching was achieved after several trials with the right hand, it might well generalize to all points in space for that hand, but it will not generalize to the left hand without further feedback concerning that limb. In this sense, visuomotor adaptations are regarded as recalibrations of the proprioceptive system responsible for maintaining a sense of limb and body position in the visual world. Such adaptations only occur if the body is actively moved or attended.

In addition to spatial distortions, novel correlations between locomotion and visual feedback can concern perceived velocity. Simply running on a treadmill, which provides none of the visual motion normally associated with forward locomotion, produces a number of aftereffects including a visual illusion of increased forward motion when walking on solid ground. On one view, such visuomotor adaptations are like contingent aftereffects in which a visual source of information is paired with specific motor signals. Both can be subsumed under a recalibration account based on adaptation to experienced regularities.

Bibliography

Anstis, S. M. (1975). What does visual perception tell us about visual coding? In M. S. Gazzaniga and C. Blakemore (Eds.), *Handbook of psychobiology* (pp. 269–323). New York: Academic Press. Analysis of use of aftereffects for investigating visual processing.

Barlow, H. B. (1990). A theory about the functional role and synaptic mechanism of visual after-effects. In C. Blakemore (Ed.), *Vision: Coding and efficiency* (pp. 363–375). Cambridge, UK: Cambridge University Press.

Durgin, F. H. (1996). Visual aftereffect of texture density contingent on color of frame. *Perception & Psychophysics, 58,* 207–233. Includes recent review of known contingent aftereffects.

Graham, N. V. S. (1989). *Visual pattern analyzers.* New York: Oxford University Press. Analysis of spatial vision. Much is based on using adaptation as an inferential tool about underlying coding.

Harris, C. S. (Ed.). (1980). *Visual coding and adaptability.* Hillsdale, NJ: Erlbaum. Harris's chapter contrasts purely visual aftereffects with visuomotor adaptation. Held's chapter provides an excellent account of adaptive nature of contingent chromatic compensations in form perception.

Helson, H. (1964). *Adaptation-level theory: An experimental and systematic approach to behavior.* New York: Harper & Row. Classic treatment of adaptation as a psychological principle.

Humphrey, G. K. (1998). The McCollough effect: Misperception and reality. In V. Walsh & J. Kulikowski (Eds.), *Visual constancies: Why things look as they do* (pp. 31–68). Cambridge, UK: Cambridge University Press. Reviews literature on McCollough's Effect.

Kohler, I. (1964). *The formation and transformation of the perceptual world.* New York: International Universities Press. Classic monograph on visuomotor adaptation.

Wallach, H. (1976). *On perception.* New York: Quadrangle. Includes a number of papers on adaptation and visual learning.

Walls, G. L. (1942). *The vertebrate eye and its adaptive radiation.* Bloomfield Hills, MI: Cranbrook Press. An evolutionary analysis of the eye as an adaptive information transducer. Helpful for understanding retinal adaptations.

Wöhlgemuth, A. (1911). On the after-effect of seen movement. *British Journal of Psychology (Monograph Supplement 1).* Classic analysis of one of the oldest known aftereffects.

Frank H. Durgin

VISUAL AND DESIGN ARTS. The psychology of visual aesthetics is the branch of psychology that is concerned with the study of the creation and contemplation of visible aesthetic objects. We can only tell that an object is aesthetic by knowing that it is the object of an aesthetic experience.

Some experiences are better exemplars of the aesthetic experience than others; that is, they have properties that make them *prototypical* aesthetic experiences. A prototypical visual aesthetic experience (1) is one in which attention is firmly fixed upon heterogeneous but interrelated components of a visual pattern; (2) excludes the awareness of other objects or events, such as noises, bodily disturbances, and distracting thoughts; (3) is one in which attention is not fixed upon an object's relation to ourselves, its relation to the artist, or to the culture from which it sprang; (4) is dominated by intense feelings or emotions evoked by the visual pattern; (5) hangs together, is coherent; and (6) involves "make-believe." While in this state we do not think of a painting as a material object; we do not believe that the scene we see in it is real; we do not respond to a lifelike statue of a person as we would to the person. The greater the number of these properties an experience bears, and the purer each of them is, the stronger—the more pleasurable—the aesthetic experience. However, the absence of any of these properties does not mean that the experience is not aesthetic.

The objects that can evoke a prototypical visual aesthetic experience differ from person to person; some love the works of Salvador Dali, and some find his oeuvre trite and bombastic. So it should come as no surprise that many people believe the saw, "beauty is in the eye of the beholder" (and the Latin proverb, "*de gustibus non est disputandum*"—taste cannot be debated). There is little evidence to support such extreme subjectivist views. Indeed during several hundred years there has been broad agreement in Western society on which objects belong in the canon of great works. Two hypotheses have been put forward to account for this agreement: (1) Beauty and art are social constructions; (2) beauty is determined by mechanisms that are common to all humans.

Beauty and Art as Social Constructions

In support of the hypothesis that beauty and art are social constructions, we note that aesthetic taste changes. For example, the Art Nouveau style of architecture and design, dominant from 1890 to 1910, was characterized by elaborate ornamentation dominated by long sinuous organic lines. The Modern movement, which started in 1910, eschewed all ornament. Such oscillations are common in all the arts. Three hypotheses have been offered to account for these oscillations: the *reflectionist*, the *developmental*, and the *functional*. According to the reflectionist hypothesis, held by eminent art historians (such as Wölfflin, Riegel, and Panofsky), the oscillations of artistic styles reflect oscillations of the *Zeitgeist* (the spirit of the age). Art Nouveau could have been an antithetical response to the rampant ugliness of nineteenth-century urban landscape, whereas the well-ordered and austere Modern movement may have been a reaction to the severe social unrest fomented by the utopian movements of its time, such as anarchism and communism. According to the developmental theory, the development of visual art from prehistory to the present parallels the Piagetian stages of cognitive development in the child. These theories are fraught with conceptual difficulties and have little credible empirical evidence to support them.

The functional hypothesis stays close to known facts. For the approximately 40,000 years that modern humans (*Homo sapiens sapiens*) have existed, they have used representations, not to reflect society, but as tools to help express the ideas of a society. The oldest known drawings, representing humans and animals, were created in caves (in Southwest Europe) around 30,000 BCE. Several hypotheses (which are not mutually exclusive) have been formulated to explain the function of these portrayals. (1) These depictions may have been produced by animists—people who believed that animals are inhabited by spirits that are separable or separate from their bodies. The drawings may have been used by shamans to mediate between the visible and spirit worlds. (2) They may have been produced in the service of rituals designed to ensure a good hunt or promote fertility. Indeed, some of these faithfully delineated images show large game mammals (not infrequently with spears and arrows embedded in them), pregnant women, and men engaged in hunting. (3) They may have been totems, representations of animals or plants as the emblem of a clan. These animals or plants may have been revered as the clan's ancestor or guardian. As spectators at the end of the twentieth century we may contemplate these drawings as aesthetic objects and enjoy the aesthetic experiences they afford. But it is unlikely that their creators viewed them just in this way. Nevertheless, since it is unlikely that the requisite representational skills were common among humans in the Upper Paleolithic (40,000 to 10,000 BCE), these people must have had high regard for the "artists" who had the talent as well as the right spiritual powers.

Since the emergence of agriculture and the domestication of animals (about 10,000 BCE), much of what we now consider art has played important roles in society. Monumental art honors rulers and heroes, demonstrates the wealth of the society, memorializes important events in its history, and provides a focus for the pride of its members. Religious art honors deities and figures from scriptures, demonstrates the wealth of the organized religion, memorializes important events in its history, and provides a focus for its rites. The people who commissioned these works may have enjoyed the aesthetic experiences afforded by the works, but these experiences were rarely the sole purpose of their creation.

Beauty and Art as Evolutionary Adaptations

The last quarter of the twentieth century saw a revival of theories about universals of the mind and the rise of evolutionary psychology. As an example of an evolutionary argument, consider the results showing that wolves do not prey on sheep after feeding on a sheep carcass spiked with an emetic that causes nausea and vomiting. This stimulus-specific learning-preparedness, that makes one-trial learning possible, is an important adaptation that decreases the likelihood of animals being poisoned. Such a mechanism is also present in humans: food consumed before a gastrointestinal illness is likely to become repellent.

The Adaptiveness of Symmetry and Beauty. The question of the innateness or the universality of aesthetic responsiveness has been the subject of much speculation. Humans share with other animals an appreciation of many animal and plant displays. For example, male bowerbirds invest much time building elaborately decorated shaded leafy enclosures called bowers. These bowers serve only one function: to be stages on which the males perform courtship displays. One such species, Archbold's bowerbird, native to Papua New Guinea, seeks out the exquisite feathers from the head of the king-of-Saxony bird of paradise to decorate its bower. These feathers are also treasured by the indigenous inhabitants of Papua New Guinea. These feathers were neither formed to please bowerbirds nor humans; they are a display that makes its bearer attractive to females of its species.

Many animal displays have a mathematical structure called symmetry, which comes in many forms (for example, Figures 1 and 2). Symmetric patterns have one important feature: They make irregularity easy to detect. Animals whose sensory systems are tuned to symmetry are particularly adept at detecting deviations from symmetry, which constitute flaws in potential mates. The more flawlessly symmetric the display of a peacock the greater the resources he must have invested in it. Ill health or having been defeated in fights with other males would have damaged the display and caused deviations from symmetry. Thus the perfection of a peacock's display demonstrates to a selective peahen that he has resources to spare, is in good health, and dominates other peacocks. He therefore is likely to be a good mate.

Why is it that flowers or the peacock's tail, which evolved to attract species very different from our own, appeal to humans? If one could show that humans are universally attracted to certain forms, we could surmise that art is an adaptation; that the possession of art by human beings enables them to survive and reproduce in their natural environment better than if they lacked art. There is reason to believe that symmetry patterns of the type shown in Figures 1 and 2 are universally produced and appreciated. For example, the women of Mozambique weave straw handbags decorated with patterns that conform to the seven types of symmetry shown in Figure 2. The Alhambra (built in Cordoba during the fourteenth century by Muslim princes of Spain) has examples of all 17 types of so-called wallpaper patterns. A theory of human attraction to such patterns and how it increases human fitness has yet to be formulated. It is likely to be a more complex version of the explanations offered for the attractiveness of symmetry to nonhuman animals.

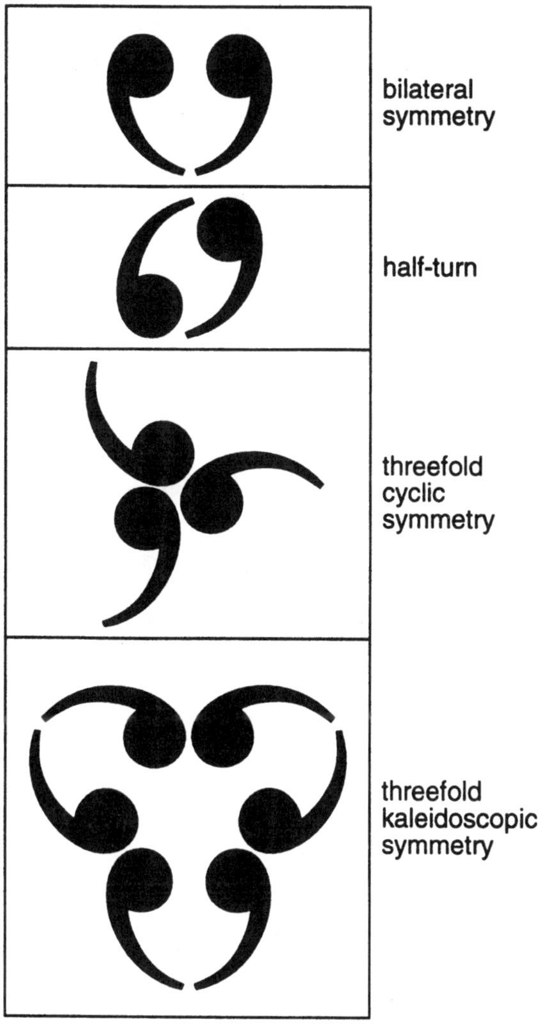

VISUAL AND DESIGN ARTS. Figure 1. Four types of point symmetry.

Is the Appeal of the Golden Section Universal? Attempts to find universals of beauty other than sym-

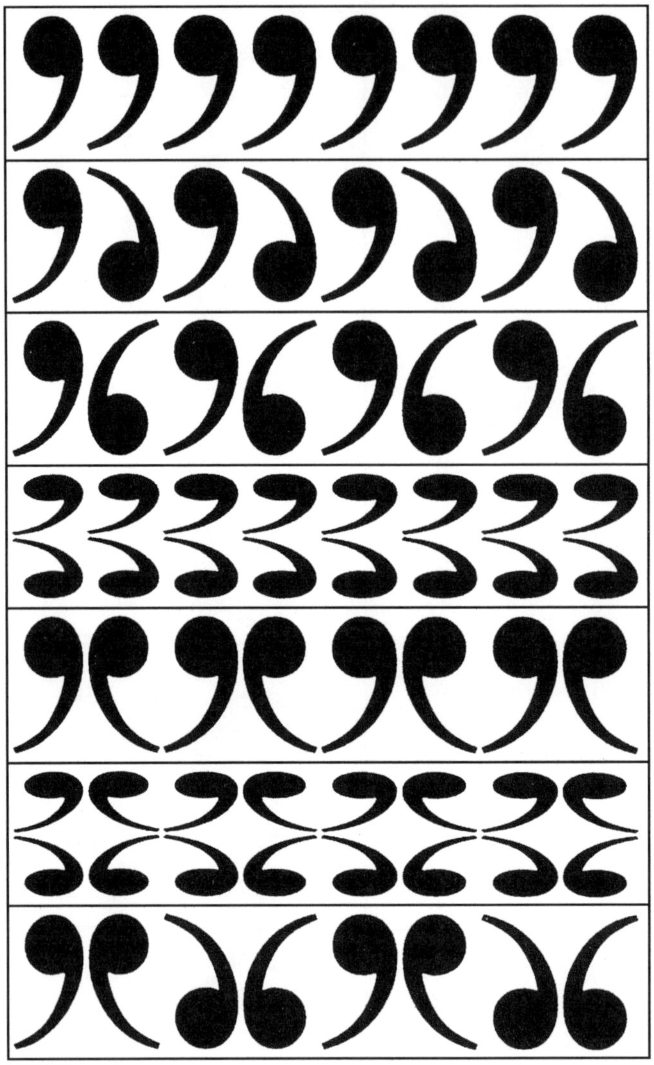

VISUAL AND DESIGN ARTS. Figure 2. The seven types of frieze symmetry.

metry have not been particularly successful. The first such effort was undertaken by the founder of psychophysics, Gustav Theodor Fechner (1801–1887). In 1865, he published the first paper on experimental aesthetics, on the golden section. The golden section, ϕ, is a ratio that divides a line segment into two so that the ratio of the smaller part to the larger part is equal to the ratio of the larger part to the whole

$$\phi = \frac{1+\sqrt{5}}{2} = 1.61803\ldots$$

The ratio ϕ manifests itself in many types of plant growth, was used extensively in ancient Greek sculpture and architecture, and has many interesting mathematical properties. Impressed by the ubiquity of this ratio, Fechner produced data in support of the claim that the most attractive rectangles are those whose sides stand in the ratio ϕ. Unfortunately, those who have tried to confirm Fechner's data have produced a mixed bag of results. Currently scholarly opinion favors the view that people *do not* prefer ϕ over other proportions.

Is Optimal Arousal the General Principle of Aesthetic Appeal? Another attempt to propose a universal principle of aesthetic pleasure was proposed in the late 1950s by Daniel E. Berlyne. The theory appeared to shift away from the explanation of attractiveness by appealing to the properties of objects and toward the intensity of the *arousal* the objects produce. Arousal is a general state of the organism that affects the vigor and organization of its behavior. Its lowest degree represents sleep; its highest degree represents disorganization and frenzy. It can be affected by internal influences (drugs, hormones, and deprivation levels) or by external influences (the sight or smell of food, or painful stimuli). Berlyne and his followers came to believe that the stimulus arousal potential of a work of art is determined to a large extent by its complexity. He defined the complexity of stimuli on an ordinal scale: he would create a set of stimuli that were similar in structure, but differed only in the number or the variability of elements they comprised. In doing so, his theory became another theory of preferred stimulus properties rather than a theory of responses.

Experimentalists have had mixed success in obtaining evidence in support of Berlyne's theory. It would appear that complexity does not strongly influence preference. This conclusion should be reached with caution: It is warranted only if one accepts Berlyne's conception of complexity. He mistakenly thought that complexity is a measurable feature of *single stimuli.* When John looks at a geometric abstract painting by Mondrian, he sees black intersecting perpendicular lines bounding rectangles of primary colors. If he says that his 4-year-old niece could have done as well, he means that the painting is simple because all the artist could have done differently was to fail to stay within the lines or use different primary colors. John thinks that this painting is simple because he thinks that all Mondrian's paintings are alike. He is not aware of the subtle choices Mondrian made in creating a balanced organization of forms. On the other hand, when John sees a television program that teaches how to do landscape paintings, he sees the picture of a unique landscape. If he says that this painting is complex, he means that what differentiates it from other paintings by the same artist is its subject matter, each detail of which requires different strokes of the paintbrush. Each of these brushstrokes appears to be the result of a choice. He is not aware that this skill requires a few tricks; it has fewer alternatives than it may seem. As Wendell R. Garner and Daniel Kahneman have argued, complexity is not a property of single objects; it is a property of an imagined—or inferred—set of alternatives. A person's construal of the set to which an object belongs determines her judgment of the object's complexity. It remains to be seen whether a better version of this theory can be formulated.

Artistic Production in Children

We have pointed out that the enjoyment of representation and decoration appear to be ancient and universal human pleasures. If the production of art (broadly conceived) is an evolved adaptation, we should observe regularities in the development of artistic skills, just as there are regularities in the development of linguistic skills. Note that until they reach kindergarten age, children's drawing is part of make-believe play. They draw *enactively*, accompanying rather than illustrating what they are imagining. In other words, the desire to *represent* emerges relatively late in the development of the child.

The drawings of preschool children go through a fixed series of stages, leading to the first representational drawing of a human being. The stages are (1) basic scribbles, (2) diagrams, (3) aggregates, (4) suns with rays, (5) sun faces, (6) arms and legs attached to the head, derived by extending sun rays, (7) arms and legs attached to torso.

The naturalism of representations is of little concern to small children. It is teachers who instill in children the goal of representing accurately. Eventually, the assessment that one has the skill to draw disappears in all but a few children. And so the desire to draw or paint fades too. Seymour B. Sarason has attributed this phenomenon to two damaging misconceptions in contemporary society in general, and in the educational and psychological establishments in particular: (1) all children have artistic abilities, and (2) artistic activity is not a special feature of special people (although not all people can become great artists). He sees this problem as "the challenge of art to psychology."

Further reinforcement of the idea that humans have evolved an ability to draw comes from the study of children with autistic disorder. A number of cases of extraordinary drawing ability have been documented among these children. One such case was Nadia, who was studied by Lorna Selfe. At age 3½ Nadia began drawing horses, roosters, and human figures, which were more complex versions of illustrations she had seen in picture books.

Making before Matching

At first children do not use drawings to represent or depict reality. As they mature, they create increasingly complex patterns, which eventually suggest to them the likeness of a face. Then, by degrees, they discover how to modify what they have drawn to look more like a face. Little by little they discover how to add arms and legs to the face. This process characterizes not only the development of children's drawings; it is true of the development of all depictions. Sir Ernst Gombrich (1972), in what may be the greatest treatise on psychology of art, *Art and Illusion*, coined two slogans to describe the development of depiction: (1) *making before matching*, and (2) *schema plus correction*. Artists do not just copy reality, any more than children do. Artists (like children) start out with a number of drawing techniques. Medieval painters did not know about drawing in perspective, but they knew about occlusion: one cannot see a distant object through a closer one. Florentine painters of the early fifteenth century knew about perspective, but did not use atmospheric perspective, the technique by which an impression of space is conveyed by correlating the blueness and the blurriness of objects with their distance. Gombrich calls the rules of

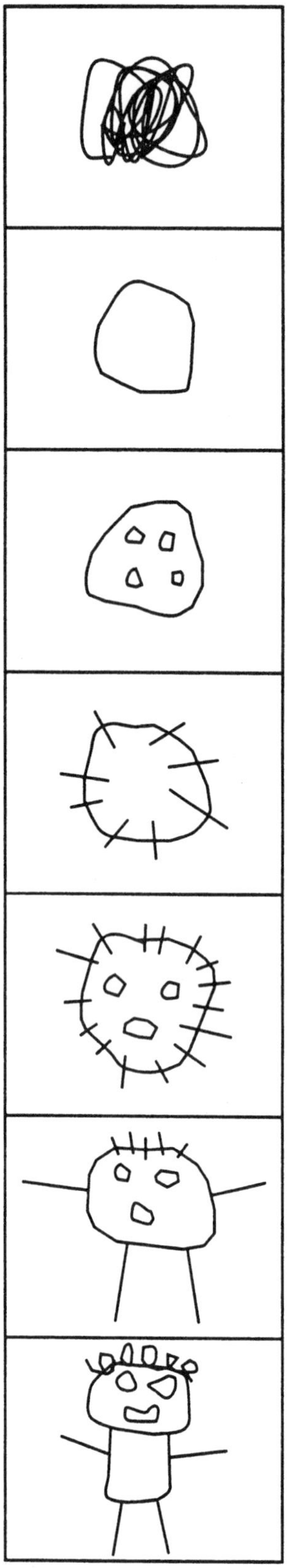

VISUAL AND DESIGN ARTS. Figure 3. Stages of development of children's drawings. (After Rhoda Kellogg.)

thumb and techniques available to the artist *schemas* (for example, "to draw a head, draw an oval; place the eyes about halfway between the top and the bottom of the oval"). Once the schema has been applied, the *making*, the *matching* phase begins. The artist tests the drawing against her perception of reality. Even if she sees that the drawing does not match the scene well, she cannot call upon what nineteenth-century art historian John Ruskin called "the innocent eye" to better depict the scene. All she can do is to look for a way to modify the schema, creating a *schema plus correction*.

The Difficulty of Experimental Aesthetics

We have seen tantalizing evidence that both the appreciation of visual art and its production are deeply embedded in human nature. Unfortunately, empirical research on this topic is difficult, and therefore there is little reason to expect rapid progress in this area. In fact, empirical research on any aspect of aesthetics is fraught with methodological difficulties that have prevented this field from maturing as rapidly as other areas of psychology.

The greatest weakness of psychological aesthetics (which Fechner called *aesthetics from below*) is that it inevitably starts from general phenomena that are in themselves of secondary aesthetic interest, such as the golden section. Psychological aesthetics is not well suited to the more captivating study of particular works of art because particular works of art are inextricably bound to a culture. The allusions of a painting may be understood only by a minority of the population; for example, those who know Greek mythology or Christian hagiography. Could responses to eleventh-century calligraphy from northern China be studied with typical Western experimental participants—college students, few of whom are conversant with this form of art? So perhaps one should recruit experts on this visual art as experimental participants. But this strategy would give rise to new problems. Although the experts would have the requisite cultural background to appreciate the calligraphy, they might know too much: They may have studied the artistry of Ts'ai Hsiang or Huang T'ing-chien. Their responses to the work might then reflect art historical theories about the painting and would therefore be of little value to the psychologist.

[*See also* Arts Therapy; Creativity; Environmental Design Research; *and* Environmental Psychology.]

Bibliography

Arnheim, R. (1974). *Art and visual perception: The psychology of the creative eye* (Rev. ed.). Berkeley: University of California Press.

Berlyne, D. E. (1971). *Aesthetics and psychobiology.* New York: Appleton-Century-Crofts.

Gombrich, E. H. (1972). *Art and illusion: A study in the psychology of pictorial representation.* Princeton, NJ: Princeton University Press.

Kahneman, D., & Miller, D. T. (1986). Norm theory: Comparing reality to its alternatives. *Psychological Review, 93*, 136–153.

Kellogg, R. (1969). *Analyzing children's art.* Palo Alto, CA: Mayfield.

Kennedy, J. M. (1993). *Drawing and the blind: Pictures to touch.* New Haven, CT: Yale University Press.

Kubovy, M. (1986). *The psychology of perspective and renaissance art.* New York: Cambridge University Press.

Sarason, S. B. (1990). *The challenge of art to psychology.* New Haven, CT: Yale University Press.

Selfe, L. (1983). *Normal and anomalous representational drawing ability in children.* London, UK: Academic Press.

Washburn, D. K., & Crowe, D. W. (1988). *Symmetries of culture: Theory and practice of plane pattern analysis.* Seattle: University of Washington Press.

Willats, J. (1997). *Art and representation: New principles in the analysis of pictures.* Princeton, NJ: Princeton University Press.

Michael Kubovy

VISUAL DEFECTS. *See* Vision and Sight.

VISUAL ILLUSIONS. It is hard to define "illusion." Illusions are various kinds of departures from truth, but how should we define, or indeed recognize, truth? There are very different accounts of truth and reality, in science, in the arts, in religions and mysticism, and in many flavors of metaphysics. One person's illusion may be another's truth.

It is important to note that science's professed realities have changed many times throughout its history—recently from the "mechanistic" physics of the nineteenth century to the quantum physics and relativity theories of the twentieth century—as science departs ever further from common sense. Should we say that, as everyday commonsense perception differs from modern physics, *all* our experience is illusion? This is what Plato thought two and a half millennia ago; but this is not what artists and brain scientists, including psychologists, mean by "visual illusions" as found in children's books and texts of psychology.

The fact that there are illusions is strong evidence that perceptions are indirectly related to the world of objects. This was pointed out very clearly by the English philosopher John Locke (1632–1704), whose greatest work is *The Essay Concerning Human Understanding* (1690). Locke described perceptions as being, like words, related to objects but quite different from them. Perceptions and words stand for objects, generally without being at all similar to the objects they represent. Thus the word *cat* may be used (at least by convention) correctly or incorrectly, though it is not, in shape or anything else, at all like a cat. Just how far this is so for perceptions is a central question for philosophy and psychology. Experiments on illusions give it an empirical basis. The problem is to agree on what *references* should be accepted as nonillusions.

There are phenomena of illusion for all the senses, including touch, which seems so simple and direct. As vision is our richest sense, and is the most studied (and easiest to illustrate in a book!), we will concentrate here on visual illusions. The well-known examples are discrepancies from measurements of lengths and curvatures of lines. Many illusions are, however, impossible to measure as simple mismatches from a reference "reality." For some illusions are fictions, but others paradoxes, which do not exist in the physical world though we see them.

There are four principal kinds of visual illusions. They may be named *ambiguities, distortions, paradoxes,* and *fictions.* It may be no accident that these correspond to errors of language—for language may have developed from ancient, indeed prehuman, perceptual classification of the world of objects and actions. Let's look at each kind in turn.

Ambiguities

Any retinal image is infinitely ambiguous. For it could correspond to or represent an infinity of possibilities of shapes and sizes and distances of objects. Thus an ellipse, in an image or a drawing, could come from or represent an elliptical object or a tilted circle—which might be small and near, or more distant and correspondingly larger to give the same image in the eyes. The possibilities are endless, yet we generally see just one of the infinite range of possibilities of what might be out there. How the visual brain selects just a few, usually only one possibility, is still not fully understood.

There are well-known illusion figures that flip between just a few possibilities. Known as "ambiguous figures" they are important for showing the dynamics of perception, searching for hypotheses of what might be out there in the external world. The brain's best guess, or selected hypothesis, is psychologically projected into the external world of objects—which are never experienced directly. The perception is never certain, and probably always has some errors. There are flipping ambiguities between shapes, between depths, and even between different kinds of objects. The best known illusion of ambiguity is the Necker cube (Figure 1). The young/old women illusion (Figure 2) illustrates change of object.

Ambiguities are particularly useful for perceptual research, as perception changes, though the input to the

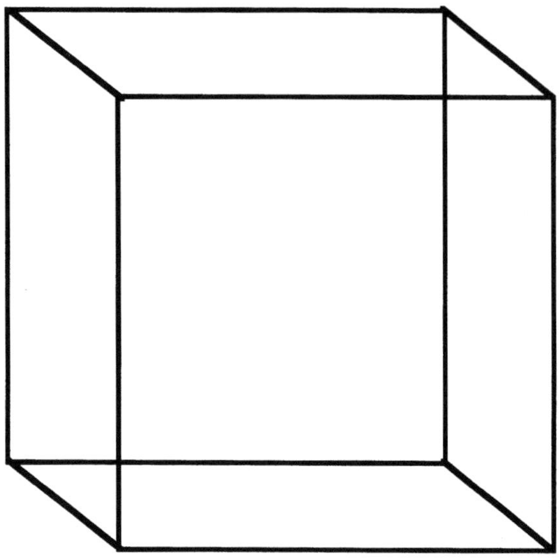

VISUAL ILLUSIONS. Figure 1. Necker cube.

eyes remains unchanged. So we can see what is going on inside our visual brain, to separate effects of "bottom-up" signals from the eyes from "top-down" knowledge and assumptions for reading sensory signals in terms of possible objects. This is an important distinction. Top-down knowledge is essential for giving images the richness of perceptions of objects (e.g., hard and heavy) though images are merely insubstantial ghosts. Yet it is nonsensed properties of objects that are vital for behavior.

It may be said that light physically enters the eyes, but visual perceptions are psychological projections from the brain, into an external world that is never directly known. It is projection of object knowledge as hypotheses of what is out there that gives objects and pictures significance.

A dramatic demonstration that knowledge and probabilities are important is the *hollow face*, or inside of a mask (Figure 3). From a viewing distance of a meter or so, the hollow inside will appear as a normal face with nose sticking out. When slowly rotated, it goes through the most astonishing transformations. As the hollow inside appears, the direction of rotation reverses (as motion parallax is wrongly attributed to near and far) so the two perceptions kind of slide into each other, like the changing faces of Jekyll and Hyde.

Distortions

It is well known that size and shape may be distorted, even in the lines of simple illusion figures. Many were discovered by physicists and astronomers in the nineteenth century when designing hairlines for the eye pieces of optical instruments—to make their measurements more accurate! Figure 4 shows six well-known distortion illusions. Among the best known and easiest to measure is the Müller-Lyer illusion (Figure 4a). The outgoing looks longer than the ingoing arrow, though both are the same length, as may be checked with a ruler (though the ruler may become distorted!). As for all illusions, for explanation it is important to distinguish between errors of "hardware" (physiology) and "software" (cognition). The illusions in Figure 4 are all cognitive errors, associated with seeing depth in flat pictures. For the Müller-Lyer illusion, the outgoing fins would typically represent the *inside* corner, say of a room; the ingoing fins would represent an *outside* corner, say of a building. The Ponzo illusion, Figure 4b, is a typical perspective of receding parallel lines, such as a road. In all these cases, features represented as *further* are seen as *larger*. Evidently this compensates for the usual shrinking of retinal images with increasing distance. As the pictures are flat, this normally useful compensation produces an opposite distortion.

Although these figures are typical flat projections of three dimensions, each could represent something quite different. The arrow figures might represent a steeplejack's view of a roof; the converging lines (as physically in the picture) rather than parallel lines shrinking with distance. These illusion figures are typical perspective views; but they could be drawings of something quite different.

These corners and converging lines and so on are normally useful cues to distance. A pilot uses convergence of lines from the converging image of the parallel runway (with other cues such as relative motion) for judging his landing. This depends upon assuming that the runway really is parallel. The neighboring buildings should have simple square shapes, to avoid confusion. It is just these normally useful cue-shapes that become misleading—generating distortion illusions—when they are present without their normal depths, as in illusion figures.

It is curious that the illusions figures are distorted, though they appear flat. This is because the depth-cues, such as perspective shapes, set the compensation known as *size constancy scaling*, which for normal three-dimensional objects compensates for shrinking of their retinal images with increasing distance (i.e., bottom-up scaling).

A different and much simpler kind of bottom-up distortion (Figure 5) is the café wall illusion (discovered on the tiles of a nineteenth-century café, in Bristol, hence its name.) The long illusory wedges occur with no perspective or other depth features, being caused by the brightness contrast across the narrow gaps of the mortar lines, pulling the edges together for half of each "tile"—so forming small wedges—which integrate to

VISUAL ILLUSIONS. Figure 2. Young/old woman.

VISUAL ILLUSIONS. Figure 3. Hollow face (the left face is a hollow mold of the right face, but does not look hollow).

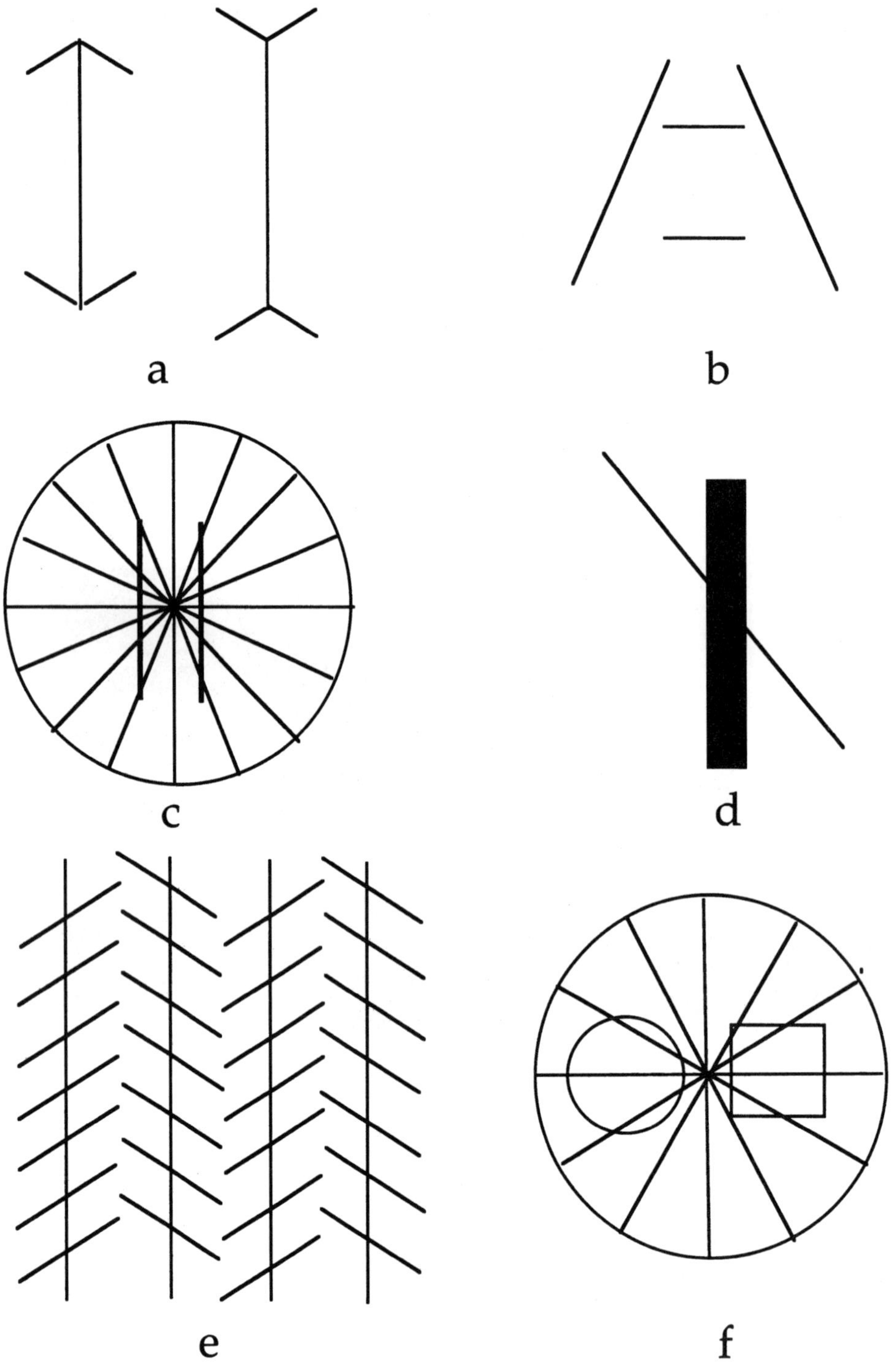

VISUAL ILLUSIONS. Figure 4. Distortion illusions. (a) Muller-Lyer; (b) Ponzo; (c) Hering; (d) Poggendorff; (e) Zollner; (f) Orbison (2 combined).

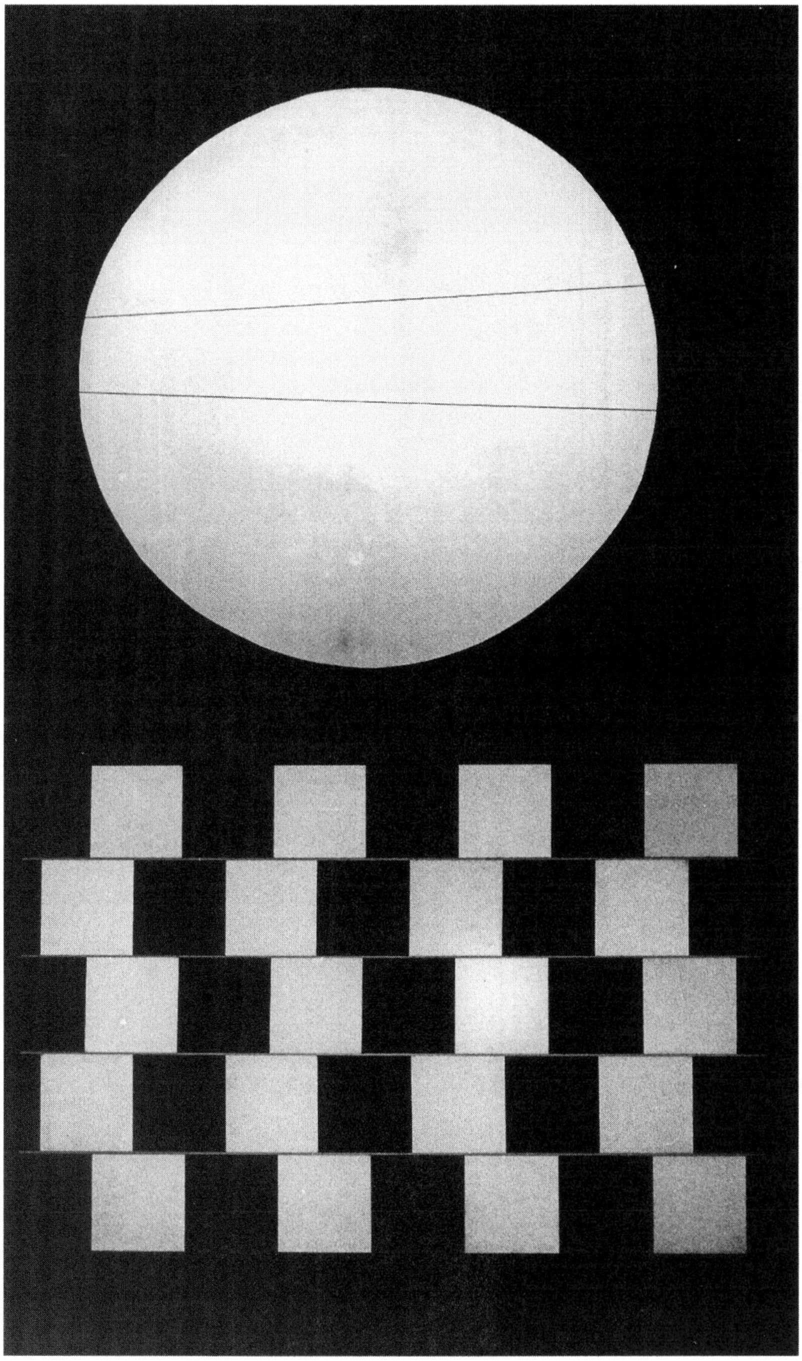

VISUAL ILLUSIONS. Figure 5. Café wall (showing how the wedge distortion can be measured with comparison lines).

give the long wedges across the figure. So two processes are involved, both very different from the cognitive distortions from perspective depth cues of Figure 4.

Paradoxes

Many perceptions are unlikely; but some are impossible. This needs an explanation because likely alternatives of ambiguous figures are generally favored by being probable. The explanation is that perceptions are *hypotheses*, which can be generated by *rules*. Hypotheses of science can be extremely unlikely in the same way, as when based on incorrect assumptions. Then rules for generating hypotheses of science or perceptions can be highly unlikely or logically impossible—paradoxes. The visual paradox the impossible triangle (designed by the English geneticist Lionel Penrose and his nephew the cosmologist Roger Penrose in 1958) can be a three-dimensional object made of wood. This appears paradoxical when seen from certain positions when features at different distances touch in the image—to be

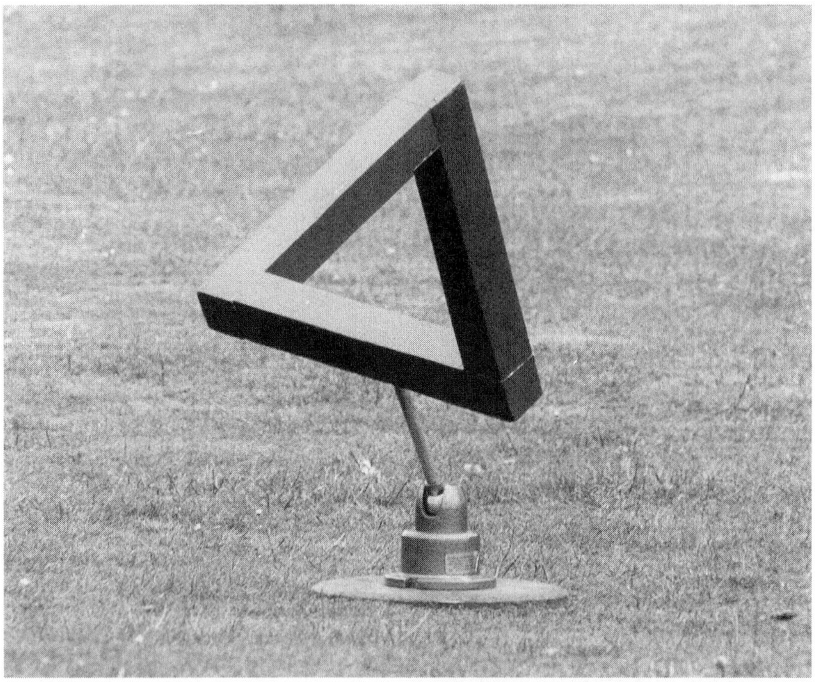

VISUAL ILLUSIONS. Figure 6a. Impossible object (appears impossible).

VISUAL ILLUSIONS. Figure 6b. Impossible object (the same as 6a, from a different point of view, now looks possible).

wrongly assumed to be the same distance (Figure 6). This illustrates how following rules from false assumptions can generate paradoxes, both for *conceptual* and *perceptual* hypotheses.

Fictions

Vision can take off from "reality" to create fictions, The most famous "fiction" illusion is the ghostly triangle, of the Italian artist and psychologist Gaetano Kanizsa (Figure 7). This process is generally useful, for parts of objects are often hidden. Also, small blind regions of the eye—including the blind spots where the optic nerves leave the retina—are normally invisible, as the brain fills in what "ought" to be there, by copying the surrounding pattern. Much of what we see every day is fiction, though not necessarily false.

Classifying Illusions

Classifying phenomena is important in science: surely illusions are no exception. They may be classified by

VISUAL ILLUSIONS. Figure 7. Kanizsa "fictional" triangle.

appearances and by *causes*. We attribute causes according to how we approach the nature of perception and its relation to the object world. Here we have assumed a particular approach—that perceptions are indirect, made much richer than the eyes' images by employing knowledge, which may be wrong or inappropriate to the situation. A different theory might demand a different kind of classification.

Some "optical" illusions are caused by physical effects between objects and the eyes. Others by physiological disturbances of neural signals. Others by the visual brain misreading, or wrongly interpreting, sensory signals. These cognitive illusions may be because inappropriate *general rules* (such as perspective and the Gestalt laws of perceptual organization) are misleading (Figure 4), or because of inappropriate *object knowledge*. Knowledge that faces are convex makes the highly unusual hollow face almost impossible to see correctly (Figure 3).

Most of these illusions are classified in Table 1. Others include retinal rivalry—different pictures in each eye producing dynamic changes and confusion when the brain is unable to combine them into a sensible perception. The Pulfrich pendulum is worth trying: Swing a mug on a string, across the line of sight, and look at it with a dark glass (from sunglasses) over one eye with both open. The mug seems to move in an ellipse, in and out. The size-weight effect is also worth trying: Fill a large and a small can with, for example, sugar, so that both are the same scale weight. The smaller will feel heavier. The aftereffect of motion is apparent movement after looking steadily at a rotating spiral: It seems to expand (or contract) yet not change its size, as the visual movement channel is adapted but not the position channel. Magritte's painting of a man in a mirror shows the back of his head in the mirror though he is looking into it—so it is paradoxical, once one recognizes it as a mirror. It is our knowledge of mirror images that produces this paradox.

Bibliography

Gregory, R. L. (1968). Perceptual illusions and brain models. *Proceedings of the Royal Society, B171*, 179–296.

Gregory, R. L (1997). *Mirrors in mind.* New York: W. H. Freeman.

Gregory R. L. (1998). *Eye and brain* (5th ed.). Oxford: Oxford University Press.

VISUAL ILLUSIONS. Table 1. Tentative illusions, classified by kinds and causes

	CAUSES			
KINDS	Optics	Signals	Rules	Knowledge
Ambiguity	Cataract Mist	Red+green or monochromatic yellow lights (look the same)	Figure-ground (Gestalt Laws)	Vase-faces Hollow face (looks normal)
Distortion	Astigmatism Mirages	Café Wall Pulfrich pendulum	Ponzo Müller-Lyer Poggendorff	Size-weight (smaller object feels heavier)
Paradox	Looking-glass (one is doubled)	Rotating spiral (expands, but no size change)	Impossible triangle Devil's fork	Magritte mirror (back of head instead of face in mirror)
Fiction	Rainbows Moiré patterns	After images Mach bands	Kanizsa Triangle Filling scotomas	Faces-in-the-fire Ink blots

Gregory, R. L., & Heard, P. (1979). Border locking and the café wall illusion. *Perception 8*, 365–380.
Ittleson, W. H. (1952). *The Ames demonstrations in perception*. Princeton, NJ: Princeton University Press.
Kanizsa, G. (1979). *Essays on Gestalt perception*. New York: Praeger.
Penrose, L. S., & Penrose, R. (1958). Impossible objects: A special type of visual illusion. *British Journal of Psychology, 49*, 31–33.
Ramachandran, V. S., & Gregory, R. L. (1991). Perceptual filling-in of artificially induced scotomas in human vision. *Nature, 350* (6320), 699–702.
Robinson, J. O. (1972). *The psychology of visual illusions*. London: Hutchinson.
Rock, I. (1984). *Perception*. New York: Scientific American Library.

Richard L. Gregory

VISUAL IMPAIRMENT. [*This entry comprises two articles:* Physical Causes *and* Psychological Implications. *The first article covers the causes of blindness and visual impairment. The second article describes the conditions, psychological and behavioral factors, prevalence, and incidence of visual impairment.*]

Physical Causes

Visual impairment is a term that has taken on many meanings over the years. Some of these diverse meanings can be understood by looking at two landmark studies that estimated the prevalence of visual impairment in the United States. The first was the National Center for Health Statistics' Health Interview Survey, initiated in 1977 (Kirchner & Peterson, 1985). A nationwide random sample of over 100,000 adults were interviewed at home regarding a variety of health issues. Respondents were considered to have "severe vision impairment" if they reported that they could not read newsprint, and "other vision impairment" if they reported difficulty seeing with one or both eyes even when wearing glasses. The results of this survey indicated that about 1.5 million American adults had severe vision impairment and 10 million had other vision impairment. Another study, the Baltimore Eye Survey (BES), interviewed 5,300 adults in defined geographical regions of the city (Tielsch, Sommer, Witt, Katz, & Royall, 1990). Visual impairment was determined during an ophthalmologic screening exam and was defined as a visual acuity worse than 20/40 in the better-seeing eye. National projections of the BES data indicated that approximately 3 million Americans were visually impaired.

The Health Interview Survey prevalence estimates were based on the respondent's perceived difficulty with everyday tasks. The Baltimore Eye Survey's definition of visual impairment was based on a psychophysical measure of visual function (visual acuity). There is growing consensus that *impairment* be reserved for loss or abnormality of organ function, while a restriction or an inability to perform a task is referred to as a disability. But even where there is agreement regarding the definition of terms, there remains disagreement concerning the level of abnormality that constitutes impairment. In the United States, a 20/40 cutoff is most often used. This is the level at which most states impose restrictions on driver's licenses. The World Health Organization has proposed a detailed classification system for vision loss that imposes a 20/60 cutoff for visual impairment. This definition is derived from data showing that it becomes difficult to read ordinary newsprint when acuity falls below 20/60. Curiously, both definitions of impairment are tied to related disabilities (inability to drive or read newsprint), showing how closely these two concepts are intertwined.

Epidemiologic data indicate that the prevalence of visual impairment is similar for men and women, however, there are dramatic differences by age and race. By U.S. standards, visual impairment occurs in fewer than 1% of individuals under the age of 60, but rapidly increases to more than 10% by age 80 (Tielsch, Sommer, Witt, Katz, & Royall, 1990). Moreover, visual impairment is twice as common in African Americans as in Whites (Rubin et al., 1997; Tielsch, Sommer, Witt, Katz, & Royall, 1990).

The causes of visual impairment can be divided into optical, retinal, and neural disorders.

Optical Disorders as Causes of Visual Impairment

Optical disorders include refractive errors, cataracts, and corneal opacification. The refractive state of the eye changes throughout the life span. During infancy, the eye is often hyperopic (farsighted), unable to bring near objects into sharp focus. As the eye grows and develops it tends to lose this hyperopia through a process known as emmetropization. However, if this process does not work correctly the eye may progress to myopia (nearsightedness), making it unable to sharply focus distant objects. Myopia typically develops in the teen years and is thought to be influenced by a combination of genetic and environmental factors. An environmental factor of particular interest is the influence of near work, such as reading. According to one theory, accommodation, or focusing the lens for near objects, causes the eye to grow slightly longer from front to back. A longer eye will naturally be more myopic, since light from distant objects will come to a focus in front of the retinal surface.

As the lens matures, its ability to focus on near objects markedly diminishes. This loss of accommodation, or presbyopia, is an unwelcome harbinger of middle age, especially for those who have not had to depend on glasses throughout their youth. The cause of presbyopia has been debated for most of the century, with various theorists attributing the loss of accommodation to changes in the elastic properties of the lens, changes in the action of the ciliary muscle, which is responsible for accommodation, or both. But whatever its cause, there is an inevitable reduction in the amplitude of accommodation such that an emmetropic child can focus on objects as close as 10 cm while an older adult must move objects at least a meter or more away to see them in clear focus.

Eyeglasses and contacts are such simple and effective treatments that discussions of visual impairment often exclude refractive error. However, it is estimated that as much as one third of all visual impairment in the U.S. adult population is caused by uncorrected refractive error (Rubin et al., 1997; Tielsch, Sommer, Witt, Katz, & Royall, 1990).

As the lens ages its transparency also changes. Short wavelength light is much more highly attenuated with age than long wavelength light, causing the aged lens to appear yellow. There is also a marked increase in light scatter, causing the lens to appear opalescent. Light scattered from the lens toward the retina casts a veil over the retinal image, thereby reducing its contrast and hence its visibility.

The lenticular changes described thus far are considered representative of the normal aging process. When these changes become severe enough they are considered pathological and earn the designation of cataract. Aside from refractive error, cataracts are the most common cause of visual impairment. It is estimated that over 1 million cataract surgeries are performed in the United States every year, making it the most frequent surgical procedure. The lens consists of a central nucleus surrounded by layers of cortex and enclosed by an elastic capsule. Cataracts are typically classified according to location as nuclear, cortical (anterior), or subcapsular (posterior). In nuclear cataracts there is an accelerated yellowing of the lens and an increase in diffuse scatter throughout the nucleus. Cortical cataracts tend to be more localized, with areas of turbidity sequestered in annular rings or wedges of the lens cortex. Posterior subcapsular cataracts are the most highly localized and typically appear as a small opaque region near the center of the posterior pole of the lens. Given these differences in morphology among cataract types, one might expect there to be differences in the transmission and scattering properties. While clinicians report that posterior subcapsular cataracts (PSCs) are more visually disabling than nuclear or cortical cataracts, there is no evidence for differences in optical properties of PSCs compared to other cataract types. For example, PSCs and nuclear and cortical cataracts show similar light-scattering behavior (van den Berg, 1995).

The last category of visual impairments of the optical pathway are those related to loss of corneal transparency. While far less common in the United States than refractive error or cataracts, corneal disorders are a major cause of severe vision loss in developing nations. Onchocerciasis, or river blindness, affects more than 20 million people in Africa and South and Central America. Trachoma is even more widespread and is often described as the leading cause of world blindness. Both diseases cause opacification of the cornea.

Disorders of the optical pathway can cause the image to be blurred, distorted, desaturated, or reduced in contrast. These changes are reflected as deficits in visual acuity, contrast sensitivity, and increased sensitivity to glare.

Visual acuity loss, regardless of its cause, has a dramatic effect on everyday tasks that require good resolution, such as reading fine print. As would be expected, acuity loss increases the letter size required for reading and generally reduces reading speed even for text of optimal letter size. However, the maximal achievable reading speed tends to be higher when the decline in acuity is caused by optical factors, such as cataracts, as compared to retinal disorders, discussed later (Legge, Rubin, Pelli, & Schleske, 1985).

No aspect of spatial vision has received as much attention as contrast sensitivity. Unlike acuity, which measures the limits of resolution of fine detail, contrast sensitivity is a measure of the eye's ability to detect subtle differences between light and dark objects of a fixed size. Individuals with normal contrast sensitivity can tolerate substantial reductions in the contrast of printed text with little effect on reading speed. But people with reduced contrast sensitivity require high contrast text in order to read well, and may be severely handicapped by low contrast text, such as colored letters on colored papers (Rubin & Legge, 1989).

Photographic simulations of the world as seen though a cataract suggest that the loss of contrast sensitivity makes the world appear hazy or washed out (Hess & Woo, 1978). This loss of contrast sensitivity makes it difficult to navigate safely and efficiently through unfamiliar environments (Marron & Bailey, 1982), reduces postural stability, and increases falls and fear of falling (Turano, Dagnelie, & Herdman, 1996)

Glare can refer to a variety of phenomena, including discomfort glare, the sensation one experiences when overall illumination is too bright, and glare recovery, the speed with which the visual system regains function following exposure to a bright light. Optical disorders usually do not increase discomfort glare or glare recovery. However, they often lead to disability glare, which is the reduced visibility of a target due to the presence of a light source elsewhere in the visual field.

A common example is the reduced visibility of road signs in the presence of oncoming headlights. Disability glare occurs when light from the glare source is scattered by the ocular media. This scattered light forms a veiling luminance that reduces the contrast and thus the visibility of the target. Increased sensitivity to glare is a common complaint among older individuals, especially those with cataracts.

Retinal Disorders as Causes of Visual Impairment

The two leading retinal causes of visual impairment are diabetic retinopathy and macular degeneration. Diabetic retinopathy is an eye disease affecting diabetics in which the blood vessels inside the retina may proliferate and break through the retinal surface. These vessels are fragile and tend to leak blood into the gelatinous vitreous in front of the retina. Prior to the proliferative stage just described, there is often a buildup of fluid that elevates and distorts the retinal surface. The disease is treated by applying a grid or ring of small laser burns to the retina. This slows the proliferation of new blood vessels and reduces the buildup of fluid. Leaky blood vessels can also be sealed with laser photocoagulation.

Macular degeneration comes in two forms. In the more common "dry" (atrophic) form, there is a gradual atrophy of the retinal cells that transduce the light stimulus. The atrophy often follows a characteristic pattern, beginning as a horseshoe that surrounds the macula. The horseshoe gradually coalesces into a ring, and then spreads both in toward the fovea and out toward the periphery. The less common "wet" (exudative) form is characterized by the growth of new blood vessels from behind the retina that break through into the retinal tissues. These vessels also leak blood and eventually scar over. In both types of macular degeneration there is a complete loss of visual sensitivity (scotoma) in the affected area. Macular degeneration is the leading cause of severe vision loss in older adults (where it is referred to as age-related macular degeneration or AMD), but related diseases with similar consequences can also affect children and young adults. Exudative AMD can be treated with laser photocoagulation, which limits the spread of new vessels. However, the treatment itself creates a scotoma wherever it is applied. At present there is no treatment for atrophic AMD or the juvenile forms of the disease.

Diabetic retinopathy and macular degeneration are most disabling when their effects encroach upon the foveal region in the very center of the retina. The fovea is the area of greatest spatial resolution and highest contrast sensitivity. Loss of foveal vision causes acuity and contrast sensitivity to decline, however, foveal scotomas disrupt many visual tasks to an extent that far outweighs the loss of resolution and contrast. For example, individuals with macular degeneration seldom read faster than about 50 words per minute, while those with equivalent acuity loss caused by optical disorders may reach 150 words per minute or more with adequate magnification (Legge, Rubin, Relli, & Schleske, 1985). One explanation for the disproportionate effect of foveal scotomas is that saccadic and smooth pursuit eye movements are driven by visual processes at the fovea. Loss of foveal vision disrupts eye movement patterns, and this results in the inefficient processing of visual information (Rubin & Turano, 1994). A second possibility is that peripheral vision may be less well suited for processing text and other images because of its relative insensitivity to spatial position information and increased sensitivity to lateral masking (crowding) and metacontrast masking (Bouma, 1970).

There are many other retinal diseases that cause visual impairment, however, they are relatively uncommon and space does not permit a comprehensive discussion. One disorder worth noting is retinitis pigmentosa, which is a disease of the retinal pigment epithelium that lies at the back of the retina. The disease is characterized by atrophy of the photoreceptors, usually beginning with the rods, resulting in night blindness and peripheral field loss. With progression of the disease, the cone photoreceptors become more involved and the field loss migrates toward the fovea. Early in the disease it is not uncommon to find individuals with good visual acuity and contrast sensitivity, but severely restricted fields, or "tunnel vision." In such cases, the afflicted individual may be able to read and recognize objects without difficulty, but navigating independently in unfamiliar places becomes especially challenging.

Neural Disorders as Causes of Visual Impairment

The distinction between retinal and neural disorders is somewhat arbitrary, since the retina is composed of multiple layers of neurones. The conventional boundary is drawn at the level of the retinal ganglion cell from which neural impulses are carried to the brain via the optic nerve. The most common neural cause of visual impairment is glaucoma, which is estimated to affect 3 million Americans, of whom 120,000 are severely visually impaired. Moreover, glaucoma is the leading cause of visual impairment in African Americans. Glaucoma is an insidious disease that destroys the optic nerve fibers and may go undetected for many years. If left untreated, glaucoma will cause peripheral field loss that progresses slowly toward the fovea, culminating in blindness. The treatment for glaucoma is to lower the pressure inside the eye, although the mechanism by which elevated eye pressure destroys the optic nerve is not well understood.

Although glaucoma is classically described as causing a peripheral field impairment, recent evidence suggests that central vision is also affected early in the disease. However, this is not apparent when measuring static visual function, such as acuity or contrast sensitivity. Instead, there are deficits in the processing of dynamic stimuli, such as flickering patterns or moving objects. For example, people with glaucoma are unable to detect the coherent motion of random dot patterns unless the patterns move further or faster than the normal threshold (Bullimore, Wood, & Swenson, 1993). These dynamic vision deficits are believed to contribute to the difficulties with orientation, mobility, and navigation that accompany glaucoma (Geruschat, Turano, & Stahl, 1998).

Optic neuritis is an inflammation of the optic nerve that most often affects middle-aged adults. Although the condition may be transient without permanent loss of function, it can also be a precursor of multiple sclerosis, in which case the optic nerve becomes demyelinated. In its acute phase, optic neuritis causes visual field loss, color vision deficits, and reduced acuity and contrast sensitivity. If demyelination occurs, there is a slowing of neural transduction that reduces the person's ability to resolve rapidly flickering stimuli. Patients with multiple sclerosis often have visual symptoms that are hard to describe because they do not involve acuity-type problems, which are most common in other types of visual impairment.

The final class of neural disorders to be discussed are those resulting from brain injury. This includes trauma and stroke. It is well-known that people recovering from brain injury often experience symptoms of visual dysfunction. A common deficit is visual field loss, but this may be accompanied by abnormalities of dynamic visual processing, oculomotor dysfunction, and higher-order visual processing deficits. The complex set of vision abnormalities associated with stroke are referred to as posttrauma vision syndrome, or PTVS (Padula & Argyris, 1996). The prevalence of PTVS is not well documented, but one study estimated that about one half of stroke patients exhibit visual processing deficits (Gianutsos, Ramsey, & Perlin, 1988). While it has been shown that stroke reduces walking ability and increases the risk of falls, it is difficult to separate the contribution of visual impairment from other impairments that accompany stroke. There is good reason to expect there to be a link between vision loss and mobility problems, given that other studies have shown similar types of vision loss to increase the risk of falls in the elderly and severely limit the mobility of persons with visual field loss due to eye disease (Geruschat, Turano, & Stahl, 1998). Moreover, clinical observations suggest that PTVS may be associated with unilateral spatial inattention (neglect), a lack of spatial orientation and attention for one half of interpersonal space. The individual may collide with obstacles or miss doorways on the unattended side, and when walking or driving a wheelchair veer toward the attended space rather than navigate in a straight line. Following a stroke, individuals who do not exhibit symptoms of spatial inattention may still show abnormalities of ambient visual processing (Padula & Argyris, 1996). The ambient process is used for spatial localization and provides general information used for balance, movement, and posture.

Visual impairment is seldom life-threatening. Nevertheless, compared to other chronic medical conditions, visual impairment is among the most disabling; more disabling than arthritis, pulmonary disease, or hearing impairment in young adults, and more disabling than all conditions except diabetes and cancer in the oldest adults (Verbrugge & Patrick, 1995). The limitations in employment, education, and recreation imposed by vision loss are disproportionate to health-care expenditures for vision impairment research and rehabilitation.

Bibliography

Bouma, H. (1970). Interaction effects in parafoveal letter recognition. *Nature, 226*, 177–178.

Bullimore, M. A., Wood, J. M., & Swenson, K. (1993). Motion perception in glaucoma. *Investigative Ophthalmology and Visual Science, 34(13)*, 3526–3533.

Geruschat, D., Turano, K., & Stahl, J. (1998). Traditional measures of mobility performance and retinitis pigmentosa. *Optometry and Vision Science, 75*, 525–537.

Gianutsos, R., Ramsey, G., & Perlin, R. R. (1988). Rehabilitative optometric services for survivors of acquired brain injury. *Archives of Physical Medicine and Rehabilitation, 69*, 573–578.

Hess, R., & Woo, G. (1978). Vision through cataracts. *Vision Research, 17*, 428–435.

Kirchner, C., & Peterson, R. (1985). *The latest data on visual disability from NCHS.* New York: American Foundation for the Blind.

Legge, G. E., Rubin, G. S., Pelli, D. G., & Schleske, M. M. (1985). Psychophysics of reading. 2. Low vision. *Vision Research, 25*, 253–266.

Marron, J. A., & Bailey, I. L. (1982). Visual factors and orientation-mobility performance. *American Journal of Optometry and Physiological Optics, 59*, 413–426.

Padula, W. V., & Argyris, S. (1996). Posttrauma vision syndrome and visual midline shift syndrome. *Neuro Rehabilitation, 6*, 165–171.

Rubin, G. S., & Legge, G. E. (1989). Psychophysics of reading: The role of contrast in low vision. *Vision Research, 29*, 79–91.

Rubin, G. S., & Turano, K. (1994). Low vision reading with sequential word presentation. *Vision Research, 34*, 1723–1733.

Rubin, G., West, S., Muñoz, B., Bandeen-Roche, K., Zeger, S., Fried, L., & SEE Project Team. (1997). A comprehensive assessment of visual impairment in an older American population: SEE study. *Investigative Ophthalmology and Visual Science, 38*, 557–568.

Tielsch, J. M., Sommer, A., Witt, K., Katz, J., & Royall, R. M. (1990). Blindness and visual impairment in an American urban population. The Baltimore Eye Survey. *Archives of Ophthalmology, 108*, 286–290.

Turano, K. A., Dagnelie, G., & Herdman, S. J. (1996). Visual stabilization of posture in persons with central visual field loss. *Investigative Ophthalmology and Visual Science, 37*, 1483–1491.

van den Berg, T. J. T. P. (1995). Analysis of intraocular straylight, especially in relation to age. *Optometry and Vision Science, 72*, 52–59.

Verbrugge, L. M., & Patrick, D. L. (1995). Seven chronic conditions: Their impact on U.S. adults' activity levels and use of medical services. *American Journal of Public Health, 85*, 173–182.

Gary S. Rubin

Psychological Implications

Normal vision is basic for human action. Among the most important functions that normally rely on visual capacity are orientation in space as well as the recognition and coordination of behavioral options to be executed in an environment. Reading is also among the most prominent capabilities that depend on visual capacity. Although there are genuine functions of the visual system within the human perceptual architecture, it should also be noted that one crucial aspect of this architecture is the intermodality of the different sense systems in everyday life, particularly the integration of vision and hearing.

Vision can be regarded as a typical environment-related capability in all organisms, that is, vision is essential for the transaction between the person and her or his environment, especially the physical environment. In contrast, hearing is more concerned with communication, that is, the social environment. From a historical perspective, the connotations of losing the capacity for vision are both positive (e.g., a prerequisite for the gift of prophecy given to Teresias) as well as negative (e.g., a punishment for sin in the medieval age). Survey data indicate that the loss of vision is experienced as one of the most fear-provoking conditions within a range of given illnesses and disabilities; it is ranked fourth behind AIDS, cancer, and Alzheimer's disease (Horowitz & Silverstone, 1991).

The rich literature focusing on the question of what it means to suffer from blindness and severe visual loss supports the assumption that this chronic condition is a real threat and existential challenge for those affected (e.g., Ainlay, 1988). Available clinical evidence points to severe emotional and behavioral consequences, such as feelings of incompetence, helplessness, anxiety, and depression, as well as the undermining of action routines in the activities of daily living, professional life, and leisure time. However, this one-sided picture must be complemented by other evidence underscoring the individual's capacity to cope effectively, for instance, in the case of jazz and pop musicians Ray Charles, Lennie Tristano, or Stevie Wonder. Obviously, a highly differential view is needed in which the negative impact of visual impairment has to be juxtaposed against a variety of coping and compensation efforts.

Terminological Issues and Epidemiology

Terms that are most often, and sometimes interchangeably, used in the literature as well as in the practical field are *visual impairment, blindness, legal blindness*, and *low vision* (Orr, 1992). The term *legal blindness* denotes individuals eligible for government and agency benefits and services. Legal blindness is defined as a visual acuity of 20/200 or less in the better eye with the best correction, or a visual field of no more than 20 degrees. ("Normal" visual acuity is defined as 20/20, that is, a person with a visual acuity of 20/200 must be 20 feet away to see what a person with normal sight sees at 200 feet; the "normal" visual field is 175 to 180 degrees.) Visual impairment not meeting these criteria can nevertheless interfere with independent functioning and the activities of daily living. This has been underscored by terms such as *low vision* or being *severely visually impaired*. One feature of low vision is that it cannot be corrected by normal eyeglasses or contact lenses. Frequently, a visual acuity of 20/70 or less is used as a criterion for low vision; also, difficulty or disability in reading newspaper print using the best possible correction has been applied in survey and epidemiology research as a more functional definition of low vision.

It should also be noted that about 70% of those affected by visual impairment are beyond the age of 60 years, and about 90% of these have experienced their loss only late in their lives. The positive age correlation persists into old age: While 14% of those 65 and older suffer from visual impairment, the percentage grows to about 28% in those aged 85 years and over (National Center for Health Statistics, 1989). Furthermore, it is estimated that (depending on the criteria used) up to 50% of the nursing home population is visually impaired but the majority of older visually impaired persons continue to live in their communities. The general demographic situation makes visual impairment particularly burdensome for aging women. Aging minorities and elderly African Americans reveal higher-prevalence data due to higher percentages in some other chronic conditions that are associated with visual impairment (e.g., diabetes). To sum up from an epidemiological point of view, visual impairment is predominantly a challenge for older adults who experience this chronic condition late in life and frequently with an irreversible and progressive course. Because of the multimorbidity of old age, visual impairment often is accompanied by other chronic impairments and disabilities as well. Also, as a consequence of the general demographic trend, the absolute number of older visually impaired persons will steadily increase during the forthcoming decades. Demographic projections state that there will be 3,203,000 older visually impaired persons by the year 2000, which will climb to nearly 6 million in the year 2030 due to the aging of the baby boom generation (Orr, 1992).

Need for a Life Span Perspective of Visual Impairment

There is a need to employ a life-span perspective of visual impairment. A couple of reasons underlie the assumption that the experience of visual impairment in childhood and youth, or even since birth, is qualitatively different from the experience of a later life onset of the condition. With respect to childhood, visual impairment can be expected to interfere with psychomotor and cognitive development that heavily relies on the visual channel in "normal" development (Warren, 1984). Furthermore, educational processes and decisions for professional career tracks are probably influenced by the presence of visual impairment. Thus, visual impairment already existing in early stages of the life span must be seen as a rare but powerful influencing factor that will shape the further course of life-span development with respect to the professional as well as the private domain. However, the life-span perspective—in conjunction with the rehabilitation potential available for early life visual impairment and the resulting adaptational processes (e.g., special school and professional training, training in mobility, and in the performance of everyday tasks)—also leads to the insight that the critical influence of this chronic condition may become steadily weaker as life goes on.

Regarding late-life visual impairment, and thus with respect to the majority of persons affected by visual impairment, the situation is different. The elderly person is challenged by the occurrence of "old age," a situation normally associated with significant role losses (such as the professional role) and critical life events (such as the death of a loved one), as well as by visual impairment after decades of a "seeing" life. In particular, action that may compensate for some of the role losses associated with "old age," such as new or more extensive leisure activities in the domain of reading or traveling, may become more difficult or impossible due to visual impairment. Also, feelings of becoming incompetent, dependent, and unproductive, which frequently rise during old age, will probably find further reinforcement from the permanent loss of vision.

Psychological Theories and Empirical Results

Based on the life-span framework just described, visual impairment can be seen from diverse psychological approaches: theories of psychological development (psychomotor, cognitive, and social) predominantly find application on early-life visual impairment (Kalloniatis & Johnston, 1994; Warren, 1984). According to the so-called visual frame of reference hypothesis, the availability of visual experience in early stages of the life span may facilitate adaptation to vision loss (Warren, 1984). However, there is also evidence that points in the opposite direction, founded on the premise that the earlier the onset of the visual impairment, the better the chances of maximizing environmental control over the course of development. Furthermore, Jean Piaget's developmental stages seem to apply to children who are visually impaired as well, with the only difference being that they pass through the stages more slowly than their sighted peers. [*See the biography of Piaget.*] By and large, no severe deviations from normal psychological development should be expected in visually impaired children; potential deficits present at a certain period early in childhood must always be viewed from a larger perspective. For example, compensations such as the development of a haptic frame of reference as well as better use of the hearing system (both of which are systematically trained in rehabilitation) are normally very effective tools for managing a "good" life in adulthood. A very high degree of professional expertise relying on computer-based supportive technical environments can currently be achieved by visually impaired and even blind persons (Kooijman, Looijestijin, Welling, & van der Wildt, 1994).

Theories of stress and coping are especially helpful to consider the consequences of age-related visual impairment. In these theories, the onset of visual impairment is seen as a permanent stressor that warrants coping in order to minimize negative psychological consequences. According to a body of empirical evidence, there can be no doubt that age-related visual impairment is associated with negative consequences in the behavioral and emotional domain (e.g., Branch, Horowitz, & Carr, 1989; Wahl, Schilling, Oswald, & Heyl, 1999). With respect to the former, lower functioning in the activities of daily living, and especially the more difficult instrumental activities, such as cooking, shopping, or banking, were found; also, leisure activities in and particularly outside the home reveal shrinkage as well. In the emotional domain, a heightened rate of depression and lower subjective well-being are the most frequently replicated findings. Regarding the most successful coping strategies in dealing with these negative consequences, the best current research answer is that this process is a highly individual one. Problem-focused coping is not always most effective, and escape strategies may be helpful in some cases as well. Additional variables to explain interindividual differences in psychosocial adaptation are comorbidity and subjective evaluations of the vision loss, whereas the objectively measurable visual impairment reveals less stronger association.

Theories of person-environment transactions are principally important for visually impaired persons of all ages due to the general impact that vision loss has on the person-environment relation. Nevertheless, person-environment transactions may be particularly worth considering in the later years because it is generally assumed that older adults are more strongly affected by the "press" of the physical environment (Lawton & Nahemow, 1973; Wahl & Oswald, in press; Wahl, Oswald, & Zimprich, 1999). However, empirical evidence has revealed that visually impaired older adults are very creative in person- and environment-related compensation efforts to counteract their visual loss and thus should not be seen as mere "pawns" of environmental conditions. Nevertheless, the relationship to the environment can be taken as a good example to underline the importance of the time of onset in a life-span perspective; typically, older persons who suffer from severe visual impairment or blindness since their early childhoods are better adapted with respect to their inside and outside person-environment relationships, compared to the elderly suffering from visual impairment only late in life.

Rehabilitation and Intervention Issues

There are very effective rehabilitation strategies for visual impairment in all periods of the life span. Most critical is training in orientation and mobility, as well as the performance of day-to-day tasks. Both of these skills are very important in maintaining the highest possible level of independent functioning and autonomy; self-help groups also significantly contribute to the maintenance of rehabilitative success and coping with the daily challenges caused by vision loss. However, there is reason to assume that comprehensive ophthalmological rehabilitation, which includes the best visual correction aids as well as the systematic improvement of everyday competence, is broadly applied in the earlier years, yet this is still not the rule in the later years of life. Among the reasons for this are the negative image of old age, information deficits both in patients as well as their doctors, as well as the simple fact that often no rehabilitation site is readily accessible (e.g., for the elderly living in rural areas). Probably, this situation is still more unsatisfactory with respect to African American older adults and the elderly from minority populations. As a positive development in the field, one ought to mention the shift in the literature toward low vision and severe visual impairment from a mere consideration of blindness or legal blindness. The acknowledgement is an important one, because it allows a much greater number of persons, particularly older adults, increased access to rehabilitation programs. Another promising development is the recognition that rehabilitation can be very effective with older adults as well, with the clear consequence of a significant and persisting increase in independence and general quality of life (Wahl & Tesch-Römer, 1996).

[*See also* Rehabilitation Psychology.]

Bibliography

Ainlay, S. C. (1988). Aging and new vision loss: Disruptions of the here and now. *Journal of Social Issues, 44*, 79–94.

Branch, L. G., Horowitz, A., & Carr, C. (1989). The implications for everyday life of incident self-reported visual decline among people over age sixty-five living in the community. *Gerontologist, 29*, 359–365.

Horowitz, A., & Silverstone, B. (1991). *The paradox of "blindness": Implications for adaptation to aging and disability in later life.* Paper presented at the symposium entitled "The Influence of Traumatic Life Threatening Illness on Adult Development, Coping, and Well Being." Forty-fourth Annual Scientific Meeting of the Gerontological Society of America, San Francisco, California.

Kalloniatis, M., & Johnston, A. W. (1994). Visual environmental adaptation problems of partially sighted children. *Journal of Visual Impairment and Blindness, 88*, 234–243.

Kooijman, A. C., Looijestijn, P. L., Welling, J. A., & van der Wildt, G. J. (Eds.). (1994). *Low vision: Research and new developments in rehabilitation.* Amsterdam: IOS Press.

Lawton, M. P., & Nahemow, L. (1973). Ecology and the aging process. In C. Eisdorfer & M. P. Lawton (Eds.), *The psychology of adult development and aging* (pp. 619–674). Washington, DC: American Psychological Association.

National Center for Health Statistics. (1989). *The National Nursing Home Survey 1985. 1985 summary for the United States.* Vital and Health Statistics. (Series 13, No. 97. DHHS. No. PHS.) Public Health Service. Washington: U.S. Government Printing Office.

Orr, A. L. (1992). Aging and blindness: Toward a system approach to service delivery. In A. L. Orr (Ed.), *Vision and aging: Crossroads for service delivery* (pp. 3–31). New York: American Foundation for the Blind.

Wahl, H.-W., & Oswald, F. (2000). The person/environment perspective of visual impairment. In B. Silverstone, M. A. Lang, B. Rosenthal, & E. Faye (Eds.), *The Lighthouse handbook on vision impairment and vision rehabilitation.* New York: Oxford University Press.

Wahl, H.-W., & Tesch-Römer, C. (1996). Über die Technik hinaus—Psychosoziale Aspekte der Rehabilitation bei Hör—und Seheinbußen im Alter. [Beyond technique—psychological aspects of rehabilitation with hearing and vision impaired elderly]. In C. Tesch-Römer & H.-W. Wahl (Eds.), *Seh-und Höreinbußen älterer Menschen.*

Herausforderungen in Medizin, Psychologie, und Rehabilitation [Vision and hearing impairment in old age: Challenges for medicine, psychology, and rehabilitation] (pp. 203–232). Darmstadt, Germany: Steinkopff.

Wahl, H.-W., Oswald, F., & Zimprich, D. (1999). Everyday competence in visually impaired older adults: A case for person-environment perspectives. *Gerontologist, 39*, 140–149.

Wahl, H.-W., Schilling, O., Oswald, F., & Heyl, V. (1999). Psychosocial consequences of age-related visual impairment: Comparison with mobility-impaired older adults and long-term outcome. *Journal of Gerontology: Psychological Sciences, 54B*, P304–P316.

Warren, D. (1984). *Blindness and early childhood development* (2nd ed.). New York: American Foundation for the Blind.

Hans-Werner Wahl

VISUAL PERCEPTION. *See* Vision and Sight.

VISUAL SEARCH is an important visual behavior. Whenever we look for the mustard in the pantry, the exit sign on the highway, or the missile launcher in the aerial photograph, we are performing a visual search task. We may need to search for several reasons: (1) the object of desire may be outside of the visual field. (2) The object may be in the field but unrecognizable because it is too far from the center of gaze. Visual functions like visual acuity fall off rapidly away from the center of gaze. Thus, even though the word *exit* is presently in your visual field (in the second sentence of this article), you cannot read it unless you move your eyes to fixate it. Finally, (3) the object may be clearly visible but, in a field filled with other distracting objects, it may not be recognized until you direct attention to it. This third case is interesting because it suggests that we cannot fully process everything we see at one time. Ulric Neisser (1967) proposed that visual processes could be divided into two classes. Preattentive processes have the capacity to operate over the entire visual field at once. Other processes have more limited capacity and can operate on only a small portion of the visual field at one time—perhaps only on one object at a time.

This distinction is reflected in the results of visual search experiments. Figure 1 shows some common visual search experiments. In a visual search experiment, an observer is asked to search for a specific target in a display containing a number of distracting items. The total number of items (the "set size") is varied from trial to trial, and the amount of time required to make a response (the "reaction time" or "RT") is recorded. In the top row of Figure 1 are examples of displays where the target is present (a vertical line in the first panel, a black vertical line in the second, and a "2" in the third). The second row shows examples of displays containing only distractors. The measure of most interest is the slope of the function relating reaction time to set size. Idealized data are shown in the third row. Some search tasks, like the search for a vertical line among horizontals, produce slopes near 0 milliseconds per item. A flat slope of this sort suggests that all of the items could be processed in parallel—with no more effort or resource required to process 20 items than would be required for 5 items. In most cases, search tasks that produce slopes near 0 milliseconds per item involve a target defined by a unique feature. This has given rise to the idea that a limited set of basic features can be processed preattentively, in parallel across the visual field. The precise features remains open to debate, but the list includes color, motion, size, orientation, and a variety of cues to depth (e.g., binocular stereo vision). Other candidates with support in the literature include curvature, shininess, line termination, and closure (an O is a closed curve; a C is not).

The basic features in visual search have already received substantial processing beyond processing of simple luminance. Orientation serves as a good example. As noted, search for a vertical line among horizontal lines produces a slopes near 0 milliseconds per item. As Figure 2 shows, we can define those oriented lines in many different media. Part A shows lines defined by luminance, whereas part B shows lines defined by texture. One can even define oriented line by regions of different orientation (part C). Efficient search remains possible in these and other cases. Detection of stimuli like those in parts B and C of Figure 2 relies on visual centers beyond the primary visual cortex.

Similarity relationships between items have a predictable impact on feature search (e.g., Duncan and Humphreys, 1989). The greater the difference between target and distractors, the more efficient the search. The greater the similarity between the distractors, the more efficient the search. This is illustrated in Figure 3. There is considerable debate as to whether the list of basic preattentive features is fixed or whether extensive practice can add new features to an individual's preattentive processing abilities. It is possible that individuals can develop an ability to search in parallel for overlearned stimuli like letters. Alternatively, it is possible that the development of efficient search for stimuli such as letters involves learning to make better use of existing basic feature information.

When feature information is inadequate, the slopes of RT × set size functions become steeper. The third column of Figure 1 shows a typical result in which RT for a search for a 2 among 5s increases about 20 to 30 milliseconds for each additional item on target-present

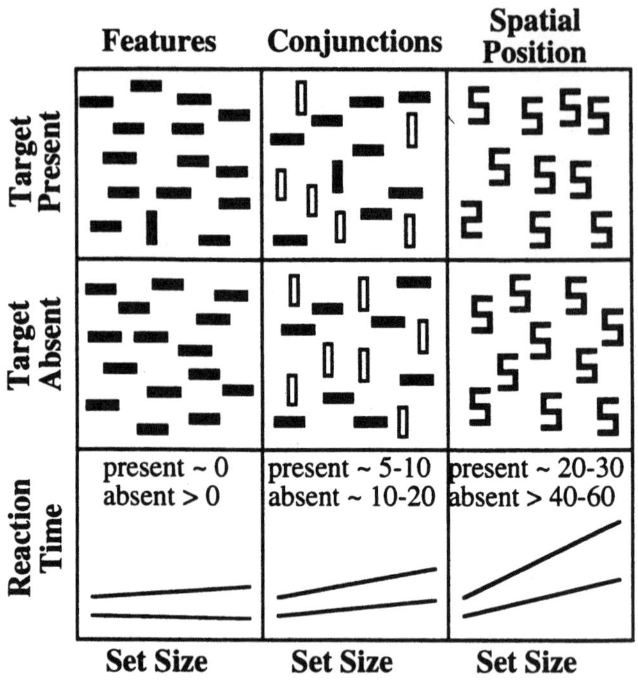

VISUAL SEARCH. Figure 1. Examples of stimuli and idealized data for three categories of visual search task.

trials and about 40 to 60 milliseconds per item for target-absent trials. These results are consistent with an item-by-item or "serial" search at a rate of about one item every 40 to 60 milliseconds. It could also be the case that all items are processed at once but that processing capacity is limited, so that the time required to process 20 items would be greater than the time needed to process 5.

In most real-world searches, basic feature information is available but is not a perfect guide to the target. A laboratory version is shown in the middle column of Figure 1. The black vertical target is neither uniquely black nor uniquely vertical, but a search process that could make use of preattentive feature information could be used to guide attention toward the target. In practice, these "conjunction" tasks tend to produce results that lie between those of simple feature searches and the least efficient searches, such as the search for the 2 among 5s.

Attention in visual search seems to be directed from object to object rather than from location to location. This suggests that preattentive processes must be capable of dividing the visual scene into a set of objects in parallel. Object identity, however, is not processed

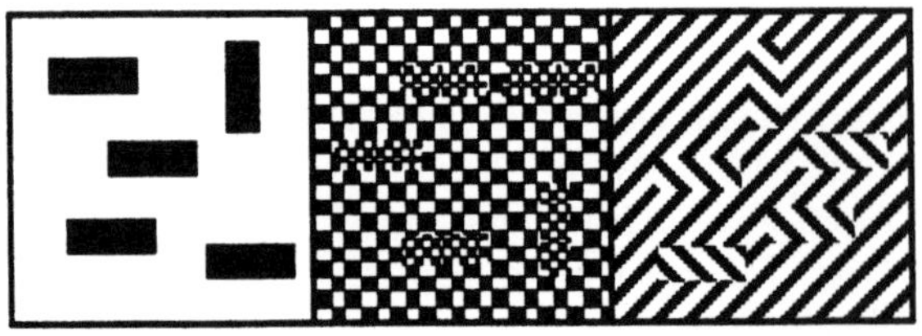

A B C

VISUAL SEARCH. Figure 2. Three ways to make oriented lines.

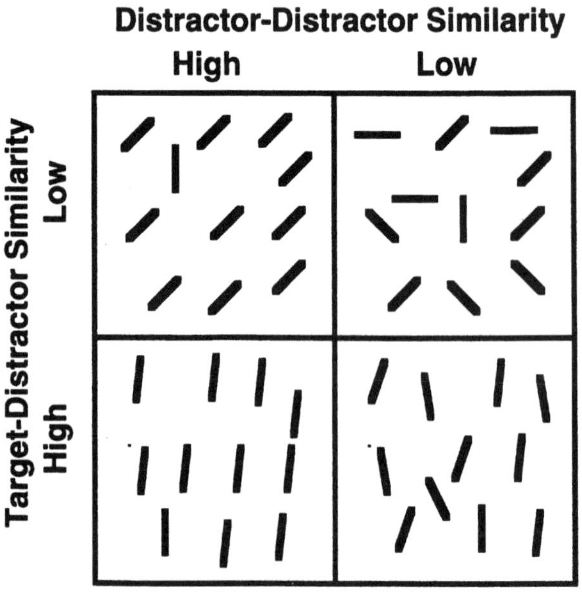

VISUAL SEARCH. Figure 3. The role of similarity in visual search.

preattentively. In most real-world visual searches, the search will combine overt movements of the eyes with covert deployments of attention. The mechanisms governing deployment of attention and movements of the eyes appear to be closely related. For instance, one cannot normally move the eyes in one direction while shifting attention in another. The two processes are not identical. It is possible to fixate at one location while deploying covert attention to another location. Moreover, if attention is being deployed on an item-by-item basis in visual search, then the rate of deployment (at least 20 times per second) is substantially greater than the rate of voluntary eye movements (3 to 5 times per second).

Bibliography

Classic Sources

Neisser, U. (1967). *Cognitive psychology*. New York: Appleton-Century-Crofts. The basic source for the two-stage preattentive/attentive model.

Treisman, A., & Gelade, G. (1980). A feature-integration theory of attention. *Cognitive Psychology, 12*, 97–136. Historically, the most influential theory of visual search.

Some Modern Theories of Search

Bundesen, C. (1990). A theory of visual attention. *Psychological Review, 97*, 523–547.

Duncan, J., & Humphreys, G. W. (1989). Visual search and stimulus similarity. *Psychological Review, 96*, 433–458. Contains a discussion of the role of similarity in search.

Grossberg, S., Mingolla, E., & Ross, W. D. (1994). A neural theory of attentive visual search: Interactions of boundary, surface, spatial and object representations. *Psychological Review, 101*(3), 470–489.

Logan, G. D. (1996). The CODE theory of visual attention: An integration of space-based and object-based attention. *Psychological Review, 103*(4), 603–649.

Treisman, A. (1988). Features and objects: The 14th Bartlett memorial lecture. *Quarterly Journal of Experimental Psychology, 40A*, 201–237.

Wolfe, J. M. (1994). Guided Search 2.0: A revised model of visual search. *Psychonomic Bulletin and Review, 1*(2), 202–238.

Useful Reviews

Bundesen, C. (1996). Formal models of visual attention: A tutorial review. In A. Kramer, G. H. Cole, & G. D. Logan (Eds.), *Converging operations in the study of visual selective attention* (pp. 1–44). Washington, DC: American Psychological Association.

Kinchla, R. A. (1992). Attention. *Annual Review of Psychology, 43*, 711–742.

Pashler, H. (1997). *The psychology of attention*. Cambridge, MA: MIT Press.

Shiffrin, R. M. (1988). Attention. In R. Atkinson, R. J. Herrnstein, G. Lindzey, & R. D. Luce (Eds.), *Steven's handbook of experimental psychology* (Vol. 2, 2nd ed., pp. 739–812). New York: Wiley.

Treisman, A. (1986). Properties, parts, and objects. In K. R. Boff, L. Kaufmann, & J. P. Thomas (Eds.), *Handbook of human perception and performance* (Vol. 2, pp. 37.1–35.70). New York: Wiley.

Jeremy Wolfe

VIVES, JUAN LUIS (1492–1540), philosopher. René Descartes is usually acknowledged as the "father of psychology," an honor that has been challenged more than once. In a most illuminating article, Foster Watson (1915) argued that a Spaniard, Juan Luis Vives, should properly be credited with this title. Similarly, the noted historians of medical psychology, Zilboorg and Henry (1941), concur with Watson in attributing a more significant role to Vives than he is given in texts on the history of psychology.

Vives was born in Valencia, Spain, on 6 March 1492, and studied in that city until he went to Paris to pursue further studies at the age of 17 (Zilboorg & Henry, 1941). Academically, he was steeped in the Greek classics, conversant with the scholasticism of St. Thomas Aquinas, and fluent in the rhetoric of Quintilian, Seneca, and Cicero (Swift & Block, 1974). Vives was a vigorous scholar and an adventurous thinker who was dissatisfied with the authority of Aristotle and the conventions of scholasticism. His contributions to both psychology and education are prolific. However, this analysis will concentrate on his contributions to modern psychology.

Empirical Psychology

Watson (1915) points out that Vives was a forerunner to Descartes and Francis Bacon in the "*self-conscious emphasis on induction* as a method of inquiry and discovery in philosophical, and particularly in psychological questions" (p. 334). Vives also believed in testing his hypotheses pragmatically. He was convinced of the importance of observation in understanding behavior and was an astute observer of his own actions.

In *De Anima et Vita* (1538), Vives argues that questions concerning the soul's essence are of little importance relative to questions of knowing "the *manifestations* of the soul in all the activities of consciousness" (Watson, 1915, p. 337). From this position, Vives then proceeded to observe the results of mental activity in the form of the association of ideas and memory as well as of the effects of various passions (or emotions) on behavior. This empirical psychology is not so distant from the introspective interrogation of consciousness that occupied such thinkers as Wundt and Titchener some 350 years later.

Association of Ideas

Watson (1915) acknowledges that the doctrine of association of ideas can be traced to Aristotle, but argues that Vives's work marks the Renaissance advance:

> No other author as early as Vives contributed so strong and comprehensive an exposition of it, as Vives. Indeed, Sir William Hamilton, the most erudite of all British philosophers, in the history of psychology, said: "Vives's observations comprise in brief, nearly all of principal moment that has been said upon this subject (of mental association) *either before or since*. (p. 339)

In his exposition of the laws of association, Vives was quick to note individual differences in memory. He believed that memory must be exercised to be good and was a strong advocate of techniques to improve memory. Vives noted that a chain of association could exist between memories so that one event could trigger other memories as well as their associated emotions. He recognized the role that emotions play in the connections between thoughts and feelings and that memory is inextricably bound up with the emotion with which it is paired.

Emotions as Psychological Drives

Vives built a descriptive psychology of emotions with the following major premises: Life in its entirety is regulated by emotions; emotions can obscure perceptions and are not subordinate to intellect, and they can, in fact, hinder or destroy intellectual activities; emotions are rooted in dispositions, so that a dominant emotion can color an individual's thoughts either continuously or periodically; and emotions can be changed physically by diet or mentally by training.

In Vives's scheme, all emotions could be dichotomized as either good (love) or evil (hate). Specifically, he recognized the emotions of good will, respect, sympathy, gaiety, hope, laughter, annoyance, scorn, anger, hatred, envy, jealousy, indignation, vengeance, cruelty, sadness, mourning, fear, shame, and pride. Brett (1953) noted that "His work on the passions marks a new era in the history of the troublesome subject, not by virtue of a new classification, but rather on account of the careful way in which the phenomena are described" (p. 319).

One aspect of Vives's thoughts on emotions merits our attention: the role that he has assigned to emotions in influencing somatic effects (Clements, 1967). According to Vives, emotional life corresponds to physiological life to such an extent that the two are capable of influencing each other. In this treatment, an individual's physiological state can predispose that person to a particular emotion; similarly, a person's emotional state can alter the somatic state of the individual. Clements (1967), however, cautions that "it would be erroneous to regard Vives as an innovator in the field of psychosomatic illness since the phenomena cited by Vives are drawn from traditional sources" (pp. 233–234). Yet Clements points out that Vives is "unique in the sense of emphasizing them as psychological phenomena, and not merely in connection with other disciplines or topics" (p. 234).

In sum, Vives's writings on emotions as psychological drives bear a close resemblance to conceptualizations of dynamic psychology. Emotions could aid or hinder the process of remembering and forgetting. They were described as the basis for associations that were acquired without awareness (Zilboorg & Henry, 1941). Finally, emotions were perceived as the basis for human appetites, feelings, and actions.

Mental Illness and Care of the Afflicted

Vives was, above all, a humanist who argued that the state had a responsibility to care for the less fortunate members of society. This is revealed in his belief that the mentally ill were above all human beings and should be treated with compassion. He proposed that the mentally ill be given medical attention, gentle care, and instruction. Interestingly, he argued that if chains were necessary, they should be used in such a way as to not make patients more violent. Tranquility was the key to the successful treatment of the mentally ill (Zilboorg & Henry, 1941). Zilboorg and Henry (1941) state that psychiatry would find little to add to or subtract from Vives's approach to the treatment of the mentally ill. Vives died on 6 May 1540 in Bruges, Flanders.

Bibliography

Brett, G. S. (1953). *History of psychology* (R. S. Peters, Ed. & Abridger). London: George Allen & Unwin.

Clements, R. D. (1967). Physiological-psychological thought in Juan Luis Vives. *Journal of the History of the Behavioral Sciences, 3*, 219–235.

Swift, L. J., & Block, S. L. (1974). Classical rhetoric in Vives' psychology. *Journal of the History of the Behavioral Sciences, 10*, 74–83.

Watson, F. (1915). The father of modern psychology. *Psychological Review, 22*, 333–353.

Zilboorg, G., & Henry, G. W. (1941). *A history of medical psychology*. New York: Norton.

Amado M. Padilla

VOCATIONAL PSYCHOLOGY. *See* Counseling Psychology; *and* Industrial and Organizational Psychology.

VOLITION. Kurt Lewin, a German social psychologist in the 1920s and 1930s, suggested that there are at least two distinct aspects of being motivated to pursue a desired goal: goal setting and goal striving. Whereas goal setting relates to the motivational issue of what goals a person will adopt and thus to how the person considers the feasibility and desirability of the available choice options, goal striving entails the volitional issue of behaving with respect to set goals and thus of how a person moves most effectively toward a chosen goal. Noticing the distinct nature of both of these issues, the first being primarily motivational (i.e., what does the person want to attain) and the second primarily volitional (i.e., how does the person exert her will to attain what she wants), Lewin adopted a distinct theoretical perspective for each of them. He referred to an expectancy *x* value model when goal setting was at issue—people are expected to choose goals that appear as both highly desirable and feasible. Issues of goal striving (i.e., the willful implementation of chosen goals), on the other hand, were explained in terms of his theory of tension systems, which tried to elucidate the forces that move a person toward a chosen goal.

Lewin proposed a need theory of goal striving and assumed that goals, like needs, assign a valence to objects and events in people's social and nonsocial surroundings. For a person who intends to mail a letter, Lewin's favorite example, a mailbox entices her to deposit the letter much as food entices a hungry person to eat. Because needs can be satisfied by various types of behaviors, which may all substitute for each other in reducing need tension (e.g., eating fruit, vegetables, or bread), many different goal-directed behaviors qualify for satisfying the quasi-need associated with a goal. The amount of the tension associated with the quasi-need was assumed to directly relate to the intensity of a person's goal striving.

The exact amount of tension may vary, however. First, it is affected by the degree of quasi-need fulfillment (i.e., tension comes to a final rest only when the goal is achieved). Second, it is thought to depend on the strength of relevant real needs (i.e., superordinate drives and general life goals) and how strongly these are related to the quasi-need. For a person with strong affiliative needs but weak achievement needs (or professional goals) a mailbox, for example, acquires more valence when that person intends to send off letters inviting people to a party than when he plans to send out job applications.

Lewin's tension state metaphor effectively accounts for the flexibility of goal striving. It is assumed that people commonly see more than just one route to goal achievement (e.g., contacting a friend) and that all these routes may substitute for each other (e.g., phone, fax, e-mail, letter). In other words, a goal can be realized in many different ways, and the blocking of one of them should readily lead to attempts to realize the goal through alternative routes.

In his tension state theory of volition, Lewin still employed classic motivational variables, such as needs and incentives (valences), and attempted to predict the effects of goals on the basis of these variables. Narziss Ach, a member of the German Würzburg school that specialized in the analysis of thought processes and was most productive in the early twentieth century, established a scientific analysis of phenomena of volitional action or willing that was devoid of any motivational concepts. Ach employed a simple experimental paradigm. Subjects were trained to respond repeatedly and consistently to specific stimuli (e.g., numbers, meaningless syllables) with certain responses (e.g., to add or rhyme them). When these responses had habituated, subjects were instructed to employ their will and execute antagonistic responses (e.g., to subtract or read them). Ach discovered that setting oneself the goal of responding to critical stimuli with an antagonistic response helps one to impose one's will.

The theorizing on how one achieves the reliable execution of an intended action was based on the concept of determination. Ach assumed that linking in one's mind an anticipated situation to a concrete intended behavior creates what he called a *determination* and that this determination in turn would push the person to execute the intended action when encountering the specified situational stimulus. The strength of the determination should depend on how concretely people specify the anticipated situation; concreteness was thought to intensify determination. Moreover, the intensity of the act of intending (willing) should also increase determination, because intensive willing induces a heightened commitment. When presented with the specific stimulus, determination was expected to directly elicit the intended behavior without a person's needing to become conscious again of the intent to get started. Ach speculated that determination may affect perceptual and attentional processes, so that the specified situation is cognized in a way that favors the initiation of the intended action.

Further roots of the psychological analysis of the will can be found by the American psychologist William James in his *Principles of Psychology* (New York, 1890). James discussed questions such as: How is it possible that a behavior that a person intends to perform (i.e., has been set as a goal by this person) fails to be executed? James referred to such problems as *issues of the obstructed will*, but he also raised questions related to what he called issues of the explosive will (i.e., how is it possible that an undesired behavior is performed even though we have set its suppression as our goal?) James's analysis of the will is based on the assumption that behavior can potentially be regulated by a person's resolutions (or intentions, subjective goals), even though in certain situations and at certain times this may be difficult.

A further prominent historical figure in the theorizing about subjective goals and their effects on behavior is William McDougall. In his *Social Psychology* (London, 1908) he was so intrigued by the issue of purposeful or goal-directed behavior that he proposed a novel psychological theory (i.e., hormic psychology) to account for its uniqueness. He postulated that subjective goals guide a person's behavior, whereby this guidance is achieved through cognitive activity that pertains to the analysis of the present situational context and the envisioned event or goal-state to be realized. Progress toward and attainment of the goal are seen as pleasurable experiences, and thwarting and failure are seen as painful or disagreeable.

Modern Theories of Volition

With the triumphant progress of expectancy *x* value models of motivation in the 1950s to 1970s, traditional theorizing on volition fell into oblivion. Only in the 1980s did new research emerge on the many questions of willful goal realization. This research was stimulated by the observation that failure experiences often do not lead to retreat but to an invigoration of goal pursuit, an observation that speaks against expectancy *x* value theorizing, which hypothesizes that the perception of reduced feasibility leads to a reduced motivational tendency to act. Apparently, the motivational tendency to choose a certain course of action or goal does not account for the person's successfully pursuing it. Explaining the successful pursuit of goals requires adding further explanatory concepts, as in modern theorizing on volition.

Action control theory offered by Julius Kuhl (Kuhl & Beckmann, 1994) postulates that self-regulatory processes contribute to goal achievement in the face of competing action tendencies. It is assumed that at any given point in time many different action tendencies coexist, waxing and waning in strength. For an orderly action sequence to occur Kuhl assumes that a current guiding goal has to be shielded from competing intentions or goals (e.g., the goal of making an important phone call from the competing intention to tidy up one's messy desk). He terms this shielding mechanism *action control*. A number of different action control strategies is distinguished: selective attention, encoding control, emotion control, motivation control, environment control, parsimonious information processing, and context matching. Selective attention, for example, helps goal achievement by putting relevant information into the center of attention. Through environmental control, as another example, the individual prevents the derailing of an ongoing goal pursuit by removing competing temptations or enticements from the situational context in which goal pursuit is to occur.

Whether and how effectively these strategies are employed depends on the current control mode of the individual. An action-oriented person concentrates on the planning and initiating of goal-directed action, responds flexibly to the respective situational demands, and makes effective use of the listed control strategies. Things are quite different with a state-oriented person, because this person cannot disengage from competing incomplete goals, is caught up in uncontrollable perseveration of thoughts related to aversive experiences or dysfunctional thoughts about future successes. State orientation may be induced by situational variables (e.g., a surprising event, persistent failure), but the term is also applied to a corresponding enduring, personal disposition.

The model of action control has seen many refinements and has arrived at a high level of complexity. It is suggested that action control cannot be understood without considering the many different mental subsystems (e.g., a memory system specialized on the retention of goals) involved. In addition, experimental research on state orientation as a personality attribute has discovered a further volitional handicap called *self-infiltration*. State-oriented individuals readily misperceive assigned goals as self-generated, and the degree of such false self-ascriptions is closely associated with a reduced enactment of self-chosen as compared with assigned goals. Action control theory has stimulated numerous studies related to the likelihood of goal attainment, to decision making under time pressure, and coping with performance-related threats. The samples of these studies included schoolchildren, high-performance athletes, mental patients (e.g., depressed individuals, individuals with obsessive–compulsive disorders), and people in the workplace.

A further attempt to analyze issues of volition was made by Heinz Heckhausen (1991) and Peter M. Gollwitzer (1996). In their model of action phases they postulated that the course of successfully attaining a goal can be separated into four distinct phases, each presenting a different task to be solved by the individual. The model takes a comprehensive temporal (horizontal) view of goal pursuit, which extends from the origin of a person's wishes and desires to the evaluation of attained outcomes.

Accordingly, the first of these tasks, which is to be accomplished in the predecisional phase, is to weigh their wishes and desires in light of feasibility and desirability so as to arrive at a decision on whether to act on them. A positive decision transfers a wishful desire into a binding goal accompanied by a feeling of determination or obligation.

The second task to be solved is promoting the initiation of goal-directed action. This may be simple when the necessary goal-directed actions are well practiced or routine, or difficult when the person is still undecided as to when, where, and how to act. In the latter case the execution of goal-directed action needs to be prepared. The action-phases model refers to this period as the preactional phase, where the individual creates plans by reflecting and deciding on when, where, how, and how long to implement action.

With the initiation of goal-directed actions, the individual enters the actional phase, and faces a third task: bringing goal-directed behaviors to a successful conclusion. For this purpose, the individual should readily respond to situational opportunities and demands, should jump at all opportunities that allow progress to the goal, and, when encountering difficulties and hindrances, should readily increase effort expenditure. The final action phase, the postactional phase, is associated with the fourth task of evaluating goal achievement by comparing what has been achieved with what had been desired. The action-phases model considers the first and the fourth task to be motivational in nature, whereas the second and the third task are said to be volitional in nature.

To analyze the volitional processes involved in solving the first and second task, the model suggests two theoretical concepts, the concept of mind-set and the concept of implementation intention. The concept of mind-set led to the distinction between so-called deliberative and implemental mind-sets. Deliberative mind-sets originate when people become heavily involved in choosing between various wishes and desires, trying to solve the task of deciding which desires to pursue. Implemental mind-sets originate when people become involved with planning the when, where, and how of initiating actions that are geared toward goal attainment, trying to solve the task of getting started with one's goal pursuit. Both mind-sets are associated with a general cognitive orientation that helps to solve the task at hand. Accordingly, the implemental mind-set is perceived as a volitional tool that promotes goal attainment.

Analogously, implementation intentions are also conceptualized as volitional tools. Implementation intentions are acts of will that link anticipated future situational contexts to intended goal-directed actions ("When situation *x* arises, I will perform the goal-directed behavior *y*"). Forming implementation intentions has been found to facilitate the initiation of goal-directed actions once the specified situation is encountered. In this way, implementation intentions assure that goal-directed actions are initiated even when action initiation is hampered because people are involved in competing goal pursuits, absorbed with ruminating thoughts or intense feelings, or are simply tired.

Solving Volitional Problems

Problems of volition can be classified into two categories. The first set of problems involves getting started. For a number of reasons, people continue to miss good opportunities to act, and thus delay goal attainment. The second set of problems involves bringing started goal pursuits to successful completion. People often give up in the face of difficulties, fail to ward off distractions, and have trouble resuming the pursuit of goals once problems have occurred. An intensive program of research analyzed how implemental mind-sets and implementation intentions alleviate these problems.

Implemental mind-sets facilitate action initiation via a number of different processes. Implemental mind-sets were found to increase positive illusions about one's invulnerability to controllable and uncontrollable risks, the possession of valuable skills and abilities, and the behavioral control of desired outcomes. Positive illusions of this kind are known to promote a person's readiness to act on a given goal. Implemental mind-sets also tune a person's thoughts toward implementational issues (e.g., available opportunities and means) and produce a more effective processing of implementation-related information (i.e., information on when, where, and how to act on a given goal). Finally, implemental mind-sets create an unequivocal behavioral orientation in the sense that people no longer ruminate about the pros and cons of pursuing a given goal, but solely focus on the pros of the chosen goal pursuit.

Implementation intentions also facilitate initiation of goal-directed action, albeit by a number of different processes. First, implementation intentions produce a heightened perceptual readiness for the specified situational cues. Even when the intended opportunities are hidden in the larger situational context and are thus easily overlooked, implementation intentions make for easy detection. Second, having formed implementation intentions assures that attention that is focused on other things is easily disrupted when the critical stimuli appear. This assures that people can make use of opportunities to get started, even at times when they are absorbed with other issues. Finally, forming implementation intentions creates a behavioral readiness to immediately respond to the specified situational cues. This immediacy is observed even under conditions where people are busied with an ongoing second task. Apparently, the immediate response to the critical stimuli is highly efficient in the sense of occupying few cognitive resources. Moreover, responding to a specified situational cue with the intended goal-directed behavior does not need a conscious intent. In summary, by forming implementation intentions, the initiation of intended actions can be turned into automatic action control. Recent research that builds on this discovery shows that patients with a frontal lobe injury, who are known to be deficient in conscious action control, greatly benefit from being assigned implementation intentions.

Implemental mind-sets and implementation intentions further not only the initiation of goal pursuit but also its completion. When it comes to warding off distractions, implemental mind-sets are helpful by reducing cognitive receptiveness to the available information, which allows the person to focus on the ongoing goal pursuit. In addition, the positive illusions associated with an implemental mind-set should help people to persist when hindrances and failures are encountered, and to resume goal pursuits that have become derailed. Implementation intentions, on the other hand, facilitate the completion of goal pursuit via a number of different processes. By forming implementation intentions people can effectively ward off distractions if they are framed in a temptation-inhibiting way: "Whenever distraction *x* arises, I will ignore it." However, implementation intentions framed in a task facilitating format ("Whenever distraction *x* occurs, I will concentrate on performing the ongoing task") are observed to be less effective. These findings are in line with Walter Mischel's work conducted in the 1970s exploring how, by forming various plans, children can escape temptations while performing a boring task.

These findings are particularly noteworthy as they suggest that willpower should not be construed as an issue of intensification of effort. Rather, effective willing seems more closely associated with the flexible and skillful use of cognitive strategies than with the determined mobilization of effort. It speaks for the effectiveness of cognitive strategies of willing that the completion rate of difficult goal projects (e.g., to write a paper, to diet, to exercise, to solve an interpersonal conflict) could be tripled when people were asked to furnish these goal projects with implementation intentions. In addition, implementation intentions have even been found to effectively block bad habits, no matter whether these referred to unwanted thoughts or to unwanted behaviors (e.g., gender stereotypes or eating unhealthy food, respectively).

Bibliography

Ach, N. (1935). *Analyse des Willens* [The analysis of willing]. Berlin: Urban & Schwarzenberg. Presents a summary of the traditional psychology of volition.

Atkinson, J. W., & Birch, D. (1970). *The dynamics of action.* New York: Wiley.

Gollwitzer, P. M. (1996). The volitional benefits of planning. In P. M. Gollwitzer & J. A. Bargh (Eds.), *The psychology of action* (pp. 287–312). New York: Guilford Press. Discusses how implemental mind-sets and implementation intentions are effective tools for solving volitional problems.

Heckhausen, H. (1991). *Motivation and action.* Heidelberg: Springer Verlag. Describes classic motivational and volitional issues and discusses their differences.

Klinger, E. (1977). *Meaning and void: Inner experience and the incentives in people's lives.* Minneapolis: University of Minnesota Press. Points to the shortcomings of motivational theorizing and presents a plea and a theoretical framework for a psychology of volition.

Kuhl, J., & Beckmann, J. (Eds.). (1994). *Volition and personality.* Göttingen: Hogrefe. Documents the importance of action control theory and considers volition as a personality disposition.

Lewin, K. (1926). Vorsatz, Wille und Bedürfnis [Intention, will, and need]. *Psychologische Forschung, 7,* 330–385. Presents a need theory of the volitional pursuit of chosen goals.

Mischel, W., Cantor, N., & Feldman, S. (1996). Principles of self-regulation: The nature of will power and self-control. In E. T. Higgins & A. W. Kruglanski (Eds.), *Social psychology: Handbook of basic principles.* New York: Guilford Press. Discusses the various issues of self-control in terms of the concept of willpower.

Peter M. Gollwitzer

VOLUNTARY AND INVOLUNTARY HOSPITALIZATION. The first patient hospitalized in the United States for the treatment of mental illness was admitted to the Pennsylvania Hospital in 1752. Few formalities attended his admission: His family requested hospitalization, and a physician approved it. For the next century, such informal procedures predominated almost everywhere, with patients themselves largely excluded from hospitalization decisions. It was assumed that anyone so disturbed as to require hospital admission was not capable of making a competent decision and that families would represent patients' interests.

After the Civil War, growing public concern about possible abuses by family members and physicians led to the introduction of procedural protections. These procedures included requirements for judicial review and, in some cases, jury trials.

Throughout the twentieth century, procedures have been alternately tightened and relaxed as public attention has switched between fear of abuses and concern that persons with mental illness were going untreated. Voluntary admission, now the most prevalent mechanism for hospitalization, was not explicitly authorized until New York State did so by statute in 1881.

Voluntary Hospitalization

Voluntary admission to psychiatric facilities is governed by statute in every state. Adults can sign themselves into a hospital with the concurrence of an admitting clinician. Two types of voluntary status exist: true voluntary (sometimes called informal) and conditional voluntary admissions. Patients entering on the former basis are free to leave at will. Conditional voluntary patients can be held against their will for a statutorily determined period (often 72 hours) while an evaluation of their eligibility for involuntary commitment takes place. Many states require that information be given to prospective voluntary patients describing this limitation on their ability to leave and enumerating their rights in the facility.

Commentators have questioned the extent to which voluntary admissions actually reflect patients' free choice. Many patients elect voluntary hospitalization only to avoid involuntary commitment; indeed, some states' statutes require that they be given this option. Attention has also focused on the competence of patients to make admission decisions following a 1990 decision by the U.S. Supreme Court challenging Florida's practices (*Zinermon v. Burch*). However, no good alternative exists at present for dealing with noncommittable patients who desire hospitalization but whose competence may be in doubt.

Involuntary Hospitalization

All U.S. jurisdictions permit involuntary hospitalization of certain categories of persons with mental illness. Until the 1970s, most state statutes permitted emergency commitment of persons judged by a physician to be in need of treatment, with judicial review after an initial period of confinement. During that decade, every state adopted more restrictive criteria, based on persons' dangerousness to themselves or others or their inability to meet basic needs. This remains the dominant approach, although a few states have relaxed their criteria somewhat—for example, allowing commitment of persons whose deterioration to the point of dangerousness appears predictable. Increasingly, states have authorized psychologists, social workers, and psychiatric nurses, in addition to physicians, to initiate commitment proceedings.

As part of the statutory reforms of the 1970s, states also adopted more rigorous procedures for effecting commitment, often borrowing them from the criminal justice model. Thus, patients have been afforded rights to timely notice, probable cause hearings soon after initial detention, frequent judicial review, representation by attorneys, exclusion of hearsay evidence, and in some states the right to remain silent during examinations or at hearings. The burden of proof of commitability rests with the state or treatment facility. A U.S. Supreme Court decision in 1977 (*Addington v. Texas*) held that the minimum standard of proof acceptable under the Constitution is "clear and convincing evidence," but some states mandate that commitability be demonstrated "beyond a reasonable doubt."

Although the more rigorous procedures generally have been well accepted, the proper criteria for commitment remain a matter of contention. Objections to dangerousness-based statutes come from those who are skeptical of the ability of clinicians to predict violence or suicidal acts, as well as from those who contend that the laws unfairly exclude from hospitalization nondangerous persons who are nonetheless in need of care. Studies tend to show that the reforms of the 1970s have had only modest effects on the number and type of persons being committed, with families, clinicians, and judges generally finding ways around restrictive statutes when patients appear to need inpatient care. The "grave disability" standard—related to an inability to meet one's basic needs—often provides flexibility in such situations.

Hospitalization of Children

Historically, children have been hospitalized "voluntarily" by their parents or those acting *in loco parentis*, a practice upheld in 1979 by the U.S. Supreme Court (*Parham v. J. R.*) on the grounds that the admitting clinician serves as a "neutral fact finder," thus protecting children's interests. States vary in setting the age at which adolescents can consent to their own hospitalization, ranging from 12 to 18 years of age. Children and adolescents can also be committed under involuntary hospitalization statutes, but this occurs infrequently. The 1980s saw skyrocketing rates of admission for children and adolescents as some private facilities allegedly took advantage of available insurance reimbursement. This problem faded with the introduction of tightly managed mental health care rules in the 1990s.

Future Developments

Periodic discussions of major reforms in commitment criteria have produced few changes since the early 1980s. Large-scale modifications appear unlikely in the foreseeable future. Recent attention has centered on models of involuntary outpatient commitment, in which patients can be ordered to undergo treatment outside of a facility. The intent of such statutes is multiple: to allow earlier discharge from inpatient facilities, to provide an alternative to hospitalization for those who can be treated in the community, and to break the cycle of rehospitalization by intervening with noncompliant patients before they decompensate again. Eligibility criteria range from standards identical to those for inpatient commitment to broader criteria focused on a history of repeated decompensation. Studies of the efficacy of outpatient commitment are still in their infancy.

The impact of changes in the organization and financing of the mental health system on voluntary and involuntary hospitalization remains to be determined. Many payers and managed care companies have adopted dangerousness-based criteria similar to those found in commitment statutes as the basis for authorizing even voluntary admissions. The rigorous review of the need for initial and continued hospitalization that characterizes most managed mental health care may replace legal rules as the primary determinant of the duration of hospitalization. Use of residential and holding facilities in lieu of hospitalization raises unaddressed issues regarding the legal basis for admission and patients' rights while there.

Bibliography

American Psychiatric Association. (1987). *Involuntary commitment to outpatient treatment. Task force report #26.* Washington, DC: Author. A good discussion of outpatient commitment and a model law.

American Psychological Association. (1984). *A model act for the mental health treatment of minors.* Washington, DC: Author.

Appelbaum, P. S. (1994). *Almost a revolution: Mental health law and the limits of change.* New York: Oxford University Press. Analyzes the mental health law reforms of the 1970s and considers their impact.

Appelbaum, P. S., & Anfang, S. A. (1996) Civil commitment. In R. Michels (Ed.), *Psychiatry.* Philadelphia: Lippincott. A thorough overview of the topic.

Bagby, R. M., & Atkinson, L. (1988). The effects of legislative reform on civil commitment rates: A critical analysis. *Behavioral Sciences and the Law, 6*, 45–62. An important study demonstrating the less-than-anticipated impact of commitment law reforms.

Parry, J. (1994). Survey of standards for extended involuntary commitment. *Mental and Physical Disability Law Reporter, 18*, 329–336.

Stromberg, C. D., & Stone, A. A. (1983). A model state law on civil commitment of the mentally ill. *Harvard Journal on Legislation, 20*, 275–396. An influential discussion of the American Psychiatric Association's model statute.

Swartz, M. S., Burns, B. J., Hiday, V. A., George, L. K., Swanson, J., & Wagner, H. R. (1995). New directions in research on involuntary outpatient commitment. *Psychiatric Services, 46*, 381–385.

Warren, C. A. B. (1982). *Court of last resort: Mental illness and the law.* Chicago: University of Chicago Press. Based on a sociological study; provides the best look at how commitment law functions in practice.

Weithorn, L. A. (1988). Mental hospitalization of troublesome youth: An analysis of skyrocketing admission rates. *Stanford Law Review, 40*, 773–838. The leading description of the abuses of the 1980s.

Paul S. Appelbaum

VOLUNTEERISM. *See* Prosocial Behavior.

VOTING BEHAVIOR. *See* Political Behavior, Individual; *and* Political Decision Making.

VOYEURISM is defined as the act of becoming sexually aroused by watching some form of nudity or sexual activity of unsuspecting, unconsenting individuals, either adult or child, male or female. The *Diagnostic and Statistical Manual of Mental Disorders* (*DSM–IV*; American Psychiatric Association, 1994) criteria for voyeurism are: (a) over a period of 6 months, recurrent, intense sexually arousing fantasies, sexual urges, or behavior involving the act of observing an unsuspecting person(s) who is naked, in the act of disrobing, or engaging in sexual activity; and (b) the fantasies, sexual urges, or behavior cause clinically significant distress or impairment in social, occupational, or other important areas of functioning. In the typical case, no contact with the observed individual is sought, but these individuals may have a fantasy of sexual activity with the observed individual, although in reality this rarely occurs. Orgasm is typically produced by masturbation, during the observation or later in response to memory of the event.

For a few individuals, voyeurism is the exclusive form of sexual activity. For others, these fantasies are the preferred but not the only manner of achieving sexual arousal. In some individuals these fantasies and urges become more intense during periods of stress and are episodic. Since watching or observing is a part of the sequence of normal or deviant sexual activity (i.e., rape), a major issue in diagnosing these cases is whether "peeping" is a step to normal or deviant sexual activity or if it has supplanted or replaced it. In other words, is the goal only to watch or to participate?

According to the *DSM–IV* (1994), the onset of voyeuristic behavior is usually before age 15, which is consistent with clinical data noted by Abel and Rouleau (1990). The average age of first criminal conviction is 23.8 years. The median number of reported voyeuristic acts per voyeur was 17 as reported by Abel and Rouleau (1995). Two thirds of voyeurs are unmarried, one fourth are married, and the rest are either separated, divorced, or widowed. Alcohol and drugs are rarely involved; only about 16% practice voyeurism while drinking alcohol and none under the influence of drugs from a sample taken by Gebhard, Gagon, Pomeroy, and Christenson (1965). The prevalence of voyeurism is unknown, but it must be fairly common, since approximately 20% of women claim to have been victims of this behavior.

Is Voyeurism a Discrete, Unique, Clinical Disorder?

As noted above, a major issue in discussing and understanding voyeurism is the overlap of this concept with normal behavior on the one hand and with paraphilia on the other. Is becoming aroused to undressing, lovemaking, strip teasers, pornographic materials, and nudity abnormal? The answer is no. Furthermore, is the seeking and observing of an unsuspecting, nonconsenting individual unique to voyeurism? From the available research, the answer is no.

Of 62 individuals diagnosed as voyeurs in the Abel and Rouleau study, all revealed histories of other paraphilia, such as rape (37%), female nonincestuous pedophilia (52%), exhibitionism (63%), and sadism (11%). Furthermore, many other type of paraphilia, such as pedophilia, report a history of voyeurism. For example, Bradford, Boulet, and Pawlak also found that voyeurism was commonplace among men who had committed rape (1992). This issue is perhaps best illustrated by two studies of voyeurs conducted by Langevin, Paitich, and Russon and reported by Langevin (1983), who compared voyeurs (a minimum of 10 times), multiple anomaly controls (no history of peeping) and normal controls (peeping was fortuitous and nonorgasmic). In the first study there were no exclusive voyeurs, and only 17% of 45 cases had peeped as their dominant, sexual outlet. In the second study, only 23% of 31 cases were predominantly voyeurs. Langevin concludes that voyeurism, as a discrete clinical entity, is very rare and seldom exists alone. This fact, well documented by other studies, as well as the lack of significant research on this disorder, make evaluation of theories and treatment of this disorder very difficult.

Theories of Voyeurism

Few theoretical approaches specifically target voyeurism, but they tend to explain paraphilia in general. Psychoanalytic theory emphasizes the complexity of the perverse formation in terms of conscious and unconscious components, the role of guilt and conscience, the contribution of both aggressive and libidinal interests, the symbolic representation of developmental missteps, and adaptive functions. In voyeurism, the emphasis is on separation and castration. The voyeur watches a woman to note the true nature of her genitals and identify with her. However, through masturbation he reassures himself that his penis is intact. There are other variations on psychodynamic explanation, but as Abel and Rouleau (1995) note, if specific emotional conflicts produce specific sexual, deviant acts, why do paraphiliacs engage in such a variety of deviant sexual behavior? Abel and Rouleau suggest that a general deficit of control over deviant sexual behavior is more likely the problem.

Ford and Beach (1951) first proposed a general social-learning theory explanation of sexual deviance. They note that the kinds and types of situations that become capable of evoking sexual excitation are determined by learning, and the overt sexual behavior of the individual is largely based on the individual's previous experiences. Numerous other researchers also maintain that social learning is important in the development of both normal and abnormal forms of sexual behavior. As noted by Laws and Marshall (1990), sexual arousal patterns are acquired and maintained by operant and respondent conditioning, modeling, and observation, and shaped through differential reinforcement. Most social-learning approaches emphasize the role of masturbation and masturbation fantasies as a major reinforcer in the development of sexual preferences.

Sociobiological theory, as described by Symons (1979) and others, emphasizes the evolutionary factors as it relates to natural selection in the development of sexual arousal and interest. He notes that a male's desire to look at female genitals, particularly those he has not seen before, and to seek out opportunities to do so, is part of the motivational process that maximizes male reproductive opportunities. He further notes that selection favors the basic male tendency to become aroused by the sight of females because a male can potentially impregnate a female at almost no cost to himself in terms of time and energy. The problem with this theory is that there is little or no description of what goes awry in sexual deviation generally or voyeurism specifically.

In his discussion of "love maps," Money (1993) has stated that a paraphilia is a mental template or love map that, in response to neglect, suppression, or traumatization of its normphilic formation, has developed with distortions (omissions, displacements, and inclusions) that otherwise have no place in it. Thus, voyeurism is a displacement paraphilia, a love map gone awry, that involves a segment of the preparatory phase of an erotic and sexual activity before genital intercourse begins, which becomes attached to the phase that leads to the climax or orgasm (Money, 1984). However, as with other theories, what events cause sexual development to go awry is not well documented.

Freund and Blanchard (1986), in their discussion of courtship disorders, described four phases of erotic interaction: (1) location and first appraisal of a suitable partner; (2) pretactile interaction with a prospective partner (looking, smiling, or talking); (3) tactile interaction; and (4) genital union. According to them, voyeurism is an exaggeration and distortion of the first phase of normal sexual interaction. Supporting this theory is the coexistence of other disorders with voyeurism, which is predicted by this theory, which assumes that voyeurism is one of several courtship disorders.

While the psychoanalytic, social learning, and sociobiological theories are informative, the more specific theories of Money and Freund appear to be more practical and useful in developing research strategy, devising assessment procedures, and developing treatment procedures.

Assessment and Treatment of Voyeurism

Careful assessment of any disorder is a prerequisite for diagnosis, research, and treatment. With voyeurism, there are no well-established measures, and clinicians typically rely on clinical interviews and reports of past behavior. Sexual questionnaires, such as the Multiphasic Sex Inventory or the popular Abel/Becker Card Sort, usually have a few items related to voyeurism. However, the development of scales, norms, or data on how voyeurs fare on these items have not been reported. One exception is the Erotic Preference Examination Scheme (EPES), developed by Freund, Watson, and Rienzo (1988), which contains six items addressing voyeurism. These authors used the EPES to compare 60 well-defined voyeurs with 221 nonvoyeur sex offenders, 69 student controls, and 35 nonstudent controls. Each question significantly differentiated the voyeurs from each of the control groups. Eighty-five percent of the voyeurs endorsed both the item concerning excessive time spent peeping and the question concerning masturbating while observing unsuspecting women undressing, as compared to only 20% of the control groups. The internal consistency (alpha) of the total scale was .83. These are promising results, but more work is needed.

The phallometric procedure so useful with other sexual disorders has not been directly used with well-defined voyeur groups. Of course, the stimulus materials would have to be auditory descriptions rather than visual, because nearly all males respond to visual slides of nudes. This is a promising procedure with this group but not yet evaluated and developed.

As with other issues of voyeurism, little treatment research has been conducted with voyeurs. Most research consists of single-case studies conducted by behavior therapists. Since peeping is a natural part of sexual interaction, the goal of decreasing arousal to the deviant activity, per se, is not feasible in this disorder. Jackson (1969) used orgasmic reconditioning (masturbating to "Playboy-type" pictures) when he had the urge to peep. After eight sessions, the patient reported an increase in heterosexual activity and a decrease in the urge to peep, which was maintained after 9 months. Several other case studies have been published, largely using behavioral techniques, such as electrical aversion and anxiety relief, although Maltin (1991) successfully used a humanistic approach in one case, and Emmanuel, Lydiard, and Ballenger (1991) successfully used fluoxetine, a drug reported to be successful with compulsive disorders, with one case. There is no standard, accepted treatment program for this disorder, and the clinician has to rely on his own judgment. However, from an evaluation of the case studies, the most feasible approach would appear to be behavior therapy after a careful case formulation and the selection of appropriate treatment procedures. Certainly, there should be a heavy emphasis on relapse prevention to ensure that the individual does not return to exposing.

In conclusion, we know very little about voyeurism because of its rarity in pure form and a lack of research information.

[*See also* Sexual Disorders.]

Bibliography

Abel, G. G. & Rouleau, J. L. (1995). Sexual abuse: Special issue: Clinical sexuality. *Psychiatric Clinics of North America, 18*, 139–153.

Abel, G. G. & Rouleau, J. L. (1990). The nature and extent of sexual assault. In W. L. Marshall, D. R. Laws, & H. E. Barbaree (Eds.), *Handbook of sexual assault: Issues, theories and treatment of the offenders* (pp. 9–21). New York: Plenum Press.

American Psychiatric Association. (1994). *Diagnostic and statistical manual of mental disorders* (4th ed.). Washington, DC: Author.

Bradford, J. M., Boulet, J., & Pawlak, A. (1992). The paraphilias: A multiplicity of deviant behaviour. *Canadian Journal of Psychiatry, 37*, 104–108.

Emmanuel, N., Lydiard, R. B., & Ballenger, J. (1991). Fluoxetine treatment of voyeurism. *American Journal of Psychiatry, 148*, 950.

Ford, C., & Beach, F. (1951). *Patterns of sexual behavior.* New York: Harper & Row.

Freund, F., & Blanchard, R. (1986). The concept of courtship disorders. *Journal of Sexual and Marital Therapy, 12*, 79–82.

Freund, F., Watson, R., & Rienzo, D. (1998). The value of self report in the study of voyeurism and exhibitionism. *Annals of Sexual Research, 1*, 243–262.

Gebhard, P. H., Gagon, J. H., Pomeroy, W. B. & Christenson, C. V. (1965). *Sex offenders.* New York: Harper & Row.

Jackson, B. T. (1969). A case study of voyeurism treated by counter-conditioning. *Behaviour Research and Therapy, 7*, 133–134.

Langevin, R. (1983). *Sexual strands: Understanding and treating sexual anomalies in men.* Hillsdale, NJ: Erlbaum.

Laws, D. R., & Marshall, W. L. (1990). A conditioning theory of the etiology and maintenance of deviant sexual preference and behavior. In W. L. Marshall, D. R. Laws, & H. E. Barbaree (Eds.), *Handbook of sexual assault: Issues, theories, and treatment of the offender.* New York: Plenum Press.

Malkin, D. (1991). Individuation in a voyeur recidivist. *Australian Journal of Clinical and Experimental Hypnosis, 19*, 117–131.

Money, J. (1993). *Lovemaps: Clinical concepts of sexual/erotic health and pathology, paraphilia and gender transposition in childhood, adolescence and maturity.* New York: Irvington Publishers.

Symons, D. (1979). *The evolution of human sexuality.* New York: Oxford University Press.

Henry E. Adams

VYGOTSKY, LEV SEMENOVICH (1896–1934), Russian psychologist. Vygotsky was born in Orsha and grew up in Gomel in the western provinces of the Russian Empire. He graduated with honors from Gomel's Jewish High School in 1913 and in the same year left for Moscow where he studied social sciences at Shaniavsky University and law at Moscow University. Vygotsky started publishing literary reviews and essays on Jewish history and culture in 1916–1917. During the same period he wrote an essay on *Hamlet* that was later included in his "Psychology of Art," submitted in 1925 as a doctoral dissertation to the Psychological Institute in Moscow. In 1924, he was invited to join the research staff of the Institute. The range of his activities included research on the history of psychology, experimental study of child language and concept formation, and research and development projects in the areas of special education and psychopathology. In addition to Moscow, Vygotsky also lectured and supervised research projects in Leningrad (Saint Petersburg) and Kharkov. In 1931–1932, Vygotsky, with his colleague Alexander Luria, organized a pioneering cross-cultural study of cognition in Central Asia. Vygotsky died of tuberculosis in 1934. For political reasons his works were banned in the Soviet Union from the mid-1930s to the mid-1950s.

Vygotsky proposed that psychology should concern itself with what is distinctive in human behavior. What distinguishes human psychology from that of animals is its determination by social and cultural forces. For this reason Vygotsky called his psychological theory sociocultural or cultural-historical. The sociocultural theory emerged as a possible answer to the protracted crisis in psychology associated with the uncompromising confrontation between biologically oriented "scientific" psychology and philosophically oriented descriptive psychology. The analysis of this crisis was offered by Vygotsky in *The Historical Meaning of the Crisis in Psychology* (1927; reprinted in Vygotsky, 1997). The sociocultural theory proposed to consider two types of psychological functions: "natural" functions reflecting the maturational processes in the child's mind and "cultural" functions dependent on the use of symbolic tools available in a given culture. Vygotsky presented the developmental process as a process of gradual mastery by children of their own "natural" psychological functions with the help of these symbolic "psychological tools." Psychological tools included signs, symbols, oral and written language, formulae, and graphic-symbolic organizers. In *Thought and Language* (1934; Cambridge, Mass., 1986) Vygotsky outlined the mediational role played by speech in the transformation of children's thinking, concept formation, and problem-solving. The role of psychological tools can also be seen on the macro level in the diversity of human thinking dependent on the symbolic mediators available in a given culture. In *Studies on the History of Behavior* (1930; Hillsdale, N.J., 1993) Vygotsky and Luria explored historical and ontogenetic differences in cognition dependent on symbolic mediators and literacy practices characteristic of a given society in a specific historical period.

Vygotsky (1978) rejected the popular belief, associated with Piagetian theory, that instruction should follow the child's cognitive development. He claimed that on the contrary, instruction and learning constitute an important factor in, or "a motor" of, the child's development. Thus, from the Vygotskian point of view, learning and development are just two aspects of one and the same process of "development-generating education." Instead of conceiving instruction as a mere provision of information and rules to be processed by already existent psychological functions, Vygotsky suggested that instruction and learning are responsible for the development of higher psychological functions that are absent in the "natural" cognitive endowment of the child. To make education truly "developing," instruction should be carried on in what Vygotsky defined as the zone of proximal development (ZPD).

The ZPD constitutes an "area" within which the child's functions are in a state of development. They cannot be displayed by children themselves because they have not been formed yet, but if the child receives help from an adult or more competent peer, these functions can be displayed as an outcome of such a cooperative action. The notion of ZPD can also be conceptualized as a meeting place between experientially rich but unsystematic and sometimes erroneous spontaneous concepts of the child and systematically organized "scientific" concepts taught by educators. The notion of ZPD can be used for both assessment and instructional purposes. ZPD based assessment (Lidz, 1987) permits a distinction between children's learning potential and their manifest level of functioning. Teaching based on ZPD takes into account children's ability to benefit from assistance and cooperation and charts the course of development from spontaneous to "scientific" concepts. Although Vygotsky's ideas reached the West with much delay, they have informed a wide range of educational (Moll, 1990), cross-cultural (Cole, 1996), and assessment (Lidz, 1987) studies.

[*See also* the biography of Luria.]

Bibliography

Works by Vygotsky

Vygotsky, L. (1978). *Mind in society* (M. Cole, S. Scribner, V. John-Steiner, & E. Souberman, Eds.). Cambridge, MA: Harvard University Press.

Vygotsky, L. (1987). *Problems of general psychology* (N. Minick, Trans.). New York: Plenum Press.

Vygotsky, L. (1993). *The fundamentals of defectology: Abnormal psychology and learning disabilities* (J. Knox & C. Stevens, Trans.). New York: Plenum Press.

Vygotsky, L. (1994). *The Vygotsky reader* (R. Van der Veer & J. Valsiner, Eds.). Oxford, U.K.: Blackwell.

Vygotsky, L. (1997). *Problems of the theory and history of psychology* (R. Van der Veer, Trans.). New York: Plenum Press.

Works about Vygotsky

Cole, M. (1996). *Cultural psychology*. Cambridge, MA: Harvard University Press.

Daniels, H. (Ed.). (1996). *Introduction to Vygotsky*. London: Routledge.

Kozulin, A. (1990). *Vygotsky's psychology: A biography of ideas*. Cambridge, MA: Harvard University Press.

Lidz, C. (Ed.). (1987). *Dynamic assessment*. New York: Guilford Press.

Moll, L. (Ed.). (1990). *Vygotsky and education*. New York: Cambridge University Press.

Van der Veer, R., & Valsiner, J. (1991). *Understanding Vygotsky: A quest for synthesis*. Oxford: Blackwell.

Wertsch, J. (1985). *Vygotsky and the social formation of mind*. Cambridge, MA: Harvard University Press.

Alex Kozulin

W

WALES. The Principality of Wales has a distinctive Celtic tradition, but it has long been dominated by the Anglo-Saxon English. Wales is now of course part of the United Kingdom, and the political, social, and legal systems of England and Wales within the United Kingdom are common. A history of psychology in Wales is therefore essentially a regional rather than a national history, but during the last four decades psychology in Wales has developed a particularly forceful presence.

Psychology has grown as a university-based discipline in Wales in a way that essentially reflects the general history and development of the subject in the United Kingdom. Although the subject of psychology had been taught to varying extents before that, autonomous academic departments of psychology were established in constituent colleges of the federal University of Wales in Cardiff, Bangor, and Swansea in the 1960s as part of the university expansion following the Robbins report into higher education, which led, among other things, to the establishment of psychology departments in many other universities in the United Kingdom, many of which emerged from departments of philosophy.

At the then University College Cardiff, a department of psychology was established in 1962. The founding professor was George Westby, a broadly based scholar who had previously been influential in the development of the department of psychology at the University of Hull. In 1965 the then University of Wales Institute of Science and Technology (UWIST), also based in Cardiff, established a department of applied psychology under the leadership of Professor Hywel Murrell, whose reputation was in the then new research topic of ergonomics. Each department quickly became securely established both within its college and nationally. Each developed to some extent in the image of its founders: The University College Cardiff department provided degrees in no less than three faculties (science, arts, social sciences) and also taught psychology to medical students at the College; the UWIST department developed distinctive first degrees in occupational and then applied psychology (which included a pioneering interpolated year of supervised work experience for students), together with a postgraduate degree and particular research strengths in occupational psychology. The national standing of these departments was reflected by such honors as Professor Murrell serving as president of the Ergonomics Society and Professor Westby as president of the British Psychological Society. Professor Westby's successor at University College Cardiff, Professor Derek Blackman, also served as president of the British Psychological Society (1981–1982). From 1983 to 1989 Professor Blackman was also the psychology adviser to the United Kingdom University Grants Committee, the body which at that time distributed public funds to the various universities.

In 1988 University College Cardiff and UWIST merged to form what is now Cardiff University, and the two departments of the previous colleges were combined and developed to form a new School of Psychology. The school has ensured that the distinctive histories of its two parents have been respected (maintaining for example the still distinctive first degree in applied psychology), and their fusion has led to the emergence of one of the largest and best departments of psychology in the United Kingdom. Since its founding in 1988, and under the direction of Professor Hadyn Ellis, the School of Psychology at Cardiff has more than doubled its core academic staff from 19 to 36. Of these, no less than 10 are full professors, an unusually large number in British universities. The school's high standing within British psychology is evidenced, for example, by its consistently high ratings in the United Kingdom national Research Assessment Exercise. These are regular peer reviews of the research conducted in university departments, the judgments being used to provide selective research funding within the national system of university finance. Psychology at Cardiff University has been rated at the top Grade 5 in both the most recent Assessment Exercises in 1992 and 1996, reflecting the judgment of peers that it has international standing in psychological research. This is based on its research strengths in behavioral neuroscience, cognitive ergonomics, cognition and neuropsychology, personal relationships, and social cognition.

The founding professor of psychology at Swansea was Mark Hansel, best known as a forceful critic of parapsychology. In Swansea, too, the department of psychology has flourished, with a broadly based teaching program and distinctive research strengths in behavioral pharmacology, cognitive psychology, and industrial psychology. In the most recent United Kingdom Research Assessment Exercise, psychology at Swansea was rated in Grade 4.

At the University College of North Wales, Professor T. R. Miles was appointed as the founding professor of a separate department of psychology in 1963. This department also developed to some extent in the image of its first head, with distinctive strengths in philosophical analysis in psychology and in dyslexia. The department has seen impressive growth since 1987 under the direction of Professor C. F. Lowe, and it is now one of the largest and best psychology departments in the United Kingdom with seven full professors and a Grade 5 rating in the most recent national Research Assessment Exercise. The research strengths at University of Wales Bangor include child development and learning (for which the department's unique collaborative venture with a commercial sponsor of a Daycare Nursery and Centre for Child Development for 50 preschool children is a substantial resource); language development (with a continuing interest in dyslexia, and also in Welsh-English bilingualism as befits the only university department of psychology in a predominantly Welsh-speaking region); cognitive science, and health-clinical psychology.

Psychology is also currently taught at university level at two further institutions in Wales, the University of Glamorgan and University of Wales Institute, Cardiff. Though less distinguished as yet in research than are the three departments of psychology within the federal University of Wales, it is worth noting that all five psychology programs in Wales have received top-grade evaluations for the quality of their teaching in recent national reviews (Teaching Quality Assessments). Wales, therefore, has an enviable record in British academic psychology: All its departments have been rated as excellent with respect to their teaching, and, as described above, two of these (Cardiff University and Bangor) also received a Grade 5 in the most recent Research Assessment Exercise, placing them in the top 8 of some 75 university departments in terms of their research.

Wales has also been at the forefront in the United Kingdom with respect to the development of applied psychology. The master's degree in occupational psychology in Cardiff is one of the longest established and most highly regarded courses in the United Kingdom. Postgraduate training in educational psychology has also been distinctive in Wales. In the United Kingdom, entry to the profession of educational psychology is based on a number of requirements: a recognized honors degree in psychology; professional postgraduate training as a schoolteacher; at least two years' experience as a teacher; and finally a postgraduate qualification in educational psychology, for which all the preceding are required precursors. The department of education at the University of Wales, Swansea, for many years had one of only two courses in which the last four elements of this extended chain were integrated. The course, under the direction of Professor M. Chazan, was naturally popular with well-qualified applicants. However, funding uncertainties at a national level made it impossible to sustain this distinctive integrated course, and postgraduate training in educational psychology was transferred in 1997 to the School of Psychology at Cardiff University in a more traditional format, available to applicants who already have a psychology degree and experience as a qualified teacher.

Clinical psychology has also been both distinctive and pioneering in Wales. An all-Wales postgraduate in-service training course began in 1975, leading to the Postgraduate Diploma in Psychology of the British Psychological Society, and with Dr. David Griffiths as regional tutor. In 1985 the course was subdivided into courses for North and South Wales. The most novel development, however, was the emergence of these courses from master's degree to doctoral programs in the schools of psychology at the University of Wales, Bangor and Cardiff. Through the University of Wales, of which it is a member, and thanks to the pioneering work of Professor Mark Williams, the School of Psychology at Bangor was the first university institution in the United Kingdom to offer a taught doctoral program in clinical psychology that combines postgraduate teaching, clinical practice, and research training. The scheme, approved at the level of the federal University of Wales in 1992, was immediately taken up also by Cardiff University, where Dr. Griffiths was appointed an honorary professor in the School of Psychology. Though certainly pioneering, these new doctorates in clinical psychology captured the spirit of professional development in British clinical psychology at that time, and now most postgraduate courses in clinical psychology in the United Kingdom follow a similar model to that pioneered in Wales and lead to the award of a doctoral degree.

Finally we should mention the influence of the Welsh branch of the British Psychological Society, which has also been both pioneering and forceful. For more than three decades it has organized a most successful interdepartmental annual conference for students, a model that has been copied by other regional branches of the BPS. It is more widely known, however, because it has also organized a series of extremely successful international conferences, among which were Humor and Laughter (1976), Practical Aspects of Memory (1978 and 1987), Models of Man (1979), Psychology and the Arts (1979), Road Safety (1981), Psychology and Law (1982), and Face Recognition (1993). These conferences attracted large numbers of high-profile participants from all over the world, and most have led to very successful book publication.

With a population of some 2.5 million, Wales is in truth but a small part of the United Kingdom. However, both as an academic discipline and as an applied profession, psychology has flourished in Wales. It has a forceful presence in British academic and professional psychology and has also achieved international significance in research.

A pleasing endnote to this short piece is provided by noting the award by the University of Wales in 1991 of an honorary D.Sc. degree to Donald Broadbent. Broadbent worked at the Applied Psychology Unit in Cambridge and then at Oxford University, but he was always quick to remember his Welsh roots. His distinctive position in international psychology as an academic of the highest standing, whose reputation rested on research of applied significance, made it seem both pleasing and fitting for such an academic honor to be conferred on him on behalf of the University of Wales by the Prince of Wales. Though, sadly, Broadbent has since died, his particular approach to applying good psychological theory to industrial and health-related problems lives on in much of the contemporary research in Wales. Information about current research in the three major Departments of Psychology in Wales can be obtained from the following www addresses: Cardiff University: http://www.cf.ac.uk/uwcc/psych; University of Wales Swansea: http://www.swan.ac.uk/psychology; and University of Wales Bangor: http://www.psych.bangor.ac.uk.

[*See also* England.]

Derek Blackman and Hadyn Ellis

WAR AND CONFLICT. [*This entry comprises two articles:* Effects on General Population *and* Effects on Military Personnel. *The first article provides a survey of the psychological effects of war and armed conflict on civilians (both adults and children). The second article discusses the psychological effects of war and armed conflict on military personnel. For discussions related to war and conflict, see* Combat; Enemy Image; Military Culture; Military Psychology; Peace; *and* Propaganda.]

Effects on General Population

Prior to the nineteenth century, wars frequently devastated civilian populations—for example, the Punic Wars, which leveled Carthage, the Mongol invasions of North Africa and eastern Europe, and the Thirty Years' War. By contrast, the Napoleonic wars, the Franco-Prussian War, and other wars of German unification establishing Prussian dominance were essentially military conflicts that affected civilian populations only indirectly by virtue of military casualties and economic dislocation and hardship. General William Sherman's march through Georgia to the sea in the American Civil War is another good example. The aim of Sherman's campaign was to inflict economic catastrophe on the Confederacy and to stamp on the Confederate collective psyche the power of the Union armies. Civilian populations were not directly assaulted.

Advances in technology toward the end of the nineteenth century ended the relative isolation of civilians from direct military onslaught. Civilians could readily be rendered vulnerable to attack and thereby could be regarded as pawns in devising military strategy. In the Franco-Prussian War the city of Paris became the target of long-range bombardment from German artillery, and London was the target of bombs from German zeppelins in World War I. The object of these attacks was to weaken civilian morale, undermining civilian support for the war. The military value of these attacks was slight, but they presaged far more ominous actions. In the 1930s during the Spanish Civil War, Italian planes bombed the city of Guernica, which had no defenses against attack by aircraft—a sheer act of terror. In World War II German air attacks on cities (e.g., Warsaw and Rotterdam) became routine, culminating in the London blitz. Striking terror into the hearts of civilian populations in addition to causing economic and military damage was an essential part of military strategy. Germany went so far as to attach fins to bombs dropped from planes, eliciting a shrieking sound to add to the terror. British and American reprisals followed, with bombing of the major cities of Germany. The culmination of the bombing of civilians in World War II was the deployment of the atomic bombs on Hiroshima and Nagasaki. World War II was the occasion for the development of missiles, which could substitute for manned planes. Against the V-2 German missile, which was directed primarily at London, there was no defense.

By the end of World War II it was apparent that often in warfare there is only a thin margin between military and civilian participants, and terror visited on civilian populations can be an integral part of military strategy. In World War II in Asia, particularly in China,

Japanese troops murderously assaulted civilian populations. Especially in eastern Europe and the Soviet Union, not to mention the Holocaust, occupation by German troops automatically created fear and dread among civilian populations.

Surprisingly, but perhaps not so, these tactics of terror were of little significance in prosecution of the war, and if anything were perhaps a detriment. At times panic among civilian populations served Germany well, clogging roads and creating chaotic conditions that served to hamper military movements of enemy forces. By and large, however, British and German civilian morale and support for the war did not shatter under the force of bombardment, and on Germany's eastern front, harsh treatment of civilians served only to consolidate hatred of the conquerors. Disaffected citizens of the Soviet Union, potential German allies, were turned into enemies.

World War II was followed by the Cold War, during which the threat of nuclear warfare governed relationships between blocs of nations, headed by the United States and the Soviet Union. This hardly peaceable but controlled relationship was almost destroyed by the Cuban missile crisis. Particularly in the early phases of this relationship of mutual deterrence, the threat of nuclear war was immediate and powerful. Schoolchildren were drilled in safety procedures such as crouching under classroom desks in the event of a nuclear attack. Instructions for building bomb shelters in homes were disseminated, and some were built. The feasibility of developing a shield to protect the United States from missiles was the subject of great public attention. Proposals for easing tensions between the United States and the Soviet Union triggered passionate debates.

The Cold War has ended, but in recent decades civilian populations in many parts of the world have been or are being subjected to severe oppression and even large-scale massacres. Hitler, Stalin, and Mao Zedong led the way in defining fellow citizens as the enemy to be obliterated or violently oppressed. In many, perhaps the majority, of situations in recent decades, the chief danger to civilians has come from fellow citizens or their own government; examples include Cambodia, the Kurds of the Middle East, the massacres in sub-Saharan Africa, and the violent turmoil in the former nation-state of Yugoslavia. Today, many wars are likely to be intranational, not international.

In the absence of wars or mass oppression of citizenry, terrorist activities on a large scale are becoming a prominent feature of modern life. In the past, they were limited in scope—an assassination or a small-scale bombing. Now loss of life and destruction of property may be massive—for example, the destruction of a Trans World Airlines plane over Lockerbie, Scotland, as well as the bombing of the World Trade Center in New York City and the Federal Building in Oklahoma City. Although detente between the former Soviet Union and the United States has removed the threat of a catastrophe comparable to the Cuban missile crisis, nuclear menace is hardly a thing of the past. Many a Russian nuclear bomb is unaccounted for or carelessly guarded. The governments of some nation-states that now possess nuclear weapons or may in the future often do not strike notes of equanimity. To this nuclear threat is added the potential for mass biological or chemical assault, as exemplified by an event of this kind in 1998 in the Tokyo subway system.

The psychological and emotional toll of terror is considerable and is often insufficiently recognized or appreciated. Consider the following comments concerning terrorist bombings in Israel in recent years.

> Israel . . . has been treated to a form of terrorism—suicide bombing—that is more pernicious and terrifying than any form of terrorism ever encountered by a modern democracy. This suicide terrorism invades every aspect of daily life . . . the Israeli public will only act on its instinct for a settlement, if the threat of suicide terrorism is removed. (Friedman, 1997, p. A21)

Anxiety narrows the cognitive map, foreshortening perspective. Fight or flight is frequently the only alternative envisioned by a victim (Bion & Rickman, 1943).

The Persian Gulf War provided an occasion for systematic research carried out primarily by American and Israeli social and behavioral scientists. Pennebaker and Harber (1993) propose a social stage model of coping with the emotional turmoil of war based on a study of American civilians during and after the Persian Gulf War.

> Immediately after an upheaval, individuals openly talk and think about the event for approximately two weeks. Following this emergency stage, individuals progress into an inhibition stage wherein they stop talking about the upheaval but continue thinking about it for approximately six weeks. Certain indicators of distress, such as hostility and dreaming, peak during the inhibition phase. After this time, people enter an adaptation phase wherein they neither talk nor think about the upheaval.

Pennebaker (1989) concludes, "the more that individuals reported talking about their personal traumas, the better their physical and psychological health in the subsequent months and years."

Concerning threat—whether via conventional warfare, nuclear attack, or deployment of chemical or biological weapons—Milburn (1977) says:

> Threats produce some general effects; they serve as stresses. The effects of stress . . . can cumulate to produce well-known effects: shortened time span, a diminished search for alternatives, decreased planning, increased concreteness of thought, simplification of

thought processes, and diminished attention to events outside the point or area most threatened.

During the Persian Gulf War the nation-state of Israel was attacked by Iraq with missiles carrying conventional warheads. This afforded an opportunity for systematic study of civilian populations under assault. According to Milgram (1993),

> Analysis of Israel's psychiatric casualties during the Gulf War confirms the traumatic character of the use of or threat of use of unconventional weapons. Investigators . . . conclude that the specific threat of chemical attack or an actual attack . . . would increase the number of psychiatric casualties enormously, and together with the medical casualties, tax the nation's health systems to its limits. . . . There is uncertainty about the country's ability to predict such attacks in advance, to prevent them, or to cope with their consequences. . . . These kinds of uncertainty may well become debilitating at the level of the individual or the society, the policy maker or the ordinary civilian.

These considerations loom large on the global horizon in an age of potential nuclear blackmail or actual explosion, terroristic tactics utilizing chemical or biological agents, sabotage of planes, destruction of buildings.

The influence on children of intensely troubling social circumstances—war, for example—has received little systematic study. In accord with psychoanalytic theory, children's play mirrors their fears, anxieties, and attempts at control and mastery in the face of stress and trauma (Axline, 1969; Fenichel, 1945). Bat-Zion (1993) studied the play of Israeli children during the Persian Gulf War. During the most stressful period of the war, the children engaged in little play. When stress lessened, they invested energy in play unrelated to the war. When peace was secure and civilian life returned to normal, the children addressed the war in symbolic and concrete play. Zeidner, Klingman, and Itzkovitz (1993) utilized a projective technique to investigate the relationship between stress and coping among Israeli children during the Gulf War. They concluded that children who perceived themselves as recipients of strong social support used functional coping strategies and displayed low anxiety.

Erikson (1963) has delineated ways in which various powerful macrosocial events are integrated into the personality development of children, often in subtle ways that are not clearly discernible. Such experiences shared by a cohort of children may result in consequential social action a generation or two later in life. From this perspective, Bauer (1956) can discern relationships between the attitudes and behavior of bureaucrats in the Soviet Union under Communism and their experiences in infancy and childhood in the nineteenth century. Bonaparte (1947) has illuminated ways in which myths enter into the collective psyche of a nation. She describes the analogies ubiquitously prevalent in the popular art of Germany in the 1930s between Hitler and Siegfried, who slays the dragon and releases the Nibelung Ring, possession of which gives world power. "Hitler, Siegfried's avatar, must combat the sharks of capital, shut in the Nibelheim of International Jewry, and seize the treasure which the dragons—the 'haves' of this world—wrongfully hold" (p. 9). Bonaparte predicts that "Hitler, to the German imagination will remain the Siegfried who fought the Dragon, the mythic hero who conquered Mother Europe. . . . For it is not enough to kill an enemy to obliterate him: he will survive in legend." Germany is now a democracy, but from time to time various demonstrations and activities testify to the power of the Nazi myth and legend (Cowell, 1997).

Bibliography

Axline, V. M. (1964). *Dibs in search of self.* New York: Ballantine Books.

Bat-Zion, N. (1993). Do children play in extreme stress situations? The case of Israeli children under the 1991 missile attack. In E. Klugman & S. Smilansky (Eds.), *Play, politics, and practice.* Unpublished manuscript. Boston: Wheelock College.

Bauer, R. A. (1953). The psychology of the Soviet middle elite: Two case histories. In C. Kluckhohn & H. A. Murray (Eds.), *Personality in nature, society, and culture* (pp. 633–650). New York: Knopf.

Bion, W. R., & Rickman, J. (1943). Intra-group tensions in therapy. *Lancet, 2,* 678–681.

Bonaparte, M. (1947). *Myths of war.* London: Imago.

Cowell, A. (1997, November 5). Pro-Nazi incidents in German army raise alarm. *New York Times,* A4.

Erikson, E. H. (1963). *Childhood and society.* New York: Norton.

Fenichel, P. (1945). *The psychoanalytic theory of neurosis.* New York: Norton.

Friedman, T. L. (1997, October 16). *New York Times,* A21.

Milburn, T. W. (1977). The nature of threat. *Journal of Social Issues, 33,* 126–140.

Milgram, N. (1993). Stress and coping in Israel during the Persian Gulf War. *Journal of Social Issues, 49,* 103–123.

Pennebaker, J. W. (1989). Confession, inhibition, and disease. In L. Berkowitz (Ed.), *Advances in experimental social psychology* (Vol. 22, pp. 211–245). New York: Academic Press.

Pennebaker, J. W., & Harber, K. (1993). A social stage model of collective coping: The Loma Prieta earthquake and the Persian Gulf War. *Journal of Social Issues, 49,* 125–145.

Zeidner, M., Klingman, A., & Itzkovits, R. (1993). Children's affective responses to coping under threat of missile attack. *Journal of Personality Assessment, 60,* 433–457.

Mervin Freedman

Effects on Military Personnel

The psychological effects of war on participants and civilian bystanders are among the most powerful and profound known to humanity. Such effects are inherent in the nature of war, since one primary goal of any combatant force is to break the enemy's will to fight. The nature of warfare also dictates that, rather than having a single effect, war produces multiple interrelated effects. The stress of intense combat stands out as the most dramatic effect. But those who have engaged in warfare often have also undergone exposure to environmental extremes, sleep deprivation, dehydration, nutritional deficits, primitive living conditions, and prolonged separation from families and friends. They return to families and societies that may have changed in their absence. Many of the same psychological effects also occur in military operations that do not involve direct combat, such as peacekeeping operations or disaster relief.

Although the appearance of psychiatric battle casualties in large numbers is a twentieth-century phenomenon (Ingraham & Manning, 1981), psychological consequences of war have been observed over the centuries, albeit with different names and explanations in different eras. References to psychosocial reactions to war can be found in the Bible, the works of Homer, and Shakespeare's plays. Hyams, Wignall, and Roswell (1996) point out common symptom clusters that have been observed since at least the time of the U.S. Civil War. Reviewing English language literature on war-related illnesses since 1863, they found that veterans of each war exhibited poorly understood syndromes of symptoms seen as either psychological or physiological, but with the physiological symptoms being ones that are often related to psychological stress, such as fatigue, sleep disturbance, headache, or impaired memory and concentration. The labels given to these war syndromes have reflected the medical and cultural beliefs of the specific era, but the reported symptoms appear to be remarkably similar over time.

In battle, a substantial percentage of the casualties can be expected to be combat stress reactions (CSR). Estimates of the prevalence of CSR vary, but all agree that the numbers are high. Brill, Beebe, and Lowenstein (1953) report psychiatric CSRs in 28.5% of the force in American combat divisions in World War II. Glass (1973) reports CSR rates ranging between 10 and 48% of individuals wounded in action in U.S. Army engagements in that war. Noy (1991) notes that CSR rate estimates—especially when different forces and different wars are compared—are confounded by lack of a common criterion for defining a CSR casualty, and further, that rates may be underestimated because of delayed CSR reactions as well as CSR casualties appearing statistically as other effects, such as physical illness or discipline problems.

Studies consistently show that CSR rates rise with the intensity of combat and are lower among a force that is winning, or holding the initiative in combat, than among a force that is retreating or facing imminent defeat. In general, the longer a soldier is exposed to direct combat, the more likely that soldier is to develop CSR. However, this depends on the intensity of combat. There is no set minimum duration of exposure to combat before CSR starts to appear in substantial numbers of soldiers. Ingraham and Manning (1981) note that the United States experience in World War II and Korea suggested that 23 to 30 days in direct combat were required before a unit started showing large numbers of CSRs. However, in 1973 the Israelis encountered CSRs within 24 hours of intense combat, which Ingraham and Manning attribute to the terror introduced by the lethality of modern weaponry and the rapid pace of warfare.

The question of what causes one soldier to experience a CSR, whereas another who has been through similar combat does not, remains open. Research has failed to identify any preexisting personality trait or disposition that predisposes an individual to CSR, although there is evidence that personality may influence recovery from CSR (Noy, 1991). Solomon, Noy, and Bar-On (1986) did find individual differences in susceptibility to CSR among Israeli soldiers in the 1982 conflict in Lebanon, with those over age 26, reservists, those with a low level of education, those of low military rank, and those with a low score on a combat suitability composite measure (computed at the time of induction) being most vulnerable to CSR. However, this finding does not alter the more general conclusion that anyone might become a stress casualty given a sufficient duration and intensity of combat. Bartone (1996) has presented evidence that personality hardiness, a cognitive style that influences how stressful circumstances are processed and integrated into a person's life experience (Kobasa, 1979), may serve as a buffer against stress in noncombat situations and may well extend to combat. Hardiness may correlate with some of the factors identified by Solomon and colleagues. Thus, Bartone's findings, while not negating the proposition that no one is immune to CSR, suggest a potential direction for future attempts to identify individual factors leading to or mitigating against CSR.

Social and interpersonal factors appear to be better predictors of susceptibility to CSR. Starting with classic studies done after World War II (Shils & Janowitz, 1948; Weinstein, 1947), these factors have received increasing attention in the literature. The overlapping concepts of morale, cohesion, and esprit de corps are commonly mentioned as factors that protect against CSR, although, as Manning (1991) notes, these are all terms that have been defined in various ways and must be defined carefully to have any value. Manning defines morale as "the enthusiasm and persistence with which a member of a group engages in the prescribed activities of that group," noting that, in military settings at least, it is important to differentiate morale from happiness or mood and to tie the concept of morale to a goal-oriented group. Cohesion and esprit both contribute to morale. *Cohesion* is generally defined as bonding of soldiers to each other in primary groups that have face-to-face interaction, and *esprit*, a term that is harder to define precisely, refers to soldiers' sense of identification with larger groups such as their divisions, their branch of service, or the nation or cause they serve. Other protective factors include confidence in the caring and tactical proficiency of leaders and the quality of training, which serves to build confidence as well as cohesion.

Although psychiatric battle casualties are the effect of warfare that is typically identified as uniquely military, there are other potential adverse psychological effects that may not be labeled as CSR. The U.S. involvement in Vietnam is often characterized as producing a low rate of CSR, but there were substance abuse problems, disciplinary problems, including attacks on leaders ("fragging"), and evacuations for psychoses that do not appear in the statistics as CSR (Jones & Johnson, 1975). One could consider these alternative expressions of the stresses of that war, even though the causal links are not firmly established. Furthermore, some effects do not appear until later. Noy (1991) argues that CSR must be viewed as having an immediate stage, lasting for hours to days, an acute stage lasting for weeks to months, and a chronic stage that may not begin until several months after the combat exposure. The chronic stage is most often seen as posttraumatic stress disorder, but it may also include other psychiatric disorders, as well as problems of family and occupational readjustment.

One weakness in our knowledge of the effects of war on participants is the lack of long-term studies, particularly of nonclinical populations. One exception to this generalization is the work of Elder and his colleagues (Elder, Shanahan, & Clipp, 1997). Taking data from a group of U.S. World War II veterans who had been enrolled in a prospective study before the war started, they found that those who had served in combat were more likely to suffer physical decline or death in the 15 years after the war. Combat veterans were also more than twice as likely to describe themselves as heavy or problem drinkers. However, these health and mortality findings were restricted to the first 15 years after the war. No differences were found in lifetime health trajectory outside of this 15-year period, and combat veterans were similar to others in their marital and occupational lives. However, the group they studied was a narrow sample of the population, and more such longitudinal research is needed.

Another problem is that most of what is known comes from studies of individuals who have been in treatment or otherwise suffered negative consequences as a result of wartime experiences. Little attention has been paid to individuals who have coped well with their experiences and who may even have gained some benefits from their wartime experience (Antonovsky & Bernstein, 1986). As a result, our knowledge centers on pathology, without consideration of the majority of combatants who, despite the extremely stressful nature of war, have not become the focus of mental health attention. These authors note that even in studies that include successful copers, the emphasis is on absence of pathology rather than on what strengths these individuals have. Although it is understandable that research would focus on the negative aspects of participation in war, we will probably never fully understand the psychological effects of war on soldiers until we better understand those individuals who engage in intense combat and yet are able to process their experiences in a manner that leads to healthy coping, and until we take a life course perspective in our study of the effects of war.

Bibliography

Antonovsky, A., & Bernstein, J. (1986). Pathogenesis and salutogenesis in war and other crises: Who studies the successful coper? In N. A. Milgram, (Ed.), *Stress and coping in time of war: Generalizations from the Israeli experience* (pp. 52–65). New York: Brunner/Mazel.

Bartone, P. T. (1996). Family notification and survivor assistance: Thinking the unthinkable. In R. J. Ursano & A. E. Norwood (Eds.), *Emotional aftermath of the Persian Gulf War: Veterans, families, communities, and nations* (pp. 315–350). Washington, DC: American Psychiatric Press.

Brill, N. Q., Beebe, G. W., & Lowenstein, R. L. (1953). Age and resistance to military stress. *U.S. Armed Forces Medical Journal, 4*(9), 1247–1266.

Elder, G. H., Shanahan, M. J., & Clipp, E. C. (1997). Linking combat and physical health: The legacy of World War II in men's lives. *American Journal of Psychiatry, 154*(3), 330–336.

Glass, A. J. (1973). *Neuropsychiatry in World War II: Vol. 2. Overseas theaters.* (W. S. Mullins, Series Ed.) Washington, DC: Office of the Surgeon General, Department of the Army, U.S. Army.

Hyams, K. C., Wignall, F. S., & Roswell, R. (1996). War syndromes and their evaluation: From the U.S. Civil War to the Persian Gulf War. *Annals of Internal Medicine, 125*(5), 398–403.

Ingraham, L. H., & Manning, F. J. (1981). Cohesion: Who needs it, what is it, and how do we get it to them? *Military Review, 61*(6), 2–12.

Jones, F. D., & Johnson, A. W. (1975). Medical and psychiatric treatment, policy, and practice in Vietnam. *Journal of Social Issues, 31*(4), 49–65.

Kobasa, S. C. (1979). Stressful life events, personality, and health: An inquiry into hardiness. *Journal of Personality and Social Psychology, 37*, 1–11.

Manning, F. J. (1991). Morale, cohesion, and esprit de corps. In R. Gal & A. D. Mangelsdorff (Eds.), *Handbook of military psychology* (pp. 453–470). West Sussex, UK: Wiley.

Noy, S. (1991). Combat stress reactions. In R. Gal & A. D. Mangelsdorff (Eds.), *Handbook of military psychology* (pp. 507–530). West Sussex, UK: Wiley.

Shils, F. A., & Janowitz, M. (1948). Cohesion and disintegration in the Wehrmacht in World War II. *Public Opinion Quarterly, 12*, 280–315.

Solomon, Z., Noy, S., & Bar-On, R. (1986). Who is at risk for combat stress reaction syndrome? In N. A. Milgram (Ed.), *Stress and coping in time of war: Generalizations from the Israeli experience* (pp. 78–83). New York: Brunner/Mazel.

Weinstein, E. A. (1947). The function of interpersonal relations in the neurosis of combat. *Psychiatry, 10*, 307–314.

Robert K. Gifford

WARD, JAMES (1843–1925), British psychologist and philosopher. Born in Hull and raised in Liverpool, Ward was the eldest son of a merchant whose business failures forced James Jr. to leave school at 13. Largely self-taught, Ward served 4 years as an architectural apprentice, while pursuing his interest in natural history. In 1863 he began a 6-year course of studies to prepare himself for the Congregational ministry. During these studies, Ward's increasing awareness of the tension between science and religion stimulated his interest in philosophy and precipitated a crisis in his faith. After spending an unhappy year preaching at the Cambridge Congregational Chapel, Ward, at the age of 29, enrolled at Trinity College, Cambridge, where he came under the influence of Henry Sidgwick, the moral philosopher whose struggles with faith and science mirrored Ward's own.

Ward belonged to a generation of British philosophers whose German education stimulated a critique of their native empiricist tradition. From 1869 to 1870 he attended lectures by Isaac Dorner in Berlin and Hermann Lotze in Goettingen. Ward was particularly impressed by Lotze's claim that science, aesthetics, and moral inquiry all represent legitimate paths to knowledge. In 1876, Ward returned to Germany to work with the physiologist Karl Ludwig, and he continued physiological research upon his return to Cambridge. Although Ward published several physiological papers, his conviction that natural science could not provide an exhaustive account of reality was one factor that led him to insist that psychology must remain independent of physiology.

Ward's account of psychology, summarized in his famous 1886 *Encyclopedia Britannica* article "Psychology" and elaborated in his book *Psychological Principles* (1918), proclaimed a new departure for British psychology. Ward claimed psychology must examine experience from the standpoint of the active conscious subject. This claim undermined the psychological atomism of associationists such as Alexander Bain. For Ward, the conscious subject first encounters an undifferentiated presentational continuum, not a series of discrete presentations. It is the subject's power of directing attention, guided by feeling, that differentiates and elaborates mental objects. Ward insisted that mental (and motor) development is not a mechanical process of accretion or aggregation, but rather an organic process of unfolding or segmentation. The central role given to the activity of the subject and Ward's organic view of development signaled a new start for British psychology, one that made it relatively immune to the behaviorism that swept the United States in the early twentieth century.

Ward taught at Trinity College, Cambridge, until his death in 1925. He held a lectureship in moral science from 1881 to 1897, when he was appointed to the newly established Knightsbridge Chair of Mental Philosophy and Logic. Ward spearheaded the creation of Cambridge's laboratory of experimental psychology and instituted curriculum changes that established Cambridge as Britain's leading center of psychological work. During the 1880s Ward offered courses in psychology as it applied to education, including treatment of both intellectual and moral issues, at Cambridge's newly formed Teacher's Training Syndicate.

Ward's institutional and conceptual contributions to psychology and philosophy had lasting effects. Ward was a founding editor of the *British Journal of Psychology* (1904) and one of the founding members of the British Psychological Association (1901). His theoretical formulations influenced the philosophical psychology of G. H Stout, the cognitive psychology of F. C. Bartlett, and the self-psychology of Mary Whiton Calkins.

Bibliography

Bartlett, F. C. (1925). James Ward: 1843–1925. *American Journal of Psychology, 36*, 449–453.

James Ward Commemorative Number. (1926). *The Monist, 36*(1). This special issue includes several essays assessing Ward's work, as well as a fairly complete list of his writings.

Sorley, W. R. (1925). James Ward. *Mind, 34*, 273–279.
Ward, J. (1926). *Psychology applied to education* (G. Dawes Hicks, Ed.). Cambridge, UK: Cambridge University Press. This posthumously published collection of Ward's educational essays is worth consulting.
Ward, J. (1927). *Essays in philosophy* (W. R. Sorley & G. F. Stout, Eds.). Cambridge, UK: Cambridge University Press. This volume contains a memoir prepared by Ward's daughter, Olwen Ward Campbell.

Deborah F. Johnson

WARDEN, CARL JOHN (1890–1961), American comparative psychologist. Carl Warden was born in Hamilton, Missouri, and received a bachelor's degree from Cotner College in 1915 and a master's degree from the University of Nebraska the following year. After working in the personnel division of Montgomery Ward for 2 years, Warden attended the University of Chicago, where he completed his Ph.D. degree in 1922. He joined the faculty of the University of Wisconsin for 1 year in 1923 and then moved to Columbia University, where he spent the rest of his academic career.

Warden's best known research concerned studies of motivation in rats in the Columbia obstruction box, a device he designed. Rats were placed in one end of the apparatus, and an incentive was placed at the other end; the two were separated by a shock grid. The intensity of the motivation was inferred from the strength of electric shock that an animal would endure in order to reach the incentive. By comparing different incentives under different conditions, Warden could scale various motivational states.

Warden was also interested in comparative studies of intelligence and perception. He studied the manner in which rats learn mazes and was involved in controversy on that topic with Edward Tolman. [*See the biography of Tolman.*] Warden used mazes, such as the U-maze, that were simpler than the traditional mazes, such as the one at Hampton Court in England. Another topic was the effectiveness of punishment.

Warden was skeptical of claims concerning genius and human-level performance in animals. He was especially critical of authors who relied on anecdotes in estimating the capacities of animals. He studied the sensory capacities and learning abilities of dogs in an effort to provide realistic estimates of their abilities under controlled conditions.

Interested in the study of imitation, a classic problem in comparative psychology, Warden found that rhesus monkeys were capable of imitating the solutions to manipulative tasks displayed by companion monkeys in adjacent cages. He believed that the ability to imitate was orthogonal to problem-solving ability. Warden studied illusions, brightness perception, and size discrimination in ring doves. In work with humans he studied the learning of stylus mazes, effects of advertising, and motivation in the classroom.

Warden was well known as a systematizer of comparative psychology. His three-volume *Comparative Psychology: A Comprehensive Treatise* (1935), written with Thomas N. Jenkins and Lucien H. Warner, became a standard source for many years. The volumes covered historical, conceptual, and methodological principles, as well as research results for both vertebrates and invertebrates. A shortened version (Warden, Jenkins, & Warner, 1934) served as a useful textbook in the field.

In both journal articles and his books, Warden did much to advance the study of the history of comparative psychology with scholarly treatments of the development of the field.

Warden served as associate editor of both the *Journal of Genetic Psychology* and *Genetic Psychology Monographs*. He was a member of the American Psychological Association and a fellow of the American Association for the Advancement of Science and the American Eugenics Society. He died in a nursing home in DeLand, Florida.

Bibliography

Works by Warden

Warden, C. J. (1928). The development of modern comparative psychology. *Quarterly Review of Biology, 3*, 486–522.
Warden, C. J. (1931). *Animal motivation: Experimental studies on the albino rat*. New York: Columbia University Press.
Warden, C. J. (1932). *The evolution of human behavior*. New York: Macmillan.
Warden, C. J., Jenkins, T. N., & Warner, L. H. (1940). *Comparative psychology: A comprehensive treatise* (Vols. 1–3). New York: Ronald Press. (Original work published 1935)
Warden, C. J., Jenkins, T. N., & Warner, L. H. (1934). *Introduction to comparative psychology*. New York: Ronald Press.

Works about Warden

Prof. Carl Warden dies at 70; retired Columbia psychologist. (1961, March 1). *New York Times*, p. 33.

Donald A. Dewsbury

WARREN, HOWARD CROSBY (1867–1934), American psychologist. Born in Montclair, New Jersey, the second son of a successful businessman, Warren was raised in a prosperous but puritanical household. In infancy he was accidentally burned and badly scarred.

He spent much of his early life recuperating from successive operations, and the enforced isolation shaped his introspective and emotionally reticent character. Educated by private tutors and in small private schools, he entered Princeton University at the age of 18 to study civil engineering. There he read works by Spencer, Clifford, and Tyndall and spent much of his undergraduate career attempting to reconcile naturalism and mysticism, a phase that ended when he concluded that "spirituality was nothing more than earnest endeavor, plus emotion" (Warren, 1930).

Warren graduated from Princeton in 1889, winning the Mental Science Fellowship, and began graduate work at Princeton in philosophy. Although he found James McCosh an inspiring teacher, he was more attracted to the atomistic approach of the associationists. Encouraged to study the new psychology in Germany, in 1891 he traveled to Leipzig to study with William Wundt. Although he made the acquaintance of Edward Bradford Titchener and Lightner Witmer, he never became part of Wundt's inner circle. The following year he attended lectures by Ebbinghaus in Berlin, Théodule Ribot in Paris, and Carl Stumpf in Munich and began work on the two theoretical problems that would occupy him throughout his professional career—the problem of accounting for mental qualities in an atomistic universe and the double aspect view of the mind-body relation.

Warren's doctoral work was interrupted when James Mark Baldwin offered his former student a position as a psychology laboratory assistant at Princeton. Warren took the position and remained at Princeton for over 30 years, earning promotions to assistant professor (1896) and professor of psychology (1902) while serving as director of the psychological laboratory. When Baldwin moved to Johns Hopkins in 1903, Warren reluctantly assumed leadership and became embroiled in conflicts with the philosophy department. Warren created an independent department of psychology at Princeton (1920) and solicited support and funding for the construction of Enos Hall (1924), the first psychology building at an American university.

Warren's publications include a translation of G. Tarde's *Social Laws, an Outline of Sociology* (1899); *Human Psychology* (1919), a textbook that went through several editions, and *History of the Association Psychology* (1921), a classic account of associationism. Portions of this last work were accepted as his doctoral thesis work, and he was awarded his doctoral degree from Johns Hopkins on his fiftieth birthday in 1917.

Warren played a pivotal role in founding, nurturing, and financially sustaining key journals in the field. In 1893 Baldwin assigned Warren the task of compiling a bibliography for the *Psychological Review*, and the following year the first issue of the *Psychological Index* (later *Psychological Abstracts*), edited by Warren and Livingston Farrand, appeared. Warren became editor of the new journal the *Psychological Bulletin* in 1904. In 1910 he purchased the review publications *Psychological Review, Psychological Monographs*, and *Psychological Bulletin* from Baldwin and assumed the task of managing the company. A fourth journal, the *Journal of Experimental Psychology*, edited by J. B. Watson, was founded in 1916. In 1925 Warren sold the review publications to the American Psychological Association (APA) at their original price and, in 1929, when the debt was two-thirds paid, he forgave the remaining debt. Warren was an active member of the APA, chairing several committees and serving as president in 1913.

Warren's theoretical concerns and his "journey from mysticism to mechanism" mirrored those of many in his generation. Although convinced of the value of mechanism as a working hypothesis, he recognized the limitations of the mechanistic framework and argued, against the behaviorists, that introspection plays a key role in psychology. Warren's nurturing of some of the early psychology journals and his generosity in transferring them to the APA represent his most enduring contribution to psychology.

Bibliography

Fernberger, S. W. (1934). Howard Crosby Warren 1867–1934. *Psychological Bulletin, 31*, 1–4.

Langfeld, H. S. (1936). Howard Crosby Warren. In D. Malone (Ed.), *Dictionary of American biography* (Vol. 19, pp. 476–477). New York: Scribner.

Warren, H. C. (1919). *Human psychology*. Boston: Houghton Mifflin.

Warren, H. C. (1930). Howard Crosby Warren. In C. Murchison (Ed.), *A history of psychology in autobiography* (Vol. 1, pp. 443–469). Worcester, MA: Clark University Press.

Warren, H. C. (1934). *Dictionary of psychology*. Boston: Houghton Mifflin.

Woodworth, R. S. (1934). Howard Crosby Warren: Associate editor, *Psychological Review*, 1901–1909, editor 1916–1934. *Psychological Review, 41*, 105–107.

Deborah F. Johnson

WASHBURN, MARGARET FLOY (1871–1939), American psychologist. Early recognized as an eminent psychologist and one of the first women in the field, Washburn achieved enduring status as academician, experimentalist, author, theorist, and contributor to the early development of psychology as a scientific discipline and scholarly profession in the United States.

She was born in New York City and entered Vassar College in 1886, where she was introduced to the new field of psychology in a required senior course. Upon graduation in 1891, recognizing that psychology combined her strongest intellectual interests, philosophy and science, she attempted to enroll for graduate study at Columbia University. Supported by James McKeen Cattell but denied admission to regular status because of her gender, she transferred to Cornell University and became E. B. Titchener's first graduate student there. Upon completion of her doctoral thesis on the influence of visual imagery on judgments of tactual distance and direction, she received the Ph.D. degree in 1894 and was elected to membership in the newly organized American Psychological Association (APA).

Following a teaching position at Wells College (1894–1900), 2 years at Cornell as warden (i.e., dean of women) of Sage College and part-time lecturer, and a year as the only woman on the faculty at University of Cincinnati, she returned to Vassar College as associate professor of philosophy in 1903. She became head of the psychology department when it was formed in 1912 and remained at Vassar until her retirement in 1937, establishing there one of the most significant psychological centers in the country. Although she lacked graduate students and extensive laboratory facilities and regularly carried a heavy teaching load, Washburn nevertheless produced a continuous stream of experimental work by recruiting advanced undergraduate students in the study of a variety of subjects, including spatial perception by different senses, memory, experimental aesthetics, individual differences, animal psychology, emotion, and affective consciousness. These studies were published, principally in the *American Journal of Psychology*, in a series of 69 articles over a period of 35 years.

Washburn's most widely recognized publication was *The Animal Mind* (1908), the first comprehensive textbook of comparative psychology, in which she compiled, analyzed, and interpreted the rapidly expanding body of experimental studies of animal behavior and mentality. Washburn maintained throughout her career a strong adherence, evident even in the fourth edition of the book in 1936, to the position that psychology must include the study of both behavior and consciousness. Her position vis-à-vis the dominant theoretical systems of early twentieth-century psychology was stated succinctly in 1930 when she defended her own motor theory, developed earlier and based on physiological evidence and logic, that accounted for the facts of drive, emotion, learning, perception, and thinking. She believed that her independently derived approach agreed better with functional psychology than other systems, although she rejected the interactionism of the functionalists.

Despite disagreements with them on theoretical matters, Washburn developed and maintained cordial and facilitative professional relationships with leaders of the major systems, including especially Cattell and R. S. Woodworth at Columbia; Titchener, Madison Bentley, and Karl M. Dallenbach at Cornell; Robert M. Yerkes and E. G. Boring at Harvard; Howard C. Warren at Princeton; and Walter M. Pillsbury at Michigan. The respect these and other colleagues held for her was indicated by the honors they bestowed. She was the second woman elected as APA president, serving in 1921, and 10 years later was elected chair of the Society of Experimental Psychologists as well as president of the New York Branch of APA (which later became the Eastern Psychological Association). Washburn's highest honor was election to the National Academy of Sciences in 1932. She was the first woman psychologist and the second woman scientist to be awarded that distinction.

In addition to her own scholarly work, Washburn actively supported and participated in the various kinds of professional service important for establishing and maintaining psychology as a discipline. Her literary skills, mastery of subject areas, professional contacts, and critical judgment were valuable to the several journals for which she carried significant editorial responsibilities that spanned her career years at Vassar: *American Journal of Psychology* (1903–1937), *Psychological Bulletin* (1909–1915), *Journal of Animal Behavior* (1911–1917), *Psychological Review* (1916–1930), and *Journal of Comparative Psychology* (1921–1935). She served also as member of the APA Council (1912–1914), psychology representative to the National Research Council Division of Psychology and Anthropology (1919–1920, 1925–1928), vice president and chair of the psychology section of the American Association for the Advancement of Science (1927), and member of the International Committee on Psychology (1929). In addition she contributed importantly to several significant national committees addressing particular issues.

Margaret Washburn's prolonged and accomplished career was extraordinary in several ways. She was one of the most productive and influential among the first group of psychologists trained in America. That she achieved her prestige as a woman and while situated at a woman's college rather than a university research center was all the more remarkable. She overcame the obstacles that handicapped most women of her cohort (see Scarborough and Furumoto, 1987) because of the combination of several circumstances as well as her individual choices. As the only child of an educated mother, she benefited from an inheritance from her mother's family and was supported in her scholarly ambitions by both parents, thereby assuring her ability to move through undergraduate and graduate study without interruption from family obligations or economic hardship. The opening of the psychology laboratories at Columbia and Cornell at just the time she was seeking graduate work was also facilitative, as was the location of these two institutions in her home state, which permitted her to remain close to her parents. Her early experiences at Columbia and Cornell put her in close contact with men who were at the forefront of psychology's emergence as a scholarly profession and allowed the development of early contacts that she maintained and nourished in later years through frequent travel and participation in professional organizations. She was thereby able to minimize the collegial exclusion that typically worked against women's full participation. Importantly, Washburn appears not to have suffered the agony of the marriage versus career dilemma. Marriage and maternity apparently did not appeal to her as personal goals, and she gained great satisfaction in her career activities as well as rich social experiences amongst the faculty at Vassar College and her professional colleagues at other institutions.

Washburn's status as an influential psychologist was first documented in 1903 when she was ranked among the top fifty psychologists in the country. Her sustained reputation was affirmed in a 1967 study (Annin, Boring, & Watson, 1968) that placed her among the most eminent contributors to psychology who lived between 1600 and 1967.

Bibliography

Annin, E. L., Boring, E. G., & Watson, R. I. (1968). Important psychologists, 1600–1967. *Journal of the History of the Behavioral Sciences, 4*, 303–315.

Goodman, E. S. (1980). Margaret F. Washburn (1871–1939): First woman Ph.D. in psychology. *Psychology of Women Quarterly, 5*, 69–80.

Scarborough, E. (1990). Margaret Floy Washburn. In A. N. O'Connell & N. F. Russo (Eds.), *Women in psychology: A bio-bibliographic sourcebook* (pp. 342–349). New York: Greenwood Press. Includes bibliography of selected works by and on Washburn.

Scarborough, E., & Furumoto, L. (1987). *Untold lives: The first generation of American women psychologists.* New York: Columbia University Press. Discusses gender-specific issues faced by early women psychologists and includes a chapter focusing on Washburn.

Washburn, M. F. (1936). *The animal mind: A text-book of comparative psychology.* New York: Macmillan. (Original work published 1908) Successive editions in 1917, 1926, and 1936.

Washburn, M. F. (1930). A system of motor psychology. In C. Murchison (Ed.), *Psychologies of 1930* (pp. 81–94). Worcester, MA: Clark University Press.

Washburn, M. F. (1932). Some recollections. In C. Murchison (Ed.), *A history of psychology in autobiography* (Vol. 2, pp. 333–358). Worcester, MA: Clark University Press.

Elizabeth Scarborough

WATSON, JOHN B. (1878–1958), American psychologist. As the founder of behaviorism and as a publicist and popularizer of psychology, John B. Watson was perhaps the most influential American psychologist of his generation. Born in 1878 near Greenville, South Carolina, Watson grew up in a large and poor rural family. In 1890, Watson's mother, a devout Baptist, moved the children from their isolated family farm to the relatively large town of Greenville. She hoped both to distance the children from their largely absent, hard-drinking father and to give them opportunities lacking in the meager circumstances of near poverty in which they lived.

Swollen by poor white migrants drawn to the burgeoning cotton mills and torn by racial conflict, Greenville, in microcosm, mirrored the social unrest and economic turbulence experienced by larger urban centers in America. Watson's adjustment to these new surroundings was a difficult one. He later recalled that these were unpleasant and troubled years marked by indifference to schoolwork and brushes with the law.

Nevertheless, Watson prepared to enter Furman University, a small Baptist college near Greenville. There, despite an uneven academic performance, he glimpsed a wider professional world and resolved, however ambiguously, to succeed in it. Graduating in 1899 with a master's degree, Watson taught for a year in a small private academy in rural South Carolina. At that point, his mother died, and Watson determined to seek further training. Watson managed to obtain a scholarship from the University of Chicago, which he entered in the fall of 1900.

At Chicago, Watson studied with John Dewey, psychologist James Rowland Angell, neurophysiologist H. H. Donaldson, and biologist Jacques Loeb. Initially attracted to philosophy, Watson was drawn to the new science of psychology by Angell, who been instrumental in founding the functional school of psychology at Chicago. Influenced by Charles Darwin, William James, and John Dewey, functionalists opposed the elementistic psychology developed by Wilhelm Wundt in Germany and espoused in America as structuralism by British-trained psychologist E. B. Titchener. Whereas structuralism attempted to discover an underlying structure of the mind by first isolating basic elements of consciousness, functionalism was concerned with the mind in use. Following James, functionalists held that the mind was essentially a problem-solving organ and that the function of consciousness itself was its capacity to enable an organism to adapt to its environment.

Although Angell's protegé, Watson was later to reject both structuralism and functionalism. Even as a student he was particularly influenced by Jacques Loeb's insistence that all life processes could be explained in physiochemical terms. Watson's own interests lay in comparative or animal psychology. He was uncomfortable with human subjects and what he considered to be the artificiality of introspective methods, which required subjects to observe and record the sensations and perceptions of their own conscious experience. His dissertation, completed under Donaldson, was a study of the correlation between the learned behavior and the neurophysiology of the white rat. In 1903, Watson received the first Ph.D. degree in psychology awarded by the University of Chicago. With the recommendation of Angell and Dewey, he was invited to stay at Chicago as lecturer and director of the psychological laboratory, where he quickly gained a reputation as a leading figure in the relatively new field of comparative psychology.

Soon after he received his degree, Watson married Mary Ickes, who had been one of his students. Strained from the beginning, this relationship was further complicated by the fierce enmity of Watson's brother-in-law, Harold Ickes. Ickes (who, years later, became Franklin D. Roosevelt's secretary of the interior) was irked by Watson's social pretensions and was convinced of his infidelity. When Ickes attempted to have Watson dismissed from the university, however, Watson's colleagues rallied to his defense and the matter was dropped.

In the summer of 1907, Watson began what was to become a series of experiments in the Dry Tortugas of the Florida Keys. Funded by the Carnegie Institute, Watson set out to observe the behavior of noddy and sooty terns. He was interested in determining the origin of their migrating and nesting habits. He was not convinced that instincts accounted for such behavior, but believed that he could demonstrate that behavior such as the "homing instinct" was learned. He was also determined to develop techniques that could control the learning process itself.

In 1908, Watson was invited by James Mark Baldwin to develop a program in experimental psychology at Johns Hopkins University. Less than a year later, Baldwin was forced to resign. Baldwin's misfortune was a windfall for Watson, leaving him chairman of the department and editor of the *Psychological Review.* Thus, at 31, Watson became the director of psychology at a major research institution and editor of an influential journal within the profession. Now he would have access to funding for his own research and a forum for the dissemination of his ideas.

Watson became increasingly dissatisfied with the assumptions of both structuralism and functionalism. He wanted to demonstrate that psychology was a true experimental science, based upon a sound methodology, but capable of producing knowledge with practical applications. As long as psychology considered its subject matter to be the investigation of consciousness, he argued, it perpetuated a mind-body dualism that kept it beyond the pale of current scientific thought. Watson believed that he could resolve this issue by denying the existence of mind as a distinct entity. For years he had been investigating animals without referring to purely mental categories or functions. As early as 1910, he had become convinced that psychological investigations could be conducted exclusively through the observation of behavior without any reference to consciousness. At that point, however, he was not yet willing to challenge the leadership of the profession.

It was not until 1913 that Watson stated his position publicly. In a lecture at Columbia University called "Psychology as the Behaviorist Views It" he challenged psychologists' fundamental assumptions and called for radical measures to prepare the way for a science of behavior that would fulfill what he believed to be the true promise of psychology. Lamenting that psychology had failed to be fully accepted as a natural science, Watson blamed psychologists' use of the introspective method and such imprecise concepts as "consciousness." Watson considered concepts such as "mind" and "consciousness" to be as unverifiable as that of "soul" and refused to make assumptions that could not be verified from overt behavior. A behaviorist approach, argued Watson, would permit psychology to become "a purely objective natural science," with its objective being nothing less than "the prediction and control of behavior." Watson hoped to ally psychology with the positivist trend in the natural sciences. He also sought to bridge the gap between applied psychologists and experimentalists. Behaviorism, he claimed, would develop practical tools useful in such vital endeavors as business, education, medicine, and law enforcement. It was not enough for psychology to have a theoretical and methodological footing that would enable it to make an uncontested contribution to scientific knowledge. Watson had a grand vision of its applications. The fruits of psychological research would have an enormous impact on the development of humanity, he believed, for, as he emphasized at the end of his lecture, the ultimate goal of psychology should not only be to be able to understand behavior, but to predict and control it.

Rejecting the notion of consciousness or mind, Watson held all behavior to be conditioned by external experience. Watson's initial formulation of behaviorism, however, had more to do with defining psychology's purpose and function than with any specific methodology beyond a seemingly rigorous empiricism. Yet, his characterization of psychology resonated with a significant group of like-minded colleagues. Watson belonged to the first generation of American-trained psychologists—a cohort determined that psychology no longer remain a stepchild of philosophy, but an empirical science in its own right.

In 1914, Watson became the youngest president in the history of the American Psychological Association. In his presidential address the following year, he proposed the conditioned motor reflex, as described by Russian neurologist V. M. Bechterev, as the basis for an objective methodology that could be used to measure and control sensory responses. Watson was exhilarated by the range of possibilities opened up by the conditioned reflex. Continued conditioning, he discovered, made it possible to narrow the range of stimuli to which a subject will react. The conditioned reflex, then, became not only a method for gathering data, but a tool for modifying behavior. It would become the cornerstone of a science that sought to develop techniques for behavior control. It was at this point that Watson began experiments on human subjects. Adolf Meyer, a leading figure in the development of American psychiatry, had established a clinic and psychological laboratory at the Johns Hopkins Medical School. He was interested in developing reliable and objective methods for studying and treating mental disorders and invited Watson to set up a laboratory at the clinic. Watson had planned to spend the next several years trying to create and refine an objective methodology for deriving a behavioral theory of emotional response. He accepted Meyer's offer and soon began observing human infants sent over to the laboratory from the obstetrical ward of the hospital.

The alliance between Watson and Meyer proved to be a fragile one. Meyer had applauded Watson's critique of structural psychology because he believed that abstracting "mind" into structural elements maintained a mind-body dualism that precluded any functional understanding of mental disorders. He also shared Watson's misgivings about the ability of Freudians to come up with a psychodynamic theory that could be objectively verified. But Watson's exclusive reliance on the conditioned reflex soon alienated Meyer. Watson, Meyer argued, had merely turned structuralism on its head, substituting a mechanistic model of simple reflexes and perpetuating a dualism on the side of "body" that was no better than the structuralists' preoccupation with "mind."

Watson's infant work was temporarily interrupted by the mobilization for World War I. He was among a group of scientists and engineers who played a crucial role in developing wartime policies that would shape peacetime relationships among science, government, and industry for years to come. Watson served for a time on the newly formed National Research Council, then on the Committee for Classification of Personnel in the Army and was commissioned major in the Signal Corps. There, Watson conducted research on homing pigeons for the Army in Texas and Louisiana and developed tests for aviators in France. The military served as a huge laboratory as psychologists worked to coordinate and allocate manpower on a massive scale. Above all, the war underscored Watson's vision of the enormous potential for applied psychology.

When the war ended, Watson returned to his laboratory at Johns Hopkins University. There, he began a series of experiments culminating in the famous "Little Albert" experiment, by which Watson claimed to have developed techniques to condition at will specific emotional reactions in human infants. In this case, Watson sought to demonstrate that a child could be conditioned to fear harmless animals toward which it had previously shown no fear. Watson believed that he had found the key to behavior control which he had long sought.

Watson was at the apex of his academic career. But, ironically, in the midst of conducting this experiment in behavior control he became romantically involved with his graduate assistant. Watson's colleagues sought to reason with him, lest his career be jeopardized. Watson, however, refused to break off the affair. As a result, he was forced to resign from Johns Hopkins in 1920 under the cloud of a widely publicized divorce scandal.

Watson found a temporary haven in New York with his friend, sociologist William I. Thomas, who had been dismissed from the University of Chicago under similar circumstances. Thomas introduced Watson to executives of the J. Walter Thompson advertising agency, who recognized Watson as a valuable asset to their company. Watson's characterization of behaviorism as a science with broad applications to the marketplace was particularly appealing to advertisers. Watson accepted a handsome offer from J. Walter Thompson's president, Stanley Resor, who made him a vice president in 1924. For Watson and his new associates, behaviorism seemed to offer the universal key to human motivation. Behaviorism represented a departure from earlier notions of advertising psychology that emphasized matching rational appeals to distinct mental categories. The behavioral approach ignored questions of the rationality or irrationality of mind and emphasized instead the plasticity of human behavior. Watson remained in advertising until his retirement in 1945. Watson conducted research for the J. Walter Thompson company on brand appeal of cigarettes and developed the "brand X" consumer choice "test" as a marketing tool for advertisers. He developed behavioral sales platforms for Johnson & Johnson baby powder, adapted testimonial advertising for cosmetics, and pioneered in radio advertising.

Watson also struggled to continue his experimental work and maintain his academic connections. During the 1920s he taught at the New School for Social Research and supervised experiments on infants at Columbia University. He also continued to revise his behaviorist theory. But it was, ironically, through Watson's skill as a publicist and popularizer that behaviorism made its strongest impact. During the 1920s and 1930s, Watson not only brought behaviorism to the attention of a broad general readership, but also sparked lively debate among wider scientific circles. Through an enormous output of books, magazine articles, newspaper stories, and radio broadcasts, he established himself in the public eye as an expert on subjects ranging from child care to economics.

His best-selling *Behaviorism* was published in 1924. A generation mystified and apprehensive about the mysteries of science turned with relief to a popularizer like Watson. Above all, behaviorism promised to unlock the mechanism that governed human action. Its notion of a malleable human nature fired the imagination of a new meritocratic elite. Professional managerial classes saw the intractability of the "human factor" as the last obstacle to a rationally managed society. The 1920s witnessed the transformation of large foundations from charitable trusts to professionally managed enterprises. As foundation support became more problem oriented rather than discipline oriented, scientific research came to be defined more and more by issues concerning social conduct and behavior. Within this context, human behavior became the focus of a new synthesis in an increasingly integrated research community. The "social and behavioral sciences" became invariably linked.

Watsonian behaviorism, with its emphasis on the primacy of environment over instincts, held special appeal for reformers who sought a scientific basis to counter genetic-based theories linking intelligence, race, and gender. Watson, however, especially in his utopian writings, never intended for his vision of behaviorism to imply that human beings were equal, but that all human beings were—the same. By rejecting the concept of consciousness, behaviorism at once desanctified both the outer world of nature and the realm of inner experience, reducing both to manipulable objects. If behaviorism represented the freedom to remake the individual, it also raised the specter of social conditioning. Behaviorism, wrote social scientist Horace Kallen, made human beings "as equal as Fords."

As a popularizer of self-help psychology, Watson made behaviorism a household word. His *Psychological Care of Infant and Child* instructed a generation of mothers in behavioral techniques. Watson's claims to demystify human behavior and to simplify the complexities of modern life were enormously appealing to middle-class Americans. By the 1930s, behaviorism had become the dominant paradigm in American experimental psychology. Although few psychologists were willing to accept the more radical aspects of Watson's extreme materialism, behaviorism's objective methodology had a powerful impact on the direction of American psychology. Behaviorism helped legitimize experimental psychology among the natural sciences. Moreover, the popular reception of Watson's behaviorism, which characterized human beings as "organic machines" and envisioned a scientifically managed society, reflects a preoccupation with order and efficiency among those who came to shape modernist America.

[*Many of the people mentioned in this article are the subjects of independent biographical entries.*]

Bibliography

Works by Watson

Watson, J. B. (1914). *Behavior: An introduction to comparative psychology*. New York: Holt.

Watson, J. B. (1919). *Psychology from the standpoint of a behaviorist*. Philadelphia: J. B. Lippincott.

Watson, J. B. (1924). *Behaviorism*. New York: People's Institute.

Watson, J. B. (1928). *The psychological care of infant and child*. New York: Norton.

Watson, J. B. (1929). *The ways of behaviorism*. New York: Harper & Brothers.

Watson, J. B. (1936). John Broadus Watson. In Carl Murchison (Ed.), *A history of psychology in autobiography* (Vol. 3, pp. 271–281). Worcester, MA: Clark University Press.

Works about Watson

Buckley, K. W. (1989). *Mechanical man: John Broadus Watson and the beginnings of behaviorism*. New York: Guilford Press.

O'Donnell, J. M. (1985). *The origins of behaviorism: American psychology, 1870–1920*. New York: New York University Press.

Todd, J. T., Morris, E. K. (Eds.). (1994). *Modern perspectives on John B. Watson and classical behaviorism*. Westport, CT: Greenwood Press.

Kerry W. Buckley

WATT, HENRY JACKSON (1879–1925), Scottish experimental psychologist. Henry J. Watt was born in Aberdeen on 15 July 1879, the youngest son of James and Jane Watt; his schooling was at the Aberdeen Grammar School (a "grammar school" in Britain accepts only gifted students aged from about 11 to about 18). He entered the University of Aberdeen in 1896, obtaining a first-class master's degree in philosophy in 1900. In 1901 and 1902 he studied in Berlin, in particular with Carl Stumpf (1848–1936), an expert on the psychological aspects of auditory perception. He then spent the years 1902 to 1906 with Oswald Külpe (1862–1915) at the University of Würzburg, obtaining his Ph.D. degree with a thesis in German that, when published, was one of the foremost contributions to the research of the "Würzburg School" on the processes of thinking in human adults. [*See the biographies of Stumpf and Külpe.*]

Watt returned to Britain in 1907, being appointed lecturer on psychophysiology at the University of Liverpool, and then moved in 1908 to become lecturer in experimental psychology at the University of Glasgow. In 1909 he married Gertrude Nellie Smith, a pianist he had met in Berlin, and also wrote the first of several books in English on psychological topics, *The Economy and Training of Memory* (1909). This book was designed for the assistance of teachers. Later books included his *The Psychology of Sound* (1917), *The Foundations of Music* (1919), *The Sensory Basis and Structure of Knowledge* (1925), and *The Common Sense of Dreams* (1929). These last two books were published posthumously; he had died in Glasgow on 25 October 1925. His health had been impaired since 1915 when he had been sent home from Germany as an invalid following incarceration as a civilian prisoner at the outbreak of World War I in 1914; he had happened, at that time, to have been on a return visit to Würzburg.

His Würzburg thesis involved visually presenting a series of words (such as object names) to highly trained subjects; the subject's task was to classify the object in question, or to name a whole to which it belonged, or to do some other associative task related to the object name. His analysis of the subject's protocols (their reports of their thought processes during the task) led him to assert that performance was determined not only by the subject's previous experience with the object in question (that is, the subject's "associations") but also by the subject's setting himself or herself to focus explicitly on the "task" (German, *Aufgabe*). Thinking, therefore, is "directed" by the task; it does not wander from association to association in a way determined purely by habit.

In his book on sound, Watt argued that the perception of tones involves not only a sensory analysis of tone intensities and tone frequencies but also takes into account a psychological quality he called tone "volume," a quality he believed to play an intrinsic part in explaining why chords involving octaves, fourths, and fifths appear to be so perceptually unified to musical listeners. In his next book he extended this theory to the study of harmony in music. His book on dreams attempted to show that straightforward associational processes can explain some dream phenomena without recourse to the concept of a Freudian "unconscious," but Watt did accept that dreams could be disguised representations of long-held motives the subject was reluctant to confront consciously. His book on the sensory basis of knowledge incorporated detailed analyses (based on earlier papers by Watt) of the ways in which a given sensation could be described as *quantitatively* related to other sensations that were in the same modality or concerned the same object. Ogden (1926) described the 1925 book as a "swan song" of structural psychology; Watt's mentor, Külpe, had been a founder of structuralism, the attempt to base a scientific psychology on a classification of the characteristics of "sensations," "feelings," and "thoughts" and their interactions.

Bibliography

Dawson, S. (1929). Biographical sketch and bibliography of H. J. Watt. In H. J. Watt, *The common sense of dreams* (pp. vii–xii). Worcester, MA: Clark University Press. A short life of Watt followed by a listing of 31 publications (of these, his thesis and five articles were in German). Valuable summaries of three of the books in English were provided by R. M. Ogden (see below).

Humphrey, G. (1951). *Thinking: An introduction to its experimental psychology*. New York: Wiley. The best account in English of the findings and theories of the Würzburg School; chapter 3 includes a useful summary of Watt's Ph.D degree thesis. Watt himself also summarized the thesis in English in H. J. Watt (1905–1906), Experimental contribution to a theory of thinking. *Journal of Anatomy and Physiology, 40*, 257–266.

Ogden, R. M. (1917). [Review of the book *The psychology of sound*]. *Psychological Bulletin, 14*, 254–258. Ogden stressed how Watt's theory depended heavily on Watt's concept of tone volume.

Ogden, R. M. (1921). [Review of the book *The foundations of music*.] *Psychological Bulletin, 18*, 497–500. While praising Watt's opinions on musical aesthetics, Ogden was more skeptical of the value of Watt's extension of his tone volume theory to the theory of musical harmony. Watt said harmonies are of three main kinds, those based on octaves, fourths, and fifths (which are like anchors); those based on thirds and sixths (which are neutral); and those based on other intervals (which are irregular and tend to sound discordant).

Ogden, R. M. (1926). [Review of the book *The sensory basis and structure of knowledge*.] *Psychological Bulletin, 23*, 603–605. Ogden noted that this book was a near-miss in terms of being a contribution to Gestalt theory, because, in discussing how sensations are related to each other, Watt stressed that some sensory objects are processed holistically.

David J. Murray

WEBER, ERNST HEINRICH (1795–1878), German physicist and physiologist. Weber was born on 24 June 1795, the third of seven surviving children of Michael Weber, a professor of Protestant theology at the University of Wittenberg. Two of his younger brothers, Wilhelm Eduard (1804–1891) and Eduard Friedrich (1806–1871) also became famous as scientists, the former for his work on magnetism and the latter for his work on physiology. Ernst Heinrich went to school in Meissen and entered the University of Wittenberg at the age of 16 to study medicine. After some moves necessitated by his father's being transferred involuntarily from Wittenberg to Halle as a consequence of events in the Napoleonic Wars, he eventually completed a thesis on the sympathetic nervous system at the University of Leipzig in 1817. Acceptance of this thesis (German, *Habilitationsschrift*) allowed him to take a university teaching post. He was promoted in 1821 to the rank of *ordentlicher* (full) professor of anatomy; it was also in 1821 that he married Friedericke Schmidt, with whom he had eight children. In 1840, he was additionally appointed professor of physiology. He retired from the latter chair in 1866 and the former in 1871. He died on 26 January 1878 at the age of 83.

In the area of general physiology, Weber is best known for his discovery in 1845, with his brother Eduard Friedrich, that stimulation of the vagus nerve can inhibit the heartbeat. This was a milestone on the way to our understanding that in the nervous system some synapses are inhibitory as opposed to excitatory, a fact incorporated into nearly all twentieth-century models of neural functioning. Weber also made fundamental contributions to our understanding of the pulse, the spine, and the male reproductive system; he also contributed to hydrodynamics and acoustics. But for psychologists his best known discovery came to be called Weber's Law; it concerned the limits on humans' ability to detect small differences in perceived loudness, brightness, heaviness, and so forth. But this discovery emerged as a by-product of his pioneering experimental research on the touch senses and on sensations of temperature. He also studied pain, sensations from internal organs, sensations of hunger and thirst, and other general "feelings" denoted in Weber's time by the now obsolete expression *common sensibility*.

In his *On the Sensitivity of the Touch Sense (De Subtilitate Tactus*; Leipzig, 1834) and his *On the Touch Sense and Common Sensibility (Tastsinn und Gemeingefühl*, Brunswick, 1846) Weber described his measurement of the sensitivity of the "localization sense" (*Ortsinn*) of the skin surface. If two points are placed fairly close together on the skin, the subject usually reports feeling two sensations of touch. But if the two points are gradually brought even nearer, there will be a crucial distance between them at which the subject reports feeling only one sensation. Later writers called this the "two-point threshold." Weber was able to map the sensitivity of the skin surface of most of the human body in terms of this threshold, showing, for example, that the lips and fingertips are the most sensitive areas and the small of the back the least sensitive area; over a century later, Georg von Békésy, in his *Sensory Inhibition* (Princeton, NJ, 1967), argued that, when only one sensation is felt from two touches, this results from a neural inhibitory mechanism designed to reduce sensory overload.

Weber also explored the sensitivity of the "pressure sense" (*Drucksinn*). It was in this context that Weber's Law was discovered. If a weight is lifted by the fingers, the weight can be increased until the subject reports feeling a just noticeable difference (JND) in the weight's heaviness; the same experiment can be repeated but with the weight's being placed on the subject's outstretched palm instead. The actual increase in grams that is required to produce a JND in heaviness depends partly on whether the weight is lifted or placed on the palm; but in each case it also depends on the number of grams in the weight before any additions are made to the weight. If this "starting weight" has *G* grams, then in order to make it just noticeably heavier, Weber's Law asserts that the extra weight that needs to be added will be a fraction of *G*, a fraction which is always the same provided that the method of assessing the weight's heaviness remains unchanged. For example, the fraction for weights lifted by the fingers was reported by Weber to be about 1/40. So if the starting weight were 100 g, the weight that would be just noticeably heavier would be 100 + (1/40) (100), that is, 102.5 g. If the starting weight had been 500 g, then the weight that would have been just noticeably heavier would have been 500 + (1/40) (500), that is, 512.5 g. The value 1/40 is called the "Weber fraction" for lifted weights. However, the Weber fraction for weights placed on the palm is larger, about 1/30. Hence more grams need to be added to a weight placed on the palm than to a weight lifted by the fingers if the weight is to appear just noticeably heavier. Weber's Law always fails to apply at the extremes of any sensory dimension, but it can occasionally fail to apply within some sensory dimensions as well.

Weber also showed that the rapidity with which a subject could judge whether a stimulus applied to a point on the skin was "hot" or "cold" varied with the body region stimulated, but the variability of such judgments with respect to different body regions was less than that associated with the two-point threshold. He also showed that the perceived warmth or coldness was greater the larger the area of the body stimulated (this is now called "spatial summation"); and he measured how perceived warmth or coldness decreased the longer the hot or cold stimulus was applied to the body region ("sensory adaptation").

Weber's Law formed the foundation upon which Fechner, in his *Elements of Psychophysics* (Leipzig, 1860), based his attempt to found a science relating the subjective "intensity" of a sensation to the objectively measured intensity of the stimulus that evoked that sensation.

Bibliography

Dawson, P. M. (1928). The life and work of Ernst Heinrich Weber. *Phi Beta Pi Quarterly*, *25*, 86–116. This article is particularly useful for its evaluation of Weber's contribution to our understanding of inhibition in the nervous system.

Gescheider, G. A. (1997). *Psychophysics: Method, theory and application* (3rd ed.). Hillsdale, NJ: Erlbaum. A convenient introduction to the topic, including Weber's Law.

Jesteadt, W., Weir, C. C., & Green, D. M. (1977). Intensity discrimination as a function of frequency and sensation level. *Journal of the Acoustical Society of America, 61*, 169–177. A demonstration of how JND data concerning the perceived loudness of pure tones of various frequencies can provide a "near miss" to Weber's Law.

Kruta, V. (1976). Weber, Ernst Heinrich. In C. C. Gillespie (Ed.), *Dictionary of scientific biography* (Vol. 14, pp. 199–202). New York: Charles Scribner's. A particularly useful source in English about Weber's life and contributions to sciences other than psychology.

Murray, D. J. (1993). A perspective for viewing the history of psychophysics. *Behavioral and Brain Sciences, 16*, 115–186. A history of how Fechner and other psychophysicists attempted to incorporate Weber's Law into their theories.

Ross, H. E., & Murray, D. J. (Eds. & Trans.). (1996). *E. H. Weber on the tactile senses* (2nd ed.). Hove, UK: Erlbaum and Taylor & Francis. This book includes English translations of Weber's *De subtilitate tactus* (1834) and *Tastsinn und Gemeingefühl* (1846). It also includes a short biography of Weber, background information on tactile research at the time he wrote, and a summary of research carried out since his time on the two-point threshold, Weber's Law, and other matters.

Solomons, L. M. (1900). A new explanation of Weber's Law. *Psychological Review, 7*, 234–240. One of the first of many attempts to give an explanation of Weber's Law in terms of neural functioning; references to other attempts will be found in Ross and Murray's translation.

Weinstein, S. (1968). Intensive and extensive aspects of tactile sensitivity as a function of body part, sex, and laterality. In D. R. Kenshalo (Ed.), *The skin senses* (pp. 195–222). Springfield, IL: Thomas. A detailed replication of Weber's research on the two-point threshold covering almost the whole body.

David J. Murray

WECHSLER, DAVID (1896–1981), clinical psychologist. Wechsler was born in Romania. He was formally trained in experimental psychopathology, earning his master's degree in 1917 (on retention in Korsakoff's psychosis) and his doctorate in 1925 (on the psychogalvanic skin response and emotion), both at Columbia University under Robert Woodworth.

As he awaited induction into the U.S. Army in 1917, he secured a position in Long Island under Edward G. Boring, requiring him to score thousands of Army Alpha exams. After induction, he was trained to administer individual tests of intelligence such as Terman's fledgling Stanford–Binet and Yerkes' nonverbal test. Because the nonverbal tests were intended for recruits who could not read English and the Binet scale was designed for children, Wechsler became sensitive to the needs of nonmainstream individuals and to the necessity of developing adult-oriented tests for adults. These experiences paved the way for his Wechsler series of scales and his insistence that it was, indeed, essential to measure nonverbal abilities of everyone, not just those who could not speak English, and to provide a profile of IQs and subtest scores, not just one single number.

In 1919, Wechsler studied with Charles Spearman and Karl Pearson at the University of London. Upon returning to America, he went into private practice until 1932, when he became chief psychologist at Bellevue Psychiatric Hospital in New York City, where he worked until 1967.

Wechsler published his first test in 1939, the Wechsler-Bellevue, in which he introduced the Deviation IQs (standard scores) as replacements for the Stanford–Binet's MA/CA formula-driven IQs. He never wavered, however, from his deep-seated belief that standard scores, no matter how seemingly precise, must take a back seat to the clinical aspects of the assessment. Intelligence was only meaningful when interpreted in the broader context of personality. His intent was to measure these conative aspects of intelligence. Wechsler had high hopes that a new level of aspiration test, which was standardized with the 1981 revision of the Wechsler Adult Intelligence Scale (WAIS), would provide a breakthrough in this regard; it did not. At his death, he was disappointed that he had not successfully measured the nonintellective factors associated with intellectual assessment.

Pivotal influences on Wechsler's development as a clinician included Bernard Glueck, one of the first forensic psychologists; F. L. Wells, whose book with J. Ruesch (*Mental Examiners Handbook*, New York, 1945) influenced greatly Wechsler's own approach to psychodiagnosis; Augusta Bronner and William Healy, who were pioneers in multidisciplinary presentation of clinical cases; and A. A. Brill, who encouraged Wechsler to study psychoanalysis in Vienna, where he met Sigmund Freud and his daughter, Anna.

Although Wechsler developed his scales from a practical and clinical perspective, his tests and the thousands of research investigations they have generated have been influential in helping to delineate important concepts in neuropsychological theories, such as Roger Sperry's cerebral specialization theory, and theories of intelligence, notably the Horn-Cattell distinction between fluid and crystallized intelligence. Both the Wechsler Intelligence Scale for Children (WISC-III, 1991) and the Wechsler Adult Intelligence Scale (WAIS-III, 1997) remain the leading instruments for assessing the cognitive abilities of individuals between the ages of 6 and 89 years. Furthermore, the Wechsler Scales are the dominant intelligence tests worldwide, not just within the United States

[*Many of the people mentioned in this article are the subjects of independent biographical entries.*]

Bibliography

Works by Wechsler

Wechsler, D. (1939). *Measurement of adult intelligence.* Baltimore, MD: Williams & Wilkins.

Wechsler D. (1950). Cognitive, conative, and non-intellective intelligence. *American Psychologist, 5,* 78–83.

Wechsler D. (1975). Intelligence defined and undefined: A relativistic appraisal. *American Psychologist, 30,* 135–139.

Wechsler, D. (1989). *Manual for the Wechsler Preschool and Primary Scale of Intelligence-Revised (WPPSI-R).* San Antonio, TX: The Psychological Corporation.

Wechsler, D. (1991). *Manual for the Wechsler Intelligence Scale for Children-Third Edition, (WISC-III).* San Antonio, TX: The Psychological Corporation.

Wechsler, D. (1997). *Manual for the Wechsler Adult Intelligence Scale-Third Edition (WAIS-III).* San Antonio, TX: The Psychological Corporation.

Works about Wechsler

Kaufman, A. S. (1990). *Assessing adolescent and adult intelligence.* Boston, MA: Allyn & Bacon.

Kaufman, A. S. (1994). *Intelligence testing with the WISC-III.* New York: Wiley.

Matarazzo, J. D. (1972). *Wechsler's measurement and appraisal of adult intelligence* (5th ed.). New York: Oxford University Press.

Sattler, J. M. (1988). *Assessment of children* (3rd ed.). San Diego: Author.

Alan S. Kaufman

WECHSLER INTELLIGENCE TESTS. Since their introduction as the Wechsler-Bellevue Intelligence Scale in 1939, David Wechsler published versions of the test for children (Wechsler Intelligence Scale for Children, 1949, 1974, 1991), adults (Wechsler Adult Intelligence Test, 1955, 1981, 1997), and preschoolers (Wechsler Preschool and Primary Scale of Intelligence, 1967, 1989). The scales have been widely used in clinical, educational, and industrial settings around the world because of their usability and the value of the information they provide. Today, the Wechsler scales are still the most widely used individually administered measures of intelligence in psychology (Kaufman, 1990).

The Wechsler scales can be administered to individuals aged four years through adult in approximately 60 minutes. Each of the Wechsler scales were developed using state-of-the-art methods for their time. For example, the statistical methods and scaling developed for the Wechsler-Bellevue became a standard, and the methods for standardization used in the WISC-III and WAIS-III are exemplary. All of Wechsler's tests are organized into two parts: Verbal and Performance. The verbal scales are comprised of subtests that demand the comprehension and use of language. This includes subtests like Vocabulary (oral definition of words), Similarities (explanations of how words are alike), Comprehension (discussion of what should be done in various social situations), and Arithmetic (solving orally presented math word problems). The Performance scale is composed of subtests with nonverbal content such as Block Design (completion of an abstract design using blocks to match a picture), Object Assembly (completion of a puzzle), Picture Completion (identification of a missing portion in a line drawing), and Picture Arrangement (placing line drawings in the correct order to convey a logical story). The Verbal and Performance scales each yield a standardized score with a mean of 100 and standard deviation of 15, as does the Full scale, which is the overall measure of intelligence. These scales reflect David Wechsler's definition of intelligence as the "aggregate or global capacity of the individual to act purposefully, to think rationally, and to deal effectively with his environment" (Matarazzo, 1972, p. 79).

Wechsler's organization of his tests into Verbal and Performance (nonverbal) scales followed the categorization used in the Army Alpha and Beta (Matarazzo, 1972). In fact, much of Wecshler's tests are derived from the methods used by the U.S. military around the time of World War I, as described in the book *Army Mental Testing* (Yoakum & Yerkes, 1920). This testing program was developed for the examination of a large number of adults entering military service and was based substantially on the work of pioneers such as Alfred Binet. [*See the biography of Binet.*] At that time in psychology there was considerable borrowing of methods used in different intelligence tests, well documented in the various sources that describe the development of the first intelligence tests (e.g., see Pintner, 1923). There is a similarity in the content of IQ tests developed at that time as a result of extensive "borrowing from a common professional or scientific pool" (Matarazzo, 1972, p. 44). This continued for many years. The combination of subtests included in the Wechsler scales represented the best thinking of early researchers on how to measure intelligence.

The hallmark of Wechsler's contribution was his ability to transform the group and individual testing procedures of the Army Mental Testing Program into an individually administered test that psychologists could use effectively. The huge success of these efforts is apparent by the widespread use of his scales and the research results presented in many journals throughout the world. Clearly, the Wechsler scales set the standards for what IQ is and how it is measured. In addition, the scales set standards for psychometric characteristics that are often used as examples of excellence. It is only recently that new approaches have been introduced to create norms, but more importantly, some test developers have begun to question the general ability concept used in tests of intelligence like the Wechsler. [*See* Kaufman Assessment Battery for Children.]

The Wechsler scales have been the subject of literally thousands of research papers, book chapters, and books since they were published. The information that has been obtained has demonstrated that the Wechsler scales are reliable and valid measures of general intelligence. This has been shown for children of both genders, of various socioeconomic levels, different races and ethnic backgrounds, and in fact, for children in many countries around the world where the test has been used in translated form. Kaufman (1990, 1994) and Matarazzo (1972) describe much of the research on the tests' use and interpretation, as well as its limitations. Most notably, Kaufman (1994) discussed issues dealing with analysis of the subtest profiles and application of the results for educational interventions. Similarly, Naglieri (1999) and Kaufman and Kaufman (1983) suggested that verbal knowledge (i.e., the Verbal scale) should not be used to assess ability and that a modern view of intelligence and its measurement is needed.

The field of intelligence testing is beginning to change, and the age of the Wechsler scale and the concepts behind it have become subjects of concern, spawning alternatives. Whereas in the past the Wechsler scales have been evaluated in comparison to tests built at that same period, now its value is compared to newer measures based on more modern concepts. Ultimately, the ability of these approaches to meet the needs of users and withstand the critical examination of researchers will determine which instruments psychologists will use in the future.

[*See also* Testing.]

Bibliography

Kaufman, A. S. (1990). *Assessing adolescent and adult intelligence.* New York: Wiley.

Kaufman, A. S. (1994). *Intelligent testing with the WISC-III.* New York: Wiley.

Kaufman, A. S. & Kaufman, N. L. (1983). *Kaufman assessment battery for children.* Circle Pines, MN: American Guidance Service.

Matarazzo, J. D. (1972). *Wechsler's measurement and appraisal of adult intelligence* (5th ed.). Baltimore: Williams & Wilkins.

Naglieri, J. A. (1999). *Essentials of CAS assessment.* New York: Wiley.

Pintner, R. (1923). *Intelligence testing methods and results.* New York: Holt.

Yoakum, C. S., & Yerkes, R. M. (1920). *Army mental tests.* New York: Holt.

Jack A. Naglieri

WECHSLER MEMORY SCALE. Prior to 1945 there was no regularly used standardized clinical assessment tool for the evaluation of memory. Responding to this situation, David Wechsler, one of the most prominent American psychologists in the field of assessment, developed the first Wechsler Memory Scale (WMS). This scale was designed to be a brief and easily administered instrument that covered those aspects of memory thought to be of significance to the clinical examination.

As a result, the original test focused on areas traditional to the mental status evaluation of the client: orientation, mental control (e.g., serial 3s—the repeated subtraction of 3 from a fixed number such as 100), visual memory, memory for pairs of words, and paragraph memory. The original test yielded a total score that was adjusted for age to yield a Memory Quotient (MQ), which was expressed as a standard score that could be directly compared to IQ.

For many years, the WMS was considered the premiere instrument in the assessment of memory, despite such deficiencies as its overreliance on verbal memory, its emphasis on immediate memory, its inadequate normative data, and the conceptual difficulty of classifying clients with a single memory quotient. Despite these deficiencies, the WMS remained popular. However, users of the test often departed from the standard approach to it, employing local norms or adding additional tests of nonverbal memory or tests of memory retention over 30-minute delays.

As a result of the criticisms and change in the knowledge base, Wechsler began revising the WMS in the late 1970s, until the time of his death in 1981. His publisher undertook the task of the completion of this project, publishing the Wechsler Memory Scale–Revised (WMS–R) in 1987. The WMSR represented many changes over the initial battery: the addition of more nonverbal assessment tasks, the provision of 30-minute delayed memory tasks, the collection of more extensive normative data, and the calculation of separate memory indices for visual memory, verbal memory, general memory, attention/concentration, and delayed memory. The new test was longer than the WMS, often taking over an hour to administer in impaired clients.

The new test was rapidly adopted for the assessment of memory and again quickly became the premiere instrument in the field. The WMS–R has remained popular because of its excellent standardization sample and the tradition of regarding the test as the "gold standard" for the general assessment of memory. However, factor analysis of the test did not support Wechsler's five-factor memory model. Over 400 published research articles and numerous presentations have supported the use of the WMS–R as a general test of memory and delayed memory, but has been less supportive of the meaning of the specific verbal and visual indices. The length of the test has led clinicians to seek ways to abbreviate the battery.

Other tests have also become increasingly popular, decreasing the overall importance of the WMS–R. In late 1997, the publishers released a fully revised version (WMS–III), which aimed to respond to many of the criticisms of the WMS–R. The new test appears to be a more theoretically and psychometrically sound instrument, with better potential than the WMS–R. However, there is as yet limited experience with how the test will actually function in clinical settings.

[*See also* Attention; Memory; *and* Testing.]

Bibliography

Golden, C. J. (1992). *Clinical interpretation of objective psychological tests.* Boston: Taylor & Francis. This book contains a description of the interpretive strategies used with the WMS and WMS–R.

Wechsler, D. (1945). A standardized memory test for clinical use. *Journal of Psychology, 19*, 87–95. Although this is a difficult to find source, this is the basic description of and manual for the original Wechsler Memory Scale.

Wechsler, D. (1987). *Wechsler Memory Scale (Revised): Manual.* San Antonio, TX: Psychological Corp. This is the manual and description of the Wechsler Memory Scale–Revised.

Wechsler, D. (1997). *WMS–III: Administration and scoring.* San Antonio, TX: Psychological Corporation. This manual succinctly describes the newest version of the Wechsler Memory Scale.

Charles J. Golden

WEISS, ALBERT PAUL (1879–1931), American psychologist. Weiss came to the United States from Germany as a child. At age 27, he entered the University of Missouri to study science. Weiss's interests shifted to psychology after a chance encounter with the early behaviorist Max F. Meyer (1873–1967). His dissertation under Meyer, *Apparatus and Experiments on Sound Intensity*, was completed in 1916 while employed as an instructor at Ohio State University. Weiss continued at Ohio State and, in 1925, published his principal work, *A Theoretical Basis for Human Behavior* (Columbus, Ohio: 1925). This book established Weiss as an important early behaviorist whose views represented a sophisticated extension of Meyer's ideas. A heart condition claimed Weiss's life in 1931.

Meyer's major works, *The Fundamental Laws of Human Behavior* (1911) and *The Psychology of the Other One* (1921), had outlined an objective psychology in which behavior was reduced to nervous system activity. Mentalistic concepts such as consciousness were rejected, as were mentalistic terms—except when those terms were understood to refer to actual physical events. Weiss, following Meyer, formulated an objective psychology labeled biosocial behaviorism. Biosocial behaviorism rejected mentalistic concepts and proposed that behavior was the result of the interaction of the organism's physiology and environmental events. Weiss understood that physiological reductionism invited the criticism that psychology would become too distant from meaningful behavior to be useful. He answered this criticism by establishing a distinction between biophysical stimuli and biosocial stimuli. Biophysical stimuli affected the organism directly and caused a chain of physiological events that resulted in biophysical responses. Biosocial stimuli were biophysical stimuli that had social relevance (such as linguistic stimuli) and caused socially relevant biosocial responses. For Weiss, psychology was concerned primarily with biosocial events; physiology investigated biophysical reactions. The distinction between biosocial and biophysical reactions in Weiss's psychology bears some similarity to the distinction between acts and actions in Edwin R. Guthrie's psychology and foreshadowed the emphasis on the function of stimuli and responses (rather than their physical form) in B. F. Skinner's radical behaviorism. Guthrie and Skinner, however, would reject reductionism; Weiss took reductionism to an extreme—reducing behavior, conceptually at least, to the atomic level.

Weiss's book appeared at about the same time as John B. Watson's *Behaviorism* (New York: University of Chicago Press, 1924) Weiss was unable to match Watson's popular appeal and prodigious published output. A similar fate befell most of Weiss's behavioristic contemporaries such as Edwin B. Holt, Walter S. Hunter, and Knight Dunlap. By the 1930s, the behaviorisms of Guthrie, Clark L. Hull, Edward C. Tolman, and B. F. Skinner would eclipse all earlier versions of behaviorism. By the 1960s, only the interbehavioral psychologist J. R. Kantor (1888–1984) appeared to regard Weiss as a pivotal figure in the history of psychology. Although Weiss's biophysical-biosocial distinction is implicit in Kantor's system, in the *Scientific Evolution of Psychology* (1969) Kantor attached more importance to Weiss's system of postulates in which psychology was explicitly linked to the other sciences. Beyond this, Weiss's influence on modern psychology is uncertain.

[*Many of the people mentioned in this article are the subjects of independent biographical entries.*]

Bibliography

Influences on Weiss

Meyer, M. F. (1911). *The fundamental laws of human behavior.* Boston: R. G. Bager.

Meyer, M. F. (1921). *The psychology of the other one: An introductory textbook of psychology.* Columbia, MO: Missouri Book Company.

Obituaries

Bloomfield, L. (1931). Albert Paul Weiss. *Language, 7,* 219–221.

Elliot, R. M. (1931). Albert Paul Weiss. *American Journal of Psychology, 43,* 707–709.

Renshaw, S. (1932). A. P. Weiss (1879–1931). *Journal of General Psychology, 6,* 3–7. Many of the details of Weiss's early life, education, and later impact can be gleaned from these obituaries. The extent of Weiss's influence on the early history of behaviorism, and psychology in general, is evidenced by the appearance of obituaries in three the major journals of psychology and linguistics of the era.

Modern Views of Weiss's Impact

Kantor, J. R. (1969). *The scientific evolution of psychology* (Vol. 2). Chicago: Principia Press.

Kitchener, R. F. (1977). Behavior and behaviorism. *Behaviorism, 5,* 11–71.

Powell, R. P., & Still, A. W. (1979). Behaviorism and the psychology of language: An historical reassessment. *Behaviorism, 7,* 71–89.

Wozniak, R. H. (1993). Albert P. Weiss and *A theoretical basis of human behavior.* In R. H. Wozniak (Ed.), *Behaviorism: The early years.* London: Routledge/Thoemmes Press. Few modern analyses or descriptions of Weiss's work are available and he is usually only mentioned in passing, if at all, in modern histories of psychology. The titles above include works in which some aspects of Weiss's views on behavior, language, and science are discussed in depth. Wozniak's introductions to the works of Weiss, Meyer, and other early behaviorists in his reprint series are especially helpful for understanding Weiss's place in the history of psychology. Works in this specialized series can be found in some large university libraries.

James T. Todd

WELL-BEING. *See* Wellness and Illness.

WELLNESS AND ILLNESS. In the 1990s there has been a radical move in psychology away from the medical model and toward a more comprehensive view of behavioral health. Over 40% of all Americans have used some form of alternative medicine in preventing illness or restoring balance to their systems. There has been a merger of Eastern holistic methods such as acupuncture and herbal remedies with modern stress management techniques including hypnotherapy, biofeedback, imagery and relaxation techniques. The surgeon general's *Healthy 2000* report endorses the lifestyle sources of many chronic illnesses such as diabetes, heart disease, and pulmonary diseases. Thus, a role for the future of psychology is ensured. There has in fact been scientific research justifying the use of stress management in reducing immune dysfunction. Self-regulation of emotions and strong ties with other supportive individuals have been found to ameliorate the influences of chronic stress. The techniques used by psychotherapists, including meditation, dietary concern, smoking cessation, and behavioral-cognitive approaches, have won approval in managed care. Demonstrations have shown that chronic pain, infection healing, and even the common cold are responsive to the way we deal with other people and cope with our problems.

As a result, psychologists, including Robert Kaplan, Sheldon Cohen, and Janice Kiecolt-Glaser, have been involved in redefining health. The concept of subjective well-being has received attention by such psychologists as Ed Diener, Vicki Helgeson, and Kristina DeNeve. The early focus on the disease-prone personality has been replaced by concepts of the self-healing personality. We are studying healthy individuals in their 70s to evaluate how they have avoided succumbing to illnesses. Those who hold optimistic beliefs, take responsibility for their own health (internal locus of control), and have the ability to maintain diverse social ties with others are more likely to get the care they need. Thus, the focus on spirituality and importance of family has reemerged within popular psychology. The wellness movement has focused on internal balance, hardiness, the power of intimacy, and finding meaningful purpose in life. Persistence even in the face of adversity is an essential factor in resilience.

Psychological research has found that personality traits do not predict well-being. A focus on affect regulation, particularly the role of depression, hostility, and anxiety on exacerbating illness, has shown direct links with survival from heart disease, and to some extent cancer. The person who has a disease is seen as being as important as what disease they have. The ability to take advantage of early detection through mass screening, magnetic resonance techniques, and gene therapy has changed the way individuals cope. While decision making has become more complicated, the power of individuals to determine their medical outcomes has increased. The primary model in focusing on wellness is that of a stress-diathesis concept. There are genetic and environmental predispositions to becoming ill, but the individual's coping style can affect the balance. Thus, the body is viewed as a system with a variety of different causal influences that work in relationship between personality and disease. The concept of wellness is a dimension of attitudes, behaviors, thoughts, and feelings, which can enhance a subjective sense of well-being, and influence the individual's attention to self-care and compliance with medical regimens. The individual's focus includes dealing with issues of safety, homelessness, and environmental solutions to pollution.

Bibliography

DeNeve, K. & Cooper, H. (1998). The happy personality: A meta-analysis of 137 personality traits and subjective well-being. *Psychological Bulletin, 124*, 197–229.

Friedman, H. (1991). *The self-healing personality.* New York: Henry Holt.

Healthy People 2000: National Health Promotion and Disease Prevention Objectives. (1991). Washington, DC: U.S. Government Printing Office.

Moyers, B. (1993). *Healing and the mind.* New York: Doubleday.

Taylor, S. (1997). Health psychology: What is an unhealthy environment and how does it get under the skin? *Annual Review of Psychology, 48M*, 411–447.

Barbara G. Melamed

WERNER, HEINZ (1890–1964), European and American psychologist. Werner was born in Vienna, Austria, and held positions until 1933 at the universities of Munich and Hamburg. Following the advent of the Nazis, he came to the United States and held positions at the University of Michigan, Harvard University, Wayne County Training School, Brooklyn College, and Clark University.

Werner viewed the developmental principles he proposed as applicable to all areas of the life sciences. [*See* Developmental Psychology, *article on* Theories.] He believed that wherever there is life there is formation in terms of systematic, orderly sequence of progression and regression that has broad applicability. In contrast to the prevailing view of development as restricted to ontogenesis, Werner used a formal, organizational definition of development, formulated later in work with Bernard Kaplan as the orthogenetic principle: namely, that wherever development occurs, it proceeds from a state of relative globality and lack of differentiation to a state of increasing differentiation, articulation, and hierarchic integration, as described by such polarities as syncretic-discrete, diffuse-articulate, rigid-flexible, labile-stable. Werner focused on three levels of mental functioning (sensory-motor, perceptual and conceptual functioning), the relations among them, the structure of psychological worlds (spheres of reality), and the principle of spirality, where the individual may resort to lower levels of functioning though higher levels are available (for example, in creativity). Utilizing these and the orthogenetic principle, ontogenesis and other aspects of development were analyzed, including: microgenesis (for example, development of a percept or thought), pathogenesis (for example, development of neuro- and psycho-pathology), phylogenesis (development of a species), ethnogenesis (development of a culture), and the range of functioning in the "normal adult" (for example, in wide awake versus fatigued states).

Werner's views on methodology, which were in keeping with his developmental approach, focused on process rather than achievement (Werner, 1937). He was more concerned with probing and understanding than with proving and used a broad range of methods (for example, phenomenological, experimental) to learn about where, what, and how the properties of formal structures change.

After a very productive career in the European context, he completed in the United States a program of research on brain-injured children and significant work on binocular perception and then initiated two major programs of research at Clark University: one with Seymour Wapner in the field of perception; a second with Bernard Kaplan on symbolization and language. [*See* Brain Injury and Recovery; *and* Vision and Sight, *article on* Behavioral and Functional Aspects.]

The program of research on perception was developed by Werner and Wapner (1952) during the so-called new look in the analysis of perception that focused on the role of the state of the organism as well as sensory input from the "to be" constructed object. The theoretical perspective underlying this approach, the sensory-tonic field theory of perception, was based on the assumption that perception is a function of the relationship between the state of the organism (neuromuscular, emotional, and so forth) and the incoming stimuli. The program of research was concerned with analysis of space perception, physiognomic perception, perception of time, and other cognitive processes. This focus on the organismic aspect of human functioning, coupled with developmental studies (Wapner & Werner, 1957), represented a significant move toward organismic-developmental theory.

Further growth of the organismic-developmental perspective is evident in Werner and Kaplan's (1963) work on the origins and development of expressive symbolic processes. Research studies using innovative methods provided empirical material for the development of a systematic theoretical framework in which symbol formation is viewed as central to human beings' cognitive construction of the world.

Werner's conceptualization of development, along with his notions of levels of organization, a broad, flexible view of methodology, and the organismic-holistic formulation, place Werner among the major developmentalists—for example, Piaget and Vygotsky—of the twentieth century (Franklin, 1997; Glick, 1983, 1992). A review and consideration of Werner's work and perspective has the potential to provide creative directions for analyzing contemporary problems and issues in the twenty-first century.

[*See also* Brain Injury and Recovery; Creativity; Developmental Psychology, *article on* Theories; Language; Psychopathology; Vision and Sight; *and the biographies of Piaget and Vygotsky.*]

Bibliography

Works by Werner

Wapner, S., & Werner, H. (1957). *Perceptual development.* Worcester, MA: Clark University Press.

Werner, H. (1919). *Die Ursprünge der Metapher.* Leipzig: Barth.

Werner, H. (1937). Process and achievement. *Harvard Educational Review, 7,* 353–368.

Werner, H. (1940). *Comparative psychology of mental development.* New York: Harper. (1980). (Paperback ed. published 1980)

Werner, H., & Kaplan, B. (1963). *Symbol formation: An organismic-developmental approach to language and the expression of thought.* Hillsdale, NJ: Erlbaum.

Werner, H. & Wapner, S. (1952). Toward a general theory of perception. *Psychological Review, 59,* 324–338.

Works about Werner

Barten, S., & Franklin, M. B. (1978). *Developmental processes: Heinz Werner's selected writings* (Vols. 1 & 2). New York: International Universities Press.

Franklin, M. B. (1997). Constructing a developmental psychology: Heinz Werner's vision. *Contemporary Psychology, 42,* 481–485.

Glick, J. (1983). Piaget, Vygotsky & Werner. In S. Wapner & B. Kaplan (Eds.). *Toward a holistic developmental psychology* (pp. 35–52). Hillsdale, NJ: Erlbaum.

Glick, J. (1992). Werner's relevance for contemporary developmental psychology. *Developmental Psychology, 28,* 558–565.

Wapner, S., & Demick, J. (1998). Developmental analysis: A holistic, developmental, systems-oriented perspective. In R. M. Lerner (Ed.), *Theoretical models of human development. Volume 1 of the Handbook of child psychology* (5th ed.). New York: Wiley.

Witkin, H. A. (1965). Heinz Werner: 1890–1964. *Child Development, 30,* 307–328.

Seymour Wapner

WERTHEIMER, MAX (1880–1943), German American Gestalt theorist and experimental and theoretical psychologist. Wertheimer became internationally renowned during the first half of the twentieth century. Born in Prague, then part of Austria-Hungary, he studied philosophy and psychology at Charles University in Prague (with, among others, Christian von Ehrenfels), at the University of Berlin (with Carl Stumpf), and at the University of Würzburg (with Karl Marbe and Oswald Külpe), receiving his doctorate from Würzburg in 1904 with highest honors. His dissertation concerned lie detection and the determination of criminal guilt, using the techniques of experimental psychology. He held postdoctoral positions in Vienna, Berlin, and Prague, and published further work on lie detection.

A 1910 paper on the music of the Vedda, an aboriginal tribe in Ceylon (now Sri Lanka), showed that this "primitive" music had its own sophisticated internal structure and rules; early parts of a melody set up "requirements" for subsequent parts. A 1912 article on numbers and the number concepts of aboriginal peoples further developed this mode of thought, analyzing how particular number concepts for different kinds and structures of quantities may be exquisitely suitable in their natural context; for example, one horse plus one horse equals two horses, and one person plus one person equals two people—but one horse plus one person may equal a rider. Or, dividing a spear in two does not result in two meaningful units but in a broken or useless spear. Both of these articles contain a mode of analysis that, while not explicitly called Gestalt theory, was to become typical of the approach of the later formal Gestalt school of psychology.

Perception of Apparent Movement

In the fall of 1910, while on a train to the Rhineland for a vacation, Wertheimer had an insight based on work he had done earlier with the physiologist Sigmund Exner in Vienna, concerning the perception of apparent motion in stationary, successively-exposed visual stimuli. He got off the train in Frankfurt, bought a toy stroboscope, and did some experiments on himself in a hotel room. Laboratory space and more sophisticated equipment were made available to him in the psychological institute at Frankfurt Academy (later the University of Frankfurt), and he undertook systematic experiments on the perception of apparent movement. Wolfgang Köhler and Kurt Koffka joined him as participants in these experiments. The procedure typically involved successive brief exposure of two lines slightly separated in space. If the time interval was long, observers reported seeing two successive separate lines. If the time interval was very short, the typical report was simultaneity of the two lines. But intermediate exposure intervals produced the compelling perception of a single line moving from one location to another. Certain slightly shorter intervals generated yet another phenomenon—pure phi—a perception of motion without the motion appearing to be the property of any particular object.

That the perceived motion in these stationary objects could not be accounted for by the then-prevailing eye-movement theories of apparent movement was demonstrated in an experiment in which simultaneous movement in opposite directions is induced in two parts of the visual field, such as above and below the point of visual fixation. Overall, the results of the experiments refuted the "constancy hypothesis," which was almost universally taken for granted by psychologists at the time, namely, that there is a constant relationship between the local attributes of a physical stimulus and the local features of the resulting sensation. The perceived motion is nowhere in the stationary stimuli, but is a result of their tempero-spatial relationship. Perceptual qualities depend not on specific isolated physical attributes of stimuli, but on their dynamic interrelated structure and relationships, their "Gestalt" characteristics.

The German term *Gestalt* (roughly equivalent to "form," "structure," or "configuration") has no corresponding term in English, so the word was adopted as the technical name for this mode of thought. A Gestalt is an integrated whole that has dynamic properties; the whole is not merely the sum-total of its constituent parts, nor is it just "more" than the sum of its parts—it is entirely different from any sum. As in a soap bubble, the parts are not indifferent to each other but are dynamically interrelated; change in one part (such as pricking the film of the bubble) can lead to dramatic changes in the entire whole. Indeed, the properties of the parts in a Gestalt depend upon their place, role, and function in the whole of which they are constituent. The whole is ontologically and perceptually primary, not the parts.

Wertheimer's 1912 article reporting the results of the experiments on apparent motion is generally viewed as the publication that launched the Gestalt school of psychology. Köhler and Koffka joined Wertheimer in promoting the movement. One theoretical proposal in the paper, Wertheimer's "short-circuit theory," was elaborated by Köhler into the "principle of isomorophism." Wertheimer suggested that a short circuit between parts of the brain activated by the two lines in the apparent-motion experiment must be the brain correlate of the perceived movement; Köhler proposed that, in general, there must be an isomorphic correspondence between the properties of any perceptual or cognitive experience and the structural and dynamic properties of the underlying brain processes.

Principles of Perceptual Organization

During World War I, Wertheimer collaborated with Erich Moritz von Hornbostel, his former colleague at the Berlin Phonogram Archives (where he had done his work on the music of the Vedda), in developing a sound-direction finder for military use. This device, the *Wertbostel*, a forerunner of sonar, was patented. In 1916, after the founding of the Gestalt school, Wertheimer, who had stayed on in Frankfurt as a lecturer, moved to the University of Berlin, where he became a professor in 1922, when Köhler was appointed to the Berlin chair, and continued to work on perception and the psychology of thinking.

In 1923, he published an article on which he had been working for a decade, in which he proposed that psychological wholes tend to be as "good" as the prevailing conditions allow (the "principle of Prägnanz"), and elaborated on what have come to be called the principles of perceptual organization. These principles describe how and why perceptual processes integrate discrete sensory input into perceived wholes. Among the special cases of the principle of Prägnanz are similarity, proximity, closure, and common fate: parts of the sensory field that are similar to each other, that are near each other, that form a closed shape, and that have a common fate (such as moving simultaneously) tend to be perceived as parts of a common Gestalt. These principles are still discussed in most introductory textbooks in psychology, and are the focus of active interest in cognitive neuroscience and sensory psychophysiology.

In 1929, Wertheimer accepted the chair of the psychology department at the University of Frankfurt. There he and his graduate students continued experimental and theoretical work in the Gestalt tradition. In 1921, a new journal, *Psychologische Forschung*, had been founded; it became the primary outlet for articles stemming from the Gestalt perspective. Wertheimer had joined Köhler, Koffka, and others on the editorial board, and remained active in editing the journal after his move to Frankfurt. Early in 1933, sensing the menace of the Nazi movement in Germany, he fled to Czechoslovakia, and by late that summer moved to the United States to teach at the New School for Social Research in New York. He was active in American psychology as a member of the Society of Experimental Psychology, a member of a committee of the American Psychological Association designed to assist displaced foreign scholars, and as a lecturer presenting talks at many locations throughout the country. He also developed productive relationships with several prominent American psychologists, such as Edwin Garrigues Boring and Clark Leonard Hull. Among his American students and collaborators were George Katona, Edwin B. Newman, and Solomon E. Asch, all of whom were to have illustrious careers in psychology. Wertheimer died at his home in New Rochelle, New York, on 12 October 1943.

The Psychology of Productive Thinking

One of Wertheimer's primary interests throughout his career was the cognitive process of problem solving and productive thinking. It was the subject of one of his early articles. He lectured on it throughout his entire teaching career, and it was the topic of an article he published in 1920. During his last years he drafted a book-length manuscript, *Productive Thinking*, to try to do justice to his work in the area, but did not live to see it published. It was released two years after his death, and has been reissued several times since then. It continues to be cited frequently in works in a variety of areas, primarily cognitive psychology.

His main message, conveyed in detailed analyses of many examples that included how to find the area of a parallelogram through Albert Einstein's formulation of the theory of relativity, concerned the transition from a confused, "blind," meaningless concept of a problem to a clear understanding of it that does justice to its essential features and leads to its solution. This process, which involves insight into what he called the "radix," or core of the problem, requires a reorganization or restructuring of the problem that strips away its superficial attributes and concentrates instead on its central structural and dynamic features, which captures the problem's Gestalt qualities. Productive thinking of this kind contrasts sharply with merely "reproductive" thinking based on rote memorization. He argued that productive thinking is the hallmark of good teaching, learning, and education, and that pedagogical techniques based on memorization, such as drill, are inimical to productive thought. Good thinking requires a top-down approach, analysis that begins with the overall characteristics of the problem and examines how its component parts fit with each other and the attributes of the whole, rather than a bottom-up or piecemeal attempt, to understand the problem's "elements" and how they could be combined to generate the whole. The book's examples still pose a challenge to modern cognitive-science workers in the area of problem-solving, especially those who develop computer simulations of human problem-solving. It remains difficult to simulate insight, meaning, understanding, or the restructuring or reorganization that Wertheimer considered essential to such processes.

In later years, Wertheimer used the Gestalt perspective to address such fundamental human issues as truth, freedom, ethics, and democracy. His essays on these questions were reissued in a 1961 book edited by Mary Henle, and again, with commentary, in a 1991 book edited by Hans-Jürgen Walter.

[*Many of the people mentioned in this entry are the subjects of independent biographical entries.*]

Bibliography

Ash, M. G. (1995). *Gestalt psychology in German culture, 1890–1967: Holism and the quest for objectivity*. New York: Cambridge University Press. This thorough examination of the emergence of Gestalt theory in Germany contains much material on Wertheimer.

Henle, M. (Ed.). (1961). *Documents of Gestalt psychology*. Berkeley: University of California Press. Reprints Wertheimer's articles of 1934, 1935, 1937, and 1940, as well as many other articles on Gestalt psychology.

Wertheimer, M. (1905). Experimentelle Untersuchungen zur Tatbestandsdiagnostik [Experimental studies of the diagnosis of facts]. *Archiv für die gesamte Psychologie, 6*, 59–131.

Wertheimer, M. (1910). Musik der Wedda [The music of the Veddas]. *Sammelbände der internationellen Musikgesellschaft, 11*, 300–309.

Wertheimer, M. (1912a). Über das Denken der Naturvölker: Vol. I. Zahlen und Zahlgebilde [On the thinking of primitive people: Vol. I. Numbers and numerical concepts]. *Zeitschrift für Psychologie, 60*, 321–378.

Wertheimer, M. (1912b). Experimentelle Studien über das Sehen von Bewegung [Experimental studies of the perception of movement]. *Zeitschrift für Psychologie, 61*, 161–265.

Wertheimer, M. (1920). *Über Schlussprozesse im produktiven Denken* [On reasoning processes in productive thinking]. Berlin: De Gruyter.

Wertheimer, M. (1923). Untersuchungen zur Lehre von der Gestalt: II. [Investigations on the doctrine of Gestalt]. *Psychologische Forschung, 4*, 301–350.

Wertheimer, M. (1934). On truth. *Social Research, 1*, 135–146.

Wertheimer, M. (1935). Some problems in the theory of ethics. *Social Research, 2*, 353–367.

Wertheimer, M. (1937). On the concept of democracy. In M. Ascoli & F. Lehmann (Eds.), *Political and economic democracy* (pp. 271–283). New York: Norton.

Wertheimer, M. (1940). A story of three days. In R. N. Anshen (Ed.), *Freedom: Its meaning* (pp. 555–569). New York: Harcourt, Brace.

Wertheimer, M. (1982). *Productive thinking*. Chicago: University of Chicago Press. (Original work published in 1945).

Wertheimer, M. (1991). *Zur Gestaltpsychologie menschlicher Werte* [On the Gestalt psychology of human values]. (H.-J. Walter, Ed.). Opladen, Germany: Westdeutscher Verlag. Contains German translations, with commentary, of Wertheimer's 1934, 1935, 1937, and 1940 articles.

Wertheimer, M., & von Hornbostel, E. M. (1920). Über die Wahrnehmung der Schallrichtung [On the perception of the direction of sounds]. *Sitzungsberichte der Preussischen Akademie der Wissenschaften, Berlin, 20*, 388–396.

Michael Wertheimer

WESTERN PSYCHOLOGICAL ASSOCIATION. *See* Regional Psychological Associations.

WEVER, ERNEST GLEN (1902–1991), American psychologist. Wever earned his doctorate in experimental psychology in 1926 at Harvard University, where he studied with E. G. Boring and Karl Lashley. Appointed to the faculty of psychology at Princeton University in 1928, he remained there until his death. Promoted through the ranks, he held the Warren (1940–1950) and then the Higgins (1950–1970) professorships. He became professor emeritus in 1970.

In 1930, Wever, with C. W. Bray, discovered bioelectrical potentials in the inner ears of cats. This discovery led to a lifetime of research on the comparative anatomy and physiology of the auditory system, with special emphasis on its evolution. Wever was an ingenious experimenter who designed and built laboratory instruments when they were not commercially available, and he was a pioneer in developing new histological techniques to examine the finer structures of the sensory organ for hearing in a broad range of species. His interests extended to the study of neural coding of acoustic events, and in 1949 he published a comprehensive theory of hearing that combined principles of the Helmholtz place theory of hearing with those of the Rutherford frequency theory. His volley theory, as it came to be known, had a major impact in the field of sensory perception because of the detailed experimental support on which it was based, including anatomy, physiological acoustics, psychophysics, and clinical data.

In 1954, Wever and Merle Lawrence published a book that treated details of the mechanical and anatomical properties of the middle ear as a transformer. The hair cells of the cochlea were treated as proximal stimuli for the activation of neurons in the acoustic nerve.

In the late 1950s, Wever received a grant from the National Institutes of Health to establish a new large-scale research facility on the Forrestal campus of Princeton University. The precautions taken to avoid experimental artifacts from mechanical vibrations, ambient acoustic energies, and electromagnetic fields were so extensive that Wever and his students were able to record bioelectrical potentials at levels significantly below any that had been achieved elsewhere. Of their kind and time, Wever's laboratories were the best in the world.

In 1972, Wever began work on a book on the ears of reptiles, a work based on his study of 247 different species. This book was published in 1978 and was to be the first of a trilogy. In 1985, he published the second work on the ears of amphibia. Poor health prevented completion of the third work, which was to have treated the fishes. The two completed books provided crucial structural and functional evidence of the evolution of the hearing process, and they forced other investigators to consider anew the then current views of the means whereby frequency (pitch) was encoded by the acoustic nervous system.

To Wever's influence was added that of his many students. His only peer in the field of hearing was Georg von Békésy, whose works Wever translated from German into English.

Bibliography

Wever, E. G. (1949). *Theory of hearing*. New York: Wiley.

Wever, E. G. (1978). *Reptile ear: Its structure and function*. Princeton, NJ: Princeton University Press.

Wever, E. G. (1985). *Amphibian ear*. Princeton, NJ: Princeton University Press.

Wever, E. G., & Bray, C. W. (1930). Action currents in the auditory nerve in response to acoustic stimulation. *Proceedings of the National Academy of Science, 16*, 344–350.

Wever, E. G., & Lawrence, M. (1954). *Physiological acoustics*. Princeton, NJ: Princeton University Press.

W. Lawrence Gulick

WHEELER, RAYMOND H. (1892–1961), American psychologist. Wheeler was a systematic psychologist interested in mental development, human behavior, and climate and weather. Born in Berlin, Massachusetts, he completed all his formal study at Clark University, receiving a doctorate in psychology in 1915.

His faculty appointments ranged over 46 years. He served on the faculty of the University of Oregon from 1915 to 1925, directing the psychology laboratories from 1920 to 1925. He served as head of the psychology department at the University of Kansas from 1925 to 1947. That year he moved to Erskine College in South Carolina, where he was head of the psychology department. From 1948 to 1961, he served on the faculty of Babson Institute of Business Administration (in Wellesley, Massachusetts).

A proponent of Gestalt psychology, he was sometimes called a field theorist and offered a modified version of Gestalt psychology that he termed "organismic psychology." He defined human nature as a field property of societies.

In *Principles of Mental Development* (1932), coauthored with Francis Theodore Perkins, and dedicated to Kurt Koffka and Robert M. Ogden, Wheeler argued that it is the classroom teacher's responsibility to facilitate and direct the development of personality in the pupil and that the teacher's personality and attitude toward the student are powerful determinants of student learning. He viewed the teacher as a human engineer, building children's intelligence and personality. He downplayed the role of hereditary factors in the development of intelligence, arguing that intelligence is made, not born. While recognizing that genetic inheritance may limit intellectual achievement, he placed the responsibility for academic failure upon faulty or uninspired teaching. Anticipating aspects of Piagetian approaches to teaching, Wheeler suggested that the process of child learning resembles the creative process of a scientist or artist and is characterized by vivid imagination and intense feeling. In contrast to Piaget's notion of constructive repetition, Wheeler argued that repetition of response does not facilitate learning. The child's imperfect execution of a response was viewed by Wheeler as an indication that it was beyond the child's maturational level and that further attempts at mastery should be postponed. He offered an early account of the problem of hyperactivity in children in his depiction of the "over-stimulated" child.

During World War I, Wheeler served as a captain in the Sanitary Corps and was a member of committees for construction of intelligence tests. He was an instructional staff member at the School of Military Psychology, Camp Greenleaf, Georgia, and chief of psychological services, Camp Bowie, Texas.

He served as chief of staff for the Climate Research Division, Weather Forecast, Inc., and Weather Science Foundation. He was a member of the American Meteorology Society and was founder and editor of *Journal of Human Ecology* in 1951.

Wheeler may be remembered primarily for his efforts to adapt field theory principles to an understanding of educational psychology and human behavior.

Bibliography

Wheeler, R. (1929). *The science of psychology*. New York: Crowell.

Wheeler, R. (1931). *The laws of human nature*. New York: Crowell.

Wheeler, R., & Perkins, F. T. (1932). *Principles of mental development: A textbook in educational psychology*. New York: Crowell.

Linda R. Jeffrey

WHIPPLE, GUY M. (1876–1941), educational psychologist, author, editor. Born to John Frances and Cornelia Whipple in Danvers, Massachusetts, Whipple grew up in New England and finished a bachelor's degree at Brown University. A graduate student and disciple of Edward B. Titchener, Whipple completed his doctorate at Cornell University in 1900 and was on the faculties at Cornell, Illinois, Carnegie Institute of Technology, and Michigan in the first 25 years of his academic career. He was among the strong contingent of applied psychologists at Carnegie at the close of World War I.

From 1928 to 1937, he was a member of the editorial staff of D.C. Heath. He also served as editor for the National Society for the Study of Education, including two volumes about the nature and nurture of intelligence (1928 and 1940), as well as volumes such as *Adapting the Schools to Individual Differences, Education of Gifted Children, General Education in the American College*, and *Music Education*.

Whipple was a cofounder of the *Journal of Educational Psychology* and a frequent contributor of articles to scholarly journals. He was a recognized expert on the standardization of mental tests, gifted children, effective methods of studying, children's vocabularies, and discrimination of pitch and served on the editorial advisory board of several journals, including the *Journal of Applied Psychology* and the *Journal of Educational Research*.

Whipple began work on his *Manual of Mental and Physical Tests* in 1906, completed it in 1910, and revised and expanded it in 1914. This work helped change the flow of mental tests in the United States from the sensorimotor stream of Francis Galton toward the work with complex mental functions initiated by Alfred Binet and Victor Henri. Whipple's manual about tests brought together current thinking and developments in measurement, particularly measurement of children, and facilitated study of functional psychology and behaviorism. This volume is characterized by Edwin G. Boring (1929) as establishing psychological and educational measurement as a field separate from experimental psychology.

Whipple's translation of William Stern's book about intelligence testing and the concept of "mental quotient," published in 1914, facilitated acceptance of the "intelligence quotient" introduced with publication of the Stanford revision of the Binet two years later. During the next few years he was a force in helping the public and profession understand the qualifications of persons who should use psychological tests.

[*Many of the people mentioned in this article are the subjects of independent biographical entries.*]

Bibliography

Boring, E. G. (1929). *A history of experimental psychology*. New York: Appleton-Century.

Stern, W. (1914). *The psychological methods of testing intelligence* (Guy M. Whipple, Trans.). Baltimore, MD: Warwick & York.

Whipple, G. M. (1910). *Manual of mental and physical tests, a book of directions compiled with special reference to the experimental study of school children in the laboratory or classroom*. Baltimore: Warwick and York. (2nd rev. and enlarged ed., 1914)

Whipple, G. M. (1916). *How to study effectively*. Bloomington, IL: Public School.
Whipple, G. M. (Ed.). (1928). *Nature and nurture*. Twenty-seventh yearbook of the National Society for the Study of Education. Bloomington, IL: Public School.
Whipple, G. M. (Ed.). (1940). *Intelligence, its nature and nurture*. Bloomington, IL: Public School. Thirty-ninth yearbook of the National Society for the Study of Education.

Joseph L. French

WILL. *See* Volition.

WILLLIAMS SYNDROME. *See* Savant Syndrome.

WISDOM. Philosophers, sociologists, anthropologists, religious scholars, and psychologists have all spent time and effort studying wisdom, often viewed as the ideal of human achievement. Much of their work has centered on the problem of defining wisdom. The major German historical dictionary, for instance, defines wisdom as "insight and knowledge about oneself and the world . . . and sound judgment in the case of difficult life problems" (Grimm & Grimm, 1854/1984). The *Oxford English Dictionary* describes wisdom as "good judgment and advice in difficult and uncertain matters of life" (Fowler & Fowler, 1964). Both definitions reflect the late Enlightenment consensus that wisdom is fundamentally a practical, contextual, and human concept rather than a divine and philosophical one; that is, wisdom is valuable and high-level knowledge that can be used by human beings in managing difficult life situations (Assmann, 1994; Baltes, Smith, & Staudinger, 1992; Kekes, 1995).

Across history and cultures, human beings show a surprisingly high consensus about the content of important and valuable knowledge about life. This consensus emerges from studies of religious and secular texts in China, India, Egypt, Old Mesopotamia (Assmann, 1994), as well as studies of proverbs, maxims, and fairy tales (Chinen, 1987). Even the two definitions above are examples—from two different countries, but sharing much overlap in content. Such consensus implies that cultures converge in selecting knowledge that is valuable and adaptive for their members.

Psychological Approaches to Wisdom

Perhaps unique to a psychological perspective on wisdom is a focus on wisdom as embodied within individuals, and reflected in particular kinds of behavior. Although this may be viewed as a strength of psychological perspectives, an individual and behavioral focus may also be problematic. For instance, such a focus conflicts with notions of wisdom as an ideal quality of *knowledge* that is seldom found within individual people, but rather involves *collaboration between individuals* (Staudinger & Baltes, 1996). Still, individual and behavioral approaches have yielded important findings about wisdom and wise persons.

In both early theoretical writings and contemporary work, psychologists highlight intellectual, personality-related, and developmental features of wisdom in individuals, such as the late-life emergence of calm and meditative attitudes (Hall, 1922), impartiality or detachment, the search for moderation between extremes of knowledge and doubt, and the well-balanced coordination of emotion, motivation, and thinking. In fact, conceptions of wisdom usually emphasize the orchestration of high intellectual capacities and positive aspects of character (e.g., Dittmann-Kohli & Baltes in Alexander & Langer, 1990; Staudinger, Lopez, & Baltes, 1997; various chapters in Sternberg, 1990). Wisdom is viewed psychologically in terms of qualities of knowledge (moderation between knowledge and doubt) and qualities of persons (calmness and reflectiveness), and the interaction between the two (impartiality or detachment, coordination of emotion, motivation, and thought).

Empirical work in psychology has centered around two themes, one of which concerns everyday or "implicit" notions about wisdom—what people believe to be the qualities of wise knowledge and of wise persons (see Clayton & Birren, 1980; Sowarka, 1989; chapters in Sternberg, 1990). The other concerns the measurement of wisdom, as manifested in personality characteristics, styles of thinking, or problem solving (Staudinger & Baltes, 1996; chapters in Sternberg, 1990).

Implicit theories of wisdom can be studied by asking people to describe wise knowledge and wise people and analyzing these descriptions (e.g., Sternberg, 1985, 1990), or by asking people first to nominate a person they view as wise and then to describe that person (Sowarka, 1989; chapters in Sternberg, 1990). Three conclusions from this work are important. First, everyday notions of wisdom and of wise persons are closely related, with wise persons viewed as the carriers of wisdom. Second, wise people combine high intellect with qualities such as concern for others, good judgment about advice giving, interpersonal skills, and intuition; thus wisdom is more than intelligence and more than personality. Third, wisdom is implicitly viewed as interpersonal and social in its development and application, as wisdom develops in the context of being mentored, and is produced in the context of advice giving. Further, people show high levels of consensus about these three features of wisdom, consistent with cross-cultural and historical findings.

The explicit approach to wisdom attempts to measure manifestations of wisdom, whether in character (personality approaches; e.g., McAdams & de St. Aubin, 1998; chapters in Sternberg, 1990), in thinking style (postformal cognitive abilities; see chapters in Sternberg, 1990), or by an individual's response to difficult life problems (e.g., Baltes, Smith, & Staudinger, 1992; Smith, Staudinger, & Baltes, 1994; Staudinger & Baltes, 1996). All of these approaches show that, given explicit operational definitions, facets of wisdom can be empirically assessed.

Wisdom as a quality of personality is usually conceived of as an advanced stage of personality development. This approach employs two ways of exploring wisdom as a personality quality. First, people who are viewed by others as wise (wisdom nominees) can be assessed in order to define personality characteristics associated with wisdom. This approach shows that wise people have integrated oppositions and transcended their own personal agendas. Second, people of various ages and levels of functioning are asked to describe themselves, and the results can be viewed as supporting development toward an advanced stage of personality or wisdom. These findings show that people perceive themselves as wiser and more mature as they grow older, and mesh well with early psychological theories (e.g., Erikson) as well as findings from the implicit approach.

Postformal approaches (Alexander & Langer, 1990) to assessing wisdom are based on Piagetian traditions in the study of cognitive development. In such approaches, wisdom is viewed as a style of thinking or a way of processing information. Wisdom is characterized variously as the ability to specify broad problems in order to find solutions, the ability to integrate multiple discrepant accounts into a dialectic whole, the ability to deal with uncertainty and the lack of perfect knowledge, and the integration of thinking, wanting, and feeling. Researchers taking this approach first ask people to engage in the process viewed as central to wisdom, and then assess their performance in applying the process, be it problem-finding or dialectical reasoning. Findings here show that not everyone attains high levels of performance, and that such performances are related to personality (e.g., ego development) as well as intellectual ability (see various chapters in Sternberg, 1990).

The third explicit approach to wisdom is an integrative one which attempts to bring together life-span developmental research on mind and personality, research on expertise, and cultural and historical perspectives on wisdom. Wisdom is viewed as "an expert knowledge system in the fundamental pragmatics of life permitting exceptional insight, judgment, and advice involving complex and uncertain matters of the human condition" (Baltes & Smith chapter in Sternberg, 1990, p. 95). From this stance, wisdom-related knowledge and skills apply to difficult problems in managing, planning, and making sense of life. Such knowledge and skills are characterized more specifically by a family of five criteria: (1) rich factual knowledge about life; (2) rich procedural knowledge about life; (3) life-span contextualism; (4) value relativism; and (5) awareness and management of uncertainty (see Baltes et al., 1992 for an extensive definition). These criteria integrate features of both cultural-historical approaches to wisdom and people's implicit theories of wisdom. Table 1 presents a more thorough description of the criteria.

Using this approach, wisdom is assessed by asking people to think out loud about difficult life dilemmas; for example, "Sometimes when people think about their lives, they realize that they have not achieved what they had once planned to achieve. What should they do and consider in such a situation?" People's responses are then evaluated according to the five criteria presented above. People nominated as wise attain higher performances on such tasks than control samples of similar educational and professional backgrounds, demonstrating the consensual validity of this method of assessing wisdom (Baltes, Staudinger, Maercker, & Smith, 1995). Finally, performance on these wisdom-related tasks reflect the notion that wisdom involves the orchestration of intellectual ability, personality, personal experience, and additional knowledge and skills. High performances are associated with intellectual ability, openness to new experiences, and creativity and flexibility in styles of thinking, as well as life experiences such as training in clinical psychology (Smith, Staudinger, & Baltes, 1994; Staudinger, Lopez, & Baltes, 1997).

According to the Berlin wisdom paradigm (Baltes & Smith in Sternberg, 1990; Staudinger & Baltes, 1996), wisdom develops as a consequence of the cooperation of several factors, including intellect, personality, contextual factors, and expertise-specific factors associated with historical events or professional training and mentorship (see Figure 1). Thus, as noted earlier, individuals who are intelligent, open to experience, flexible in thinking styles, and creative perform more highly on wisdom-related tasks, perhaps because such individuals gain more varied experiences in life. The development of wisdom can be furthered by a motivation to learn about and master difficult problems in life, or by receiving mentorship in how to navigate a life transition. In addition, some careers, like clinical psychology, provide for rich experience with a variety of life problems and ways of managing them. All of these factors have been shown to predict an individual's performance when thinking aloud about difficult life problems. The orchestration of the ontogeny of wisdom is only begin-

WISDOM. Table 1. Criteria for evaluating wisdom-related knowledge and skills

Criteria	High Performances Are Exemplified by
Basic	
Factual knowledge	Consideration of general (human condition) and specific (e.g., life events, institutions) features of life matters as well as scope and depth in coverage of issues
Procedural knowledge	Consideration of decision strategies, goal selection, choosing means to achieve goals, people to consult with, as well as strategies of advice-giving
Meta-level	
Life-span contextualism	Consideration of past, current, and possible future life contexts and the circumstances in which a life is embedded
Value relativism	Consideration of variations in values and life priorities and the importance of viewing each person within an individual framework, but also the importance of a small set of universal values
Awareness and management of uncertainty	Consideration of the inherent uncertainty of life (in terms of interpreting the past and predicting the future) and effective strategies for dealing with uncertainty

Source: Adapted from Baltes & Smith, "Toward a psychology of wisdom and its ontogenesis," in Sternberg (1990), p. 95.

ning to be understood and remains an exciting area for further work.

Clearly, wisdom and developmental psychology have reciprocal benefits for each other. Just as developmental psychology provides paradigms for thinking about wisdom, wisdom research provides a new perspective on human developmental potential. Similar reciprocal contributions exist between wisdom research and other domains of psychological inquiry. The relation between personality and wisdom, both implicitly and explicitly, underscores the importance of personality research in approaching wisdom. Personality research has offered wisdom researchers new paradigms, and the concept of wisdom offers a new and integrative conception of optimal personality development. Cognitive psychology both informs wisdom research, in the sense of neo-Piagetian and expertise-based approaches, and is informed and enriched by wisdom research. Wisdom offers a view of cognitive performance that is explicitly ecologically valid and contextual, one that contrasts sharply with work on the fluid mechanics of intellectual functioning. Wisdom also has implications for work on well-being and adjustment. Recent findings show that individuals with more mature (wiser) styles of thinking also use more effective and adaptive strategies to cope with life's vicissitudes (Diehl, Coyle, & Labouvie-Vief, 1996). We have noted throughout that wisdom is a social and collective phenomenon. Recent work shows that participants who discuss wisdom-related dilemmas with trusted others, or who simply imagine engaging in such a discussion, show better performance than individuals thinking alone (Staudinger & Baltes, 1996). Such findings open new questions about the social foundations of wise thinking.

Conclusions

In sum, various psychological perspectives on wisdom have begun to yield empirical findings that span many areas of psychology, from developmental to clinical. These findings highlight new questions about the psychological functions and the developmental acquisition of wisdom, as well as providing new perspectives for thinking about personality development, adaptive growth, cognitive development and performance, and the role of social factors in the exploration of psychological phenomena.

In closing, we want to return to the multilevel, multidisciplinary notions of wisdom with which we opened. Wisdom research in psychology offers the possibility for integrating psychological research with other social science disciplines. The notion of wisdom as reflecting culturally selected bodies of knowledge, and of individuals as holding varying degrees of expertise in those domains of knowledge, is a good example of how psychological approaches to wisdom can be informed by anthropology, sociology, and history—disciplines which explore the cultural selection of important knowledge across time and space. A psychological understanding of wisdom can further enrich other approaches as well, by specifying how such bodies of knowledge are acquired and applied within individual human contexts. In this sense, we believe wisdom has a unique potential to contribute to the study of human lives at many levels of analysis and conceptualization.

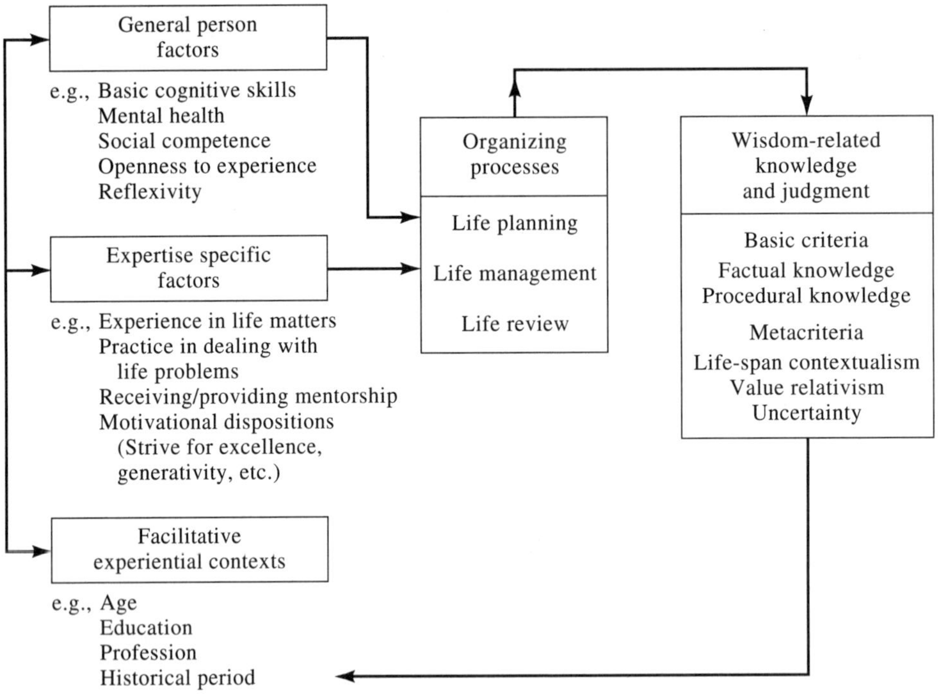

WISDOM. Figure 1. Model of the development of wisdom-related knowledge and judgment. (After Staudinger & Baltes, 1996.)

Bibliography

Alexander, C. N., & Langer, E. J. (Eds.). (1990). *Higher stages of human development: Perspectives on adult growth.* New York: Oxford University Press.

Assmann, A. (1994). Wholesome knowledge: Concepts of wisdom in a historical and cross-cultural perspective. In D. L. Featherman, R. M. Lerner, & M. Perlmutter (Eds.), *Life-span development and behavior* (pp. 187–224). Hillsdale, NJ: Erlbaum.

Baltes, P. B., Smith, J., & Staudinger, U. M. (1992). Wisdom and successful aging. *Nebraska Symposium on Motivation, 39,* 123–167.

Baltes, P. B., Staudinger, U. M., Maercker, A., & Smith, J. (1995). People nominated as wise: A comparative study of wisdom-related knowledge. *Psychology and Aging, 10,* 155–166.

Chinen, A. B. (1987). Fairy tales and psychological development in late life: A cross-cultural hermeneutic study. *Gerontologist, 27,* 340–346.

Clayton, V., & Birren, J. E. (1980). The development of wisdom across the life span: A re-examination of an ancient topic. In P. B. Baltes & O. G. Brim (Eds.), *Life-span development and behavior* (Vol. 3, pp. 103–135). New York: Academic Press.

Diehl, M., Coyle, N., & Labouvie-Vief, G. (1996). Age and sex differences in strategies of coping and defense across the life span. *Psychology and Aging, 11,* 127–139.

Fowler, H. W., & Fowler, F. G. (1964). *The concise Oxford dictionary of current English.* Oxford: Clarendon Press.

Grimm, J., & Grimm, W. (1984). *Deutsches Wörterbuch: Bd. 1–33* [German dictionary: Vols. 1–33]. Munich: Deutscher Taschenbuch-Verlag. (Original work published 1854)

Hall, G. S. (1992). *Senescence: The last half of life.* New York: Appleton.

Kekes, J. (1995). *Moral wisdom and good lives.* Ithaca, NY: Cornell University Press.

McAdams, D. P., & de St. Aubin, E. (Eds.). (1998). *Generativity and adult development.* Washington, DC: American Psychological Association.

Smith, J., Staudinger, U. M., & Baltes, P. B. (1994). Occupational settings facilitating wisdom-related knowledge: The sample case of clinical psychologists. *Journal of Consulting and Clinical Psychology, 62,* 989–999.

Sowarka, D. (1989). Weisheit und weise Personen: Common-Sense-Konzepte älterer Menschen [Wisdom and wise persons: Commonsense concepts in older people.] *Zeitschrift für Entwicklungspsychologie und Pädagogische Psychologie, 21,* 87–109.

Staudinger, U. M., & Baltes, P. B. (1996). Interactive minds: A facilitative setting for wisdom-related performance? *Journal of Personality and Social Psychology, 71,* 746–762.

Staudinger, U. M., Lopez, D., & Baltes, P. B. (1997). The psychometric location of wisdom-related performance: Intelligence, personality, and more? *Personality and Social Psychology Bulletin, 23,* 1200–1214.

Sternberg, R. J. (1985). Implicit theories of intelligence, creativity, and wisdom. *Journal of Personality and Social Psychology, 49,* 607–627.

Sternberg, R. J. (Ed.). (1990). *Wisdom: Its nature, origins, and development.* New York: Cambridge University Press.

Monisha Pasupathi and Paul B. Baltes

WITASEK, STEPHAN (1870–1915), Austrian psychologist. A member of the Austrian school of form-quality, the immediate forerunner of Gestalt psychology, Witasek conducted research that combined philosophy and empirical investigation, focusing on perception and aesthetics. His life began and ended in Graz, Austria, where he received a doctorate in philosophy in 1898 at the University of Graz. He held a faculty position there from 1900 until his death in 1915. He was a student of Alexius Von Meinong, who had established the first psychology laboratory at the University of Graz 4 years before Witasek completed his dissertation concerning geometric illusions.

Witasek wrote a textbook of psychology and a handbook on visual space perception. Combining philosophical and empirical psychology in his writings, he continued the work of Meinong and Christian von Ehrenfels. Ehrenfels, who held a faculty position at the University of Graz from 1889 to 1896, was an important leader in the Austrian school of act psychology and had developed Ernst Mach's idea that there are sensations of form. In 1890, he presented the idea that form is not a combination of other qualities, but a new one, that is, *Gestaltqualität*, or form-quality. The perception of a square, for example, is not a function of any one of the four equal lines but is experienced when all four lines are brought together.

Meinong, drawing on Franz Brentano's philosophy, had developed *Gegenstandstheorie*, or object theory. He argued that mental states have two aspects, that is, content and acts. While he concurred with Ehrenfel's notion of form-quality, he offered new terms, substituting *founding contents* for *Fundamente* and *founded contents* for *form-quality*. Founding contents were viewed as lower in the hierarchy of mental contents than founded content.

In this scheme, *complexions* were understood to be produced by the founding and founded contents. Real complexions, determined by stimulus characteristics and relationships within the perceived object, constitute perceptions. In contrast, ideal complexions or concepts are dependent on the productive process that fuses sensory elements into a whole, the act of founding, such as the fusion of four straight lines into the form of a square.

Like that of Meinong, Witasek's bipartite psychology of perception included both psychological acts and contents. His work focused on perception and the act of production. He argued that the act of production may result in simple or complex complexions, and that complex complexions are determined by both the internal mental act of production and the physical properties of the stimulus.

While the Austrian school of form-quality was a development of the 1890s, Witasek and Vittorio Benussi continued its elaboration for another generation. The members of the Austrian school criticized Wilhelm Wundt's elementarism, and claimed the discovery of a new element, form-quality. The properties of the whole were viewed as secondary elements added on to the part elements composing the whole. The Gestalt psychologists later criticized the idea of form-quality as a secondary element added on to the primary part elements and argued that the original parts disappear in the whole.

[*Many of the people mentioned in this article are the subjects of independent biographical entries.*]

Bibliography

Boring, E. (1950). *A history of experimental psychology.* New York: Appleton-Century-Crofts. Boring provides an account of Witasek's contributions to the Austrian School of Psychology and offers some biographical information.

Witasek, S. (1897). Beiträge zur Psychogie der Komplexionen [Contribution on the psychology of complexions]. *Zeitschrift für Psychologie, 14,* 401–435. Meinong edited this journal. This article contains Witasek's views on complexions and the act of producing.

Witasek, S. (1908). *Grundlinien der Psychologie* [Foundations of psychology]. Germany: Meiner. Witasek's textbook of psychology; includes a statement of his bipartite psychology of act and content, pages 222–246. See comments of E. B. Titchener, (1929), *Systematic psychology: Prolegomena.* (pp. 197–201, 226–235). New York: Macmillan.

Witasek, S. (1910). *Psychologie der Raumwahrnehmung des Auges* [Psychology of visual space perception]. Heidelberg, Germany: Winter. Witasek's psychology of visual space-perception.

Linda R. Jeffrey

WITMER, LIGHTNER (1867–1956), American psychologist. Witmer is recognized as the primary founder of clinical psychology and as the preeminent pioneer in the early history of school psychology. He also contributed in a major way to the development of special education. In addition, he was a strong vocal advocate, early in the twentieth century, for improvements in the way society treated its children.

Witmer, the eldest of four children, was born in Philadelphia, Pennsylvania. He graduated from the University of Pennsylvania in 1888 and then taught English and history for 2 years at the Rugby Academy in Philadelphia, at the same time doing graduate work at the university, with the thought of a possible career in the law. Meanwhile, the university had appointed James McKeen Cattell as its first professor of psychology. Under Cattell's influence, Witmer switched to psychology, then a new field of science. When, in 1891, Cattell moved to Columbia University, Witmer transferred to the University of Leipzig, in Germany, where he earned his doctorate under Wilhelm Wundt.

Witmer returned to the University of Pennsylvania as Cattell's successor, with the rank of lecturer, and set about developing his own program. During the early 1890s, his research was in the mainstream of experimental psychology, but gradually he developed a new perspective, emphasizing the practical applications of psychology. In March 1896, a public school teacher brought to Witmer's attention a boy who, though evidently bright enough, had great difficulty in reading and spelling. Witmer undertook intensive remedial efforts with the boy, and this case, an instance of dyslexia, stands as the first case in the history of clinical psychology. Witmer examined a number of additional problem children during the year, and in December, in a presentation to the American Psychological Association, he outlined his ideas for practical applications of psychology. For these reasons, 1896 is considered the inaugural year of the world's first psychological clinic and, in effect, of the profession of clinical psychology.

In 1902, Witmer published *Analytical Psychology: A Practical Manual for Colleges and Normal Schools* (Boston), a book notable for its lavish illustrative visual material. In 1904, he married Emma Repplier, who was on the staff of the American Philosophical Society. In 1907, Witmer received a substantial private grant that enabled him to found a journal, *The Psychological Clinic*, and to establish his own remedial clinic and school for children needing prolonged special attention. In the journal's opening article (1907), Witmer proposed and delineated a new doctoral-level profession, to be known as clinical psychology; this announcement, which can be taken to mark the formal beginning of the new profession, brought to a close Witmer's most innovative period. The remainder of his career was devoted primarily to expanding and implementing the implications of his clinical vision. In 1909, in the first of several expansions, the psychological clinic was given additional university support, and for many years thereafter the clinic saw hundreds of cases annually (Levine & Wishner, 1977). In 1931, in a ceremony celebrating the thirty-fifth anniversary of the founding of the psychological clinic, Witmer was presented with a Festschrift (Brotemarkle, 1931) including chapters by 25 of his former students, of whom the best known were Edwin Twitmyer and Morris Viteles (both, under Witmer's auspices, were pioneers—Twitmyer in speech therapy and Viteles in vocational guidance). Witmer retired in 1937.

Witmer's most original and creative idea was the insight that psychology, just recently emancipated from philosophy, could form the basis for a new, scientifically based helping profession. This conception, which was without precedent, was developed during the important child study movement in America. Witmer, in implementing his vision, worked mainly with children; however, he did see some adults, and it is clear from his writings that he envisioned the clinical method as applicable to adults as well as to children. Most of the cases seen by Witmer, particularly in the early years, were instances of mental retardation or learning deficiency, but from the first a variety of clinical problems were encountered. As a clinician, Witmer took the role of a psychological expert. His general approach was to obtain extensive information, including interview, test, family, and school data about a problem child and then make such recommendations as he deemed appropriate. His basic value was for each individual to develop his or her full potential. He developed two well-researched tests, the Witmer Formboard and the Witmer Cylinders; however, he cautioned his students against overreliance on test data, and strongly deplored what he saw as overinterpretation of measures of IQ and a tendency to emphasize assessment to the exclusion of treatment in the growing profession.

Witmer wrote over 80 articles. Most—but by no means all—of these appeared in *The Psychological Clinic*. Many of Witmer's articles were case studies, and these emphasized actual behaviors and family data. Witmer never developed a systematic conception of therapy or personality (he rejected Freudian theory), and although he wrote a number of theoretical articles, most of these were highly discursive and difficult to follow. Perhaps his most important theoretical conception concerned the nature of intelligence. Intelligence, Witmer (1922) argued, is the ability to solve new problems. He was one of the first psychologists to attempt the development of rating scales to describe personality. In the 1920s, he became particularly interested in the study of gifted children and in biochemical approaches to behavior.

Witmer was a man of strong opinions, which he expressed frequently. He emphasized the crucial importance of the early environment in child development and felt passionately that society, in particular the public schools, should take a more active role in fostering the welfare of children.

Witmer's work was a major factor in bringing a concern with practical applications into the developing field of psychology. In the area of clinical psychology his influence was paramount, and although the contributions of other pioneers, including Alfred Binet, Lewis Terman, J. E. W. Wallin, and others were also important, it was Witmer who set the original direction for the new profession.

[*Many of the people mentioned in this article are the subjects of independent biographical entries.*]

Bibliography

Works by Witmer

Witmer, L. (1897). The organization of practical work in psychology. *Psychological Review, 4*, 116–117.

Witmer, L. (1907). Clinical psychology. *The Psychological Clinic, 1*, 1–9. (Reprinted in the *American Psychologist*, [1996], *51*, 248–251).

Witmer, L. (1915). Clinical records. *The Psychological Clinic, 9*, 1–17.

Witmer, L. (1922). What is intelligence and who has it? *The Scientific Monthly, 15*, 57–67.

Works about Witmer

Brotemarkle, R. A. (Ed.). (1931). *Clinical psychology: Studies in honor of Lightner Witmer*. Philadelphia: University of Pennsylvania Press.

Fagan, T. K. (1996). Witmer's contributions to school psychological services. *American Psychologist, 51*, 241–243.

Levine, M., & Wishner, J. (1977). The case records of the Psychological Clinic at the University of Pennsylvania (1896–1961). *Journal of the History of the Behavioral Sciences, 13*, 59–66.

McReynolds, P. (1987). Lightner Witmer: Little known founder of clinical psychology. *American Psychologist, 42*, 849–858.

McReynolds, P. (1996). Lightner Witmer: A centennial tribute. *American Psychologist, 51*, 237–240.

McReynolds, P. (1997). *Lightner Witmer: His life and times*. Washington, DC: American Psychological Association.

O'Donnell, J. M. (1979). The clinical psychology of Lightner Witmer: A case study of institutional innovation and intellectual change. *Journal of the History of the Behavioral Sciences, 15*, 3–17.

Routh, D. K. (1996). Lightner Witmer and the first 100 years of clinical psychology. *American Psychologist, 51*, 244–247.

Paul McReynolds

WOLPE, JOSEPH (1915–1997), South African psychiatrist. Wolpe, who was born in Johannesburg, South Africa, and died in the United States, had a profound influence on clinical psychology and the treatment of mentally ill patients. He was, without doubt, the father of behavior therapy. Although his influence was widespread across the spectrums of psychology and psychiatry, his major influence on the model of the clinician as a scientist-practitioner was profound and contrasts strongly with the model of the clinician as an "armchair philosopher."

Excelling in academics, Wolpe enrolled in medical school at the University of Witwaterstrand and later treated "war neuroses" during World War II as a physician, using techniques loosely based on the Freudian theory of "repressed memories" and sodium pentothal. Wolpe was not satisfied with the clinical results of these techniques or the Freudian theory underlying them and began to look elsewhere for an understanding of the etiology of these conditions. He became familiar with the writings of Clark Hull and Ivan Pavlov as he was finishing his degree in psychiatry at Witwaterstrand. At approximately the same time, Leo J. Reyna, who was well versed in Hullian learning theory, joined the psychology department at Witwaterstrand and began a collaboration with Wolpe that lasted throughout Wolpe's life.

Wolpe's experimental studies centered on Pavlovian procedures that produced "experimental neuroses" in domestic cats. These cats were presented with an auditory stimulus followed by a small number of high-voltage, low-amperage shocks from an induction coil that induced the classic signs of experimental neuroses such as crouching, trembling, howling, spitting, piloerection, and defecation in most cases. Further, when the cats were confined to their cages, extinction of the anxiety responses did not occur, and they even refused to eat when meat was offered to them. Wolpe and the experimental laboratory itself elicited the anxiety response pattern, demonstrating stimulus generalization. Wolpe then began to explore, successfully, procedures that would extinguish the anxiety responses. For example, he deprived the cats of food for 48 to 72 hours and introduced food in a place different from the original conditioning situation. Using the method of counterconditioning, he made the surrounding more similar over time and found that the cats eventually ate in the original experimental situation. He concluded that if a response incompatible with anxiety occurred in the presence of anxiety-provoking stimuli, the connection between the anxiety response and its eliciting stimuli would be weakened and later eliminated. Wolpe assumed that this process was caused by *reciprocal inhibition*. This information became the basis for an effective procedure he devised to treat anxiety disorders in human patients, especially the simple phobia, labeled systematic desensitization. The notion was fairly straightforward and simple. First, find a procedure that interrupts or competes with anxiety, such as relaxation (progressive muscle relaxation, as devised by Edmund Jacobson, was probably Wolpe's technique of choice), assertive responses, sexual responses, or similar responses. Then have the patient, with the therapist's assistance, devise a hierarchy of anxiety-provoking situations ranging from those that cause mild anxiety to those that cause great anxiety. The patient is then relaxed, and the items in the hierarchy are presented in imagination, with low-anxiety starting items and gradually moving to items evoking higher levels of anxiety. After experiencing the lower level items without anxiety, the patient moves up the hierarchy until all items can be experienced without anxiety. The clinical procedure generalizes to real life, and the phobia is eliminated. Occasionally, the procedure is used with real-life situations, with gradual exposure and a competing response that seems even more effective. This technique is important because it was the first clinical technique used by psychologists to be demonstrated as uniformly effective, and it caused a flurry of research activity investigating its parameters. The procedure became the basic technique of behavior therapists. Clinical psychologists could finally say, in regard to a mental disorder (in this case, simple phobia), that they knew how to treat it and that the treatment worked. Although Wolpe's notion of reciprocal inhibition was probably wrong, there was little doubt about the effectiveness of this procedure. Although systematic desensitization was probably Wolpe's best known technique, it was only one of a variety of clinical procedures he developed.

In 1966, Wolpe came to the United States and joined the faculty of Temple University. He founded the Behavior Therapy Unit at the Eastern Pennsylvania Psychiatric Institute and participated with R. Bruce Sloan in one of the most extensive investigations of psychotherapy ever undertaken. This study, published in 1975, established behavior therapy among clinical psychologists and psychiatrists and forced psychotherapists to face directly the issue of effectiveness, which had been largely ignored in spite of the attacks of Hans Eysenck, Wolpe, and others on the effectiveness of psychodynamic psychotherapy and psychoanalysis..

Perhaps the aspect of Wolpe's career that has been most ignored is his influence as a teacher. He chaired the dissertation of Arnold Lazarus, another giant in the field, who is commonly credited with first using the term *behavior therapy*. This dissertation compared desensitization with psychodynamic psychotherapy employing direct observation as well as behavioral rating. Wolpe also had both direct and indirect influence on prominent psychologists such as David Barlow, Gordon Paul, Gerald Davidson, and Peter Lang, as well as many others. Wolpe was a kind, gentle man who was loved and admired by his colleagues as a person, as well as the nation's foremost behavior therapist.

Wolpe kept meticulous data on his clinical cases and was able to demonstrate the effectiveness of his procedures with a clinical population. In 1958 he published his classic book *Psychotherapy by Reciprocal Inhibition*, which became the bible of every young behavior therapist. His scholarly activities continued throughout his life. He published numerous articles and book chapters, started the *Journal of Behavior Therapy and Experimental Psychiatry*, and wrote several editions of *The Practice of Behavior Therapy*, an excellent handbook of clinical techniques and procedures for both experienced and novice clinicians. Wolpe's work with patients was a model of how to do clinical work; he was a master clinician.

Wolpe's professional contributions were well known. He was the second president of the Association for the Advancement of Behavior Therapy (AABT), an organization he cofounded; he received the Distinguished Scientific Award for the Application of Psychology from the American Psychological Association in 1979 and the Lifetime Achievement Award from AABT in 1995. His achievements and contributions place him the same category as Sigmund Freud and B. F. Skinner, who will be remembered in the history of psychology.

[*Many of the people mentioned in this article are the subjects of independent biographical entries.*]

Bibliography

Plaud, J. J. (1998). Joseph Wolpe: Behavior therapy pioneer, 1915–1997. *APS Observer, 11*(2), 44–45.

Poppen, R. (1995). *Joseph Wolpe*. Thousand Oaks, CA: Sage.

Wolpe, J. (1958). *Psychotherapy by reciprocal inhibition*. Stanford, CA: Stanford University Press.

Wolpe, J. (1990). *The practice of behavior therapy* (4th ed.). New York: Pergamon Press.

Wolpe, J. (1997). Thirty years of behavior therapy. *Behavior Therapy, 28*, 633–635.

Henry E. Adams

WOMEN'S HEALTH ISSUES. This entry summarizes current knowledge about key issues in women's health emphasizing information that is consistent across scientists' theoretical orientations, has endured the test of time, and is useful to psychology practitioners and educated women. Hereafter the term health connotes optimal physical health and psychological functioning. (Authors referenced in this article contributed chapters to Blechman and Brownell's *Behavioral Medicine and Women: A Comprehensive Handbook*, New York, 1998). Entries in the annotated bibliography are worth reading both for methods and findings.

Coronary heart disease (CHD), per Brownell, is the primary cause of death in U.S. women, leading to 250,000 deaths annually. One in nine women aged 45 to 64 years has evidence of clinical CHD; that proportion increases to one in three in women 65 years or older. Lifetime risks of diseases in postmenopausal women are 2.8% for hip fracture, 2.8% for breast cancer, 0.7% for endometrial cancer, but 31% for CHD. Women are more likely to die from myocardial infarction once CHD is diagnosed, their outcome is more severe, and myocardial revascularization procedures result in greater morbidity and mortality. In women, 40% of all coronary events are fatal, and 67% of sudden deaths follow no known CHD evidence. Risk factors for CHD and other debilitating diseases are strikingly prevalent among U.S. women. One fourth have elevated cholesterol; one third have hypertension or take antihypertensive medications; and one third exceed ideal body weight. Despite aggressive funding of studies of CHD in men, research on CHD in women is remarkably absent. Similar statements could be made about other major causes of women's ill health.

Reproductive changes, per Brooks-Gunn and Graber, are defining features of three life phases: puberty, pregnancy, and menopause. Environmental stressors are most likely to coincide with these life phases and obstruct physical and psychological development. Given evident physiological changes during these phases, suboptimal functioning is often mistakenly attributed exclusively to physiology. Yet stressful life events proliferate during early adolescence when 48% of female bone mass is accrued, sometimes jeopardizing lifetime bone mass accrual. Excessive exercise and disturbed eating reduce circulating estrogen, contributing to amenorrhea and delayed pubertal development. Probably via gonadal estrogen development, excessive exercise is more likely to delay breast development and menstruation than pubic hair growth. Blood lipid levels during the menopausal transition are also influenced by stressful events. Women who experience extreme premenopausal stress evidence greater increases in low-density lipoproteins and decreases in high-density lipoproteins than women with less premenopausal stress. Reproductive hormone levels, in turn, affect cardiovascular and neuroendocrine stress responses.

Coping strategies, per Blechman, determine the extent to which stressors (e.g., marital conflict) and personal attributes (e.g., ethnicity, temperament, genetic endowment, chronic illness) influence health. Thus, a woman's characteristic attachment style (how she typically copes with the frustrations of close relationships) predicts her marital satisfaction and social support. Securely attached adult women apparently cope more successfully with the frustrations inherent in marriage, providing them with more perceived support and more satisfaction with that support. A pessimistic coping style predisposes to marital distress and depression. Marital distress, in turn, contributes to poor physical health via repeated arguments that generate unrelieved physiological reactivity and impair immune system functioning. Although marital conflict is inevitable and divorce rates are high, some women prefer marriage despite persistent family violence. When depression is the product of severe but remediable marital conflict, the treatment of choice is conjoint therapy aimed at a mutually satisfying relationship. Training in improved coping strategies is in order given irremediable marital conflict or chronic dysthymia.

When coping prosocially, women consider the impact of their behavior on other people, take into account other people's opinions and expertise, and feel comfortable asking others for help and reciprocating. The resulting social support (number or perceived quality of supportive relationships) significantly benefits health. Information derived from social comparison helps women reduce uncertainty about their health, gauge the appropriateness of their reactions, regulate their emotions, and problem solve. Women who perceive more social support evidence less depression, a lower risk of mortality from diverse causes, and better illness recovery.

The least healthy coping strategies involve overreaction to mildly dangerous situations, underreaction to true threats, and excessive emotional dependence on or avoidance of others. The prototypic unhealthy coping style is the Type A behavior pattern (TABP): aggressive, competitive, and impatient responses to achievement or control-related challenges. Women who rely on TABP are inclined to cardiovascular disease through a cascade of physiological events beginning with undue sympathetic activation and concluding with myocardial infarction. The TABP may erode cardiovascular health by promoting overreactivity to daily stressors, restricting social support, and encouraging an unhealthy lifestyle. Arguably, the healthiest coping strategy involves an optimistic perspective, a willingness to persist at resolving controllable challenges while accepting the inevitability of uncontrollable challenges. Optimism may contribute to better recovery from cancer surgery, better adaptation to infertility, less morbidity, and later mortality. Pessimistic coping may have adverse effects on health because it involves fatalistic expectations of bad outcomes regardless of personal efforts and a reckless lifestyle.

Women often occupy multiple, contradictory roles: nurturing children, deferring to parents, attracting sexual partners, and inspiring confidence in coworkers. As social roles multiply, health-benefiting social and financial resources increase, as do health-draining demands for time, energy, patience, and flexibility. While subjectively positive and negative life events (e.g., marriage, job loss) can increase perceived stress, only the subjectively negative have dire health implications. Women with diversified investments in family and occupational roles may encounter more stressful life events (because they care about more people), and they may deal with these stressors with more equanimity (because they get more social support).

According to King, most of the premature morbidity and mortality caused by leading killers of U.S. women—cardiovascular disease and cancer—are preventable through behavioral changes in cigarette smoking, alcohol use, diet, physical activity, early detection, and environmental exposure. Yet less than 1% of U.S. health-care dollars are earmarked for disease prevention. Breast cancer mortality could be diminished considerably if all women aged 50 and older had regular annual mammograms. Prevention efforts should extend from early to late in life and consider high-risk, underserved groups. Homeless women are particularly vulnerable to human immunodeficiency virus (HIV)-risk behavior and in need of accessible prevention programs. African American and Hispanic women constituted 21% of all American women in 1995, but constituted 76% of women diagnosed with acquired immunodeficiency syndrome (AIDS). The majority of U.S. women do not adhere to widely supported dietary recommendations (total dietary fat below 30% energy intake, at least 5 daily servings of fruits and vegetables). Improved prenatal nutrition and elimination of prenatal cigarette smoking and substance abuse would have enduring benefit for women and children. Despite adolescents girls' concerns about body weight and image they are less likely to rely on moderate physical exercise for weight control than on cigarettes. School-based prevention programs for adolescent girls could simultaneously address eating disorders, pregnancy, depression, substance abuse, and suicide. Prevention of major causes of morbidity and mortality among women requires an equal emphasis on active prevention tactics for individuals (breast self-examination) and on social systems (reimbursement for mammograms).

The health of American women has been compromised by an overemphasis upon individual-level risk factors and a neglect of systems-level risk factors that limit access to early enough, good enough care. Gilchrist noted that receipt of prenatal care has grown since 1960, while barriers to care have declined, including excessive costs, limited system capacity, and inhospitable practices. Primary-care physicians can treat substance-abusing women rather than refer them to inaccessible specialists. At secondary schools, health clinics can provide prevention-oriented care and information. Work-site clinics can promote employees' use of substance-free strategies for coping with family and work-related stress. The military can provide specialized health care for women personnel. Health-care providers can use telephones, television, and the Internet to assist women in making informed decisions about health care, particularly those who are poor, housebound, concerned about confidentiality, or who live in remote areas. Disillusion with conventional health care has led to the proliferation of nontraditional healing approaches, broadening women's options. The Internet technology, which in early stages had led to a proliferation of choices, may in a later stage provide a clearer dissemination of information.

Brownell noted the prevalence among women of normative discontent with body weight and shape that leads to health-compromising eating disorders, substance abuse, exercise, diet, and plastic surgery. In bulimia nervosa, disabling emotional and social problems are common. The same is true of anorexia nervosa, along with life-threatening medical complications and a 5 to 15% mortality rate. With bulimia nervosa, success rates are high for cognitive-behavioral therapy or interpersonal psychotherapy. Anorexia nervosa does not respond as readily to treatment and often requires immediate medical attention. Promising comprehensive programs, some inpatient, include cognitive-behavioral therapy, family therapy, and occasional medication and group psychotherapy. It is unclear under what circumstances and for which women the benefits of plastic surgery outweigh the long-term risks and costs. Obesity compromises the health of nearly one third of U.S. women. Long-term benefits of new obesity treatments, some with biological and genetic bases, are unclear. Alcoholism and problem drinking affect a startling number of women in distinct ways. Women metabolize alcohol differently, progress more rapidly from onset of heavy drinking to dependence, increase alcohol consumption when in traditional male jobs, and endanger fetal development by prenatal alcohol use. Treatments developed specifically for women drinkers deserve wider use. Compared to men, women with opiate dependence show a telescoping pattern consisting of later onset and more rapid problem development. Illicit prenatal drug use adversely affects fetal development. The greater stigma attached to women's substance use impedes access to early, satisfactory care. Evaluations are needed of the long-term impact on women of conventional twelve-step and clinic-based programs. The prevalence of smoking in adolescent and adult women has increased dramatically since the 1950s. Smoking is now the most preventable cause of death in U.S. women, accounting for 140,000 deaths per year. Smoking prevention and cessation programs and increased taxes on tobacco products could discourage smoking initiation and continuation.

Ill health is often wrongly attributed to female physiology rather than to universal mechanisms. Williams noted that premenstrual symptoms may be specific neither to the premenstruum nor to women. Occasional benefits of placebos for premenstrual symptoms may reflect universal chronic pain mechanisms. Chronic pelvic pain responds to operant conditioning, relaxation, and cognitive strategies for coping with any chronic pain. Survivors of sexual abuse are less likely to seek regular gynecological care than women with no abuse history, yet they are at higher risk of sexually transmitted diseases (STDs) and unwanted pregnancies due to riskier sexual behavior. Birth outcomes such as length of labor, medication use, and delivery mode are favorably influenced by a socially supportive labor companion. Ethnic group differences in birth outcomes deserve investigation. Latinas are the least likely to receive prenatal care, but deliver the fewest low-birthweight babies. African American women who receive prenatal care are at higher risk of having low-birthweight infants than socially and economically comparable white women. Per Gotlib, postpartum depression may not be distinct from other forms of depression. Simply because depression follows an event such as childbirth (or occurs during the premenstrual phase) does not indicate a cause-effect relationship. Rates and symptoms of postpartum depression are equivalent to those of nonpostpartum depression among women of childbearing age. During pregnancy, approximately 8 pounds of weight gained is to provide energy stores, preparing women's bodies hormonally and anatomically to breastfeed. Only 50% of U.S. mothers breastfeed for any length of time, despite supportive evidence for lifelong health benefits to mother and child. A dose-response relationship has been shown for total months of breastfeeding and reduced risk of premenopausal breast cancer. Lactation may also lower the risk of heart disease by increasing high-density lipoprotein during breastfeeding and by lowering the risk of chronic diseases associated with obesity through greater postpartum weight loss. Not every woman should breast feed; some do not because of prior sexual abuse. Women who breast feed need accurate information regarding what to do at each stage, access to competent health-care providers when problems occur, and a coordinated approach to problem solving. The lactational amenorrhea method (LAM) of family planning or child spacing has been shown to provide 99.6% protection against pregnancy. It is an attractive but poorly publicized alternative for women who dislike other contraceptive methods. In decreasing order of effectiveness, other contraception methods include: permanent and reversible sterilization; estrogen-containing oral contraceptives and progesterone-releasing intrauterine devices; traditional male condoms and progestin-only contraceptives; female barrier methods; fertility awareness (rhythm method); and withdrawal. Therapeutic abortion involves many interested parties and engages many points of view. Women's responses to abortion are influenced by the procedure and the experience of unwanted pregnancy. Medical risks of abortion are considerably lower than childbirth with the period of greatest distress occurring prior to the procedure. After abortion, positive emotions predominate over negative ones. Risk factors for negative psychological sequelae include poor prior mental health, termination of pregnancy for medical reasons, and insufficient social support.

According to Meyerowitz and Weidner, by age 55 more than 80% of women experience at least one chronic health problem, and over half have multiple chronic problems. For every cause of mortality, annual death rates are higher for men. In contrast, for nearly two thirds of both acute and chronic causes of morbidity (excluding cancer and mental illness), women have higher rates. For men, most reported morbidity is related to injury; for women morbidity is more likely to result from illness. Since many of the most common causes of morbidity progress with age, women's longer lifespans increase gender differences. Many gender-universal chronic illnesses are more common among women, such as autoimmune disorders (e.g., rheumatoid arthritis, multiple sclerosis, and lupus) and gastrointestinal (G.I.) disorders (e.g. irritable bowel syndrome, gallstones, constipation, general gastrointestinal symptoms). Gastrointestinal disorders may be related to slower colonic transit time and inhibited gallbladder motility as well as to medication side effects. Other disorders more prevalent among women include: Alzheimer's disease, migraine headache, osteoporosis, and Raynaud's disease. Some illnesses, although not more prevalent in women, have female-specific forms such as gestational diabetes and menstrual epileptic seizures. These illnesses do not shorten life but do cause pain, disability, and disrupted quality of life. Paradoxically, the mechanisms that protect against mortality may account for morbidity. Thus, female superiority in antibody production has been implicated in autoimmune disease susceptibility. Even for universal diseases, there may be important between-gender differences in process and treatment. Although heart disease is the leading cause of death for men and women, women get the disease approximately 10 years later than men; current treatments are less effective for women; and survival rates after the first myocardial infarction are worse for women. Immune and endocrine systems function interdependently. In the presence of a universal disease, disruptions or normative changes in immune and endocrine functioning associated with the menstrual cycle, pregnancy, and menopause or with exogenous hormones (in birth control pills, hormone replacement therapy, or prescribed medication) can alter perceived stress and response to medical and psychosocial treatment. Menopause is associated with increased risk for some conditions (such as arthritis, osteoporosis, coronary heart disease, and hypertension) and with decreased risk for others (such as gastrointestinal disorders, headache, and lupus). Hormonal fluctuations associated with menstrual cycling and pregnancy appear to influence several conditions (e.g., asthma, diabetes, headache, epileptic seizures, lupus, multiple sclerosis, and pain), however, changes in symptom severity are often not uniform. Pregnancy exacerbates asthma symptoms in some women and moderates symptoms in others. Behavioral interventions (e.g., psychoeducation, social support groups, family therapy, cognitive-behavioral therapy, hypnosis, biofeedback, and progressive muscular relaxation) have been successfully adapted for women with chronic physical illnesses including multiple sclerosis, Raynaud's disease, and migraine headache. Potential benefits include improved support from and for family members, better understanding of the disease by women and their families, better response to medical care, stress management, immune functioning, pain control, quality of life, and longevity. Compared to pharmacological treatments, behavioral interventions are less likely to have negative side effects and more likely to yield lifelong, cross-situational skill generalization and maintenance.

The impact on health of comorbid physical and psychiatric symptoms may be multiplicative, not additive. Melamed noted that as many as 50% of patients with diagnosable psychiatric conditions seek medical care for comorbid symptoms. Over 16% report depression or anxiety to primary care physicians. Unexplained weakness, lethargy, sleep difficulty, appetite loss, weight fluctuation, anxiety, or chest pain cause women to question their physical health and discourage practitioners from diagnosing mood and anxiety disorders. When physical discomfort continues, women view referrals for mental-health care with suspicion and persist in their search for a rational explanation. Women receive more than 75% of all psychoactive drugs prescribed. Enduring benefits are most likely to result from individualized combinations of behavioral, environmental, and pharmacological treatments involving gradually decreased reliance on medication as new skills are developed and social support increases. For more biologically driven disorders, proper medication use is of primary significance providing the platform for optimal management of biological vulnerability. Anxiety disorders—panic disorder, agoraphobia, generalized anxiety disorder, social phobia, obsessive-compulsive disorder—are three times more prevalent in women. When women with stress-induced disorders rely on maladaptive coping strategies they often exacerbate environmental stressors and compromise immune function. Women who are overwhelmed by discomfort are most likely to benefit from interventions that enable them to generate social support, comfortably comply with prescribed medical regimens, and maintain a satisfying lifestyle. Panic symptoms may occur more often in premenstrual, perinatal, or menopausal phases. Since panic symptoms may be the result of a medical disorder, correct diagnosis and treatment may eliminate heart palpitations and dizziness and encourage proper medication use to control distress. Women genetically inclined to bipolar disorder are more likely than men to show rapid cycling with four or more annual recurrences of mania, hypomania, or depression. These mood disorders may be hormonally influenced as they predispose women to postpartum depression. Mood-regulating drugs are the primary choice for treatment. A psychoeducational family intervention improves patient-family communication and support for adherence to the medication regimen. Women with schizophrenia have relinquished mood-state regulation and either show bizarre attention to external stimuli that they attempt to incorporate into their own bodily sensations, or catatonic internal concentration to the exclusion of environmental input. Hormonal fluctuations of estrogen may lead to delayed onset of symptoms and greater susceptibility during life transitions such as menopause. The influence of estrogen on dopamine receptors and the disruption of neurotransmitters may result in disorganized thinking. Given the stronger hereditary nature of schizophrenia in women and women's greater sensitivity to medication, careful evaluation of polypharmacologic approaches is necessary. Some medication may increase susceptibility to cognitive disorganization and decrease compliance with treatment regimens. Childbearing burdens schizophrenic mothers who relate to their children as a function of their own desires. Women may be particularly inclined to confuse anxiety with fatigue or pain. Empirically based methods of differential diagnosis and treatment for chronic pain and chronic fatigue would contribute substantially to women's health.

[*See also* Abortion; Menopause; Menstruation; *and* Pregnancy.]

Bibliography

Adams, S. H. (1994). Role of hostility in women's health during midlife: A longitudinal study. *Health Psychology, 13*, 488–495. Relationships between hostility at ages 21, 27, 43, and 52 years old and general health at age 52 were investigated in 140 educated women. Hostility at each age was negatively correlated with general health at age 52, when possible mediators at age 43 (cigarette smoking, excessive alcohol intake, body mass index, negative life events, social role satisfaction) were controlled.

Avis, N. E., Brambilla, D. J., Vass, K., & McKinlay, J. B. (1991). The effect of widowhood on health: A prospective analysis from the Massachusetts Women's Health Study. *Social Science and Medicine, 33*, 1063–1070. Examined the physical and psychological effects of widowhood in a randomly sampled cohort of women, aged 45 to 55 years at baseline, followed for 5 years. Women whose spouses died during the study (76) were compared to age-matched married controls (1,625). Following the death of a spouse, the percentage of widows reporting psychological (but not physical) symptoms increased. Widows had higher rates of health-care utilization, in particular, taking prescribed medication, in part for mental-health reasons. Social support increased following widowhood and more widows reported decreased income.

Bardone, A. M., Moffitt, T. E., Caspi, A., Dickson, N., & Silva, P. A. (1996). Adult mental health and social outcomes of adolescent girls with depression and conduct disorder. *Development and Psychopathology, 8*, 811–829. Authors followed girls in complete birth cohort who at age 15 were depressed (27), conduct disordered (37), or without mental health disorder (341) to age 21. In general, depressed girls became depressed women and conduct disordered girls developed antisocial personality disorder symptoms by age 21. Conduct disorder exclusively predicted the following at age 21: antisocial personality disorder, substance dependence, illegal behavior, dependence on multiple welfare sources, early home leaving, multiple cohabitation partners, physical partner violence. Both depression and conduct disorder predicted the following at age 21: anxiety disorder, multiple drug use, early school leaving, low school attainment, any cohabitation, pregnancy, and early childbearing.

Blechman, E. A., & Brownell, K. D. (Eds.). (1998). *Behavioral medicine and women: A comprehensive handbook.* New York: Guilford Press. Documenting significant recent advances in understanding women's psychosocial and physical health, this resource covers both prevention and intervention and provides information on the links between behavior and disease. References to authors cited in the text of the article are found here.

Bruce, M. L., Takeuchi, D. T., & Leaf, P. J. (1991). Poverty and psychiatric status: Longitudinal evidence from the New Haven Epidemiological Catchment Area Study. *Archives of General Psychiatry, 48*, 470–474. Assessed the effect of poverty on psychiatric status using two waves of New Haven, CT, epidemiologic catchment area data. Poverty was defined using federal guidelines; psychiatric status was assessed by the diagnostic interview schedule (DIS). When examining the course of healthy respondents at the first interview, respondents in poverty had a twofold increased risk (controlling for demographic factors) for an episode of at least one DIS/*DSM-III* Axis I psychiatric disorder. Effects of poverty did not differ by sex, age, race, or psychiatric history. Despite the lack of sex differences in the study's findings, the implications of these findings for women's health are substantial given the fact that women and children represent the bulk of people living in poverty in the United States.

Caspi, A., & Elder, G. H. (1986). Life satisfaction in old age: Linking social psychology and history. *Journal of Psychology and Aging, 1*, 18–26. Using longitudinal data on 79 women from the 1900 generation of the Berkeley Guidance Study, they found that the consequences of adaptive resources in early adulthood vary in relation to social class. Intellectual skills in the 1930s predicted life satisfaction in old age for working-class women, while emotional health was more influential with middle-class women. Social activity in old age makes a difference only in lives of working-class women. Middle-class women in the 1930s showed gains attributable to Depression hardship, where life satisfaction of working-class women was diminished.

Colditz, G. A., Manson, J. E., & Hankinson, S. E. (1997). The nurses' health study: 20-year contribution to the understanding of health among women. *Journal of Women's Health, 6*, 49–62. The study has related use of hormones, diet, exercise, and other lifestyle practices to the development of a wide range of chronic illnesses among women. Recent findings include relations between weight gain and heart disease, diabetes, and mortality; the lack of relation between calcium and osteoporotic fractures; and the positive relation between postmenopausal use of hormones and risk of breast cancer.

Hibbard, J. H., & Pope, C. R. (1993). The quality of social roles as predictors of morbidity and mortality. *Social Science and Medicine, 36*, 217–225. The study population was randomly selected from among members of a large HMO and were part of a household interview during 1970–1971. Medical records for 2 years prior to the interview and for 15 years after indicate that for married women, equality in decision making and companionship in marriage are protective against death. Work support is protective against death, malignancy, and stroke among employed women.

Hyde, J. S., Klein, M. H., Essex, M. J., & Clark, R. (1995). Maternity leave and women's mental health. *Psychology of Women Quarterly, 19*, 257–285. Wisconsin Maternity Leave and Health Study investigated work status, maternity leave, and mental health of 570 women. Length of leave interacted significantly with marital concerns when predicting depression; women who took a short leave (6 weeks or less) and were high on marital concerns had the highest depression scores.

Matthews, K. A., Wing, R. R., Kuller, L. H., Meilahn, E. N., & Kelsey, S. F. (1990). Influences of natural menopause on psychological characteristics and symptoms of middle-aged healthy women. *Journal of Consulting and Clinical Psychology, 58*, 345–351. A longitudinal study of 541 initially premenopausal healthy women found that natural menopause led to few changes in psychological characteristics, with only a decline in introspectiveness and an increase in reported hot flashes.

Petersen, A. C., Ssarigiani, P. A, & Kennedy, R. E. (1991). Adolescent depression: why more girls? *Journal of Youth and Adolescence, 20*, 247–271. Longitudinal data on 335 adolescents randomly selected from two school districts were used to test hypotheses about gender differences in depression. Results showed that girls are at risk for developing depressed affect by the twelfth grade because they experienced more challenges than did boys. The sex difference in twelfth grade depressed affect disappeared in analyses controlling for adolescent challenges.

Repetti, R. L., Matthews, K. A., & Waldron, I. (1989). Employment and women's health: Effects of paid employment on women's mental and physical health. *American Psychologist, 44*, 1394–1401. Reviews empirical evidence concerning effects of paid employment on women's physical and mental health. Concludes that women's employment does not have a negative effect on their health, on average. Employment appears to improve the health of unmarried and married women who have positive attitudes toward employment.

Strawbridge, W. J., Camacho, T. C., Cohen, R. C., & Kaplan,

G. A. (1993). Gender differences in factors associated with change in physical functioning in old age: A 6-year longitudinal study. *The Gerontologist, 33*, 603–609. Followed 356 older men and women from 1984 to 1990. For women, each of four positive health behaviors (not smoking, exercising, regular social contacts, going out 3 days a week) was associated with a 2.5 point advantage in functioning in 1990 with age, baseline functioning, and number of chronic conditions constant. A large 48% of variance in functioning in 1990 was explained by health behavior and control variables combined.

Thompson, M. S., & Ensminger, M. E. (1989). Psychological well-being among mothers with school age children: Evolving family structures. *Social Forces, 67*, 715–730. Using longitudinal data on 833 childrearing women in an urban Black neighborhood in Chicago, findings indicate that long-term single parenting is a chronic stressor. Women who were the only adult in the household from children's early school years through their adolescence had higher levels of psychological distress than women who lived with another adult. Death of a family member or close friend, unemployment, and residence change were associated with increased distress. Emotional support, having a confidant friend, and frequent church attendance were related to less distress.

Elaine A. Blechman

WOODWORTH, ROBERT SESSIONS (1869–1962), American psychologist. Proclaimed by psychologist Edwin G. Boring as the fifth "dean" of psychology, Woodworth was the first recipient of the American Psychological Foundation's Gold Medal award in 1956 for his "unequaled contributions in shaping the destiny of scientific psychology." His influence was primarily through his systematic works and textbooks and through his eclectic and inclusive vision for psychology.

The son of a Congregationalist minister and a college mathematics teacher, Woodworth grew up in New England and attended Amherst College (bachelor of arts degree, 1891). After teaching science and mathematics, he entered Harvard University, where he studied psychology and philosophy with William James, Josiah Royce, and George Santayana, receiving a bachelor of arts degree in 1896 and a master of arts degree in 1897. Following additional work in physiology, he accepted a fellowship under James McKeen Cattell at Columbia University and was awarded a doctorate in 1899 for his dissertation on voluntary movement. He served as assistant to the noted English physiologist Charles Sherrington in 1902–1903. When Cattell invited him back to Columbia as an instructor in 1903, Woodworth accepted, and he remained at Columbia for his entire career. He was made a full professor in 1909 and succeeded Cattell as the executive officer of the psychology department. After he became professor emeritus in 1942, he continued to teach psychology at Columbia's School of General Studies until 1959.

From the beginning of his career, Woodworth's interests were wide ranging and included the control of muscular movement, reflexes, transfer of training, imageless thought, psychophysics, time perception, and psychological testing. In 1899–1900 he conducted studies of transfer of training with his close friend Edward L. Thorndike, who had just begun his appointment at Teachers College, Columbia University. They concluded that transfer was unlikely except when the two tasks contained identical elements. These findings appeared to contradict the popular notion of "formal discipline," which maintained that the study of Latin or geometry would produce general intellectual "strengthening" in a manner analogous to muscular exercise.

Convinced by Cattell of the future of psychological tests, Woodworth began work on testing in 1904, while continuing his other interests. At the 1904 St. Louis Exposition, Woodworth and Frank G. Bruner made anthropometric and psychometric assessments on 1,100 individuals in order to study "racial differences." Compared with many of his contemporaries, Woodworth was extremely cautious about interpretation of group differences in intelligence and other abilities. In 1910 he warned psychologists against overreliance on group averages and urged the proper recognition of group overlap, within-group variation, and the role of culture. He warned of the dangers of assuming a hereditary source for differences and of using group differences for selecting immigrants. His thoughtfulness in matters of heredity and environment was known and respected in subsequent decades, and the Social Science Research Council asked him to survey this topic for a widely read monograph published in 1941. At the request of the American Psychological Association, he worked with Frank Wells from 1906 to 1911 on a battery of tests for basic abilities known as the "Association Tests," which were widely used. His most important contribution to psychometrics was the development of a test of emotional stability for evaluation of World War I recruits. This self-report inventory of neurotic symptoms was not used in the war but was widely used for civilians. Known as the Woodworth Personal Data Sheet, it was an important forerunner of modern personality tests.

Woodworth authored at least 246 books, articles, and reviews. His greatest influence on the trajectory of American psychology was undoubtedly through his books rather than his research papers. He helped revise George T. Ladd's famous text, *Elements of Physiological Psychology* (New York, 1887), in 1911. Later known as "Woodworth's *Physiological Psychology*," it was the standard text in the field for many years. *Dynamic Psychology* (New York, 1918), based on a series of lectures at the American Museum of Natural History, laid the groundwork for the study of motivation. His *Contemporary Schools of Psychology* (New York, 1931, revised 1948) provided a widely read history of the major movements in the discipline. His two most influential books were his introductory text, *Psychology* (New York, 1921), and *Experimental Psychology* (New York, 1938). The introductory text was revised in 1929, 1934, 1940, and, with Donald Marquis, in 1947. The first three editions sold more than 400,000 copies, an extraordinary number for the 1920s and 1930s. The book was translated into dozens of languages and was used around the world. *Psychology* served as a model for later introductory texts, particularly in terms of the wide range of topics and openness to a variety of viewpoints.

The book that most clearly influenced generations of new psychologists was Woodworth's *Experimental Psychology*, also known as the "Columbia Bible." Although "the bible" was not formally published until Woodworth was nearly 70 years old, mimeographed versions had been used by Columbia students since about 1912. The "bible" provided comprehensive, analytical summaries of all major content areas and methods of experimental psychology. The book also helped to define the nature and scope of experimental psychology by drawing a clear distinction between experimental and correlational research in terms of manipulation of the independent variable, a distinction followed by generations of subsequent textbook authors. Although the book lacked any overall theoretical framework, it covered a very broad range of topics in a way that was eminently useful for researchers. *Experimental Psychology* was first revised in 1954 with the help of Harold Schlosberg, and in 1971, associates and students of Schlosberg brought out a third edition under the editorship of J. W. Kling and L. A. Riggs. All three editions were widely used as texts and as reference works in many countries.

Woodworth's most important conceptual contribution to psychology was his emphasis on the role of motivation. Beginning in 1918, he separated psychological inquiry into questions of "how" and "why," and he popularized the term *drives* for questions of "why." He argued that *drives* should encompass basic biological needs; neuromuscular readiness, like that of a runner poised in the starting blocks; or complex human motives, such as political ambition. This position was initially a reaction against William McDougall's instinct theory as an adequate explanation of human action. He later came to describe his dynamic approach as a *Stimulus-Organism-Response* or S-O-R model for psychology, a conceptualization widely used by subsequent textbook writers. By the inclusion of the "O," Woodworth explicitly emphasized both the active living organism and the importance of intervening processes.

Woodworth also influenced the course of psychology through many administrative positions. As Cattell's successor at Columbia, he guided the psychology department during its period of greatest prestige, when it produced many future APA presidents and leaders in both basic and applied work. The twenty-third president of the American Psychological Association (1914), he was an important figure in APA affairs and governance for decades. He served as president of the Psychological Corporation in 1929 and remained on the board of directors until 1960. While president of the Social Science Research Council in 1931–1932, he helped lay the groundwork for the founding of the Society for Research in Child Development. He edited the *Archives of Psychology*, which provided an outlet for publishing doctoral dissertations, from 1906 to 1948 and served on the editorial board of the *Psychological Bulletin* and other major journals. His advice on what should be published and who should be hired was widely sought.

Throughout his career, Woodworth promoted an antidoctrinaire, eclectic empiricism that encouraged and foreshadowed the diversity of modern psychology. He steadfastly rejected restrictions on the scope of psychology or positions that limited psychology's concern to only behavior or consciousness. His interests, activities, and authority spanned the discipline to a degree impossible for subsequent generations of psychologists. Given the extraordinarily widespread use of his textbooks, Woodworth, more than any other author, taught psychology to the world.

Bibliography

Estes, W. K. (1981). The Bible is out. *Contemporary Psychology, 26*, 327–330.

Heidbreder, E. (1933). *Seven psychologies.* New York: Appleton-Century-Crofts.

Murphy, G. (1963). Robert Sessions Woodworth, 1869–1962. *American Psychologist, 18*, 131–133. An obituary.

Poffenberger, A. (1962). Robert Sessions Woodworth: 1869–1962. *American Journal of Psychology, 75*, 677–689. An obituary. See also *The New York Times*, July 5, 1962.

Seward, G. S., & Seward, J. P. (Eds.). (1958). *Current psychological issues: Essays in honor of Robert S. Woodworth.* New York: Henry Holt.

Winston, A. S. (1990). Robert Sessions Woodworth and the "Columbia Bible": How the psychological experiment was redefined. *American Journal of Psychology, 103*, 391–401.

Winston, A. S. (1996). "As his name indicates": R. S. Woodworth's letters of references and employment for Jewish psychologists. *Journal of the History of the Behavioral Sciences, 32*, 30–43.

Woodworth, R. S. (1930). Robert S. Woodworth. In C. Murchison (Ed.), *A history of psychology in autobiography* (Vol. 2, pp. 359–380). Worcester, MA: Clark University Press.

Woodworth, R. S. (1939). *Psychological issues: Selected papers of Robert S. Woodworth*. New York: Columbia University Press. Contains a bibliography of Woodworth's publications up to 1938. A supplementary bibliography is in E. Tunnell, A bibliography of articles and books by Robert Sessions Woodworth: A continuation, 1938–1959. *American Journal of Psychology*, (1962), 75, 690–692.

Andrew S. Winston

WOOLLEY, HELEN THOMPSON (1874–1947), American psychologist. Woolley contributed to several fields within psychology, including psychology of women, child development, child assessment, and child psychology. Her work often is not well known, but it has had obvious effects in the aforementioned fields. Woolley's belief that environment was of more consequence than innate abilities and traits resonated throughout her life's work.

Woolley attended the University of Chicago under the tutelage of James Roland Angell, James H. Tufts, and John Dewey. She was a distinguished student (Rossiter, 1982), and in 1900 she became the first woman to receive a doctorate in psychology from the University of Chicago (Rosenberg, 1982). Her doctoral dissertation, "Psychological Norms in Men and Women," was published as a book entitled *The Mental Traits of Sex: An Experimental Investigation of the Normal Mind in Men and Women* (Chicago, 1903). This study was the first to use scientific investigation to support the contention that males and females are biologically complementary, in contrast to the prevailing belief of that time, that males were innately, biologically superior to females (Stevens & Gardner, 1982). Woolley's results led her to conclude that men and women were more alike than different and that socioenvironmental factors (e.g., child-rearing practices, parental/societal expectations for boys versus girls, and the different opportunities for experiences available to each gender) were largely responsible for the restricted range of personal and professional achievements then made by women. Her evidence and conclusions laid the groundwork for the field known as the psychology of women and became the basis for other studies in that field, notably those of Leta Stetter Hollingworth.

Most of Woolley's career as a psychologist was devoted to the many facets of child psychology. Her interest in this field appears to have been sparked by the birth of her first daughter in 1907 and by her ardent observations of her daughter's activities. Woolley wrote numerous articles about child development from psychophysiological, behavioral, and personality perspectives. Her work in this area influenced the professional lives of Margaret Morse Nice (Rossiter, 1982) and Lois Hayden Meek Stolz (O'Connell & Russo, 1988; Zapoleon & Stolz, 1971) to a significant degree.

Ongoing studies were conducted when Woolley worked for the Bureau for the Investigation of Conditions of Working Children in Cincinnati (1911–1921), as the staff psychologist and associate director at the Merrill-Palmer School in Detroit (1921–1925) and as director of the Institute for Child Welfare Research at Teachers College at Columbia University (1925–1929). She undertook lengthy studies of young employed children in Cincinnati and was responsible for changes in the child labor/compulsory education laws. She published reports encouraging many innovations surrounding child psychological assessment, preschool and parent education, remediation of learning difficulties, child guidance, and school/community partnerships designed to improve local and home environments.

As a psychologist, Woolley functioned as a scientist, lecturer, author, public servant, professor, innovator, and clinician. She was a member of several professional organizations and was recognized by her fellow psychologists as an important contributor to the field of psychology.

[*See also the biographies of Angell, Dewey, and Leta Stetter Hollingsworth.*]

Bibliography

O'Connell, A. N., & Russo, N. F. (Eds.). (1988). *Models of achievement: Reflections of eminent women in psychology: Vol. 2*. Hillsdale, NJ: Erlbaum.

Rosenberg, R. (1982). *Beyond separate spheres: Intellectual roots of modern feminism*. New Haven, CT: Yale University Press.

Rossiter, M. W. (1982). *Women scientists in America: Struggles and strategies to 1940*. Baltimore: Johns Hopkins University Press.

Stevens, G., & Gardner, S. (1982). *The women of psychology: Volume 1. Pioneers and innovators*. Cambridge, MA: Schenkman.

Thompson, H. B. (1903). *Mental traits of sex: An experimental investigation of the normal mind in men and women*. Chicago: University of Chicago Press.

Zapoleon, M. W., & Stolz, L. M. (1971). Helen Bradford Thompson Woolley. In E. T. James, J. W. James, & P. S. Boyer (Eds.), *Notable American women 1607–1950: A biographical dictionary* (pp. 657–660). Cambridge, MA: Belknap Press of Harvard University Press.

Elizabeth Murdoch James

WORD-ASSOCATION TEST. *See* Projective Techniques; Testing; *and the biography of Jung*.

WORK is the single most common nonbiological element cutting across both cultures and generations. It defines individuals in the most fundamental manner. People identify with their work, even if it is a humble activity. Furthermore, the adequacy of individuals' work efforts shapes their lives in terms of material, spiritual, and physical matters. It determines their finances, the kind of dwelling they possess, the way they spend their time, their family size, where they live, their friendships, their health, and even their spiritual well-being. The work products people generate contribute to the way of life of others in their community, their country, and even the world.

Most people spend about one third of their adult lives at work. Work creates a structure and rhythm to life that is sorely missed when individuals do not work for an extended period of time. When unable to work, many people experience emotional distress and a loss of the sense of self-worth. Keeping all these things in mind, it is no wonder that so much effort has been made to understand and improve the work lives of men and women. This article attempts to identify and briefly discuss some of the major elements involved in work and the effects those elements have on people.

Work Environments

Work environments can be defined and described in many ways. Some writers, such as John L. Holland, who proposed a revised theory (1997), have created theoretical models that incorporate a number of well-defined work environments. Holland has described six types of work environments: realistic, which is concrete and product oriented; investigative, which is intellectual and focused on problem solving; artistic, involving creating and transmitting aesthetic products in a variety of media; social, concerned with serving individual needs and supporting people; enterprising, which deals with risk taking and entrepreneurial activities; and conventional, emphasizing systems and detailed work.

Another approach to understanding people at work comes from the Theory of Work Adjustment of Rene Dawis and Lloyd Lofquist (1984). This theory postulates that individuals seek a correspondence between their needs and abilities and those that are satisfied and required by their work. As the correspondence between these factors increases, the person's tenure in a position increases. Dawis and Lofquist also identify a number of work styles that differentially satisfy the demands of various work environments. Examples of these styles include flexibility, activeness, reactiveness, and perseverance.

Person-Environment Fit. Because the work environment is such an important aspect of work satisfaction and success, the fit between personal characteristics and the demands of the work environment has led to considerable study of this subject. A related area of research is the impact of that fit on important outcome variables, such as satisfaction, job tenure, productivity, and career pathways.

Psychologists have long been interested in matching individuals' interests and abilities with the requirements of various work settings. Also important is the awareness of a temporal component to this match. That is, over time, the characteristics of individuals will gradually or even abruptly change, reducing or increasing the degree of fit with the work setting. In addition, work requirements change. In either circumstance, it is important to recognize that attention must be paid to the evolution of work and its requirements.

Work Role Stressors

Another variable of concern is the impact of work on well-being. In this regard, occupational stress and the reactions of the worker become important. There are many approaches to the study of occupational stress, some of which are based on the examination of ergonomics, others on life events, and still others on the perception of work environments. When an ergonomic approach is taken, attention is paid to the physical characteristics of the work setting and how they might lead to stress. Thus, factors such as proper lighting, comfortable chairs, and appropriate office arrangements are important from an ergonomic point of view. If satisfactory levels of worker comfort are not achieved, the worker will probably be stressed, and undesirable consequences will occur, affecting factors such as productivity, accuracy, and dependability.

When approaching the problem of stress from a life events perspective, one would assess the stress-producing impact of life circumstances or events. Using this method, it becomes important to identify significant changes in life circumstances. T. H. Holmes and R. H. Rahe (*Journal of Psychosomatic Research*, 1967, *11*, 213–218) developed a list of such disrupting life changes. They scaled these changes with respect to their impact on individuals. Extremely stressful events include marriage, death of a spouse, and the loss of one's job. Still high but somewhat lower on the scale is a promotion at work. On the low end are events such as a change in one's physical environment at work. Taking the past year as a basis, the observer sums the point total of stresses the worker has experienced. The higher the total score, the more stress the worker is assumed to have experienced.

The environmental perception approach focuses on how people view the same circumstances in different ways. One person may experience a heavy work schedule as particularly stressful, whereas another worker might thrive on the challenge. From this point of view, environmental stress is neither good nor bad; its impact on the worker depends on how he or she perceives the stress. As a result, stress must be separated from strain in order to assess the impact of events accurately. One approach using the perceptual model, including coping resources, has been proposed by Samuel H. Osipow and Arnold R. Spokane (1987). According to their model, environmental work stresses are moderated by coping resources that, in turn, result in strain. The level of strain experienced depends on the intensity of the perceived stress and the adequacy of the individual's coping resources to reduce the negative impact of the stress.

Barriers to Work Entry

Considerable attention has been paid to conditions that make it difficult to work, especially for women. Among the most significant barriers are conflicting demands of the workplace and the home, sexual and attitudinal harassment, and stereotyping, the notion that women are best suited for certain kinds of work and men for others.

Research has indicated that although men are somewhat involved in household duties, women still shoulder the majority of these responsibilities. For this reason, women may often experience an overload of demands at work and again when they return home. The result is that women may not be as productive at work as they might be otherwise.

Occupational Information

It has long been thought that career decision making would be improved significantly if sources of occupational information were more readily available and more accurate. To that end, those interested in helping individuals enter the workforce have used various sources of information, including the job descriptions available in the *Dictionary of Occupational Titles* (Washington, D.C., 1991), *The Occupational Outlook Handbook* (Washington, D.C., 1990–1991), and the various computer-driven occupational information sources, most commonly SIGI and DISCOVER.

Although it seems logical to assume that such information can play an important role at certain points in the decision-making process, its usefulness appears to be overrated. According to a study by Azy Barak, Clark Carney, and Robert Archibald (*Journal of Vocational Behavior*, 1975, 7, 149–159), the use of occupational information in career counseling did not seem to improve the decisions clients made.

Our intuition and that of our clients about the usefulness of occupational information might be correct if we altered our idea about what type of information is desirable and useful. Occupational information typically involves facts such as what the job market is like, how much people earn, the nature of the training required for entry, typical career ladders, and so on. That kind of information is readily available and useful but in limited ways. The kind of information that appears to be needed and is missing is affective: the lifestyle of a worker in a particular field or job, the nature of one's colleagues, and how repetitive, autonomous, or independent work in that field will be. To many people, especially young workers entering the labor market, jobs and occupations are a "black box." The exterior tells a little about the nature of what is inside the box (e.g., the size and shape) but not enough. Affective data would fill that gap to some degree. Unfortunately, affective information is usually available only on a work trial basis, and such trials have their own disadvantages because they may not provide good work samples.

Motivation to Work

The motivation to work is driven by a number of variables. Work motivations have been divided into several categories based on needs satisfaction, reinforcements, instrumentality, and balance.

Needs theory approaches are perhaps the oldest way of trying to conceive of worker motivation. It makes sense to assume that people's motivation to behave is based on their desire to meet various needs, such as those described in the work of Abraham Maslow (*Motivation and Personality*, New York, 1943), specifically their physiological needs, social needs, and need for love, esteem, and self-actualization. It is reasonable to assume that this needs satisfaction theory would apply to work motivation. Certainly, people work to earn money for food, shelter, and clothing. Satisfaction of these needs leads to the creation of a secure environment. After those needs are met, however, the degree to which needs theory helps us to understand work motivation is unclear. It does appear that for some individuals, esteem and self-actualization needs may be fulfilled by work; however, only a relatively small proportion of jobs can achieve this. It is even harder to fit the satisfaction of love needs into a work environment.

Reinforcement theories applied to understanding work motivation have also been used for many years. Their approach is straightforward: Worker productivity is directly related to income. To oversimplify these views, one might say that to the degree that workers produce and meet employers' requirements, they will meet their own needs for money.

However, other patterns of reinforcement also motivate work behavior. The simplest one is the piecework approach, in which the worker is paid for each item produced, each sale made, or each grant application approved.

Other approaches to motivating workers can alter the schedules of reinforcement. One method, called the continuous reinforcement schedule, pays workers for the time worked. Alternatively, a fixed-ratio method can be used. This is a more complicated hourly pay approach in which the worker is paid after producing a certain number of units. Related to that approach is a variable-ratio method, in which the rewards are less regular than those provided by the fixed-ratio method.

The use of instrumentality theory to understand work motivation is based on the idea that people engage in activities if these activities are likely to produce something of personal value. The key to using this approach is to identify what things particular workers value and finding ways to provide them.

The last model, balance theory, proposes that people are motivated to keep their psychological tension within acceptable limits. Workers will take action to reduce tension when it moves beyond these limits.

Work Satisfaction

Work satisfaction is an important and frequently studied aspect of the psychology of work. Work satisfaction is closely related to the individual's motivation to work. Satisfaction with work reflects a number of environmental factors interacting with the characteristics of the individual. As noted earlier, according to some theories, personality types are important predictors of the nature of satisfaction in various work environments. Thus, in Holland's theory, congruence between personality type and work environment is critical in determining work satisfaction. Similarly, in the Theory of Work Adjustment proposed by Dawis and Lofquist, correspondence between the individual and the reinforcers provided by the work setting, in combination with the ability demands of the setting, predicts work satisfaction. In Donald E. Super's theory (1957), the personal variables related to work satisfaction are summarized in one's self-concept. As a result, work satisfaction depends on the degree to which one can implement one's self-concept in work.

The motivational theories mentioned earlier can also be important in predicting work satisfaction. Thus, based on need theory, the degree to which upper level needs (e.g., esteem or self-actualization) are fulfilled will determine work satisfaction. From a reinforcement theory perspective, information on work satisfaction can confirm or fail to confirm that the particular reinforcement schedule used is working effectively. Instrumentality theory takes the position that satisfaction results from the degree to which expected and obtained rewards match.

Dual-Career Couples

The growing career commitment on the part of women has created new work-related issues, including the division of work and family responsibilities of dual-career couples. Traditionally, men have been committed to work and women to management of the home and children. However, as women have taken on increasing work responsibilities, there has not been a corresponding decrease in their responsibilities at home. Although numerous surveys indicate that men have taken on more home responsibilities, including child care, women are still the primary homemakers even if they are employed outside the home. This inequity creates a situation in which nearly all employed women work under considerable stress. This inequity remains an issue to be resolved.

Another issue dual-career couples face concerns incompatible job schedules and/or locations. Even though there might be some advantages with respect to child care if one parent works primarily during the day while the other works primarily in the evening or at night, there is a significant disadvantage: The couple has little time to spend with each other. If one spouse receives a good job offer in a location different from that of the other spouse, issues are raised about whose career takes priority or whether the couple should consider a long-distance relationship.

Retirement

The last issue to be considered is how retirement is approached. Retirement is a stressful event involving problems such as reduced income, loss of status, and decisions about how to spend the newly available time. For most people who have had busy careers, the prospect of facing endless days of unstructured time can be frightening. In addition, if work has been satisfying, the retiree faces the loss of an activity that has been a source of reward. Social connections at work are also severed at retirement, posing yet another problem for the retiree to deal with.

In today's work world, where both spouses are likely to be employed, one may be ready to retire before the other. This creates special problems in coordinating schedules and activities. The retiree may wish to travel and engage in other recreational activities, but his or her partner may be immersed in a career. This situation is especially likely to occur today because women tend to enter or reenter the labor force later than men. As a result, women may be at the peak of their work life when their partners choose to retire. On the other hand, when both partners retire at the same time, some couples face new challenges in adjusting to spending 8 more hours each day in each other's company.

Bibliography

Arthur, M. B., Hall, D. T., & Lawrence, B. S. (Eds.). (1989). *Handbook of career theory*. Cambridge, UK: Cambridge University Press. Reviews current and future directions for career research, along with new ideas for research.

Betz, N. E., & Fitzgerald, L. F. (1987). *The career psychology of women*. New York: Academic Press. Provides a review of the literature and theory dealing with how women make and implement career decisions.

Dawis, R. V., & Lofquist, L. H. (1984). *A psychological theory of work adjustment.* Minneapolis: University of Minnesota Press. A theory describing how the agreement between the satisfaction of needs in work corresponds with the degree to which work demands are satisfied.

Holland, J. L. (1997). *Making vocational choices.* Odessa, FL: Psychological Assessment Resources. Presents a theory of work choice and adjustment in terms of the match between the congruence of occupational environments and individual typologies.

Osipow, S. H., & Fitzgerald, L. F. (1996). *Theories of career development* (4th ed.). Boston: Allyn & Bacon. Describes and critically reviews the major theories of career choice and development, with their applications.

Osipow, S. H., & Spokane, A. R. (1987). *The occupational stress inventory.* Odessa, FL: Psychological Assessment Resources. Describes an approach to occupational stress measurement that describes stress in terms of perceived occupational roles and individual coping resources, and their impact on individual well-being in terms of strain.

Savickas, M. L., & Lent, R. W. (Eds.). (1994). *Convergence in career development theories.* Palo Alto, CA: Consulting Psychologists Press. Presents the views of the major career theorists with respect to the idea that the theories are growing more similar.

Savickas, M. L., & Walsh, W. B. (Eds.). (1996). *Handbook of career counseling theory and practice.* Palo Alto, CA: Davis-Black. Reviews the major approaches to career development counseling and their effectiveness.

Super, D. E. (1957). *The psychology of careers.* New York: Harper & Row. Presents a theory that describes developmental stages in vocational maturity and the role of the self-concept in selection of and satisfaction with work.

Samuel H. Osipow

WORK ADJUSTMENT THEORY. The theory of work adjustment (TWA) developed out of the empiricist, measurement, applied, individual-differences tradition of Minnesota psychology. L. Lofquist and R. Dawis originated TWA in the 1960s as a framework for their Work Adjustment Project, a long-term study of vocational rehabilitation outcomes. The first statement of TWA was published in 1964, followed by revisions and extensions in 1968, 1969, 1976, 1978, 1984, and 1991.

TWA describes the interaction between the person and the work environment, with its focus on the person. It can be summarized in one proposition: Work adjustment is the process of achieving and maintaining correspondence with the work environment. This proposition presupposes that a person seeks correspondence with a work environment. *Correspondence*—coresponsiveness—is the mutual responsiveness of a person and an environment. *Mutual responsiveness* implies that each party has requirements of the other and has some capability to meet the requirements of the other. The work environment has requirements (tasks) that the person seeks to satisfy with one's capabilities (skills), and the person has requirements (needs) that the environment seeks to satisfy with its capabilities (reinforcers). *Satisfaction* indicates the degree to which each party meets—is responsive to—the requirements of the other. To differentiate the person's satisfaction from the work environment's satisfaction, the latter is termed the "satisfactoriness" of the person, thereby keeping the focus of the theory on the person.

The correspondent situation, then, is when both person and environment are satisfied, that is, when the person is both satisfied and satisfactory—leading the person to remain in, and be retained by, the environment, termed tenure. By implication, tenure in an environment is the result of work adjustment.

Dissatisfaction in one or both parties indicates a discorrespondent situation that calls for adjustment. Adjustment can be accomplished by change at any of four locations: (a) the person's needs; (b) the person's skills; (c) the environment's reinforcers; or (d) the environment's task requirements. The person may effect change in the environment, termed active adjustment (or activeness), by influencing change in the environment's reinforcements or task requirements. Or the person may effect change in self, termed reactive adjustment (or reactiveness), by revising one's needs (in priority) or one's skills (by improvement or acquisition). How long a person tolerates dissatisfaction before doing something about it (before adjusting) defines the person's flexibility. How long a person persists in adjusting before giving up defines the person's perseverance. Flexibility, activeness, reactiveness, and perseverance describe the person's adjustment style.

As adjustment style characterizes the person's adjustment behavior, personality style characterizes the person's typical behavior in interacting with the environment. Personality style is described in terms of celerity, the quickness with which interaction is initiated; pace, the effort expended in the interaction; rhythm, the pattern of pace in the interaction; and endurance, the length of time the person stays in interaction.

Interaction between person and environment can be construed as a system, with environment providing feedback to person, and person providing feedback to environment. The reference, or ideal, condition is set by the person's satisfaction and the environment's satisfaction. Adjustment is behavior designed to reestablish the reference condition.

That adjustment results in tenure leads to an important implication: Assess the potential correspondence of a person to an environment and one can predict the potential tenure of that person in that environment. Potential correspondence may be assessed by one-to-one mapping: Does this person have the skills to do the required tasks? Does this environment have the reinforcers appropriate for the person's needs? One-to-one mapping requires commensurate measurement of person and environment characteristics, which in turn enables the prediction of potential correspondence.

However, lists of skills, tasks, reinforcers, and needs are inconveniently long. To compress this information, factor analysis is used to identify a smaller number of reference dimensions that enable definition of each variable on the reference dimensions. The reference dimensions for the person's skills are termed abilities, and for the person's needs, values. To enable commensurate measurement, the work environment's tasks are described on ability dimensions as ability requirements, and the environment's reinforcers on value dimensions as reinforcement values. Abilities and values constitute the person's personality structure, whereas ability requirements and reinforcement values constitute the environment structure. Thus, potential correspondence can be predicted by assessing the mapping of personality structure onto environment structure, and this can be done for any work environment. This predictive model constitutes TWA's basis for career exploration, planning, and choice.

TWA's predictive model finds support in the many studies in industrial-organizational psychology where: (a) rated job performance (satisfactoriness) in different occupations is predicted from different combinations of abilities; (b) turnover (the complement of tenure) is predicted from job satisfaction; and (c) job satisfaction is predicted from the correspondence of job satisfiers and dissatisfiers (reinforcers) to workers' needs and values. Support is also found in the many studies in counseling psychology where occupational tenure, satisfaction, and satisfactoriness are predicted from some mapping of personality structure onto environment structure. However, TWA's process model, involving adjustment style and personality style, have not yet been rigorously validated, in part because of the difficulty of measuring process variables.

Other problems remain: How is correspondence best measured? Are the effects of discorrespondence symmetric (is too much as bad as too little)? How are structure and style related? Can idiographic prediction improve on the normative?

TWA's model of the interaction between person and work environment can be applied to other environments (e.g., home and school). Furthermore, TWA's one-sided focus on person can be made symmetrical with a mirror-image focus on environment (e.g., environment can have needs/values and skills/abilities, and person can have task/ability requirements and reinforcers/reinforcement values). Such a fully crossed model has been recently advanced as the person-environment correspondence (PEC) model.

[*See also* Career; *and* Work.]

Bibliography

Dawis, R. V. (1994). The theory of work adjustment as convergent theory. In M. L. Savickas & R. W. Lent (Eds.), *Convergence in career development theories: Implications for science and practice* (pp. 33–43). Palo Alto, CA: Consulting Psychologists Press. Discusses TWA's foundations in psychological theory and its relation to other career development theories.

Dawis, R. V. (1996). The theory of work adjustment and person-environment-correspondence counseling. In D. Brown & L. Brooks (Eds.), *Career choice and development* (3rd ed., pp. 75–120). San Francisco, CA: Jossey-Bass. Gives the history of TWA, explicates it, and discusses its application to career counseling.

Dawis, R. V., England, G. W., & Lofquist, L. H. (1964). A theory of work adjustment. *Minnesota Studies in Vocational Rehabilitation, 15*, 1–27. The first statement of TWA primarily as a predictive model, in nine propositions.

Dawis, R. V., & Lofquist, L. H. (1984). *A psychological theory of work adjustment.* Minneapolis: University of Minnesota Press. A full explication of TWA as both a process and predictive model, in 17 propositions; presents supporting research evidence and discusses application in various fields.

Lofquist, L. H., & Dawis, R. V. (1969). *Adjustment to work.* New York: Appleton-Century-Crofts. Early book-length explication of TWA and its application in various fields.

Lofquist, L. H., & Dawis, R. V. (1991). *Essentials of person-environment-correspondence counseling.* Minneapolis: University of Minnesota Press. Generalizes TWA to other environments as PEC; discusses application in counseling.

Rene V. Dawis

WORK CONDITIONS. Work performance is a function of individual attributes and environmental conditions. The general representation of this relationship may be depicted as follows:

$$\text{Work performance} = f\,\frac{(\text{capacity} \times \text{energy}}{\text{Individual attributes}} \times \frac{\text{facilitating conditions} \times \text{inhibiting conditions})}{\text{Environmental conditions}}$$

The individual-attributes portion of the equation is the domain of motivation, learning, and individual-performance theories. These theories often represent work performance as a function of ability (capacity) and motivation (energy), which are beyond the scope of this entry. This is a general survey of work conditions that facilitate and/or inhibit work performance, and the content should be placed in this broader context of understanding work performance. In general, the physiological and psychological processes through which these conditions influence individual reactions are arousal, stress, overload, distraction, and fatigue. This survey considers four sets of facilitating and/or inhibiting conditions. These are physical conditions, psychosocial conditions, work context conditions, and work content conditions.

Physical Conditions

Five physical conditions may facilitate or inhibit work performance. These are temperature (heat and cold), indoor climate and air quality, illumination and other rays, noise and vibrations, and the physical design of the work environment.

Temperature. People vary in their physiological and psychological responses to temperature ranges and variations. People also vary with regard to the temperature zones in which their work performance is best and with regard to temperature extremes (too hot or too cold) that may interfere with effective work performance. The effects of temperature depend on the nature of the task performed (e.g., motor or mental) and the degree of task difficulty. Protections are needed to safeguard individuals working in extreme conditions, such as below 32°F or over 100°F. For example, outer garments and gloves protect individuals working in extreme cold, ice vests protect helicopter pilots flying in desert heat, and high fluid intake protects individuals from dehydration in tropical climates.

Indoor Climate and Air Quality. The World Health Organization recognizes sick building syndrome (SBS) as a cluster of work-related symptoms of unknown origin significantly more prevalent among the occupants of certain buildings in comparison with others. Sick building syndrome is a result of the 1970s energy crises, when builders included energy-efficient features such as sealed windows and heating and cooling systems that used minimal fresh air and allowed the accumulation of airborne pollutants. SBS symptoms include eye, nose, throat, sensory, and skin irritations, neurotoxic reactions (e.g., headache, nausea, and fatigue) and odor or taste complaints. The stress caused by these conditions is associated with increased aggression, irritation, and fatigue.

Illumination and Other Rays. The effects of lighting and illumination levels on productivity were originally studied at the Hawthorne Works in the 1920s. Moonlight-intensity illumination led to depressed productivity, but a linear relationship between work performance and illumination level was not found. Most work environments require 20 to 40 foot-candles of light for effective work performance, although this may need to be increased markedly for especially fine or detailed work tasks. Glare, a different lighting problem, may interfere with work performance. Rays outside the visible spectrum may have adverse health effects; yet there is no known effect on work performance, with one possible exception. The use of video display terminals (VDTs) may lead to VDT-related cumulative trauma disorder with associated adverse impacts on performance.

Noise and Vibrations. Noise at work may be a nuisance or it may interfere with essential communication, leading to work performance breakdowns. Exposure to excessive (roughly 80 decibels) and/or chronic noise and vibration can lead to temporary or permanent hearing loss with its associated adverse performance impact. Vibrations, closely associated with sound waves, typically result from a rotary or impacting motion, or a combination of the two. Choppers, ramming machines, pneumatic devices, riveting hammers, and propellers used on construction sites and in aircraft activity centers must be designed and calibrated so that the vibrations do not interfere with the work performance on the tasks in which they are being used.

Physical Design of the Work Environment. Work performance may be affected by the design of its physical setting. Physical settings fulfill one or more of six basic functions, which are to:

1. Provide shelter and security
2. Facilitate social contact
3. Provide symbolic identification
4. Enhance task instrumentality
5. Heighten pleasure
6. Stimulate growth

Hence, the physical design of the work environment should be compatible with and supportive of the work to be performed in the setting. The trend toward "virtual offices" includes offices at home used by entrepreneurs and telecommuting workers, as well as the temporary offices that some firms use to accommodate workers who travel most of the time. While traditional offices provide discipline, structure, social interaction, and the opportunity to learn from others, the virtual office eliminates this support system and creates a potentially adverse impact on performance. Physical settings and office space are thus intended to protect employees from certain demands.

Psychosocial Conditions

Four psychosocial conditions may facilitate or inhibit work performance. These are: uncertainty and ambiguity, conflicting expectations, work-nonwork conflicts, and social support systems.

Uncertainty and Ambiguity. Uncertainty and ambiguity may be among the worst conditions that inhibit work performance. There are at least four ways in which uncertainty and ambiguity may be manifested at work. One way is through the absence of essential information about a wide range of aspects of the work environment essential for good performance. A second way is when the necessary information is not provided in a clear, complete, understandable manner. A third way is if the information has inaccuracies and/or discrepancies, raising doubts about its validity and reliability. A fourth way is if the consequences of various courses of action and performance are either unspecified or confusing to a person. Future job ambiguity is a form of uncertainty that may interfere with work performance.

Conflicting Expectations. Conflicting expectations or work standards can adversely effect work performance. Discrepancies between official and unofficial expectations or the formal and informal work systems create conflict for people at work and inhibit good performance. These discrepancies develop when conflicting, inconsistent expectations about work performance are communicated to a person through one or more people or sources in the organization. Conflicting expectations may be principally manifested at work in three ways:

1. A single person, such as a supervisor, communicates conflicting expectations.
2. Two or more people, such as two different superiors, communicate conflicting expectations.
3. The expectations for a person's work performance conflict with the individual's personal values or beliefs, such as violations of personal ethical standards or religious beliefs.

Work-Nonwork Conflicts. Conflicts between expectations at work and in nonwork social roles or settings, such as at home and with family, may inhibit work performance. These conflicts may be of two forms. One is incompatible expectations between a person's work performance and his or her role as a spouse, parent, or elder care giver. For example, schedule conflicts between a work meeting with a client and a child's performance in a school concert are incompatible expectations. A second form of conflict is excessive demands from combined work and nonwork expectations. This latter form of conflict is a form of role overload.

Social Support Systems. Healthy social support systems facilitate good work performance and deficient social support systems inhibit it. The social supports and psychosocial work conditions should balance the demands for mastery and achievement at work with a supportive and nurturing concern for the person's wellbeing. There are at least five psychosocial resources provided by social support systems for people at work. These are information, instrumental support, evaluative feedback, emotional concern, and protection. Supportive relationships facilitate good work performance by offering people these resources so they may achieve psychological intimacy and integrated involvement. In exceptional cases, a person may still achieve excellent work performance in the absence of social support.

Work Context Conditions

Six work-context conditions may facilitate or inhibit work performance. These are shift systems, flexible work schedules, pacing, work breaks, safety and accidents, and alternative work sites.

Shift Systems. Shift systems are a necessity in some work environments, such as fire and police services, and they generally create risks to good work performance. Night work should be reduced, and permanent night work is not advisable for the majority of shift workers. Where night work is necessary, quickly rotating shift systems are preferred to slowing rotating ones, with forward rotation of shifts (phase delay and clockwise rotation) recommended in continuous shift systems. The performance risks in night work include reduced alertness, dampened mood, increased accident risk, fatigue, and boredom; hence, safety factors have important influence on work performance at night. Compressed work schedules of 9, 10, 12, or more hours create risks of fatigue, reduced alertness, and lack of concentration. The research is insufficient for precise guidelines for setting compressed work schedules or shift durations (i.e., how long is too long?) because individual differences are so central on that issue. However, combining a compressed work schedule through extended shifts (e.g., four 12-hour days on, four days off) may allow shift workers to better harmonize their nonwork activities with family and community rhythms.

Flexible Work Schedules. If shift systems generally inhibit work performance, flexible work schedules generally facilitate work performance. First tested at the Hawthorne Works in the 1920s, flexible work schedules allow employees to manage the conflicts discussed above that inhibit work performance. Flexible work schedules enhance employee discretion and control. The design of flexible work schedules should consider task interdependence, task autonomy, and task independence. The more independent and autonomous the work performed, the greater the feasibility of flexible work schedules.

Pacing. Pacing refers to the degree of time constraints placed on people at work. Timing at work may be either force-paced or self-paced. Force-paced work systems are designed for a fixed pace and do not consider the operator's action(s) as a determinant of pace. Very fast force-paced systems inhibit work performance by increasing the risks of errors or accidents due to inadequate operator-response opportunity time. Very slow force-paced systems inhibit work performance by increasing the risks of boredom and lack of concentration on work tasks. Force-paced systems allowing for operator discretionary control over the pace of work offer an opportunity to balance these two sets of inhibiting forces. Self-paced work systems are designed to consider the operator's action(s) as a determinant of pace. Self-paced systems allow for variability in operator behavior (e.g., efficiency), thus offering an opportunity for improved work performance.

Work Breaks. Frederick Taylor initially considered rest breaks in work as the time employees spent disengaged from strenuous, effortful activity. Work breaks, a feature of the experiments at the Hawthorne Works, were later considered as time away from task-specific activities. Work breaks may involve either restful or energizing activities. In work requiring strenuous labor leading to physical fatigue, such as steel production, work breaks of a restful nature generally facilitate work performance. In work requiring a high degree of concentration leading to psychological fatigue, such as detailed jewelry crafting, work breaks of an energizing nature generally facilitate work performance. While research supports these general guidelines on the role of work breaks, it does not provide specific guidance on their number, frequency, or duration. These are determined through experience in the specific work activities and with specific employees.

Safety and Accidents. Safety plays an important facilitating role in enhancing work performance, whereas accidents inhibit good work performance. Safety contributes to work performance by minimizing the hazards and risks to people and material in the work process. Safe work environments contribute to experienced security by employees. Accidents are one important risk factor in the work process, disrupting work, creating injuries or fatalities, and destroying materials. Accidents are the fourth leading cause of death in the United States, following heart disease, cancer, and stroke. Accident types may be single- or multicaused, event chains, process events, or complex events. Many accidents are avoidable through effective prevention.

Alternative Work Sites. Work is increasingly performed in a variety of alternative work sites other than traditional offices, factories, or stores. Information technology has made it possible to relocate many types of work, and telework is the term used to describe workers who have been relocated in this way. Increased efficiency and higher productivity resulting from high levels of employee discretion and autonomy are generally regarded as the most important benefits; however, telework requires explicit planning in order to avoid the potential problems of reduced cooperation and group cohesion. Employees in low salary categories that perform highly structured or administrative tasks tend to have the most positive attitudes toward telework. Employees who work mainly in project teams or perform tasks such as policy development and policy implementation confirm the advantages of telework, but expect fewer additional benefits from telework for their own jobs.

Work Content Conditions

Five work-content conditions may facilitate or inhibit work performance. These are: work design and overload; work demands, fatigue, and boredom; work control and high performance; stress and cognitive resources; and vigilance.

Work Design and Overload. Poor work design significantly inhibits work performance. Good work design, which considers human factors as well as engineering and nonhuman factors, facilitates work performance. Employees must be properly trained and educated to take full advantage of good work design to achieve high work performance. One major problem in work design is work overload, which contributes to poor performance. Work overload occurs when there are too many or too difficult work demands for the time and/or skill level(s) of the people intended to do the work. Work overload increases the risks of errors, exhaustion, depression, and other human dysfunctions that adversely affect work performance.

Work Demands, Fatigue, and Boredom. Work demands may vary in their intensity, duration, and frequency. Work demands that are physically and/or psychologically too high lead to fatigue and exhaustion. High-demand work, such as firefighting, requires worker relief at appropriate intervals to avoid significant and unacceptable decrements in work performance. Where people have job-relevant authority to exercise control in the work environment, the self-management of work demands to avert fatigue and exhaustion is possible. Work demands that are not physically adequate and/or psychologically challenging lead to boredom and underachievement. Work systems with low work demands and/or work standards yield low quality or low quantity work performance.

Work Control and High Performance. High work demands, combined with restricted work control or job decision latitude, have been found to adversely affect worker health and work performance due to exhaustion, fatigue, absenteeism from work for ill days, and related problems. Some researchers make a distinction between control in the work environment and perceived control. The evidence is not conclusive concerning whether lack of control in some aspects of work, such as over shift or pay schedules, may be compensated for with greater control in other aspects of the work, such as choice of tools and/or pacing within a shift. Employees require training and education to accept the responsibility associated with high control and job decision latitude.

Stress and Cognitive Resources. Stress may either facilitate or inhibit work performance. Stress caused by work overload has an inhibiting effect on work performance, at least over an extended period. Stress facilitates work performance when it arouses and stimulates people to perform at their best. In the extreme (high or low) or specific (e.g., interpersonal) forms, stress inhibits work performance by overloading or underloading the person, or by interfering with the effective use of cognitive resources. Leader intelligence has been positively correlated with performance and, under certain conditions, it has been negatively correlated with performance. Cognitive resource theory offers an explanation of these conflicting findings by introducing stress as the moderating variable. High interpersonal stress with the leader at work inhibits effective cognitive resource utilization, and therefore work performance.

Vigilance. Signal detection theory is important in work in which it is not easy to discriminate between signals and noise, such as critical events in air traffic control. Operators must be able to correctly distinguish between signals, which require a positive response, and noise, which requires a negative response. Performance errors occur when an operator responds positively to noise, constituting a false alarm, or negatively to a signal, constituting a miss, as in the case of Pearl Harbor in 1941. Signal detection theory is important in understanding the sensitivity of operators and work systems to distinctions between signals and noise. Work tasks require the vigilance of operators when they must detect intermittent, unpredictable, and infrequent signals over a relatively long period of time (the watch). Vigilance phenomena typically occur in a free response paradigm or an inspection paradigm. In the free response paradigm, target events may occur at any time, and nontarget events are not defined. In the inspection paradigm, events occur at fairly regular intervals and it is expected that targets (defects) are few and nontargets (normal items) many. Signal enhancement and methods to combat fatigue and enhance arousal are ways to combat the loss of vigilance.

Conclusion

Environmental conditions have the potential to contribute to a substantial amount of the variance in individual work performance. Managers must realize this potential and understand that employees generally have no control over this critical component of their work performance equation. While management remains ultimately accountable for work conditions, some organizations are finding that cross-functional teams composed of management, labor representatives, and employees are highly effective in developing and implementing solutions to problems. In addition to training in teams processes, improvement teams would require access to work conditions expertise and information needed for problem solving. Accomplishing changes in work conditions through employee involvement may result in significant reductions in workplace illness and injuries and overall improvements in employee health.

Bibliography

Buchanan, D. A. (1989). High performance: New boundaries of acceptability in worker control. In S. L. Sauter, J. J. Hurrell, Jr., & C. L. Cooper (Eds.), *Job control and worker health* (pp. 255–274). Chichester, England: Wiley.

Campbell, J. P., & Pritchard, R. D. (1976). Motivation theory in industrial and organizational psychology. In M. D. Dunnette (Ed.), *Handbook of industrial and organizational psychology* (pp. 63–130). Chicago: Rand-McNally.

Cooper, M. D., Phillips, R. A., Sutherland, V. J., & Makin, P. J. (1994). Reducing accidents using goal setting and feedback: A field study. *Journal of Occupational and Organizational Psychology, 67*, 219–240.

Fieldler, F. E. (1994). Leader intelligence, interpersonal stress, and task performance. In R. J. Sternberg & R. K. Wagner (Eds.), *Mind in context: Interactionist perspective on human intelligence* (pp. 152–167). New York: Cambridge University Press.

Gaustello, S. J. (1995). *Chaos, catastrophe, and human affairs: Applications of nonlinear dynamics to work, organizations, and social evolution.* Mahwah, NJ: Erlbaum.

Knauth, P. (1993). The design of shift systems. *Ergonomics, 36*, 15–28.

Luczak, H. (1992). Good work design: An ergonomic, industrial engineering perspective. In J. C. Quick, L. R. Murphy, & J. J. Hurrell, Jr. (Eds.), *Stress and well-being at work* (pp. 96–112). Washington, DC: American Psychological Association.

May, D. R., & Schwoerer, C. E. (1994). Employee health by design: Using employee involvement teams in ergonomic job redesign. *Personal Psychology, 47*, 861–876.

Ornstein, S. (1990). Linking environmental and industrial/organizational psychology. In C. L. Cooper & I. T. Robertson (Eds.), *International review of industrial and organizational psychology* (Vol. 5, pp. 195–228). Chichester, England: Wiley.

Peters, L. H., O'Connor, E. J., & Eulberg, J. R. (1985). Situational constraints: Sources, consequences, and future considerations. In K. M. Rowland & G. R. Ferris (Eds.), *Research in personnel and human resources management* (Vol. 3, pp. 79–113). Greenwich, CT: JAI Press.

Pierce, J. L., & Dunham, R. B. (1992). The 12-hour workday: A forty-eight-hour, eight-day week. *Academy of Management Journal, 35*, 1086–1098.

Quick, J. C., Quick, J. D., Nelson, D. L., & Hurrell, J. J., Jr. (1997). *Preventive stress management in organizations.* Washington, DC: American Psychological Association. (Original work published in 1984 by J. C. Quick and J. D. Quick)

Sundstrom, E. (1986). *The psychology of the physical environment in offices and factories.* New York: Cambridge University Press.

Van der Wielen, J. M. M., Taillieu, T. C. B., Poolman, J. A., & Zuilichem. (1995). Telework: Dispersed organizational activity and new forms of spatial-temporal coordination and control. In J. M. Peiró, F. Prieto, J. L. Meliá, & O. Lugue (Eds.), *Work and organizational psychology: European contributions of the nineties* (pp. 263–280). East Sussex, England: Erlbaum/Taylor & Francis.

Wickens, C. D. (1984). *Engineering psychology and human performance*. Columbus, OH: Merrill.

James Campbell Quick, Bret Simmons, and Debra L. Nelson

WORKING ALLIANCE. Although there are many different aspects to the relationship that exists between a therapist or counselor and his or her client, the working alliance is considered by many researchers and therapists to be the most fundamental. Because of its perceived importance, working alliance has been one of the most vigorously studied constructs in the field of counseling and psychotherapy over the past two decades.

Definition and Historical Review

Although somewhat differing definitions of working alliance have appeared over the years, a common feature of all of them is that of the client and therapist joining together for the purpose of fostering the therapeutic work that must occur if treatment is to be successful. Furthermore, some authors conceptualize that what is joined together is the reasonable or observing side or ego of the client, and the working or therapizing side of the therapist (cf. Gelso & Hayes, 1998). This kind of joining together allows the work of therapy to be carried out and the client-therapist relationship to survive the inevitable emotional strains that occur in a helping relationship of this sort.

In keeping with Bordin's major formulation, the working alliance may be seen as consisting of three ingredients: an implicit or explicit agreement between the client and therapist on the goals of treatment; an agreement on the in-session and extra-session tasks that will enable the client to attain those goals; and an emotional bond between the therapist and client (1979). When these three ingredients exist to a high degree, the working alliance will be strong and will facilitate therapeutic progress. However, according to Bordin and many others, when one or more of the ingredients are not operative, the alliance will falter. If a faltering alliance is not repaired, treatment itself is likely to be unsuccessful.

The idea of something like a working alliance as a key part of the therapeutic relationship has been around for a long time. Like so many therapy constructs, the roots of working alliance theory originated in Sigmund Freud's theorizing. For example, in his earliest papers on transference, Freud pointed to the friendly and affectionate aspects of the analysand's relationship to the psychoanalyst, and in 1913 he discussed the importance of the analysand's forming a healthy attachment to the analyst, one that was fostered by the analyst's interest and "sympathetic understanding" (Freud, 1913).

In Freud's writing and that of many psychoanalysts over the years, one can see the attempt to grasp an aspect of the psychotherapy relationship that is different from the neurotic transferences with which psychoanalysis was so centrally concerned. It was not until the work of Ralph Greenson, however, that the term *working alliance* was used and that the role of this alliance in psychoanalytic treatments was spelled out (1967). Since the time of Greenson's theorizing, working alliance has attained much acceptance in psychoanalytic thinking.

The Current Scene

In 1979, Bordin sought to generalize the working alliance concept beyond the domain of psychoanalysis and analytic treatments. In his seminal paper, he offered a pantheoretical definition of working alliance (see above—agreement on goals, agreement on tasks, and emotional bond) and discussed its role in a range of theoretical approaches to therapy (Bordin, 1979). Since the time of Bordin's paper and the subsequent development of a valid and convenient measure of Bordin's conception of the alliance by Adam Horvath in 1982 (Horvath & Greenberg, 1989), research and theory on this concept have mushroomed. So has research on concepts that are very similar to working alliance, for example, therapeutic alliance, helping alliance, or, simply, alliance. Although each of these concepts differs slightly from the others, they all fundamentally pertain to the client-therapist alliance that forms around doing the work of therapy. Thus, the term *working alliance* is preferred here.

Another way to think of the working alliance pertains to its fundamental elements. In this respect an analysis by Horvath, Gaston, and Luborsky of the 11 existing measures of alliance revealed that there were 2 elements common to all measures: collaboration and attachment (1993). The concept of client-therapist collaboration reflects the interactive nature of working alliance. That is, the alliance is a two-party interaction, and its formation and solidification require the efforts of both therapist and client. The collaborative element of working alliance is similar to Bordin's concept (1979) of alliance as client-therapist agreement on goals and tasks, for such agreements are essentially collaborative acts.

The concept of attachment, on the other hand, reflects Bordin's concept of the bond part of the alliance. This concept points to the fact that the alliance is an interpersonal attachment and, further, that it is the kind of attachment that provides the client a "secure base" from which to explore often painful and difficult feelings (see the discussion of working alliance in the context of Bowlby's attachment theory in Gelso & Hayes, 1998).

Is the alliance as important to the therapeutic process as the above discussion implies? In what ways does the working alliance influence treatment outcome? The answer to the first question appears to be positive. For example, in Horvath's and Symonds's synthesis of 24 studies on the effects of alliance on therapy outcome, clear and strong evidence was found for a meaningful positive impact: The stronger the alliance, the better the outcome—regardless of how long treatment lasted (1991).

Regarding the question of how the working alliance influences treatment, three ways appear most salient. First, the alliance appears to have an effect in and of itself, similar to the way in which a good relationship between client and therapist will have an effect, above and beyond the therapist's technical interventions (Gaston & Marmor, 1994). Second, Gaston and Marmor also note that the alliance fosters the client's receptivity to the therapist's interventions. Thus, when the alliance is strong the client is more likely, for example, to complete homework assignments or be receptive to good therapist interpretations.

A third way in which the alliance affects treatment is by serving as a buffer against the inevitable strains that naturally occur in the therapy relationship (e.g., due to client negative transference). To use a medical analogy, it is as if the alliance immunizes the client from infections caused by negative transference and other stresses in the relationship (Gelso & Hayes, 1998).

The Client's and the Therapist's Contributions

Because the working alliance is an interactive concept, both the client and the therapist must contribute to its formation and maintenance. What are the qualities and behaviors that each participant should exhibit in order for the alliance to develop and solidify? On the client's side, three clusters of what might be called predisposing characteristics appear to be important to alliance formation and development (see review by Horvath & Greenberg, 1994). First, clients need to have the ability and willingness to form a close attachment with another person, the therapist in this case. In order to do this, clients would likely need to have had at least some positive attachment experiences in their lives.

A second client cluster revolves around cooperativeness. As noted earlier, clients must be willing to collaborate, or, on the other side of the ledger, must at least not have such a high degree of opposition that agreement on goals and tasks would be impossible. The final cluster of predisposing characteristics pertains to clients' sense of self-efficacy. Clients must believe that they could benefit from therapy—that they themselves are capable of growth through this treatment. In the absence of such a sense, it would be difficult for clients to invest themselves in the relationship.

Regarding the therapist's contribution to the alliance, first, and perhaps most fundamentally, therapists need to possess and exhibit attitudes long ago theorized by Carl Rogers as necessary and sufficient for constructive personality change in therapy: empathic understanding, unconditional positive regard (or at least positive regard), and genuineness (1957). [*See the biography of Rogers.*] Although current thinking is that these therapist qualities are not sufficient and may not always be necessary, they do appear to be important. In considering the importance of these three attitudes, it might be helpful to visualize what kind of working alliance might be developed in their absence. It is difficult to conceive of a sound working alliance being developed by a therapist with little or no empathy, low regard for the client, and a lack of genuineness. Of the three ingredients Rogers theorized about, empathy in particular has been empirically documented to contribute to both alliance and outcome (e.g., Horvath & Greenberg, 1989).

A second cluster of therapist qualities that appear important to alliance development is what might be called responsibility taking. Especially in longer-term treatments, it appears that some problems in the alliance (often called ruptures) are very likely, and therapists who take responsibility for their contribution to those problems, as indicated in a qualitative study by Rhodes, Hill, Thompson, and Elliott (1994), are the most effective at facilitating the healing of such ruptures and in moving the alliance to higher levels.

A third therapist factor pertains to the therapist's own past relationships. Just as with clients, therapists who have a history of at least some solid and positive relationships in their lives are more likely to form positive and strong working alliances with their clients (see research by Henry & Strupp, 1994). Other hard-to-measure qualities are also likely implicated in therapists' ability to form alliances: abiding investment in the work, commitment to the client, and overall skillfulness. It will be important for future research to study these elusive concepts.

Unfolding of the Alliance

In recent years, evidence has accumulated to suggest that there is a developmental course for the working alliance and that it differs for more and less successful cases (Gelso & Hayes, 1998). As Horvath, Gaston, and Luborsky note, the first few sessions of counseling or therapy witness the initial formation of the alliance (1993). Satisfactory levels of trust and collaboration need to be developed, and the client must join the therapist in the therapeutic journey. The client must also experience some faith in the procedures that provide the framework of the therapy. With many clients, especially those with sound psychological resources, a "good enough" alliance may be formed even within the first session (Bordin, 1994).

The therapist, too, must experience a commitment to the work and a sense of empathy toward, connection to, and acceptance of the client. In this first phase, the client feels supported and helped. He or she may still be tentative about the relationship, but there is a readiness to move forward and delve further into his or her problems.

After this initial joining together, the therapist begins to challenge, however gently, the client's neurotic patterns. As this occurs, the client feels less supported, and this may reactivate old interpersonal beliefs and fears, thus instigating a weakening or rupture in the alliance. In successful cases, this rupture is then worked through and the alliance matures into a solid collaboration. In less successful cases, on the other hand, it appears that either the rupture is not resolved or never occurs to begin with. In the latter instances, as Horvath, Gaston, and Luborsky suggest, the therapy may be coasting or the client may idealize the process and not deal with core issues (1993).

Finally, although the above characterization of how the alliance unfolds may create the image of a uniform process, in reality it is likely that once the initial alliance is formed, periodic ruptures and repairs will occur. At the same time, over the entire course of successful counseling, the alliance is likely to strengthen. Although it is not yet clear just how strong the alliance must be for therapy to be successful, it is hard to imagine successful psychological treatment in the face of a very weak alliance.

In this article, some general principles of and research findings about working alliance have been presented. Future research will aim at uncovering many of the subtleties and complexities related to what kinds of alliances are needed, to what degree, with what kinds of clients, in what phases of treatment, and of what kinds of therapies.

[*See also* Psychotherapy.]

Bibliography

Bordin, E. S. (1979). The generalizability of the psychoanalytic concept of the working alliance. *Psychotherapy: Theory, Research, and Practice, 16,* 252–260. The first major paper that examined the role of working alliance across theoretical approaches rather than in psychoanalytic treatments.

Bordin, E. S. (1994). Theory and research on the therapeutic working alliance: New directions. In A. O. Horvath & L. Greenberg (Eds.), *The working alliance: Theory, research, and practice* (pp. 13–37). New York: Wiley.

Freud, S. (1913). On the beginning of treatment: Further recommendations on the technique of psychoanalysis. In J. Strachey (Ed.), *Standard edition of the complete works of Sigmund Freud* (pp. 122–144). London: Hogarth.

Gaston, L., & Marmor, C. R. (1994). The California Psychotherapy Alliance Scales. In A. O. Horvath & L. Greenberg (Eds.), *The working alliance: Theory, research, and practice* (pp. 85–108). New York: Wiley.

Gelso, C., & Hayes, J. A. (1998). *The psychotherapy relationship.* New York: Wiley.

Greenson, R. R. (1967). *Technique and practice of psychoanalysis.* New York: International Universities Press. The most significant psychoanalytic examination of the working alliance. Presents the history of the concept, shows its importance in psychoanalysis, and differentiates it from processes like transference.

Henry, W. P., & Strupp, H. H. (1994). The therapeutic alliance as interpersonal process. In A. O. Horvath & L. Greenberg (Eds.), *The working alliance: Theory, research, and practice* (pp. 51–84). New York: Wiley.

Horvath, A. O., Gaston, L., & Luborsky, L. (1993). The therapeutic alliance and its measures. In N. E. Miller, L. Luborsky, J. P. Barber, & J. P. Docherty (Eds.), *Psychoanalytic treatment research: A handbook for clinical practice* (pp. 247–273). New York: Basic Books.

Horvath, A. O., & Greenberg, L. (1989). The development and validation of the Working Alliance Inventory. *Journal of Counseling Psychology, 36,* 223–232.

Horvath, A. O., & Greenberg, L. (Eds.). (1994). *The working alliance: Theory, research, and practice.* New York: Wiley. A book of readings that represents the most thorough and integrative review of the working alliance theory and research.

Horvath, A. O., & Symonds, B. D. (1991). Relation between working alliance and outcome in psychotherapy: A meta-analysis. *Journal of Counseling Psychology, 38,* 133–138.

Rhodes, R. H., Hill, C. E., Thompson, B. J., & Elliott, R. (1994). Client retrospective recall of resolved and unresolved misunderstanding events. *Journal of Counseling Psychology, 41,* 473–483.

Rogers, C. R. (1957). The necessary and sufficient conditions of therapeutic personality change. *Journal of Consulting Psychology, 21,* 95–103.

Charles J. Gelso

WORKING MEMORY. The term *working memory* is commonly used to refer to a system responsible for the temporary storage and manipulation of information necessary for such complex tasks as learning, comprehension, and reasoning. However, as is common with many psychological terms, its usage is not entirely uniform, since the term is also used in the animal learning literature in connection with tasks that require the animal to maintain information acquired on that particular day, discarding it and starting again on the next. However, such tasks probably reflect aspects of long-term memory rather than the temporary storage systems implied by the term *working memory* in literature on human participants.

A third use of the term *working memory* comes from artificial intelligence, where the production systems approach developed by Newell and Simon (1972) utilizes a series of conditional rules known as productions. The system that holds these, and given the appropriate conditions causes them to fire, is also termed working memory, although there is no suggestion that it resembles the working memory of the human participant. Fortunately, in practice these different meanings are rarely confusable, since they operate in very different domains.

Origins of the Concept

Although the term *working memory* appears to have been first proposed by Miller, Galanter, and Pribram in their influential book *Plans and the Structure of Behavior* (1979), the idea that memory might be split into a durable long-term component and a briefer short-term element extends back at least to the nineteenth century, when William James proposed the distinction between a long-term secondary memory and a brief primary memory. While primary memory has links with later concepts, it was most closely associated with the phenomenological experience of time, and in particular of what James termed "the specious present," referring to the sense in which the experience of "now" extends over time.

Short-Term Memory

Despite earlier suggestions that memory might be differentiable into different subsystems, until the late 1950s it tended to be treated as a unitary faculty. This changed with the demonstration by John Brown in England, and Lloyd and Margaret Peterson in Indiana, that even a small amount of information such as a consonant triplet would show rapid forgetting, provided the subject was prevented from active rehearsal by a concurrent task such as counting backward.

The claim that this rapid forgetting reflected a separate short-term memory system led to a spirited controversy, resulting in a flood of evidence attempting to fractionate memory into subcomponents. This included the suggestion that primary or short-term verbal memory depended more heavily on the sound of words than their meaning, and evidence that many tasks might be split into separable short-term and long-term components. Perhaps the strongest evidence however, came from the study of neurological patients.

Brenda Milner described the case of patient HM, who had the misfortune to be treated for intractable epilepsy by bilateral surgical removal of his hippocampus and related brain areas, resulting in a profound amnesia. Despite grossly impaired long-term learning capacity, however, his performance on short-term memory tasks (such as repeating back a telephone number) was normal. In 1970, Tim Shallice and Elizabeth Warrington reported a patient showing the opposite pattern; his capacity for short-term memory performance appeared to be grossly impaired despite excellent long-term learning. Taken together, the neuropsychological evidence represents a double-dissociation, arguing strongly for two memory systems.

Therefore, by the late 1960s the evidence seemed to be favoring a division of human memory into separate stages. One of the most influential models of this period was that developed by Atkinson and Shiffrin (1968). Because it resembled a whole range of similar models, it became known as the modal model. Within this model, the short-term memory system plays a crucial role not only in temporarily storing information, but in feeding information into and out of long-term memory, in short, serving as a working memory. A conceptual link between short-term storage and a multipurpose working memory has continued to play an important role in the study of working memory.

A Multicomponent Model of Working Memory

While the modal model gave a good account of a wide range of results, it encountered at least two problems. The first concerned its assumptions about the process of learning, namely that the probability of an item being committed to long-term memory was a simple function of how long it was held in the short-term store. Evidence began to accumulate suggesting that simple maintenance in short-term storage was a very poor way of committing something to memory, whereas processing information more elaborately and more deeply led to much better learning, leading Craik and Lockhart to propose the levels of processing hypothesis (1972); material processed in a simple sensory way was rapidly forgotten, whereas a somewhat deeper processing in terms of recoding, for example, a printed word into its sound, led to a rather more durable memory trace. The most effective method of learning, however, was to process information richly and deeply in terms of its associations with existing knowledge. The levels of processing hypothesis proved capable of giving a good account of a wide range of data, although it has probably been rather less successful in leading to further insights into the processes underlying learning.

A second problem with the modal model came from the neuropsychological evidence, where it may be recalled that some patients combine very poor short-term memory performance with apparently normal long-term learning. According to the modal model, impairment in the operation of the short-term system should have major knock-on effects, resulting not only in poor long-term learning and retrieval, but also in substantial difficulties in a wide range of cognitive tasks that are assumed to depend upon the limited-capacity working memory system. In fact, the individuals observed with a profound but very pure short-term memory deficit appeared to have few cognitive problems in their everyday lives.

A possible solution to this was suggested by Baddeley and Hitch (1974), who proposed to abandon the idea of a simple unitary short-term memory system in favor of a tripartite system comprising an attentional controller, the central executive, aided by two subsidiary or slave systems, namely the phonological loop, a system for holding auditory or speech-based information, and its visual equivalent, the visuo-spatial sketchpad. The previously described patients with short-term memory deficits were assumed to have an impairment to the phonological loop system, resulting in very poor performance on tasks like digit span, in which the participant is required to repeat back a string of unrelated numbers; however, since the remainder of the working memory system was intact, overall intellectual performance was far less disrupted than would otherwise be assumed.

Baddeley and Hitch went on to investigate the nature of the two slave systems in greater detail, proposing that the phonological loop could be split into two components, a store that would hold memory traces of acoustic information for a few seconds before the trace decayed, coupled with an articulatory rehearsal system that could maintain information by a process analogous to saying the items to oneself.

Evidence that the store is phonological or acoustic in nature comes from the effect of similarity on performance. Items that are similar in sound, such as the words *man, cad, mat, cap,* and *can,* tend to be very poorly recalled in contrast to dissimilar sequences, such as *pit, day, cow, pen,* and *hot*. If the words are stored in terms of sound, then acoustically similar words will tend to be confused with each other when forgetting occurs, while dissimilar words will still be recallable. In contrast, similarity of meaning, as in a sequence such as *huge, big, large, wide,* and *tall,* has a relatively small effect on immediate memory span. In the case of long-term learning exactly the opposite pattern occurs, with semantic similarity being much more important than similarity of sound, suggesting that such learning relies on a system that reflects meaning rather than one that reflects sound.

Although the concept of a phonological loop appeared to give a good account of the data, the problem still remained as to why patients with a deficit in this system appeared to suffer from few general everyday problems; did it mean that the system was of little practical significance?

One answer to this question was to suggest that the phonological loop was important, but in children rather than in adults. It is assumed that its function is to help with the long-term learning of the sound of new words, which would be likely to be crucial during childhood when language was being acquired but less so as an adult—unless, of course, a second language was being learned. This hypothesis was tested by attempting to teach the vocabulary of a new language, Russian, to an individual with a very pure deficit to the phonological loop system. The individual had no difficulty in learning to link together pairs of words in her native language, a task that is assumed to depend on semantic coding, but had enormous difficulty in learning a list of eight Russian vocabulary items. Subsequent research showed that normal participants also had difficulty in second language learning if the phonological loop system was experimentally disrupted, again supporting the idea that it plays a crucial role in language acquisition. Furthermore, the vocabulary level of young children proved to be related to their capacity to repeat back unfamiliar sounds, with children showing language impairment being particularly poor at this task (Baddeley, Gathercole, & Papagno, 1998).

The visuospatial sketchpad has been less extensively explored, and while it seems likely that there is a rehearsal process analogous to that in the articulatory loop, it is not clear what form it takes. There appears to be evidence for a distinction between the subsystem storing visual information, such as the shape or color of an object, and that responsible for spatial encoding. Immediate visual memory appears to be best measured using a task called pattern span, in which participants are required to reproduce a matrix of black and white squares immediately after being presented with visual memory span being determined by the maximum number of squares that can accurately be reproduced. On the other hand, spatial memory span is typically measured in terms of the block-tapping task developed by Corsi, in which the tester taps out a pattern of movement involving an array of nine blocks, starting with just two blocks, and increasing the number of blocks tapped in series to a point at which the participant can no longer accurately reproduce the sequence.

The most complex and least understood component of working memory is the central executive. One way of analyzing the executive is by postulating individual executive processes, leaving the task of working out how the individual subcomponents interact to control the working memory system till later. So far the capacity for dividing attention in order to perform two tasks simultaneously is the process that has been most extensively explored, particularly using sufferers from Alzheimer's disease, who appear to have a particularly marked deficit in this function.

An alternative approach has been to define working memory as a capacity to combine storage and processing, and then to investigate the extent to which the capacity to perform such dual tasks predicts performance on complex activities such as comprehension and reasoning, which are assumed to depend on working memory. A good example of this is the working memory span task developed by Daneman and Carpenter (1980), in which the participant has to read out a series of brief sentences and is subsequently required to recall the last word from each. Working memory span is the maximum number of sentences for which final word recall is perfect, and tends to range between 2 and 4. Daneman and Carpenter showed that this is an excellent predictor of reading comprehension, while subsequent research has shown that tasks of this kind correlate very highly with more traditional measures of intelligence, typically based on reasoning tasks (Kyllonen & Christal, 1990). Not only do such working memory tasks provide a good measure of general intelligence, they have the further advantage that they are less dependent upon educational background, making them practically useful in situations where it is necessary to assess the capacity of people from a wide range of subcultures.

While working memory span measures are of some potential practical value, they can be criticized for being theoretically very difficult to interpret, since they probably involve not only central executive functioning but also other skills and components of working memory. Attempts are therefore being undertaken to try to understand the processes underlying performance, notably by Engle and his coworkers (Engle, 1996).

At the same time, a number of attempts are being made to produce a more direct model of executive processes, often as part of computational approaches to the analysis of human cognition. Examples of this include the work of Walter Schneider, who is interested in the way in which the cognitive system coordinates a range of subsystems, David Meyer and David Kieras, who are interested in modeling the performance of humans interacting with complex systems, and Anders Ericsson and Walter Kintsch, who are interested in what they call "long-term working memory," which reflects the way in which the working memory system can be extended to take advantage of long-term memory structures, particularly in the case of experts performing a well-learned task. Examples of all of these and other approaches to the executive control of working memory are given in *Models of Working Memory*, edited by A. Miyake and P. Shah (1999).

Finally, in recent years the development of neuroradiological scanning methods has been applied to the analysis of working memory with considerable success. In general, the localization data appear to be broadly consistent with the earlier data based on cognitive and neuropsychological studies, with evidence for a clear separation of the phonological loop and the visuospatial sketchpad, together with evidence of separate locations of subcomponents of the slave systems. However, the area in which brain scanning is likely to prove most productive is in analyzing the central executive component, where a number of locations within the frontal lobes appear to be implicated in different aspects of executive processing, including those involved in coding, retrieval, and dual task performance (for a review of this see Smith & Jonides, 1995).

[*See also* Memory.]

Bibliography

Atkinson, R. C., & Shiffrin, R. M. (1968). Human memory: A proposed system and its control processes. In K. W. Spence (Ed.), *The psychology of learning and motivation: Advances in research and theory* (pp. 89–195). New York: Academic Press.

Baddeley, A. D., Gathercole, S. E., & Papagno, C. (1998). The phonological loop as a language learning device. *Psychological Review, 105*, 158–173.

Baddeley, A. D., & Hitch, G. (1974). Working memory. In G. A. Bower (Ed.), *The psychology of learning and motivation* (pp. 47–89). New York: Academic Press.

Craik, F. I. M., & Lockhart, R. S. (1972). Levels of processing: A framework for memory research. *Journal of Verbal Learning and Verbal Behavior, 11*, 671–684.

Daneman, M., & Carpenter, P. A. (1980). Individual differences in working memory and reading. *Journal of Verbal Learning and Verbal Behavior, 19*, 450–466.

Engle, R. W. (1996). Working memory and retrieval: An inhibition resource approach. In J. T. E. Richardson (Ed.), *Working memory in human cognition* (pp. 89–119). New York: Oxford University Press.

Kyllonen, P. C., & Christal, R. E. (1990). Reasoning ability is (little more than) working memory capacity. *Intelligence, 14*, 389–433.

Miller, G., Galanter, E., & Pribram, K. (1979). *Plans and the structure of behavior*. New York.

Miyake, A., & Shah, P. (Eds.). (1999). *Models of working memory: Mechanisms of active maintenance and executive control*. New York: Cambridge University Press.

Newell, A., & Simon, H. A. (1972). *Human problem-solving*. Englewood Cliffs, NJ: Prentice Hall.

Smith, E. E., & Jonides, J. (1995). Working memory in humans: Neuropsychological evidence. In M. Gazzaniga (Ed.), *The cognitive neurosciences* (pp. 1019–1020). Cambridge, MA: MIT Press.

Alan Baddeley

WORK PERFORMANCE. Measures of criterion work performance are important for many personnel research applications. Examples are evaluating the effects of a training program or a job redesign effort on job performance, and assessing the validity of a selection system for predicting performance. For these and other personnel-related interventions, what is needed is accurate measures of work performance to assess the effectiveness of the intervention. As an example of the importance of accurate performance measurement, suppose we were interested in assessing the effectiveness of a new technical skills training program for increasing the job performance of trainees. As part of the design, we would measure work performance before and after the training (e.g., perhaps with supervisory ratings) to see if performance improves. If the measures of performance are inaccurate, the training program evaluation will provide misinformation on the success or failure of the training intervention.

Criterion Relevance and Other Criteria for Criteria

What distinguishes a good criterion measure from a poor one? That is, what are the most important criteria for good criteria? The most important is relevance. Relevance can be defined as the correspondence between criteria and the actual performance requirements of the job. Criterion measures should reflect all important job performance requirements. Useful in this context are the terms *contamination* and *deficiency*. Contamination refers to a criterion measure that taps variance in performance beyond the control of the organization member. For example, sales volume for account executives may be based in part on their performance, but also on how easy it is to sell the product in their territory. Deficiency for a set of criterion measure occurs when the set is relevant to only part of the criterion domain. A job knowledge test for an insurance agent will probably fail to cover the interpersonal skill part of the job. A perfectly relevant set of criterion measures is neither contaminated nor deficient.

The second most important standard for good criterion measurement is reliability. Criterion scores should be consistent in that the rank order of employees on a criterion measure does not vary widely over at least relatively short time intervals. For example, if a criterion measure for fast-food servers is ratings of customer service quality by multiple customers, we would like to see consistency (i.e., reliability) in how different customers rated the servers, with good performers in this area rated consistently high, poorer performers consistently lower, and so forth. There are other criteria for criteria that some authors have mentioned (e.g., accessibility of criterion data and acceptability of measures to the sponsor) but relevance and reliability are clearly the most important.

Multiple and Composite Criteria

An issue in measuring work performance is whether a single criterion can represent the performance requirements of a job or whether multiple criteria are required. Advocates for a single-composite criterion see criteria as economic in nature, whereas supporters of multiple criteria view them more as psychological constructs. Probably the best way to resolve the issue is to recognize that the purpose of performance measurement has a lot to do with the appropriateness of the two views (Schmidt & Kaplan, 1971). For example, when making compensation decisions for a unit's members based on performance, it is necessary to obtain a single performance score at some point for each employee. To make these decisions, we need an index of overall performance, worth to the organization, or some similar summary score. On the other hand, if the goal is to understand predictor-criterion links in personnel selection research, then using multiple criteria and examining relationships between each predictor (e.g., ability, personality, and other measures) and each criterion (e.g., technical proficiency and organizational citizenship behavior) is probably most appropriate.

A related issue is the empirical question of how highly correlated multiple criteria for a job are likely to be. If correlations between criterion measures are high, then a single composite measure will be sufficient to represent the multiple criteria. On balance, research suggests that most jobs have multiple performance requirements. Performance on these multiple dimensions may be positively correlated but not so high that distinctions between dimensions are impossible.

In fact, an attempt has been made to identify the criterion constructs underlying performance across jobs. Campbell, McCloy, Oppler, and Sager (1993) argue that eight dimensions (e.g., written and oral communication and maintaining personal discipline) reasonably summarize the performance requirements for all jobs in the U.S. economy. Not every job has every dimension as relevant, but the eight dimensions as a set reflect all performance requirements across these jobs. Criterion research in Project A, a large-scale selection study in the U.S. Army, empirically confirmed several of these dimensions for 19 jobs in the army. More will be said about these kinds of criterion models in the "Future" section.

A final issue in this area focuses on the boundaries of work performance. How should we define performance? Recent attention has been directed to organizational citizenship behavior (OCB), prosocial organizational behavior, and related constructs (e.g., Organ, 1997) as criterion concepts that go beyond task performance and the technical proficiency-related aspects of performance. For example, the OCB concept includes behavior related to helping others in the organization with their jobs and conscientiously supporting and defending the organization. Research has shown that supervisors making overall performance judgments about employees weigh OCB and similar constructs about as highly as these employees' task performance (e.g., Motowidlo & Van Scotter, 1994). Also, a link between OCB on the part of organization members and organizational effectiveness has some empirical support.

The Distinctions Among Behavior, Performance, and Effectiveness

More than 25 years ago, Campbell, Dunnette, Lawler, and Weick (1970) made the highly useful and important distinction between behavior, performance, and effectiveness. Behavior is what organization members actually do. Behaviors have no evaluative component; they are tasks and activities engaged in by employees (e.g., drives a vehicle or writes a memo). Performance is behavior that includes the evaluative element (e.g., drives a vehicle effectively, writes a short misleading memo). Thus, performance reflects members' contributions to organizational goals, behaviors that lead to or detract from organizational effectiveness. Effectiveness has to do with outcomes. Effectiveness includes both an individual's performance and factors beyond his or her control. For example, such indices as promotion rate and salary level often reflect an organization member's own efforts (i.e., performance) but also organizational factors controlled by others.

Campbell's and colleagues' main point in making this distinction was that the proper focus of criterion development efforts should be on performance. As an example, criteria that are "bottom-line" results oriented for measuring an individual's performance (i.e., measures of effectiveness) are inappropriate for this purpose. Referring to a term used previously, effectiveness indices are likely to be contaminated, including elements beyond one's control.

Methods of Measuring Criterion Performance

Two major types of measures are used to assess criterion performance: ratings and so-called objective measures. We will spend the most time on ratings—estimates of individuals' job performance made by supervisors, peers, or others familiar with their performance. This is because ratings are by far the most often used criterion measure (Landy & Farr, 1980). Objective measures such as turnover, absences, and production rates will also be discussed.

Performance Ratings. Performance ratings can be generated for several purposes, including salary administration, promotion and layoff decisions, employee development and feedback, and as criteria in validation research. Most of the research on ratings has focused on the latter for-research-only ratings. Research discussed here is in the areas of evaluating the quality of ratings, format effects on ratings, different sources of ratings (e.g., supervisors, peers), and the effects of rater training on ratings.

Evaluation of Ratings. Ratings of job performance sometimes suffer from psychometric errors, such as distributional errors or the "illusory halo." Distributional errors include leniency/severity, where raters evaluate ratees either too high or too low in comparison to their actual performance level. Restriction-in-range is another distributional error. With this error, a rater may rate two or more ratees on a dimension such that the spread (i.e., variance) of these ratings is lower than the variance of the actual performance levels for these ratees. The illusory halo occurs when a rater makes ratings on two or more dimensions such that the correlations between the dimensions are higher than the between-dimension correlations of the actual behaviors relevant to those dimensions.

A second common approach for evaluating ratings is to assess interrater reliability, either within rating source (e.g., peers) or across sources (e.g., peers and supervisor). The notion here is that high interrater agreement implies that the ratings are accurate. Unfortunately, this does not necessarily follow. Raters may agree in their evaluations because they are rating according to ratee reputation or likability, even though these factors have nothing to do with actual performance. In addition, low agreement between raters at different organizational levels may result from these raters' viewing different samplings of ratee behavior or having different roles related to the ratees. In this scenario, each level's raters might be providing valid evaluations but for different elements of job performance (Campbell Dunnette, Lawlor, & Weick, 1970). Accordingly, assessing the quality of ratings using interrater reliability is somewhat problematic. On balance, however, high interrater reliability is desirable, especially within rating source.

A third approach sometimes suggested for evaluating ratings is to assess their validity or accuracy. The argument made is that rating errors and interrater reliability are indirect ways of estimating what we really want to know. How accurate are the ratings at reflecting actual ratee performance? Unfortunately, evaluating rating accuracy requires comparing them to some kind of "true score," a characterization of each ratee's actual performance. Because determining true performance scores in an employment setting is typically impossible, research on the accuracy of performance ratings has proceeded in the laboratory. To evaluate accuracy, written or videotaped vignettes of hypothetical ratees have been developed and target performance scores on multiple dimensions have been derived using expert judgment. Ratings of these written vignette or videotaped performers can then be compared to the target scores to derive accuracy scores (Borman, 1977).

Rating Formats. A variety of different rating formats have been developed to help raters evaluate the performance of individuals in organizations. Over the years, some quite innovative designs for rating formats have been introduced.

It may seem like an obvious approach now, but the notion of assigning numerical ratings in evaluating organization members was an important breakthrough. Previously, evaluations were written descriptions of the ratee's performance. The breakthrough was that with numerical scores, ideally, well-informed raters could quantify their perceptions of individuals' job performance, and the resulting scores provided a way to compare employees against a standard or with each other. This notion can be seen as analogous to developing structured job analysis questionnaires to replace job descriptions, allowing empirical comparisons between jobs.

One potential disadvantage of numerical scales is that there is no inherent meaning to the numbers on the scale. On a 1–7 scale, for example, a 3 to one rater may mean the same thing as a 2 or a 4 to another. To address this difficulty, Smith and Kendall introduced the notion of behaviorally anchored rating scales (BARS, 1963). These authors reasoned that different levels of effectiveness on rating scales might be anchored by behavioral examples of job performance. The behavioral examples are each scaled according to their effectiveness levels by persons knowledgeable about the job and then placed on the scale at the points corresponding to their respective effectiveness values, helping raters to compare the observed performance of a rater with the behavioral anchors on the scale, leading in turn to more objective behavior-based evaluations.

Selecting Raters. Supervisors are the most often used rating source in obtaining performance evaluations of organization members. An advantage of supervisory ratings is that supervisors typically are experienced in making evaluations and have a good frame of reference from observing large numbers of subordinates. A disadvantage is that in at least some organizations, supervisors do not directly observe ratee performance on a day-to-day basis. In addition, coworker or peer ratings are sometimes used to evaluate performance. A positive feature for peer ratings is that coworkers often observe employee performance closer and more regularly than supervisors. A difficulty is that coworkers are less likely than supervisors to have experience evaluating ratee performance.

Other rating sources may also be involved in assessing job performance. In fact, a recent emphasis has been toward the concept of "360-degree ratings," augmenting supervisory ratings with evaluations from peers, subordinates, self-ratings, and even customers' assessments. The general idea is to assess performance from multiple perspectives so that a balanced evaluation of job performance might be obtained.

Rater Training. Rater training provides a promising approach to improving the accuracy of performance ratings. Two general kinds of training programs have emerged to help raters generate more error free and accurate ratings. Rater error training simply seeks to alert raters to certain psychometric or perceptual errors, such as leniency/severity, halo, and restriction-in-range effects. Training often takes the form of a demonstration of the error and instructions to avoid such errors when making performance ratings. Frame-of-reference training attempts to convey to raters that performance has multiple dimensions, and it thoroughly familiarizes them with the actual content of each performance dimension, often providing opportunities for practice ratings and feedback on their accuracy.

Researchers have conducted studies comparing the psychometric properties and accuracy of ratings made by raters trained to use one of the approaches just discussed and ratings generated by untrained raters. The main results are that (1) error training does not improve the quality of ratings when interrater reliability or accuracy is used as a criterion (Murphy & Balzer, 1989); and (2) frame-of-reference training increases rating accuracy (Smith, 1986).

Objective Criteria. A second major measurement method for criterion performance involves use of objective criteria. Objective criteria employed in personnel research include turnover, absences, production rates, and work samples of employee performance. At first glance, one may presume that objective criteria are more desirable than ratings, which are inherently subjective. Unfortunately, judgment often enters into the assignment of objective criterion scores. Also, objective measures are often contaminated as criteria, with problems such as factors beyond the assessee's control influencing these outcome measures. Nonetheless, when they are relevant to important performance areas and are reasonably reliable and uncontaminated, objective measures can be useful in indexing some criterion dimensions.

Turnover. Turnover or attrition is often an important criterion because the cost of training replacement personnel is usually high; also, having people, especially key people, leave the organization can be disruptive and adversely affect organizational effectiveness. Turnover is sometimes treated as a single dichotomous variable—a person is either a "leaver" or a "stayer." This treatment fails to distinguish between very different reasons for leaving the organization (e.g., being fired for a disciplinary infraction versus leaving voluntarily for health reasons). Clearly, turnover for such different reasons will have different patterns of relationships with individual difference or organizational factor predictors. Prediction of turnover with any substantive interpretation requires examining the categories of turnover. For example, it may be that employees fired for disciplinary reasons have reliably different scores on certain personality scales, for example, lower socialization compared to stayers, whereas prior health status is the only predictor of leaving the organization for health reasons. This approach in dealing with turnover as a criterion variable appears to offer the most hope for learning more about why individuals leave organizations and what can be done to reduce unwanted turnover.

Absences. For most jobs, having employees at work regularly is important for individual and organizational effectiveness. Accordingly, issues of absences and attendance are legitimate criteria to consider. Unfortunately, at least two problems plague measures of absences or attendance. First, criterion contamination is often a factor in measuring absences. Distinctions should be made between involuntary and voluntary absence, for example, with the latter being the more important to predict and then reduce. In fact, involuntary absences (e.g., being out sick) should not count as a negative behavior because they are typically beyond the employee's control. A second problem in measuring absences is the serious skewing of distributions. Severe truncation, with many sample members having no absences, causes difficulties when absences are correlated with scores on another variable, such as a predictor measure.

In sum, voluntary absences should be the focus of study regarding absences in criterion development. This class of absence is presumably a function of employee motivation and willingness to work. Accordingly, it should be predictable from measures of individual differences in employees and organizational factors.

Production Rates. For jobs that have observable, countable products that result from individual performance, a production-rate criterion is a compelling bottom-line index of performance. However, considerable care must be taken in gathering and interpreting production data. For example, work-related dependencies on other employees' performance or on equipment for determining production rates may create bias in these rates. Also, production standards and quota systems (e.g., in data entry jobs) create problems for criterion measurement.

Work Sample Tests. Work sample or performance tests are sometimes developed to provide criteria, especially for training programs. For example, to help evaluate the effectiveness of training, work samples may be used to assess performance on important tasks before and after training. Such tests can also be used for other personnel research applications, such as criteria in selection studies.

Some argue that work sample tests have the highest fidelity for measuring criterion performance. In a sense, the argument is compelling: What could be more direct and fair than to assess employees' performance on a job by having them actually perform some of the most important tasks associated with it? In fact, some researchers and others may view work samples as ultimate criteria, that is, the best and most relevant criterion measures. Performance tests should not be thought of in this light. First, they are clearly maximum performance rather than typical performance measures. As such, they tap the "can-do" more than the "will-do" performance-over-time aspects of effectiveness. Yet "will-do," longer-term performance is certainly important for assessing effectiveness in jobs. Accordingly, these measures are deficient when used exclusively in measuring performance. Nonetheless, work samples can be a useful criterion for measuring aspects of maximum performance.

Conclusions About Objective Criteria. The following conclusions can be made about criteria and criterion measurement methods.

Performance Ratings. Ratings have the inherent potential advantage of being sensitive to ratee performance over time and across a variety of job situations. Ideally, raters can average performance levels observed, sampling performance-relevant behavior broadly over multiple occasions. Provided that observation and subsequent ratings are made on all important dimensions, ratings can potentially avoid problems of contamination and deficiency. Of course, these are potential advantages of the rating method. Rater error, bias, and other inaccuracies must be reduced in order for ratings to realize this potential. Both basic and applied research are needed to learn more about what performance ratings are measuring and how to improve on that measurement. Rater-training research appears especially promising for reducing rating errors and enhancing the accuracy of evaluations.

Objective Measures. Like other methods of measuring criterion performance, objective measures can be quite useful. However, these are almost always deficient, contaminated, or both. Indices such as turnover, absences, and production rates produce data pertinent to only a portion of the criterion domain. In addition, some of these indices are often determined in part by factors beyond the employee's control.

Regarding work sample tests, the point was made that these measures should not be considered ultimate criteria in any sense. Nonetheless, well-conceived and competently constructed performance tests can be valuable measures of maximum, "can-do" performance.

The Future of Objective Criteria. An encouraging development in criterion measurement is the consideration of models of work performance (e.g., Campbell, McCloy, Oppler, & Sager, 1993). As mentioned, models of performance seek to identify criterion constructs that reflect broadly relevant performance requirements for jobs (e.g., communication and personal discipline). Such criterion models can help to organize accumulating research findings that link individual differences (e.g., ability and personality), organizational variables (e.g., task characteristics), and the individual criterion constructs identified in the models. In addition, efforts should continue toward learning more about what performance ratings and objective performance indexes are measuring, with the goal of improving the accuracy of these measures. Improving the measurement of work performance is critically important for enhancing the science and practice of industrial/organizational psychology toward the broad and compelling objective of increasing the effectiveness of organizations.

[*See also* Work.]

Bibliography

Borman, W. C. (1977). Consistency of rating accuracy and rater errors in the judgment of human performance. *Organizational Behavior and Human Performance, 20*, 238–252.

Campbell, J. P., Dunnette, M. D., Lawler, E. E., & Weick, K. E. (1970). *Managerial behavior, performance, and effectiveness.* New York: McGraw-Hill.

Campbell, J. P., McCloy, R. A., Oppler, S. H., & Sager, C. E. (1993). A theory of performance. In N. Schmit & W. C. Borman (Eds.), *Personnel selection in organizations* (pp. 35–70). San Francisco: Jossey-Bass.

Landy, F. J., & Farr, J. L. (1980). Performance rating. *Psychological Bulletin, 87*, 72–107.

Motowidlo, S. J., & Van Scotter, J. R. (1994). Evidence that task performance should be distinguished from contextual performance. *Journal of Applied Psychology, 79*, 475–480.

Murphy, K. R., & Balzer, W. K. (1989). Rater errors and rating accuracy. *Journal of Applied Psychology, 74*, 619–624.

Organ, D. W. (1997). Organizational citizenship behavior: It's construct clean-up time. *Human Performance, 10*(2), 85–97.

Schmidt, F. R., & Kaplan, L. B. (1971). Composite versus multiple criteria: A review and resolution of the controversy. *Personnel Psychology, 24*, 419–434.

Smith, D. E. (1986). Training programs for performance appraisal: A review. *Academy of Management Review, 11*, 22–40.

Smith, D. E., & Kendall, L. M. (1963). Retranslation of expectations: An approach to the construction of unambiguous anchors for rating scales. *Journal of Applied Psychology, 47*, 149–155.

Walter C. Borman

WORLD FEDERATION FOR MENTAL HEALTH. The world's only international, nongovernmental, voluntary mental health association of organizations and individuals, representing citizen volunteers, professionals of all disciplines, and users of mental health services is the World Federation for Mental Health (WFMH). There are approximately 170 national or international organization members, 170 regional affiliate members, and 2,350 individual members. The WFMH is accredited as a mental health consultant to all of the major agencies of the United Nations. Its ecumenical membership is bound together by dedication to the goal of improving global mental health in its broadest sense. Its mission, described in its articles of incorporation, is "to promote the mental health of all of the world's peoples in its social, educational, medical, and biological aspects."

The WFMH pursues its mission mainly through the work of topic-oriented committees, advocacy, and education, aimed at the United Nations, governments, and the general public. It acts through regional conferences, biennial world congresses, consultation, the International Committee of Women Leaders and First Ladies, volunteer representatives at major United Nations offices, an annual World Mental Health Day cosponsored with the World Health Organization (WHO), and a quarterly newsletter. Major themes are preventing mental illness, promoting positive mental health, particularly of minority groups including women, protecting the human rights of people defined as mentally ill, and improving the delivery of mental health services.

Much work is sponsored within WFMH regions, some of which have developed regional councils. The regions are Africa, the eastern Mediterranean, Mexico-Central America-the Caribbean, Europe, North America, Southeast Asia, the Western Pacific, and Oceania. The European Council is unique in that its development is tied to that of the European Union. The WFMH also engages in service and research through university-based collaborating centers. These currently focus on prevention, traumatized refugees, women's health, torture victims, aging, and sociocultural issues in mental health in southern Africa.

The forerunner of the WFMH was the International Committee for Mental Hygiene (ICMH), founded in the United States of America in 1919 by Clifford Beers, a sufferer from recurrent episodes of depression and mania. The ICMH sponsored the first International Congress for Mental Hygiene, in Washington, D.C. in 1930. After a second congress in Paris in 1937, World War II interrupted the movement. Its revival came at the suggestion of the WHO and UNESCO, agencies of the new United Nations, founded in 1945. The new federation's name was suggested in 1946 by Canadian psychiatrist George Brock Chisholm, just prior to his becoming the WHO's first director general. It was formally founded during the Third International Congress on Mental Hygiene in London, in August 1948, following a plan developed by a preparatory commission, including such well-known figures as anthropologist Margaret Mead, social psychologist Otto Klineberg, clinical psychologist Eomonn O'Doherty, and psychiatrist Harry Stack Sullivan. They contributed to the organization's founding document, "Mental Health and World Citizenship." The chief organizer and chairman of the 1948 congress, named by the national mental health association in Britain, was English psychiatrist John R. Rees, who became the WFMH's first president from 1948 to 1949, and then its director from 1949 to 1962.

The elected officers comprise a board of directors headed by a president who serves a 2-year, nonrenewable term. There are nine regional vice presidents, some of whom function as chairs of WFMH regional councils.

Bibliography

Brody, E. B. (1998). *The search for mental health: A history and memoir of the World Federation for Mental Health, 1948–1997*. Baltimore: Williams & Wilkins. Details of the human and organizational story of the federation's first half century, written by the federation's president from 1981 to 1983 and secretary general from 1983 to 1999.

World Federation of Mental Health. Available Web site: www.wfmh.com.

Eugene B. Brody

WORLD HEALTH ORGANIZATION. The United Nations established the World Health Organization (WHO) in 1948 as a specialized agency with primary responsibility for international health matters. When the League of Nations, a forerunner of the United Nations, was founded in 1919, it was charged with, among other things, taking steps in matters of international concern for the prevention and control of disease, and a Health Organization of the League was set up in Geneva, Switzerland. When WHO was established in 1948, its headquarters was sited in Geneva, where it remains. WHO now has 191 member states and six regional offices. In fact, the forerunner of what is now the Regional Office for the Americas was set up in 1902 in Washington, D.C., long before WHO itself was established. Founded as the International Sanitary Bureau, it is now called the Pan American Health Organization.

The constitution of WHO made it clear that mental health was included in its mission. For instance, health was defined as "a state of complete physical, mental and social well-being and not merely the absence of disease or infirmity." The functions of WHO included many general items, such as "to act as the directing and coordinating authority on international health work," but in addition it was specifically directed "to foster activities in the field of mental health, especially those activities affecting the harmony of human relations."

Soon after its foundation, WHO began publishing documents on mental health issues. In fact, the first two works in its monograph series, both published in 1951, were on mental health topics: *Psychiatric Aspects of Juvenile Delinquency*, followed by *Maternal Care and Mental Health* by John Bowlby, at that time a little-known psychiatrist in the United Kingdom. These were followed quickly by other publications on malaria, nutrition, and other subjects, but they also included issues on mental health topics.

Mental health, however, did not have a strong position within the WHO secretariat at that time. It existed only as a "section," "unit," or "office" before being established in 1977 as a division and, as such, one of 12 major technical programs of WHO. The division included a program on drug dependence and one on psychosocial aspects of health, as well as one on the prevention and treatment of mental and neurological disorders. In addition, each of the six regional offices appointed a staff member as a regional adviser for mental health, with some regions having a separate adviser on drug abuse.

The activities dealing with mental health and with substance abuse have now been separated into two departments within a cluster named Social Change and Mental Health. The Department of Mental Health operates as three teams: Mental Health Promotion, Mental and Neurological Disorders Control, and Nations for Mental Health. The last is a relatively new program on mental health for underserved populations, which funds and oversees the implementation of country-level projects, as opposed to the more traditional global and regional coordination type of activities that have been carried out by WHO in the past. The Department of Mental Health also shares some responsibilities with another program (Assessment, Classification and Epidemiology, ACE) within the same cluster. ACE deals, among other things, with the Mental Disorders within the *International Classification of Diseases* (*ICD*), and related international classifications. The Department of Substance Abuse deals with controlled and illegal drugs as well as with the abuse of alcohol. For a few years recently, it also included tobacco control, but this is now dealt with separately within WHO.

As with most organizations, the working structure of WHO changes, and the WHO Web site should be consulted for up-to-date information, as well as more details about the content of the various programs, including published and unpublished documentation.

Bibliography

World Health Organization. Available Web site: http://www.who.int. Complete information about WHO.

World Health Organization. Available Web site: http://www.who.int/msa/mnh. Provides detailed information about the work of the WHO Department of Mental Health.

John Orley

WRITING. Psychological research on writing has lagged behind that on reading. One reason is that language production, whether through speaking or writing, poses serious methodological obstacles. In experiments on language comprehension, the input can be controlled and the output carefully measured, as Kathryn Bock explained in the *Psychonomic Bulletin and Review* (1996). By contrast, what someone says or writes in response to an experimenter's prompt is unpredictable. Therefore, the natural observation of speech errors or slips of the tongue, not experimentation, has largely shaped theories of speech production. Similarly, a common method of investigating text production has been to observe the location and timing of pauses in handwriting and the verbal protocols of writers as they think aloud.

The origins of some contemporary psychological research on writing lie in the composition research of the 1970s from the fields of rhetoric and education and in the extensive research on discourse processing from psychology and linguistics. This line of work addresses how writers formulate the structure of a text and what role the social context of writing plays. A second line of research examines the detailed processes and codes required in the production of a sentence and links the work on spoken sentence production to writing. An increasingly important source of evidence about these production processes comes from neuropsychological studies of aphasic and agraphic patients. A third line addresses the cognitive, emotional, and behavioral dimensions of writing in the context of mental health. Included in this final line of research are studies ranging from the use of writing in psychotherapy to the treatment of writer's block.

Writing involves formulating, executing, and monitoring text. The seminal model of writing processes was concerned with formulation and monitoring only. In a classic book, *Cognitive Processes in Writing* (1980), John R. Hayes and Linda Flower proposed that formulation involves planning content and generating sentences based on knowledge drawn from the writer's long-term memory. Planning a text entails generating ideas, organizing them, and setting goals to be achieved in the structure of the text. Translating ideas into sentences includes many subprocesses that occur in producing speech, such as selecting appropriate lexical entries, assigning grammatical roles, and assembling the constituents in the proper order. Reviewing the text involves reading and editing operations that detect faults at multiple levels of text structure, ranging from local mechanics to the coherence of the whole text. According to Hayes and Flower's model, an executive monitor establishes priorities about which writing process to engage at a given moment and provides metacognitive awareness of how things are going. Often a writer must juggle simultaneous demands and risks overloading available attentional or working-memory capacity. To cope with these demands, one writer may translate ideas into sentences as they occur and delay review for later. Another writer may generate, organize, and edit ideas before attempting to translate a perfect first draft. With either strategy, the writer must monitor whether the processes are successful and alter priorities as needed.

Writing processes are constrained by the task environment and the writer's long-term memory. The topic, the type of text, the intended readership, and the text produced thus far all constitute elements of the task environment. The tools available to the writer and the deadlines for finishing also shape the task environment. It is fruitful to conceive of the writer as a problem solver. The task environment and long-term memory together pose the problems of content (what to say) and rhetoric (how to say it) that must be solved in order to produce a text.

Besides an act of problem solving, writing is inherently a social act. Texts are created to be read within a discourse community, as explained by Bennett A. Rafoth and Donald L. Rubin in *The Social Construction of Written Communication* (1988). The social aspects of creating texts may be explicit, as in collaborative writing, or they may be implicit, as in the way the imagined reader shapes the writer's ideas and manner of expression. Expert writers conform their texts to the expectations of their readers. This point is well illustrated in the publication style requirements of the American Psychological Association. The style demands an allegiance to the empirical method and so defines the psychologist's task as a writer. Conclusions must be hedged so as to avoid stepping beyond the limits of the data, creating an air of uncertainty atypical in the humanities. Disagreements are couched in terms of differences about appropriate methods or interpretations of data, never in the personal terms seen at times in literary criticism.

Recursively planning, translating, and reviewing a

text are characteristic of mature writing. The writer gains insight into the ideas being formulated as a consequence of expressing them as text. Carl Bereiter and Marlene Scardamalia called this loop "knowledge-transforming" in their book *The Psychology of Written Composition* (1987). What one thinks is then shaped by what one writes and then reads. Unlike the reflective problem solving of mature writers, young children fail to elaborate their thinking through the act of writing. They instead engage in what Bereiter and Scardamalia call "knowledge-telling." The task environment automatically cues children to retrieve material from long-term memory and then translate it into sentences. Writing continues in this manner until retrieval fails to provide relevant material. During adolescence, the skill of writing as knowledge transforming begins to emerge as a complement to the more basic knowledge telling.

Data based on verbal protocols and other forms of introspection indicate that adult writers recursively attend to the planning, translating, and reviewing processes through prewriting, first draft, and subsequent draft phases of text development. Although planning generally occurs more frequently in the earlier stages and reviewing occurs more frequently in the later stages, the three kinds of operations are called upon by the writer at any point. One effective strategy for coping with the multiple demands of writing on working memory is to delay concerns about how ideas are expressed and focus on planning. This increases the number of ideas generated during planning. Another effective strategy is to prepare an outline of ideas and their organization before composing a first draft. Advance outlining permits the writer to focus on translating ideas into sentences and increases both the fluency of writing and the quality of the resulting text.

Limitations of working memory create problems for children learning to write. Young writers often forget the ideas recently generated and so repeat them again. Sentence generation is also constrained by working memory by limiting the number of linguistic units that may be coordinated in young writers. Furthermore, handwriting or typing is not as effortless in children as it is in adults. The transcription demands that confront children divert working-memory capacity from formulation and monitoring to motor execution.

Learning to revise effectively is especially challenging, perhaps in part because of working-memory limitations. Just reading the text typically takes more effort for a young writer than for an adult. The lack of thorough revision seen in immature writers may also stem from a failure to establish clear plans initially. Without explicit goals for a text under development, it is not possible to detect problems in how the text meets those goals. Revising becomes little more than editing problems with spelling, punctuation, and other concerns of mechanics. Furthermore, a skilled writer must be able to criticize a text from the perspective of a potential reader. Taking the perspective of another individual is an important accomplishment in the cognitive development of many domains and must be acquired in written language production.

The translation of ideas into production has been extensively investigated in speech. Five levels of processing can be distinguished. Message-level processing involves planning the ideas to be conveyed. Functional processing reflects the translation of ideas into the words or lexical items along with the grammatical roles to be played by various phrases. Positional processing continues translation by retrieving the lexical (e.g., phonological segments) and grammatical morphemes (e.g., inflections) and positioning these constituents in a hierarchical syntactic structure. Next, phonological processing completes translation into speech by specifying all aspects of the sound structure of the sentence, including its prosodic features such as stress patterns. Phonological segments or phonemes are translated into phonetic segments, setting the stage for articulation. The final level of processing is the motor programming required for execution. Specifications for activating speech musculature include programs for vibrations of the larynx and articulatory movements of the tongue and lips, for instance.

In writing, the planning of message content is often more extensive than in speaking, and the reviewing of output may go through numerous drafts, in distinct contrast to the real-time nature of speech production. Also, writing requires a graphemic representation. Graphemes can be computed either from the visual appearance or orthographic code of a whole word or by applying rules for converting phonology to orthography in spelling out the word. Once the order of graphemes is specified for spelling a word, the programming necessary for typing or handwriting may begin. The musculature for handwriting or typing differs from that of speech, but the required motor programming is no less intricate. In handwriting, for example, the size of the letters and their allographic form must be selected as well as the force and muscles to be used in writing with pen and paper as opposed to chalk and blackboard.

Writing the words of a sentence, then, is a highly complex affair. Agraphia, the inability to express a thought in writing, usually occurs to some degree as a consequence of significant brain damage regardless of its location; specific disorders of central language systems, as in aphasia, or motor systems, as in Parkinson's disease, cause agraphia, as does widely spread pathology, as in Alzheimer's disease. The details of how working memory supports planning, sentence generation, reading, and editing are not yet clear. A general working memory system akin to Baddeley's central executive appears to be critical to all writing processes and affects both the efforts of children to learn to write as well as the skills of adult writers (1986). However, the role of peripheral systems of working memory that specialize in the processing and storage of phonological, semantic, or visuospatial information is not yet well understood.

Composing an extended text poses major challenges in thinking and self-regulation that go beyond language production per se. For serious writing, one must start and sustain demanding cognitive activities over lengthy intervals of time, coping with the emotional trials of such work. Successful writers set goals and monitor their output to maintain motivation in their often solitary work environment. When a writer is unable to meet the demands of the task and the words fail to come, apprehension builds to high levels as the production deadline approaches. Avoidance behavior may follow as a means of coping with the anxiety. In extreme cases of writer's block, text production halts altogether. Procrastination, excessive worrying, impatience, perfectionism, and evaluation anxiety are hallmarks of writer's block, according to Robert Boice (1985). Students and professionals suffering from writer's block may find help in cognitive-behavior therapy and writing-process training.

Writing fluently and effectively is important in many jobs; it is a basic component of functional literacy in the contemporary knowledge economy. Writing may also be an important tool for mental health. The self-disclosure of writing about important psychological problems improves mental and even physical health, according to James M. Pennebaker (1997). When individuals write about their deepest thoughts and feelings concerning events, relationships, and emotional experiences in their lives, they often disclose information about traumatic experiences, including deaths, accidents, abuses, and failures. Expressing emotional difficulties appears to improve their ability to cope. Although the use of writing in psychotherapy looks promising, important questions remain about why self-disclosure works.

In conclusion, research on writing is now rapidly expanding along multiple fronts, despite the special difficulties of experimentally studying the production of language. Psychologists are just beginning to understand in detail the processes involved in formulating, executing, and monitoring a text. To be sure, even the production of a single sentence is a remarkably complex affair. Writing extended texts engages not only cognitive and social processes but emotional ones as well that are of interest to both clinicians and scientists.

[*See also* Literature.]

Bibliography

Baddeley, A. D. (1986). *Working memory*. Oxford: Oxford University Press.

Bereiter, C., & Scardamalia, M. (1987). *The psychology of written composition*. Hillsdale, NJ: Erlbaum. Reviews the development of writing skill and contrasts knowledge-training with knowledge-transforming models of text production.

Beringer, V. W., Fuller, F., & Whitaker, D. (1996). A process model of writing development across the life-span. *Educational Psychology Review, 8*, 193–218.

Bock, K. (1996). *Psychonomic Bulletin and Review, 3*, 395–421.

Bock, J. K., & Levelt, W. (1994). Language production: Grammatical encoding. In M. A. Gernsbacher (Ed.), *Handbook of psycholinguistics* (pp. 945–984). San Diego: Academic Press. Summarizes contemporary models and research on sentence generation.

Boice, R. (1985). Cognitive components of blocking. *Written Communication, 2*, 91–104.

Caramazza, A., & Miceli, G. The structure of graphemic representations. *Cognition, 37*, 243–297. Illustrates the use of neuropsychological case studies to test models of written sentence production.

Fitzgerald, J. (1987). Research on revision in writing. *Review of Educational Research, 57*, 481–506.

Garrett, M. F. (1980). Levels of processing in sentence production. In B. Butterworth (Ed.), *Language production* (pp. 177–220). London: Academic Press. A classic presentation on the various levels of cognitive representations involved in sentence generation.

Glynn, S. M., Britton, B. K., Muth, D., & Dogan, N. (1982). Writing and revising persuasive documents: Cognitive demands. *Journal of Educational Psychology, 74*, 557–567. Experimental results showing that idea production suffers when writers attempt to do too many things at once.

Graham, S., & Harris, K. R. (1994). The role of self-regulation in the writing process. In D. Schunk & B. Zimmerman (Eds.), *Self-regulation of learning and performance: Issues and educational applications* (pp. 203–228). Mahwah, NJ: Erlbaum.

Hayes, J. R., & Flower, L. (1980). *Cognitive processes in writing* (L. W. Gregg & E. R. Sternberg, Eds.). Hillsdale, NJ: Erlbaum. A classic presentation of the processes involved in formulating and monitoring a text.

Kellogg, R. T. (1994). *The psychology of writing*. New York: Oxford University Press. Reviews research on the effects of knowledge, personality, strategies, tools such as word processors, and work habits on writers' performance.

Levy, M. C., & Ransdell, S. (Eds.). (1996). *The science of writing: Theories, methods, individual differences, and applications*. Mahwah, NJ: Erlbaum.

Lorch, M. P. (1995). Disorders of writing and spelling. In H. S. Kirshner (Ed.), *Handbook of neurological speech and language disorders* (pp. 295–324). New York: Marcel Dekker.

Madigan, R., Johnson, S., & Linton, P. (1995). The language of psychology: APA style as epistemology. *American Psychologist, 50*, 428–436. Illustrates the characteristics of the psychological discourse community.

McCutchen, D. (1996). A capacity theory of writing: Working memory in composition. *Educational Psychology Review, 8*, 299–325. Reviews research on individual differences in writing skill traceable to working-memory limitations with a focus on developmental psychology.

Pennebaker, J. M. (1997). Writing about emotional experiences as a therapeutic process. *Psychological Science, 8*, 162–166.

Rafoth, A., & Rubin, D. L. (1988). *The social construction of written communication*. Norwood, NJ: Ablex.

Salovey, P., & Haar, M. D. (1990). The efficiency of cognitive-behavior therapy and writing process training for alleviating writing anxiety. *Cognitive Therapy and Research, 14*, 515–528.

Van Galen, G. P. (1991). Handwriting: Issues for a psychomotor theory. *Human Movement Science, 10*, 165–191.

Ronald T. Kellogg

WUNDT, WILHELM MAXIMILIAN (1832–1920), German psychologist. Although his own origins in a south German village were modest, Wilhelm Wundt's roots reflect a family heritage rich with distinguished scholars, scientists, and administrators. His dreams and fantasies in the fields and forests of his youth were supplied by romantic novels, history, and religion—passions that poured forth late in his life into volumes on cultural psychology.

Family privations sent young Wilhelm into a medical career after his uninspired beginnings in stifling classrooms at Tübingen and Heidelberg universities. Yet the youthful dreams for greater adventures steadily drew him back from medicine's humdrum world into pure science. His true destiny was met when Germany's great scientist Herman Von Helmholtz hired him as a personal assistant at Heidelberg (1858). This opened Wundt's intellectual horizons to an extent rarely matched. While absorbing a grounding in Helmholtz's physical science, Wundt simultaneously threw himself, privately, into cultural studies and then into psychology. By 1860, he was building a private laboratory in which a new science of reaction-time measurement unfolded, the results of which he would use to challenge basic tenets of the prevalent Herbartian philosophy of mind. Soon Gustav Fechner's groundbreaking work on psychophysics appeared (1860), and Wundt rushed to enlarge and reinterpret it, recasting Fechner's equations in terms of purely psychological processes rather than external physical events. Although he progressed steadily toward theoretical interests, his apparatus collection expanded continuously during his long career. It was his students and assistants, however, who served as the active experimenters.

In 1864, Wundt was made Professor Extraordinarius at Heidelberg, giving him time to follow new ambitions, one of which was politics. He won elective office in the Baden parliament and championed liberal causes, challenging the antidemocratic forces rising in Prussia. In 1874, he was called to a professorship at Zurich and, with cratefuls of paraphernalia, he embarked for Switzerland. Barely had he unpacked when a call came from Leipzig offering a more distinguished professorship there at Germany's largest university. He never looked back. Leipzig for the remainder of his life (1875–1920) provided the energy that drove the great Wundt of history, the Wundt that scholars to this day struggle to interpret, to unravel, to vilify, or to justify.

Those years at Leipzig were the golden years of the university as well as of the German university professorship. Wundt granted more doctorates in psychology than were given at any other institution. Students flocked there because of his fame in establishing psychology as a new discipline. They came because of his popularity as a lecturer—the rare professor who always spoke without using notes. They came because of his innovative use of apparatus for demonstrations while lecturing. And some came because of his sense of humor that thrilled or agitated young ears with its sarcastic tone that left few academic luminaries unscathed.

Leipzig was infused with Wundt's presence. He was everywhere in its life, even serving a term as university *Rektor*. In the 1880s, he became curator of a mathematical institute, which explains why he sponsored a number of doctorates in theoretical mathematics during that decade. It explains the advanced level of mathematics found in his handbook of psychology, *Grundzüge der physiologischen Psychologie* [Characteristics of physiological psychology], (1873–1874, 1911). He also arrived at Leipzig teaching linguistics, then a rapidly growing discipline. A Wundtian school of linguistics with an international following was in full flower by the end of the century.

Problems of Historical Interpretation

Historians of psychology today often regard the accounts of Wundt written in the early twentieth century as flawed and discomfiting. But there should be little wonder that distortions arose in that earlier literature. Wundt's intellectual development faithfully followed his origins in German *idealism* and *romanticism*, and they led him along a path of opposition to Anglo American empiricism, associationism, and materialism, including manifestations of those philosophies in German-speaking areas. Wundt faced a looming opposition in the early twentieth century. The rise of behaviorism and other empiricist trends was antithetical to his psychology. On his horizon there was a series of contentious intellectual revolutions forever descending (Machian positivism, behaviorism, psychoanalysis, Gestalt psychology), each struggling to distance its adherents from psychology's past, in which Wundt was prominent.

Another obstacle was translation, particularly into English, of German philosophical and psychological terms and the cultural contexts of those terms. Within the uncompromising polemical movements there was soon little care for any sympathetic study of Wundt's demanding writings. The painfully poor translation into English of his textbook *Outlines of Psychology* (1907) did nothing to help. Furthermore, in his twilight years Wundt became a vocal German patriot with respect to World War I and published inflammatory allegations of flaws in English and American culture. Among later generations of psychologists in English- and also in Russian-speaking areas, Wundt was the symbol of a tyrannical father figure who had to be displaced.

Then, finally, the catastrophe of the Nazis and the horrors of the world wars merged in many Anglo-American academic minds with fanciful images of Wundtian psychology. All this meant that the field of historical scholarship was ripe for the distortion, neglect, and emotional avoidance of Wundtian psychology. Research on Wundt became the quintessential taboo for the psychology student (see Brock's sad account, 1992). And so the unexamined Wundtian corpus lay fallow for years. As a result, it is a fertile field for historical study today.

Wundt's Psychology

The scientific investigation of *consciousness* was the great and final subject. Wundt found a scientific approach to consciousness through his *actuality principle*, the assertion that consciousness is *activity*, rather than *substance*. In this he saw the avoidance of Cartesian mind-body dualism.

Historical texts often portray early modern psychology as a disciplinary separation from philosophy. For Wundt, the new psychology constituted a separation from physiology or from substance-based approaches to the study of mind. The title of his influential work (*Grundzüge der physiologischen Psychologie*) misled some later historians because of the adjective *physiologischen* (physiological). That word had, in mid-nineteenth century Germany, enjoyed a brief vogue in which it indicated merely the experimental treatment of a subject matter, not a reduction to physiology. The early successes of experimental *physiology* had inspired that parochial usage.

Central to Wundt's notion of consciousness is the operation of volition, or self-control. Volition, he claims, originates in the process of selective focal attention, a process that is constructive, or that has the power of *creative synthesis*, to use his preferred term. That term indicates that attentional focusings bring forth products beyond the sum of any sensory elements. A romanticist aspect of this mental activity is found in Wundt's description of the power of emotionally based urges and impulses said to underlie all mental activity.

The Early Background

Psychological themes have a nearly sacred place in German philosophy and culture. In mid-nineteenth century Germany, the spreading new thought on mental processes resided in the works of Johann Herbart, whose philosophy of mind was no less than radically mechanistic—a system of mental elements and a dynamics of interaction among them, all described in an elaborate discursive mathematics. Herbart's approach permeated the social sciences. Wundt's entire academic life, including his work in linguistics, philosophy, cultural studies, and ethics, sprang from his rejection of the foundations of the Herbartian edifice.

A first spark in that opposition was Wundt's earliest experimental investigations, delicate reaction-time measures taken in milliseconds that gave him the hard evidence, he felt, that the Herbartians could not overcome. He had measured the processes of focal attention (then named by the archaic term *apperception* from German philosophy). The lack of a motivationally guided volitional process was, in Wundt's view, the fatal flaw in all Herbartian mechanistic conceptions of mental and social processes. Further, in the Herbartian model of mental mechanics emotion is conceived as a disruption or disturbance of the machinery—a side effect of the mechanical processes. Going against Herbart, Wundt found emotion to be primary in timing and causation for all mental processes. As he wrote in his *Grundzüge* (1880, 2nd ed.), "desire or urges are the fundamental psychological phenomena from which all mental processes originate" (Vol. 2, p. 455).

The Voluntarist School

Throughout his study of volitional processes Wundt distinguishes between *controlled* actions and *automatized* actions, and he examines how self-control passes from one of those states to the other. Eventually those questions led him into writings on the psychology of ethics. And because of those interests, his school of thought was known in Europe as the *voluntarist school of psychology*, a title that failed to transfer to American textbooks owing partly to the Oxford-educated English psychologist Edward Titchener, who named his Cornell school of psychology *structuralism*. Titchener's disciples mistakenly assumed that Titchener's school represented Wundt's psychology. Titchener had spent 2 years at Leipzig for his doctorate. But he had spent his time there under the tutelage of Oswald Külpe, who had trained primarily with the Herbartian G. E. Müller at Prussia's Goettingen University, a background that had Külpe and other Müller students at odds with Wundt. A former Prussian army officer, Müller was much more representative of the minds who were to dominate American psychology a generation later. We find in his style and personality the tough-minded approach characteristic of the later Clark Hull and S. S. Stevens.

Wundt never used Titchener's term *structuralism* to describe his own school of thought, and he wrote polemically against Titchener's teaching of a particular introspectionist research technique derived from British philosophy. Yet Wundt was mistranslated as advocating that same school of introspectionism. As D. K. Robinson revealed (1987), Wundt blocked the admission of Titchener to the editorial boards of research journals.

The follower with whom Wundt maintained the longest intellectual association was Emil Kraepelin, judging by the quantity and duration of their correspondence. A founding father of modern psychiatry, Kraepelin's attentional theory of schizophrenia is an application of Wundtian psychology, an explanation of the abnormality in terms of the attention-deployment process.

Constructivism

Describing his own intellectual emergence in a position paper on *psychological causality* in 1894, Wundt writes that he first approached psychological problems with a prejudice natural to physiologists, namely that perception is merely the mechanics of sense organs. Wundt's early interest in perception drove him steadily away from that view and toward the central *creative synthesis*. He preached against the sharp distinction usually made between perceptions, memories, thoughts, or other mental representations, claiming them to be variations of one central process. He counseled against concepts of reproduced memories or actions, reasoning that the past is never exactly reduplicated, that memory is not merely a retrieval of stored items; it is a reconstruction of experiences. In consequence, he found the classical associationist psychology untenable. All mental phenomena, he said, are transient and fleeting as feelings or acts of will. In giving up the stable connections of associations, Wundt offered context-dependent relational processes and a system of rudimentary feelings or affective colorings that direct the stream of consciousness.

At the conclusion of his later theoretical summations, Wundt spelled out a system of interlocking principles that describe the stream of consciousness as well as longer spans of mental development. Those principles are all subdivisions and expansions of his first principle of creative synthesis.

Cultural Psychology and Emotion Studies

Another encyclopedic body of work is Wundt's cultural psychology. Little of it was translated for the English-speaking world, and it remained mostly unknown there. It stemmed from his conception that the study of cultural systems and products gives insight into the functioning of higher mental processes. The one cultural system that was by far his most successful topic was *language*. In the first part of his 10-volume work on cultural psychology (*Voelkerpsychologie*, 1900–1920), you read of linguistics, language acquisition, language and thought, and comparative language studies, chapters that triggered a productive, if brief, period of psycholinguistic (or *sprachpsychologische*) research at the beginning of the twentieth century. Wundt's approach emphasized the syntactic structure of sentences and the mental processes that determined that structure.

Research on emotion grew apace. It connected with the language studies in that the evolutionary beginnings of languages and language development in the infant were seen as originating in emotional gestures. Much of the work on emotion was fundamentally a multidimensional scaling of variations in emotion qualities, with the outcome showing three prominent dimensions: arousal, pleasure-pain, and self-control. In later work, emotion studies took the appearance of an aesthetics of perception, memory, thought, and other processes, invoking notions of harmonious or dissonant feelings, of rhythmical qualities in mental processes, of tensions, and of relaxations.

The Rise and Fall of Wundtian Psychology

The first mention of Wundt's experimental psychology in a Leipzig catalogue occurred in 1879. As his fame in psychology grew, the university enlarged his psychological research institute, with the final lavish expansion coming just when the first shots of World War I were fired. The then world-famous Leipzig Psychological Institute was a multistoried affair with separate departments covering subdisciplines of psychology. It was being replicated, or its activities imitated, from Calcutta to Tokyo, but the once numerous American students had by then disappeared owing to the growth of American graduate schools and the changes in the definitions of psychology there.

The Leipzig Psychological Institute was depopulated by the World War I and was ravaged by the economic chaos that followed. It was further ravaged at the hands of Nazi leaders in the 1930s. It was destroyed by a joint Anglo-American bombing raid on the night of 4 December 1943. Most of Wundt's private library survives today at Tohoku University in Japan.

[*Many of the people mentioned in this article are the subjects of independent biographical entries.*]

Bibliography

Blumenthal, A. L. (1970). *Language and psychology: Historical aspects of psycholinguistics*. New York: Wiley. A summary with translations and excerpts from turn-of-the-century Wundtian psycholinguistics.

Blumenthal, A. L. (1985). Wilhelm Wundt: Psychology as the propaedeutic science. In C. Buxton (Ed.), *Points of view in the modern history of psychology* (pp. 11–50). Orlando, FL: Academic Press.

Blumenthal, A. L. (1998). Leipzig, Wundt, and psychology's gilded age. In G. Kimble & M. Wertheimer (Eds.), *Portraits of pioneers in psychology* (pp. 31–48). Hillsdale, NJ: Erlbaum. A brief description of the social and physical surroundings of Wundt's life in Leipzig.

Bringmann, W. G. & Tweney, R. D. (1980). *Wundt studies.* Toronto: Hogrefe. A broad collection of studies by Wundt scholars and commentators.

Brock, A. (1992). Was Wundt a "Nazi"? Voelkerpsychologie, racism and anti-Semitism. *Theory and Psychology, 2*, 205–223.

Danziger, K. (1980). Wundt's theory of behavior and volition. In R. Rieber (Ed.), *Wilhelm Wundt and the making of a scientific psychology* (pp. 81–115). New York: Plenum Press.

Kusch, M. (1995). *Psychologism: A case study in the sociology of philosophical knowledge.* London: Routledge. At this time, the most thorough study of controversies involving Wundt that arose at the turn of the century regarding psychologistic explanations and the opposing positivistic and physicalistic philosophie.

Metge, A. (1983). The experimental research conducted at Wundt's institute and its significance in the history of psychology. In G. Ekardt & L. Sprung (Eds.), *Advances in historiography of psychology*. Berlin: Deutscher Verlag der Wissenschaften.

Petersen, P. (1927). *Wilhelm Wundt und seine Zeit* [Wilhelm Wundt and his times]. Stuttgart, Germany: Fromanns.

Robinson, D. K. (1987). *Wilhelm Wundt and the establishment of experimental psychology, 1875–1914: The context of a new field of scientific research.* Unpublished doctoral dissertation, University of California, Berkeley, CA. The most detailed study by far of Wundt's institutionalization of psychology and of his relations with academic colleagues.

Wundt, W. (1880–74). *Grundzüge der physiologischen Psychologie* [Characteristics of physiological psychology] (2nd ed.). Leipzig: Englemann. (Original work published 1873–1874)

Wundt, W. (1894). Ueber psychische Causalität und das Prinzip des psycho-physichen Parallelismus [On psychic causality and the principle of psychophysical parallelism]. *Philosophische Studien, 10*, 1–124. Many of the best written and most readable statements in German of Wundt's basic views are found in this journal of his many position papers on theory and method. It was published between 1881 and 1903.

Wundt, W. (1987). *Ethics* (2nd ed., E. Titchener, M. Gulliver, & M. Washburn, Trans.). New York: Macmillan.

Wundt, W. (1900–1920). *Voelkerpsychologie: Eine Untersuchung der Entwicklungsgezetze von Sprache, Mythus, und Sitte* [Cultural psychology: An analysis of the development of language, myth, and custom] (Vols. 1–10). Leipzig: Englemann.

Arthur L. Blumenthal

X

XENOPHOBIA refers to the fear of foreign things, usually people, but by extension, cultural artifacts. The term is derived from the Greek word χηνός (stranger or guest) and Φοβοζ (aversion). The term has a direct equivalent in many languages, such as the Japanese word *hitomishiri*, suggesting that the fear of strangers is a universal characteristic of early childhood. In contemporary usage, xenophobia is an attitude complex with cognitive, motivational, and behavioral properties that is applied to groups of outsiders, such as immigrants, members of other races, ethnic groups, and countries. Berger (1979) has argued that people from such groups of strangers induce both uncertainty and anxiety because their behavior is more difficult to predict.

The cognitive component of xenophobia may be found in the negative stereotypes about the character, beliefs, values, and behaviors ascribed to outsiders belonging to different groups. Attributions made for their behaviors will evidence out-group derogation by the ascription of positive behaviors to external factors like social pressure and negative behaviors to internal traits like meanness. Expectations for the likely behaviors of these outsiders are that they will actively promote their group interests at the expense of others. A protective response may be to promote beliefs about the natural superiority of one's group over others, a constellation Sidanius (1993) calls the "social dominance orientation." Staub (1989) refers to all these cognitive representations of out-groups as "ideologies of antagonism" because they promote and sustain intergroup conflict.

Such feelings may lead to forms of withdrawal or of attack. Motivationally, xenophobia is experienced as an anxiety or anger associated with foreigners or symbols of their group, like language, dress, religion, and so forth.

Behaviorally, xenophobic thoughts and feelings may result in dissociative behaviors like avoidance, gossip, and physical abuse directed toward outsiders and their property. At the group level, these tendencies may be evidenced by the phenomena of segregation, systematic discrimination, and genocide. Individual personality dynamics, social support, and cultural norms supporting violence (Cohen, 1996) will influence the strength of hostility expressed toward the out-group and its members.

Personality measures of ethnocentrism, such as right wing authoritarianism (RWA), are often used to assess xenophobia (Altemeyer, 1981). The connection between believing out-group members are opposed to one's group traditions and discrimination toward these out-group members is strengthened by RWA, for example. It is also associated with a social dominance orientation in intergroup relations.

However, appreciation of one's own group, as in patriotism, is distinguishable from aversion to outsiders, as in nationalism (Feshback, 1987). Intergroup integration appears to require both appreciation of one's own group and positive attitudes toward other groups, as Berry (1997) has shown. This readiness for out-group contact is found in persons high in openness to experience and in those who believe that the out-group members hold similar values to one's own. Economic prosperity, an immigrant tradition, and multicultural policies reinforced by law help sustain these individual attitudes, undercutting xenophobia.

Bibliography

Altemeyer, R. A. (1981). *Right wing authoritarianism*. Minneapolis: University of Minnesota Press. Carefully evaluates previous instruments for measuring ethnocentrism and develops a psychometrically defensible and valid alternative.

Brewer, M., & Campbell, D. T. (1976). *Ethnocentrism and inter-group attitudes: East African evidence.* New York: Halsted/Wiley. Elaborates the concept of ethnocentrism and documents its pervasiveness in many tribal groups.

Smith, M. B. (1992). Nationalism, ethnocentrism, and the new world order. *Journal of Humanistic Psychology, 32,* 76–91. Examines the psychology of ethnocentrism from an evolutionary perspective, distinguishing its positive from its negative features.

Michael Harris Bond

Y

YERKES, ROBERT MEARNS (1876–1956), American psychobiologist. Robert Yerkes was among the leading movers and shakers of American psychology in the twentieth century. He was deeply involved in the administration and development of many aspects of psychology as it evolved during this period. Although he may be best known for his work in intelligence testing with the U.S. Army during World War I, his primary accomplishment was the conceptualization and founding of a primate research station, later named the Yerkes Laboratories of Primate Biology, that became the leading facility in the world for research on the great apes.

Robert Yerkes was born on a farm in Bucks County, near Philadelphia, Pennsylvania. Familiarity with and love of animals came very early in this setting. Yerkes later wrote lovingly of his mother but felt that he and his father had little in common and were never close. Older than any of his siblings, the young Robert Yerkes spent much time alone and was basically a shy man his whole life. Early admiration for his family physician led Yerkes to point toward a career in medicine. He attended the State Normal School at West Chester and, with the support of an uncle, Ursinus College, graduating in 1897. That fall, he entered Harvard University, but needed to complete a second bachelor's degree to demonstrate adequate preparation for graduate study.

Yerkes decided to forgo medical training but was torn between zoology and psychology. When Josiah Royce suggested study in comparative psychology under Hugo Münsterberg, Yerkes chose that path and completed his doctoral degree in 1902 under the influence of Münsterberg, G. H. Parker, C. B. Davenport, W. E. Castle, and others. He then stayed on at Harvard with an instructorship in comparative psychology until World War I. In 1905, he married Ada Watterson; the couple had two children, David and Roberta. [*See the biographies of Münsterberg and Royce.*]

In addition to his teaching responsibilities, Yerkes conducted a wide range of research projects during this early period. These dealt generally with sensory function, habit formation, and problem solving. Among his subjects were the behavior of fiddler crabs, learning in turtles, the nervous systems of various invertebrate species, sensory function in frogs, and mouse killing by kittens. Among the apparatus developed during this period was an instrument for testing vision in animals, developed with John B. Watson, and the multiple-choice apparatus for testing animal intelligence. Yerkes published a textbook, *Introduction to Psychology* (1911), and a comprehensive book on the characteristics and behavior of mutant house mice, *The Dancing Mouse* (1907). [*See the biography of Watson.*]

Although Yerkes's career brought him a national reputation, work in comparative psychology was not greatly valued by the Harvard administration and he was advised to do more applied work. Yerkes largely resisted this advice, though he did begin five years of work at the Boston Psychopathic Hospital with Ernest E. Southard. There he developed a point-scale method of measuring intelligence.

In 1917 Yerkes accepted an appointment to the faculty of the University of Minnesota, a position he would never fill. When the United States entered World War I, Yerkes, as president of the American Psychological Association, initiated efforts to aid in the war effort. The primary result was the development and use by a group of psychometricians under Yerkes's leadership of the army alpha and beta intelligence tests; these were given to 1.75 million recruits and helped establish psychology as an important discipline.

At the end of the war Yerkes remained in Washington serving in various capacities under the aegis of the National Research Council of the National Academy of Sciences. He chaired its Division of Research Information, Committee for Research in Problems of Sex, and Committee on Scientific Problems of Human Migration.

Beginning as a graduate student, Yerkes developed an interest in research on great apes and dreamed of establishing a facility for such study. Throughout this whole period at Harvard and in Washington Yerkes took steps to advance this possibility, purchasing a New Hampshire farm where he could study chimpanzees, spending a sabbatical in Montecito, California where he could study primates, purchasing four chimpanzees with personal funds, and conducting research on captive animals in Cuba. Together with James Rowland Angell, president of Yale University, Yerkes developed a plan for an Institute of Psychology and Yerkes moved to Yale in 1924. The next year Yerkes obtained funding for a primate facility in New Haven and in 1929 the Rockefeller Foundation provided funding for a primate field station.

The Yale Laboratories of Primate Biology, later the Yerkes Laboratories, opened in Orange Park, Florida in 1930 and became a world-class facility. Perhaps the most notable accomplishment was the very demonstration that chimpanzees could be bred, maintained, and studied in such a facility. Yerkes had to develop methods as he went along. His own research dealt primarily with learning and intelligence, social behavior, and sexual behavior in chimpanzees. Yerkes was responsible for getting H. C. Bingham, Henry Nissen, and C. R. Carpenter to initiate pioneering field studies of primate behavior, thus beginning a field that has been most fertile.

Yerkes retired from Yale in 1944 but remained active in aiding the World War II mobilization effort, helping in restructuring the American Psychological Association, and writing his autobiography.

Yerkes' primate work produced several books, including *Almost Human* (1925), *Chimpanzee Intelligence and Its Vocal Expressions* (Yerkes & Learned, 1925), *The Great Apes* (Yerkes & Yerkes, 1929), and *Chimpanzees: A Laboratory Colony* (1943). In addition, he published many research articles. Many important psychologists worked as his students or associates at Yale and Orange Park.

Robert Yerkes was a member of the National Academy of Sciences and of the American Philosophical Society and was a fellow of the American Academy of Arts and Letters. He was elected president of the American Psychological Association in 1916 and of the American Society of Naturalists in 1938. Yerkes received honorary degrees from Ursinus College and Wesleyan University and was awarded the Gold Medal of the New York Zoological Society. Russian scientists placed a bust of Yerkes in the Darwinian Museum in Moscow.

Bibliography

Works by Yerkes

Yerkes, R. M. (1907). *The dancing mouse: A study in animal behavior.* New York: Macmillan.

Yerkes, R. M. (1925). *Almost human.* New York: Century.

Yerkes, R. M. (1943). *Chimpanzees: A laboratory colony.* New Haven, CT: Yale University Press.

Yerkes, R. M., & Learned, B. W. (1925). *Chimpanzee intelligence and its vocal expressions.* Baltimore: Williams & Wilkins.

Yerkes, R. M., & Yerkes, A. W. (1929). *The great apes: A study of anthropoid life.* New Haven, CT: Yale University Press.

Articles about Yerkes

Boring, E. G. (1956). Robert Mearns Yerkes (1876–1956). In *Year book of the American Philosophical Society* (pp. 133–140). Philadelphia, PA: American Philosophical Society.

Dewsbury, D. A. (1998). Robert M. Yerkes: A psychobiologist with a plan. In G. A. Kimble, C. A. Boneau, & M. Wertheimer (Eds.), *Portraits of pioneers in psychology* (Vol. 2, pp. 87–105). Washington, DC: American Psychological Association.

Elliott, R. M. (1956). Robert Mearns Yerkes, 1876–1956. *American Journal of Psychology, 69,* 487–494.

Hilgard, E. R. (1965). Robert Mearns Yerkes, May 26, 1876–February 3, 1956. In *Biographical memoirs of the National Academy of Sciences of the United States of America* (Vol. 38, pp. 385–425). New York: Columbia University Press.

Yerkes, R. M. (1930). Robert Mearns Yerkes, psychobiologist. In C. Murchison (Ed.), *A history of psychology in autobiography* (Vol. 2, pp. 381–407). Worcester, MA: Clark University Press.

Yerkes, R. M. (1950). *The scientific way.* Unpublished manuscript, Robert M. Yerkes Papers, Manuscripts and Archives, Yale University Library, New Haven, CT.

Donald A. Dewsbury

YOUNG, PAUL THOMAS (1892–1978), American psychologist. Young holds a secure place in the development of our understanding of the role of hedonic processes in motivation, emotion, and action. After receiving his doctorate in 1918 under Edward B. Titchener at Cornell University, he spent most of his career at the University of Illinois until retirement in 1960, with significant sabbatical study in Berlin, Germany, with Wolfgang Köhler, Kurt Lewin, and Max Wertheimer in 1926. In his three books going through several editions, and in his voluminously reported research, Young's approach drew on three traditions. These were Titchenerian and Gestalt introspectionism in his use of phenomenological reports of pleasantness-unpleasantness, the dominant behaviorism of the era in his analyses of food preferences in the rat, and a growing neuropsychology, in particular James Olds and Peter Milner's electrical stimulation of "pleasure centers" (*Journal of Comparative and Physiological Psychology*, 1954, 47, 419–427) and Donald Lindsley's examination of the reticular activation system (S. S. Stevens, Ed., *Handbook of Experimental Psychology*, New York, 1951).

In his work on hedonic theory, Young's aim was to understand affective arousal and its place in the organization of factors controlling action. On the basis of introspective reports, pleasantness–unpleasantness was viewed as a dimension of conscious experience; and for stimuli such as odors, the dimension was shown to correlate strongly across age levels. Both his human and animal studies showed strong lawfulness of preferences. For example, determination of isohedons for stimulus mixtures of different affective polarities led to the principle that positive and negative affects combine algebraically. Young viewed findings such as these as showing that affect could be studied objectively. At the neurophysiological level, positive and negative affects were viewed as incompatible and governed by a principle of reciprocal innervation, while affective activation was thought to give direction to general arousal. Furthermore, his hedonic theory proposed that motivation followed from nonspecific arousal together with specific direction reflecting memory of past affective experiences, as integrated by higher level cognitive control. In this way, Young emphasized the distinction between affect and cognition. He also maintained that emotion reflects cognitive appraisals, producing a temporary breakdown in that organization and leading to reorganization, and that learning occurs by contiguity, not drive reduction—but what is learned and how it is used are guided by affective activation. Furthermore, learning could to some degree modify affective evaluations leading to social values.

With his development of the "pseudophone," a device for reversing input to the ears, Young (1928) reported his classical work on auditory localization, including the surprising finding that front-back reversals accompanied the expected left-right reversals.

It is commonly said that much of Young's hedonic theory has been assimilated into our general view of the roles of affect but that the behavioristic atmosphere limited the influence of his work at the time. During his lifetime, Young saw confirmation of his approach, especially in the Olds-Milner work on "pleasure centers" and in the work of Charles Osgood and collaborators on the affective dimensions of meaning (*The Measurement of Meaning*, Champaign, Ill., 1957).

[*Many of the people mentioned in this article are the subjects of independent biographical entries.*]

Bibliography

O'Kelly, L. I. (1979). Paul Thomas Young: 1892–1978. *American Journal of Psychology, 92*, 551–553. This obituary contains several quotations from Young in which he sums up his work and assesses its contribution.

Young, P. T. (1928). Auditory localization with acoustical transposition of the ears. *Journal of Experimental Psychology, 32*, 399–429. The original report of Young's classical work with the "pseudophone," work begun during his sabbatical year in Berlin in 1926.

Young, P. T. (1961). *Motivation and emotion: A survey of the determinants of human and animal activity*. New York: Wiley. This book systematically presents Young's hedonic view and applies it to general questions about motivation and emotion.

Young, P. T. (1965). Distinguished Scientific Contributions Awards (Personal statement). *American Psychologist, 2*, 1085–1088. In acknowledging his award from the American Psychological Association, Young's personal statement contains the fullest available chronicle of his education and academic career.

Young, P. T. (1973). *Emotion in man and animal: Its nature and dynamic basis* (2nd rev. ed.). New York: Wiley. His last book, revised and published several years after his formal retirement.

Donelson E. Dulany

Z

ZHANG, YAO-XIANG (1893–1964), Chinese psychologist. One of the founders of modern Chinese psychology, Yao-xiang Zhang was born 23 February 1893 in Hankou, Hubei Province, China, and died 9 July 1964 in Shanghai. Zhang was one of the first Chinese students who studied psychology abroad and returned to develop psychology in his own country. After graduating from Qing Hua College in Beijing in 1915, he went to the United States in the same year and studied at Columbia University, receiving his B.A. degree in 1918 and his M.A. degree in 1919. Zhang returned to China in 1920 and was appointed professor and director of the Department of Education, Beijing Normal College, where he established one of the earliest psychological laboratories in China. In 1921 he founded the Chinese Psychological Society and became its first president. In 1922 he published the first Chinese psychology journal, *Psychology*, and became its first editor. However, this journal ended after publication of 14 issues, which contained a total of more than 150 articles; among these he himself wrote 29 articles and made annotations of all psychological articles published in China at that time. He strongly advocated experimental and scientific study in psychology. Though short-lived, this journal had a great impact on the subsequent development of psychology in China.

Yao-xiang Zhang was one of the pioneers in using psychological tests in China. As early as 1922 he conducted a public opinion study by distributing questionnaires to about 1,000 participants; this marked the beginning of the use of psychological measurement in China. After 1928 Zhang moved to Shanghai and was professor and dean of the School of Arts at Jinan University, as well as professor at Hujiang, Fudan, and other universities. In 1930 he joined the Commercial Press, a famous publisher in China, and edited the *Dictionary of Education*.

Yao-xiang Zhang was not only a leader in modern Chinese psychology, he was also active in the political scene in the early days of the Republic of China. In 1923, together with famous scholar activists Li Dazhao, Liang Qichao, and others, he founded the Nonreligious Union, which advocated science and opposed superstition. This organization attracted many young intellectuals in the movement against feudalism, which was important for China's social progress.

After the founding of the People's Republic of China in 1949, Yao-xiang Zhang became head of the Department of Education at East China Normal University in Shanghai and research professor at the Institute of Psychology, Chinese Academy of Sciences. He showed wide interest in many fields of psychology, published extensively in general psychology, child and adolescent psychology, educational psychology, social psychology, and psychological testing, and also collected data on the ancient history of Chinese psychology. In addition to approximately 90 published papers, his major works include: *Brief History of the Development of Chinese Psychology* (1940), *Sensory Psychology* (1947), *Psychology of Emotions* (1947), *Language and Thinking of Children* (1948).

Qicheng Jing

ZUBIN, JOSEPH (1900–1990), American psychologist. Zubin received his bachelor's degree in chemistry from Johns Hopkins University (1921) and his doctorate degree in educational psychology from Columbia University (1932). His primary academic affiliations were Columbia University (1930–1990) and the University of Pittsburgh (1977–1990). Zubin made significant contributions to experimental psychopathology and to conceptualizations of the etiology of schizophrenia.

Joseph Zubin played a key leadership role in the

adoption of quantitative methods by the field of psychopathology. At the time of his presidential address to the American Psychopathological Association in 1954, qualitative or descriptive approaches were the principal methods used in clinical psychology and psychiatry research. In that 1954 presidential address, Zubin argued that for scientific progress in psychopathology to occur, "the models around which the concepts and facts of psychopathology are to be fitted must eventually be of the quantitative variety, rather than of the impressionistic variety which is encountered so often in the clinical field" (Zubin, 1954, p. 123). The emphasis that he placed on quantitative methods was a logical outgrowth of his early work (1930s to 1940s), which was devoted primarily to statistical techniques and research designs applicable to psychological investigations. Throughout the 1950s and 1960s, Zubin consistently challenged psychopathologists to adopt a biometrics approach, which he defined as "the science which applies measurement to the structures and functions of living organisms" (Zubin, 1954, p. 123). With his empirical work, Zubin provided a model of how a biometrics of psychopathology was to be achieved. Over the six decades of his prolific career, Zubin's collaborations with scientists from diverse disciplines resulted in studies of a wide range of psychological issues, such as functions of the human frontal lobe (Columbia-Greystone Topectomy Studies organized in 1946); effects of electroconvulsive and drug (insulin, antihistamine, metrazol, dexedrine, phenobarbital) treatments on psychological functions (motor responding, perception, attention, memory, concept formation) (1940s); quantitative methods applied to projective (Rorschach) techniques (1940s to 1950s); information processing in general and clinical populations (1960s to 1980s), which included the discovery, with Samuel Sutton and colleagues, of the P300 component of the event-related brain potential (Sutton, Braren, Zubin, & John, 1965).

Consideration of the combined effects of genes and environment in determining psychological outcomes consistently appeared in Zubin's theoretical formulations of mental disorder. As early as 1938, he proposed that a class of variables may exist that "depend on social as well as biological forces" (Zubin, 1938, p. 240). Over the next four decades, efforts to systematize the findings about psychopathology from diverse areas of investigation (ecology, learning and development, genetics, internal environment, and brain function) eventually led Zubin and his colleagues to formulate the vulnerability model of schizophrenia. Similar to previous diathesis-stress theories, the primary assumption of the vulnerability model was that all individuals are "endowed with a degree of vulnerability that under suitable circumstances will express itself in an episode of schizophrenic illness" (Zubin & Spring, 1977, p. 109). Vulnerability was conceived as an enduring trait, as well as an empirical probability that an individual will experience an episode of mental disorder. In addition, three novel aspects were included in vulnerability theory. First, numerous contributions to an individual's degree of vulnerability were assumed to exist, ranging from genetic to acquired characteristics. Second, measurement of vulnerability was identified as a crucial and feasible goal. Third, a distinction was made between vulnerability to schizophrenia and episodes of schizophrenic disorder. Thus, the vulnerability model was conceived as a second-order or superordinate model that integrates the contributions from a range of influences, and provides for their interaction (Zubin & Steinhauer, 1981). A classification scheme was additionally developed for distinguishing indicators or markers of vulnerability from markers of episodes of disorder (Zubin & Steinhauer, 1981). At the close of the twentieth century, psychopathologists are engaged in empirical efforts to determine the presence of putative markers in schizophrenic patients and in individuals who vary in degree of genetic relationship to a schizophrenic individual. Consistent with the aims of Zubin and his colleagues, the ultimate goal of such efforts is to provide a strong empirical foundation that will inform future theories of etiology.

Bibliography

Sutton, S., Braren, M., Zubin, J., & John, E. R. (1965). Evoked-potential correlates of stimulus uncertainty. *Science, 150*, 1187–1188.

Zubin, J. (1938). Socio-biological types and methods for their isolation. *Psychiatry, 1*, 237–247.

Zubin, J. (1954). Presidential address—biometrics methods in psychopathology. In P. H. Hoch & J. Zubin (Eds.), *Depression* (pp. 123–143). New York: Grune & Stratton.

Zubin, J., & Spring, B. (1977). Vulnerability—a new view of schizophrenia. *Journal of Abnormal Psychology, 86*, 103–126.

Zubin, J., & Steinhauer, S. R. (1981). How to break the logjam in schizophrenia: A look beyond genetics. *Journal of Nervous and Mental Disease, 169*, 477–492.

Ruth Condray

DIRECTORY OF CONTRIBUTORS

DIRECTORY OF CONTRIBUTORS

Achenbach, Thomas M.
Professor of Psychiatry and Psychology, and Director of the Center for Children, Youth, and Families, University of Vermont, Burlington
Child Behavior Checklist

Achenbaum, W. Andrew
Professor of History, and Dean of the College of Humanities, Fine Arts, and Communication, University of Houston, Texas
Gerontology

Ackerman, Phillip L.
Professor of Psychology, Georgia Institute of Technology, Atlanta
Aptitude Tests

Adair, John G.
Professor Emeritus of Psychology, University of Manitoba, Winnipeg, Canada
Hawthorne Effect

Adams, Henry E.
Research Professor of Psychology, University of Georgia, Athens
Behavior Therapy; Voyeurism; Wolpe, Joseph

Aditya, Ram N.
Assistant Professor and Coordinator, I/O Psychology Program, Louisiana Tech University, Ruston
Artifact, *article on* Artifact in Research

Adler, Helmut E.
Professor Emeritus of Psychology, Yeshiva University, Jamaica, New York
Messer, August

Adler, Leonore Loeb
Professor Emerita of Psychology, and Director of the Institute of Cross-Cultural and Cross-Ethnic Studies, Molloy College, Jamaica, New York
Morgan, Conwy Lloyd

Agras, W. Stewart
Professor of Psychiatry, Stanford University, California
Anorexia; Eating Disorders

Agresti, Alan
Professor of Statistics, University of Florida, Gainesville
Analysis of Counts

Aiken, Leona S.
Professor of Psychology, Arizona State University, Tempe
Multiple Regression

Ajzen, Icek
Professor of Psychology, University of Massachusetts, Amherst
Theory of Reasoned Action

Albano, Anne Marie
Assistant Professor of Psychiatry, Child Study Center, New York University School of Medicine, New York
Intervention

Albrecht, Duane G.
Professor of Psychology, University of Texas at Austin
Spatial Vision

Alford, Geary S.
Professor and Director of the Division of Psychology, Department of Psychiatry and Human Behavior, University of Mississippi Medical Center, Jackson
Psychosis

Alhamad, Abdulrazzak M.
Associate Professor of Psychiatry, King Saud University, Riyadh, Saudi Arabia
Arab States, *article on* Saudi Arabia and Kuwait

Allaire, Jason C.
Predoctoral Trainee, Institute of Gerontology and Department of Psychology, Wayne State University, Detroit, Michigan
Terminal Decline

Allan, Lorraine
Professor of Psychology, McMaster University, Hamilton, Ontario, Canada
Time Perception

Altman, Irwin
Distinguished Professor of Psychology, University of Utah, Salt Lake City
Privacy; Territoriality

Amsel, Abram
Ashbel Smith Professor Emeritus of Psychology and Neuroscience, University of Texas at Austin
Spence, Kenneth Wartinbee

Andersen, Barbara L.
Professor of Psychology, The Ohio State University, Columbus
Cancer

Anderson, Barton L.
Assistant Professor of Brain and Cognitive Sciences, Massachusetts Institute of Technology, Cambridge
Depth Perception

Anderson, Craig A.
Professor of Psychology, and Chair of the Department of Psychology, Iowa State University, Ames
Violence and Aggression

Anderson, David E.
Chief of the Section on Behavioral Hypertension, National Institute on Aging, Baltimore, Maryland
Hypertension

Antoni, Michael H.
Professor of Psychology, University of Miami, Coral Gables, Florida
Psychoneuroimmunology

Antonucci, Toni C.
Professor of Psychology, The University of Michigan, Ann Arbor
Adulthood and Aging, *article on* Social Processes and Development

Antrobus, John S.
Professor of Psychology, City College of the City University of New York
Dreams, *article on* Theories and Research

Appelbaum, Paul S.
A. F. Zeleznik Professor and Chair, Department of Psychiatry, University of Massachusetts Medical School, Worcester
Voluntary and Involuntary Hospitalization

Apter, Michael J.
Visiting Researcher in Psychology, Georgetown University, Washington, D.C.
Reversal Theory

Aragón, Ángela Pattatucci
Health Scientist Administrator, National Institutes of Health, Division of Clinical and Population-Based Studies, AIDS and Related Research, Bethesda, Maryland
Bisexuality

Archer, Sally L.
Professor of Psychology, The College of New Jersey, Ewing
Intimacy

Ardila, Rubén
Research Professor of Psychology, National University of Colombia, Bogotá
Bolivia; Colombia; Ecuador; Ingenieros, Jose; Mouchet, Enrique; Peru

Arian, Gretchen
Consumer Research Analyst, University of Illinois at Chicago
Instructional Theories

Ariel, Mira
Department of Linguistics, Tel Aviv University, Israel
Pragmatics

Aries, Elizabeth
Professor of Psychology, Amherst College, Massachusetts
Sociolinguistics

Aron, Arthur
Department of Psychology, State University of New York at Stony Brook
Love, *article on* An Overview

Aronoff, Mark
Professor of Linguistics, State University of New York at Stony Brook
Morphology

Aronson, Elliot
Professor Emeritus of Psychology, University of California, Santa Cruz
Cognitive Dissonance

Asendorpf, Jens B.
Professor of Psychology, Humboldt-Universität Berlin, Germany
Personality Development, *article on* Middle Childhood and Adolescence

Aurelio, David N.
Manager of User Interface Design, Bose Corporation, Framingham, Massachusetts
Consumer Products Design

Austin, James T.
Research Specialist 2, The Ohio State University, Columbus
Industrial and Organizational Psychology, *article on* History of the Field

Baber, Ceola Ross
Associate Professor of Curriculum and Instruction, University of North Carolina at Greensboro
Multicultural Education

Baddeley, Alan
Professor of Psychology, University of Bristol, England
Working Memory

Baker, David B.
Director of the Archives of the History of American Psychology, and Associate Professor of Psychology, University of Akron, Ohio
Kiesow, Federico; Strong, Edward Kellogg, Jr.

Baker, Rodney R.
Chief of Psychology, South Texas Veterans Health Care System, San Antonio
United States Department of Veterans Affairs

Balota, David A.
Professor of Psychology, Washington University, Saint Louis, Missouri
Cognition; Cognitive Psychology, *article on* Theories; Cognitive Psychology, *article on* Research Methods; Cognitive Psychology, *article on* Research Methods

Baltes, Paul B.
Director of the Center for Life-Span Psychology, Max Planck Institute for Human Development; and Professor of Psychology, Free University of Berlin, Germany
Life Span Psychology Theory; Wisdom

Bandura, Albert
David Starr Jordan Professor of Social Science in Psychology, Stanford University, California
Self-Efficacy; Social-Cognitive Theory

Barberis, Daniela S.
Doctoral Candidate in Conceptual Foundations of Science, The University of Chicago, Illinois
Spencer, Herbert

Barbiero, Daniel
Archivist, The National Academies, Washington, D.C.
National Academy of Sciences

Bargh, John A.
Professor of Psychology, New York University, New York
Automaticity

Barling, Julian J.
Professor of Organizational Behavior and Psychology, School of Business, Queen's University, Kingston, Ontario, Canada
Unions

Barr, William B.
Assistant Professor of Neurobiology and Psychiatry, Neuropsychology Laboratory, Long Island Jewish Medical Center, New Hyde Park, New York
Epilepsy

Barratt, Barnaby B.
Professor of Family Medicine, Psychiatry and Behavioral Neuroscience, Wayne State University, Detroit, Michigan
Psychoanalysis, *article on* Psychoanalysis and Philosophy

Barrett, Gerald V.
Professor of Psychology, University of Akron, Ohio
Personnel Selection, *article on* Selection and the Law

Barsalou, Lawrence W.
Professor of Psychology, Emory University, Atlanta, Georgia
Concepts, *article on* Structure

Batchelder, William H.
Director of the Institute for Mathematical Behavioral Sciences, University of California, Irvine
Mathematical Psychology

Baum, Andrew
Deputy Director of the University of Pittsburgh Cancer Institute; Director of Behavioral Medicine and Oncology; and Professor of Psychiatry and Psychology, University of Pittsburgh, Pennsylvania
Genetic Disorders; Social Psychology, *article on* Applied Social Psychology; Stress, *article on* Impact on Health

Bear, George G.
Professor of School Psychology, School of Education, University of Delaware, Newark
School Suspension and Expulsion

Beasley, Daniel S.
Professor, and Special Assistant to the Dean of the College of Arts and Sciences, University of Memphis, Tennessee
Auditory Impairment

Beatty, Barbara
Associate Professor of Education, Wellesley College, Massachusetts
Montessori, Maria

Beauvais, Frederick
Senior Research Scientist, Tri-Ethnic Center for Prevention Research, Colorado State University, Fort Collins
Cultural Disintegration

Beck, Aaron T.
University Professor of Psychiatry, University of Pennsylvania, Philadelphia
Cognitive Therapy

Beck, J. Gayle
Professor of Psychology, State University of New York at Buffalo
Treatment

Becker, Judith V.
Professor of Psychology and Psychiatry, University of Arizona, Tucson
Exhibitionism

Beckham, E. Edward
Clinical Associate Professor, Department of Psychiatry and Behavioral Sciences, Oklahoma University, Oklahoma City
Depression

Beer, Michael
Cahners-Rabb Professor of Business Administration, Harvard Business School, Boston, Massachusetts
Organizational Theories

Behrens, John T.
Associate Professor of Psychology in Education, Arizona State University, Tempe
Exploratory Data Analysis

Beidel, Deborah C.
Professor of Psychology, University of Maryland, College Park
Anxiety Disorders

Bélanger, David
Professor Emeritus of Psychology, University of Montreal, Quebec, Canada
International Congress of Psychology

Bellack, Alan S.
Professor of Psychiatry and MIRECC Director, University of Maryland School of Medicine, Baltimore
Bipolar Disorder

Bellezza, Francis S.
Professor of Psychology, Ohio University, Athens
Mnemonic Devices

Bemak, Fred
Professor of Counselor Education, and Section Head for Wellness and Human Services, The Ohio State University, Columbus
Migrants

Benjamin, Ludy T., Jr.
Professor of Psychology, Texas A&M University, College Station
Hollingworth, Harry L.; Münsterberg, Hugo; Scott, Walter Dill

Benson, Ciarán
Professor of Psychology, University College Dublin, Ireland
Republic of Ireland

Benson, Herbert
Associate Professor of Medicine, Mind/Body Medical Institute, Beth Israel Deaconess Medical Center, Boston, Massachusetts
Meditation

Bent, Russell J.
Former Dean and Professor of Psychology, Wright State University, Dayton, Ohio
American Board of Professional Psychology

Bergin, Allen E.
Professor Emeritus of Psychology, Brigham Young University, Provo, Utah
Religious Values and Mental Health

Bergman, Erik T.
Human Factors Engineer, Pitney Bowes Technology Center, Shelton, Connecticut
Data Collection, *article on* Laboratory Research

Berkowitz, Bill
Associate Professor of Psychology, University of Massachusetts, Lowell
Suburban Communities

Berkowitz, Leonard
Vilas Research Professor Emeritus of Psychology, University of Wisconsin-Madison
Antisocial Behavior

Berman, William H.
Associate Professor, Fordham University, Bronx, New York; and President, BHOS, Incorporated
Managed Care

Bernstein, Ilene L.
Professor of Psychology, University of Washington, Seattle
Taste Aversion Learning

Berntson, Gary G.
Professor of Psychology, The Ohio State University, Columbus
Social Neuroscience

Berry, David T. R.
Professor of Psychology, University of Kentucky, Lexington
Malingering

Berry, John W.
Department of Psychology, Queen's University, Kingston, Ontario, Canada
Culture, *article on* Cultural Foundations of Human Behavior; Marginalization; Modernization

Berscheid, Ellen
Regents' Professor of Psychology, University of Minnesota, Minneapolis
Attraction

Bersoff, Donald N.
Director of Law and Psychology Program, Villanova Law School, Pennsylvania
Case Law; Confidentiality

Bertini, Mario
Professor of Psychophysiology, University of Rome "La Sapienza," Dipartimento di Psicologia, Rome, Italy
Field Dependence and Independence

Best, Phillip J.
Professor of Psychology, Miami University, Oxford, Ohio
Olds, James

Beutler, Larry E.
Professor, Counseling/Clinical/School Psychology Program, University of California, Santa Barbara
Eclectic Psychotherapy

Biaggio, Angela
Professor of Psychology, Federal University of Rio Grande do Sul, Porto Alegre; and Senior Researcher, Brazilian Research Council
Brazil

Birbaumer, Niels
Professor of Medical Psychology, Institute of Medical Psychology and Behavioral Neurobiology, University of Tübingen, Germany
Neuromuscular Disorders

Bizer, George Y.
Graduate Research Assistant and Doctoral Candidate, The Ohio State University, Columbus
Political Behavior

Bjorklund, David F.
Professor of Developmental Psychology, Florida Atlantic University, Boca Raton
Middle Childhood, *article on* Cognitive Development

Black, James E.
Assistant Professor of Psychiatry and Neuroscience, Departments of Psychiatry and Psychology, University of Illinois at Urbana-Champaign
Learning, *article on* Molecular and Cellular Aspects

Black, Maureen M.
Professor of Pediatrics, University of Maryland School of Medicine, Baltimore
Prevention, *article on* Prevention for Infants and Young Children

Blackman, Derek
Professor Emeritus of Psychology, Cardiff University, United Kingdom
Wales

Blackmore, John T.
Independent Scholar, Bethesda, Maryland
Mach, Ernst

Blake, Randolph
Professor of Psychology, Vanderbilt University, Nashville, Tennessee
Vision and Sight, *article on* Structure and Function

Blanchard, Christina G.
Professor of Medicine and Psychiatry, Division of Hematology and Oncology, Albany Medical College, New York
Doctor-Patient Relationship

Blanchard, Edward B.
Distinguished Professor of Psychology, Center for Stress and Anxiety Disorders, University of Albany, New York
Biofeedback; Headaches

Blanchard, Ray
Head of the Clinical Sexology Program, Center for Addiction and Mental Health, Clarke Division, Toronto, Ontario, Canada
Transsexualism; Transvestism

Blasco, Elizabeth
Gaithersburg, Maryland
Educational Testing Service

Blascovich, Jim
Professor of Psychology, University of California, Santa Barbara
Society of Experimental Social Psychology

Blashfield, Roger K.
Professor of Psychology, Auburn University, Alabama
International Classification of Diseases

Blass, Thomas
Professor of Psychology, University of Maryland, Baltimore County
Milgram, Stanley

Blatt, Sidney J.
Professor of Psychiatry and Psychology, Yale University, New Haven, Connecticut
Projective Techniques

Blechman, Elaine A.
Professor of Psychology, University of Colorado at Boulder
Resilience; Women's Health Issues

Blieszner, Rosemary
Professor of Gerontology and Family Studies, Virginia Polytechnic Institute and State University, Blacksburg
Parent-Child Relationship, *article on* Adulthood

Blowers, Geoffrey H.
Senior Lecturer and Director of the P.C. Psychology Program, University of Hong Kong
China; Hong Kong

Blumenthal, Arthur L.
Chairman of the Division of Liberal Arts and Sciences, Berkeley College of New York; and Lecturer, The New School, New York
Jastrow, Joseph; Judd, Charles Hubbard; Miller, George Armitage; Wundt, Wilhelm Maximilian

Bochner, Stephen
Visiting Professor of Psychology, School of Psychology, University of New South Wales, Sidney, Australia
Australia; Culture Shock

Boeschen, Laura
Doctoral Candidate, Department of Psychology, University of Arizona, Tucson
Rape

Bogdan, Robert
Director of the Social Science Project; and Professor of Sociology and Cultural Foundation of Education, Syracuse University, New York
Qualitative Research

Bogner, Marilyn Sue
Independent Scholar, Bethesda, Maryland
Medical Technology Design

Bond, Charles F., Jr.
Professor of Psychology, Texas Christian University, Fort Worth
Social Facilitation

Bond, Michael Harris
Professor of Psychology, Chinese University of Hong Kong
Xenophobia

Bondarovska, Valentyna M.
Director of the International Humanitarian Center, Rozrada, Kyiv, Ukraine
Russia and the Former Soviet Republics

Bongar, Bruce
Calvin Professor of Psychology, Pacific Graduate School of Psychology, Palo Alto, California; and Consulting Professor of Psychiatry and the Behavioral Sciences, Stanford University School of Medicine, California
Suicide

Booij, Geert
Professor of General Linguistics, Vrije University, Amsterdam, The Netherlands
Phonology

Bootzin, Richard R.
Professor of Psychology, University of Arizona, Tucson
Insomnia

Borgida, Eugene
Professor of Psychology and Law, University of Minnesota, Minneapolis
Social Motivation

Borman, Walter C.
Professor of Psychology, Department of Psychology, University of South Florida, Tampa
Work Performance

Bornstein, Marc H.
Senior Research Scientist, Child and Family Research, National Institutes of Health and Human Development, Bethesda, Maryland
Infancy, *article on* Emotions and Temperament

Bottoms, Bette L.
Associate Professor of Psychology, University of Illinois, Chicago
Children's Eyewitness Testimony

Bourguignon, Erika
Professor Emeritus of Anthropology, The Ohio State University, Columbus
Consciousness and Unconsciousness, *article on* Cross-Cultural Experience; Dreams, *article on* Cross-Cultural Perspectives

Boyle, Mary
Professor of Clinical Psychology, Department of Psychology, University of East London, United Kingdom
Kraepelin, Emil

Boynton, David M.
Assistant Professor, Department of Psychology, Western Connecticut State University, Danbury
Gibson, James Jerome

Brabeck, Mary M.
Professor of Counseling, Developmental, and Educational Psychology; and Dean, Boston College, Chestnut Hill, Massachusetts
Kohlberg, Lawrence

Braden, Jeffery P.
Professor of Educational Psychology, University of Wisconsin-Madison
Deafness and Hearing Loss

Brady, James D.
Doctoral Candidate, Department of Psychology, University of California, San Diego
Neuropsychology, *article on* Theories

Brady, Joseph V.
Professor of Behavioral Biology, and Professor of Neuroscience, Behavioral Biology Research Center, Johns Hopkins University School of Medicine, Baltimore, Maryland
Placebo Effect in Research Design

Brady, Linda S.
Chief of the Neuropharmacology and Drug Discovery Program, National Institute of Mental Health, Bethesda, Maryland
Opiates

Braithwaite, Ronald L.
Professor, Department of Behavioral Sciences and Health Education, Rollins School of Public Health, Emory University, Atlanta, Georgia
Empowerment

Branch, Marc N.
Professor of Psychology, University of Florida, Gainesville
Operant Conditioning, *article on* An Overview; Punishment, *article on* Research

Bransford, John D.
Centennial Professor of Psychology and Education; and Co-Director, Learning Technology Center, Vanderbilt University, Nashville, Tennessee
Learning Technologies

Breedlove, S. Marc
Professor of Psychology, University of California, Berkeley
Reproductive System

Brehm, Jack W.
Professor of Psychology, University of Kansas, Lawrence
Festinger, Leon; Reactance

Brewer, Marilynn B.
Professor of Psychology, and Ohio State Eminent Scholar in Social Psychology, The Ohio State University, Columbus
Campbell, Donald Thomas

Briere, John
Associate Professor of Psychiatry and Psychology, University of Southern California School of Medicine, Los Angeles
Incest

Bringmann, Wolfgang G.
Professor Emeritus of Psychology, University of Southern Alabama, Mobile
Ebbinghaus, Hermann; Klemm, Otto August

Brislin, Richard W.
Professor, Department of Management and Industrial Relations, College of Business Administration, University of Hawaii, Honolulu
Back-Translation; Cross-Cultural Training

Brody, Eugene B.
Visiting Professor, Harvard Medical School, Boston, Massachusetts; and Secretary General, World Federation for Mental Health, Baltimore, Maryland
World Federation for Mental Health

Brody, Nathan
Professor of Psychology, Wesleyan University, Middletown, Connecticut
Intelligence

Bronfenbrenner, Urie
Jacob Gould Schurman Professor Emeritus of Human Development and Family Studies and of Psychology, Cornell University, Ithaca, New York
Ecological Systems Theory

Bronson, Martha B.
Associate Professor of Developmental and Educational Psychology, Boston College, Chestnut Hill, Massachusetts
Preschool Education

Brooks, G. P.
Dean of Arts, and Professor of Psychology, Saint Francis Xavier University, Antigonish, Nova Scotia, Canada
Biran, Maine de

Brophy, Jere
University Distinguished Professor of Teacher Education, Michigan State University, East Lansing
Classrooms, *article on* Processes and Management

Brown, Barbara B.
Professor of Environment and Behavior, Department of Family and Consumer Studies, University of Utah, Salt Lake City
Privacy; Territoriality

Brown, John Lott
Tampa, Florida
Graham, Clarence Henry

Brown, Scott C.
Doctoral Student, Department of Psychology, University of Toronto, Ontario, Canada
Memory, *article on* Coding Processes

Brownell, Kelly D.
Professor of Psychology, Epidemiology and Public Health Director, Yale Center for Eating and Weight Disorders; and Master of Silliman College, Yale University, New Haven
Dieting

Brožek, Josef
Professor of Psychology, Bethlehem, Pennsylvania
Dolezal, Jan; Henning, Hans; Lindner, Gustav Adolf; Purkinje, Johannes

Bruce, Darryl
Professor of Psychology, Saint Mary's University, Halifax, Nova Scotia, Canada
Bartlett, Frederic C.; Lashley, Karl Spencer

Buckelew, Susan P.
Adjunct Associate Professor of Psychology, University of Missouri, Columbia
Fibromyalgia Syndrome

Buckley, Kerry W.
Northampton, Massachusetts
Watson, John B.

Buckner, Randy L.
Assistant Professor of Psychology, Radiology, and Neurobiology, Washington University, Saint Louis, Missouri
Brain Imaging Techniques

Budman, Simon
President of Innovative Training Systems, Inc., Newton, Massachusetts
Brief Therapy

Bugental, James F. T.
Professor Emeritus, Saybrook Graduate School, San Francisco, California
Maslow, Abraham Harold; May, Rollo

Bulka, Reuven P.
Rabbi, Congregation Machzikei Hadas; and Fellow, Institute of Logotherapy, Ottawa, Canada
Logotherapy

Bundesen, Claus
Professor of Cognitive Psychology, University of Copenhagen, Denmark
Attention, *article on* Models of Attention

Burger, Jerry M.
Professor of Psychology, Santa Clara University, California
Compliance

Burgess, Kim B.
Research Assistant Professor of Human Development, University of Maryland, College Park
Middle Childhood, *article on* Social and Emotional Development

Burlew, A. Kathleen Hoard
Professor of Psychology, University of Cincinnati, Ohio
Ethnic and Racial Identity, *article on* Racial Identity

Burlingame, Gary M.
Professor of Clinical Psychology, Brigham Young University, Provo, Utah
Group Therapy

Burns, Melissa
Postdoctoral Research Associate, Department of Psychology, University of Texas, Austin
Learning Theories

Burston, Daniel
Associate Professor of Psychology, Duquesne University, Pittsburgh, Pennsylvania
Rank, Otto

Buskist, William
Professor of Psychology, Auburn University, Illinois
Behaviorism and Neobehaviorism

Buss, David M.
Professor of Psychology, University of Texas, Austin
Evolutionary Psychology; Natural Selection

Buss, William G.
O. K. Patton Professor of Law, University of Iowa College of Law, Iowa City
Measures of Intelligence, *article on* Legal Issues

Butcher, James N.
Professor of Psychology, University of Minnesota, Minneapolis
Clinical Psychology, *article on* Assessment; Computerized Assessment; Minnesota Multiphasic Personality Inventory

Cacioppo, John T.
Tiffany and Margaret Blake Distinguished Service Professor, University of Chicago, Illinois
Social Neuroscience

Cahill, Larry
Assistant Professor, Department of Neurobiology and Behavior, University of California, Irvine
Emotional Learning

Calabrese, Raymond L.
Professor of Educational Leadership, University of Texas, San Antonio
Alienation

Calfee, Robert C.
Professor and Dean, University of California, Riverside
Educational Psychology

Campbell, James L.
Department of Counseling, Indiana State University, Terre Haute
American Psychological Association of Graduate Students

Capaldi, E. J.
Professor of Psychology, Purdue University, West Lafayette, Indiana
Animal Learning and Behavior, *article on* History of the Field; Animal Learning and Behavior, *article on* Methods of Study; Learning, *article on* Cognitive Approach for Animals; Learning and Memory, *article on* Learning and Memory in Animals

Caplan, David
Professor of Neurology, Harvard Medical School, Boston, Massachusetts
Aphasia

Caplan, Robert D.
Independent Consultant, Redondo Beach, California
Job Loss and Unemployment

Cardeña, Etzel
Professor, Uniformed Services University of the Health Sciences, Bethesda, Maryland
Dissociative Disorders

Care, Norman S.
Professor of Philosophy, Oberlin College, Ohio
Moral Discourse

Carey, Joseph
Public Information Director, Society for Neuroscience, Washington, D.C.
Society for Neuroscience

Carlson, Neil R.
Professor of Psychology, University of Massachusetts, Amherst
Neuron; Synapse

Carlston, Donal E.
Associate Professor of Psychology, Purdue University, West Lafayette, Indiana
Impression Formation

Carnevale, Peter
Professor of Psychology, University of Illinois at Urbana-Champaign
Negotiation

Carson, Robert C.
Professor of Psychology, Duke University, Durham, North Carolina
Electroconvulsive Therapy; Psychosurgery

Carstensen, Laura
Professor of Psychology, Stanford University, California
Social Gerontological Theories

Cartwright, Rosalind D.
Chairman, and Professor of Psychology, Rush-Presbyterian-Saint Luke's Medical Center, Chicago, Illinois
Sleep Apnea

Carver, Charles S.
Professor of Psychology, University of Miami, Coral Gables, Florida
Coping; Optimism and Pessimism

Casas, J. Manuel
Professor of Counseling, Clinical, and School Psychology, Graduate School of Education, University of California, Santa Barbara
Multicultural Counseling

Cascio, Wayne F.
Professor of Management, Graduate School of Business, University of Colorado, Denver
Test Utility

Cash, Thomas F.
Old Dominion University, Department of Psychology, Norfolk, Virginia
Body Image

Castellino, Domini R.
Research Scholar, Center for Child and Family Policy, Duke University, Durham, North Carolina
Parent-Child Relationship, *article on* Childhood

Catania, A. Charles
Professor of Psychology, University of Maryland, Baltimore County
Behavior Analysis; Cumulative Record; Law of Effect

Cauce, Ana Mari
Professor of Psychology and American Ethnic Studies, University of Washington, Seattle
Homelessness

Caudle, Fairfid M.
Professor of Psychology, The College of Staten Island, City University of New York
Gibson, Eleanor J.

Ceccoli, Velleda C.
Clinical Faculty, New York University Medical Center, New York
Breuer, Josef

Ceci, Stephen J.
The Helen L. Carr Professor of Developmental Psychology, Cornell University, Ithaca, New York
Bronfenbrenner, Urie; Determinants of Intelligence, *article on* Schooling and Intelligence; Memory, *article on* Constructive Processes

Cella, David
Research Professor, Institute for Health Services Research and Policy Studies, Northwestern University, Evanston, Illinois
Quality of Life

Chambers, Mark J.
The Sleep Clinic of Nevada, Las Vegas
Sleepwalking

Chaplin, James P.
Professor Emeritus of Psychology, Saint Michael's College, Colchester, Vermont
Functionalism

Chartrand, Judy
Director of Research, Consulting Psychologists Press, Lindstrom, Minnesota
Career, *article on* Career Assessment

Chatelaine, Kenneth L.
Professor of Psychology, and Research Scholar and Specialist in Childhood Disorders, Glen Burnie, Maryland
Sullivan, Harry Stack

Chaves, John F.
Professor of Behavioral Medicine and Bioethics, Department of Oral Biology, School of Dentistry, Indiana University, Indianapolis
Hypnosis

Cheek, Jonathan M.
Professor of Psychology, Wellesley College, Massachusetts
Shyness

Chesir-Teran, Daniel
Fellow in the Department of Psychology, New York University, New York
Community Prevention and Intervention, *article on* Prevention with School-Aged Children

Chi, Michelene T. H.
Professor of Psychology, and Senior Scientist, University of Pittsburgh, Pennsylvania
Cognitive Understanding Levels

Chirban, John T.
Clinical Instructor, Harvard Medical School, Carlisle, Massachusetts
Hellenistic Psychology

Choi, Sang-Chin
Department of Psychology, Chung-Ang University, Seoul, South Korea
Korea

Christensen, Andrew
Professor of Psychology, University of California, Los Angeles
Computerized Psychotherapy

Church, Russell M.
Edgar J. Marston Professor of Psychology, Brown University, Providence, Rhode Island
Schlosberg, Harold

Churchill, Scott D.
Chair and Associate Professor of Psychology, University of Dallas, Irving, Texas
Phenomenological Psychology; Phenomenology

Clark, Eve V.
Professor of Linguistics and Symbolic Systems, Stanford University, California
Language, *article on* Language Acquisition

Clark, Herbert H.
Professor of Psychology, Stanford University, California
Conversation

Clark, Margaret S.
Professor of Psychology, Carnegie Mellon University, Pittsburgh, Pennsylvania
Altruism

Clements, Carl B.
Professor of Psychology, The University of Alabama, Tuscaloosa
Prisons and Correctional Institutions

Clifton, Charles, Jr.
Professor of Psychology, University of Massachusetts, Amherst
Psycholinguistics, *article on* Syntax and Grammar

Coates, Thomas J.
Professor of Medicine and Epidemiology, AIDS Research Institute, University of California, San Francisco
Acquired Immune Deficiency Syndrome

Cobb, Paul
Professor of Mathematics Education, Vanderbilt University, Nashville, Tennessee
Constructivism

Cohen, David
Professor of Social Work, Université de Montréal, Canada
Critical Psychiatry

Cohen, Sheldon
Professor of Psychology, Carnegie Mellon University, Pittsburgh, Pennsylvania
Social Support

Coleman, S. R.
Professor of Psychology, Cleveland State University, Ohio
Hall, Marshall; Hunter, Walter S.; Skinner, Burrhus Frederic

Collins, Kathleen
Assistant Professor of Psychology, University of San Diego, California
Learning Skills

Collins, W. Andrew
Morse Alumni Professor of Child Psychology, Institute of Child Development, University of Minnesota, Minneapolis
Middle Childhood, *article on* Socialization and Social Contexts

Colman, Rebecca A.
Graduate Student, Department of Psychology, University of Nebraska, Lincoln
Infancy, *article on* Early Experience and Socialization

Colyer, Peter J.
Executive Secretary, Academia Europaea, London
Academia Europaea

Compton, Carolyn L.
Co-Director, Morrissey-Compton Educational Center, Palo Alto, California
Sears, Pauline S.

Comrey, Andrew L.
Professor Emeritus of Psychology, University of California, Los Angeles
Guilford, Joy Paul

Condray, Ruth
Assistant Professor of Psychiatry, University of Pittsburgh School of Medicine, Western Psychiatric Institute and Clinic, Pittsburgh, Pennsylvania
Zubin, Joseph

Conway, Kevin
Associate Research Scientist, Department of Epidemiology and Public Health, Yale University School of Medicine, New Haven, Connecticut
Alcoholism

Conway, Martin A.
Professor of Psychology, Department of Experimental Psychology, University of Bristol, England
Repressed Memory

Coolidge, Frederick L.
Professor of Psychology, University of Colorado at Colorado Springs
Art Therapy; Assessment

Cooper, Steven H.
Training and Supervising Analyst, The Boston Psychoanalytic Society and Institute; and Associate Clinical Professor of Psychology, Harvard Medical School, Cambridge, Massachusetts
Drive; Id

Corcoran, Mary
The University of Michigan, Ann Arbor
Poverty, *article on* Adulthood Poverty

Corr, Philip J.
Lecturer in Psychology, Goldsmiths College, University of London, United Kingdom
Psychoticism

Corral, Carla V.
Postdoctoral Fellow, Stanford Center for Research in Disease Prevention, Stanford University School of Medicine, California
Multicultural Counseling

Cortese, Michael J.
Postdoctoral Research Associate, Department of Psychology, Washington University, Saint Louis, Missouri
Cognitive Psychology, *article on* Theories

Costa, Paul T.
Baltimore, Maryland
NEO Personality Inventory

Cottam, Martha
Department of Political Science, Washington State University, Pullman
Enemy Image

Cowles, Michael
Professor of Psychology, York University, Toronto, Canada
Fisher, Ronald Aylmer; Quetelet, Lambert Adolphe Jacques

Cox, Richard H.
Professor of Educational and Counseling Psychology, University of Missouri-Columbia
Sport Psychology, *article on* History of the Field

Coyne, James C.
Professor of Psychology, University of Pennsylvania School of Medicine, Philadelphia
Mood Disorders

Cozzarelli, Catherine
Associate Professor of Psychology, Kansas State University, Manhattan
Abortion

Crabtree, Adam
Core Faculty, Centre for Training in Psychotherapy, Toronto, Ontario, Canada
Braid, James; Charcot, Jean-Martin; Flournoy, Théodore; Lavater, Johann Caspar; Mesmer, Franz Anton

Craig, James C.
Chancellors' Professor of Psychology, Indiana University, Bloomington
Touch, *article on* Behavioral and Functional Aspects

Craik, Fergus I. M.
University Professor of Psychology, University of Toronto, Ontario, Canada
Broadbent, Donald E.; Memory, *article on* Coding Processes

Craik, Kenneth H.
Professor, Institute of Personality and Social Research, University of California, Berkeley
Personality Psychology, *article on* Methods of Study

Cramer, Phebe
Professor of Psychology, Williams College, Williamstown, Massachusetts
Thematic Apperception Test

Craske, Michelle G.
Professor of Psychology, University of California, Los Angeles
Panic Disorder

Cravens, Hamilton
Professor of History, Iowa State University, Ames
Boas, Franz

Crawford, Meredith P.
Chevy Chase, Maryland
Flanagan, John C.; Human Resources Research Organization

Creemers, B. P. M.
Professor of Educational Research, GION, Groningen Institute for Educational Research, University of Groningen, The Netherlands
School Effectiveness and Improvement

Creer, Thomas L.
Professor Emeritus of Psychology, Ohio University, Athens
Asthma

Crenshaw, Martha
John E. Andrus Professor of Government, Department of Political Science, Wesleyan University, Middletown, Connecticut
Terrorism

Croce, Paul Jerome
Associate Professor of American Studies, Department of American Studies, Stetson University, DeLand, Florida
Peirce, Charles S.

Crocker, Jennifer
Professor of Psychology, Research Center for Group Dynamics, Institute for Social Research, The University of Michigan, Ann Arbor
Stigma

Crowder, Robert G.
Professor of Psychology, Yale University, New Haven, Connecticut
McGeoch, John A.; Melton, Arthur; Sensory Stores

Crowne, Douglas P.
Distinguished Professor Emeritus of Psychology, University of Waterloo, Ontario, Canada
Social Desirability

Croyle, Robert T.
Associate Director for Behavioral Research, Division of Cancer Control and Population Sciences, National Cancer Institute, Bethesda, Maryland
Genetic Counseling

Csikszentmihalyi, Mihaly
C. S. and D. J. Davidson Professor of Management, Claremont Graduate University, California
Boredom; Creativity, *article on* An Overview; Flow; Talent

Curran, Patrick J.
Assistant Professor of Quantitative Psychology, University of North Carolina at Chapel Hill
Factor Analysis

Dahlstrom, W. Grant
Kenan Professor Emeritus of Psychology, University of North Carolina at Chapel Hill
Dashiell, John Frederick; Hathaway, Starke R.

Damon, William
Professor of Education, Stanford University, California
Moral Development

Danoff-Burg, Sharon
Assistant Professor, University at Albany, State University of New York at Albany
Arthritis

Dantzer, Robert
Professor of Psychobiology; Director of Research; and Director of the Laboratory of Integrative Neurobiology of the French National Institute of Health and Medicine Research, Bordeaux, France
Immune System

Darley, John M.
Dorman T. Warren Professor of Psychology, Princeton University, New Jersey
Bystander Phenomenon

Das, Ajit K.
Professor of Psychology, University of Minnesota, Duluth
Compulsive Gambling

Das, J. P.
Emeritus Professor, J. P. Das Developmental Disabilities Centre, University of Alberta, Edmonton, Canada
Mental Retardation

D'Augelli, Anthony R.
Professor of Human Development, The Pennsylvania State University, University Park
Sexual Orientation

Davidson, Emily S.
Associate Professor of Psychology, Texas A&M University, College Station
Pestalozzi, Johann Heinrich

Davidson, Janet E.
Assistant Professor of Psychology, Lewis and Clark College, Portland, Oregon
Giftedness

Davidson, T. L.
Professor of Psychology, Purdue University, West Lafayette, Indiana
Endorphins; Latent Learning

Davies, Scott A.
Research Specialist 2, Center on Education and Training for Employment, The Ohio State University, Columbus
Industrial and Organizational Psychology, *article on* History of the Field

Davis, James H.
Professor Emeritus of Psychology, University of Illinois at Urbana-Champaign
Group Performance

Davis, John M.
Professor of Psychology, Southwest Texas State University, San Marcos
International Council of Psychologists

Davis, Richard L.
Professor of Domestic Violence, Criminal Justice, and Sociology, Quincy College at Plymouth, Massachusetts
Domestic Violence

Davis, Stephen F.
Professor of Psychology, Emporia State University, Kansas
Psi Chi

Davison, Gerald C.
Professor of Psychology, University of Southern California, Los Angeles
Case Study

Dawes, Robyn
Charles J. Queenan, Jr. University Professor, Department of Social and Decision Sciences, Carnegie-Mellon University, Pittsburgh, Pennsylvania
Coombs, Clyde H.; Tversky, Amos

Dawis, Rene V.
Professor Emeritus of Psychology, University of Minnesota, Minneapolis, and Senior Research Fellow, The Ball Foundation, Glen Ellyn, Illinois
Work Adjustment Theory

Dazzi, Nino
Dean of the Faculty of Psychology, University of Rome La Sapienza, Italy
Benussi, Vittorio; Buccola, Gabriele; de Sanctis, Sante; Gemelli, Agostino; Lombroso, Cesare

Deaux, Kay
Distinguished Professor of Psychology, Graduate Center, City University of New York
Identity

Deegan, Mary Jo
Professor of Sociology, University of Nebraska, Lincoln
Mead, George Herbert

Deese, Wynelle S.
Independent Scholar, Saint Petersburg, Florida
Kirkbride, Thomas S.

Deffenbacher, Jerry L.
Professor of Psychology, Colorado State University, Fort Collins
Social Skills Training

DeGrandpré, Richard J.
Independent Scholar, Burlington, Vermont
Behaviorism and Neobehaviorism

De Leon, George
Director of the Center for Therapeutic Community Research, National Development and Research Institutes, Inc., New York; and Clinical Professor of Psychiatry, New York University School of Medicine, New York
Therapeutic Communities

DeLeon, Patrick H.
Administrative Assistant to United States Senator Daniel K. Inouye, Washington, D.C.
Prescription Privileges

Delis, Dean C.
Professor of Psychiatry, University of California, San Diego
Neuropsychology, *article on* Testing

De-Nour, Atara Kaplan
Professor of Psychiatry, Hadassah University Hospital, Jerusalem
Endstage Renal Disease

De Raad, Boele
Associate Professor of Personality Psychology, University of Groningen, The Netherlands
Differential Psychology

Deręgowski, J. B.
Anderson Professor of Psychology, University of Aberdeen, Scotland
Scotland

Derogatis, Leonard R.
Professor and Director, Office of Research, School of Nursing, University of Maryland, Baltimore
Hopkins Symptom Checklist; SCL-90-R

Detterman, Douglas K.
Louis D. Beaumont University Professor, Case Western Reserve University, Cleveland, Ohio
Determinants of Intelligence, *article on* Heritability of Intelligence

Deutsch, Diana
Professor of Psychology, University of California, San Diego
Music

Devonis, David C.
Assistant Professor of Psychology, Graceland College, Lamoni, Iowa
Dessoir, Max; Lipps, Theodor; Troland, Leonard Thompson

Dewsbury, Donald A.
Professor of Psychology, University of Florida, Gainesville
Beach, Frank A.; Carmichael, Leonard; Comparative Psychology; Harlow, Harry Frederick; Lehrman, Daniel Sanford; Miller, Neal Elgar; Nissen, Henry Wieghorst; Psychonomic Society; Tinbergen, Nikolaas; Warden, Carl John; Yerkes, Robert Mearns

Diamond, Shari S.
Professor of Law and Psychology, Northwestern University Law School, Chicago, Illinois
Expert Testimony

Díaz-Guerrero, Rogelio
Research Professor Emeritus of Psychology, Universidad Nacional Autonoma de Mexico
Mexico

Diehl, Kim A.
Doctoral Candidate, Department of Psychology, University of Kansas, Lawrence
Item Response Theory; Rasch Model

Diehl, Lesley A.
Emerita Professor of Psychology, State University of New York College at Oneonta
Hall, Granville Stanley

Dileo, Cheryl
Professor of Music Therapy, Esther Boyer College of Music, Temple University, Pennsylvania
Music Therapy

DiLillo, Vicki
Assistant Professor of Medicine, University of Alabama, Birmingham
Cancer

Dion, Kenneth L.
Professor of Psychology, University of Toronto, Ontario, Canada
Canada

Dixon, David N.
Professor of Psychology-Counseling, Ball State University, Muncie, Indiana
Parsons, Frank

Dixon, Roger A.
Department of Psychology, University of Victoria, British Columbia, Canada
Memory, *article on* Memory and Aging

Dodge, George E.
Senior Research Fellow, Institute for Leadership Research, Texas Tech University, Lubbock
Organizational Management

Doherty, William J.
Professor of Family Social Science, University of Minnesota, Saint Paul
Systems Theory

Domjan, Michael
Professor of Psychology, University of Texas, Austin
Animal Learning and Behavior, *article on* Theoretical Issues; Avoidance Learning; Learning, *article on* An Overview; Learning Theories; Sexual Conditioning

Donahey, Karen M.
Director of the Sex and Marital Therapy Program; Assistant Professor in Psychiatry, Northwestern University Medical School, Chicago, Illinois
Sexual Disorders

Donaldson, Gail
Visiting Assistant Professor of Psychology, Union College, Schenectady, New York
Freud, Anna; Klein, Melanie

Donnerstein, Edward
Dean of Social Sciences; and Professor of Communication, Communication Studies Program, University of California, Santa Barbara
Pornography

Doty, Richard L.
Professor of Psychology in Otorhinolaryngology, Head and Neck Surgery; and Director of the Smell and Taste Center, School of Medicine, University of Pennsylvania, Philadelphia
Smell

Dougall, Angela Liegey
Graduate Student Researcher, University of Pittsburgh
Stress, *article on* Impact on Health

Dovidio, John F.
Charles A. Dana Professor of Psychology, Colgate University, Hamilton, New York
Prosocial Behavior; Racism

Doyle, Charlotte L.
Professor of Psychology, Sarah Lawrence College, Bronxville, New York
Baltic Countries; Psychology, *article on* Definition

Draguns, Juris G.
Professor Emeritus of Psychology, The Pennsylvania State University, University Park
Baltic Countries

Drenth, Pieter J. D.
Professor of Psychology, Vrije Universiteit, Amsterdam, The Netherlands
Netherlands

DuCette, Joseph P.
Professor of Educational Psychology, Temple University, Philadelphia, Pennsylvania
School Dropout

Duffy, Jennifer R.
Statistical Assistant, Law School Admission Council, Newtown, Pennsylvania
Elementary Education

Dulany, Donelson E.
Professor Emeritus of Psychology, University of Illinois at Urbana-Champaign
Young, Paul Thomas

Durgin, Frank H.
Professor of Psychology, Swarthmore College, Pennsylvania
Visual Adaptation

Durlach, Nathaniel
Senior Research Scientist, Sensory Communications Group, Massachusetts Institute of Technology, Cambridge
Virtual Reality

Durlak, Joseph A.
Professor of Psychology, Loyola University, Chicago
Paraprofessionals; Prevention, *article on* Prevention for School-Aged Children and Adolescents; Social Competence Programs

Dwyer, Johanna T.
Professor of Medicine and Nutrition, Tufts University School of Medicine; and Senior Scientist, Jean Mayer Human Nutrition Research Center on Aging, Tufts University, Boston, Massachusetts
Nutrition

d'Ydewalle, Géry
Professor of Psychology, University of Leuven, Belgium
Belgium

Eagle, Morris N.
Professor of Psychology, Derner Institute of Advanced Psychological Studies, Adelphi University, Garden City, New York
Psychoanalysis, *article on* History of the Field; Rapaport, David

Eagly, Alice
Professor of Psychology, Northwestern University, Evanston, Illinois
Attitudes, *article on* Attitude Change; Conformity; Gender, Sex, and Culture, *article on* Sex Differences and Gender Differences; Gender Roles

Early, Charles E.
Professor of Psychology, Roanoke College, Salem, Virginia
Ebbinghaus, Hermann; Klemm, Otto August

Eccles, Jacquelynne S.
Wilbert McKeachie Collegiate Professor of Psychology, Institute for Social Research, The University of Michigan, Ann Arbor
Adolescence, *article on* Social Patterns, Achievements, and Problems; Gender Socialization

Egeth, Howard
Department of Psychology, Johns Hopkins University, Baltimore, Maryland
Attention, *article on* An Overview

Eichenbaum, Howard
Professor of Psychology, Boston College, Massachusetts
Long-Term Potentiation

Eifert, Georg H.
Eberly Family Distinguished Professor of Clinical Psychology, West Virginia University, Morgantown
Aversion Therapy

Eisenberg, Nancy
Regents' Professor of Psychology, Arizona State University, Tempe
Empathy; Prosocial Development in Childhood and Adolescence; Sympathy

Eisenbruch, Maurice
Associate Professor, School of Medical Education, University of New South Wales, Sydney, Australia
Eastern Religions and Philosophies; France

Eisenbruch, Renata Volich
University of Paris VII
France

Eisner, Elliot W.
Professor of Education and Art, Stanford University, California
Curriculum Development

Ekerdt, David J.
Professor of Sociology, and Senior Scientist, Gerontology Center, University of Kansas, Lawrence
Retirement

Ekman, Paul
Professor of Psychiatry, University of California, San Francisco
Emotion, *article on* An Overview; Emotion, *article on* Methods of Study

Elder, Glen H., Jr.
Howard W. Odum Distinguished Professor of Sociology, and Research Professor of Psychology, University of North Carolina, Chapel Hill
Life Course Theory

Elkind, Jerome I.
Chairman, Lexia Institute, Portola Valley, California
Technology, *article on* Technology and Disabilities

Ellis, Albert
President, Albert Ellis Institute, New York
Rational Emotive Behavior Therapy

Ellis, Hadyn D.
Professor of Psychology, Cardiff University, United Kingdom
Wales

Ellis, Stephen R.
Research Scientist, NASA Ames Research Center, Moffett Field, California
Information Display

Elmes, David G.
Professor of Psychology, and Head of the Department of Psychology, Washington Lee University, Lexington, Virginia
Experimental Psychology

Elms, Alan C.
Professor of Psychology, University of California, Davis
Literature

Embretson, Susan E.
Professor of Psychology, University of Kansas, Lawrence
Item Response Theory; Rasch Model

Emmons, Robert A.
Professor of Psychology, University of California, Davis
Motivation, *article on* Assessment

Emmorey, Karen
Senior Staff Scientist, Laboratory for Cognitive Neuroscience, The Salk Institute for Biological Studies, La Jolla, California
Sign Languages

Erdelyi, Matthew Hugh
Professor of Psychology, Brooklyn College and the Graduate School of the City University of New York
Repression

Ericsson, K. Anders
Conradi Eminent Scholar, and Professor of Psychology, Florida State University, Tallahassee
Simon, Herbert Alexander

Ernst, John M.
Assistant Professor of Psychology, Illinois Wesleyan University, Bloomington
Social Neuroscience

Evans, Gary W.
Professor of Design and Environmental Analysis, Cornell University, Ithaca, New York
Crowding

Evans, Rand
Tarboro, North Carolina
Dallenbach, Karl M.; Pillsbury, Walter B.

Evans, Richard I.
Distinguished Professor of Psychology, Department of Psychology, University of Houston, Texas
Fromm, Erich

Fabrigar, Leandre R.
Assistant Professor of Psychology, Queen's University, Kingston, Ontario, Canada
Attitudes, *article on* An Overview

Faenza, Michael
President and Chief Executive Officer, National Mental Health Association, Alexandria, Virginia
National Mental Health Association

Fagan, Thomas K.
Professor of Psychology, University of Memphis, Tennessee
Gesell, Arnold Lucius; Hobbs, Nicholas; School Psychology

Fagot, Beverly
Oregon Social Learning Center, University of Oregon, Eugene
Gender Schema

Fairchild, Halford H.
Professor of Psychology and Black Studies, Pitzer College, Claremont, California
African American Psychology

Falmagne, Jean-Claude
Professor of Cognitive Sciences, University of California, Irvine
Suppes, Patrick

Fancher, Raymond E.
Professor of Psychology, York University, Toronto, Ontario, Canada
Binet, Alfred; Brentano, Franz; Darwin, Charles R.; Freud, Sigmund; Galton, Francis; James, William; Leibniz, Gottfried Wilhelm; Locke, John; Mill, James; Mill, John Stuart; Spinoza, Baruch (Benedictus de)

Farag, M. Samir
Professor of Psychology, Institute for Strategic Sciences, Cairo, Egypt
Arab States, *article on* Egypt and the Arab States

Farah, Martha J.
Professor of Psychology, University of Pennsylvania, Philadelphia
Agnosias

Farberman, Rhea K.
Associate Executive Director, Public Communications, American Psychological Association, Washington, D.C.
Consumerism of Psychological Services

Farreras, Ingrid G.
Doctoral Candidate in History and Theory of Psychology, University of New Hampshire, Durham
Hume, David; Rousseau, Jean-Jacques

Farrington, David P.
Professor of Psychological Criminology, Cambridge University, United Kingdom
Delinquency

Farthing, G. William
Professor of Psychology, University of Maine, Orono
Consciousness and Unconsciousness, *article on* An Overview

Fearing, Thomas G.
Doctoral Candidate in Clinical Psychology, University of Louisville, Kentucky
Intervention

Fehr, Beverley
Professor of Psychology, University of Winnipeg, Manitoba, Canada
Friendship

Feinstein, David
Ashland, Oregon
Archetypes

Fekken, G. Cynthia
Associate Professor of Psychology, Queen's University, Kingston, Ontario, Canada
Reliability

Feldman, Laurie B.
Professor of Psychology, State University of New York at Albany
Morphology

Feldman, Pamela J.
Research Scientist, Department of Epidemiology and Public Health, University of London, United Kingdom
Social Support

Ferdman, Bernardo M.
Associate Professor, Organizational Psychology Programs, California School of Organizational Psychology, San Diego
Interamerican Society of Psychology

Fernández-Alvarez, Héctor
President, Fundacion AIGLE, Buenos Aires, Argentina
South America, South Cone Zone of

Ferrari, Joseph R.
Associate Professor of Psychology, DePaul University, Chicago
Hotline Services

Field, Tiffany
Dean of the Family and School Center, and Director of the Touch Research Institutes, Nova Southeastern University, Fort Lauderdale, Florida
Child Abuse and Neglect

Finger, Stanley
Professor of Psychology, Washington University, Saint Louis, Missouri
Broca, Paul; Ramón y Cajal, Santiago

Finkelstein, Jordan W.
Professor of Biobehavioral Health, Human Development, and Pediatrics, Pennsylvania State University, University Park
Middle Childhood, *article on* Physical and Biological Development

Fischhoff, Baruch
University Professor of Social and Decision Sciences, and Professor of Engineering and Public Policy, Carnegie Mellon University, Pittsburgh, Pennsylvania
Decision Making

Fiske, Donald W.
Professor Emeritus of Psychology, University of Chicago, Illinois
Artifact, *article on* Artifact in Assessment; Research Methods, *article on* Concepts and Practices

Fiske, Susan T.
Professor of Psychology, Princeton University, New Jersey
Schema

Fitzgerald, Louise F.
Professor of Psychology, University of Illinois, Urbana-Champaign
Sexual Harassment

Flesher, Mary Mosher
Research Associate, History of Science, Smith College, Northampton, Massachusetts
Bain, Alexander

Fonagy, Peter
Freud Memorial Professor of Psychoanalysis, University College, London, United Kingdom
Personality Development, *article on* Infancy and Early Childhood; Psychosexual Stages

Foote, Stephen L.
Chief of the Behavioral and Integrative Neuroscience Research Branch, National Institute of Mental Health, Rockville, Maryland
Arousal; Neuroscience

Ford, J. Kevin
Professor of Psychology, Michigan State University, East Lansing, Michigan
Employee Training

Ford, Martin E.
Professor of Education, and Associate Dean, Graduate School of Education, George Mason University, Fairfax, Virginia
Personality and Intelligence

Forness, Steven R.
Professor of Psychiatry, and Director of the Neuropsychiatric Institute, University of California, Los Angeles
Exceptional Students

Fowler, Floyd Jackson, Jr.
Senior Research Fellow, Center for Survey Research, University of Massachusetts, Boston
Survey Methodology

Fowler, Raymond D.
Executive Vice-President and Chief Executive Officer, American Psychological Association, Washington, D.C.
American Psychological Association, *article on* Structure; Professional Organizations

Fox, Ronald E.
Executive Director of the Consulting Group, a Division of Human Resource Consultants, PA, Chapel Hill, North Carolina
Prescription Privileges

Foxx, Richard M.
Professor of Psychology, The Pennsylvania State University, Harrisburg, Middletown, Pennsylvania
Enuresis

Franck, Karen A.
Professor of Architecture, New Jersey Institute of Technology, Newark
Environment Research Design

Fraser, Barry J.
Professor of Education, Curtin University of Technology, Perth, Australia
Instructional Environment

Freedheim, Donald K.
Professor of Psychology, Case Western Reserve University, Cleveland, Ohio
Clinical Psychology, *article on* Theories; Psychiatry

Freedman, Mervin B.
Professor Emeritus of Psychology, San Francisco State University, California
War and Conflict, *article on* Effects on General Population

Freedman, Robert R.
Professor of Obstetrics and Gynecology; Professor of Psychiatry and Behavioral Neurosciences; and Director of Behavioral Medicine Division, Wayne State University School of Medicine, Detroit, Michigan
Raynaud's Disease

Freeman, Linton C.
Research Professor, Department of Sociology and Institute for Mathematical Behavioral Sciences, School of Social Sciences, University of California, Irvine
Social Network Analysis, *article on* Definition and History

French, Joseph L.
Professor Emeritus of Education, The Pennsylvania State University, University Park
Itard, Jean-Marie-Gaspard; Seguin, Edouard; Whipple, Guy M.

French, Sabine E.
Project Director of the Adolescent Pathways Project, New York University, New York
School Transitions

Frensch, Peter A.
Professor of Psychology, Max-Planck Institute for Human Development, Berlin, Germany
Max Planck Institute for Human Development and Education

Frese, Michael
Professor of Psychology, University of Giessen, Germany
Job Stress

Freund, Joel S.
Associate Professor of Psychology, University of Arkansas, Fayetteville
Underwood, Benton J.

Frick, Robert W.
Adjunct Assistant Professor of Psychology, Department of Psychology, State University of New York at Stony Brook
Statistical Significance

Friedman, Maurice
Professor Emeritus of Religious Studies, Philosophy, and Comparative Literature, San Diego State University, and Co-Director of the Institute for Dialogical Psychotherapy, California
Existentialism

Friedman, Richard
Professor of Psychiatry and Behavioral Science, State University of New York at Stony Brook
Meditation

Friedman, Steven
Professor of Clinical Psychiatry, State University of New York Health Science Center, Brooklyn, New York
Dermatological Disorders

Frueh, B. Christopher
Assistant Professor, Department of Psychiatry and Behavioral Sciences, Medical University of South Carolina and Veterans Affairs Medical Center, Charleston, South Carolina
Posttraumatic Stress Disorder

Fuchs, A. H.
Professor Emeritus of Psychology, Bowdoin College, Brunswick, Maine
Hunter, Thomas Alexander; Porter, Noah; Postman, Leo Joseph; Upham, Thomas Cogswell

Fuchs, Lynn S.
Professor of Special Education, Vanderbilt University, Nashville, Tennessee
Academic Assessment–Intervention Link

Fuhriman, Addie
Dean of Graduate Studies, Brigham Young University, Provo, Utah
Group Therapy

Furumoto, Laurel
Professor of Psychology, Wellesley College, Massachusetts
Calkins, Mary Whiton; Ladd-Franklin, Christine

Gabbard, Glen O.
Bessie Walker Callaway Distinguished Professor of Psychoanalysis and Education, Karl Menninger School of Psychiatry and Mental Health Sciences, The Menninger Clinic, Topeka, Kansas
Ego Psychology Theory; Superego

Gade, Paul A.
Chief of the Organization and Personnel Resources Research Unit, United States Army Research Institute, Alexandria, Virginia
Military Service

Gaenslen, Fritz
Associate Professor of Political Science, Gettysburg College, Pennsylvania
Political Decision Making

Galano, Joseph
Associate Professor of Psychology, College of William and Mary, Williamsburg, Virginia
Public Service

Galanter, Eugene
Professor of Psychology, Director of the Psychophysics Laboratory, Columbia University, New York
Psychophysics

Galanter, Marc
Professor of Psychiatry, Division of Alcoholism and Drug Abuse, New York University, New York
Cults

Gallo, David A.
Graduate Student in the Department of Psychology, Washington University, Saint Louis, Missouri
False Memory

Gannon, Linda R.
Professor of Psychology, Southern Illinois University, Carbondale
Menopause

Gardiner, Harry W.
Professor Emeritus of Cross-Cultural Psychology, University of Wisconsin, La Crosse
Ethnopedagogy

Gardiner, John M.
Professor of Psychology, City University, London, United Kingdom
Retrieval Processes

Gardner-Bonneau, Daryle J.
Human Factors Specialist, Independent Consultant, Kalamazoo, Michigan
Machine Design

Garfield, Sol L.
Professor Emeritus of Psychology, Washington University, Saint Louis, Missouri
Scientist-Practitioner Model

Garman, Michael
Professor of Linguistics, University of Reading, United Kingdom
Psycholinguistics, *article on* An Overview

Garofalo, John P.
Assistant Professor of Psychology, University of Pittsburgh, Pennsylvania
Genetic Disorders

Gavin, Eileen A.
Professor of Psychology, College of Saint Catherine, Saint Paul, Minnesota
Bühler, Charlotte M.; Michotte, Albert Edouard

Gavin, Joanne H.
Otto Alois Faust Doctoral Fellow in Health and Character, University of Texas at Arlington
Stress, *article on* Measurement

Gawlick, Ute
Doctoral Candidate, Laboratory of Immunophysiology, Neurosciences Program, Department of Animal Sciences, University of Illinois at Urbana-Champaign
Immune System

Gearon, Jean S.
Assistant Professor of Psychiatry, University of Maryland School of Medicine, Baltimore
Bipolar Disorder

Geisler, Wilson S.
Professor of Psychology, University of Texas at Austin
Spatial Vision

Gelso, Charles J.
Professor of Psychology, University of Maryland, College Park
Working Alliance

Gentile, J. Ronald
State University of New York Distinguished Teaching Professor, Department of Counseling and Educational Psychology, State University of New York at Buffalo
Learning, Transfer of

Georgas, James
Professor of Social Psychology, University of Athens, Greece
Greece

Gergen, Mary M.
Professor of Psychology and Women's Studies, The Pennsylvania State University, Delaware County
Feminism, *article on* Feminist Psychology

Germans, Marja K.
Graduate Student, Department of Psychology, Vanderbilt University, Nashville, Tennessee
Anhedonia

Gettinger, Maribeth
Professor of Educational Psychology, University of Wisconsin, Madison
Mainstreaming and Inclusion

Geuter, Ulfried
Lecturer in Clinical Psychology, Free University of Berlin, Germany
Krueger, Felix

Gibbs, Peter R.
Director of the Center for Adoption Research and Policy, University of Massachusetts, Worcester
Adoption; Foster Care

Gifford, Robert K.
Colonel, United States Army, Walter Reed Army Institute of Research, Washington, D.C.
War and Conflict, *article on* Effects on Military Personnel

Gilbert, Andrew
Professor of Psychology, Rhodes University, East London, South Africa
South Africa

Gilbert, Daniel
Professor of Psychology, Harvard University, Cambridge, Massachusetts
Jones, Edward Ellsworth

Gill, Michele
Research Manager, Department of Psychiatry and Behavioral Sciences, Stanford University School of Medicine, California
Somatoform Disorders

Gillam, Barbara J.
Professor of Psychology, University of New South Wales, Sydney, Australia
Perceptual Constancies

Gilmore, Rick O.
Assistant Professor of Psychology, The Pennsylvania State University, University Park
Infancy, *article on* Biological Processes

Gilstrap, Livia L.
Graduate Student, Department of Human Development, Cornell University, Ithaca, New York
Determinants of Intelligence, *article on* Schooling and Intelligence

Ginzler, Joshua Aaron
Research Coordinator, Alchohol and Drug Abuse Institute, University of Washington, Seattle
Homelessness

Giora, Rachel
Professor of Linguistics, Tel Aviv University, Israel
Pragmatics

Gleason, Jean Berko
Professor of Psychology, Boston University, Massachusetts
Language, *article on* An Overview

Glenberg, Arthur M.
Professor of Psychology, University of Wisconsin-Madison
Melton, Arthur

Glickman, Stephen E.
Professor of Psychology and Integrative Biology, University of California, Berkeley
Ethology; Hebb, Donald Olding

Glisky, Elizabeth L.
Professor of Psychology, University of Arizona, Tucson
Neuropsychology, *article on* Interventions

Glynn, Laura M.
Postdoctoral Fellow, Department of Psychiatry and Human Behavior, University of California, Irvine
Field Study

Goldberg, Joel O.
Associate Professor, Department of Psychiatry, McMaster University, Hamilton, Ontario, Canada
Eysenck Personality Questionnaire

Golden, Charles J.
Professor of Psychology, Nova Southeastern University, Fort Lauderdale, Florida
Wechsler Memory Scale

Golden-Kreutz, Deanna M.
Research Associate, Department of Psychology, The Ohio State University, Columbus, Ohio
Cancer

Goldin-Meadow, Susan
Professor of Psychology, University of Chicago, Illinois
Language, *article on* Language Development, Syntax, and Communication

Goldstein, Julius L.
Professor of Electrical Engineering, Washington University, Saint Louis, Missouri
Pitch Perception

Goldstein, Suzanne G.
Doctoral Candidate, Department of Clinical and Health Psychology, MCP Hahnemann University, Philadelphia, Pennsylvania
Day Treatment

Gollwitzer, Peter M.
Professor of Psychology, University of Konstanz, Germany
Goals; Volition

Good, Thomas L.
Professor and Head, Department of Educational Psychology, University of Arizona, Tucson
Teachers, *article on* Assessment of Teacher Effectiveness

Goodale, Melvyn A.
Professor of Psychology and Neuroscience, University of Western Ontario, London, Canada
Perception and Action

Goodman, Gail S.
Professor of Psychology, University of California, Davis
Family Violence

Goodman-Delahunty, Jane
Administrative Judge, United States Equal Employment Opportunity Commission, Los Angeles, California
Employment Discrimination

Goodwin, C. James
Professor of Psychology, Wheeling Jesuit University, West Virginia
Miles, Walter Richard; Sanford, Edmund Clark

Gopher, Daniel
Yigal Allon Professor for the Study of Humans at Work, Technion-Israel Institute of Technology, Haifa, Israel
Mental Workload

Gordon, Claire C.
Senior Research Anthropologist, United States Army Natick Research, Development, and Education Center, Massachusetts
Anthropometry

Gordon, Wayne A.
Professor and Associate Director, Department of Rehabilitation Medicine, The Mount Sinai School of Medicine, New York
Rehabilitation Psychology

Gormezano, Isidore
Kenneth W. Spence Professor of Psychology, University of Iowa, Iowa City
Learning, *article on* Conditioning Approach

Gosling, Samuel D.
Professor of Psychology, University of Texas, Austin
Personality Traits

Gottlieb, Gilbert
Research Professor of Psychology, University of North Carolina at Chapel Hill
Nature and Nurture Theories

Gough, Harrison G.
Professor Emeritus of Psychology, University of California, Berkeley
Adjective Checklist

Gould, Herbert Jay
Associate Professor of Audiology, School of Audiology and Speech Language Pathology, University of Memphis, Tennessee
Auditory Impairment

Grad, Héctor M.
Associate Lecturer in Social Psychology, Universidad Autonoma de Madrid, Spain
Spain

Grant, Elizabeth R.
Doctoral Candidate, Cornell University, Ithaca, New York
Memory, *article on* Constructive Processes

Grau, James W.
Professor of Psychology, Texas A&M University, College Station
Avoidance Learning

Greenberg, Leslie S.
Department of Psychology, York University, North York, Ontario, Canada
Gestalt Therapy

Greenberg, Roger P.
Professor, and Head of Psychology Division, Department of Psychiatry and Behavioral Science, State University of New York Health Science Center, Syracuse
Psychoanalysis, *article on* Methods of Study

Greene, Beverly A.
Professor of Psychology, Saint John's University, Jamaica, New York
Gender, Sex, and Culture, *article on* Gender and Culture; Gender, Sex, and Culture, *article on* Sex and Culture; Homophobia

Greene, George J.
Assistant in Psychology, University of Illinois at Chicago
Community Psychology, *article on* History of the Field

Greenfield, Patricia Marks
Professor of Psychology, University of California, Los Angeles
Culture, *article on* Culture and Development

Greenough, William T.
Swanlund and Center for Advanced Study Professor of Psychology, Psychiatry, and Cell and Structural Biology, University of Illinois at Urbana-Champaign
Brain Development; Learning, *article on* Molecular and Cellular Aspects

Greer, Scott
Independent Scholar, Milton, Ontario, Canada
Nietzsche, Friedrich W.

Gregg, Aiden P.
Postdoctoral Fellow, Department of Psychology, University of Southampton, United Kingdom
Attitudes, *article on* Attitude Structure

Gregory, Richard L.
Professor Emeritus of Neuropsychology, University of Bristol, United Kingdom
Visual Illusions

Grenke, Heidi M.
Project Coordinator, Center for Psychotherapy Research, Department of Psychiatry, Medical School of the University of Pennsylvania, Philadelphia
Interpersonal Psychotherapy

Grigorenko, Elena L.
Research Scientist, Department of Psychology and Child Study Center, Yale University, New Haven, Connecticut; and Associate Professor, Moscow State University
Cognitive Styles, *article on* Intelligence

Grove, William M.
Professor of Psychology, Department of Psychology, University of Minnesota, Minneapolis
Actuarial Prediction

Guignon, Charles
Professor of Philosophy, The University of Vermont, Burlington
Philosophy, *article on* An Overview

Gulick, W. Lawrence
Resident Scholar and Professor of Psychology, University of Delaware, Newark
Wever, Ernest Glen

Gully, Stanley M.
Professor of Human Resource Management, Rutgers University, Piscataway, New Jersey
Group Cohesiveness

Gundlach, Horst
Professor of Psychology, Institut für Geschichte der Psychologie, Passau University, Germany
Henning, Hans

Gurman, A.
Professor of Psychiatry, University of Wisconsin Medical School, Madison
Family Therapy

Guthrie, Robert V.
Professor Emeritus of Psychology, Southern Illinois University
Clark, Kenneth Bancroft; Sumner, Francis Cecil

Gutkin, Terry B.
Professor of Educational Psychology, University of Nebraska, Lincoln
Buros Mental Measurements Yearbook

Gyueseog, Han
Korea

Haas, Leonard J.
Professor of Family and Preventive Medicine; and Director of Behavioral Science, University of Utah, Salt Lake City
Ethics, *article on* Ethics in Practice

Haber, Lyn
Adjunct Professor of Psychology, University of California, Riverside, and University of California, Santa Cruz
Eidetic Imagery

Haber, Ralph Norman
Adjunct Professor of Psychology, University of California, Riverside, and University of California, Santa Cruz
Eidetic Imagery

Hackenberg, Timothy D.
Associate Professor of Psychology, University of Florida, Gainesville
Loeb, Jacques; Schedules of Reinforcement

Haertel, Geneva D.
Senior Educational Researcher, SRI International, Menlo Park, California
Teachers, *article on* Teacher Relationships

Hagen, John W.
Professor of Psychology, The University of Michigan, Ann Arbor; and Executive Officer, Society for Research in Child Development, Ann Arbor, Michigan
Society for Research in Child Development

Hagenaars, Jacques A.
Professor of Methodology of the Social Sciences, Tilburg University, The Netherlands
Cohort Effects

Hagglund, Kristofer J.
Associate Professor of Physical Medicine and Rehabilitation, University of Missouri, Columbia
Fibromyalgia Syndrome

Hakel, Milton D.
Regents' Eminent Scholar, and Professor of Psychology, Bowling Green State University, Ohio
American Psychological Society

Hakuta, Kenji
Professor of Education, Stanford University, California
Bilingualism

Halford, Kim
Chair of the Department of Psychology, Griffith University, Australia
Marriage

Hall, Felicia D.
Graduate Student in the Department of Psychology, University of Virginia, Charlottesville
Cultural Diversity

Hall, Gordon C. Nagayama
Professor of Psychology, The Pennsylvania State University, University Park
Fetishism; Pedophilia; Sexual Masochism; Sexual Sadism

Hall, Judy E.
Executive Officer of the National Register of Health Service, Providers in Psychology, Washington, D.C.
National Register of Health Service Providers in Psychology

Hamann, Stephan B.
Assistant Professor of Psychology, Emory University, Atlanta, Georgia
Amnesia

Hambleton, Ronald K.
Distinguished University Professor, Laboratory of Psychometric and Evaluative Research, University of Massachusetts, Amherst
International Test Commission

Hamilton, David L.
Professor of Psychology, University of California, Santa Barbara
Illusory Correlation; Stereotypes

Hampton, Keith
Doctoral Student, Department of Sociology, University of Toronto, Ontario, Canada
Virtual Communities

Han, Kyunghee
Assistant Professor of Educational Psychology, University of Mississippi, University
Construct Validity

Handel, Stephen
Professor of Psychology, University of Tennessee, Knoxville
Auditory Pattern Recognition

Hans, Valerie P.
Professor of Criminal Justice and Psychology, University of Delaware, Newark
Juries

Hansen, Jo-Ida C.
Professor of Psychology, University of Minnesota, Minneapolis
Strong Interest Inventory

Haque, Abdul
Professor of Psychology, University of Sindh, Pakistan
Pakistan

Hargrove, David S.
Professor of Psychology, and Chair of the Department of Psychology, University of Mississippi, University
Rural Communities

Harkness, Sara
Professor in the School of Family Studies, University of Connecticut, Storrs
Developmental Agenda

Harper, Dennis C.
Professor of Pediatrics and Graduate Studies in Rehabilitation, University of Iowa College of Medicine, Iowa City
Developmental Disorders

Harris, Richard J.
Professor of Psychology, University of New Mexico, Albuquerque
Analysis of Variance

Harrow, Martin
Professor of Psychology, Departments of Psychiatry and Psychology, University of Illinois at Chicago
Delusions

Hartley, Eugene L.
Dean Emeritus, University of Wisconsin-Green Bay, and Professor Emeritus of Psychology, The City College of New York
Murphy, Gardner

Hartup, Willard W.
Regents' Professor Emeritus of Child Psychology, Institute of Child Development, University of Minnesota, Minneapolis
International Society for the Study of Behavioural Development; Middle Childhood, *article on* Socialization and Social Contexts

Harvey, O. J.
Professor Emeritus of Psychology, University of Colorado, Boulder
Sherif, Muzafer

Hatcher, Robert L.
Director of the Institute of Human Adjustment, The University of Michigan, Ann Arbor
Cathexis; Libido

Hatfield, Gary
Adam Seybert Professor of Moral and Intellectual Philosophy, University of Pennsylvania, Philadelphia
Descartes, René

Hattie, John
Head of the School of Education, University of Auckland, New Zealand
Instructional Treatments

Haugtvedt, Curtis P.
Professor of Marketing, Fisher College of Business, The Ohio State University, Columbus
Consumer Psychology

Haupt, Edward J.
Professor of Psychology, Montclair State University, Upper Montclair, New Jersey
Jaensch, Erich R.; Katona, George; Katz, David; Lotze, Hermann; Marbe, Karl; Meumann, Ernst; Müller, Georg Elias; Schumann, Friedrich

Hauser, Stuart T.
Professor of Psychiatry, Harvard Medical School, and President, Judge Baker Children's Center, Boston, Massachusetts
Ego

Hauser-Cram, Penny
Associate Professor of Developmental and Educational Psychology, Boston College, Chestnut Hill, Massachusetts
Preschool Education

Hayes, Steven C.
Foundation Professor of Psychology, and Chair of the Department of Psychology, University of Nevada, Reno
Applied Behavior Analysis

Haynes, Stephen N.
Professor of Psychology, University of Hawaii at Manoa, Honolulu
Direct Observation; Health Psychology, *article on* Assessments and Interventions

Haywood, H. Carl
Dean of the School of Education, Touro College, New York; and Professor Emeritus of Psychology, Vanderbilt University, Nashville, Tennessee
Hunt, J. McVicker

Healy, Alice F.
Professor of Psychology, University of Colorado, Boulder
Estes, William Kaye

Hedges, Larry V.
Stella M. Rowley Professor of Education, Psychology, and Sociology, University of Chicago, Illinois
Meta-Analysis

Heesacker, Martin
Professor of Psychology, University of Florida, Gainesville
Counseling Psychology, *article on* Theories

Heinrichs, R. Walter
Associate Professor of Psychology, York University, Toronto, Ontario, Canada
Bleuler, Eugen

Held, Barbara S.
Barry N. Wish Professor of Psychology and Social Studies, Bowdoin College, Brunswick, Maine
General Systems Theory and Philosophy

Helkama, Klaus
Professor of Social Psychology, University of Helsinki, Finland
Finland

Helmers, Karin F.
Department of Exercise and Health Sciences, York University, North York, Ontario, Canada
Impulsivity

Helson, Ravenna
Research Psychologist and Adjunct Professor of Psychology, University of California, Berkeley
Personality Development, *article on* Adulthood and Aging

Hendry, Cheryl N.
Doctoral Student in Educational Psychology, University of Georgia, Athens
Learning Disabilities

Henin, Aude
Department of Psychiatry, Massachusetts General Hospital, Boston
Cognitive-Behavioral Therapy

Henle, Mary
Professor Emerita of Psychology, Graduate Faculty, New School for Social Research, New York
Köhler, Wolfgang

Heppner, Mary J.
Associate Professor, Counseling Psychology, University of Missouri, Columbia
Career Counseling

Herber, Christiane
Academic Program Advisor, University of Texas, El Paso
Nightmares

Herbert, James D.
Associate Professor, Department of Clinical and Health Psychology, MCP Hahnemann University, Philadelphia, Pennsylvania
Day Treatment

Herek, Gregory M.
Professor of Psychology, University of California, Davis
Homosexuality

Herkenham, Miles
Chief of the Section on Functional Neuroanatomy, National Institute of Mental Health, Bethesda, Maryland
Marijuana

Herring, K. Lee
Director of Public Affairs, American Consulting Engineers Council, Washington, D.C.
American Psychological Society

Hetherington, E. Mavis
Professor Emeritus of Psychology, University of Virginia, Charlottesville
Divorce

Heyd, Thomas
Visiting Assistant Professor of Philosophy, and Faculty Fellow, Centre for Studies in Religion and Society, University of Victoria, British Columbia, Canada; and 1999 Research Fellow, Japan Foundation, Konan University
Hamilton, William

Hickman, Larry A.
Director of the Center for Dewey Studies, Southern Illinois University, Carbondale
Dewey, John

Higgins, E. Tory
Professor of Psychology, Columbia University, New York
Category Accessibility; Self-Regulation

Hill, Clara E.
Professor of Psychology, University of Maryland, College Park
Client-Centered Therapy

Hills, Michael D.
Senior Lecturer in Psychology, University of Waikato, Hamilton, New Zealand
New Zealand

Hilsenroth, Mark J.
Assistant Professor, Department of Psychology, University of Arkansas, Fayetteville
Rorschach Test

Hineline, Philip N.
Professor of Psychology, Temple University, Philadelphia, Pennsylvania
Single-Case Experimental Design

Hobson, J. Allan
Professor of Psychiatry, Harvard Medical School, Boston, Massachusetts
Dreams, *article on* Physiology

Hofer, Barbara K.
Assistant Professor of Psychology, Middlebury College, Vermont
Middle Childhood, *article on* Education and Schooling

Hofstede, Geert
Professor Emeritus and Senior Research Fellow, Institute for Research on Intercultural Cooperation, Tilburg University, The Netherlands
Masculine and Feminine Cultures

Hogan, John D.
Professor of Psychology, Saint Johns University, Jamaica, New York
Anastasi, Anne; Developmental Psychology, *article on* History of the Field

Holbrook, Allyson L.
Graduate Research Associate, Center for Survey Research, Department of Psychology, The Ohio State University, Columbus
Political Behavior

Holden, Ronald R.
Professor of Psychology, Queen's University, Kingston, Ontario, Canada
Psychometrics

Hollander, Edwin P.
University Distinguished Professor Emeritus of Psychology, Bernard M. Baruch College and University Graduate Center, New York
Klineberg, Otto

Hollon, Steven D.
Professor of Psychology, Vanderbilt University, Nashville, Tennessee
Antidepressants; Cognitive Therapy

Holtzman, Wayne H.
Hogg Professor of Psychology and Education, University of Texas, Austin
International Psychology

Hood, Ralph W., Jr.
Professor of Psychology, University of Tennessee, Chattanooga
Mysticism

Hopkins, J. Roy
Associate Provost for Academic Services, and Professor of Psychology, Saint Mary's College of Maryland
Brown, Roger William; Erikson, Erik H.

Horn, John L.
Professor of Psychology; and Head of the Adult Development and Aging Department, University of Southern California, Los Angeles
Cattell, Raymond B.

Hornstein, Gail A.
Professor of Psychology, Mount Holyoke College, South Hadley, Massachusetts
Fromm-Reichmann, Frieda

Horowitz, Mardi J.
Professor of Psychiatry, University of California, San Francisco
Abreaction; Associationism; Compromise Formation; Self-Concept and Self-Representation

Horvat, Erin McNamara
Assistant Professor of Urban Education, Temple University, Philadelphia, Pennsylvania
School Dropout

Hoshmand, Lisa Tsoi
Professor of Psychology, and Director of the Division of Counseling and Psychology, Lesley College, Cambridge, Massachusetts
Narrative Psychology

Hoskovec, Jiří
Professor of Psychology, Charles University, Prague, Czech Republic
Doležal, Jan

Howard, George S.
Professor of Psychology, University of Notre Dame, Indiana
Philosophy, *article on* Philosophy of Science

Howard, Kenneth I.
Professor of Psychology, Northwestern University, Evanston, Illinois
Psychotherapy, *article on* Research

Howard, Natasha M.
Graduate Student, School of Education, Boston College, Massachusetts
Disruptive Behavior Disorders

Howe, Michael J. A.
Professor of Psychology, University of Exter, United Kingdom
Genius; Prodigies

Hoy, Anita Woolfolk
Professor of Education, The Ohio State University, Columbus
College Teaching and Learning

Hsiang, Simon M.
Liberty Mutual Research Center for Safety and Health, Hopkinton, Massachusetts
Biomechanics and Kinematics

Huesmann, Graham R.
Doctoral Candidate, Beckman Institute for Advanced Science and Technology, Neuronal Pattern Analysis, University of Illinois, Urbana-Champaign
Immune System

Humphreys, Keith
Assistant Professor of Psychiatry, Stanford University School of Medicine, California
Alcoholics Anonymous; Twelve-Step Programs

Hunt, James G. "Jerry"
Paul Whitfield Horn Professor of Management, Institute for Leadership Research, Texas Tech University, Lubbock
Organizational Management

Hunter-King, Edna J.
Research Professor Emeritus, United States International University, San Diego, California
Prisoners of War

Hurvich, Leo M.
Professor Emeritus of Psychology, and Member of the Mahoney Institute of Neurological Sciences, University of Pennsylvania, Philadelphia
Society of Experimental Psychologists

Hwang, Kwang-Kuo
National Chair, and Professor of Psychology, National Taiwan University, Taipei
Taiwan

Hynd, George W.
Research Professor of Special Education and Psychology, University of Georgia, Athens
Dyslexia

Ickes, William
Professor of Psychology, University of Texas at Arlington
Empathic Accuracy; Heider, Fritz

Ilgen, Daniel R.
John A. Hannah Professor of Psychology and Management, Michigan State University, East Lansing
Industrial and Organizational Psychology, *article on* Theories and Methods of Study

Imada, Hiroshi
Professor of Psychology, Kwansei Gakuin University, Nishinomiya, Japan
Japan

Imhoff, Anne R.
Psychologist at the University of Albany, State University of New York
Career, *article on* Career Interventions

Infanti, Helen
Doctoral Student, Department of Educational Psychology, University of Arizona, Tucson
Discipline

Innis, Nancy K.
Professor of Psychology, University of Western Ontario, London, Canada
Krech, David; Tolman, Edward Chace

Innis, Robert E.
Professor and Chairman, Department of Philosophy, University of Massachusetts, Lowell
Bühler, Karl

Iscoe, Ira
Ashbel Smith Professor Emeritus of Psychology, The University of Texas at Austin
Crisis Intervention

Ito, Tiffany A.
Assistant Professor of Psychology, University of Colorado, Boulder
Social Neuroscience

Izard, Carroll
Unidel Professor of Psychology, University of Delaware, Newark
Affect; Interest; Joy; Sadness

Jääskeläinen, Manu
Doctor of Philosophy, and Independent Scholar, Kerava, Finland
Kaila, Eino

Jackson, Douglas N.
Professor Emeritus of Psychology, University of Western Ontario, London, Canada
Scale Development

Jackson, Thomas L.
Professor and Director of Clinical Training, Department of Psychology, University of Arkansas, Fayetteville
Prevention, *article on* Prevention for Adults

Jacobs, Barry L.
Professor and Director of the Program in Neuroscience, Princeton University, New Jersey
Hallucinogens

Jacobson, Mark
Postdoctoral Fellow in Neuropsychology, University of California, San Diego, School of Medicine
Neuropsychology, *article on* Testing

James, Elizabeth Murdoch
Psychologist in Private Practice, and Independent Scholar, Las Vegas, Nevada
Woolley, Helen Thompson

Jeffery, Sarah E.
Doctoral Candidate, Department of Psychological and Brain Sciences, University of Louisville, Kentucky
Specific Phobia

Jeffrey, Linda R.
Professor of Psychology, Rowan University, Glassboro, New Jersey
Rubin, Edgar; Wheeler, Raymond H.; Witasek, Stephan

Jennings, Jerry L.
Clinical Director, Liberty Healthcare Corporation, Narberth, Pennsylvania
Husserl, Edmund

Jensen, Arthur R.
Professor Emeritus of Educational Psychology, University of California, Berkeley
Elementary Cognitive Tasks; Twins

Jensen, Donald D.
Professor of Psychology, University of Nebraska, Lincoln
Jennings, Herbert Spencer

Jing, Qicheng
Professor of Psychology, Institute of Psychology, Chinese Academy of Sciences, Beijing
Pan, Shu; Zhang, Yao-xiang

Jobe, Thomas H.
Professor of Psychiatry, and Associate Director of the Division of Neuropsychiatry, University of Illinois at Chicago
Delusions

John, Oliver P.
Professor of Psychology, University of California, Berkeley
Personality Traits

Johnson, David H.
Executive Director, Federation of Behavioral, Psychological, and Cognitive Sciences, Washington, D.C.
Federation of Behavioral, Psychological, and Cognitive Sciences

Johnson, Deborah F.
Associate Professor of Psychology, University of Southern Maine, Portland
Plato; Socrates; Ward, James; Warren, Howard Crosby

Johnson, Mark H.
Professor of Psychology, Birkbeck College, University of London, United Kingdom
Infancy, *article on* Biological Processes

Johnson-Laird, Phillip N.
Stuart Professor of Psychology, Princeton University, New Jersey
Thinking, *article on* Reasoning

Johnston, Marie
Professor of Psychology, University of Saint Andrews, Fife, United Kingdom
Physical Disabilities

Jolliffe, Darrick M.
Research Associate, Institute of Criminology, University of Cambridge, United Kingdom
Millon Clinical Multiaxial Inventory

Jones, James W.
Professor of Religion, and Adjunct Professor of Clinical Psychology, Rutgers University, New Brunswick, New Jersey
Religious Experience, *article on* Belief and Faith

Jones, Lyle V.
Research Professor of Psychology, University of North Carolina at Chapel Hill
Thurstone, Louis Leon

Jones, Lynette A.
Principal Research Scientist in Mechanical Engineering, Massachusetts Institute of Technology, Cambridge
Kinesthesis; Proprioception

Jones, Stanley E.
American Psychological Association, Washington, D.C.
Ethics, *article on* An Overview

Jones, Stanton L.
Provost, and Professor of Psychology, Wheaton College, Illinois
Religion and Psychology, *article on* Theories and Methods

Jopp, David A.
Assistant in Psychology, University of Illinois at Chicago
Community Psychology, *article on* History of the Field

Joravsky, David
Department of History, Northwestern University, Evanston, Illinois
Marx, Karl

Judge, Timothy A.
Professor of Management and Organizations, Henry B. Tippie College of Business, University of Iowa, Iowa City
Job Satisfaction

Kaas, Jon H.
Centennial Professor of Psychology, Vanderbilt University, Nashville, Tennessee
Touch, *article on* Biological Organization

Kagan, Jerome
Professor of Psychology, Harvard University, Cambridge, Massachusetts
Temperament

Kagitcibasi, Cigdem
Professor of Psychology, Koç University, Istanbul, Turkey
School Readiness; Turkey

Kahn, Robert L.
Professor Emeritus of Psychology and Public Health; and Research Scientist Emeritus, Institute for Social Research, The University of Michigan, Ann Arbor
Campbell, Angus; Institute for Social Research

Kalikow, Theodora J.
President of the University of Maine at Farmington
Lorenz, Konrad

Kamphaus, R. W.
Professor of Educational Psychology, University of Georgia, Athens
Learning Disabilities

Kantowitz, Barry H.
Director and Professor of Industrial and Operations Engineering, The University of Michigan, Ann Arbor
Transportation Systems Design

Kaplan, Kalman J.
Professor of Psychology, Wayne State University, Detroit, Michigan; Director, Suicide Research Center, Michael Reese Hospital and Medical Center, Chicago, Illinois; and Editor, Journal of Psychology and Judaism: *Religion, Culture, and Personality Section*
Judaism and Psychology

Kaplan, Robert M.
Professor, and Chair of the Department of Family and Preventive Medicine, University of California, San Diego
Chronic Obstructive Pulmonary Disease

Karau, Steven J.
Assistant Professor of Management, Southern Illinois University, Carbondale
Deindividuation; Psychosis

Karns, Leslie
School of Dentistry, University of Mississippi Medical Center, Jackson
Psychosis

Kastenbaum, Robert
Professor Emeritus, Hugh Downs School of Human Communication, Arizona State University, Tempe
Death and Dying

Katz, Albert N.
Professor of Psychology, University of Western Ontario, London, Canada
Mental Imagery

Kaufman, Alan S.
Clinical Professor of Psychology, Yale University School of Medicine, New Haven, Connecticut
Wechsler, David

Kaufmann, Paul M.
Chief Operating Officer of the Choate Mental Health and Developmental Center, Anna, Illinois; and Adjunct Associate Professor of Psychiatry, Southern Illinois University School of Medicine, Carbondale
Head Injury

Kazdin, Alan E.
Professor and Chairman of Psychology, Yale University, New Haven, Connecticut
Child and Adolescent Psychotherapy; Experimental Neurosis; Parent Management Training; Token Economy

Keith, Kathy W.
Doctoral Candidate, Experimental Psychology, University of North Texas, Denton
Helson, Harry

Kelley, Harold H.
Professor Emeritus of Psychology, University of California, Los Angeles
Thibaut, John W.

Kelley, Keith W.
Professor of Immunophysiology, University of Illinois at Urbana-Champaign
Immune System

Kellogg, Ronald T.
Professor of Psychology, University of Missouri, Rolla
Writing

Kelly, James G.
Professor of Psychology and Public Health, University of Illinois at Chicago
Community Psychology, *article on* History of the Field; Professional Consultation

Kelly, Jeffrey A.
Professor of Psychiatry and Behavioral Medicine, and Director, Center for AIDS Intervention Research, Medical College of Wisconsin, Milwaukee
Sexually Transmitted Diseases

Keltner, Dacher
Associate Professor of Psychology, University of California, Berkeley
Emotion, *article on* An Overview

Kemp, Simon
Associate Professor of Psychology, University of Canterbury, Christchurch, New Zealand
Psychology, *article on* The Middle Ages

Kendall, Philip C.
Professor of Psychology; and Head of the Division of Clinical Psychology, Temple University, Philadelphia, Pennsylvania
Cognitive-Behavioral Therapy

Kenny, Maureen E.
Associate Professor, Department of Counseling, Developmental and Educational Psychology, Lynch School of Education, Boston College, Chestnut Hill, Massachusetts
Oppositional Defiant Disorder

Keogh, Barbara K.
Professor Emerita, Graduate School of Education, and Professor, Department of Psychiatry, University of California, Los Angeles
Exceptional Students

Keyser, Barbara Whitney
Professor of Painting Conservation, Queens University, Kingston, Ontario, Canada
Kries, Johannes Von; Müller-Lyer, Franz Carl; Révèsz, Geza

Khan, Hassan Kassim
President of The Yemeni Psychological Society, Kormachsar, Yemen
Arab States, *article on* Yemen, Oman, and Sudan

Kiang, Nelson Yuan-sheng
Eaton-Peabody Professor Emeritus, Harvard-MIT Division of Health Sciences and Technology; Professor Emeritus of Physiology, Department of Otology and Laryngology, Harvard Medical School; Founding Director, Eaton-Peabody Laboratory, Massachusetts Eye and Ear Infirmary; and Neurophysiologist Emeritus, Neurology Service, Massachusetts General Hospital, Boston
Hearing, *article on* Behavioral and Functional Aspects

Kier, Frederick J.
Postdoctoral Fellow in Geropsychology, Houston Veterans Affairs Medical Center, Houston, Texas
Pressey, Sidney Leavitt

Kihlstrom, John
Professor, Department of Psychology, University of California, Berkeley
Parapsychology

Kimble, Gregory A.
Professor Emeritus of Psychology, Duke University, Durham, North Carolina
Sechenov, Ivan Mikhailovich

Kimmel, Allan J.
American University of Paris, France
Rumors

King, Abby C.
Associate Professor of Health Research, Policy and Medicine, Stanford University School of Medicine, Palo Alto, California
Exercise and Physical Activity

King, Alison
Professor of Educational Psychology, California State University, San Marcos
Situated Cognition

King, Laura A.
Associate Professor, Department of Psychology, Southern Methodist University, Dallas, Texas
Motivation, *article on* Assessment

Kingsbury, Sherman
Palo Alto, California
NTL Institute for Applied Behavioral Science

Kirk, Roger E.
Distinguished Professor of Psychology and Statistics, Baylor University, Waco, Texas
Randomized Experiments

Kirmayer, Laurence J.
Professor and Director of the Division of Social and Transcultural Psychiatry, McGill University, Montreal, Quebec, Canada
Epidemiology

Kirschner, Suzanne R.
Assistant Professor of Psychology, College of the Holy Cross, Worcester, Massachusetts
Postmodern Psychology

Kish, Leslie
Professor Emeritus of Sociology, and Research Scientist, Institute for Social Research, The University of Michigan, Ann Arbor
Sampling

Kiss, György
Budapest, Hungary
Ranschburg, Pal

Kitsantas, Anastasia
Assistant Professor, Department of Educational Research and Educational Psychology, Florida State University, Tallahassee
Student Characteristics

Kitzinger, Celia
Reader in Lesbian and Feminist Psychology, Loughborough University, United Kingdom
Heterosexism; Heterosexuality

Kivlighan, Dennis M.
Professor, and Chair of the Department of Educational and Counseling Psychology, University of Missouri, Columbia
Counseling Process and Outcome

Klatzky, Roberta L.
Professor, and Head of Psychology; and Professor of Human-Computer Interaction, Carnegie Mellon University, Pittsburgh, Pennsylvania
Cognitive Maps

Kleckler, Diane M.
Adjunct Professor of Psychology, Northern Illinois University, DeKalb
Play Therapy

Klein, Malcolm W.
Professor Emeritus of Psychology, University of Southern California, Los Angeles
Gangs

Klimoski, Richard J.
Professor of Psychology, George Mason University, Fairfax, Virginia
Handwriting Analysis; Industrial and Organizational Psychology, *article on* Assessments and Interventions

Kline, Paul
Department of Psychology, University of Exeter, United Kingdom
Rigidity

Kling, Kristen C.
Postdoctoral Researcher in Psychology, University of Minnesota, Minneapolis
Self-Report; Validity

Klinger, Eric
Professor of Psychology, University of Minnesota, Morris
Commitment; Daydreams

Knapp, Samuel J.
Professional Affairs Officer, Pennsylvania Psychological Association, Harrisburg
Licensure

Knapp, Terry J.
Professor of Psychology, University of Nevada, Las Vegas
Shepard, Roger N.

Kobayashi, Mireika
Doctoral Candidate, Department of Psychology, University of Cincinnati, Ohio
Psychotherapy, *article on* Clinical Practice

Kodama, Seiji
Professor of Psychology, Nihon University, Tokyo, Japan
Matsumoto, Matataro; Motora, Yujiro

Koenig, Kathryn
Associate Professor Emeritus of Psychology, York University, Toronto
Newcomb, Theodore Mead

Kokoszka, Andrzej
Professor of Psychiatry, Medical University of Warsaw, Poland
Altered States of Consciousness

Koku, Emmanuel
Doctoral Candidate, Department of Sociology, University of Toronto, Ontario, Canada
Virtual Communities

Kolko, David J.
Associate Professor of Child Psychiatry and Psychology, Pittsburgh, Pennsylvania
Conduct Disorder

Koopman, Cheryl
Associate Research Professor in Psychiatry and Behavioral Science, Stanford University, California
Somatoform Disorders

Koppes, Laura L.
Associate Professor of Psychology, Eastern Kentucky University, Richmond
Gilbreth, Lillian

Korn, Marcella E.
Doctoral Candidate, University of Arizona, School of Family and Consumer Resources, Family Studies and Human Development Program, Tucson
Developmental Psychology, *article on* Theories

Kornfeld, Alfred D.
Professor of Psychology, Eastern Connecticut State University, Willimantic
Dunlap, Knight

Kosmicki, Frank X.
Doctoral Candidate, Department of Psychology, Georgia State University, Atlanta
Catharsis

Koss, Mary P.
Professor of Public Health, Family and Community Medicine, Psychiatry, and Psychology, Arizona Prevention Center, University of Arizona College of Medicine, Tucson
Rape

Kowal, Dennis
Annandale, Virginia
Brainwashing

Kowalski, Robin M.
Associate Professor of Psychology, Western Carolina University, Cullowhee, North Carolina
Anxiety

Kozulin, Alex
Research Director, International Center for the Enhancement of Learning Potential, Jerusalem, Israel
Luria, Alexander R.; Vygotsky, Lev Semenovich

Kraemer, Helena Chmura
Professor of Biostatistics in Psychiatry, Stanford University, California
Measures of Association

Krain, Amy L.
Doctoral Candidate in Clinical Psychology, Temple University, Philadelphia, Pennsylvania
Cognitive-Behavioral Therapy

Kral, Michael J.
Associate Professor of Psychology, University of Windsor, Ontario, Canada
Pintner, Rudolf

Krantz, David L.
Professor of Psychology, Lake Forest College, Illinois
McDougall, William

Kreppner, Kurt
Senior Research Scientist in Psychology, Max Planck Institute for Human Development, Berlin, Germany
Parent-Child Relationship, *article on* Adolescence

Kring, Ann M.
Associate Professor of Psychology, University of California, Berkeley
Anhedonia

Krosnick, Jon A.
Professor of Psychology and Political Sciences, The Ohio State University, Columbus
Political Behavior

Krueger, Gerald P.
Colonel, United States Army (retired), and Krueger Ergonomics Consultants, Alexandria, Virginia
Military Culture

Krueger, Richard A.
Professor and Evaluation Leader, University of Minnesota, Saint Paul
Focus Group

Krueger, Robert F.
Assistant Professor of Psychology, University of Minnesota, Minneapolis
Self-Report; Validity

Krug, Samuel E.
President, MetriTech, Incorporated, Champaign, Illinois
Sixteen Personality Factor Questionnaire

Krumhansl, Carol L.
Professor of Psychology, Cornell University, Ithaca, New York
Music Perception

Ksir, Charles
Dean of the College of Education, and Professor of Psychology and Counselor Education, University of Wyoming, Laramie
Drugs

Kubovy, Michael
Professor of Psychology, University of Virginia, Charlottesville
Visual and Design Arts

Kuhn, Deanna
Professor of Psychology and Education, Teachers College, Columbia University, New York
Adolescence, *article on* Adolescent Thought Processes

Kurpius, Sharon E. Robinson
Professor of Counseling Psychology, Division of Psychology in Education, Arizona State University, Tempe
Peer Counseling

Kusch, Martin
Lecturer in History and Philosophy of Science, University of Cambridge, United Kingdom
Külpe, Oswald

Lachman, Margie E.
Professor of Psychology, Brandeis University, Waltham, Massachusetts
Agency, *article on* Agency and Control Theory

Lack, Leon C.
Associate Professor of Psychology, Flinders University, School of Psychology, Adelaide, South Australia
Circadian Rhythms, *article on* Circadian Rhythm Disorders

LaFrance, Marianne
Professor of Psychology, and Professor of Women's and Gender Studies, Yale University, New Haven, Connecticut
Nonverbal Communication

Lafuente, Enrique
Professor of History of Psychology, Universidad Nacional de Educacion a Distancia, Madrid, Spain
Germain, José; Giner de los Ríos, Francisco; Simarro, Luis

Lakin, Martin
Professor Emeritus of Psychology, Duke University, Durham, North Carolina
Rogers, Carl Ranson

Lamb, Michael E.
Senior Research Scientist, National Institute of Child Health and Human Development, Bethesda, Maryland
Attachment; Fathering

Lambert, Michael J.
Professor of Psychology, Brigham Young University, Provo, Utah
Beck Depression Inventory

Lamiell, James T.
Professor of Psychology, Georgetown University, Washington, D.C.
Stern, Louis William

Landy, Frank J.
Chief Executive Officer of Litigation Support Services, SHL, Incorporated, Boulder, Colorado
Ghiselli, Edwin E.; Myers, Charles S.

Lansford, Jennifer E.
Doctoral Candidate, The University of Michigan, Ann Arbor
Adulthood and Aging, *article on* Social Processes and Development

Lattal, Kennon A.
Arts and Sciences Centennial Professor of Psychology, West Virginia University, Morgantown
Operant Conditioning, *article on* Operant Conditioning Chamber; Single-Case Experimental Design

Lawton, M. Powell
Senior Research Scientist, Polisher Research Institute, Philadelphia Geriatric Center, Pennsylvania
Clinical Geropsychology

Lazarus, Arnold A.
President of the Center for Multimodal Psychological Services, Princeton, New Jersey
Multimodal Therapy

Leahey, Thomas Hardy
Professor of Psychology, Virginia Commonwealth University, Richmond
Psychology, *article on* Nineteenth Century through Freud; Psychology, *article on* Renaissance through the Enlightenment

Leamon, Tom B.
Director of the Liberty Mutual Research Centers, Boston, Massachusetts
Biomechanics and Kinematics

Leary, David E.
Dean of Arts and Sciences, and Professor of Psychology, University of Richmond, Virginia
Brunswik, Egon; Herbart, Johann Friedrich; Koch, Sigmund

Leary, Mark R.
Professor of Psychology, Wake Forest University, Winston-Salem, North Carolina
Self-Consciousness

Lefcourt, Herbert M.
Distinguished Professor Emeritus, University of Waterloo, Ontario, Canada
Locus of Control

Lejuez, Carl W.
Graduate Research Associate, Department of Psychology, West Virginia University, Morgantown
Aversion Therapy

Lent, Robert W.
Professor of Counseling Psychology, University of Maryland, College Park
Educational Counseling

Léon, Rámon
Associate Professor, Universidad Ricardo Palma, Lima, Peru
Delgado, Honorio

Leong, Frederick T. L.
Associate Professor of Psychology, The Ohio State University, Columbus
Asian American Psychology; Cultural Pluralism

Lerner, Jacqueline V.
Professor of Developmental and Educational Psychology, Boston College, Chestnut Hill, Massachusetts
Human Origins; Parent-Child Relationship, *article on* Childhood

Lerner, Melvin J.
Distinguished Professor Emeritus of Psychology, University of Waterloo, Ontario, Canada
Just World Belief

Lerner, Richard M.
Bergstrom Chair in Applied Developmental Science, Tufts University, Medford, Massachusetts
Developmental Psychology, *article on* Theories

Lesgold, Alan M.
Professor of Psychology and Intelligent Systems, Learning Research and Development Center, University of Pittsburgh, Pennsylvania
Cognitive Science Society

Leslie, Alan M.
Professor of Psychology and Cognitive Science, Rutgers University, Piscataway, New Jersey
Theory of Mind

LeUnes, Arnold
Professor of Psychology, Texas A&M University, College Station
Griffith, Coleman Roberts

Levant, Ronald F.
Dean and Professor of Psychology, Nova Southeastern University, Fort Lauderdale, Florida
Psychology of Men

Levelt, Willem J. M.
Professor of Psycholinguistics, Max-Planck-Institut fur Psycholinguistik, Nijmegen, The Netherlands
Speech Production

Levin, Henry M.
William Heard Kilpatrick Professor of Economics and Education, Teachers College, Columbia University, New York
Alternative Schools

Levin, Robert A.
Assistant Professor of Foundations of Education, Youngstown State University, Ohio
American Educational Research Association

Levine, John M.
Professor of Psychology, University of Pittsburgh, Pennsylvania
Groups, *article on* Group Processes

Levine, M.
Distinguished Service Professor of Psychology, and Adjunct Professor of Law, State University of New York at Buffalo
Labeling; Mandated Reporting

Levinson, Edward M.
Professor of Educational and School Psychology, Indiana University of Pennsylvania
Technical and Professional Education

Levy, J.
Professor of Psychology, University of Chicago, Illinois
Hemispheric Functions

Lichstein, Kenneth L.
Professor of Psychology, University of Memphis, Tennessee
Relaxation Training

Lickel, Brian
Doctoral Candidate, Department of Psychology, University of California, Santa Barbara
Illusory Correlation

Liddle, Howard A.
Professor of Psychiatry and Psychology, University of Miami School of Medicine, Florida
Family Psychology, *article on* History of the Field; Family Psychology, *article on* Assessments and Interventions

Lilienfeld, Scott O.
Assistant Professor of Psychology, Emory University, Atlanta, Georgia
Psychopathology

Lin, Keh-Ming
Professor of Psychiatry, Research Center on the Psychobiology of Ethnicity, Harbor-University of California Los Angeles Medical Center, Torrance
Psychopharmacology, *article on* Ethnopsychopharmacology

Lind, E. Allan
Thomas A. Finch Professor of Business Administration, Fuqua School of Business, Duke University, Durham, North Carolina
Social Justice

Lindahl, Kristin
Associate Professor of Psychology, University of Miami, Florida
Marriage

Lindenberger, Ulman
Senior Research Scientist, Max Planck Institute for Human Development, Center for Lifespan Psychology, Berlin (Dahlem), Germany
Life Span Psychology Theory

Lindenfeld, David F.
Professor of History, Louisiana State University, Baton Rouge
Meinong, Alexius

Lindzey, Gardner
Director Emeritus, Center for Advanced Study in the Behavioral Sciences, Stanford, California
Center for Advanced Study in the Behavioral Sciences

Linehan, Marsha M.
Professor of Psychology, University of Washington, Seattle
Borderline Personality Disorder

Littman, Richard A.
Professor of Psychology, University of Oregon, Eugene
Piéron, Henri; Preyer, Wilhelm

Loewenstein, George
Professor of Economics and Psychology, Carnegie Mellon University, Pittsburgh, Pennsylvania
Curiosity

Logan, Cheryl A.
Professor of Psychology and Biology, University of North Carolina at Greensboro
Small, Willard S.

Logan, Gordon D.
Professor of Psychology, University of Illinois at Urbana-Champaign
Information Processing Theories

Lohman, David F.
Professor of Educational Psychology, University of Iowa, Iowa City
Measures of Intelligence, *article on* Cognitive Theories

LoLordo, Vincent M.
Professor of Psychology, Dalhousie University, Halifax, Nova Scotia, Canada
Classical Conditioning; Solomon, Richard Lester

LoPiccolo, Joseph
Professor of Psychology, University of Missouri, Columbia
Sexual Dysfunctions

Lord, Robert G.
Professor of Psychology, University of Akron, Ohio
Leadership

Lorion, Raymond P.
Professor, and Chair of the Department of Psychology, Ohio University, Athens
Prevention, *article on* Prevention for Adults; Public Policy

Lovie, Pat
Senior Lecturer in Statistics for the Social Sciences, University of Keele, Staffordshire, United Kingdom
Brett, George S.; Hovland, Carl Iver; Kelley, Truman Lee; Spearman, Charles Edward; Sully, James

Lovie, Sandy (A. D.)
Senior Lecturer in Psychology, University of Liverpool, United Kingdom
Brett, George S.; Hovland, Carl Iver; Kelley, Truman Lee; Spearman, Charles Edward; Sully, James

Lubinski, David
Associate Professor of Psychology and Human Development, Vanderbilt University, Nashville, Tennessee
Measures of Intelligence, *article on* Intelligence Tests

Luborsky, Lester
Professor of Psychology in Psychiatry, University of Pennsylvania, Philadelphia
Psychoanalysis, *article on* Psychoanalytic Psychotherapies

Luebbert, Michael C.
Postdoctoral Fellow, Saint Louis Behavioral Medicine Institute, Missouri
Schopenhauer, Arthur

Lunt, Ingrid
Reader in Educational Psychology, University of London Institute of Education, United Kingdom
European Federation of Professional Psychologists' Associations

Lyman, Robert D.
Professor of Psychology, University of Alabama, Tuscaloosa
Residential Treatment Programs

Lyon, David R.
Graduate Student in Law and Forensic Psychology, Simon Fraser University, Burnaby, British Columbia, Canada
Criminality

MacLean, William E., Jr.
Associate Professor of Psychology, University of Wyoming, Laramie
Down Syndrome

MacLin, Otto H.
Research Associate, The University of Texas at El Paso
Cognitive Psychology, *article on* History of the Field

Mae, Lynda
Research Assistant, Department of Psychological Sciences, Purdue University, West Lafayette, Indiana
Impression Formation

Magnusson, David N.
Olof Eneroth Professor Emeritus of Psychology, Stockholm University, Sweden
Developmental Science

Mahrer, Alvin R.
Professor Emeritus of Psychology, University of Ottawa, Ontario, Canada
Experiential Psychotherapy

Maier, Steven F.
Professor of Psychology, University of Colorado, Boulder
Learned Helplessness

Main, Mary
Professor of Psychology, University of California, Berkeley
Attachment Theory

Major, Brenda
Professor of Psychology, University of California, Santa Barbara
Abortion

Malatesta, Victor J.
Clinical Associate Professor of Psychology in Psychiatry, Pennsylvania Hospital and University of Pennsylvania School of Medicine, Wynnewood
Inpatient Treatment

Malchiodi, Cathy A.
Director of the Institute for the Arts and Health, Salt Lake City, Utah
Art Therapy

Malony, H. Newton
Senior Professor of Psychology, Fuller Theological Seminary, Pasadena, California
Christianity and Psychology

Malt, Ulrik Fredrik
Clinical Director and Professor, Department of Behavioral and Psychosomatic Medicine, The National Hospital, Oslo, Norway
Accidents

Manber, Rachel
Associate Professor of Psychiatry and Behavioral Sciences, Stanford University, California
Night Terrors

Mangelsdorff, A. David
Professor, Graduate Program in Healthcare Administration, U.S. Army-Baylor University Graduate Program in Healthcare Administration, Fort Sam Houston, Texas
Military Psychology

Marhaba, Sadi
Professor of History of Psychology, Università degli Studi di Padova, Italy
Italy

Markman, Howard J.
Professor of Psychology and Director of the Center for Marital and Family Studies, University of Denver, Colorado
Marriage

Marsella, Anthony J.
Professor of Psychology, University of Hawaii, Honolulu
Culture, *article on* Culture and Mental Health; Culture-Bound Disorders; Refugees

Marshall, Marilyn E.
Professor of Psychology, Carleton University, Ottawa, Ontario, Canada
Fechner, Gustav Theodor

Marsiske, Michael
Assistant Professor of Gerontology and Psychology, Wayne State University, Detroit, Michigan
Terminal Decline

Martin, Carol Lynn
Professor, Department of Family Resources and Human Development, Arizona State University, Tempe
Gender Identity

Martin, Rod A.
Professor of Psychology, University of Western Ontario, London, Canada
Humor and Laughter

Martindale, Colin
Professor of Psychology, University of Maine, Orono
Aesthetics

Mason, DeWayne A.
Assistant Superintendent of Educational Services, Jurupa Unified School District, Riverside, California
Teachers, *article on* Assessment of Teacher Effectiveness

Massarik, Fred
Professor Emeritus, Anderson School, University of California, Los Angeles; and Executive Consultant, Behavior Science Research Associates, Los Angeles, California
Field Theory

Matarazzo, Joseph D.
Professor and Chairman, Department of Medical Psychology, Oregon Health Sciences University, Portland
Hunt, William Alvin

Maton, Kenneth I.
Professor of Psychology, University of Maryland, Baltimore County
Mutual-Help and Self-Help

Matsumoto, David
Professor of Psychology, San Francisco State University, California
Cross-Cultural Communication

Maxwell, Christine B.
Program Coordinator, Department of Curriculum and Instruction, University of Wisconsin, Milwaukee
Head Start

Maxwell, Scott E.
Matthew A. Fitzsimons Professor of Psychology, University of Notre Dame, Indiana
Data Analysis

Mayer, Richard E.
Professor of Psychology, University of California, Santa Barbara
Conceptual Change

Maynard, Ashley E.
Postdoctoral Fellow, Department of Psychology and Biobehavioral Sciences, University of California, Los Angeles
Culture, *article on* Culture and Development

McAdams, Dan P.
Professor of Human Development and Psychology, Northwestern University, Evanston, Illinois
Extraversion and Introversion; Generativity; Personality Psychology, *article on* History of the Field

McAnulty, Richard D.
Associate Professor of Psychology, University of North Carolina at Charlotte
Sex Therapy

McCalmont, Elizabeth M.
Research Programmer Analyst, Center for Psychotherapy Research, Department of Psychiatry, Medical School of the University of Pennsylvania, Philadelphia
Hamilton Rating Scale

McCaslin, Mary
Associate Professor of Psychology, Department of Educational Psychology, University of Arizona, Tucson
Discipline

McCauley, Clark
Professor of Psychology, Bryn Mawr College, Pennsylvania
Asch, Solomon E.

McCrae, Robert R.
Research Psychologist, Section on Stress and Coping, Gerontology Research Center, National Institute on Aging, Baltimore, Maryland
NEO Personality Inventory

McCubbin, James A.
Professor and Chair of Psychology, Clemson University, South Carolina
Psychoneuroendocrinology

McDargh, John
Associate Professor of Religion and Psychology, Boston College, Chestnut Hill, Massachusetts
Love, *article on* Spiritual Conceptions of Love

McDermott, Kathleen B.
Research Assistant Professor, Washington University, Saint Louis, Missouri
Implicit Memory

McEwen, Bruce S.
Alfred E. Mirsky Professor, and Head of the Harold and Margaret Milliken Hatch Laboratory of Neuroendocrinology, Rockefeller University, New York
Endocrine Systems

McFarland, Pamela T.
Postdoctoral Fellow in Neuropsychology, Veteran's Affairs Medical Center, Veteran's Hospital, Long Beach, California
Computerized Psychotherapy

McGaugh, James L.
Director of the Center for the Neurobiology of Learning and Memory; and Research Professor, Department of Neurobiology and Behavior, University of California, Irvine
Emotional Learning

McGuinness, Carol
Senior Lecturer, Queens University Belfast, Department of Psychology, Northern Ireland
Northern Ireland

McGuire, William J.
Professor Emeritus of Psychology, Yale University, New Haven, Connecticut
Cognitive Consistency Theories; Research Methods, *article on* History of the Field

McKeachie, Wilbert J.
Professor Emeritus of Psychology, The University of Michigan, Ann Arbor
American Institutes for Research in the Behavioral Sciences

Mcloughlin, Caven S.
Associate Professor, School of Psychology, Kent State University, Ohio
Burt, Cyril Lodowic; Eysenck, Hans Jurgen

McLoyd, Vonnie C.
Professor of Psychology, Center for Human Growth and Development, The University of Michigan, Ann Arbor
Poverty, *article on* Childhood Poverty

McNally, Richard J.
Professor of Psychology, Harvard University, Cambridge, Massachusetts
Fear and Terror

McNeil, Daniel W.
Associate Professor and Director of Clinical Training, Department of Psychology, West Virginia University, Morgantown
Systematic Desensitization

McNulty, John L.
Visiting Assistant Professor of Psychology, The University of Tulsa, Oklahoma
Five-Factor Model of Personality

McReynolds, Paul
Professor Emeritus of Psychology, University of Nevada, Reno
Witmer, Lightner

Meade, Michelle L.
Graduate Student in the Department of Psychology, Washington University, Saint Louis, Missouri
Learning, *article on* Cognitive Approach for Humans

Meaney, Michael J.
Professor, Departments of Psychiatry and Neurology and Neurosurgery, McGill University, Douglas Hospital Research Center, Montréal, Québec, Canada
Stress, *article on* Definition and Physiology

Mecacci, Luciano
Professor of Psychology, Universitá degli Studi di Firenze, Italy
Ferrari, Giulio Cesare

Medin, Douglas L.
Professor of Psychology, Northwestern University, Evanston, Illinois
Concepts, *article on* An Overview

Megargee, Edwin I.
Professor of Psychology, Florida State University, Tallahassee
Testing

Melamed, Barbara G.
Professor of Psychology, Ferkauf Graduate School of Psychology, Albert Einstein College of Medicine, Department of Psychiatry, Epidemiology, and Social Medicine, Yeshiva University, Bronx, New York
Chronic Fatigue Syndrome; Wellness and Illness

Melia, Kathleen R.
Clinical Instructor, Department of Psychiatry, Harvard University Medical School, Boston, Massachusetts
Veterans

Meltzoff, Andrew N.
Professor of Psychology, University of Washington, Seattle
Infancy, *article on* Learning and Cognitive Development

Mensh, Ivan N.
Professor Emeritus of Medical Psychology, Department of Psychiatry and Biobehavioral Sciences, University of California, Los Angeles
Mental Health Care

Mergendoller, John R.
Director of Research and Evaluation, Buck Institute for Education, Novato, California
Classrooms, *article on* Technology

Merikangas, Kathleen R.
Director of the Genetic Epidemiology Research Unit, Yale University School of Medicine, New Haven, Connecticut
Alcoholism

Merikle, Philip
Professor of Psychology, University of Waterloo, Ontario, Canada
Consciousness and Unconsciousness, *article on* Processes; Subliminal Perception

Mesibov, Gary B.
Professor and Director of TEACCH, University of North Carolina at Chapel Hill
Autistic Disorder

Metcalfe, Janet
Professor of Psychology, Columbia University, New York
Intuition

Mikkelsen, Jon Mark
Associate Professor of Philosophy and Humanities, Missouri Western State College, Saint Joseph, Missouri
Kant, Immanuel

Milgram, Noach
Professor of Clinical Psychology, Tel Aviv University, Israel
Israel; Propaganda

Miller, Alison B.
Doctoral Candidate in Clinical Psychology, University of Illinois at Chicago
Professional Consultation

Miller, Arthur G.
Professor of Psychology, Miami University of Ohio, Oxford
Obedience

Miller, Chris (*translator*)
Freelance Editor, Translator, and Critic; and Founding Member of the Oxford Amnesty Lectures, United Kingdom
Fraisse, Paul; Meyerson, Ignace; Taine, Hippolyte

Miller, Eric J.
Senior Consulting Social Scientist, The Tavistock Institute, London, United Kingdom
Tavistock Institute

Miller, Harold R.
Associate Professor of Psychiatry and Behavioral Neurosciences, McMaster University, Hamilton, Ontario, Canada
Millon Clinical Multiaxial Inventory

Miller, Ronald B.
Professor of Psychology, and Director of the Graduate Program in Clinical Psychology, Saint Michael's College, Colchester, Vermont
Epistemology of Practice

Millon, Theodore
Dean and Scientific Director, Institute for Advanced Studies in Personology and Psychopathology, Coral Gables, Florida
Obsessive-Compulsive Personality Disorder

Mills, Eugene S.
President Emeritus and Professor Emeritus of Psychology, Whittier College, Tustin, California
Ladd, George Trumbull

Minton, Henry L.
Department of Psychology, University of Windsor, Ontario, Canada
Hooker, Evelyn; Terman, Lewis Madison

Miserandino, Marianne
Assistant Professor of Psychology, Beaver College, Glenside, Pennsylvania
Frankl, Viktor Emil.

Mitchell, Stephen A.
Founding Editor, Psychoanalytic Dialogues, *New York*
Object Relations Theories

Mitler, Merrill M.
Professor, Department of Neuropharmacology, The Scripps Research Institute, La Jolla, California
Narcolepsy

Mobilio, Lynne
Doctor of Philosophy, Department of Psychology, University of Minnesota, Minneapolis
Social Motivation

Mogil, Jeffrey S.
Assistant Professor of Psychology, University of Illinois at Urbana-Champaign
Pain, *article on* Mechanisms

Moldawsky, Stanley
Faculty Member, Institute for Psychoanalysis and Psychotherapy of New Jersey, South Orange
Private Practice

Monahan, John
Henry and Grace Doherty Professor of Law, University of Virginia, Charlottesville
Violence Risk Assessment

Monk, Timothy H.
Professor of Psychiatry, Western Psychiatric Institute and Clinic, University of Pittsburgh, Pennsylvania
Circadian Rhythms, *article on* An Overview

Monte, Christopher F.
Professor of Psychology, Manhattanville College, Purchase, New York
Personality Psychology, *article on* Theories

Monteiro Neto, Felix Fernando
Professor of Psychology, University of Porto, Portugal
Portugal

Monteith, Margo J.
Associate Professor of Psychology, University of Kentucky, Lexington
Prejudice

Montero, Maritza
Professor of Social Psychology, Universidad Central de Venezuela, Caracas
Sociohistorical Process

Montville, Joseph V.
Director of the Preventive Diplomacy Program, Center for Strategic and International Studies, Washington, D.C.
Peace

Moore, Carmella C.
Assistant Research Anthropologist, University of California, Irvine
Cognitive Anthropology

Moos, Rudolf H.
Research Career Scientist and Professor, Department of Veteran Affairs Health Care System, and Stanford University, Palo Alto, California
Social Settings

Mor, Vincent
Professor of Medical Science; Chair, Department of Community Health; and Director, Center for Gerontology and Health Care Research, Brown University School of Medicine, Providence, Rhode Island
Hospice

Moras, Karla
Assistant Professor of Psychology in Psychiatry, Center for Psychotherapy Research, Medical School of the University of Pennsylvania, Philadelphia
Hamilton Rating Scale; Interpersonal Psychotherapy

Morawski, Jill
Professor of Psychology, Wesleyan University, Middletown, Connecticut
Ellis, Henry Havelock; Feminism, *article on* Feminism and Philosophy; Psychology, *article on* Early Twentieth Century

Moray, Neville
DERA Professor of Applied Cognitive Psychology, University of Surrey, United Kingdom
Human Error Analysis

Morris, Edward K.
Professor of Human Development, University of Kansas, Lawrence
Association for Behavior Analysis; Keller, Fred Simmons

Morris, Tracy L.
Associate Professor of Psychology, West Virginia University, Morgantown
Covert Conditioning

Morse, Stephen J.
Ferdinand Wakeman Habbell Professor of Law, and Professor of Psychology and Law in Psychiatry, University of Pennsylvania, Philadelphia
Criminal Responsibility

Moughrabi, Fouad
Professor of Political Science, University of Tennessee at Chattanooga
Islam and Psychology

Mountjoy, Paul T.
Professor Emeritus of Psychology, Western Michigan University, Kalamazoo
Kantor, Jacob R.

Mowbray, Carol T.
Associate Professor, and Associate Dean for Research, School of Social Work, The University of Michigan, Ann Arbor
Deinstitutionalization

Moxley, D. P.
Associate Professor of Social Work, The University of Michigan, Ann Arbor
Deinstitutionalization

Mueser, Kim T.
Professor of Psychiatry, Dartmouth Medical School, Concord, New Hampshire
Paranoia or Delusional Disorder

Multon, Karen D.
Professor of Counseling Psychology, University of Missouri, Columbia
Career, *article on* Career Development

Muñoz, Ricardo F.
Professor of Psychology, University of California, San Francisco
Community Prevention and Intervention, *article on* Prevention of Depression

Munroe, Robert L.
Research Professor of Anthropology, Pitzer College, Claremont, California
Anthropology; Cognitive Anthropology; Ethnography

Murphy, Lawrence R.
Senior Research Psychologist, National Institute for Occupational Safety and Health, Cincinnati, Ohio
Employee Assistance Programs

Murray, David J.
Professor Emeritus of Psychology, Queen's University, Kingston, Ontario, Canada
Beebe-Center, John Gilbert; Békésy, Georg von; Koffka, Kurt; Ogden, Robert Morris; Watt, Henry Jackson; Weber, Ernst Heinrich

Murray, John P.
Professor and Interim Associate Vice Provost for Research, Kansas State University, Manhattan
Media Effects

Murrell, Audrey J.
Associate Professor of Business Administration, Psychology, and Women's Studies, The Katz School, University of Pittsburgh, Pennsylvania
Discrimination

Mussen, Paul Henry
Professor Emeritus of Psychology, and Director Emeritus of the Institute of Human Development, University of California, Berkeley
Jones, Mary Cover

Myambo, Kathleen
Senior Lecturer in Psychology, University of Zimbabwe, Harare
Sub-Saharan Africa

Myers, Patricia
Senior Research Associate, Harvard Medical School, Boston, Massachusetts
Meditation

al-Naboulsi, Mohamed Ahmed
President of the Center for Psychological and Psycho-Somatic Studies, Tripoli, Lebanon
Arab States, *article on* Lebanon, Syria, Jordan, and Iraq

Naglieri, Jack A.
Independent Scholar, Dublin, Ohio
Kaufman Assessment Battery for Children; Peabody Picture Vocabulary Test; Stanford–Binet Intelligence Scale; Wechsler Intelligence Tests

Nairne, James S.
Professor of Psychology, Purdue University, West Lafayette, Indiana
Forgetting

Neath, Ian
Associate Professor of Psychology, Purdue University, West Lafayette, Indiana
Learning and Memory, *article on* In Humans

Neimeyer, Robert A.
Professor of Psychology, University of Memphis, Tennessee
Constructivist Psychotherapy; Kelly, George Alexander

Nelson, Debra L.
CBA Associates Professor of Business Administration, and Professor of Management, Oklahoma State University, Stillwater
Work Conditions

Nelson, Elizabeth L.
Associate Professor, Department of Psychology, California State University, Stanislaus, Turlock
American Psychological Association of Graduate Students

Nelson, Linda D.
Associate Professor of Neurology, University of California, Irvine
Bender–Gestalt Visual Motor Test

Nelson, Paul D.
Deputy Executive Director for Education, American Psychological Association, Washington, D.C.
Doctoral Degree

Neumann, Jean E.
Senior Consulting Social Scientist, The Tavistock Institute, London, United Kingdom
Tavistock Institute

Newman, Colin V.
Executive Secretary, The British Psychological Society, Leicester, United Kingdom
British Psychological Society

Nezami, Elahe
Research Assistant Professor of Preventive Medicine, and Associate Director of Undergraduate Training in Health Promotion and Disease Prevention, University of Southern California School of Medicine, Los Angeles
Standardized Tests

Nicholson, Ian A. M.
Assistant Professor of Psychology, University of Prince Edward Island, Charlottetown, Canada
Allport, Floyd Henry; Langfeld, Herbert Sidney; Stevens, Stanley Smith

Nickerson, Raymond S.
Senior Vice President (retired), Bolt Beranek & Newman Incorporated, Cambridge, Massachusetts
Determinants of Intelligence, *article on* Teaching of Intelligence; Human Behavior and the Natural Environment; Technology, *article on* Technology and Communication

Nicolas, Serge
Assistant Professor of Experimental Psychology and History of Psychology, University René Descartes, Paris
Delboeuf, Joseph-Léopold-Rémi; Ribot, Théodule Armand; Simon, Théodore

Nielsen, Kathleen H.
Pediatric Neuropsychologist Intern, Center for Clinical and Developmental Neuropsychology, University of Georgia, Athens
Dyslexia

Nietzel, Michael T.
Professor of Psychology and Dean of the Graduate School, University of Kentucky, Lexington
Police Psychology

Nigh, Margaret S.
Research Assistant, Missouri Arthritis Rehabilitation Research and Training Center, University of Missouri, Columbia
Fibromyalgia Syndrome

Niit, Toomas
Professor of Psychology, Tallinn Pedagogical University, Estonia
Baltic Countries

Nilsson, Lars-Göran
Olof Eneroth Professor of Psychology, Stockholm University, Sweden
Sweden

Norcross, John C.
Professor of Psychology, University of Scranton, Pennsylvania
Psychotherapy, *article on* Clinical Practice

Norman, Kent L.
Associate Professor of Psychology, University of Maryland, College Park
Human-Computer Interface Design

Northover, Mehroo
Lecturer, University of Ulster, Newtownabbey, Northern Ireland
Northern Ireland

Novaco, Raymond W.
Professor of Psychology and Social Behavior, University of California, Irvine
Anger

Nye, Robert A.
Thomas Hart and Mary Jones Horning Professor of Humanities and Professor of History, Oregon State University, Corvallis
Le Bon, Gustave

Oakes, Jeannie
Professor of Education, and Associate Dean for Outreach and Research, University of California, Los Angeles
Grouping and Tracking

Oatley, Keith
Professor of Applied Psychology, Centre for Applied Cognitive Science, University of Toronto, Ontario, Canada
Emotion, *article on* Theories

O'Brien, William H.
Department of Psychology, Bowling Green State University, Ohio
Direct Observation

Ogloff, James R. P.
University Endowed Professor of Law and Forensic Psychology, Simon Fraser University, Burnaby, British Columbia, Canada
Criminality

Ohala, John J.
Professor of Linguistics, University of California, Berkeley
Phonetics

O'Hara, Maureen
Acting President, Saybrook Graduate School, San Francisco, California
Humanistic Psychology

O'Hara, Michael W.
Professor of Psychology, University of Iowa, Iowa City
Pregnancy

Okagaki, Lynn
Associate Professor of Child Development and Family Studies, Purdue University, West Lafayette, Indiana
Determinants of Intelligence, *article on* Socialization of Intelligence

Okifuji, Akiko
Research Assistant Professor of Anesthesiology, University of Washington, Seattle
Pain, *article on* Models and Management

Olson, David R.
University Professor, Ontario Institute for Studies in Education, University of Toronto, Canada
Literacy

Olson, Heather Carmichael
Research Assistant Professor, School of Medicine, University of Washington, Seattle
Fetal Alcohol Syndrome

Olweus, Dan
Research Professor of Psychology, Research Center for Health Promotion, University of Bergen, Norway
Bullying

O'Neill, Ynez Violé
Professor of Medical History, Department of Neurobiology, University of California, Los Angeles
Galen

Orff, Henry
Laboratory and Project Coordinator, Sleep Research Laboratory, University of Rochester School of Medicine, New York
Sleeptalking

Orley, John
Independent Consultant, Divonne-les-Bains, France
World Health Organization

Orlinsky, David E.
Professor of Human Development and Social Sciences, Committee on Human Development, University of Chicago, Illinois
Psychotherapy, *article on* Research; Society for Psychotherapy Research

Orne, Martin T.
Professor Emeritus of Psychiatry and Psychology, University of Pennsylvania, Philadelphia
Demand Characteristics

Osipow, Samuel H.
Professor Emeritus of Psychology, The Ohio State University, Columbus
Work

Ostrow, Andrew C.
Professor and Program Coordinator, School of Physical Education, West Virginia University, Morgantown
Sport Psychology, *article on* Assessment

Otto, Michael W.
Director of the Cognitive Behavior Therapy Program, Massachusetts General Hospital; and Associate Professor of Psychology, Harvard Medical School, Boston
Antianxiety Medication

Ozer, Daniel J.
Associate Professor of Psychology, University of California, Riverside
Nomothetic and Idiographic Orientations

Padilla, Amado M.
Professor of Education, Stanford University, California
Hispanic Psychology; Vives, Juan Luis

Palincsar, Annemarie
Jean and Charles Walgreen Professor of Literacy, School of Education, The University of Michigan, Ann Arbor
Learning Skills

Palmer, Stephen E.
Professor of Psychology, University of California, Berkeley
Perceptual Organization

Pandey, Janak
Director of the G. B. Pant Social Science Institute, Allahabad, India
India

Paolitto, Anthony W.
Assistant Professor, School Psychology, The Ohio State University, Columbus
Stanford–Binet Intelligence Scale

Paquin, Anthony R.
Assistant Professor of Industrial and Organizational Psychology, Illinois Institute of Technology, Chicago
Drever, James

Parekh, Priti I.
Research Assistant, Department of Psychiatry and Behavioral Sciences, Duke University Medical Center, Durham, North Carolina
Diabetes

Pargament, Kenneth I.
Professor of Psychology, Bowling Green State University, Ohio
Interventions Based in Religious Congregations

Paris, Bernard J.
Professor Emeritus of English, University of Florida, Gainesville
Horney, Karen D.

Parlee, Mary Brown
Visiting Professor of Women's Studies, Massachusetts Institute of Technology, Cambridge
Teuber, Hans-Lukas

Parrott, W. Gerrod
Professor of Psychology, Georgetown University, Washington, D.C.
Jealousy and Envy

Pasupathi, Monisha
Assistant Professor of Developmental Psychology, University of Utah, Salt Lake City
Wisdom

Pate, James L.
Professor of Psychology, Georgia State University, Atlanta
Regional Psychological Associations, *article on* Regional Psychological Associations in the United States

Patterson, Michael
Graduate Student, Rutgers University, Newark, New Jersey
Language, *article on* Language and Brain Systems

Paul, Gordon L.
Cullen Distinguished Professor, Department of Psychology, University of Houston, Texas
Milieu Therapy

Paul, Robert A.
Charles Howard Caudler Professor of Anthropology, Institute of Liberal Arts, Emory University, Atlanta, Georgia
Oedipus Complex

Paulus, Paul B.
Professor of Psychology and Chair, University of Texas, Arlington
Brainstorming

Pedersen, Paul B.
Professor, Department of Human Studies, School of Education, University of Alabama at Birmingham
Cross-Cultural Counseling; Non-Western Therapies

Pelham, William E., Jr.
Professor of Psychology, and Director of the Attention-Deficit/Hyperactivity Disorder (ADHD) Program, State University of New York at Buffalo
Stimulants

Penn, David L.
Assistant Professor, Department of Psychology, University of North Carolina at Chapel Hill
Hallucinations

Perdue, Charles W.
Professor of Psychology, West Virginia State College, Institute
Ageism

Perlis, Michael L.
Assistant Professor of Psychiatry and Psychology; Assistant Director of the University of Rochester Sleep Research Laboratory; and Co-Director of the Sleep Disorders Center of Rochester—Insomnia Clinic, New York
Sleeptalking

Perlman, Daniel
Professor of Family Studies, University of British Columbia, Vancouver, Canada
Affiliation

Pervin, Lawrence A.
Professor of Psychology, Rutgers State University of New Jersey, Piscataway
Personality

Peterman, Amy
Research Assistant Professor, Institute for Health Services Research and Policy Studies, Northwestern University, Evanston, Illinois
Quality of Life

Petersen, Anne C.
Senior Vice President for Programs, W. K. Kellogg Foundation, Battle Creek, Michigan
Adolescence, *article on* Puberty and Biological Maturation

Peterson, Beverly
Associate Professor of English and American Studies, The Pennsylvania State University, Fayette
Public Service

Peterson, Donald R.
Professor Emeritus of Psychology, Rutgers University, Piscataway, New Jersey
Practitioner Model; Training, *article on* An Overview

Peterson, Roger L.
Chair of the Department of Clinical Psychology, Antioch New England Graduate School, Keene, New Hampshire
Doctor of Psychology Degree

Pettifor, Jean L.
Adjunct Professor of Applied Psychology, Clinical Psychology, University of Calgary, Alberta, Canada
Canadian Psychological Association

Pew, Richard W.
Principal Scientist, BBN Corporation, Cambridge, Massachusetts
Human Factors Psychology; Situation Awareness

Phillips, David P.
Professor of Sociology, University of California, San Diego
Field Study

Phillips, Susan D.
Professor of Psychology, University at Albany, State University of New York
Career, *article on* Career Interventions

Philogène, Gina
Assistant Professor of Psychology, Sarah Lawrence College, Bronxville, New York
Social Representations

Phinney, Jean S.
Professor of Psychology, California State University, Los Angeles
Ethnic and Racial Identity, *article on* Ethnic Identity

Picciano, Anthony G.
Professor, Department of Education Administration and Supervision Program, School of Education, Hunter College of the City University of New York
Computer Learning

Pickren, Wade E.
Director of Archives and Library Services, American Psychological Association, Washington, D.C.
Goldstein, Kurt; Piotrowski, Zygmunt A.; Stone, Calvin P.

Pintrich, Paul R.
Professor of Education and Psychology, The University of Michigan, Ann Arbor
Learning and Motivation

Pittenger, David J.
Professor of Psychology, Marietta College, Marietta, Ohio
Stout, George Frederick; Thomson, Godfrey Hilton

Plas, Régine
Lecturer of the History of Psychology, Institute de Psychologie, Université René Descartes, Boulogne Billancourt, France
Fraisse, Paul; Meyerson, Ignace; Taine, Hippolyte Adolphe

Platte, Petra
Independent Scholar, Trier, Germany
Obesity

Plaut, David C.
Associate Professor of Psychology and Computer Science, Carnegie Mellon University, Pittsburgh, Pennsylvania
Connectionism

Polich, John
Associate Professor, Department of Neuropharmacology, The Scripps Research Institute, La Jolla, California; and Adjunct Professor of Psychology, University of California, San Diego
Cognitive Electrophysiology

Polkinghorne, Donald E.
Professor of Counseling Psychology, University of Southern California, Los Angeles
Hermeneutics; Narrative Therapy

Pollack, Mark H.
Director of the Anxiety Disorders Program, Massachusetts General Hospital; and Associate Professor of Psychiatry, Harvard Medical School, Boston
Antianxiety Medication

Pollard, C. Alec
Professor of Community and Family Medicine, Saint Louis University; and Director, Anxiety Disorders Center, Saint Louis Behavioral Medical Institute, Missouri
Flooding

Pollard, Diane S.
Professor of Educational Psychology, University of Wisconsin-Milwaukee
Secondary Education

Pollatsek, Alexander
Professor of Psychology, University of Massachusetts, Amherst
Reading

Pols, Hans
Lecturer in History of Psychology, University of New Hampshire, Durham
Baldwin, James Mark; Beers, Clifford Whittingham; Meyer, Adolf

Pomerleau, Ovide F.
Director of Behavioral Medicine, and Professor of Psychology in Psychiatry, The University of Michigan School of Medicine, Ann Arbor
Smoking

Poortinga, Ype H.
Professor of Cross-Cultural Psychology, Tilburg University, The Netherlands; and University of Lenven, Belgium
Cross-Cultural Test Adaptation

Porter, Stephen
Assistant Professor of Psychology and Chair of Forensic Psychology Area, Dalhousie University, Halifax, Nova Scotia, Canada
Deception

Porter, Theodore M.
Professor of History of Science, University of California, Los Angeles
Pearson, Karl

Prentice, Deborah A.
Associate Professor of Psychology, Princeton University, New Jersey
Norms; Values

Prenzel-Guthrie, Peter M.
Professor Emeritus of Psychology, Carleton College, Northfield, Minnesota
Guthrie, Edwin R.

Pribram, Karl H.
Professor Emeritus of Psychology, Stanford University, California; Distinguished Professor of Psychology and Director of the Center for Brain Research, Radford University, Virginia; Distinguished Research Professor of Psychology, Georgetown University, Washington, D.C.
Philosophy, *article on* Philosophy of Mind

Price, Richard H.
Professor of Psychology, and Senior Research Scientist, The University of Michigan, Ann Arbor
Community Prevention and Intervention, *article on* Prevention with Adults; Community Psychology, *article on* Prevention and Intervention; Prevention, *article on* An Overview

Proffitt, Julia Beth
Doctoral Candidate, Department of Psychology, Northwestern University, Evanston, Illinois
Concepts, *article on* An Overview

Pruitt, Dean G.
Distinguished Professor of Psychology, State University of New York at Buffalo
Alternative Dispute Resolution; Conflict Resolution

Puente, Antonio E.
Professor of Psychology, University of North Carolina at Wilmington
Sperry, Roger Wolcott; Varona y Pera, Enrique José

Puente, Krista L.
Student, University of the South, Sewanee, Tennessee
Varona y Pera, Enrique José

Pulver, Sydney E.
Training and Supervising Analyst, Philadelphia Psychoanalytic Society, Pennsylvania
Narcissism

Purdie, Nola
Senior Lecturer in Education, Queensland University of Technology, Australia
Instructional Treatments

Quas, Jodi A.
Postdoctoral Fellow, MacArthur Foundation Research Network on Psychopathology and Development, Institute of Human Development, University of California, Berkeley
Family Violence

Quick, James Campbell
Professor of Organizational Behavior, University of Texas, Arlington
Stress, *article on* Measurement; Work Conditions

Quick, Jonathan D.
Director of Essential Drugs and Other Medicines (EDM), World Health Organization, Geneva, Switzerland
Stress, *article on* Measurement

Rabi, Moubarak
Dean of the Ben Msik College of Arts and Humanities, and Professor of Psychology, University Hassan II, Mohammedia, Rabat, Morocco; and Researcher, Moroccan Ministry of Higher Education, Vocational Training and Scientific Research
North Africa

Ramirez, Sylvia Z.
Assistant Professor of Educational Psychology, University of Texas–Pan American, Edinburg
School Refusal

Randel, Bruce
Doctoral Candidate, Department of Psychology, University of Michigan, Ann Arbor
Middle Childhood, *article on* Education and Schooling

Randi, Judi
Adjunct Assistant Professor, Teachers College, Columbia University, New York
Apprenticeship

Rapoport, Amnon
Department of Marketing, Hong Kong University of Science and Technology, Kowloon, China
Game Theory

Rappaport, Julian
Professor of Psychology, University of Illinois at Urbana-Champaign
Community Psychology, *article on* Theories

Ray, William J.
Professor of Psychology, The Pennsylvania State University, University Park
Dissociative Identity Disorder

Rayner, Keith
Distinguished Professor of Psychology, University of Massachusetts, Amherst
Reading

Rebec, George V.
Chancellors' Professor of Psychology, and Director of the Program in Neural Science, Indiana University, Bloomington
Cocaine

Reed, Stephen K.
Professor of Psychology, San Diego State University, California
Thinking, *article on* Problem Solving

Reezigt, Gerry J.
Educational Researcher, GION, Groningen Institute for Educational Research, University of Groningen, The Netherlands
School Effectiveness and Improvement

Reich, Darcy A.
Doctoral Student in Social Psychology, The Ohio State University, Columbus
Attribution Theories

Reich, Jill N.
Vice President for Academic Affairs and Dean of the Faculty, Bates College, Lewiston, Maine
Careers in Psychology

Reicher, Stephen
Reader in Psychology, University of Saint Andrews, Fife, United Kingdom
Crowd Behavior

Reid, R. Clay
Associate Professor, Department of Neurobiology, Harvard Medical School, Boston, Massachusetts
Sensory Systems

Reis, Harry T.
Professor of Psychology, Department of Clinical and Social Sciences in Psychology, University of Rochester, New York
Self-Disclosure

Reisenzein, Rainer
Professor of Psychology, University of Bielefeld, Germany
Stumpf, Carl

Reisman, John M.
Professor Emeritus of Psychology, DePaul University, Chicago, Illinois
Shakow, David

Reiss, Steven
Professor of Psychology and Psychiatry, and Director of the Nisonger Center UAP for Mental Retardation and Developmental Disabilities, The Ohio State University, Columbus
Psychopharmacology, *article on* Pharmacotherapy

Rensink, Ronald A.
Research Scientist, Cambridge Basic Research, Nissan Research and Development, Massachusetts
Scene Perception

Reppucci, Nicholas Dickon
Professor of Psychology, University of Virginia, Charlottesville
Child Custody

Reskin, Barbara F.
Professor of Sociology, Harvard University, Cambridge, Massachusetts
Sex Segregation; Sex Stratification

Retschitzki, Jean
Professor of Psychology, University of Fribourg, Switzerland
Switzerland

Revelle, William
Professor of Psychology, Northwestern University, Evanston, Illinois
Individual Differences

Revenson, Tracey A.
Professor of Psychology, Graduate School of the City University of New York
Arthritis

Reynolds, David
Professor of Education, University of Newcastle upon Tyne, United Kingdom
School Effectiveness and Improvement

Rhodes, Jean
Associate Professor of Psychology, University of Illinois at Urbana-Champaign
Mentoring Programs

Rhodes, Nancy
Lecturer in Psychology, Texas A&M University, College Station
Kretschmer, Ernst

Richard, Jaqui R.
Doctoral Candidate, Department of Educational Psychology, University of Utah, Salt Lake City
School Consultation

Richards, P. Scott
Associate Professor of Counseling Psychology, Brigham Young University, Provo, Utah
Religious Values and Mental Health

Richardson, Mary Sue
Professor of Applied Psychology, School of Education, and Director of the Counseling Programs, New York University, New York
Transference

Richer, Paul
Associate Professor of Psychology, Duquesne University, Pittsburgh, Pennsylvania
Phenomenology

Richman, Lynn C.
Professor and Director of Pediatric Psychology, University of Iowa, Iowa City
Speech and Language Disorders

Rieber, Robert W.
Professor of Psychology, John Jay College of Criminal Justice, City University of New York
Head, Henry; Mowrer, O. Hobart; Osgood, Charles Egerton

Ries, Andrew L.
Professor of Medicine, and Director of Pulmonary Rehabilitation, University of California, San Diego School of Medicine
Chronic Obstructive Pulmonary Disease

Rilling, Mark
Professor of Psychology, Michigan State University, East Lansing
Kuo, Zing-Yang

Riskin, Jessica
Leo Marx Career Development Assistant Professor of the History and Culture of Science and Technology, Massachusetts Institute of Technology, Cambridge
Condillac, Etienne Bonnot de; La Mettrie, Julien Offray de

Ritchie, Pierre L.-J.
Professor of Psychology, University of Ottawa, Ontario, Canada
Regional Psychological Associations, *article on* Regional Psychological Associations in Canada

Roazen, Paul
Professor Emeritus of Political and Social Science, York University, Toronto, Ontario, Canada
Ferenczi, Sandor

Robbins, Steven B.
Management Consultant, Richmond, Virginia
Countertransference

Roberts, Michael C.
Professor and Director of the Clinical Child Psychology Program, University of Kansas, Lawrence
Pediatric Psychology

Robinson, Daniel N.
Distinguished Research Professor, Georgetown University, Washington, D.C.
Berkeley, George; Hobbes, Thomas; Psychology, *article on* Classical Antiquity; Reid, Thomas

Rockland, Kathleen S.
Professor of Neurology, University of Iowa, Iowa City
Brain

Rodgers, Carie
Researcher, Oregon Social Learning Center, Eugene
Gender Schema

Rodgers, Joseph Lee
Professor of Psychology, University of Oklahoma, Norman
Birth Order

Roe, Daniel
Doctoral Candidate, Department of Psychology, Washington University, Saint Louis, Missouri
Broca, Paul

Roediger, Henry L. III
James S. McDonnell Distinguished Professor of Psychology, Washington University, Saint Louis, Missouri
Data Collection, *article on* Laboratory Research; False Memory; Learning, *article on* Cognitive Approach for Humans

Roehrs, Timothy A.
Research Director, Sleep Disorders and Research Center, Henry Ford Hospital; and Adjunct Professor of Psychiatry, Wayne State University, Detroit, Michigan
Depressants, Sedatives, and Hypnotics

Roesch, Ronald
Professor of Psychology, Simon Fraser University, Burnaby, Canada
Forensic Psychology

Rook, Karen S.
Professor, Program in Social Ecology, University of California, Irvine
Loneliness

Rosen, David H.
McMillan Professor of Analytical Psychology, Texas A&M University, College Station
Jung, Carl Gustav

Rosenberg, Erika L.
Assistant Professor of Psychology, College of William and Mary, Williamsburg, Virginia
Emotion, *article on* Methods of Study

Rosenberg, Richard S.
Associate Professor of Neurology, Evanston Hospital, Northwestern University, Illinois
Sleep Disorders

Rosenblith, Judy F.
Professor Emerita of Psychology, Wheaton College, Massachusetts
Bayley, Nancy

Rosenblum, Kristina
Research Associate in Developmental Psychology, Florida Atlantic University, Boca Raton
Middle Childhood, *article on* Cognitive Development

Rosenfield, Sylvia
Professor of School Psychology, University of Maryland, College Park
School-Based Collaboration and Teaming

Rosenstock, I. M.
Professor Emeritus of Health Behavior, University of Michigan, Ann Arbor, and California State University, Long Beach
Health Belief Model

Rosenthal, Robert
Distinguished Professor of Psychology, University of California, Riverside, and Edgar Pierce Professor Emeritus, Harvard University, Cambridge, Massachusetts
Expectancy Effects; Replication in Research

Rosenzweig, Mark R.
Professor of Graduate Studies in Psychology, University of California, Berkeley
Biological Psychology; Ethology; International Union of Psychological Science

Rosenzweig, Saul
Professor Emeritus of Psychology and Psychiatry, Washington University, Saint Louis, Missouri
Kinsey, Alfred C.

Rosnow, Ralph L.
Thaddeus Bolton Professor of Psychology, Temple University, Philadelphia, Pennsylvania
Artifact, *article on* Artifact in Research; Longitudinal Research; Rumors; Semantic Differential

Ross, Brian H.
Professor of Psychology, University of Illinois at Urbana-Champaign
Concepts, *article on* Learning

Roth, Thomas
Chief and Division Head of the Sleep Disorders and Research Center, Henry Ford Hospital Sleep Center, Detroit, Michigan
Depressants, Sedatives, and Hypnotics

Rothman, Alexander J.
Assistant Professor of Psychology, University of Minnesota, Minneapolis
Guttman Scale; Likert Scale

Roussalov, Vladimir M.
Professor of Psychology, Institute of Psychology, Russian Academy of Sciences, Moscow, Russia
Lomov, Boris Fydorovich

Routh, Donald K.
Professor of Psychology, University of Miami, Coral Gables, Florida
Clinical Psychology, *article on* History of the Field

Royden, Constance S.
Visiting Assistant Professor of Computer Science, Wellesley College, Massachusetts
Motion Perception

Rozin, Paul
Edmund J. and Louise W. Kahn Professor of Psychology, University of Pennsylvania, Philadelphia
Asch, Solomon E.; Richter, Curt Paul

Rubin, Gary S.
Helen Keller Chair of Ophthalmology, University College, London, United Kingdom
Visual Impairment, *article on* Physical Causes

Rubin, Kenneth H.
Professor of Human Development, and Director of the Center for Children, Relationships, and Culture, University of Maryland, College Park
Middle Childhood, *article on* Social and Emotional Development

Ruble, Diane N.
Professor of Psychology, New York University, New York
Gender Constancy

Rumbaugh, Duane M.
Regents' Professor of Psychology and Biology, and Director, Language Research Center, Georgia State University, Atlanta
Nonhuman Intelligence

Runco, Mark A.
California State University, Fullerton
Creativity, *article on* Research on the Processes of Creativity; Performing Arts

Runyan, William McKinley
Professor, School of Social Welfare, and Research Psychologist, Institute of Personality and Social Research, University of California, Berkeley
History; Psychobiography

Rusbult, Caryl E.
J. Ross MacDonald Professor of Psychology, University of North Carolina at Chapel Hill
Interdependence, *article on* Interdependence Theory

Rushall, Brent S.
Professor of Exercise Science, San Diego State University, California
Athletic Coaching

Rychlak, Joseph F.
Professor Emeritus of Psychology, Loyola University of Chicago, Illinois
Agency, *article on* An Overview; Psychology, *article on* Post–World War II

Ryff, Carol
Director of the Institute on Aging, and Professor of Psychology, University of Wisconsin, Madison
Meaning of Life

Saatkamp, Herman J., Jr.
Dean of the School of Liberal Arts, Indiana University Purdue University, Indianapolis
Royce, Josiah; Santayana, George

Sabshin, Melvin
Professor of Psychiatry, University of Maryland, Baltimore
American Psychiatric Association

Sackett, Paul R.
Professor of Psychology, University of Minnesota, Minneapolis
Personnel Selection, *article on* Techniques and Instruments

Saegert, Susan
Director of the Center for Human Environments, and Professor of Psychology, City University of New York Graduate School and University Center
Urban Communities

Salazar, José Miguel
Emeritus Researcher, Instituto de Psicologia, Universidad Central de Venezuela, Caracas
Venezuela

Šalkovskis, Paul M.
Professor of Cognitive Psychology, University of Oxford, United Kingdom
Hypochondriasis

Sallis, James F.
Professor of Psychology, San Diego State University, California
Health Promotion

Salmela, John H.
Professor in Human Kinetics, University of Ottawa, Ontario, Canada
Athletes

Salmon, D.
Professor of Neurosciences, University of California, San Diego
Alzheimer's Disease

Salthouse, Timothy A.
Regents' Professor of Psychology, Georgia Institute of Technology, Atlanta
Adulthood and Aging, *article on* Cognitive Processes and Development

Samejima, Fumiko
President of the Psychometric Society, Department of Psychology, University of Tennessee, Knoxville
Psychometric Society

Sammons, Morgan Taylor
Head of the Mental Health Department, United States Naval Hospital, Keflavik, Iceland
Prescription Privileges

Sandell, Julie H.
Associate Professor of Anatomy and Neurobiology, Boston University School of Medicine, Massachusetts
Vision and Sight, *article on* Behavioral and Functional Aspects

Sanders, Andries F.
Professor of Psychology, Vrije Universteit, Amsterdam, The Netherlands
Human Performance Theory

Sandler, Howard M.
Professor of Psychology, Peabody College of Vanderbilt University, Nashville, Tennessee
Hypothesis Testing

Sanford, Anthony J.
Professor of Psychology, University of Glasgow, Scotland
Psycholinguistics, *article on* Semantics

Santor, Darcy A.
Assistant Professor, Departments of Psychology and Psychiatry, Dalhousie University, Halifax, Nova Scotia, Canada
Center for Epidemiologic Studies of Depression

Sarigiani, Pamela A.
Associate Professor, Human Development and Family Studies, Central Michigan University, Mt. Pleasant
Adolescence, *article on* Puberty and Biological Maturation

Saunders, Katherine N.
Graduate Student, Texas A&M University, College Station
Sears, Robert R.

Savickas, Mark L.
Professor of Behavioral Sciences, Northeastern Ohio Universities College of Medicine, Rootstown
Super, Donald Edwin

Sayrs, David M.
Educational Advisor/Transfer Coordinator, Pierce College, Lakewood, Washington
Applied Behavior Analysis

Scarborough, Elizabeth
Dean of Liberal Arts and Sciences, and Professor of Psychology, Indiana University, South Bend
Donders, Franciscus Cornelis; Washburn, Margaret Floy

Scarr, Sandra
Professor Emerita of Psychology, University of Virginia, Charlottesville; and Retired Chairman and Chief Executive Officer of KinderCare Learning Centers, Incorporated, Portland, Oregon
Day Care

Schacter, Daniel L.
Professor, and Chair of Psychology, Harvard University, Cambridge, Massachusetts
Memory, *article on* Memory Systems

Schantz, Susan L.
Associate Professor of Toxicology and Psychology, University of Illinois at Urbana-Champaign
Behavioral Teratology

Scharff, Robert C.
Professor of Philosophy, University of New Hampshire, Durham; and Editor, Continental Philosophy Review
Comte, Auguste

Schauer, Margarete
Assistant Professor of Psychology, University Konstanz, Germany
Neuromuscular Disorders

Schiffman, Ellen
Bachelor of Arts, Department of Psychology, Duke University, Durham, North Carolina
Gulliksen, Harold

Schiffman, Harold
Professor Emeritus of Psychology, Duke University, Durham, North Carolina
Gulliksen, Harold O.

Schiffman, Susan S.
Professor of Medical Psychology, Department of Psychiatry, Duke University Medical School, Durham, North Carolina
Taste, *article on* Biological Organization

Schklar, Jason
Graduate Student, University of Illinois at Chicago
Expert Testimony

Schlenker, Barry R.
Professor of Psychology, University of Florida, Gainesville
Impression Management

Schliemann, Analúcia
Professor of Education, Tufts University, Medford, Massachusetts
Informal Learning

Schmaus, Warren
Professor of Philosophy, Department of Humanities, Illinois Institute of Technology, Chicago
Durkheim, Émile

Schmidt, Lyle D.
Professor of Psychology, The Ohio State University, Columbus
Counseling Psychology, *article on* History of the Field

Schneider, Stanley F.
Associate Director of Research Training and Career Development (retired), National Institute of Mental Health, Kensington, Maryland
National Institute of Mental Health

Schneiderman, Neil
James L. Knight Professor of Psychology, Medicine, and Psychiatry, University of Miami, Coral Gables, Florida
Coronary Heart Disease

Schoggen, Phil H.
Professor Emeritus of Human Development, Cornell University, Ithaca, New York
Barker, Roger G.

Schooler, Tonya Y.
Research Principal, University of Pittsburgh, Pennsylvania
Stress, *article on* Impact on Health

Schopler, John
Professor of Psychology, University of North Carolina at Chapel Hill
Power

Schut, Henk A. W.
Assistant Professor, Research Institute for Psychology and Health, Faculty of Social Sciences, Utrecht University, The Netherlands
Grief and Loss

Schwartz, Gary E.
Professor of Psychology, Neurology, Psychiatry, and Medicine; Director of the Human Energy Systems Laboratory; and Co-Facilitator in Energy Medicine, Program in Integrative Medicine, University of Arizona, Tucson
Psychosomatic Illness

Schwartz, Hillarie C.
Doctoral Candidate, Department of Psychology, Northwestern University, Evanston, Illinois
Concepts, *article on* An Overview

Schwartz, Matthew
Adjunct Professor, Department of History and Department of Near East, Wayne State University, Detroit, Michigan
Judaism and Psychology

Schwarz, Norbert
Professor of Psychology, The University of Michigan, Ann Arbor
Attitudes, *article on* Attitude Measurement

Scott, Thomas R.
Professor of Psychology, University of Delaware, Newark
Taste, *article on* Behavioral and Functional Aspects

Searight, H. Russell
Adjunct Professor of Psychology and Community and Family Medicine, Saint Louis University, Missouri
Family Psychology, *article on* Theories of Family Dynamics

Sechrest, Lee
Professor of Psychology, University of Arizona, Tucson
Unobtrusive Measures

Sechzer, Jeri Altneu
Visiting Professor of Psychology, Pace University, New York
Stellar, Eliot

Segal, Daniel L.
Assistant Professor of Psychology, University of Colorado, Colorado Springs
Assessment

Seidman, Edward
Professor of Psychology, New York University, New York
Community Prevention and Intervention, *article on* Prevention with School-Aged Children; School Transitions

Sekuler, Allison B.
Associate Professor of Psychology, University of Toronto, Ontario, Canada
Vision and Sight, *article on* Age-Related Changes, Optical Factors, and Neural Processes

Sekuler, Robert
Frances and Louis H. Salvage Professor of Psychology, and Member, Volen Center for Complex Systems, Brandeis University, Waltham, Massachusetts
Vision and Sight, *article on* Age-Related Changes, Optical Factors, and Neural Processes

Sera, Maria D.
Associate Professor of Child Psychology, University of Minnesota, Minneapolis
Psycholinguistics, *article on* Linguistic Determinism

Serpell, Robert
Professor of Applied Developmental Psychology, University of Maryland, Baltimore County
Determinants of Intelligence, *article on* Culture and Intelligence

Severy, Lawrence J.
R. David Thomas Professor of Psychology, University of Florida, Gainesville
Menstruation

Sewell, Trevor E.
Professor of School Psychology, Temple University, Philadelphia, Pennsylvania
School Dropout

Shadish, William R.
Dunavant University Professor, Department of Psychology, University of Memphis, Tennessee
Nonrandomized Designs

Shaffer, Howard J.
Associate Professor, and Director of the Division on Addictions, Harvard Medical School, Boston, Massachusetts
Addictive Personality

Shafranske, Edward P.
Professor of Psychology and Luckman Distinguished Teaching Fellow, Pepperdine University, Southern California Psychoanalytic Institute, Irvine, California
Religion and Psychotherapy, *article on* Beliefs and Training of Psychotherapists; Religious Experience, *article on* Religious Experiences and Practices; Religious Symbol, Myth, and Ritual

Shapiro, Edward S.
Professor, School Psychology Program, Lehigh University, Bethlehem, Pennsylvania
Academic Assessment of Performance

Shelton, Richard C.
Associate Professor of Psychology, Vanderbilt School of Medicine, Nashville, Tennessee
Antidepressants

Sheridan, Susan M.
Professor of Educational Psychology, University of Nebraska, Lincoln
School Consultation

Sheridan, Thomas B.
Professor of Engineering and Applied Psychology, Massachusetts Institute of Technology, Cambridge
Robotics

Sherman, Steven J.
Professor of Psychology, Indiana University, Bloomington
Counterfactual Thought

Shevell, Steven K.
Professor of Psychology and Ophthalmology and Visual Science, University of Chicago, Illinois
Color Vision

Shields, Stephanie A.
Professor of Psychology and Women's Studies, The Pennsylvania State University, University Park
Hollingworth, Leta Stetter

Shinn, Marybeth
Professor of Psychology, New York University, New York
Community Psychology, *article on* Methods of Study

Shively, Carol A.
Professor of Pathology (Comparative Medicine) and Psychology, Wake Forest University School of Medicine, Winston-Salem, North Carolina
Hormone Replacement Therapy

Shuman, Daniel W.
Professor of Law, Southern Methodist University, Dallas, Texas
Government Regulation, *article on* State Regulation

Sieber, Joan E.
Professor of Psychology, California State University, Hayward
Ethics, *article on* Ethics in Research

Sigman, Marian D.
Professor of Psychology and Psychiatry, University of California, Los Angeles
Determinants of Intelligence, *article on* Nutrition and Intelligence

Silverman, Phyllis R.
Professor Emerita, MGH Institute of Health Professions, Boston, Massachusetts
Bereavement Programs

Silverstein, Albert
Professor of Psychology, University of Rhode Island, Kingston
Aristotle

Sim, Catherine Q. E.
Assistant Professor of International Studies, Thunderbird, The American Graduate School of International Management, Glendale, Arizona
Austria

Simmons, Bret
Assistant Professor of Business Administration, University of Alaska, Fairbanks
Work Conditions

Simon, Herbert A.
Richard King Mellon University Professor of Computer Science and Psychology, Carnegie Mellon University, Pittsburgh, Pennsylvania
Artificial Intelligence; Newell, Allen

Simonton, Dean Keith
Professor of Psychology, University of California, Davis
Archival Research

Simpson, Jeffry A.
Professor of Psychology, Texas A&M University, College Station
Schachter, Stanley

Singer, Jefferson A.
Professor of Psychology, Connecticut College, New London
Peak Experiences

Singer, Jerome L.
Professor of Psychology, Yale University, New Haven, Connecticut
Imagination

Singer, Murray
Professor of Psychology, University of Manitoba, Winnipeg, Canada
Psycholinguistics, *article on* Discourse Comprehension

Singh, Ramadhar
Professor of Psychology, Department of Social Work and Psychology, National University of Singapore
Southeast Asia

Slife, Brent D.
Professor of Psychology, Brigham Young University, Provo, Utah
Theoretical and Philosophical Psychology

Slobodin, Richard
Professor Emeritus, Department of Anthropology, McMaster University, Hamilton, Ontario, Canada
Rivers, William Halse

Smith, Andrew J. A.
Head of Communication and Information, European Science Foundation, Strasbourg, France
European Science Foundation

Smith, Eliot R.
Professor of Psychological Sciences, Purdue University, West Lafayette, Indiana
Social Cognition; Social Psychology, *article on* Methods of Study

Smith, Laurence D.
Associate Professor of Psychology, University of Maine, Orono
Bacon, Francis; Holt, Edwin Bisell; Hull, Clark Leonard

Smith, M. Brewster
Professor Emeritus of Psychology, University of California, Santa Cruz
Cook, Stuart W.; Frenkel-Brunswik, Else

Smith, Steven M.
Graduate Fellow, Department of Psychology, Queen's University, Kingston, Ontario, Canada
Attitudes, *article on* An Overview

Smith, Steven R.
Dean and Professor of Law, California Western School of Law, San Diego
Malpractice

Smoot, Tracine Y.
Department of Educational Psychology, University of Utah, Salt Lake City
School Consultation

Snowdon, Charles T.
Hilldale Professor of Psychology, University of Wisconsin, Madison
Nonhuman Communication

Snyder, Douglas K.
Professor of Psychology, and Director of Clinical Training, Texas A&M University, College Station
Couples Therapy

Snyder, Mark
Professor of Psychology, University of Minnesota, Minneapolis
Self-Fulfilling Prophecy

Sobell, Linda C.
Professor of Psychology, Nova Southeastern University, Fort Lauderdale, Florida
Drug Abuse

Sobell, Mark B.
Professor of Psychology, Nova Southeastern University, Fort Lauderdale, Florida
Drug Abuse

Sokal, Michael M.
Professor of History, Worcester Polytechnic Institute, Department of Humanities and Arts, Massachusetts
Cattell, James McKeen; Scripture, Edward Wheeler; Seashore, Carl Emil; Stratton, George M.

Sollod, Robert N.
Professor of Psychology, Cleveland State University, Ohio
Religious Experience, *article on* Religious Experiences and Practices

Solomon, Zahava
Dean of the Bob Schapell School of Social Work, Tel Aviv University, Ramat Aviv, Israel
Combat

Solso, Robert L.
Professor of Psychology, University of Nevada, Reno
Cognitive Psychology, *article on* History of the Field

Spencer, Margaret Beale
Board of Overseers Professor of Education, University of Pennsylvania, Philadelphia
Ethnocentrism

Spieler, Daniel H.
Assistant Professor of Psychology, Stanford University, California
Reaction Time

Spilka, Bernard
Professor Emeritus of Psychology, University of Denver, Colorado
God Concepts

Spokane, Arnold
Professor of Education and Psychology, Department of Counseling Psychology, School Psychology, Lehigh University, Bethlehem, Pennsylvania
Career, *article on* Career Choice

Sprung, Helga
Assistant Professor of Psychology, Free University of Berlin, Germany
Stumpf, Carl

Sprung, Lothar
Professor Emeritus of Psychology, Humboldt University of Berlin, Germany
Germany

Stam, Henderikus J.
Professor of Psychology, University of Calgary, Alberta, Canada
Lewin, Kurt

Stanley, Melinda A.
Professor of Psychiatry and Behavioral Sciences, University of Texas, Houston Health Science Center, Mental Sciences Institute
Obsessive-Compulsive Disorder; Trichotillomania

Stanley-Hagan, Margaret M.
Chair of the Department of Psychology, and Associate Professor of Psychology, University of North Carolina, Charlotte
Divorce

Starker, Steven
Chief of the Psychology Service, and Professor of Psychology in Psychiatry, Portland Veterans Administration Medical Center, Oregon Health Science University
Fantasy

Staub, Ervin
Professor of Psychology, University of Massachusetts, Amherst
Genocide

Steenbarger, Brett N.
Assistant Professor, and Director of Student Counseling, Department of Psychiatry and Behavioral Sciences, State University of New York Health Science Center, Syracuse
Brief Therapy

Stein, Donald G.
Asa G. Candler Professor of Neurology and Psychobiology, Departments of Neurology and Psychology, Emory University, Atlanta, Georgia
Brain Injury and Recovery

Stein, Janice Gross
Harrowston Professor of Conflict Management and Negotiation, and Director of the Munk Centre for International Studies, University of Toronto, Ontario, Canada
International Relations

Steinberg, Laurence
Laura H. Carnell Professor of Psychology, Temple University, Philadelphia, Pennsylvania
Punishment, *article on* Developmental Perspectives

Stephan, Walter G.
Professor of Psychology, New Mexico State University, Las Cruces
Intergroup Relations

Stephenson, Annette
Research Associate, Brigham Young University, Provo, Utah
Beck Depression Inventory

Sternberg, Robert J.
IBM Professor of Psychology and Education, Yale University, New Haven, Connecticut
Research Dissemination; Thinking, *article on* An Overview

Stevens, Robert J.
Associate Professor of Educational Psychology, The Pennsylvania State University, University Park
Elementary Education

Stevenson, Harold W.
Professor of Psychology, The University of Michigan, Ann Arbor
Middle Childhood, *article on* Education and Schooling

Stewart, Alan E.
Assistant Professor of Psychology, University of Florida, Gainesville
Adler, Alfred

Stocker, Clare M.
Assistant Research Professor of Psychology, University of Denver, Colorado
Sibling Relationships

Stoiber, Karen Callan
Professor of Educational Psychology, University of Wisconsin, Milwaukee
Academic Intervention

Stokols, Daniel
Professor of Social Ecology, University of California, Irvine
Environmental Psychology

Stone, Philip J.
Professor of Psychology, Harvard University, Cambridge, Massachusetts
Content Analysis

Straus, Elisabeth R.
Director of the American Psychological Foundation, Washington, D.C.
American Psychological Foundation

Stricker, Edward M.
University Professor of Neuroscience, University of Pittsburgh, Pennsylvania
Motivation, *article on* Physiological Aspects

Stricker, George
Distinguished Research Professor of Psychology, Adelphi University, Garden City, New York
Clinical Psychology, *article on* Interventions

Stroebe, Margaret S.
Associate Professor of Psychology, Research Institute for Psychology and Health, Utrecht University, The Netherlands
Grief and Loss

Stroebe, Wolfgang
Professor of Psychology, Utrecht University, The Netherlands
Grief and Loss

Strohmetz, David B.
Assistant Professor of Psychology, Monmouth University, West Long Branch, New Jersey
Artifact, *article on* Artifact in Research

Strong, Stanley R.
Professor of Psychology, Virginia Commonwealth University, Richmond
Social Influence Theory

Struckman, Andrea
Student in the Master's Program in the Department of Clinical Psychology, Saint Michael's College, Winooski, Vermont
Psychology, *article on* Post–World War II

Strunk, Orlo C., Jr.
Professor Emeritus of Psychology of Religion and Pastoral Psychology, Boston University, Massachusetts
Pastoral Counseling

Stryker, Sheldon
Distinguished Professor of Sociology, Indiana University at Bloomington
Symbolic Interaction Theory

Stukas, Arthur A., Jr.
Assistant Professor of Psychology, University of Northern Colorado, Greeley
Self-Fulfilling Prophecy

Stunkard, Albert J.
Professor of Psychiatry, University of Pennsylvania, Philadelphia
Obesity

Sue, Stanley
Professor of Psychology and Psychiatry, and Director of the Asian American Studies Program, University of California, Davis
Ethnocultural Psychotherapy

Suedfeld, Peter
Professor of Psychology, University of British Columbia, Vancouver, Canada
Cognitive Styles, *article on* Personality

Sundberg, Norman
Department of Psychology, University of Oregon, Eugene
Tyler, Leona E.

Surprenant, Aimée M.
Assistant Professor of Psychology, Purdue University, West Lafayette, Indiana
Sensory Stores

Surwit, Richard S.
Professor, and Chair of the Division of Medical Psychology, Department of Psychiatry and Behavioral Sciences, Duke University Medical School, Durham, North Carolina
Diabetes

Sutton-Smith, Brian
Professor Emeritus of Education Psychology and Folklore, University of Pennsylvania, Philadelphia
Play

Suzuki, Lalita K.
Doctoral Candidate, Department of Psychology, University of California, Los Angeles
Culture, *article on* Culture and Development

Swanson, Dena Phillips
Assistant Professor of Human Development and Family Studies, The Pennsylvania State University, University Park
Ethnocentrism

Swim, Janet K.
Associate Professor of Psychology, The Pennsylvania State University, University Park
Sexism

Tallal, Paula
Professor of Neuroscience, and Co-Director of the Center for Molecular and Behavioral Neuroscience, Rutgers University, Newark, New Jersey
Language, *article on* Language and Brain Systems

Tan, Siang-Yang
Professor of Psychology, Fuller Theological Seminary, Pasadena, California
Religion and Psychotherapy, *article on* An Overview

Tangney, June
Professor of Psychology, George Mason University, Fairfax, Virginia
Guilt; Shame

Tanzer, Norbert K.
Associate Professor of Psychology, University of Graz, Austria
Austria

Tarr, Michael
Associate Professor of Cognitive and Linguistic Sciences, Brown University, Providence, Rhode Island
Pattern Recognition

Tattersall, Andrew J.
Professor of Psychology, Liverpool John Moores University, United Kingdom
British Association for the Advancement of Science

Taylor, Eugene
Professor of Psychology, Saybrook Graduate School, San Francisco, California
Cannon, Walter Bradford; Edwards, Jonathan; Humanistic Psychology; Murray, Henry Alexander; Prince, Morton

Taylor, Steven J.
Professor, Syracuse University, New York
Qualitative Research

Teigen, Karl Halvor
Professor of Psychology, University of Tromso, Norway
Norway

Teo, Thomas
Assistant Professor of Psychology, York University, Toronto, Ontario, Canada
Ach, Narziss K.; Holzkamp, Klaus; Spranger, Eduard

Tesser, Abraham
Professor Emeritus of Psychology, University of Georgia, Athens
Self-Esteem

Thacher, Ilisa
Research Associate, Department of Psychology, University of Hawaii at Manoa, Honolulu
Health Psychology, *article on* Assessments and Interventions

Thayer, Robert E.
Professor of Psychology, California State University, Long Beach
Mood

Thelen, Esther
Professor of Psychology, Indiana University, Bloomington
Infancy, *article on* Perception and Motor Development

Thomas, Elwyn
Senior Lecturer in Education, University of London, United Kingdom
England

Thomas, Jeanne L.
Dean of the College of Health and Human Services, and Professor of Psychology, Southwest Missouri State University, Springfield
Grandparenting

Thomas, Roger K.
Professor of Psychology, University of Georgia, Athens
Bekhterev, Vladimir Mikhailovich; Franz, Shepherd Ivory; Klüver, Heinrich; Morgan, Clifford Thomas; Romanes, George John

Thompson, Charles P.
Professor of Psychology, Kansas State University, Manhattan
Mnemonists

Thompson, Dennis N.
Professor of Educational Psychology, Georgia State University, Atlanta
Goodenough, Florence Laura; Murchison, Carl

Thompson, Richard F.
Director of the Neuroscience Program, University of Southern California, Los Angeles
Habituation; Memory, *article on* Brain Systems

Thompson, Ross A.
Professor of Psychology, University of Nebraska, Lincoln
Infancy, *article on* Early Experience and Socialization

Thompson, Travis
Director of the John F. Kennedy Center for Research on Human Development, and Professor of Psychology, Vanderbilt University, Nashville, Tennessee
Bernard, Claude

Tindale, R. Scott
Department of Psychology, Loyola University of Chicago, Illinois
Groups, *article on* Groups and Group Structure

Tinsley, Howard E. A.
Assistant Professor of Psychology, University of Florida, Gainesville
Counseling Psychology, *article on* Assessments and Interventions

Tjosvold, Dean
Chair Professor of Management and Head of the Department of Management, Lingnan University, Hong Kong, China
Team Training

Todd, James T.
Department Head and Professor of Psychology, Eastern Michigan University, Ypsilanti
Weiss, Albert Paul

Tolchinsky, Liliana
Research Associate, Institute of Educational Sciences, University of Barcelona, Spain
Representational Tools

Tolman, Charles W.
Emeritus Fellow, Centre for Studies in Religion and Society, University of Victoria, British Columbia, Canada
Angell, James Rowland; Bentley, Madison; Carr, Harvey A.

Tomkins, Alan J.
Professor of Psychology and Law, University of Nebraska, Lincoln
Government Regulation, *article on* State Regulation

Topmiller, Donald A.
Director of Aviation Psychology, and Human Factors Consultant, Topmiller and Associates, Fairborn, Ohio
System Error Analysis

Torff, Bruce
Assistant Professor of Education, Hofstra University, Hempstead, New York
Multiple Intelligences

Tracy, Carol
Executive Director, Psi Beta, Chattanooga, Tennessee
Psi Beta

Tranel, Daniel
Professor of Neurology and Psychology, University of Iowa, Iowa City
Frontal Lobe Disorders

Treffert, Darold A.
Psychiatrist, Saint Agnes Hospital Behavioral Health Services, Fond du Lac, Wisconsin
Savant Syndrome

Triandis, Harry C.
Professor Emeritus of Psychology, University of Illinois at Urbana-Champaign
Affective Universals; Allocentrism-Idiocentrism; Collectivism and Individualism; Cross-Cultural Psychology, *article on* History of the Field; Data Collection, *article on* Field Research; Social Distance

Trickett, Edison J.
Professor of Psychology, University of Maryland, College Park
Community Ecology

Trimble, Joseph E.
Professor of Psychology, Western Washington University, Bellingham
American Indian Psychology

Trommsdorff, Gisela
Professor of Developmental Psychology, Universität Konstanz, Germany
Germany

Trull, Timothy J.
Professor of Psychology, University of Missouri, Columbia
Paranoid Personality Disorder

Tulving, Endel
Tanenbaum Chair in Cognitive Neuroscience, Rotman Research Institute, Baycrest Centre for Geriatric Care, North York, Ontario, Canada
Memory, *article on* An Overview

Turk, Dennis C.
John and Emma Bonica Professor of Anesthesiology and Pain Research, University of Washington School of Medicine, Seattle
Pain, *article on* Models and Management

Turkaan, Jaylan S.
Chief of the Behavioral Sciences Research Branch, National Institute on Drug Abuse, Bethesda, Maryland
Placebo Effect in Research Design

Turner, John C.
Professor of Psychology, Australian National University, Canberra
Social Identity

Turner, R. Steven
Professor of History of Science, University of New Brunswick, Fredericton, Canada
Helmholtz, Hermann von; Hering, Ewald

Turner, Ralph H.
Professor Emeritus of Sociology, University of California, Los Angeles
Role Theory

Turner, Samuel M.
Professor of Psychology, and Director of Clinical Training, University of Maryland, College Park
Social Phobia

Tversky, Barbara
Professor of Psychology, Stanford University, California
Mental Models

Tweney, Ryan D.
Professor of Psychology, Bowling Green State University, Ohio
Newton, Isaac; Titchener, Edward Bradford

Tyler, Tom R.
Professor of Psychology, New York University, New York
Justice

Uhles, A. Neville
Doctoral Candidate, Department of Psychology, University of California, Santa Barbara
Stereotypes

Useda, J. David
Graduate Student, Department of Psychology, University of Missouri, Columbia
Paranoid Personality Disorder

Vaillant, George E.
Professor of Psychiatry, Harvard Medical School, Boston, Massachusetts
Defense Mechanisms

Valentine, Elizabeth R.
Reader in Psychology, University of London, United Kingdom
Metaphysics

Valsiner, Jaan
Professor of Psychology, Clark University, Worcester, Massachusetts
Cultural Psychology

Vande Kemp, Hendrika
Professor of Psychology, Fuller Theological Seminary, Pasadena, California
Höffding, Harald; Psyche and Soul

VandenBos, Gary R.
Publisher, American Psychological Association, Washington, D.C.
Schizophrenia

van de Vijver, Fons J. R.
Lecturer in Psychology, Tilburg University, The Netherlands
Bias and Equivalence; Cross-Cultural Psychology, *article on* Theories and Methods of Study

Vandewater, Elizabeth A.
Assistant Professor, Department of Human Ecology, University of Texas at Austin
Adulthood and Aging, *article on* Social Processes and Development

Van Lange, Paul A. M.
Professor of Psychology, Free University, Amsterdam, The Netherlands
Cooperation and Competition; Interdependence, *article on* Interdependence Structure

Van Male, Lynn M.
Doctoral Candidate, Department of Psychology, University of Missouri, Columbia
Sexual Dysfunctions

van Strien, Pieter J.
Professor Emeritus of Psychology, University of Groningen, The Netherlands
Buytendijk, Frederik J. J.; Heymans, Gerardus

Vaughan, Frances E.
Psychologist and Independent Scholar, Mill Valley, California
Transpersonal Psychology

Venne, Vickie L.
Director of Support Services, High Risk Cancer Clinics, Huntsman Cancer Institute, Salt Lake City, Utah
Genetic Counseling

Vernon, Philip A.
Professor of Psychology, University of Western Ontario, London, Canada
Measures of Intelligence, *article on* Biological Theories

Vidal, Fernando
Research Scholar, Max-Planck Institute for the History of Science, Berlin, Germany
Claparède, Édouard; Janet, Pierre; Piaget, Jean

Viney, Wayne
Professor of Psychology, Colorado State University, Fort Collins
Dix, Dorothea Lynde; Rush, Benjamin

von Mayrhauser, Richard T.
Independent Scholar, Gibsonia, Pennsylvania
Bingham, Walter Van Dyke; Thorndike, Edward Lee

Waas, Gregory A.
Associate Professor of Psychology, Northern Illinois University, DeKalb
Play Therapy

Wachtel, Paul L.
City University of New York Distinguished Professor of Psychology
Integrative Psychotherapy

Wagner, John A. III
Professor and Chairperson of Management, Michigan State University, East Lansing
Organizations

Wagner, Richard K.
Professor of Psychology, Florida State University, Tallahassee
Practical Intelligence

Wahl, Hans-Werner
Professor of Social and Environmental Psychology, The German Center for Research on Aging, University of Heidelberg, Germany
Visual Impairment, *article on* Psychological Implications

Wahlsten, Douglas
Professor of Psychology, University of Alberta, Edmonton, Canada
Behavioral Genetics

Walberg, Herbert J.
Research Professor of Education and Psychology, University of Illinois, Chicago; and Distinguished Visiting Fellow (1999–2005), Hoover Institution on War, Revolution, and Peace, Stanford University, California
Instructional Theories

Waldo, Craig R.
Research Specialist, Center for AIDS Prevention Studies, University of California, San Francisco,
Acquired Immune Deficiency Syndrome

Walker, C. Eugene
Professor Emeritus of Psychiatry and Behavioral Sciences, University of Oklahoma Medical School, Edmond
Encopresis; Training, *article on* Special Training Issues

Walker, Pamela
Research Associate, Center on Human Policy, Syracuse University, New York
Qualitative Research

Walsh, Mary E.
Professor of Psychology, Boston College, Lynch School of Education, Chestnut Hill, Massachusetts
Disruptive Behavior Disorders

Walsh, Roger
Professor of Psychiatry, Philosophy, and Anthropology, University of California, Irvine
Transpersonal Psychology

Walsh, W. Bruce
Professor of Psychology, The Ohio State University, Columbus
Career, *article on* Career Assessment

Walter, Maila L.
Independent Scholar, Laguna Nigel, California
Bridgman, Percy Williams

Wandersman, Abraham
Professor of Psychology, University of South Carolina, Columbia
Citizen Participation

Wang, Margaret C.
Professor of Psychology and Director, Temple University, Philadelphia, Pennsylvania
Teachers, *article on* Teacher Relationships

Wankel, Leonard M.
Professor Emeritus of Physical Education and Recreation, University of Alberta, Edmonton, Canada
Sport Psychology, *article on* Social Psychology Perspectives

Wapner, Seymour
Chair of the Executive Committee, Heinz Werner Institute for Developmental Analysis, Clark University, Worcester, Massachusetts
Werner, Heinz

Wardlaw, Dana Meritt
Doctoral Candidate, Division of Community and Prevention Research, University of Illinois at Chicago
Community Psychology: History of the Field

Washburn, David A.
Deputy Director of the Sonny Carter Life Sciences Laboratory, Language Research Center, Georgia State University, Decatur
Nonhuman Intelligence

Wasserman, Stanley
Professor of Psychology, Statistics, and Sociology, University of Illinois, Champaign
Social Network Analysis, *article on* Concepts, Applications, and Methods

Watkins, C. Edward, Jr.
Professor of Psychology, University of North Texas, Denton
Psychotherapy, *article on* Approaches

Watkins, Linda R.
Professor of Psychology, University of Colorado, Boulder
Learned Helplessness

Watson, Jason M.
Doctoral Candidate in Cognitive Psychology, Washington University, Saint Louis, Missouri
Cognitive Psychology, *article on* Research Methods

Weary, Gifford
Professor of Psychology, The Ohio State University, Columbus
Attribution Theories

Webb, Wilse B.
Professor Emeritus of Psychology, University of Florida, Gainesville
Sleep

Wegener, Duane T.
Associate Professor of Psychological Studies, Purdue University, West Lafayette, Indiana
Attitudes, *article on* Attitude Structure

Weinberg, Robert S.
Professor of Physical Education, Health, and Sports Studies, Miami University, Oxford, Ohio
Sport Performance Interventions; Sport Psychology, *article on* Research

Weiner, Bernard
Professor of Psychology, University of California, Los Angeles
Motivation, *article on* An Overview

Weiner, Dora B.
Professor of the Medical Humanities and History, University of California, Los Angeles
Pinel, Philippe

Weiss, Stephen M.
Professor of Psychiatry and Behavioral Sciences, University of Miami School of Medicine, Florida
Health Psychology, *article on* History of the Field

Weithorn, Lois A.
Adjunct Professor of Law, University of California, San Francisco
Informed Consent

Weizmann, Fredric
Associate Professor of Psychology, York University, Toronto, Ontario, Canada
Bowlby, John

Wellman, Barry
Professor of Sociology, University of Toronto, Ontario, Canada
Social Network Analysis, *article on* Concepts, Applications, and Methods; Virtual Communities

Wellman, Henry M.
Professor of Psychology, The University of Michigan, Ann Arbor
Early Childhood

Wells, Gary L.
Distinguished Professor of Liberal Arts and Sciences, and Professor of Psychology, Iowa State University, Ames
Eyewitness Testimony

Wenk, Gary L.
Professor of Psychology and Neurology, University of Arizona, Tucson
Drugs and Intelligence

Werner, Carol M.
Professor of Psychology and Director of Environmental Studies, University of Utah, Salt Lake City
Privacy; Territoriality

Wertheimer, Michael
Professor Emeritus of Psychology, University of Colorado, Boulder
American Psychological Association, *article on* History; Duncker, Karl; Ehrenfels, Christian von; Fernberger, Samuel W.; Gestalt Psychology; Wertheimer, Max

West, Stephen G.
Professor of Psychology, Arizona State University, Tempe
Multiple Regression

Westen, Drew
Director of the Adult and Adolescent Personality Program, Center for Anxiety and Related Disorders; and Research Associate Professor of Psychology, Boston University, Massachusetts
Psychoanalysis, *article on* Theories

Wetmore, Karin E.
Independent Scholar, Boston, Massachusetts
McCosh, James

Wexler, David B.
Lyons Professor of Law and Professor of Psychology, University of Arizona; and Professor of Law and Director of the International Network on Therapeutic Jurisprudence, University of Puerto Rico
Mental Health Law; Right to Refuse Treatment

Whalen, Carol K.
Professor of Psychology and Social Behavior, University of California, Irvine
Attention-Deficit/Hyperactivity Disorder

Wheaton, George R.
Vice President, American Institutes for Research, Washington, D.C.
American Institutes for Research in the Behavioral Sciences

Whitaker, Harry A.
Professor, and Head of the Department of Psychology, Northern Michigan University, Marquette
Flourens, Pierre; Phrenology

Whitbourne, Susan Krauss
Professor of Psychology, University of Massachusetts, Amherst
Adulthood and Aging, *article on* Biological Processes and Physical Development; Adulthood and Aging, *article on* Personality Process and Development; Differential Aging

Whitehead, William E.
Professor of Medicine, and Adjunct Professor of Psychology, University of North Carolina at Chapel Hill
Irritable Bowel Syndrome and Functional Disorders

Whitehouse, Wayne G.
Research Associate, Department of Psychiatry, University of Pennsylvania School of Medicine, Philadelphia
Demand Characteristics

Whitten, Lisa
Associate Professor of Psychology, State University of New York, College at Old Westbury; and Membership Chair of the Association of Black Psychologists, Washington, D.C.
Minority Psychology

Whyte, Glen
Professor of Organizational Behavior, University of Toronto, Ontario, Canada
Groupthink

Wickens, Christopher D.
Professor of Psychology, and Head of the Aviation Research Laboratory, University of Illinois at Urbana-Champaign
Aviation Psychology; Driving and Highway Safety; Multiplc Task Performance

Wickesberg, Robert E.
Associate Professor of Psychology, University of Illinois at Urbana-Champaign
Hearing, *article on* Biological Organization

Widaman, Keith F.
Professor of Psychology, University of California, Davis
Developmental Psychology, *article on* Research Methods

Widiger, Thomas A.
Professor of Psychology, University of Kentucky, Lexington
Antisocial Personality Disorder; Diagnostic and Statistical Manual of Mental Disorders; Narcissistic Personality Disorder; Personality Disorders

Wigfield, Allan
Professor of Human Development, University of Maryland, College Park
Adolescence, *article on* Social Patterns, Achievements, and Problems

Wiggins, Elizabeth C.
Senior Research Associate, Federal Judicial Center, Washington, D.C.
Government Regulation, *article on* Federal Regulation

Wight, Randall D.
Professor of Psychology and Biology, Ouachita Baptist University, Arkadelphia, Arkansas
Müller, Johannes Peter; Sherrington, Charles Scott

Wilcox, Rand
Professor of Psychology, University of Southern California, Los Angeles
Nonparametric Statistics

Williams, Richard N.
Professor of Psychology, Brigham Young University, Provo, Utah
Epistemology

Williams, Susan M.
Senior Research Associate, Learning Technology Center, Vanderbilt University, Nashville, Tennessee
Learning Technologies

Williamson, Donald A.
Professor of Psychology, Louisiana State University, Baton Rouge
Bulimia

Williges, Robert C.
Ralph H. Bogle Professor of Industrial and Systems Engineering; Professor of Psychology and Computer Sciences, Virginia Polytechnic Institute and State University, Blacksburg
Person-Machine Systems

Wilpert, Bernhard
Professor of Psychology, Institute of Psychology, Berlin University of Technology, Germany
International Association of Applied Psychology

Wilson, Glenn F.
Senior Research Psychologist, Air Force Research Laboratory, Wright-Patterson Air Force Base, Dayton, Ohio
Aerospace Systems

Wilson, Melvin N.
Professor of Psychology, University of Virginia, Charlottesville
Cultural Diversity

Windholz, George
Professor Emeritus of Psychology, University of North Carolina at Charlotte
Pavlov, Ivan Petrovich

Wingfield, Nancy Poe
Assistant Professor of Social Work, University of Maryland, Baltimore County
Parent-Child Relationship, *article on* Adulthood

Winick, Bruce J.
Professor of Law, and Director of the University of Miami School of Law, Institute on Law, Psychiatry, and Psychology, Florida
Competency; Mental Health Law; Right to Refuse Treatment

Winston, Andrew S.
Professor of Psychology, University of Guelph, Ontario, Canada
Boring, Edwin Garrigues; Woodworth, Robert Sessions

Winter, David G.
Professor of Psychology, The University of Michigan, Ann Arbor
Achievement Motivation; Allport, Gordon Willard; Authoritarianism; McClelland, David C.; Political Leadership; Power Motivation

Wise, Steven P.
Research Biologist, National Institute of Mental Health, Bethesda, Maryland
Motor System

Wisniewski, Edward
Associate Professor of Psychology, University of North Carolina at Greensboro
Concepts, *article on* Combinations

Wittig, Michele Andrisin
Professor of Psychology, California State University, Northridge
Action Research

Wolery, Mark
Investigator at the Frank Porter Graham Child Development Center, University of North Carolina at Chapel Hill
Special Education

Wolf, Elizabeth B.
Professor Emerita of Psychology, Florida Institute of Technology, Melbourne, Florida
Rorschach, Hermann

Wolf, Rosalie S.
Executive Director of the Institute on Aging, University of Massachusetts Memorial Health Care, Worcester
Elder Abuse and Neglect

Wolfe, Jeremy M.
Associate Professor of Ophthalmology, Harvard Medical School, Boston, Massachusetts
Visual Search

Wolfe, Jessica
Associate Professor of Psychiatry and Psychology, Boston University School of Medicine, Massachusetts
Veterans

Wolfle, Dael
Professor Emeritus, Evans School of Public Affairs, University of Washington, Seattle
American Association for the Advancement of Science

Wood, James M.
Associate Professor of Psychology, University of Texas, El Paso
Nightmares

Wood, Joanne V.
Associate Professor of Psychology, University of Waterloo, Ontario, Canada
Social Comparison

Woodruff-Borden, Janet
Associate Professor of Psychology, Department of Psychological Brain Sciences, University of Louisville, Kentucky
Specific Phobia

Woodworth, Joan Bryant
Professor of Psychology, Appalachian State University, Boone, North Carolina
Hartley, David

Worell, Judith
Professor Emeritus, Department of Educational and Counseling Psychology, University of Kentucky, Lexington
Feminism, *article on* Feminist Psychotherapy

Wright, Rogers H.
Executive Officer, Association for Advancement of Psychology, Spring Valley, California
Association for the Advancement of Psychology

Wrightsman, Lawrence S.
Professor of Psychology, University of Kansas, Lawrence
Law and Psychology

Wulff, David M.
Professor of Psychology, Wheaton College, Norton, Massachusetts
Religion and Psychology, *article on* An Overview

Wyatt, James K.
Assistant Professor of Psychology, Rush-Presbyterian–St. Luke's Medical Center/Rush Medical College, Chicago, Illinois
Seasonal Affective Disorder

Yates, Brian T.
Professor of Psychology, American University, Washington, D.C.
Cost-Benefit Analysis

Yoshikawa, Hirokazu
Assistant Professor of Psychology, New York University, New York
Community Prevention and Intervention, *article on* Prevention with Young Children

Young, Joseph L.
Program Director for Cross-Directorate Activities, Division of Social and Economic Sciences, National Science Foundation, Arlington, Virginia
National Science Foundation

Yuille, John C.
Assistant Professor of Psychology, Dalhousie University, Halifax, Nova Scotia, Canada
Deception

Zahn, Theodore P.
Senior Research Psychologist, Laboratory of Brain and Cognition, National Institute of Mental Health, Bethesda, Maryland
Antipsychotic Medication

Zarin, Deborah A.
Deputy Medical Director, American Psychiatric Association, Washington, D.C.
American Psychiatric Association

Zarit, Steven H.
Professor of Human Development, and Assistant Director of the Gerontology Center, Pennsylvania State University, University Park
Elder Care

Zellou, Aziz (*translator*)
Foreign Affairs Counselor and Translator/Interpretor, Moroccan Ministry of Foreign Affairs and Cooperation, Ottawa, Ontario, Canada
North Africa

Zenderland, Leila
Professor of American Studies, California State University, Fullerton
Goddard, Henry Herbert

Zilber, Suzanne M.
Staff Psychologist, Iowa State University, Ames
Tyler, Leona E.

Zillmann, Dolf
Professor of Psychology and Communication, University of Alabama, Tuscaloosa
Excitement

Zimmerman, Barry J.
Distinguished Professor of Educational Psychology, City University of New York
Student Characteristics

Zimmerman, Marc A.
Associate Professor of Health Behavior and Health Education and Psychology, The University of Michigan, Ann Arbor
Public Health

Zola, Stuart M.
Professor in Residence, Departments of Psychiatry and Neurosciences, University of California, San Diego
Neuropsychology, *article on* Theories

Zuckerman, Marvin
Professor of Psychology, University of Delaware, Newark
Sensation Seeking

Zvolensky, Michael J.
Doctoral Candidate in Clinical Psychology, West Virginia University, Morgantown
Systematic Desensitization

Zwick, Rami
Associate Professor of Marketing, and Director of the Center for Experimental Business Research, Hong Kong University of Science and Technology, Kowloon, China
Game Theory

SYNOPTIC OUTLINE OF CONTENTS

SYNOPTIC OUTLINE OF CONTENTS

The entries in the *Encyclopedia of Psychology* pertain to the general conceptual categories listed on this page, often within hierarchical clusters that begin with broad, synthetic overviews and that end with relatively short entries on specialized topics. Thus, entries that broadly define key topics within a conceptual category are often collected under the heading "Principal Entries," while smaller-scale entries that "break out" from or "amplify" the principal entries are usually listed as "Supporting Entries." These sub-groups are followed occasionally by "Related Entries," which examine a topic area from a different disciplinary perspective or focus on an aspect of the topic that may be of special interest to the reader. In addition, several conceptual categories begin with a list of "Primary Field Surveys"—that is, a brief selection of those entries in the encyclopedia that, in exploring major fields of psychological inquiry (for example, clinical psychology, social psychology, and so on), provide the primary disciplinary context for understanding the principal, supporting, and/or related entries that follow them in the outline.

The subsequent pages in this section provide a detailed synoptic outline of the contents, organized by these conceptual categories. Because the categories are not necessarily mutually exclusive, several field surveys—and indeed several other types of entries—are listed more than once. Such multiple listings, although not exhaustive, are intended to convey the central notion of the "circle of knowledge" and cross-relatedness implicit in the field of psychology.

Professional Training, Employment, and Ethics

• *Principal Entries*

• *Supporting Entries*

International Psychology

• *Principal Entry*

• *Supporting Entries*

• *Related Entries*

RESEARCH DESIGN AND STATISTICS

• *Principal Entries*

Behavioral and Mental Disorders

Physical Illnesses and Conditions

Social Issues and Problems

INTERVENTIONS

Primary Field Surveys

Prevention

Psychosocial Interventions

Biological Interventions

Institutional Care

PSYCHOLOGY AND OTHER DISCIPLINES

Psychology and Law

• *Principal Entry*

• *Supporting Entries*

• *Related Entries*

Psychology and Politics

Psychology and the Military

• *Principal Entry*

• *Supporting Entries*

Psychology and Religion

• *Principal Entries*

• *Supporting Entries*

Psychology and Sports

• *Principal Entry*

• *Supporting Entries*

Psychology and Other Areas of Study

INDEX

INDEX

Volume numbers are printed in boldface type, followed by a colon and relevant page numbers. Page numbers printed in boldface indicate a major discussion.

A

B

D

E

F

G

H

I

K

L

M

N

O

P

Q

S

T

U

V

W

X

Y

Z